Situational Awareness in Computer Network Defense:

Principles, Methods and Applications

Cyril Onwubiko
Research Series Limited, UK

Thomas John Owens
Brunel University, UK

Managing Director:	Lindsay Johnston
Senior Editorial Director:	Heather Probst
Book Production Manager:	Sean Woznicki
Development Manager:	Joel Gamon
Development Editor:	Myla Harty
Acquisitions Editor:	Erika Gallagher
Typesetter:	Jennifer Romanchak
Cover Design:	Nick Newcomer, Greg Snader

Published in the United States of America by
Information Science Reference (an imprint of IGI Global)
701 E. Chocolate Avenue
Hershey PA 17033
Tel: 717-533-8845
Fax: 717-533-8661
E-mail: cust@igi-global.com
Web site: http://www.igi-global.com

Library of Congress Cataloging-in-Publication Data

Situational awareness in computer network defense: principles, methods and applications / Cyril Onwubiko and Thomas Owens, editors.
    p. cm.
  Includes bibliographical references and index.
    ISBN 978-1-4666-0104-8 (hbk.) -- ISBN 978-1-4666-0105-5 (ebook) -- ISBN 978-1-4666-0106-2 (print & perpetual access) 1. Cyberinfrastructure--Security measures. 2. Computer networks--Security measures. 3. Computer security. 4. Situational awareness. I. Onwubiko, Cyril, 1972- II. Owens, Thomas.
  TK5105.59S566 2012
  005.8--dc23

                                    2011043980

British Cataloguing in Publication Data
A Cataloguing in Publication record for this book is available from the British Library.

All work contributed to this book is new, previously-unpublished material. The views expressed in this book are those of the authors, but not necessarily of the publisher.

Editorial Advisory Board

Table of Contents

Preface xvi

Section 1
Principles of SA CND

Chapter 1
Review of Situational Awareness for Computer Network Defense 1
    Cyril Onwubiko, Research Series Limited, UK
    Thomas John Owens, Brunel University, UK

Chapter 2
The Contributions of Information Security Culture and Human Relations to the Improvement of
Situational Awareness 10
    Janne Merete Hagen, Norwegian Defence Research Establishment, Norway

Chapter 3
Cyber Command and Control: A Military Doctrinal Prospective on Collaborative Situation
Awareness for Decision Making 29
    Michael E. Ruiz, Deloitte Consulting, USA
    Richard Redmond, Virginia Commonwealth University, USA

Chapter 4
A Proactive Defense Strategy to Enhance Situational Awareness in Computer Network Security 48
    Yi Luo, The University of Arizona, USA
    Ferenc Szidarovszky, The University of Arizona, USA

Chapter 5
An Alternative Framework for Research on Situational Awareness in Computer
Network Defense 71
    Eric McMillan, The Pennsylvania State University, USA
    Michael Tyworth, The Pennsylvania State University, USA

Chapter 6
Information Security for Situational Awareness in Computer Network Defense 86
> *Uri Blumenthal, MIT Lincoln Laboratory, USA*
> *Joshua Haines, MIT Lincoln Laboratory, USA*
> *William Streilein, MIT Lincoln Laboratory, USA*
> *Gerald O'Leary, MIT Lincoln Laboratory, USA*

Chapter 7
Designing Information Systems and Network Components for Situational Awareness 104
> *Cyril Onwubiko, Research Series Limited, UK*

Section 2
Methods in SA CND

Chapter 8
Cyber Situation Awareness through Instance-Based Learning: Modeling the Security Analyst in a
Cyber-Attack Scenario 125
> *Varun Dutt, Carnegie Mellon University, USA*
> *Cleotilde Gonzalez, Carnegie Mellon University, USA*

Chapter 9
Information Data Fusion and Computer Network Defense 141
> *Mark Ballora, The Pennsylvania State University, USA*
> *Nicklaus A. Giacobe, The Pennsylvania State University, USA*
> *Michael McNeese, The Pennsylvania State University, USA*
> *David L. Hall, The Pennsylvania State University, USA*

Chapter 10
Usefulness of Sensor Fusion for Security Incident Analysis 165
> *Ciza Thomas, College of Engineering, India*
> *N. Balakrishnan, Indian Institute of Science, India*

Chapter 11
GCD: A Global Collaborative Defense Approach to Thwart Internet Attacks 181
> *Subrata Acharya, Towson University, USA*

Chapter 12
DNSSEC vs. DNSCurve: A Side-by-Side Comparison 201
> *Marios Anagnostopoulos, University of the Aegean, Greece*
> *Georgios Kambourakis, University of the Aegean, Greece*
> *Elisavet Konstantinou, University of the Aegean, Greece*
> *Stefanos Gritzalis, University of the Aegean, Greece*

Chapter 13
IEEE802.21 Assisted Fast Re-Authentication Scheme over GSABA 221
    Qazi Bouland Mussabbir, Brunel University, UK
    Thomas John Owens, Brunel University, UK

Section 3
SA CND Applications

Chapter 14
Modelling Situation Awareness Information and System Requirements for the Mission using
Goal-Oriented Task Analysis Approach 245
    Cyril Onwubiko, Research Series Limited, UK

Chapter 15
On Situational Aware En-Route Filtering against Injected False Data in Wireless Sensor
Networks 263
    Xinyu Yang, Xi'an Jiaotong University, P. R. China
    Jie Lin, Xi'an Jiaotong University, P. R. China
    Wei Yu, Towson University, USA
    Xinwen Fu, University of Massachusetts Lowell, USA
    Genshe Chen, Independent Consultant Professional, USA
    Erik P. Blasch, Air Force Research Laboratory, USA

Chapter 16
Attack Graphs and Scenario Driven Wireless Computer Network Defense 284
    Peter J. Hawrylak, The University of Tulsa, USA
    George Louthan IV, The University of Tulsa, USA
    Jeremy Daily, The University of Tulsa, USA
    John Hale, The University of Tulsa, USA
    Mauricio Papa, The University of Tulsa, USA

Chapter 17
Advanced Security Incident Analysis with Sensor Correlation 302
    Ciza Thomas, College of Engineering, India
    N. Balakrishnan, Indian Institute of Science, India

Chapter 18
PITWALL: Tools, Techniques and Metrics for the Optimization of Enterprise Network Defense
Systems 320
    Subrata Acharya, Towson University, USA

Chapter 19
Forensic Investigative Process for Situational Awareness in Information Security 344
Khidir Mohamed Ali, Jubail University College, Saudi Arabia
Thomas John Owens, Brunel University, United Kingdom

Compilation of References 357

About the Contributors 381

Index 390

Detailed Table of Contents

Preface xvi

Section 1
Principles of SA CND

Chapter 1
Review of Situational Awareness for Computer Network Defense 1

Cyril Onwubiko, Research Series Limited, UK
Thomas John Owens, Brunel University, UK

The importance of situational awareness to air traffic control, and hence the safety and security of aircraft, is evident, demonstrable, and has been hugely significant. The main purpose of this book is to convey an understanding of the impact of situational awareness on the design of the next generation computer systems, network architectures, and platform infrastructures. The book achieves its purpose by presenting principles, methods, and applications of situational awareness for computer network defense; in doing so, it makes clear the benefits situational awareness can provide for information security, computer security and computer network defense. This book contributes to cross-multidisciplinary discussion among researchers, academia, and practitioners who are engaged objectively in sharing, contributing, and showcasing how situational awareness can be adapted to computer systems, network infrastructure designs, and architecture patterns. The goal of this chapter is to explain situational awareness for computer network defense from the point of view of its most basic foundations as a spring board to discuss how situational awareness can be relevant to computer network defense, whose operations and environment are similar to air traffic control where the application of situational awareness has been hugely successful.

Chapter 2
The Contributions of Information Security Culture and Human Relations to the Improvement of
Situational Awareness 10

Janne Merete Hagen, Norwegian Defence Research Establishment, Norway

The chapter gives an overview of business practices and how people and human relations influence situational awareness and information security in an organization. There is still a long way to go in training employees in information security and improving employees' information security awareness. Motivated and trained employees have the ability to detect and report security weaknesses and breaches, including near-miss incidents, and in this way, they may provide a valuable defense-in-depth-capability that is often lacking. The chapter discusses two approaches to overcome the barriers to building situational awareness promulgated in the general deterrence theory and socio-technical theory.

Chapter 3
Cyber Command and Control: A Military Doctrinal Prospective on Collaborative Situation
Awareness for Decision Making 29
        Michael E. Ruiz, Deloitte Consulting, USA
        Richard Redmond, Virginia Commonwealth University, USA

Cyber-space is emerging as the fifth domain of warfare and a crucial operational concern for commercial industry. As such, it requires a command and control system that enables defensive and operational capabilities within cyber-space. This chapter describes a research and development project aimed at discovering solutions for a Cyber Command and Control both for commercial and military environments. The chapter identifies challenges and provides solutions rooted in the body of knowledge composed of Command and Control and Situation Awareness Theory.

Chapter 4
A Proactive Defense Strategy to Enhance Situational Awareness in Computer Network Security 48
        Yi Luo, The University of Arizona, USA
        Ferenc Szidarovszky, The University of Arizona, USA

With the development of situational awareness in intrusion defense, a proactive response is a realistic and effective approach against the attackers. It is assumed that each player can update knowledge of the opponent and assess possible future scenarios of the dynamic game based on their previous interactions. Therefore, finding the best current move of the defender is modeled as a discrete-time stochastic control problem. An on-line, convergent, scenario based proactive defense (SPD) algorithm considering adaptive learning is developed based on differential dynamic programming (DDP) to solve the associated optimal control problem. Numerical experiment shows that the new algorithm can help the defender in finding the best dynamic strategies quickly and efficiently. Moreover, the SPD algorithm can provide optimal defensive efforts against possible future attacks within an appropriate time window, so the success of the attack in the possible future interactions can be assessed, improving situational awareness in computer network security.

Chapter 5
An Alternative Framework for Research on Situational Awareness in Computer
Network Defense 71
        Eric McMillan, The Pennsylvania State University, USA
        Michael Tyworth, The Pennsylvania State University, USA

In this chapter the authors present a new framework for the study of situation awareness in computer network defense (cyber-SA). While immensely valuable, the research to date on cyber-SA has overemphasized an algorithmic level of analysis to the exclusion of the human actor. Since situation awareness, and therefore cyber-SA, is a human cognitive process and state, it is essential that future cyber-SA research account for the human-in-the-loop. To that end, the framework in this chapter presents a basis for examining cyber-SA at the cognitive, system, work, and enterprise levels of analysis. In describing the framework, the authors present examples of research that are emblematic of each type of analysis.

Chapter 6

Information Security for Situational Awareness in Computer Network Defense 86

    Uri Blumenthal, MIT Lincoln Laboratory, USA
    Joshua Haines, MIT Lincoln Laboratory, USA
    William Streilein, MIT Lincoln Laboratory, USA
    Gerald O'Leary, MIT Lincoln Laboratory, USA

Situational awareness – the perception of "what is going on" – is crucial in every field of human endeavor, especially so in the cyber world where most of the protections afforded by physical time and distance are taken away. Since ancient times, military science emphasized the importance of preserving your awareness of the battlefield and at the same time preventing your adversary from learning the true situation for as long as possible. Today cyber is officially recognized as a contested military domain like air, land, and sea. Therefore situational awareness in computer networks will be under attacks of military strength and will require military-grade protection. This chapter describes the emerging threats for computer SA, and the potential avenues of defense against them.

Chapter 7

Designing Information Systems and Network Components for Situational Awareness 104

    Cyril Onwubiko, Research Series Limited, UK

Operators need situational awareness (SA) of their organisation's computer networks and Information Systems in order to identify threats, estimate impact of attacks, evaluate risks, understand situations, and make sound decisions swiftly and accurately on what to protect against, and how to address incidents that may impact valued assets. Enterprise computer networks are often huge and complex, spanning across several WANs and supporting a number of distributed services. Understanding situations in such dynamic and complex networks is time-consuming and challenging. Operators SA are enhanced through a number of ways, one of which is through the use of situation-aware systems and technology. Designing situation-aware systems for computer network defence (CND) is difficult without understanding basic situational awareness design requirements of network applications and systems. Thus, this chapter investigates pertinent features that are foundation, essential, and beneficial for designing situation-aware systems, software, and network applications for CND.

Section 2
Methods in SA CND

Chapter 8

Cyber Situation Awareness through Instance-Based Learning: Modeling the Security Analyst in a
Cyber-Attack Scenario 125

    Varun Dutt, Carnegie Mellon University, USA
    Cleotilde Gonzalez, Carnegie Mellon University, USA

In a corporate network, the situation awareness (SA) of a security analyst is of particular interest. The current work describes a cognitive Instance-Based Learning (IBL) model of an analyst's recognition and comprehension processes in a cyber-attack scenario. The IBL model first recognizes network events based upon events' situation attributes and their similarity to past experiences (instances) stored in the model's memory. Then, the model comprehends a sequence of observed events as being a cyber-attack or not, based upon instances retrieved from its memory, similarity mechanism used, and the model's risk-tolerance. The execution of the model generates predictions about the recognition and comprehension processes of an analyst in a cyber-attack. A security analyst's decisions in the model are evaluated based upon two cyber-SA metrics of accuracy and timeliness. The chapter highlights the potential of this research for design of training and decision support tools for security analysts.

Chapter 9

Information Data Fusion and Computer Network Defense 141
    Mark Ballora, The Pennsylvania State University, USA
    Nicklaus A. Giacobe, The Pennsylvania State University, USA
    Michael McNeese, The Pennsylvania State University, USA
    David L. Hall, The Pennsylvania State University, USA

Computer networks no longer simply enable military and civilian operations, but have become vital infrastructures for all types of operations ranging from sensing and command/control to logistics, power distribution, and many other functions. Consequently, network attacks have become weapons of choice for adversaries engaged in asymmetric warfare. Traditionally, data and information fusion techniques were developed to improve situational awareness and threat assessment by combining data from diverse sources, and have recently been extended to include both physical ("hard") sensors and human observers (acting as "soft" sensors). This chapter provides an introduction to traditional data fusion models and adapts them to the domain of cyber security. Recent advances in hard and soft information fusion are summarized and applied to the cyber security domain. Research on the use of sound for human-in-the-loop pattern recognition (sonification) is also introduced. Finally, perspectives are provided on the future for data fusion in cyber security research.

Chapter 10

Usefulness of Sensor Fusion for Security Incident Analysis 165
    Ciza Thomas, College of Engineering, India
    N. Balakrishnan, Indian Institute of Science, India

Intrusion Detection Systems form an important component of network defense. Because of the heterogeneity of the attacks, it has not been possible to make a single Intrusion Detection System that is capable of detecting all types of attacks with acceptable levels of accuracy. In this chapter, the distinct advantage of sensor fusion over individual IDSs is proved. The detection rate and the false positive rate quantify the performance benefit obtained through the fixing of threshold bounds. Also, the more independent and distinct the attack space is for the individual IDSs, the better the fusion of Intrusion Detection Systems performs. A simple theoretical model is initially illustrated and later supplemented with experimental evaluation. The chapter demonstrates that the proposed fusion technique is more flexible and also outperforms other existing fusion techniques such as OR, AND, SVM, and ANN, using the real-world network traffic embedded with attacks.

Chapter 11

GCD: A Global Collaborative Defense Approach to Thwart Internet Attacks 181
Subrata Acharya, Towson University, USA

With the tremendous growth in the dependence of services on the Internet, service disruption has become less and less tolerable. The greatest threat to service availability is the rapid growth in the complexity and frequency of large-scale distributed attacks. These attacks cause economic losses due to unavailability of services and potentially serious security concerns by the incapacitation of critical infrastructures. Despite the tremendous attention by the research community to find distributed attack countermeasures, a practical and comprehensive solution is yet to see the light of the day. In this research, the authors present a research direction aimed at finding a solution to the above problem.

Chapter 12

DNSSEC vs. DNSCurve: A Side-by-Side Comparison 201
Marios Anagnostopoulos, University of the Aegean, Greece
Georgios Kambourakis, University of the Aegean, Greece
Elisavet Konstantinou, University of the Aegean, Greece
Stefanos Gritzalis, University of the Aegean, Greece

Without a doubt, Domain Name System (DNS) security is a complicated topic of growing concern. In fact, it can be argued that the whole Internet infrastructure depends on the smooth operation of the DNS service. Despite this fact, the original DNS design concentrated on availability, not security, and thus included no authentication. Nowadays, this security gap has been addressed by two cryptographic mechanisms: DNSSEC and DNSCurve. They both utilize public key cryptography and extend the core DNS protocol. Although the second mechanism is still in its infancy while the first is well-standardized, they are both promising and are quite likely to compete with each other in the near future to gain acceptance. This work aims to provide a comprehensive and constructive comparison between the aforementioned security mechanisms. Towards this direction, the authors theoretically cross-evaluate and assess the benefits and the drawbacks of each particular mechanism based on several distinct criteria. This is necessary in order to decide which mechanism is the best fit for each particular deployment.

Chapter 13

IEEE802.21 Assisted Fast Re-Authentication Scheme over GSABA 221
Qazi Bouland Mussabbir, Brunel University, UK
Thomas John Owens, Brunel University, UK

To satisfy customer demand for a high performance "global" mobility service, network operators are facing the need to evolve to a converged "all-IP" centric heterogeneous access infrastructure. However, the integration of such heterogeneous access networks brings major mobility issues. Dynamic service bootstrapping and authorization mechanisms must be in place to efficiently deploy a mobility service, which will allow only legitimate users to access the service. Authentication, access, and accounting based authentication mechanisms like Extensible Authentication Protocol (EAP) incur signalling overheads due to large Round Trip Times (RTTs). As a result, overall handover latency also increases. A fast re-authentication scheme is presented in this chapter, which utilizes IEEE802.21 Media Independent Handover (MIH) services to minimize the EAP authentication process delays and reduce the overall handover latency. In this way, it is shown that the demands mobility places on availability can broadly be met, leaving only the generic issues of Internet availability.

Section 3
SA CND Applications

Chapter 14

Modelling Situation Awareness Information and System Requirements for the Mission using
Goal-Oriented Task Analysis Approach..245

Cyril Onwubiko, Research Series Limited, UK

This chapter describes work on modelling situational awareness information and system requirements for the mission. Developing this model based on Goal-Oriented Task Analysis representation of the mission using an Agent Oriented Software Engineering methodology advances current information requirement models because it provides valuable insight on how to effectively achieve the mission's requirements (information, systems, networks, and IT infrastructure), and offers enhanced situational awareness within the Computer Network Defence environment. Further, the modelling approach using Secure Tropos is described, and model validation using a security test scenario is discussed.

Chapter 15

On Situational Aware En-Route Filtering against Injected False Data in Wireless Sensor
Networks 263

Xinyu Yang, Xi'an Jiaotong University, P. R. China
Jie Lin, Xi'an Jiaotong University, P. R. China
Wei Yu, Towson University, USA
Xinwen Fu, University of Massachusetts Lowell, USA
Genshe Chen, Independent Consultant Professional, USA
Erik P. Blasch, Air Force Research Laboratory, USA

Cyber-physical systems (CPS) are systems with a tight coupling of the cyber aspects of computing and communications with the physical aspects of dynamics and engineering that abide by the laws of physics. The real-time monitoring provided by wireless sensor networks (WSNs) is essential for CPS, as it provides rich and pertinent information on the condition of physical systems. In WSNs, the attackers could inject false measurements to the controller through compromised sensor nodes, which not only threaten the security of the system, but also consume significant network resources and pose serious threats to the lifetime of sensor networks. To mitigate false data injection (FDI) measurement attacks, a number of situation aware en-route filtering schemes to filter false data inside the networks have been developed. In this book chapter, the authors first review those existing situation aware en-route filter mechanisms such as: Statistical En-route Filtering (SEF), Location-Based Resilient Secrecy (LBRS), Location-ware End-to-end Data Security (LEDS), and Dynamic En-route Filtering Scheme (DEFS). The authors then compare the performance of those schemes via both the theoretical analysis and simulation study. These extensive simulations validate findings that most of the schemes can filter out false data within few hops, and the filtering efficiency increases as the number of hops increases and the filtering efficiency of most schemes decreases rapidly as the number of compromised nodes increases.

Chapter 16
Attack Graphs and Scenario Driven Wireless Computer Network Defense.......................................284
    Peter J. Hawrylak, The University of Tulsa, USA
    George Louthan IV, The University of Tulsa, USA
    Jeremy Daily, The University of Tulsa, USA
    John Hale, The University of Tulsa, USA
    Mauricio Papa, The University of Tulsa, USA

This chapter describes how to use attack graphs to evaluate the security vulnerabilities of an embedded computer network and provides example cases of this technique. Attack graphs are powerful tools available to system administrators to identify and manage vulnerabilities. Attack graphs describe the steps an adversary could take to reach a desired goal and can be analyzed to quantify risk. The systems investigated in this chapter are embedded systems that span hardware, software, and network communication. The example cases studied will be (1) radio frequency identification (RFID), (2) vehicle networks, and (3) the Smart Grid (the next generation power and distribution network in the USA).

Chapter 17
Advanced Security Incident Analysis with Sensor Correlation...302
    Ciza Thomas, College of Engineering, India
    N. Balakrishnan, Indian Institute of Science, India

This chapter explores the general problem of the poorly detected attacks with Intrusion Detection Systems. The poorly detected attacks reveal the fact that they are characterized by features that do not discriminate them much. The poor performance of the detectors has been improved by discriminative training of anomaly detectors and incorporating additional rules into the misuse detector. This chapter proposes a new approach of machine learning method where corresponding learning problem is characterized by a number of features. This chapter discusses the improved performance of multiple Intrusion Detection Systems using Data-dependent Decision fusion. The Data-dependent Decision fusion approach gathers an in-depth understanding about the input traffic and also the behavior of the individual Intrusion Detection Systems by means of a neural network learner unit. This information is used to fine-tune the fusion unit since the fusion depends on the input feature vector. Thus fusion implements a function that is local to each region in the feature space. It is well-known that the effectiveness of sensor fusion improves when the individual IDSs are uncorrelated. The training methodology adopted in this work takes note of this fact. For illustrative purposes, the DARPA 1999 data set as has been used. The Data-dependent Decision fusion shows a significantly better performance with respect to the performance of individual Intrusion Detection Systems.

Chapter 18
PITWALL: Tools, Techniques and Metrics for the Optimization of Enterprise Network Defense
Systems 320
    Subrata Acharya, Towson University, USA

The continuous growth in the Internet's size, the amount of data traffic, and the complexity of processing this traffic give rise to new challenges in building high performance network devices. Such an exponential growth, coupled with the increasing sophistication of attacks, is placing stringent demands on the performance of network Information Systems. These challenges require new designs, architecture, and algorithms for raising situational awareness, and hence, providing performance improvements on current network devices and cyber systems. In this research, the author focuses on the design of architecture and algorithms for optimization of network defense systems, specifically firewalls, to aid not only adaptive and real-time packet filtering but also fast content based routing (differentiated services) for today's data-driven networks.

Chapter 19

Forensic Investigative Process for Situational Awareness in Information Security 344
    Khidir Mohamed Ali, Jubail University College, Saudi Arabia
    Thomas John Owens, Brunel University, United Kingdom

As a starting point for the development of a common visualization of the forensics process by the members of an investigating team, this chapter provides algorithms that provide guidance and step by step instructions on how to deal with computer forensics and the investigations they carry out. A general introductory overview of computer forensics is provided, and the framework of a forensic investigation is summarized. On the basis of this framework, three algorithms are provided, one for each phase of a forensic investigation, which cover the different aspects of computer forensics and address key elements to be considered when attacked systems are investigated.

Compilation of References 357

About the Contributors 381

Index 390

Preface

This book addresses three broad aspects of situational awareness in computer network defense: principles, methods, and applications, with six chapters devoted to each area.

PRINCIPLES

The principles section of the book is comprised as follows:

The in depth coverage of situational awareness rightly begins in chapter 2 by addressing the human factor component of situational awareness. The greatest threat to information security is generally considered to be the insider. This chapter gives an overview of business practices and how people and human relations influence situational awareness and information security in an organization. It highlights the need to train employees in information security with a view to improving their information security awareness. It shows the relevance of socio-technical theory and the general deterrence theory to investigations into the effectiveness of implemented organizational information security measures.

The effective conduct of warfare requires command and control systems for defensive and operational capabilities. Cyber-space is now considered to be the fifth domain of warfare after land, sea, air, and space. For national security it requires a Cyber Command and Control environment that is suitable for military and civilian use. Chapter 3 describes research undertaken to lay the foundations for the development of a Cyber Command and Control environment and identifies the challenges faced in realising that environment based on the body of knowledge in Command and Control and Situation Awareness Theory. The chapter presents a Cyber Command and Control reference architecture and a Collaborative Situational Awareness for Decision Making framework. It draws attention to the fact that the field of cyber security analytics requires extensive research in the interests of national security.

With the development of situational awareness in intrusion defense, the adoption a proactive defense strategy to combat a multi-stage attack is a realistic option. At its current stage, a multi-stage attack seeks to use intelligence gathered in previous stages of the attack to break the defense of the system. At a given stage of a multi-stage attack, a proactive defense strategy uses knowledge of the attack gained in previous stages of the attack to improve the defense of the system. The resulting situation can be modelled using classical game theory. In chapter 4 the best current move of the defender is modelled as a discrete-time stochastic control problem. An on-line scenario based proactive defense algorithm based on differential dynamic programming (DDP) is presented, which can solve the associated optimal control problem. The algorithm is validated through numerical experiment.

Chapter 5 proposes an alternative, more contextually-grounded framework for cyber-situational awareness that seeks to more fully account for the interaction of the human agent with the cyberspace environment. The framework is applicable to multiple levels of analysis by human agents. The knowledge dimension describes the internal cognitive processes and structures of the agent. The action component describes the interaction of the agent with the environment. and the environment dimension accounts for system, enterprise, and operational factors.

Chapter 6 describes the security needs of a Situational Awareness system, mentions the basic techniques that can be applied to achieve these goals, and discusses some of the issues. It discusses advantages and benefits of certain approaches and solutions, and weighs them against the cost of maintaining them, the difficulty of implementing them, or obtaining the desired degree of reliability. This chapter is not aimed at the IT manager or Network Security administrator, but at scientists seeking to expand the boundaries of the Computer Network Defense field and designers evaluating their options to decide on the acceptable set of compromises for the system they are working on.

Chapter 7 investigates task and system requirements that Computer Network Defense systems should meet to support enhanced operator situational awareness. Task requirements are human operator-specific tasks such as risk assessment, protective monitoring, and decision making. System requirements are automated system-specific tasks completed by computer systems and network appliances. There are two main categories of requirements: non-functional and functional. Non-functional requirements are concerned with the quality of the system. Functional requirements are functions the system performs such as processing, display, tasks, and analysis. The chapter provides a comprehensive assessment of pertinent factors to be considered when designing modern computer and network systems for situational awareness in a Computer Network Defense environment. It is highlighted that few contributions in the published literature discuss qualitative task and system requirements.

METHODS

The methods section of the book is comprised as follows:

Chapter 8 presents a cognitive Instance-Based Learning (IBL) model of a security analyst's recognition and comprehension processes in a cyber-attack scenario. The IBL model recognizes network events based upon events' situation attributes and their similarity to past experiences (instances) stored in the model's memory. Then, the model comprehends a sequence of observed events as being a cyber-attack or not, based upon instances retrieved from its memory, the similarity mechanism used, and the model's risk-tolerance. The model generates predictions about the recognition and comprehension processes of an analyst in a cyber-attack. It is proposed that computational models based on the IBL theory can be used to make predictions of a security analyst's cyber-situational awareness in a cyber-attack scenario. Simulation results indicate that the cyber-situational awareness of an analyst is a function of their memory of threat and non-threat events, risk-tolerance, and the methods they use to compare network events to prior experiences of events. The predictions obtained indicate that it might be helpful to devise security analyst job training that makes analysts cautious about the possibility of cyber threats and less risk-tolerant, which enables them to look for features in attributes of network events that communicate the indication of potential threats.

Research into information fusion for multi-sensor data in support of military operations has led to the development of process models, creation of algorithms for signal and image processing, pattern recognition, state estimation, automated reasoning, and dynamic resource allocation. Chapter 9 adapts these models to the domain of cyber security and presents a novel means of situational awareness involving an auditory representation (sonification) of network traffic. The chapter suggests that effective information data fusion for computer network defense will require multi-disciplinary efforts and work on multiple areas including algorithms and techniques "inside the machine" and "outside the machine" to improve the ability of analysts to understand a) An evolving cyber situation, b) Identify and predict threats, and c) Develop collaborative decision making methods. It is asserted that success in this domain will require simultaneously addressing both areas, from both directions.

Chapter 10 reports work on quantitatively detecting threats and targeted intruder activity using sensor fusion Intrusion Detection Systems (IDSs), which are composed of several constituent IDSs. The more independent and distinct the attack space is for the constituent IDSs, the better the fusion IDS performs. A simple theoretical model is provided for the purpose of showing the improved performance of fusion IDSs. The detection rate and the false positive rate quantify the performance benefit obtained through the fixing of threshold bounds. The theoretical analysis is supplemented with experimental evaluation, and the detection rates, false positive rates, and F-score were measured. Preliminary experimental results support the correctness of the theoretical analysis. The chapter also demonstrates that sensor fusion based intrusion detection is more flexible and outperforms other existing fusion techniques using real-world network traffic embedded with attacks.

Chapter 11 presents the design of a dynamic collaborative defense infrastructure to detect and limit distributed denial of service attacks. The Collaborative Defense Architecture (CDA) introduces the design of a separate security plane to manage and pass information between the various network elements. The decision logic for the security mechanisms is distributed in a small set of active security guards (Active sentinels), each responsible for a set of core routers. The Active sentinels collaborate both by proactive and reactive mechanisms to mitigate attacks. The task of the Active sentinels is to actively probe packets sent probabilistically by routers in the network. Upon the detection of an attack, the Active sentinels send messages to the Edge firewall nodes to filter the attack traffic by changing their rule set. The design and evaluation study confirms that such a global and coordinated approach would be real-time and cost-effective with very minimal changes to the current network infrastructure.

The Domain Name System (DNS) is probably the most critical service in the Internet as it translates domain names into the numerical IP address of any network host. Any DNS security breach could cause severe problems to affected network domains, and in the worst case, to the Internet as a whole. However, the original DNS design was concentrated on availability, not security, and thus included no authentication. This security gap has been addressed by two cryptographic mechanisms: DNSSEC and DNSCurve. They both utilize public key cryptography and extend the core DNS protocol. Although the second mechanism is still in its infancy, while the first is well-standardized, they are both promising and quite likely to compete with each other in the near future. Chapter 12 provides a comprehensive and constructive comparison of DNSSEC and DNSCurve and concludes that a mechanism that combines the advantages of both methods; namely the high speed Elliptic Curve Cryptography of DNSCurve and the end-to-end security of DNSSEC would be highly appreciated.

For situational awareness, authentication of all users of the network is an absolute requirement. For users accessing company provided resources out of the office on a Next Generation Network (NGN), there will be two steps to authenticating users. First the user must be authenticated by the NGN, and then, the corporate network must authenticate users of resources it provides who are accessing those resources over a NGN. In NGNs, the use of real-time applications in mobility will be critically dependent on stringent Quality of Service requirements being met. Roaming often implies a temporary service disruption due to handover from one Point of Attachment to another. Authentication, Access, and Accounting (AAA) based authentication mechanisms like Extensible Authentication Protocol (EAP) incur signalling overheads due to large Round Trip Times, and as a result, overall handover latency also increases. Such disruption is unacceptable for potentially business-critical applications such as Voice over IP (VoIP), video conferencing, streaming media, et cetera. In chapter 13, a fast re-authentication scheme is presented, which utilizes IEEE802.21 Media Independent Handover (MIH) services to minimize the EAP authentication process delays, and as a result, reduce the overall handover latency. Therefore, it is shown that the demands mobility places on availability can be broadly met, leaving only the generic issues of Internet availability.

APPLICATIONS

The applications section of the book is comprised as follows:

Chapter 14 describes work on modelling situational awareness information and system requirements for the mission based on Goal-Oriented Task Analysis using an Agent Oriented Software Engineering methodology called Secure Tropos. The security enhanced actor diagram used to model the mission's security operational capability requirements represents each stakeholder's objectives and demonstrates how these objectives can be modelled to achieve enhanced situational awareness for each stakeholder in the Computer Network Defense environment. This work provides valuable insight on how to effectively achieve the mission's goal-orientated (high-level) and task-orientated (low-level) requirements. Model validation is done using security attack scenario testing. It is shown how a simulated attack can be assessed using the proposed model. The outcome of the security scenario testing is a security test case, which shows that the model has the capability to detect and dispel the type of attacked launched.

Cyber-physical systems (CPS) are systems with a tight coupling of the cyber aspects of computing and communications with the physical aspects of dynamics and engineering. Real-time monitoring provided by wireless sensor networks (WSNs) is essential for CPS, as it provides information on the condition of physical systems. In WSNs, the attackers could inject false measurements through compromised sensor nodes, which not only threaten the security of the system, but also consume significant network resources, reducing the lifetime of sensor networks. To mitigate this type of attack, a number of situation aware en-route filtering schemes to filter false data inside the networks have been developed. However, there is lack of a systematic strategy to evaluate these schemes and establish a foundation for designing en-route filtering techniques. In chapter 15, a taxonomy of en-route filters is developed by categorizing the existing en-route filtering schemes and comparing their advantages and disadvantages. To fairly compare the schemes, a theoretical analysis is conducted, from which, a set of closed formulae for each of the schemes is derived. Extensive simulations validate the reported findings.

Chapter 16 describes how to use attack graphs to evaluate the security vulnerabilities of embedded systems and provides examples of the use of this technique. The systems investigated in this chapter are embedded systems that span hardware, software, and network communication. The example cases studied are (1) radio frequency identification (RFID), (2) vehicle networks, and (3) the Smart Grid (the next generation power and distribution network in the USA). Attack graphs describe the steps an adversary could take to reach a desired goal and can be analyzed to quantify risk. Attack graphs enable the discovery of new and unknown vulnerabilities. Armed with this, Information System designers can redesign the system to address and remove these vulnerabilities. System administrators can use this information to apply patches and other defensive measures to secure existing or deployed systems. Currently, most work in attack graphs focuses on development of the attack graph and not on the analysis of the resulting attack graph. The chapter concludes that methods for the analysis of attack graphs that are both accurate and computationally efficient must be developed and formalized.

Chapter 17 proposes a new machine learning method for intrusion detection. The method improves the performance of multiple Intrusion Detection Systems (IDSs) using Data-dependent Decision fusion. The Data-dependent Decision fusion approach gathers an in-depth understanding about the input traffic, and also the behavior of the individual IDS by means of a neural network learner unit. The method adapts and extends notions from the field of multi-sensor data fusion for the Data-dependent Decision Fusion. The extensions are principally in the area of generalizing feature similarity functions to comprehend observances in the intrusion detection domain. The approach has the ability to fuse decisions from multiple, heterogeneous, and sub-optimal IDSs. The test results reported using of the Data-dependent Decision Fusion method are better than those predicted by the Lincoln Laboratory after the DARPA IDS evaluation.

Chapter 18 focuses on the design of architecture and algorithms for optimization of network defense systems, specifically firewalls, to aid not only adaptive and real-time packet filtering but also fast content based routing (differentiated services) for today's data driven networks. It presents various algorithmic and architectural techniques that seek to overcome shortcomings in terms of adaptation, speed of operation (under attack or heavily loaded conditions), and overall operational cost-effectiveness of current network defense systems. Approaches for Tier-I Internet Service Provider networks, and filtering routers are presented to correlate the dynamic metrics and achieve situational awareness required to protect critical network infrastructure and data driven operations over the Internet. The tools proposed also aim to offer the flexibility to include new approaches, and provide the ability to migrate or deploy additional entities for attack detection and defense. The design aspects presented in the proposed automated tool PITWALL assist network administrators in gaining real-time network dynamic information and hence in enhancing the overall security of any typical enterprise network system.

As a starting point for the development of a common visualization of the forensics process by the members of an investigating team, chapter 19 provides algorithms that provide guidance and step by step instructions on how to deal with computer forensics and the investigations they carry out. A general introductory overview of computer forensics is provided, and then the framework of a forensic investigation is summarized. On the basis of this framework, three algorithms are provided, one for each phase of a forensic investigation, which cover the different aspects of computer forensics and address key elements to be considered when attacked systems are investigated. Algorithms that provide a complete model of the forensics process are unlikely to be created, but they are a starting point, from which additional guidance can be provided to analysts on the basis of their particular expertise that leverages their existing understanding of the workspace.

Section 1
Principles of SA CND

Chapter 1
Review of Situational Awareness for Computer Network Defense

Cyril Onwubiko
Research Series Limited, UK

Thomas John Owens
Brunel University, UK

ABSTRACT

The importance of situational awareness to air traffic control, and hence the safety and security of aircraft, is evident, demonstrable, and has been hugely significant. The main purpose of this book is to convey an understanding of the impact of situational awareness on the design of the next generation computer systems, network architectures, and platform infrastructures. The book achieves its purpose by presenting principles, methods, and applications of situational awareness for computer network defense; in doing so, it makes clear the benefits situational awareness can provide for information security, computer security and computer network defense. This book contributes to cross-multidisciplinary discussion among researchers, academia, and practitioners who are engaged objectively in sharing, contributing, and showcasing how situational awareness can be adapted to computer systems, network infrastructure designs, and architecture patterns. The goal of this chapter is to explain situational awareness for computer network defense from the point of view of its most basic foundations as a spring board to discuss how situational awareness can be relevant to computer network defense, whose operations and environment are similar to air traffic control where the application of situational awareness has been hugely successful.

SITUATION AWARENESS

Situation awareness (SA) is made up of two words 'situation' and 'awareness'. According to Chambers 21st Century Dictionary (Chambers, 1997), *Situation* (noun) is defined as:

1. A set of circumstances or state of affairs.
2. A place, position or location.
3. A job; employment. Example, *situations vacant*.
4. A critical point in the action of a play or in the development of the plot of a novel.

DOI: 10.4018/978-1-4666-0104-8.ch001

Situational is *adjective of situation*. **ETY-MOLOGY:** 15c. *Awareness* (noun) is defined as the fact or state of being aware, or conscious, especially of matters that are particularly relevant or topical (Chambers 1997). Putting these two words together, we define *Situational Awareness* as the state of being aware of circumstances that exist around us, especially those that are particularly relevant to us and which we are interested about. By this definition, situational awareness means, as people, we seek to be aware of situations around us, particularly those that we are interested in. For example:

- Every driver wants to know about obstacles along their way, especially those that may lead to an accident. For instance, when reversing, drivers usually look into the rear and side mirrors of their car to ensure they are aware of any impeding situation, for instance objects, or obstacles, or onward moving vehicles so as to be apprised of the risk of such situations and avoid them.
- A nursing mother wants to maintain situational awareness of the environment which her crawling baby is in, especially; she wants to keep the baby away from any objects that can be of harm to the baby such as breakable (glass) cups, scissors, photo frames, table knives, etc.
- Politicians want to be aware of how popular their government is, for instance, by checking what the polls say. Moreover they do this especially when new legislation or bills have been passed.
- In computer network security and information security organizations want to be aware of the vulnerabilities of their assets and weaknesses that may exist in the mechanisms used to protect their assets, and the risks that may result should vulnerabilities be exploited. More importantly, organizations want to know about the vulnerabilities of assets which if exploited could have

a significant or even catastrophic impact on the organization.
- In computer network defense the mission (agency or organization) wants to be aware of the vulnerabilities that may exist in its systems and any weakness that may exist in the systems defense controls, including possible threats and threat actors (such as, foreign intelligence services) that may be interested in compromising, breaching or circumventing its defense systems and wants to be aware of the motivation and capability of such threat actors.

Evolution of SA Definitions

Recorded accounts of SA definitions began in the mid 1980s, but the use of the term 'SA' can be traced back to World War I. This is not surprising, because as one samples through some of the existing SA definitions in the literature, one realizes that situational awareness's foundational development stems from psychology, human factors and military warfare operations. For example, Hamilton 1987, Endsley 1988, Regal et al. 1988, Beringer and Hancock 1989, Taylor 1990, Carol 1992, Vidulich 1994, Billings 1995, and Endsley 1995 all defined SA in relation to human factors, pilots, aviation, warfare and air traffic control (ATC).

A general purpose definition of SA, we believe, was provided in 1998. According to Endsley (1998), SA describes "the perception of the elements in the environment within a volume of time and space, the comprehension of their meaning and the projection of their status in the near future". This definition has become the most quoted, cited and accepted definition for situational awareness, alongside Endsley's (Endsley 1995b) proposed abstract model for situation awareness (See Figure 1) which has since been extended by McGuinness and Foy (2000) to include a fourth level of situational awareness called *Resolution*.

Figure 1. Network security situation awareness model (Onwubiko, 2011b)

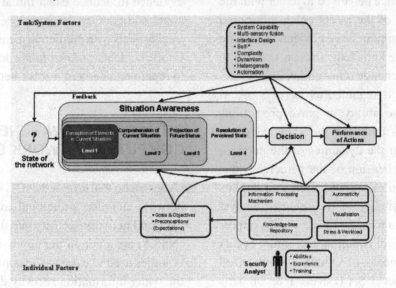

It was not until recently that the application of SA to Cyber security, information security, network computer security and computer network defence (CND) began to emerge, Grégoire and Beaudoin, 2005, Lefebvre et al, 2005, Onwubiko, 2009, Jajodia et al. 2009, and Barford et al, 2009.

Figure 1 is adapted from Endsley's situation awareness reference model (Endsley, 1995b), which presents three levels of situation awareness, *perception*, *comprehension* and *projection*. In addition McGuinness and Foy's (2000) extension of Endsley's SA model includes *resolution* as a fourth level of situation awareness.

- **Perception** is regarded as Level 1 SA. In relation to CND, perception refers to knowledge of the elements in the network that security analysts (operators) must be aware of, such as alerts reported by intrusion detection systems, firewall logs, scan reports, as well as the time these pieces of security evidence occurred and the specific controls that reported the alerts or generated the logs (Onwubiko, 2009). Perception also relates to observed and unprocessed low-level data. According to Salerno et al

(2004), *perception* provides information about the status, attributes and dynamics of the relevant elements in the environment. It extends the classification of information into meaningful representations that offer the basis for comprehension, projection and resolution.

- **Comprehension** is regarded as Level 2 SA. To understand the true nature of the perceived threats, and ascertain the threat level, security logs and alerts must be analysed, assessed and synthesized. At the comprehension level, a number of techniques, methodologies, processes and procedures are used by security analysts to analyze, synthesize, correlate and aggregate pieces of evidence perceived in the network in order to deduce the level of perceived threats or to determine if the network has been compromised. Hence, *comprehension* involves a determination of the relevance of the pieces of evidence captured to the underlying goal of resolution of the situation (Salerno et al, 2004). Thus, comprehension offers an up-to-date picture of the current situation by determining the significance of the evidence perceived together with the importance of the assets being monitored so that when new sets of evidence become available the knowledge-base is updated to reflect this change (Onwubiko, 2009).

- **Projection** is regarded as Level 3 SA. It refers to the ability to make predictions or forecasts based on the knowledge extracted from the dynamics of the network and comprehension of the perceived situation (Onwubiko, 2009). Hence, it implies the responsibility of the security analyst (operator) to forecast future events, or predict patterns of occurrence of future events based on pieces of evidence synthesized from low level SA (Levels 1 & 2). This enables decision makers and security analysts to forecast future network states and provide preventive controls to address potential situations. In this respect, *Projection* tries to answer questions such as, what network attacks are possible on our network? And what controls may be needed to address, prevent, or respond to such attacks should vulnerabilities be exploited?

- **Resolution** is regarded as Level 4 SA. It refers to applicable and possible countermeasure controls required to manage risks inherent in or dependent on the networks being monitored. *Resolution* was first discussed in situation awareness by McGuinness and Foy, 2000 as an extension to Endsley's SA abstract model. Resolution is concerned with the provision of the necessary actions and controls required to resolve a perceived network situation.

These terms (*perception, comprehension, projection* and *resolution*) are discussed in this chapter in relation to situational awareness for computer network defence (Cyber SA).

In summary, *perception* deals with the gathering of evidence of situations in the network, *comprehension* deals with the analysis of sets of

evidence to deduce exact threat levels, types of attack and associated or interdependent risks. *Projection* deals with predictive measures to estimate future incidents, and *resolution* deals with controls to repair, recover and resolve network situations.

SITUATIONAL AWARENESS FOR COMPUTER NETWORK DEFENSE

Cyber situational awareness (Cyber SA), computer network defence situational awareness (CND SA), and network security situational awareness (NSSA) are some of the newly emerging terminologies used to express the application of SA to the wider information security domain.

Situational awareness is described as knowing what is going on around you and with that knowledge of your surroundings being able to identify which events in those surroundings are important. SA is very complex and involves very dynamic states, e.g. of a computer network with hundreds of network objects (firewalls, IDSs, routers, switches, servers, PADs etc). Maintaining a consistently high level of situational awareness over these objects can be challenging (Onwubiko and Owens, 2010). Thus, the underpinning of situational awareness in computer networks is to assist operators to identify adversaries, estimate impact of attacks, evaluate risks, understand situations and make sound decisions on how best to protect valued assets swiftly and accurately (Onwubiko, 2009). By this proposition, we believe that, the application of SA to CND will yield unprecedented benefits akin to SA for safety and security in aircraft, flight operation, ATC and safety controls.

In many respects, SA is comparable to the OODA (observe, orient, deduce and act) loop (Onwubiko, 2011b). The OODA decision control was first proposed by Boyd, (1987) for use in Command and Control (C2) environments. This means operators need to observe network situations, evaluate the situation, deduce the impact it may have and decide possible mitigation controls to effectively and accurately address the situation. By continually following the OODA loop, an operator or group of operators are able to act in accordance to the situation they are in. The operator may use technology, in this case protective monitoring, interfaces, HCI interactions, and other methods, (see Onwubiko, 2011b) to enhance situational awareness of the network being monitored and then decide the best possible cause of action to be taken.

Whether SA or OODA, the approach for CND is:

- First, the network should be monitored by trained and experienced network security operators;
- Second, these operators through the use of tools and technologies are able to observe, analyse and resolve abnormal situations (faults, errors and attacks) in the network;
- Third, operator SA is enhanced through the use of technologies that are swift and accurate in processing and analysis of perceived situations in networks. Thus, operators gain enhanced situational awareness of the environment by monitoring networks and ensuring network activities (alerts, logs, volumetric statistics and abnormal behaviour) are visualised, whilst using techniques (correlation and fusion techniques) that are able to combine and analyze data from a number of distributed sensors deployed in and around the network;
- Fourth, using their mental models (past knowledge of network behaviours, experience and training) operators are able to make projections about future network states. For example, based on observed network traffic and volumetric statistics an experienced operator could make an accurate estimation of when the network is under attack from an evolving computer worm mutant or variants of self-propagating malicious code.

BACKGROUND

Computer crimes around the world cost organisations and governments billions of dollars each year. In response, organisations use a plethora of heterogeneous security devices and software such as firewalls, Intrusion Detection Systems (IDS), Security Information and Event Management (SIEM) to monitor networks in conjunction with Computer Security Incident Response Teams (CSIRT), that are responsible for ensuring availability, integrity and confidentiality of network services. Their primary challenge is to maintain situational awareness over many critical network objects some of which include critical national infrastructures, the impact of a cyber attack on which could result in a breakdown in national communications networks or essential support services, which may impact on citizens' safety or livelihoods. Maintaining consistent high-level situational awareness over such objects requires that the CSIRT has the knowledge and ability to perceive and analyse situations that may have security related implications, make sound decisions on how to protect organisations' valued assets and offer accurate predictions of future states in dynamic and complex environments. This is the underpinning of situational awareness in computer network defence (Onwubiko, 2009).

In the last fifteen years the application of SA has been revolutionary, particularly in ATC, Defence and Military operations where SA has been extensively researched. ATC operation, for instance, can be compared to CND operation; unfortunately, while the application of SA to CND is still in its embryonic stage, its application to ATC is mainstream (Onwubiko, 2009).

Computer Network Defense

Cyber attacks on computer networks are growing and evolving. For example, from code-driven attacks, deliberate malicious software attacks, espionage, distributed denial of service attacks,

5

Table 1. ATC compared to CND

Features	ATC	CND
Human operator	Service is provided by ground-based controllers (human operators) who direct aircraft on the ground and in the air	Service is provided by security analysts (human operators) who monitor systems and networks for abnormal traffic, behaviour, signs, events and alerts
Goal	Primary goal is to prevent aircraft collisions, organize and expedite the flow of traffic and to provide information and other support to the pilot when required	Primary goals are to ensure systems and networks are protected, and services are availability to users or consumers when required.
Activities	Requires information of varying nature ranging from weather information to longitudinal and latitudinal information (location information)	Requires information on the ICT systems being infected, and the sensors or defence systems that detected the issue. For example, an IDS (intrusion detection system) detected an intrusion against a critical asset
Information	Issue instruction that pilots are required to follow or mere flight advisory to assist pilots operate in the airspace	Provide information to the organisation (security manager) about perceived threat level, on-going attacks and risks, so that the manager can advise on CoA (cause of action)
Security	Provide security or defence role to the aircraft	Provide security and defence function for the organisation by ensuring alerts, event and attacks are identified, addressed and resolved.
Use of Technology	Uses collision avoidance systems, GPS (global positioning systems), GIS (Geographic information systems), GNSS (Global Navigation Satellite System) and location tracking and monitoring systems to inform the pilot of changing weather conditions, incoming aircraft and navigation information and NOTAMs (NOtices To Air Men)	Uses IDS, firewall, AV (anti-virus), sensors, guards file and log integrity violation tracker and security event and information monitoring systems to monitor the systems and networks
Environment	Usually dynamic and complex in nature involving the monitoring and coordination of various activities such as weather information, collision avoidance information, ground-based activities and air-based activities, which require swift and instantaneous response	Usually dynamic and complex in nature. Involving monitoring of a myriad of toolkits used to monitor the network such as protective monitoring of servers, traffic utilisation, network traffic (normal and abnormal), threshold and threat and vulnerability advisories including intelligence about threat actors.
Coordination	Controller coordinates numerous other operators who assist to ensure that the ATC operations are successful, such as GIS technicians, backroom and backoffice operators, pilots, flight crews etc.	Security analysts work with security administrators, network engineers, system support and IT support to ensure that systems and network infrastructure of the mission is protected.
Impact	Failure to coordinate ATC operations and activities leads to significant impact, first aircraft will not be allowed to fly, and those already in the air may witness severe disruption in service and accidents may occur as a result.	Failure to monitor network and systems will impact the organisation as security incidents may not be resolved, this may impact service level agreements, resulting in significant financial penalties, and consequently putting the network at risk.

phishing to the recent computer electronics attacks, such as Stuxnet. All these contribute to demonstrate how complex and challenging the CND environment is (Onwubiko, 2008).

CND is a growing field which is geared towards measures to protect and defend computer networks and information systems from cyber attacks that could cause disruption, denial of service, degradation and destruction (Onwubiko and Owens, 2010). A CND environment is one that ensures that vulnerabilities that exist in computer networks are addressed, threats to the environment are identified and controls and risks inherent to this environment are managed to an acceptable level in relation to the organisation (Onwubiko, 2011b).

Figure 2 is a basic model of a CND environment. It shows that security mechanisms (such as a firewall) can be decomposed into several sub-security mechanisms, such as an access control list (ACL), and that the security mechanisms contribute to achieving the protection objectives (such as allow only authorised access). However, security threats can lead to the compromise of or breach of security features by threat actors exploiting vulnerabilities that may exist in assets. The security administrator (operator) who monitors the CND environment must maintain situational awareness over these systems, which in itself is demanding and challenging, however, the operator shall assess the existence of vulnerabilities in the protection of assets, and whether existing vulnerabilities can be exploited. The operator must check if protection objectives are achieved, and whether security features can be breached, compromised or violated. Finally, the operator must assess the impacts threats may have should a security attack be realised.

One of the primary purposes of CND is to ensure that systems and networks are secure, reliable and operational. This includes actions taken via computer networks to protect, monitor, analyse, detect and respond to cyber attacks, computer network intrusions, disruptions or other perceived unauthorized actions that could compromise or impact network defense and information systems. CND is achieved through a collective effort by personnel (a.k.a. 'human' operators) who monitor, manage and maintain defence systems, networks and infrastructures, such as network operators, security analysts, systems administrators and network engineers. These personnel are faced with the onerous tasks of coordinating, maintaining, monitoring and ensuring the necessary actions required in keeping defence systems and network infrastructures operational, whilst ensuring that appropriate protection from cyber-attacks is provided on a daily basis (Onwubiko, 2011).

CONCLUSION

The goal of this chapter is to explain situational awareness for computer network defense from the point of view of its foundations and use this as a spring board to discuss how SA can be relevant to CND whose operations and environment are similar to ATC where the application of SA has been hugely successful.

Figure 2. Operator monitors a CND environment

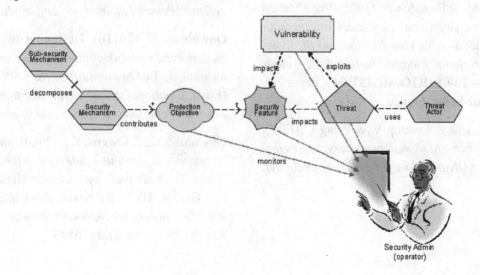

REFERENCES

Barford, P., Dacier, M., Dietterich, T. G., Fredrikson, M., Giffin, J., & Jha, S. … Yen, J. (2009). Cyber SA: Situational awareness for cyber defense. In S. Jajodia, P. Liu V. Swarup & C. Wang (Eds.), *Cyber situational awareness: Issues and research (Advances in information security)*.

Boyd, J. (1987). *Organic design for command and control*. Presentation Slides, May 1987. Retrieved from www.ausairpower.net/JRB/organic_design.ppt

Chambers Dictionary. (1997). *Chambers 21ˢᵗ century dictionary*. Retrieved from http://www.chambersharrap.co.uk/chambers/features/chref/chref.py/main

Endsley, M. R. (1995b). Toward a theory of situation awareness in dynamic systems. *Human Factors Journal, 37*(1), 32–64. doi:10.1518/001872095779049543

Endsley, M. R. (2000). Errors in situation assessment: Implications for system design. In Elzer, P. F. K. R. H. B. B. (Ed.), *Human error and system design and management (Lecture Notes in Control and Information Sciences (Vol. 253, pp. 15–26)*. London, UK: Springer-Verlag. doi:10.1007/BFb0110451

Grégoire, M., & Beaudoin, L. (2005). Visualisation for network situational awareness in computer network defence. In *Visualisation and the Common Operational Picture Meeting Proceedings* (pp. 20-1 – 20-6). (RTO-MP-IST-043, Paper 20). Neuilly-sur-Seine, France.

Jajodia, S., Liu, P., Swarup, V., & Wang, C. (Eds.). (2009). *Cyber situational awareness: Issues and research (Advances in information security)*. Springer.

Lefebvre, J. H., Grégoire, M., Beaudoin, L., & Froh, M. (2005). *Computer network defence situational awareness*. Information Requirements, Defence R&D Canada – Ottawa, Technical Memorandum, DRDC Ottawa TM 2005-254, December 2005.

McGuinness and L. Foy. (2000). A subjective measure of SA: The crew awareness rating scale (CARS). *Proceeding of the First Human Performance, Situation Awareness, and Automation Conference, Savannah, Georgia, 2000*.

Onwubiko, C. (2008). Data fusion in security evidence analysis. *Proceeding of the 3rd International Conference on Computer Security and Forensics, 2008*.

Onwubiko, C. (2008). *Security framework for attack detection in computer networks*. VDM Verlag.

Onwubiko, C. (2009). *Functional requirements of situational awareness in computer network security*. IEEE International Conference on Intelligence and Security Informatics, ISI '09, Dallas, TX, USA, 8-11 June 2009.

Onwubiko, C. (2011). Modeling situation awareness information and system requirements for the mission using goal-oriented task analysis approach. In Onwubiko, C., & Owens, T. J. (Eds.), *Situational awareness in computer network defense: Principles, methods and applications*.

Onwubiko, C. (2011b). Designing Information Systems and network components for situational awareness. In Onwubiko, C., & Owens, T. J. (Eds.), *Situational awareness in computer network defense: Principles, methods and applications*.

Onwubiko, C., & Owens, T. J. (2010). *Situational awareness in computer network defence: Principles, methods and applications*. Hershey, PA: IGI Global, USA. Retrieved from http://www.wikicfp.com/cfp/servlet/event.showcfp?eventid=11783&copyownerid=16539

Salerno, J., Hinman, M., & Boulware, D. (2004). *Building a framework for situation awareness. AFRL/IFEA*. Rome, NY: AF Research Lab.

Tadda, G. P., & Salerno, J. S. (2009). Overview of cyber situation awareness. In *Cyber situational awareness: Issues and research (Advances in information security)*. Springer.

Wang, H., Liu, X., Lai, J., & Liang, Y. (2007). Network security situation awareness based on heterogeneous multi-sensor data fusion and neural network, *Second International Multi-Symposiums on Computer and Computational Sciences. IMSCCS, 2007*, 352–359.

Chapter 2
The Contributions of Information Security Culture and Human Relations to the Improvement of Situational Awareness

Janne Merete Hagen
Norwegian Defence Research Establishment, Norway

ABSTRACT

The chapter gives an overview of business practices and how people and human relations influence situational awareness and information security in an organization. There is still a long way to go in training employees in information security and improving employees' information security awareness. Motivated and trained employees have the ability to detect and report security weaknesses and breaches, including near-miss incidents, and in this way, they may provide a valuable defense-in-depth-capability that is often lacking. The chapter discusses two approaches to overcome the barriers to building situational awareness promulgated in the general deterrence theory and socio-technical theory.

INTRODUCTION

While the internet exposes our computer networks to threats from all over the world, it is still insiders that are considered to be the greatest threat to information security, either alone or in combination with people outside the organization. Insiders can be trusted people like employees, hired consultants and sub-contractors. These persons and trusted people have much easier access to computers and IT systems than outsiders. Both US reports about insider threats (e.g. Keeney, Kowaski, Capelli, Moore, Shimeall and Rogers, 2005) and the Norwegian Computer Crime Surveys (NCCS, 2006; Hagen, 2007) document a significant threat to an organization's IT systems from insiders like employees that should not be neglected. Insider threats are likely to increase in the coming years

DOI: 10.4018/978-1-4666-0104-8.ch002

as the number of people using social networks is expanding. Personal preferences, interests and relations are published; this facilitates more than ever social engineering attacks, including automated social engineering attacks (Huber, Kowalski, Nohlberg and Tjoa, 2009).

The question is what can be done in order to detect and mitigate the threats from inside? There are two ways to deal with the insider threat: By searching research databases and scientific articles we find that the most common approach is to regard insiders as malicious or unintentional threats and by technical and administrative means restrict their access rights in accordance with the-need-to-know principle. They are given just as much access as needed, and nothing more than this. Their actions are also supervised and logged. This regime will restrict their freedom and their opportunities to commit illicit actions without detection, and subsequently reduce the risk of failures and vulnerability to malicious actions. If an insider should commit an illegal action, then that breach will be reported to the police. This approach is in line with the general deterrence theory, which is a well established social theory explaining activities that deviate from accepted norms and emphasizes disincentives. According to this theory, potential offenders will refrain from illicit actions if the risk of being subjected to disciplinary action is high and the punishment severe (Straub, Carlson and Jones, 1992). The effectiveness of the disincentives depends on the applied sanctions and punishment. The other approach focuses on employees and regards them as a resource as opposed to a threat. Here, employees are considered to be loyal to the company and constitute a defense capability against malicious attacks and illegal actions. While the first approach has strong relations with the general deterrence theory, the latter approach is linked to the social-technical theory which is more common in Scandinavia. The socio-technical theory emphasizes: the development of humane working conditions, employee participation, and democracy. The roots

go back to the 1950s and the close link between technical aspects and the social systems in British coal mines (Trist and Bambort, 1951). The social-technical theory takes a positive view of humans and their contributions, in stark contrast to the negative view taken by Taylor with respect to a more scientific form of management (Taylor, 1911). It is the socio-technical view that influenced the development of industrial democracy that is widespread in the Scandinavian countries.

How these two theories relate to information security becomes clearer if we study roles of human beings within the context of information security. Human beings as insiders can adopt different roles in organizations, spanning from good to unfortunate and malicious. The two theoretical approaches offer advice on mitigating measures and how to influence security awareness and behaviour, and as this chapter will show, the socio-technical theory approach has a broader application than the general deterrence theory.

The detection and reporting of incidents and near-miss incidents is one key to increasing situational awareness. In order to detect and report abnormalities, normal conditions and security requirements must be well known among all employees. Employees and other insiders must therefore be educated to see, and react, if they observe anything abnormal. There must also be guidelines or instructions on what is permitted and what is not. Trust among management and employees is also necessary in combination with the acceptance that everyone can make an occasional mistake or error. Ideally, the reporting of incidents and near-miss incidents should be a normal activity, guiding and aiding security managers in reducing the risk of serious failures and malicious attacks. The way towards building a human situational awareness capability is however both curved and narrow. Several barriers must be overcome. Nevertheless many managers are not aware of these barriers or else they are stuck behind them themselves. While most organizations have emphasized the implementation of technical security measures and building a formal organization with policies and routines, the human element appears to have been neglected. This is exemplified by the fact that merely half of all Norwegian enterprises give some kind of education or training in information security to their employees, and while there is a significant difference between large and small enterprises when it comes to application of technical-administrative measures, it is not the case for education and training of employees with respect to situational awareness.

The objectives of the chapter are first to give an overview of business security practices and the barriers that must be overcome in order to raise situational awareness, and second to present and discuss how situational awareness in organizations can be improved through educating employees and developing in them and the organization a sound security culture.

BACKGROUND

What does the Literature tell us about Insiders?

Insiders are trusted persons. They can be employees, partners, managers, or consultants; anyone who has access to sensitive information and knowledge about computer and IT systems. Indeed, employees, previous employees, vendors, and customers are said to be responsible for 70% of the losses of sensitive information. However, due to the sensitivity of this information, the loss of information is not reported (Boni and Kovacich, 2000). The insiders' role is also confirmed by the Norwegian Computer Crime Survey (2006), which documents that about half of the detected incidents were committed by insiders. The consequences of insider attacks are claimed to be worse than the consequences of external attacks (Baker, Hylender and Valentine, 2008). One famous insider attack was the Omega Engineering case. In mid-1996, three weeks after Omega's degraded computer

systems manager Tim Lloyd was fired, all of the programs running the company's manufacturing machines were erased. The attack resulted in eighty workers being laid off, two million dollars spent in reprogramming, and a loss of 10 million dollars in other expenses and lost sales. The jury in Lloyd's trial found him guilty of sabotaging Omega's network. This was the first U.S. federal criminal prosecution of a computer sabotage case (Jones, Kowacich and Luswich, 2002). Since then, many cases of computer sabotage have been reported to the police around the world.

Because newer operating systems such as Windows Vista have more embedded security than the old ones, the old methods of compromising computers through networks have become more difficult, while social engineering attacks against IT-users have increased. In this context, it is unrealistic to expect that the average IT-user will understand all the security mechanisms and numerous accompanying configurations. Rather, the IT-users should learn to manage attacks at the cognitive level, because when technological measures fail, system users become the last line of defense. They must be able to identify an incident when a system is attacked (Biros, 2004). To date, however, most research in information security has been directed towards security technologies; thus more research is required to study the relation between information security and the human factor (Sipponen, 2007). In this chapter the human factor is understood as being humans and their impact on information security and situational awareness through their knowledge, attitude and behaviour.

The human factor can have an influence upon information security. *Information security* has moved away from its strict technical image and now includes a wide range of facets; organizational, technical, legal etc., all of which must be considered in creating a secure environment (Von Solms, 2001). In the Information Security Management Standards ISO/IEC 27001 and ISO/IEC 27002, information security is based on three integral elements: confidentiality, integrity and availability. The standard provides a list of different controls that can be implemented and advises also on how to establish and run a process with a steady focus on risk management, continual improvement, change management and management commitment, all of which are important for information security and situational awareness. Among the different controls, particularly four of them are relevant in building situational awareness:

- **An Information Security Policy** should be approved and reviewed by the management, published and communicated to employees and other collaborating partners. The policy should be in accordance with business objectives and relevant laws and regulations.
- **Organization of information security** covers the following important issues: management commitment, the authorization process and confidentiality agreements, coordination, roles and job functions, the maintenance of contact with authorities and independent review.
- **Human Resources Security**: documentation in accordance with the organization's policy on employee roles and responsibilities, background check, terms and conditions of employment including responsibilities with respect to information security, training and disciplinary processes, and termination of employment.
- **Information Security Incident Management:** this important topic is about reporting and reacting to security weakness and security violations. This control also covers learning from the incidents through monitoring and evaluation of lessons learnt.

Several authors have studied the effectiveness of the policy on information security. The effectiveness of the policy is dependent on the way the security content is addressed in the policy document and how the content is communicated to the users (Höne and Eloff, 2002). Thompson and von Solms (2006) add that effectiveness is created when a policy is adopted by employees in practical situations. Karyda, Kiountouzis, and Kokolakis (2005) claim that the criterion for success is having a coherent policy in which employees follow a code of best practice, or alternatively, a corporate culture in which employees participate in security work.

The importance of properly educating IT-users in information security is emphasized by several authors. People are an important resource in assuring information security, as the success of an information security programme depends on the commitment of all IT-users. If this commitment is not in place, the security mechanisms could be bypassed or diminished by the employees (Ward and Smith, 2002; Schneier, 2000). Measures that are designed for the purpose of improving skills and knowledge consist of either experience-based learning activities or systematic training and education. The former involve learning by personal on-the-job-experience; the latter involve learning through participation in formal education (Hale and Glendon, 1987). Research shows that most people learn better by actually being involved and doing a particular job than by sitting in a classroom listening to a lecturer (Wang and Yestko, 2005).

Identifying and measuring abuse by insiders can be done by applying both leading and lagging indicators. Lagging indicators are measurements of a system taken after the incident has occurred. They measure outcomes and occurrences (Grabowski et al, 2007; Beatham et al, 2004). In contrast, leading indicators aim to measure events that precede an undesirable event and have some value in predicting the occurrence of the event. Leading and lagging indicators differ in granularity and focus. Leading indicators often have a focus on an individual and perhaps departmental level, while lagging indicators have their focus on the company or site level (Grabowski et al, 2007).

A typical leading indicator would be a change in employees' attitudes or behaviour that could precede for instance computer crime. If colleagues observe such a change and report it, the reporting could work as an early warning signal to the security manager and a positive contribution to the organization's overall situational awareness. Such early warnings could also contribute to increasing the resilience of the organization, enabling the organization to react before an incident occurs.

The Human Factor in Information Security: Six Roles

Human beings can take six roles in relation to information security (Hagen, 2009). The first role is that of a resource person and contributor, the one positive role that is very important to nurture and develop in relation to situational awareness. In this role, both tacit and explicit knowledge of threat characteristics and IT vulnerabilities constitute important assets for detecting security breaches and system weaknesses. The ensuing five roles regard humans as a negative contributor and a threat to information security. In role two, it is humans who cause unintentional failures. The role is partly explained by human nature itself and by a lack of competence and awareness. The third role deals with how humans handle conflicting goals. At work, security is usually a secondary goal. That is, people do not usually sit down for the purpose of managing security. Rather, they typically intend to send emails, browse web pages, or download software, and they want security in place to protect them while they do those things (Whitten and Tygar, 2005). IT users will overlook or ignore security concerns when such tasks interfere with or prohibit the completion of their work tasks; such omissions simply make it easier to do their job (Besnard and Arief, 2004). The fourth role occurs in situations where employees are victims of social engineering attacks, such as when a hacker manipulates the natural human tendency to trust and thereby deceives and tricks them into giving away access to, or actual confidential information (Mitnick, 2002). Human's ability to detect deception is poor, estimated to 18% by the researchers Qin and Burgoon (2007). They explain this poor ability first of all by the humans' tendency to normally trust others because honest behaviour is most frequently observed, secondly, by humans' stereotypical thinking and finally by the processing ability with an embedded lack of ability to systemic thinking. While hacking into a computer may be considered an illegal action, using a phone to ask for sensitive information is not illegal. In that case, it is the informant and not the caller who breaks the law. It is a combination of factors that facilitates the attack: a lack of security awareness, including a lack of understanding of the value of information, and weak plans, procedures and controls to protect information (Winkler, 1996). The fifth role is that of an opportunistic hacker or a disgruntled employee who wants attention, revenge, or to cover vandalism or gain personal profit (Keeney, Kowalski, Capelli, Moore, Shimeall, and Rogers, 2005). These researchers studied forty-nine incidents that were carried out between 1996 and 2002 across critical infrastructure sectors. They purposely limited cases to those in which an insider's primary goal was to sabotage some aspect of the organization or to cause direct specific harm of an individual. Their study revealed that a negative work-related event had triggered most of the insiders' actions. The sixth and final role is that of a planted spy or attacker. One famous industrial espionage case in the US was when Hitachi tried to get an IBM employee to sell the drawings for a next generation computer (Boni and Kovacich, 2000). Other examples are criminals placing agents in security companies to explore the security routines of money transportations and the famous leakage of secret documents to Wiki Leaks.

The challenge is that on one hand one must trust insiders to get the job done, and normally trusted people are loyal. But people can fill different roles, and it takes just one disloyal person or one unfortunate incident to commit a security breach.

The general deterrence theory is the most commonly applied approach within information security. But it is the socio-technical theory that covers broadest with regard to the six roles. It is through initiatives such as empowerment, involvement, education, training and motivation that the human mind and way of thinking can be altered and loyalty established and nurtured. Sanctions and punishment work only in some cases. However, it should also be stated that both approaches are needed. As this chapter will describe, today's management approach is mainly based on the socio-technical theory, but for many cases it fails with respect to all the factors mentioned above: empowerment, involvement, education, training and motivation of employees in the matter of information security. It is also a paradox in this context that while there is a lot of research on the humans' malicious side of information security, much less research has been done on how insiders and in particular employees can become a resource and a capability for building situational awareness. This chapter endeavours to close some of that gap.

The literature provides some recommendations on how to improve situational awareness and information security. Two approaches are in particular relevant. The first is inspired by quality management and ISO standards (ISO 27001 and ISO 27002) and the second by the Health, Safety and Environment field. Both approaches include advice on how to reduce unwanted incidents and the subsequent risk. In both regimes humans are considered an important resource in increasing situational awareness through the reporting of incidents and near-miss incidents.

HUMANS AS A SITUATIONAL AWARENESS CAPABILITY

Current Practices

Modern societies make extensive use of financial, commercial- and news services on the Internet. Almost all households have access to the Internet and are connected to the Internet by broadband. The development of computers and the growth of the Internet have changed the way we live and work, but they have also exposed the population and enterprises to new risks. Remote working and outsourcing of IT systems give new opportunities for businesses, but introduces new risks as well, and situational awareness thus becomes increasingly more important. Charles Perrow (1984) introduced the notion of the risk society and described large-scale accidents. He demonstrates that failures are inevitable due to the complexity of large systems such as airplanes and chemical plants and close interconnections. The human factor and the different roles human beings can take within information security add complexity to this. What strategies do enterprises choose to use to mitigate the broad specter of risks?

The Norwegian Computer Crime Survey (2006) addresses a number of different security measures spanning from technical to organizational measures including the education of employees. Analyzing the 749 answers from the 2006 survey reveals two important tendencies. First, it is a trend that large enterprises have implemented more security measures than smaller concerns. This is not surprising due to the increased complexity of large organizations. Large organizations also possess more resources. Another obvious pattern is that the use of mature preventive measures is more widespread than measures that tend to detect and react if incidents occur. The same tendency may also be observed in outsourcing practices: Liability and sanctions are rarely embedded in outsourcing contracts, in contrast to preventive measures. This makes the buyer vulnerable to potential failures and weaknesses of the outsourcing partners. These findings can also be connected with the low percentage of enterprises which have routines for calculating the economic losses from computer crime. Compensation for potential losses is not emphasized. A few organizational security measures are emphasized in the survey and these are used in a lesser extent compared to many preventive security technologies. User education and exercises in particular are implemented by few enterprises. Compared with good security principles such as defense in breadth and depth, the results reveal holes in corporate security strategies, particularly in depth behind the security perimeter. Furthermore, organizational measures have inherent weaknesses as few enterprises train or educate their employees in information security (Hagen, 2007).

The study of Hagen, Albrechtsen and Hovden (2008) confirmed that enterprises participating in the study have emphasized developing and applying formal systems such as security policies, procedures and controls, whereas awareness creating activities are less applied in the organizations. This indicates a formal, mechanical view on information security as argued by Dhillon and Backhouse (2001). The study also reveals the following paradox: The least implemented of the security measures, the creation of information security awareness, is assessed to be the most effective group of organizational measures. Technical-administrative measures such as policy, procedures, control and administrative tools are the most implemented measures, but are at the same time assessed to have lower effectiveness than awareness creation. There is an inverse relationship between the implementation of organizational information security measures and how the effectiveness of the measures is assessed.

Lack of Incident Reporting and Situational Awareness

The most difficult questions for the Norwegian Computer Crime Survey 2006 respondents to answer are related to estimates of security incidents in the last 12 months. Questions have been raised about the validity of the numbers. Security incidents are sensitive data, and accurate reporting would require a high degree of situational awareness in the whole organization as well as a reporting system and a culture for information safety. Few enterprises register incidents systematically. This combined with the fact that few enterprises have their logs frequently checked or have implemented Intrusion Detection Systems, and only half of the enterprises provide some introduction or training of their employees in information security, indicate that far from all incidents are detected. The Norwegian computer crime surveys state that the "dark numbers" are probably higher than the result of the survey shows. The non-transparency of electronic communication and the cyberspace makes it possible to distribute sensitive information to unauthorized recipients without leaving visible foot prints for the management under attack. The only way they might detect that something is amiss is perhaps through reduced market shares or identity thefts. Hagen, Sivertsen and Rong (2008) discuss this challenge with incident reporting. The visible incidents are those that are reported to the police. The Norwegian Computer Crime Survey (2006) estimates that there must be a number of unrecorded cases of computer crime based on the survey results. These are incidents that the IT staff and managers detect and report through the survey. We can regard this as partly visible, but what about all the incidents that are never detected, even by IT staff and management or employees, due to a lack of awareness? While only 11 incidents of abuse are reported to the police as a criminal offence, the survey registered 8900 IT abuse incidents. Correspondingly we have 61 hacking incidents reported to the police in contrast to 3900 hacking incidents reported through the survey. What about the undetected incidents that occur that no one is aware of? They probably constitute the majority of incidents, including numerous near-miss incidents. Hagen and Spilling (2009) explain that the low rate of reporting follows from employees that deal with incidents personally or just neglect them. The following reasons are given for this kind of behaviour: Employees are reluctant to report a colleague because they lack knowledge, they judge the consequences to be too small or the incident to not be malicious. Also, when employees fear the personal consequences of reporting an incident or if the manager is the perpetrator, they refrain from reporting. Increased situational awareness could help visualizing the risks, both near-miss and real incidents. While formal technical-administrative procedures may increase the organization's ability to detect threats to security, this is not a sufficient condition to reduce the risk. There is still the human dimension to consider, and the next section deals with some barriers that employees must get through in order to report the detected near-miss and real incidents.

The Cultural Challenges, Knowledge, Attitudes and Actions

The role of employees in the internalization of security policies and procedures is studied by Hagen (2009). Comparative case studies were conducted in four organizations, of which two were private and two were public and all were regulated by the Norwegian Security Act. A total of 74 employees were interviewed.

The Norwegian Security Act requires the existence of a formal security organization with a security manager and a data security manager. The informal organization, which consists of the relationship among the contributing members of the organization and their actual behaviour, is however more difficult to study. But it can be done through interviews and personal observations.

Since all four organizations in the Hagen study (2009) fall legally under the Norwegian Security Act, it can be expected that their security measures will comply with the multi-level security regime required by the act. However, the study documented differences in how the four organizations had adapted and implemented their organizational security policies. While all four organizations required employees to know the company's security instructions and security organizations and report security breaches, the practical implementation varied with respect to the ways measures pertaining to computer security, internet publication of private information, participation in internet societies and how protection against human-to-human information leakages were dealt with. In all organizations new employees had to meet personally with the security manager for a security brief; in addition to this, security was included in the organizations' introductory programme, which all employees were required to attend. In general the study showed that for the most part, employees have good attitudes and intentions to comply with the security policy.

Returning to the previous discussion about the ISO standards 27001 and 27002 and the four important controls for situational awareness, it becomes apparent that the first three bullets are well covered. Focus is then turned to the last one concerning "Information Security Incident Management", which is about reporting and reacting to security weaknesses and security violations. This control also covers learning from the incidents through monitoring and quantification. The research documents significant differences among the four case studies of employee attitudes regarding reporting. One of the public organizations has higher security awareness than the other three organizations. This finding is also reflected in the detected security breaches; those employees who are more eager to report incidents also detect more incidents. These employees had some kind of experience or good knowledge about the subject and security was also part of their job. However, there are no significant differences among the four cases when it comes to the actual reporting of security violations. This means that good intentions and the ability to detect incidents do not guarantee accurate reporting of incidents. The question to be asked then is: why do employees who detect incidents not report them?

The study referred to use a simple methodology. A number of statements were developed covering issues mentioned by the organization's security instructions and security policy, which the employees were expected to read. The statements covered knowledge, attitudes and behaviour with respect to the requirements given by the security instructions or policy. The statements were mixed together to make it difficult to give strategic answers. The respondents were then asked to give their opinion on the statements on a scale: totally agree, agree, neither agree nor disagree, disagree, and strongly disagree. The respondents were also encouraged to think aloud and reflect upon the statements, and these reflections yielded additional information explaining the barriers that employees experience when endeavouring to comply with security policy and security instructions. Responses such as "Why should I report security incidents when nobody else does?", and "I would not report my boss", or "The security measures are stupid" tell something about the security culture within an organization. Here it is important to emphasize that such explanations might not have been forthcoming in a web-based survey. Interviewing employees from different parts of the organization in person, people with different skills and in various positions, and analyzing the data gives indicators on security knowledge, attitudes and behaviour. It also provides some guidance on what changes should be made: Building knowledge, increasing security awareness or influencing unwanted behaviour.

The qualitative data collected from this survey gave the opportunity to identify and study the barriers that employees must get through in order to comply with the security policy and instructions. One of the questions asked was why employees do not report detected incidents. The explanations are as follows:

First there is the low security usability of security measures. This barrier is well illustrated by Whitten and Tygar (2005) in the article "Why Johnny can't encrypt". Also the Norwegian data confirm that low security usability is an important issue: One respondent replied: "You know, it was too hard – even the person who designed the security measure had to omit the measure, if not, the job would not be done." Another person said: "It is so difficult to work with classified information because of the strict security regime, therefore we reduce the classification level temporarily, and this makes it possible to work". These statements clearly illustrate the importance of usability if the organization's security measures offer humans the opportunity to choose. Turning back to security incident reporting, low usability was not an issue. It is fairly easy to send an email or make a phone call. In this case other barriers came into force.

The next barrier is an important one. It is lack of knowledge. Knowledge is a basic precondition if employees are to see and report incidents. Unfortunately, the quality of the training and education employees receive in information security is poor. Respondents in the study stated that they probably would not be able to detect unwanted incidents. Knowledge about the security requirements stated in the policy is a basic skill that is needed in order to report incidents, but few employees read the guidelines, and any kind of education is usually given only to newcomers as part of the introduction programme. On average, it is only every other employee who receives some kind of education and training in information security. Social engineering attacks and how to mitigate that threat is not a big part of the training, if it is emphasized at all.

The next barrier is that of awareness and the lack of good attitudes. Even if employees know the security rules a lax personal attitude towards security could ruin everything. The following quotes are examples of how it works when attitudes are not synchronized with knowledge: " I would not report a newcomer, how should she know what is the right thing to do?" and "No, I would not report because I disagree with the security controls that this company has implemented – the security controls are stupid and of no use". There are also attitudes that show a total lack of risk awareness, and this is often linked with lack of knowledge. Employees need to know what to look for. This is particularly challenging when it comes to technological vulnerabilities as new technologies and working methods often come first, and security comes next.

If, however, knowledge and good attitudes are in place, employees could still be influenced by the organizational security culture. This may be observed in former policemen and military officers. When they later take employment in private businesses or in other areas of the public sector with less focus on security, they typically adjust their attitudes towards the existing culture and practices. This barrier is easily observed when studying the attitude towards the use of memory sticks. Memory sticks can represent an important security risk. Nevertheless, the following attitude is quite common: "I am well aware about the risks, but why should I not use those sticks when everyone else uses them?"

Even when a good organizational security culture is present within a concern, management and line managers may set working conditions that make it impossible to comply with security guidelines. The main explanation given by interviewed employees is related to short deadlines. There is simply not enough time to comply with the security routines. Thus, security controls are omitted in order to deliver on time. The basic problem is that compliance with security guidelines is not measured and reported up the hierarchy, as for example productivity and budget compliance are. Managers in both the private and the public sector are assessed on how well they achieve their economic objectives. Their performance is measured against the economic objectives or other measures of productivity, while security measurements are absent or merely conducted within the IT department. Managers are therefore not aware themselves of all the security risks, not to mention all the near-miss incidents that occur within the organization, and that could provide important information about coming risks.

The existing literature documents four approaches on how to measure the effectiveness of information security measures and controls. These are: a) evaluating risk compliance (e.g Aven, 2007); b) evaluating economic compliance (Sonnenreich, Albanese and Stout, 2006); c) assessing legal compliance (Spears and Cole, 2006); and d) evaluating how well employees comply with the security policy (Furnell, 2007; Albrechtsen, 2008). Interviewing IT leaders and managers about their interpretation of security objectives and the effectiveness of information security measures revealed that most of them consider information security to fall within the sphere of risk management and thereafter as a legal matter. Fewer think about information security as a security culture issue or an economic issue where security contributes to the economic performance of the organization. Studying the position adopted by security managers and data security managers in the organizations reveals that information security as a topic seems to be buried in the IT-department in the lower levels of the organization, and that it is a matter that is for the most part handled by IT personnel. The paradox is that information security is much more than technical IT security, and hence the risks should be a concern and well understood by the upper levels of management as well. However, even the top managers themselves can introduce serious information security risks to the company. Their decisions can have direct impact for instance on how reorganizations are handled, or how the company deals with questions from journalists.

Finally, if all these barriers to a good organizational security culture are removed, there is still one that remains and that is the human tendency to sometimes, often quite unintentionally just fail anyway. It is all too human to forget, to occasionally click the link, to open the attachment in the email and to be cheated. Therefore security or no security is not a zero-one relationship. It is more about being aware of a multitude of risks and being able to handle the existing and upcoming risks and balancing the objectives of return on investment and risk management. The human factor is one of the primary keys to improved situational awareness and security. The next section deals with how organizations can turn employees into a situational awareness capability.

Strategies for Closing the Gaps and Turning Employees into a Situational Awareness Capability

Table 1 gives some ideas on how to deal with each human role and the theoretical relationship.

As pinpointed already, most research seems to be focused on the bad deportment of humans. Humans can be disgruntled employees or spies, attacking and destroying computer network and systems. The way to deal with these challenges is laid out in the general deterrence theory, and in essence consists of punishment and sanctions so that employees refrain from committing crime. However, this is not sufficient. Regarding spies for instance, screening those applicants who have been offered a job could be a good measure of reliability and loyalty since studies show that many of those who commit computer crime already had a criminal record before being employed. Similarly, sanctions alone are not enough to prevent disgruntled employees from attacking the systems. In this case management should examine the reasons that trigger such incidents. Why are employees not satisfied? Why do they change from loyal to disgruntled? Some companies carry out working environmental studies to gauge the satisfaction of employees. Such studies could provide an insight to the security work in the organization, as for instance alerting management when tendencies change over time. Special attention should be paid to this dimension in times of restructuring organizations, in particular when the organization has to get through huge changes and some employees are laid off while others are promoted. Such reorganizations increase the risk of creating disgruntled employees. The qualitative answers confirm that work environment is an issue in relation to information security and loyalty to the organization. Fair treatment builds loyalty, while the feeling of being mistreated results in negative feelings and disloyalty.

The next role is that of the human being that has been fooled. It is so easy to fool people through social engineering attacks, and Kevin Mitnick and others have well proved that no ac-

Table 1. Measures needed to address each of the six information security roles of humans and related theoretical fundament

Roles	Measures needed to improve/deal with each role and its theoretical connection	
	Socio-technical theory	**General deterrence theory**
Resource person and contributor	Education, empowerment and training	
Causing unintentional failures	Awareness and training Improved working conditions	
Dealing with conflicting goals	Management follow-up	
Victim of social engineering	Awareness and training	
Disgruntled employee and/or opportunistic attacker	Management and follow up work	Sanctions and punishment
Spy or planted criminal	Screening and background checks	Sanctions and punishment

cess to computers or the organization's network is needed to obtain desired sensitive information. Why hack the technical systems when you can hack the humans? There are different strategies that may be used. So-called "phishing" attacks are easy precisely because human beings are so unaware and easily fooled (Qin and Burgoon, 2007). The growth of people using social networks such as Facebook, combined with people's low security awareness in general and the availability of automated easy-to-use attack tools, provide a great opportunity for hackers stealing personal and business information. When the awareness is low, even too good to be true offers that are distributed by email are successful in collecting bank accounts and passwords. The way to deal with this role and mitigate social engineering attacks is through raising awareness and training. Employees must become aware of their own vulnerability and the tricks utilised by hackers to fool people; well known attack vectors include utilizing trust (sending a link from a friend), fear (sending warnings, fake viruses and account updates) and desire (promising money or rewards). When people understand this, awareness may follow, and they may be able to detect some attacks, but not all of them, since new methods and techniques are continuously being developed. The attacker comes first, then the defensive measures to counter him.

Two further aspects are not much dealt with within information security literature. These are how humans deal with conflicting objectives and the risk of unintentional failure. Among the solutions that may be applied to redress the first aspects by management is to improve working conditions and give clear guidance. The risk of unintentional failure can be dealt with by implementing activities and training to raise awareness. It is important to note that management should also become aware of the importance of information security and how the lack of information security can reduce the return of investment through information leakages or by reduced quality and reliability of information that is used in production processes or to promote the services of the organization.

Research on the human factor as a positive contributor to information security is lacking. Eirik Albrechtsen (2008) has identified a digital divide between employees and IT personnel: employees view themselves as a resource while IT personnel regard employees as a risk factor. An organization's employees can however be a last line of defense if they are well educated and trained and education or training measures work.

Different organizations may apply different strategies for education and awareness campaigns. Small organizations have far fewer resources than larger ones, but they are on the other hand more transparent. In some organizations maybe nobody is in possession of sound knowledge on information security. In Norway, the Norwegian Centre for Securing Information (NorSIS) provides information security advice to organizations. NorSIS activities are directed towards small and medium sized enterprises, and the aim is to raise information security awareness. NorSIS supervises security risks and trends and provides practical guidance on how to handle upcoming risks as soon as they are detected.

How information security education can be provided in large multinational organizations is illustrated by the WW Group, a leading maritime industry group that delivers logistics solutions and maritime services worldwide. The WW Group developed the ISA program (Information Security Awareness) program in order to raise security awareness among the employees. This program consists of six modules focusing on different aspects of security. It uses vocal presentation, pictures, music and text to illustrate the risks and then provides exercises and quizzes to motivate reflection. Employees can freely choose which module to take. Each one requires about ten minutes to complete the training.

The effect of the program was studied by Hagen and Albrechtsen (2009). Web-based surveys/questionnaires were developed and distributed to all 3994 employees at the WW Group before and after the test group had been introduced to the ISA program. The researchers received 1896 answers from employees responding to both surveys, and their answers became input to the evaluation of the effect of ISA on security knowledge, awareness and behaviour.

The results showed that the ISA program had a significant short-term effect on employees' security knowledge, awareness and behaviour, and there were significant differences between the intervention subgroups, too. Changes were also found in the control group. These changes might be explained by the Hawthorne effect; the awareness and behaviour of control group members also changed in a positive direction. The introduction of the ISA program probably brought about some change in everyone, and this change (even a negative one like excluding the control group from use of ISA) had some impact, even though it was not expected to have any influence. It is not possible to fully separate the test groups in a living organization as can be done in a laboratory. This is one of the limitations of field experiments. The conclusion is that e-learning can provide an inexpensive way to educate employees in organizations and that e-learning can also have effect on improving knowledge, changing security attitudes and behaviour.

Solutions and Recommendations: Building a Situational Awareness and Defense in Depth Capability

This chapter has presented two theories which provide some guidance on how to deal with information security and how to increase situational awareness. The first one is the general deterrence theory, the ideas of which are widely applied within information security. This approach emphasizes the use of punishment and sanctions in order to deter people from committing crime. The second theory is the socio-technical theory, an approach which is common in the Scandinavian countries and that emphasizes humane working conditions and democracy.

The two theories are both relevant and cover different theoretical aspects of information security and how to approach the six identified roles that humans can have with respect to information security (spy/planted criminal, disgruntled employee, victim of social engineering attacks, failure in handling conflicting objectives, committing unintentional errors and the employee as a resource as opposed to a risk, see Table 1). The lessons learned are that each employee should be conscious about the risks and the element of human vulnerability, including the different roles that humans can play in the life of an organization. This heightened awareness of the employee's own role is a necessary condition if the aim is to increase situational awareness within organizations. The condition will not be met if employees are not educated and trained to see and be aware of the risks and to react whenever they detect abnormalities.

The second recommendation is that an information security management system (ISMS) should be implemented. ISO 27001 and ISO 27001 provide guidelines and best practices on how to design such a system. The standard describes four important processes: risk management, continual improvement, change management and management commitment, all of which are important in the continual improvement of situational awareness and information security. The ISMS should be adjusted to the actual need to protect information and tailored to fit the size of the organization, which means that certification is not the solution for every single business. Many businesses are small and could benefit from simply applying the standard as a guideline. The Norwegian petroleum industry has adopted this approach. An important outcome from implementation of the ISMS should be clear information security guidelines which employees should adhere to. The guidelines should also provide clear advice on how to report near-miss incidents and computer crime incidents, and they should state why this is important. Nevertheless, this will not work if trust does not permeate through the whole organization and it is more or less normal to err occasionally and report failures and incidents. It is a matter of fostering an organizational culture that allows people to make an honest mistake without fearing for their jobs and their reputations, while simultaneously imprinting upon them the importance of reporting malicious and harmful activities. It is about cultivating a certain kind of attitude and not least, a sense of loyalty and the feeling that the employees have a stake in the wellbeing and prosperity of the organization – not that they are just slaves and tools.

Third, regularly updated user guidelines are of no use if they are not communicated to and adopted by all employees. This is where employees can turn into a positive contributor to information security. In large multicultural organizations, e-learning can provide a good and inexpensive starting point to increase awareness. The training in information security should include an introduction to risks, own vulnerabilities, the organization's IT guidelines and pointers on how each employee can contribute to the improvement and strengthening of security. Awareness can also be improved by using information channels such as the Intranet or emails to publish newsletters about security and security risks. This can in particular be useful for communicating novel social engineering attack risks. What is most efficient depends on the organizational culture, and what information sources employees prefer to use. Table 2 shows some communication strategies that the organization could use.

Finally, management should pay attention to the six barriers mentioned earlier in this chapter. Each one of these barriers can reduce an organization's ability to improve situational awareness among its personnel. As stated previously, employees must adopt and accept the security measures. If they feel that the security measures are of no use, or that the measures have the effect of

Table 2. Measures for dealing with the six information security roles of humans and related theoretical fundament

Communication strategies for information security	On regular basis	Driven by individual need
Passive	Intranet	Clicking links
Active	Emails/news letters	Meeting with security manager Reporting incidents

reducing their productivity, employees might try to omit or circumvent the security measures. Involving employees in developing new security measures could be a fruitful approach in reducing potential barriers such as low usability and the risk of no-acceptance of security measures. Another idea might be to establish project groups where employees are invited and encouraged to participate.

CONCLUSION

This chapter deals with employees' contribution to information security and situational awareness. Two theories, the socio-technical theory and the general deterrence theory, are both relevant in this context; to understand how humans can become an added value to situational awareness, information security and computer network defense.

Most organizations have emphasised the development of a good formal security system consisting of security policy, systems and routines. Indeed, a good formal system contributes to the capability of detecting security violations, and is thus important, but awareness creation by educating the employees is considered by managers and IT security managers to be an even more effective measure to further strengthen the overall security. The detection and reporting of security violations can be further improved by training the employees in information security, but attention should also be directed towards the six barriers that employees must overcome in order to report security incidents. These are related to low security usability, lack of knowledge, employee attitudes, conflicting objectives, the dominant organizational security culture and the human tendency to fail sometimes, anyway.

The research also shows that employee compliance with security policies and guidelines is taken for granted in many companies, and that a formalistic approach to security is the preferred one. This provides some guidelines on where extra resources should be directed if the ambition is to improve security. Additional resources should be used to strengthen the employees as the last line of defense by continuous education, awareness raising, involvement and empowerment. Management engagement is also important, and information security should be integrated into all business processes. This might sound overwhelming, and some readers may ask for priorities, since resources are scarce. The Pareto principle, also known as the 80-20 rule, or the law for the vital few, states that as much as 80% of the effect comes from 20% of the investment or effort (Muzea, 2005). Maybe, we are here now; 20% are already invested in technical security measures and formal controls, hence protecting against 80% of the threats from Internet, like spam and viruses? It is extremely resource demanding to continuously educate and change human minds and behaviour, but unless this is done, we are still stuck with the weakest link in security, the human factor. Our network will still be under attack and challenging and undermining the trust we have to digital and web based services. Information security and situational awareness require implementation of both strategies: defense in breadth and depth. There is still room for improvements when it comes to enhancing the contributions from humans. In the future, social engineering attacks and phishing might turn into an even more important threat, nurtured by the growing amount of data available on the Internet and social networks.

A sound security regime could be designed through the use of ISO standards 27001 and 27002 which provide guidelines for an information security management system. A management system is a necessity for facilitating the reporting of security incidents and building situational awareness. Such a regime can only be developed if employees are involved in its development. This goes straight back to the socio-technical theory which emphasizes humane working conditions, employee participation and democracy. Important to note, however, is that this does not mean that the approach given by the general deterrence theory is not relevant; it simply means that there is a need for a mental shift in order to increase situational awareness, and the general deterrence theory alone does not provide the solution. Neither do the ISO standards.

REFERENCES

Albrechtsen, E. (2008). *Friend or foe? Information Security management of employees*. Ph.D. dissertation. NTNU, Trondheim, March 2008.

Aven, T. (2007). A unified framework for risk and vulnerability analysis covering both safety and security. *Reliability Engineering & System Safety*, *92*, 745–754. doi:10.1016/j.ress.2006.03.008

Baker, W. H., Hylender, D. C., & Valentine, A. J. (2008). Four years of forensic research: More than 500 cases: One comprehensive report. *Verizon Data Breach Investigation Report*, (pp. 2-27).

Besnard, D., & Arief, B. (2004). Computer security impaired by legitimate users. *Computers and Security 23*(3), 253-264. doi:10.1.1.95.9210

Biros, D. P. (2004). Scenario-based training for deception detection. *InfoSecCD Conference*, Kennesaw, GA, October 8, (pp. 32-36). doi:10.1145/1059524.1059531

Boni, W., & Kovacich, G. L. (2000). *Netspionage: The global threat to information*. Boston, MA: Butterworth-Heinemann.

Dhillon, G., & Backhose, J. (2001). Current directions in IS security research: Towards socio-organizational perspectives. *Information Systems Journal, 11*(2), 127–153. doi:10.1046/j.1365-2575.2001.00099.x

Furnell, S. (2007). IFIP workshop: Information security culture. *Computers & Security, 26*(1), 35. doi:10.1016/j.cose.2006.10.012

Grabowski, M., Ayyalasomayajula, P., Merrick, J., Harrald, J. R., & Roberts, K. (2007). Leading indicators of safety in virtual organizations. *Safety Science, 45*, 1013–1043. doi:10.1016/j.ssci.2006.09.007

Hagen, J. M. (2007). *Evaluating applied information security measures: An analysis of the data from the Norwegian Computer Crime Survey, 2006*, (pp. 1-66). Norwegian Defense Research Establishment (FFI), FFI-rapport 02558

Hagen, J. M. (2009). *The human factor behind the security perimeter. Evaluating the effectiveness of organizational information security measures and employees' contributions to security*. Doctoral Dissertation, Faculty of Mathematics, University of Oslo.

Hagen, J. M., Albrechtsen, E., & Hovden, J. (2008). Implementation and effectiveness of organizational information security measures. *Journal of Information Management and Computer Security, 16*(4), 377–397. doi:10.1108/09685220810908796

Hagen, J. M., Sivertsen, T. K., & Rong, C. (2008). Protection against unauthorized access and computer crime in Norwegian businesses. *Journal of Computer Security, 16*, 341–366.

Hagen, J. M., & Spilling, P. (2009). Do organisational security measures contribute to the detection and reporting of IT-system abuses? In *Proceedings of the Third International Symposium on Human Aspects of Information Security & Assurance*, (pp. 71-81).

Hale, A. I., & Glendon, O. (1987). *Individual behavior in the control of danger*. Amsterdam, The Netherlands: Elsevier.

Höne, K., & Eloff, J. H. P. (2002). Information security policy: What do international security standards say? *Computers & Security, 21*(5), 402–409. doi:10.1016/S0167-4048(02)00504-7

Huber, M., Kowalski, S., Nohlberg, M., & Tjoa, S. (2009). Towards automating social engineering using social networking sites. *Computational Science and Engineering, CSE '09*, (vol. 3, pp. 117-123). doi: 10.1109/CSE.2009.205

ISO IEC 27002. (2005). *Information technology – Security techniques – Code of practice for information security management.*

ISO/IEC 27001. (2005). *Information technology – Security techniques – Information security management systems – Requirements.*

Jones, A., Kovacich, G. G., & Luzwick, P. G. (2002). *Global information warfare: How businesses, governments, and others achieve objectives and attain competitive advantages* (pp. 3–75). New York, NY: Auerbach Publications. doi:10.1201/9781420031546

Karyda, M., Kiountouzis, E., & Kokolakis, S. (2005). Information systems security policies: A contextual perspective. *Computers & Security, 24*(3), 246–260. doi:10.1016/j.cose.2004.08.011

Keeney, M., Kowalski, E., Capelli, D., Moore, A., Shimeall, T., & Rogers, S. (2005). *Insider threat study: Computer system sabotage in critical infrastructure sectors*, (pp. 2-45). Carnegie Mellon, Software Engineering Institute.

Lobree, B. (2002). Impact of legislation on information security management. *Security Management Practices,* (November/December), 41-48.

Mitnik, K. D., Simon, W. L., & Wozniak, S. (2002). *The art of deception: Controlling the human element of security*. John Wiley & Sons.

Muzea, G. (2005). *The vital few. The trivial many. Invest with the insiders. Not the masses* (pp. 200–203). John Wiley and Sons.

NCCS. (2006). *Mørketallsundersøkelsen om datakriminalitet 2006 (The Norwegian Computer Crime Survey 2006)*. Oslo, Norway: Næringslivets sikkerhetsråd (in Norwegian).

Perrow, C. (1984). *Normal accidents: Living with high-risk technologies*. New York, NY: Basic Books.

Qin, T., & Burgoon, J. (2007). An investigation of heuristics of human judgment in detecting deception and potential implications in countering social engineering. *Intelligence and Security Informatics, 2007 IEEE*, (pp. 152-159). Doi: 10.1109/ISI.2007.379548

Ruighaver, A. B., Maynard, S. B., & Chiang, S. (2007). Organizational security culture: Extending the end-user perspective. *Computers & Security, 26*(1), 56–62. doi:10.1016/j.cose.2006.10.008

Schneier, B. (2004). *Secrets and lies: Digital security in a networked world, with new information about post-9/11 security* (2nd ed.). Wiley Publishing.

Siponen, M. T., & Oinas-Kukkonen, H. (2007). A review of information security issues and respective research contributions. *The Data Base for Advances in Information Systems, 38*(1), 60–81.

Sonnenreich, W., Albanese, J., & Stout, B. (2006). Return on security investment (ROSI): A practical quantitative model. *Journal of Research and Practice in Information Technology, 38*(1), 55–66.

Spears, J. L., & Robert, J. C. (2006). A preliminary investigation of the impact of the Sarbanes-Oxley Act on information security. *Proceedings at the 39th Hawaii International Conference on System Sciences*, (p. 218.c). doi:10.1109/HICSS.2006.24

Straub, D. W., Carlson, P. J., & Jones, E. H. (1992). Deterring highly motivated computer abusers: A field experiment in computer security. In Gable, G. G., & Caelli, W. J. (Eds.), *IT security: The need for international cooperation* (pp. 309–324). Holland: Elsevier Science Publishers.

Taylor, F. W. (1911). *The principles of scientific management*. New York, NY: Harper.

Thomson, K.-L., & von Solms, R. (2006). Towards an information security competence maturity model. *Computer Fraud & Security, 5*, 11–15. doi:10.1016/S1361-3723(06)70356-6

Trist, E., & Bamforth, K. W. (2001). Some social and psychological consequences of the longwall method of coal getting. *Human Relations, 4*(1), 3–38. doi:10.1177/001872675100400101

Von Solms, B. (2001). Information security: A multidimensional discipline. *Computers & Security, 20*(6), 501–508. doi:10.1016/S0167-4048(01)00608-3

Wang, A. J. A., & Yestko, K. (2005). Building reusable information security courseware. *Information Security Curriculum Development Conference,* September 23-24, Kennesaw, GA, USA. doi: 10.1145/1107622.1107642

Ward, P., & Smith, C. (2002). The development of access control policies for information technology systems. *Computers & Security, 21*(4), 365–371. doi:10.1016/S0167-4048(02)00414-5

Whitten, A., & Tygar, J. D. (2005). Why Johnny can't encrypt: A usability evaluation of PGP 5.0. In Cranor, L., & Simson O'Reilly, G. (Eds.), *Security and usability: Designing secure systems that people can use* (pp. 679–702).

Winkler, I. S. (1996). The non-technical threat to computing systems. *Computing Systems, 9*(1), 3–14.

ADDITIONAL READING

Albrechtsen, E., & Hagen, J. (2009). Information Security Measures Influencing User Performance. In Martorell, (Eds.), *Proceedings of Safety, Reliability, and Risk Analysis: Theory, Methods, and Applications, 2649-2656.*

Albrechtsen, E., & Hovden, J. (2009). The information security digital divide between information security managers and users. *Computers & Security, 26,* 276–289. doi:10.1016/j.cose.2006.11.004

Barret, N. (2003). Penetration testing and social engineering: Hacking the weakest link. *Information Security Technical Report, 8*(4), 56–64. doi:10.1016/S1363-4127(03)00007-4

Berghel, H. (2005). The two sides of RoI: Return on investment vs. risk of incarceration. *Communications of the ACM, 48*(4), 15–20. doi:10.1145/1053291.1053305

Blakely, B., McDermott, E., & Geer, D. (2001). Information Security is Information Risk Management. In: *Proceedings of the 2001 Workshop on New Security Paradigms,* New York: ACM Press, 97-104. doi:10.1145/508171.508187

Campbell, K., Gordon, L. A., Loeb, M. P., & Zhou, L. (2003). The economic cost of publicly announced information security breaches: Empirical evidence from the stock market. *Journal of Computer Security, 11*(3), 431–448.

Detert, J., Schroeder, R., & Mauriel, J. (2000). A framework for linking culture and improvement initiatives in organizations. *Academy of Management Review, 25*(4), 850–863.

Dhillon, G., & Gholamreza, T. (2006). Value-focused assessment of information system security in organizations. *Information Systems Journal, 16,* 293–314. doi:10.1111/j.1365-2575.2006.00219.x

Doherty, N. F., & Fulford, H. (2006). Aligning the information security policy with the strategic information systems plan. *Computers & Security, 25*(1), 55–63. doi:10.1016/j.cose.2005.09.009

Hagen, J., & Albrechtsen, E. (2009). Effects on employees' information security abilities by e-learning. *Information Management & Computer Security, 17*(5), 388–408. doi:10.1108/09685220911006687

Hagen, J. M., & Albrechtsen, E. (2008). Regulation of information security and the impact on top management commitment: A comparative study of the energy supply sector and the finance sector. In Martorell et al. (Eds). *Proceedings of: Safety, Reliability, and Risk Analysis: Theory, Methods, and Applications,* 407-413.

Halibozek, E. P., & Kovacich, G. L. (2005). *Mergers and Acquisitions Security.* Burlington: Elsevier Butterworth-Heinemann.

Hollnagel, E. (2008). Risk + barriers = safety? *Safety Science, 46*(2), 221–229. doi:10.1016/j.ssci.2007.06.028

ISO IEC 27002 (2005). Information technology – Security techniques – Code of practice for information security management.

ISO/IEC 27001 (2005). Information technology – Security techniques – Information security management systems – Requirements.

Karyda, M., Kiountouzis, E., & Kokolakis, S. (2005). Information systems security policies: A contextual perspective. *Computers & Security, 24*(3), 246–260. doi:10.1016/j.cose.2004.08.011

Person, F., & Weiner, N. A. (1985). Toward an integration of criminological theories. *The Journal of Criminal Law & Criminology, 76*(1), 116–150. doi:10.2307/1143355

Sangkyun, K., & Lee, H. J. (2005). *Cost-benefit Analysis of Security Investments: Methodology and Case Study. LNCS 3482, ICCSA 2005* (pp. 1239–1248). Berlin, Heidelberg: Springer-Verlag.

Schultz, E. E. (2002). A framework for understanding and predicting insider attacks. *Computers & Security, 21*(6), 526–531. doi:10.1016/S0167-4048(02)01009-X

Siponen, M. (2000). A conceptual foundation for organizational information security awareness. *Information Management & Computer Security, 8*(1), 31–41. doi:10.1108/09685220010371394

Sundt, C. (2006). Information security and the law. *Information Security Technical Report, 11*(1), 2–9. doi:10.1016/j.istr.2005.11.003

Torres, J. M., Sarriegi, J. M., Santos, J., & Serrano, N. (2006). Managing Information Systems Security: Critical Success Factors and Indicators to Measure Effectiveness. *Information Security, Procceedings of the 9th International Conference, ISC, LNCS 4176*, 530-545. doi: 10.1007/978-3-540-89173-4_27

Weeks, M. R. (2007). Organizing for disaster: Lessons from the military. *Business Horizons, 50*(6), 479–489. doi:10.1016/j.bushor.2007.07.003

Wiant, T. L. (2005). Information security policy's impact on reporting security incidents. *Computers & Security, 24*(6), 448–459. doi:10.1016/j.cose.2005.03.008

Wienche, H., Aven, T., & Hagen, J. (2006). A framework for selection of methodology for risk and vulnerability assessments of infrastructures depending on ICT. In: Guedes Soares and Zio, eds., *Proceedings of the European Safety and Reliability Conference 2006: Safety and Reliability for Managing Risk,* Vol. I, 2297-2304.

Zhang, D., Oh, L.-B., & Teo, H. H. (2006). An Experimental Study of the Factors Influencing Non-Work-Related Use of IT Resources at Work Place. *Proceedings of the 39th Hawaii International Conference on System Science 8,* 206.1. doi:10.1109/HICSS.2006.56

KEY TERMS AND DEFINITIONS

Dark Numbers: Hidden statistics or unrecorded cases of computer crime incidents.

Human Factor: Understood as being the humans and their impact on information security and situational awareness by their knowledge, attitude and behaviour.

Information Security: Based on three integral elements: confidentiality, integrity and availability.

Insiders: People with special access to IT systems, such as employees, consultants and hired staff.

Risk: A function of the probability of being attacked, the system vulnerability and the consequences that might occur if the attack succeeds.

Technical-Administrative Security Measures: Measures such as security policy, plans and procedures.

The Hawthorne Effect: Refers to the tendency of some people to work harder and perform better when they are participants in an experiment, first discovered in 1950 by Henry A. Landsberger when analysing older experiments from 1924-1932 at the Hawthorne Works, a Western Electric factory outside Chicago.

Chapter 3
Cyber Command and Control:
A Military Doctrinal Perspective on Collaborative Situation Awareness for Decision Making

Michael E. Ruiz
Deloitte Consulting, USA

Richard Redmond
Virginia Commonwealth University, USA

ABSTRACT

Cyber-space is emerging as the fifth domain of warfare and a crucial operational concern for commercial industry. As such, it requires a command and control system that enables defensive and operational capabilities within cyber-space. This chapter describes a research and development project aimed at discovering solutions for a Cyber Command and Control both for commercial and military environments. The chapter identifies challenges and provides solutions rooted in the body of knowledge composed of Command and Control and Situation Awareness Theory.

INTRODUCTION

Cyberspace is officially the fifth domain of warfare. On June 23, 2009, US Secretary of Defense, Robert Gates, in a memorandum to the Joint Chiefs of Staff and Military Service leadership, established the US Cyber Command (USCYBERCOM) (Jackson, 2009). This came as no surprise to those in the US military industrial complex, because the Air Force and the other military services were all competing for leadership of this new mission area (Clarke & Knake, 2010). The Gates Memo, for the first time, positioned cyber as the fifth domain of warfare along side of Air, Land, Maritime, and Space; giving the US military the authority and the duty to conduct defensive and offensive missions in cyberspace (Fry, 2010; Jackson, 2009; Staff Writer, 2010). Like the other four domains, cyber requires a command and control system that is able to integrate with existing command and

DOI: 10.4018/978-1-4666-0104-8.ch003

control systems in an operational environment, while providing supporting capability to those operating in cyber space.

Prior to the official announcement many firms in the military industrial complex actively conducted research in this emerging domain. BearingPoint Public Service (now Deloitte Federal Services), performed research and development in the information sharing domain dating back to mid-2007; applying their efforts to the maritime domain awareness (MDA) problem. In mid-2008, the research team decided that the solutions created for MDA could be applied to the Cyber Command and Control (Cyber C2) problem.

In the early stages of this research it was important to understand how security operation centers (SOC) were conducting business. Visits to several security operations centers revealed similar results to those articulated in Visualizing Cyber Security: Usable Workspaces (Fink, North, Endert, & Rose, 2009). Many of the cyber analysts working in the SOC were former systems administrators, network engineers, and hardware technicians. The analysts' comfort with hands-on operations of the physical system coupled with their years of experience in dealing with systems at the system console level, created an environment where only a minimum set of automation and analytical tools existed. The sheer volume of information that the analysts were processing on any given day was of particular interest. It was on the order of three million alerts indicating possible threats every day.

This chapter articulates the outcomes associated with the Cyber C2 R&D effort and the lessons learned from that research endeavor. In order to provide the most complete analysis the chapter starts with the theoretical underpinning of command and control, as well as situation awareness. The chapter then progresses into a description of the technical solution and aligns that solution with its theoretical foundation.

BACKGROUND

The Challenge

Command and Control Systems today, have a limited perception as it pertains to Situation Awareness. Traditional C2 systems situational awareness elements are typically focused on a geospatial understanding of the battlefield. This can be seen, most notably, in red force/blue force tracking systems and many other command and control sub-systems. Capabilities, not on the battlefield, are considered in the context of readiness but are typically not an integrated part of the situation awareness picture (i.e. Common Operating Picture). While this separate tracking of human capital and other capabilities is effective in traditional three-dimensional warfare (land, air, and maritime), it is not effective in today's five-dimensional battlefield.

Superior communication and information systems once offered commanders a distinct advantage on the battlefield. Today, that advantage creates a more complex and vulnerable environment to manage and understand (Builder, Bankes, & Nordin, 1999; Krulak, 1996). Specifically, the operational problem faced by commanders in the field is to understand the real- time situation as it pertains to the current health and status of individual C2 resources (including sensors and actuators both on and off the battlefield). This understanding is required in order to dramatically reduce the iteration time for each OODA[1] loop associated with mission planning or re-planning based on detected failures or degraded operational states of the C2 systems (Joint Chiefs of Staff, 2006; 2007; 2008; 2010a; 2010b). Furthermore, commanders on the battlefield require greater accuracy as it relates both to situation assessment and awareness of the current health and status of individual C2 resources, including cyber assets. Increasing accuracy and, by default, increasing a commander's confidence in the expanded situation awareness picture necessitates monitoring of the monitoring system itself (Thoms, 2003).

Communications and information systems are an integral part of operations (Joint Chiefs of Staff, 2006; 2007; 2008; 2010a; 2010b; Krulak, 1996); therefore a resilient command and control system requires both an expanded view on situation awareness and a mechanism to implement more effective situation awareness and assessment systems. Effective C2 must compress the amount of information and project courses of action that a commander may act upon (Builder et al., 1999; Endsley, 1995).

The Military Aspects

Military literature on the doctrinal aspects of Cyber Security and Operation evolves daily. Existing disciplines, such as Information Operation, continue to change based on the reality associated with each new attack. Attacks such as Titan Rain[2] prove the reality of the threat. The cyber doctrine is evolving in the wake of fundamental changes to asymmetric warfare; although much debate exists on the topic and progress is slow (Hayden, 2011).

Based on the challenges articulated above, all command and control systems share a common set of issues and challenges. However, Cyber C2 may possess some additional challenges not encountered with systems for land, air, and maritime. Specifically, cyber is the domain in which information for all other systems is transported. A degraded cyber space affects the ability of a military organization to conduct operations effectively. Further the cyber domain creates an environment where the battle lines are not clearly understood (Clarke & Knake, 2010). In the book "Unrestricted Warfare", two Chinese People's Liberation Army Officers generate a manifesto for nation-states with inferior forces to wage effective war against nation states with superior military capability. This type of warfare involves attacks against the infrastructure and economic system of the adversary (Qiao & Xiangsui, 2002).

More importantly, these attacks differ from traditional attacks in that identification as to who is attacking you is difficult, if not impossible. Cyber warriors are a highly decentralized fighting force that operates in the shadows of networks and improperly protected computer systems. A highly centralized force must adapt if it is to have any hope of winning versus a decentralized adversary (Brafman & Beckstrom, 2008).

It is important to note since the battlefield for cyber war is the same space used for global commerce, commercial organizations and national critical infrastructures are vulnerable to attacks. Just as the disciplines of physical security, espionage, and communications evolved from military operation and doctrine to civilian applications, cyber defense mechanisms gained from military efforts will permeate the commercial and civilian domains.

The Theoretical Aspects of Command and Control

Command and control, as a field of practice, dates back to the days of Sun Tzu and other military theorists. In 1981, Lawson and Wohl, separately, published research on the topic of command and control. Lawson articulated command and control as a well-defined control process that senses, processes, compares, decides, and acts (Lawson, 1981). Wohl took a very different approach based on a cognitive relationship between stimulus, hypothesis, options, and response (Wohl, 1981). Lawson's work depicts the systematic and methodical aspect of command and control, while Wohl exposes the complexity associated with decision-making. In 1995, Boyd articulated his OODA loop, a process for real-time decision-making in the cockpit of an airplane during a dogfight (Boyd, 1995). These three works are the basis for command and control today. Future command and control systems must implement both the process and cognitive aspects described by Lawson and Wohl, respectively. This increases the complexity of the system and would fundamentally change the way systems are built today.

The Theoretical Aspects of Situational Awareness

The State of the Art in Situation Awareness (SA) dates back to Endsley's work, "Toward a Theory on Situation Awareness in Dynamic Systems", published in 1995 by the Human Factors and Ergonomics Society. This seminal work is often referenced in the discourse of situation assessment and situation awareness. In 2003 Salerno et al, based on their work at Air Force Research Lab (AFRL), published several articles that expanded upon Endsley's work and leveraged work from the Joint Director's Laboratories (JDL). The expansion combined Endsley's Situation Awareness Model and JDL's Fusion Model into a Framework for Cyber Situation Awareness (Endsley, 1995; Matheus, M.M. Kokar, & Baclawski, 2003; Salerno, 2008; Salerno, Hinman, & Boulware,

2002; Salerno, Hinman, Boulware, & Bello, 2003; Tadda, 2008).

In Figure 1, three levels of situation awareness are depicted. These include Level-1 Perception of Elements; Level-2 Comprehension of Disjoint Elements, and Level-3 Projection of the Future State. Further, the situation awareness reference model when decomposed, as depicted in Figure 2, illustrates three key constructs which include Short-term, Working, and Long Term memory (Endsley, 1995). This paper will define an instantiation of these concepts specifically for Cyber C2.

REQUIREMENTS FOR CYBER COMMAND AND CONTROL

This section codifies the theory presented briefly above into a set of requirements useful for the instantiation of Cyber C2 systems. When this research project first started, the requirements for the system were not well understood. At a high-level, the requirements described a system that would share large quantities of information from disparate sources; would analyze that information

Figure 1. Endsley's Situation awareness reference model (Endsley, 1995)

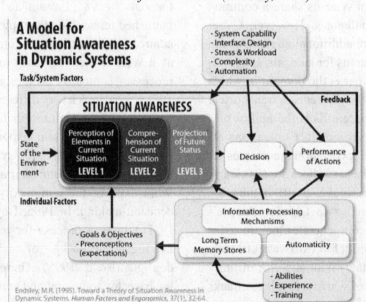

Figure 2. Endsley's decomposition of the SA reference model (Endsley, 1995)

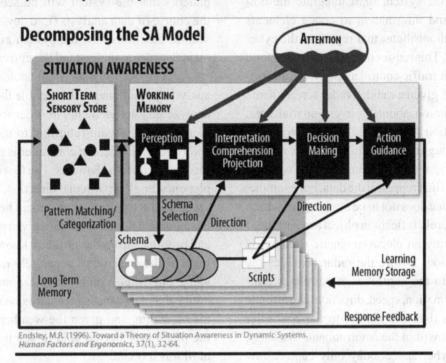

Endsley, M.R. (1996). Toward a Theory of Situation Awareness in Dynamic Systems. *Human Factors and Ergonomics*, 37(1), 32-64.

to find anomaly or signature based vulnerabilities; and provide a mechanism for collaboration, as well as decision-making. Over time the research team refined these requirements based on lessons learned and further investigation into the field of study. These requirements are presented here in 4 categories. The first 3 categories align with the three levels of situation awareness, as described by Endsley, 1995. The fourth category describes the decision-making and resource management aspects of command and control (Holley, 2004; Kometer, 2010). These requirements implicitly describe the use of a Lawson model of command and control as a process.

Level 1 Situation Awareness Requirement: Perception of the Elements in the Environment

The perception level of situation awareness is the level where data and information are collected, processed, and correlated to create fully attributed elements. These elements are representative of the environment (Endsley, 1995). This section articulates a set of requirements within this context.

A Cyber C2 system shall collect large quantities of data and information from a diverse sources and providers. The data processed by a Cyber C2 will come from a varied population of cyber sensors placed throughout the enterprise. These sensors may include audit logs from desktops, servers, specialized appliances, firewalls, routers, HIDS/NIDS devices, and various others sensors that collect state data about the cyber environment. While sensors, provide the greatest amount of aggregate information, other information sources that require integration into the environment include vulnerability alerts / reports from external organizations. These external sources may include malware signature providers, such as Symantec, McAfee, and various other malware research centers. Other information sources that may provide vulnerability information include organizations such as US-CERT, USCYBERCOM-IAVA, and academic research centers.

A Cyber C2 system shall integrate the collected data and information to create elements complete with attributes that represent the cyber environment. This requirement is best understood through an air traffic control analogy. An air traffic controller, given a radio, a radar screen, some basic information about their geo-spatial area, and information from a field flight plan moves airplanes through an area. However, the controller is not working with raw data; they are working with elements that represent the data. For example, the radar device does not have a concept of what a plane is, it merely reflects an object at a particular distance casting an electromagnetic shadow on its transmission. Before the radar provides the information to the controller, it correlates transponder information, speed, direction, and altitude and provides that information to the controller as an element within the environment. Similarly, sensors in cyber space today only capture raw data. For example a net-flow sensor, captures the originating address of a packet, the protocol, and the destination address. However one packet of information is not necessarily an element that would be of interest to cyber analysts. Therefore the short-term memory store and the working memory for the system must create meaningful elements for the environment.

Once sensor data and external provider information is collected, interpreted, and assembled into elements, it transcends to Level 2 in the situation awareness model (Endsley, 1995). The next section describes the key components required in Level 2.

Level 2 Situation Awareness Requirement: Comprehension of the Current Situation

The comprehension aspect of situation awareness is decomposed into two distinct components. The first component resides in the working memory of the system and provides a mechanism for correlating disjoint elements in the environment. The second component resides in the long-term memory of the system and provides the known patterns that the system will be seeking out in the course of data analysis (Endsley, 1995). This section describes how the system analyzes element in order to understand the current situation.

A Cyber C2 system shall include a set of analytical components that enable the system to analyze disjoint elements in order to create element patterns. Again returning to the air traffic controller example, the controller is provided, in this case, with two elements. The first element is a plane heading in a particular direction, at particular speed, and at a particular altitude. The second is a tall mountain that is located at a given geo-position and protrudes from the surface a known distance. Each of these elements separately provide little value but when combined the controller may notice that the plane is on a collision course with the mountain, and given the weather conditions the plane may not be able to see the mountain until it is too late.

A Cyber C2 system shall possess a long-term memory component that manages the creation and index of schemas for known situations. These schemas are composed of known element patterns and a description of courses of action (Endsley, 1995). Returning to the controller and the plane heading into the side of the mountain, the controller recognizes that element pattern based on their experience. Once that pattern is recognized, the controller sets into motion a set of corrective actions that allow the plane to navigate around the mountain. From past experience, the controller knows that it is simpler for the plane to take one set of actions versus several sets of actions. Given this historical (long term) knowledge, the controller will always respond with a preferred course of action.

Just as level 1 bridges the divide between the short-term sensor memory and the working memory of the system level 2 bridges the divide between the long-term knowledge and working memory processes of the system. At this point one has the humble beginnings of a situation awareness system.

Level 3 Situation Awareness Requirement: Projection of Future Status

Level 3 is undoubtedly the most difficult aspect to both conceive and implement. In this aspect the system is trying to predict the future state of a particular element with some degree of certainty. In most situation awareness systems there exists a mathematical model that allows one to extrapolate possible future states (Endsley, 1995). In the cyber domain, the laws of physics do not apply, at least not at the concept/element level. As an example, one can label an element within a Cyber C2 system as a "session". This session has a set of attributes that includes its cyber address, the identity of the user, and other information important to the operation of the session. But how does one predict the future state of that session at varying time frames? There may be a particular system policy that says the session must update at certain intervals or it will no longer be considered a valid session. The challenge becomes the complexity associated with mathematically predicting the future is beyond what is available to security experts today. This section will articulate one broad sweeping requirement for the consideration of the reader. However, creating an adequate projection mechanism is a topic that still requires a great deal of research.

A Cyber C2 system shall articulate a mechanism that allows the mathematical extrapolation of the current state of elements within an environment to possible future states. To understand this better, one may consider the example of an airplane in mid-air flight. At any given time the flying airplane, from the earlier examples, is defined by a set of attributes that may include its speed, location, and direction, along with many others. From one moment to the next the airplane may change any one or more of those attributes within a bounded set of possible changes. This suggests an airplane may start to climb or descend, turn right or left, or accelerate or decelerate. However, the sheer physics of aerodynamics that govern the flight of the airplane will not allow the plane to disappear from a given position and reappear at another position. Furthermore, given that the airplane exhibits physical limitations, it can only change its attributes at a given maximum rate. These physical limitations bound the possible future states that an airplane may assume given a particular point in time.

A projection mechanism within a Cyber C2 space must operate at Internet speed. A rudimentary definition of real-time control includes the execution of all aspects of processing in a sufficiently expeditious time frame so as to preclude failure of the system. Therefore, a real-time system may adequately measure in microseconds, seconds, or minutes depending how fast the system must operate to accommodate the processing requirements imposed on the system. In a Cyber C2 system, the real-time nature of the system operates at Internet speed; this is to say that packets flying through the cyber may change certain elements many times a second. In a worse possible scenario, the magnitude of the number of elements that the systems must track may be overwhelming. It is for these reasons that the Cyber Command and Control System must leverage parallel processing of data and distributed computing.

The level 3 requirement imposes a need for a great deal of computational power and further research before a mature Cyber C2 system can be created. At minimum, more research is needed to in order to create an effective projection mechanism; this would include: (a) gaining a greater understanding of the type and quality of cyber elements needed to detect threats; the development of (b) algorithms for projecting the future state of the cyber elements and (c) a visualization mechanism that would aid the cyber analyst in working with the massive amounts of data being generated by the system.

Command and Control Requirements

The literature is replete with text that describes the design of and requirements for Command and Control Systems (Andriole & Halpin, 1991; Builder et al., 1999; İnce, 1997; Kometer, 2010; Morris, 1983; Walker, Stanton, & Salmon, 2009). This section focuses on the aspects of Command and Control that are novel to the emerging Cyber C2 domain. It is important to note that control is the mechanism for command, while command is the method by which the commander: delegates authority, standardizes requirements, allocates resources, measures performance, and correct deviations (Joint Chiefs of Staff, 2010c; Kometer, 2010). The command and control process is hinged on the idea of centralized control and decentralized execution (Kometer, 2010). This section is decomposed into subsections that articulate specific command requirements and explicit control requirements. The command requirements focus on the decision making process and the mechanism for tracking performance. The control requirements focus on the tools that commanders and their subordinates use to execute decisions made in the command process.

Command Requirements: Decision Making and Progress Monitoring

The fundamental function of any commander is to make decisions. Clausewitz said it best in his book, *On War*:

"War is the province of uncertainty; three quarters of the factors on which action in war is based are wrapped in a fog of greater or lesser uncertainty... The commander must work in a medium which his eyes cannot see; which his best deductive powers cannot always fathom and with which, because of constant changes, he can rarely become familiar." *(Clausewitz, 1832) By Carl von Clausewitz*

No medium better exemplifies this reality than cyber. Moreover, Martin van Creveld articulates an axiom relating to information and organization as follows:

"... having less information available than is needed to perform [a] task, an organization may react in either of two ways. One is to increase its information-processing capacity, the other to design the organization, and indeed the task itself, in such a way as to enable it to operate on the basis of less information." (van Creveld, 1985) By Martin van Creveld

These quotes epitomize the importance of decision-making as it relates to the command aspects of command and control. It is for these reasons that one must be careful, when designing a command and control system, to closely scrutinize how the system is used for decision-making. Situation awareness provides the commander information about the situation, but the decision-making requires the ability to manipulate the information in a more complex manner. A cyber command and control system must provide cyber intelligence and a cyber analytics mechanism, both emerging fields of study.

Once a decision is made, the commander requires a mechanism to monitor progress and any changes in situation, if necessary. As stated above, the commander must be able to recognize when a course correction is necessary.

Control Requirements: Visualization and Collaboration

Visualization and collaboration are key enablers of the command and control process. Visualization tools help the commander, and their staff, understand complex information in a more intuitive manner. Visualization within a Cyber C2 system must include a geo-spatial representation, a logical representation, and a physical representation of the system and its elements. Information must be summarized and drill-down functionality is essential. To the extent possible the visualization must endeavor to provide the decision maker with an understanding of how the information was aggregated. Visualization aids collaboration by providing a common operating picture for common situation awareness. However, collaboration serves two main purposes in the Cyber C2 domain. First collaboration, through the use of technology such as crowd sourcing and knowledge mining provides the system with additional context sensitive data and information that is typically not available in other command and control systems. This is because many disparate organizations may be working on the same problem and collaboration facilitates finding a solution faster. In this mode collaboration is bi-directional or omni-directional, all users effectively work together to find a solution. Command and control collaboration is also used in a uni-directional mode, where the commander-- having made a decision-- communicates that decision to subordinates with force as orders and missions they must accomplish.

One Possible Reference Architecture Based on Requirements

Below is a depiction of the reference architecture for a Cyber C2 system in which large amounts of structured and unstructured data are gathered, analyzed, and processed. The system is designed under a service-oriented paradigm, so new capabilities are easily added and evolving data formats are updated as needed. The next section will articulate the framework and the logical architecture that was developed during the course of this research.

A FRAMEWORK FOR IMPLEMENTING CYBER C2

This section describes the Collaborative Situation Awareness for Decision Making (CSA-DM) framework, depicted in Figure 4. This framework asserts the types of services required for situation awareness systems, in the context of the theory discussed in previous sections. The CSA-DM was founded on a set of principles, which allow for timely and informed decision-making. These principles are listed below:

Figure 3. Reference architecture for Cyber C2 (Deloitte, 2009)

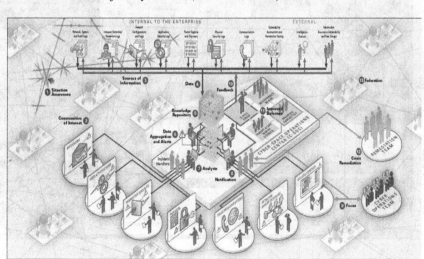

1. Process automation is crucial to working with the amount and speed of the data that is provided by the system.
2. The system will be composed of formal and informal processes. Formal process must be codified and accessible to the appropriate stakeholder. Informal process should receive input from formal processes and return results to the formal.
3. Context aware information relating to the interaction of the system must be maintained in order to assess the performance of existing formal processes and to determine if informal processes should be formalized.
4. The collaboration functionality of the system must enable the ability to implement crowd sourcing or shared problem solving, through the use of such mechanisms as common operating picture and knowledge repositories.

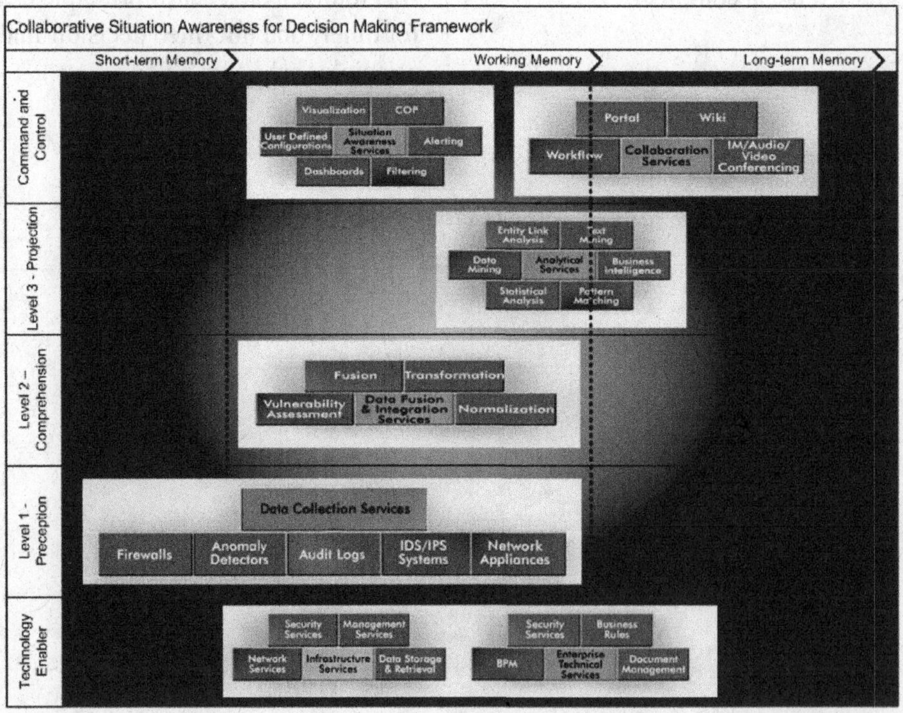

The following sections explain the services described in the framework in more detail.

Data Collection Services and Tools

The data collection services provide a mechanism for gathering information from disparate sensors in the environment. In the context of cyber, these sensors may include Firewall logs; HIDS/NIDS alerts; audit logs from computers, network devices, and applications, or other indicators and alerts from monitoring devices. The sole function of the data collection service is to aggregate information and to make it available to the rest of the system. Data collection services produce the systems perceptions and are the first step in the creation of system entities. In the cyber domain, these entities may be users, sessions, packets, computers, devices, or other entities that may be of interest given the mission of the organization.

Figure 4. Collaborative situation awareness

The Cyber C2 proof of concept developed within this IR&D effort leveraged Tivoli's Security Operations Manager (TSOM) as the mechanism for both short-term and working memory. In short-term memory a series of agents polled the sensors in the environment for updated information. The information captured from the sensors underwent preliminary processing and was then stored in working memory for further process by the data fusion and analytical services.

Data Fusion Service and Tools

The data fusion services supplied a means by which information stored in the working memory was normalized and then correlated. These services included normalization and transformation services that performed data cleansing. This included time zone conversion, character set conversion, and other data harmonization processes to ensure that the data from the various sensors was interoperable. Once the information was normalized these services commenced with the task of fusing disjoint entities. This represents the first step in an iterative process associated with situation comprehension. Vulnerability assessment services use this fused information as a starting point for the process of identifying threats and / or vulnerabilities based on patterns stored in long-term memory.

The data fusion services were instantiated in Tivoli's Security Information and Event Manager (TSIEM) and Tivoli's Security Operation Manager. These products, used in conjunction, allowed the research team to create a long-term memory of searchable patterns based on known exploits and attack vectors. Later one will see that the collaboration service exposed a mechanism for updating the long-term memory based on newly identified exploits and attack vectors.

Analytical Services and Tools

The analytical services were the first point at which the end-user interacted with the system. The very nature of cyber situation awareness required that policies and rules defined for use by the data fusion services evolve quickly over time. The analyst using the prescribed services and tools analyzed information in the working memory to identify new patterns associated with a threat or vulnerability. Services for entity link analysis, data mining, text mining, and statistical analysis were coupled with Palantir to create a platform in which entities were enriched with attributes from other data sources and patterns were investigated by a team to identify new threat and vulnerabilities. The ability to project future events based on an understanding of the current events was limited, due to a lack of tools and devices.

A key finding during the research was the complete lack of analytical tools for evaluating cyber security data. The research team's discussions with large software product vendors found that many product vendors are not interested in adding capabilities such as machine learning, probabilistic algorithms, or other non-deterministic forms of computation to their product roadmap. This may be due to viewpoints such as Tadda's: "In order for human to trust automated decision making, the decision process has to be deterministic" or Dieterich's viewpoint on cyber situation awareness that current machine learning approaches yield far too many false-positives, rendering their utility ineffective (Jajodia, Liu, & Swarup, 2009). In either case, it was clear that the volume of information, to be processed and the rate at which that volume increased, require that process automation and machine processing be added to the research agenda.

Situational Awareness Service and Tools

The situation awareness services were the primary set of services utilized by the end-user. These service included (a) portals and portlets, (b) GIS visualization, (c) dashboards, (d) user-defined operating picture (UDOP) based on filtering services, and (e) the ability for shared situation awareness through a common operating picture. These situation awareness services allowed decision makers and analyst to review the pertinent information in an intuitive and easy to follow format. These services compressed that data visualization while allowing users to drill down into finer grain data elements.

The tools used in to instantiate these service included tools from Google, Oracle, Adobe, and IBM. Google Earth was used as the GIS visualization. Its ability to consume KML and HTML allowed the research team to quickly integrate the product. The portal used for this proof of concept was the old BEA portal more; this allowed for seamless integration into the workflow engine addressed in the following sections. Additionally, the IBM TSOM, TSIEM, and NetCool products allowed us to integrate rich user interfaces with Adobe Flash through the use of Representational State Transfer (REST) calls. While the end product created for the proof of concept was not integrated into one user interface, all the user interfaces were interconnected through open standards such as XML, REST, or SOAP. Proving that a single user interface is possible as either a thick or thin client; however, developing an integrated user interface was outside the scope of the research.

Collaboration Services and Tools

The collaboration services worked closely with the situation awareness service to provide a robust end-to-end capability. In the context of collaboration service many of the capabilities that the team sought to integrate already existed. Capabilities such (a) SMTP, (b) XMPP Chat, (c) Collaborative White Boarding for marking up maps in a shared SA environment were integrated as a matter of best practice. Additionally, the team decided on the use of an open-source wiki as the knowledge repository that served as the long-term memory for the system. Two key areas that the researchers looked into included the use of context-aware collaboration and the use of workflow for situation awareness associated with incident response.

Context-aware collaboration referred to the practice of encoding patterns of interaction with context about the incident or investigation. For example, the scenario used to demonstrate the proof of concept involved a "spear-phishing" attack. When the system identified that an internal IP address was connected to a potentially harmful external IP address, an investigation workflow was initiated. From that point forward all SMTP, XMPP, and other forms of messaging traffic about that incident was coded with meta-data that allowed the system to aggregate the information exchanged into the wiki knowledge repository. This capture of information served two purposes. The first purpose was as an audit trail that is used for process improvement and refinement; the other was as a mechanism to share information with other parts of the organization that are not currently experiencing the problem. Over time analysts refined the latter into a well-defined set of patterns with policies that are enforceable by sensors on the network. Context-aware collaboration started a feature that would only serve to simplify the work of the analyst. However, the research yielded far more interesting utility for this information.

Another, key aspect of the collaboration service was the use of a workflow engine to drive the execution of formal business process. In the military, formal business processes are referred to as the tactics, techniques, and procedures (TTPs) associated with the execution of a particular doctrinal area. While command and control was extensively covered in the doctrinal literature, cyber security and operations were devoid of codified doctrine. It was widely thought that cyber command and control would be an extension of existing command and control systems, as an additional layer in the common operating picture. Recently, an article by LTG Hayden reaffirmed that line of thinking and proposed that cyber is different from the physical domains and required its own doctrine (Hayden, 2011). Without doctrine, it was impossible to implement real-world formal business processes. The research team defined its own pseudo military doctrine and codified those notional TTPs within a workflow engine. This allowed decision makers to understand exactly where in the process and how much information was available on a particular incident. In some cases the decision maker was forced to make a decision with incomplete information because of the severity of the situation. In other cases the decision maker was able to wait for more information to make a more informed decision. The research team noted that future research in this space should capture the decision that would be made with less information and then how the decision is affected by more information. But that research question was not in scope for this particular IR&D.

Clearly the literature is replete with examples of the evolving nature of how information-centric organizations make decisions. Books such as Wikinomics point to crowd-sourcing and intelligent mobs as the way organizations solve problems (Tapscott & Williams, 2008). Books such as The Social Like of Information and The Power of Pull point to how information changes the nature of how people and organizations interact. The collaboration services created in the research sought to incarnate those ideas into a practical application for decision-making.

Technology Enablers

Infrastructure service and enterprise technical service are the enabling services that allow the entire system to function, the research team utilized Oracles (formerly BEA) application server and business process engine to integrate the various applications. A REST approach was followed for most of the integration as it was felt to be less costly and timelier to use. Services such as security were implemented to prove that a secure application was possible although the security was kept minimal, as that was not a key focus of the research and the enterprise and infrastructure service were implemented at the most basic level merely to prove interoperability. The focus of this research was not to determine if a robust Cyber C2 system could be built, but to determine if a Cyber C2 system could be built that can truly provide situation awareness and more effective decision-making. In this respect, the researchers learned a great deal. The following section describes the issue and design concerns, while the concluding section describes the key lessons learned.

ISSUE AND DESIGN CONCERNS

Issues and design approaches in Situation Awareness are widely researched areas of study; from the work by Zahid Qureshi et al, in 1999 to the more recent research of Erik Blasch et al. in 2006. The common issues are categorized into the following areas, User, Process Models, Context, Meaning, and Metrics. The key challenges include the following: (Blasch et al., 2006; Qureshi & Urlings, 2002).

1. Process Explanation
    a. How is evidence accumulated?
    b. How are contradictions resolved?

c. How is reasoning (based on machine learning) articulated to user?

d. How is automation best leveraged?

2. User Interface

a. How is Collaboration facilitated?

b. How is knowledge best represented and presented?

Approaches to solving some of these key challenges include, hypothesis based reasoning, model based understanding, Collaborative Situational Awareness, and human-in-the-loop interpretation (Jajodia et al., 2009). Each of these approaches exhibit issues and challenges as identified above. Of note, a paper by Thoms published in 2003 through the International Society of Information Fusion, titled "Situation Awareness – A Commander's View", rightfully points out that "Robust inference requires a language that affords precise description of relevant entities …" Thoms goes on in the paper to state that "Steady progress in situation awareness cannot be made until semantic inconsistencies are resolved" (Thoms, 2003). A great deal of work in the area of semantics for systems interoperability is currently on-going in the U.S. Air Force but only limited success can be claimed.

The research described in this chapter focused on a subset of the above stated issues; specifically, automation, representation, collaboration, and evidence accumulation. Some of the design concerns that the research team identified are detailed in the following sections.

Automation

The research team found that the problem of automation is less about the technological challenges associated with automation than with the human perspective. One key challenge pointed out by Tadda in 2008 and verified by participants in the research, is the deterministic nature of the decision making process. Decision makers want to understand the rationale associated with a particular decision or outcome. The second issue

with automation was the lack of codified process. This issue of codified processes is one requiring research and over time the processes will emerge from lessons learned and best practices. However, trust in the systems, will continue to plague developers of the command and control systems.

To alleviate this concern the research team implemented the following design feature. First, the business process itself was monitored so as to provide not only the situation awareness related to the observable environment, but also maintain situation awareness of the command and control system. This allowed the decision maker to understand how much information the decision was being based on and to what degree the analysis process was complete. Future issues may include providing the validity associated with the information evaluated and / or an understanding of the reliability of the analytical method used. Decision makers must be trained to use this form of information as it less intuitive in the cyber realm than it is in other more physically linked domains.

COLLABORATION

The issue of collaboration is another well-studied field. The research team sought to introduce concepts from social networking to advance the understanding of how crowd sourcing improved collaborative decision-making. One of the main challenges identified in the research included the extremely short time frames in which decisions must be made with a cyber domain. However, collaboration using web 2.0 technologies created a mechanism for capturing information and using that information for process improvement. Future research in this area may find it useful to measure the performance gains associated with web 2.0 technologies over time. For example, as the wiki knowledge repository grows with incidents, does the communication channel reach a saturation point where additional information ceases to be useful or timely?

Evidence Accumulation

In the context of evidence accumulation, the challenge within a cyber command and control system is infinitely more difficult than in environments that have a linkage with a physical environment. In physical systems there exists a physics that drives the behavior of the entities in the systems. The entities themselves are intuitively more recognizable in a physical environment (i.e. a plane, a mountain, a runway). In a cyber environment the physics are not well understood, and the dynamic nature of the system exacerbates the problem. An issue identified for further research is: What are the entities that provide the best understanding of the systems? For this research IP addresses and sub-nets were the prevalent entities used. However, other entities such as sessions or users may make more sense given a different use cases or environment. Additionally, evidence accumulation is well suited to having more analytic approaches taken based on machine learning and other adaptive technologies. These present further issues but are essential for scalability in large complex environments.

CONCLUSION

The Cyber C2 proof of concept was an internal research and development project that sought to integrate the theory of Command and Control, as well as situation awareness, into an operational system for either military or civilian. The system enabled timely and effective decision making in the realm of cyber security by integrating technology from various disciplines. This research explored the various levels of situation awareness and the key components of C2 for application to the cyber domain. In the process, the researchers learned a great deal and identified several important gaps.

Lessons learned are reflected in the creation of Cyber C2 reference architecture and the CSA-DM framework. These artifacts drive the creation not only of Cyber C2 systems but are applicable to the broader C2 body of knowledge. Several novel outcomes included the use of a wiki as a knowledge repository that the research team easily integrated due to its open standards and open architecture. This type of knowledge repository allowed for integration with analytical COTS products.

Several areas identified as requiring significant research included the need for more cyber security analytical tools that enable a projection functions for bounding possible future states based on current situation. Further, the research recognized the need for well defined TTPs and Cyber Security and Operation Doctrine. Without this strategic understanding decision making became inconsistent and often lacking in utility.

Most importantly, the proof of concept accomplished its intended goal of understanding whether a Cyber C2 system built of COTS products, integrated using service orientation principles, and social decision making would be effective for future C2 systems, specifically in the cyber domain. Like in most systems today, many of the most difficult challenges are not technological; they are at the interface between human cognition and machine computation.

While the researchers answered many of the open questions, more questions and additional research areas are still left open. The field of cyber analytics and more specifically cyber security analytics is ripe for research.

ACKNOWLEDGMENT

The authors pause a moment to acknowledge the various contributions of those key to this research. LTG Peter Cuviello, former US Army CIO, and Dr. Greg Lomow, author and thought leader in SOA, provided the impetus for this internal research and development project. Their contributions to the foundational idea were crucial to the success of the project. We acknowledge and appreciate the technical team, but specifically, Andy Suchoski,

Security Architect, and Dilip Rane, Systems Architect, whose countless hours in the lab were the lifeblood of the project. And to Stacey Camp whose various contributions allowed the team to excel in all aspects of the project. Special thanks to the leadership of Deloitte Consulting for allowing us to continue this research after the acquisition. And, finally we thank the Information System department at VCU for their contributions to the theoretical aspects of this work.

REFERENCES

Andriole, S. J., & Halpin, S. M. (1991). *Information Technology for command and control: Methods and tools for systems development and evaluation* (pp. 1–576). IEEE Press.

Blasch, E., Kadar, I., Salerno, J., Kokar, M., Powell, G. M., & Corkill, D. D. (2006). Issues and challenges in situation assessment (level 2 fusion). *Journal of Advances in Information Fusion, 1*(2), 122–139.

Boyd, J. R. (1995). *The essence of winning and losing key statements*. Retrieved from http://pogo-archives.org/m/dni/john_boyd_compendium/essence_of_winning_losing.pdf

Brafman, O., & Beckstrom, R. A. (2008). *The starfish and the spider: The unstoppable power of leaderless organizations* (p. 240). Penguin Group USA.

Builder, C. H., Bankes, S. C., & Nordin, R. (1999). *Command concepts: A theory derived from the practice of command and control* (pp. 1–144). Washington, DC: RAND Corporation.

Clarke, R. A., & Knake, R. (2010). *Cyber war: The next threat to national security and what to do about it* (pp. 1–304). Washington, DC: Harper Collins.

Endsley, M. R. (1995). Toward a theory of situation awareness in dynamic systems. *Human Factors, 37*(1), 32–64. doi:10.1518/001872095779049543

Fink, G. A., North, C. L., Endert, A., & Rose, S. (2009). *Visualizing cyber security: Usable workspaces.* Workshop on Visualization for Cyber Security - VizSec.

Fry, R. (2010, July). Fighting wars in cyberspace. *Wall Street Journal*.

Hayden, M. V. (2011). The future of things "cyber". *Strategic Studies Quarterly*. Maxwell AFB, AL: Air University Press. Retrieved from http://www.au.af.mil/au/ssq/2011/spring/hayden.pdf

Holley, I. B. (2004). *Technology and military doctrine: Essays on a challenging relationship* (pp. 1–160). Air University Press.

İnce, A. N. (1997). *Planning and architectural design of modern command control communications* (p. 301). Springer. Jackson, W. (2009). DOD creates cyber command as U. S. strategic command sub-unit. *Federal Computer Week*. Washington, DC. Retrieved from http://fcw.com/Articles/2009/06/24/DOD-launches-cyber-command.aspx?p=1

Jajodia, S., Liu, P., & Swarup, V. (2009). *Cyber situational awareness: Issues and research* (p. 249). Springer.

Joint Chiefs of Staff. (2006). *Personnel support to joint operations*. US Department of Defense Joint Publication. Department of Defense.

Joint Chiefs of Staff. (2007). *Joint publication 2-0 joint intelligence*. US Department of Defense Joint Publication. Department of Defense.

Joint Chiefs of Staff. (2008). *Command and control for joint maritime operations*. US Department of Defense Joint Publication. Department of Defense.

Joint Chiefs of Staff. (2010a). *Command and control for joint land operations*. US Department of Defense Joint Publication. Department of Defense.

Joint Chiefs of Staff. (2010b). *Joint publication 3-30 command and control for joint air operations*. US Department of Defense Joint Publication. Department of Defense.

Joint Chiefs of Staff. (2010c). *Department of Defense dictionary of military and associated terms*. US Department of Defense Joint Publication. US Department of Defense.

Kometer, M. W. (2010). *Command in air war: Centralized versus decentralized control of combat airpower* (p. 348). Maxwell AFB, AL: Air University Press.

Krulak, C. C. (1996). Command and control. *Marine Corps Doctrinal Publication, 6* (pp. 1-156). Washington, DC: Wildside Press LLC. Retrieved January 30, 2011, from http://books.google.com/books?id=FiyX-ARjwDMC&pgis=1

Lawson, J. (1981). Command control as a process. *IEEE Control Systems Magazine, 1*(1), 5–11. doi:10.1109/MCS.1981.1100748

Matheus, C. J., Kokar, M. M., & Baclawski, K. (2003). A core ontology for situation awareness. *Proceedings of the Sixth International Conference on Information Fusion* (pp. 545-552).

Morris, D. J. (1983). *Communication for command and control systems* (p. 506). Pergamon Press.

Qiao, L., & Xiangsui, W. (2002). *Unrestricted warfare: China's master plan to destroy America* (p. 197). Panama City, Panama: Pan American Publishing Company.

Qureshi, Z., & Urlings, P. (2002). Situation awareness and automation: Issues and design approaches. *Proceedings Information. Decision and Control, 1999*, 605–610.

Salerno, J. (2008). Measuring situation assessment performance through the activities of interest score. *2008 11th International Conference on Information Fusion* (pp. 1-8).

Salerno, J., Hinman, M., & Boulware, D. (2002). Building a framework for situation awareness. In V. S. Naipaul (Ed.), *Proceedings of the Fifth International Conference on Information Fusion, 2002* (pp. 680-686). Sunnyvale, CA: International Society of Information Fusion.

Salerno, J., Hinman, M., Boulware, D., & Bello, P. (2003). Information fusion for situational awareness. *Proceedings of the Sixth International Symposium on Information Fusion (Fusion 2003)*, Cairns, Queensland, Australia (pp. 507-513).

Tadda, G. P. (2008). Measuring performance of cyber situation awareness systems. *2008 11th International Conference on Information Fusion* (pp. 1-8).

Tapscott, D., & Williams, A. D. (2008). *Wikinomics: How mass collaboration changes everything* (pp. 1–368). Portfolio Hardcover.

Thoms, G. A. (2003). Situation awareness - A commander's view. *Proceedings of the Sixth International Symposium on Information Fusion (Fusion 2003)*, Cairns, Queensland, Australia (pp. 1094-1101).

van Creveld, M. L. (1985). *Command in war* (pp. 1–339). Cambridge, MA: Harvard University Press.

von Clausewitz, C. (1832). *On war: Vom Kriege*. Forgotten Books. Retrieved from http://books.google.com/books?id=eVjotAEMyRwC&pgis=1

Walker, G., Stanton, N. A., & Salmon, P. M. (2009). *Command and control: The sociotechnical perspective* (p. 198). Ashgate Publishing, Ltd.

Wohl, J. G. (1981). Force management decision requirements for Air Force tactical command and control. *IEEE Transactions on Systems, Man, and Cybernetics, 11*(9), 618–639. doi:10.1109/TSMC.1981.4308760

Writer, S. (2010). War in the fifth domain. *Economist, 396*(8689), 25–28.

ADDITIONAL READING

Alberts, D. S., Garstka, J. J., Hayes, R. E., & Signori, A. (2001). *Understanding Information Age Warfare. Knowledge Creation Diffusion Utilization* (p. 319). Command and Control Research Program Publications.

Goodall, J. R., & Sowul, M. (2009). VIAssist: Visual Analytics for Cyber Defense. *Integration The Vlsi Journal*, 143-150.

İnce, A. N. (1997). *Planning and architectural design of modern command control communications* (p. 301). Springer.

Joint Chiefs of Staff. (2006). Joint Publication 3-13 Information Operations. *US Department of Defense Joint Publication*. Department of Defense.

McMorrow, D. (2010). *Science of Cyber-Security* (pp. 1–83). Washington, DC.

Stanton, N. A., Stanton, N., Baber, C., & Harris, D. (2008). *Modelling command and control: event analysis of systemic teamwork* (p. 249). Ashgate Publishing, Ltd. Retrieved January 31, 2011, from http://books.google.com/books?id=chqJM48ZBBkC&pgis=1.

Ten, C.-W., Manimaran, G., & Liu, C.-C. (2010). Cybersecurity for Critical Infrastructures: Attack and Defense Modeling. *IEEE Transactions on Systems, Man, and Cybernetics. Part A, Systems and Humans, 40*(4), 853–865. doi:10.1109/TSMCA.2010.2048028

KEY TERMS AND DEFINITIONS

Command and Control: The exercise of authority and direction by a properly designated commander over assigned and attached forces in the accomplishment of the mission. Command and control functions are performed through an arrangement of personnel, equipment, communications, facilities, and procedures employed by a commander in planning, directing, coordinating, and controlling forces and operations in the accomplishment of the mission.(Joint Chiefs of Staff, 2010c)

Situation Assessment: Is the set of processes and best practices for achieving situation awareness.

Situation Awareness Level 1 – Perception: The level where data and information are collected, processed, and correlated to create fully attributed elements.

Situation Awareness Level 2 – Comprehension: The aspect of situation awareness composed of two distinct components. The first component resides in the working memory of the system and provides a mechanism for correlating disjoint elements in the environment. The second component resides in the long-term memory of the system and provides the known patterns that the system will be seeking out in the course of data analysis

Situation Awareness Level 3 – Projection: The level of situatin awareness where current state is extrapoloated to possible future states. Within Cyber data the lack of "virtual physics" creates difficulty in understanding and defining projection functions.

Situation Awareness: The perception of elements in a given environment within a volume of time and space (being either physical or virtual), the comprehension of their meaning, and the projection of their near-future status. (Endsley, 1995)

ENDNOTES

[1] The OODA Loop as articulated by John Boyd in his presentation within the US Department of Defense describes the human cognitive process that occurs in the cockpit of a fighter plane during battle. A pilot Observes, Orients, Decides, and Acts. This process is performed in quick iteration many times during the course of a battle. This process has gained wide acceptance as foundational in Command and Control over the years.

[2] Titan Rain was the U.S. government's designation given to a series of coordinated attacks on American computer systems since 2003. The attacks were labeled as Chinese in origin, although their precise nature and their real identities remain unknown.

Chapter 4
A Proactive Defense Strategy to Enhance Situational Awareness in Computer Network Security

Yi Luo
The University of Arizona, USA

Ferenc Szidarovszky
The University of Arizona, USA

ABSTRACT

With the development of situational awareness in intrusion defense, a proactive response is a realistic and effective approach against the attackers. It is assumed that each player can update knowledge of the opponent and assess possible future scenarios of the dynamic game based on their previous interactions. Therefore, finding the best current move of the defender is modeled as a discrete-time stochastic control problem. An on-line, convergent, scenario based proactive defense (SPD) algorithm considering adaptive learning is developed based on differential dynamic programming (DDP) to solve the associated optimal control problem. Numerical experiment shows that the new algorithm can help the defender in finding the best dynamic strategies quickly and efficiently. Moreover, the SPD algorithm can provide optimal defensive efforts against possible future attacks within an appropriate time window, so the success of the attack in the possible future interactions can be assessed, improving situational awareness in computer network security.

BACKGROUND

With the development of information technology and computer network systems, cybersecurity is one of the most critical issues in almost every aspect of our society such as administration, business, finance, personal life, etc. Attackers often launch multi-stage attacks which can last several days, weeks and even months (Stewart, 2010).

They are the most dangerous types of attacks, since the attackers use intelligence to break the defense of the system to reach their goals. Therefore, defense strategies against these attacks are becoming more and more important in cyber space and they had been intensively studied recently (Foo et al., 2005; Foo et al., 2008; Stakhanova et al., 2007; Toth and Kruegel, 2002). The accurate and timely situational awareness can help

DOI: 10.4018/978-1-4666-0104-8.ch004

the defender find its efficient response strategies against multi-stage attacks quickly. On the other hand, a well-designed response strategy with an appropriate way to model the attacker's and the defender's decision processes and their interactions can affect current situational awareness, and it is the main objective of this chapter. Classical game theory examines decision making problems with more than one decision maker and conflicting interests. In cyber security, the outcomes of the attack and the defense depend on the efforts of both of them, therefore game theoretic analysis is the most appropriate approach to model and analyze their interactions. Many scholars used multi-player sequential decision making models as stochastic (Markovian) games (Lye and Wing, 2005; Shen et al., 2007), while others applied partially observable Markov decision processes (POMDP) to model the attacker's actions (Carin et al., 2008; Luo et al., 2009b; Zhang and Ho, 2009). However, the main disadvantage of the Markovian and the POMDP models is the extremely large state space, and therefore the solutions are hard to compute. Some scholars in the intrusion defense research community claim that the dynamic game approach is more efficient than the application of Markovian games under many situations (Liu and Zang, 2003; Siever et al., 2007), and proactive defense strategies need to be considered for intrusion defense system (Wood et al., 2000) as well. Therefore, a discrete-time dynamic evolutionary game and proactive response mechanisms are employed in this chapter to enhance situational awareness in computer network defense.

INTRODUCTION

In this chapter, the interactions between an attacker and the defender of a computer network are modeled as a system of two-person non-zero-sum non-cooperative dynamic evolutionary games with incomplete information. In the dynamic evolutionary games, the type of the players, their strategy sets, the prediction of future interactions, etc. are uncertain. The payoffs of the players are therefore random at each interaction of the game. The classical equilibrium approach has its limitations to find the solutions under this situation, so risk analysis is used often to complement the equilibrium approach to capture the uncertainty of the random elements in the players' payoff functions (Hausken, 2002; Banks and Anderson, 2006; Bier and Azaiez, 2008).

The nature of the distribution of a random variable mathematically can be described by the central moments (Samuelson, 1970). Clearly, the characterization of a random variable becomes more accurate if higher moments are employed. However, the complexity of the computation process increases as well. The first moment is usually used by researchers to describe the payoffs of the players leading to expected value analysis (Bier et al., 2005; Azaiez and Bier, 2007; Levitin, 2007; Zhuang and Bier, 2007), while a linear combination of the expectation and variance is considered as the certain equivalent of the random payoff value. A risk attitude coefficient is assigned to the variance and can be learned by the opponent along the evolutionary game. This is a well-known approach to describe the uncertainty of the dynamic system in economic literature. However, the probability distribution of the players' future possible activities is a concern in our response strategies. For updating the defender's knowledge and for the evaluation of the probability distributions of possible future attacks, we refer to our earlier works (Luo et al., 2009a; 2010; 2011). In this chapter, we assume that the players are able to update their knowledge of the opponent after each interaction, they can predict on-line the opponents' activities and the probabilities of their occurrences. Finding the best proactive defense strategy at any time period of the game is therefore modeled as an optimal control problem.

At each time period of the game, instead of assuming that the attacker is the leader and the defender is the follower, the defender considers all future possible interactions with the attacker and finds its best prevention strategy before detecting the current attack. In other words, the attacker and the defender are assumed to play a simultaneous game. The predicted possible attacks and their probabilities in future time periods can be illustrated in a scenario tree (ST).

Figure 1 shows an ST that the defender considers for its best move at the beginning of time period 1. Any node and its associated arc in each time period describe one possible interaction of the simultaneous game. The nodes represent the possible future decision points of the attacker and the defender along the game, and the arcs represent the possible interactions between them. The attacks and the defensive actions are quantified by the values of the attacker's and the defender's efforts, respectively. After obtaining its best current efforts, the defender is able to interpret them as the corresponding defensive moves against the attacker.

In Figure 1, the numbers given in the parenthesis of each arc show the effort of the attacker and the probability of that attack. In comparison to the game tree, the ST shows the possible alternatives as well as describes the efforts on each choice. Therefore, the ST has more compact tree structure and can lead to more accurate best de-

fensive efforts. Due to limited time the defender cannot search the entire ST, however he/she is able to find an appropriate time window with the attacker by balancing computation capacity and the accuracy of the best efforts. For example, in Figure 1 the time window considered by the defender is two. Therefore, a partial scenario tree (PST) with the depth of the length of the time window can be obtained and used.

In order to find its best move, the defender needs to optimize its payoff based on the updated PST, which requires the solution of a discrete-time optimal control problem. Dynamic programming (DP), which has the characteristics of a stage-wise decomposition, is an efficient way to solve control problems (Murray and Yakowitz, 1981). However, the special form of the variance makes it very difficult to use because of the nonseparability of the squared term (Li and Ng, 2000). Therefore, we propose a good approximation of the first two central moments of the defender's payoff by using the first two raw moments to overcome this difficulty. However, it is still very hard to use regular dynamic programming because of the large size of the problem and the nonlinearity of the payoffs.

Differential Dynamic Programming (DDP) is a successive approximation technique, where second-order Taylor series are used to estimate the complex nonlinear objective functions (Jacobson and Mayne, 1970). This methodology has many successful applications (Heidari, 1970; Murray

Figure 1. A scenario tree starting at time period 1

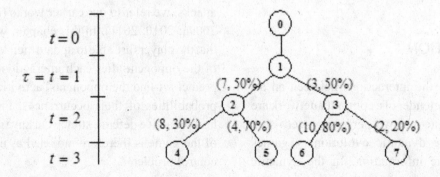

and Yakowitz, 1979; Chang et al., 1990; Morimoto et al., 2003) and it is known that the DDP guarantees quadratic convergence (Yakowitz, 1989). Therefore, the basic idea of our SPD algorithm is to enhance initial nominal defensive effort trajectories on a PST using the DDP, consider the updated effort trajectories as new nominal trajectories and improve them again. The process will not terminate until best effort trajectories are found. After implementing current response and observing current attack, the defender's knowledge of the attacker can be updated for more accurate prediction of future possible attacks. In the next time period of the game, a new PST is constructed and the nominal effort trajectories are kept updating again.

This chapter focuses on the determination of optimal effort trajectories based on a PST. The attacker's possible future strategy set can be predicted based on attack path analysis (see for example, Lye and Wing, 2005). The equilibrium analysis of the evolutionary game will be presented in our future papers.

The rest of the chapter is organized as follows. Section 2 introduces the optimal control model for the dynamic game. The new SPD algorithm is introduced in Section 3 and an illustrative example is shown in Section 4. Conclusions and future research directions are outlined in the final section.

OPTIMAL CONTROL MODEL

The State of Stochastic Discrete-Time Dynamic System

It is assumed that the attacker launches its multi-stage attack in the network system to one objective with value v. The attack-defense game can be modeled as an optimal control problem and represented by a discrete-time dynamic system, where the states of the system depend on the cumulative efforts of both the attacker and the defender along the game. Let S be the set of discrete time periods in the game, and t be the index of the time periods ($t \in S$, $t = 0, 1, 2, \ldots$). The total number of time periods depends on the time when the attacker stops its actions. Suppose the defender needs to make decision at the beginning of time period $\tau(\tau \in S)$.

Figure 2 shows the previous and possible future interactions of the two players considered by the defender, which is also an extension of the dynamic system shown in Figure 1.

At time period t ($t < \tau$) let a_t and u_t be the efforts of the attacker and the defender, w_t^A and w_t^D the relative effectiveness of the attacker's and the defender's efforts which can be assessed based on technology information. A ST is developed at the beginning of time period τ.

Let T be the length of the time window that the defender will consider for its decision at this moment. The future possible attacks can be represented by a PST (τ, T) shown in Figure 2, the properties of which can be described as follows. Let N_t be the total number of nodes starting at time period t, n_t be the index of these nodes ($n_t = 1, 2, \ldots, N_t$ for $t = \tau, \tau+1, \ldots, \tau+T-1$). The defender can identify I_t different attack intensity levels at time period t, which are denoted by $i_t = 1, 2, \ldots, I_t$. It is assumed that the attacker's possible strategies and their probabilities can be predicted by the defender. Let a_{i_t} denote the predicted effort of the attacker with intensity level i_t in time period t. In addition let $p_{i_t}^{i_{t+1}}$ be the predicted transition (Markovian) probability of attack intensity levels from i_t to i_{t+1} between the adjacent time periods t and t + 1. The decision variables of the defender are its defending efforts u_{i_t} on the arcs originating from node n_t. Their optimal values can be obtained by using the SPD algorithm to be outlined in the next section. Let x_{i_t} be the future state of the system which represents the success of the attack following a possible realiza-

Figure 2. A stochastic dynamic system starting at time period τ

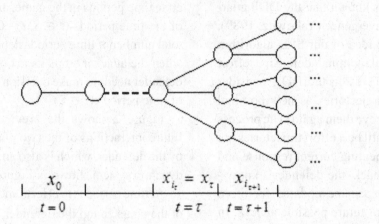

tion in the PST (τ, T). It can be obtained from the accumulative efforts of the attacker and the defender along the realization from the previous t-1 time periods as follows:

$$x_{i_t} = \frac{\sum_{k=0}^{\tau-1} w_k^A a_k + \sum_{k=\tau}^{t-1} w_k^A a_{i_k}}{\sum_{k=0}^{\tau-1} w_k^A a_k + \sum_{k=\tau}^{t-1} w_k^A a_{i_k} + \sum_{k=0}^{\tau-1} w_k^D u_k + \sum_{k=\tau}^{t-1} w_k^D u_{i_k}}.$$
$(i_t=1, 2, ..., I, t = \tau+1, \tau+2, ..., \tau+T-1)$ \qquad (1)

where the initial state depends on the time period when decision is made:

$$x_{i_\tau} = x_\tau = \begin{cases} \dfrac{\sum_{k=0}^{\tau-1} w_k^A a_k}{\sum_{k=0}^{\tau-1} w_k^A a_k + \sum_{k=0}^{\tau-1} w_k^D u_k} & \text{if } \tau > 1 \\[2ex] \dfrac{w_0^A a_0}{w_0^A a_0 + w_0^D u_0} & \text{if } \tau = 1. \\[2ex] 0 & \text{if } \tau = 0 \end{cases}$$

In order to avoid zero denominator, we can add a very small positive number to it. However, for the sake of notational simplicity, we ignore this term in the rest of the chapter. The recursive relationship between states x_{i_t} and $x_{i_{t-1}}$ along a realization can be described by Equation

$$\frac{\sum_{k=0}^{\tau-1} w_k^A a_k + \sum_{k=\tau}^{t-1} w_k^A a_{i_k}}{x_{i_t}} =$$
$$\frac{\sum_{k=0}^{\tau-1} w_k^A a_k + \sum_{k=\tau}^{t-2} w_k^A a_{i_k}}{x_{i_{t-1}}} + w_{t-1}^A a_{i_{t-1}} + w_{t-1}^D u_{i_{t-1}}.$$
$(i_t=1, 2, ..., I, t = \tau+1, \tau+2, ..., \tau+T-1)$ \qquad (2)

Let $A_{i_t} = \sum_{k=0}^{\tau-1} w_k^A a_k + \sum_{k=\tau}^{t} w_k^A a_{i_k}$, then this Equation can be re-written as

$$x_{i_t} =$$
$$f(x_{i_{t-1}}, u_{i_{t-1}}) = \frac{x_{i_{t-1}} A_{i_{t-1}}}{A_{i_{t-2}} + x_{i_{t-1}}(w_{t-1}^A a_{i_{t-1}} + w_{t-1}^D u_{i_{t-1}})}.$$
$(i_t=1, 2, ..., I, t = \tau+1, \tau+2, ..., \tau+T-1)$ \qquad (3)

COST FUNCTIONS

In the dynamic game, it is assumed that the attacker is rational, launches multi-stage attacks to maximize its impact. The defender tries to minimize the impact of the attack by its defense. The payoffs of the attacker and the defender are not necessary equal because they have their own values of system vulnerabilities and costs of their actions. The defender's payoff consists of the actual damage, the defending cost within the PST and the potential future damage/cost after the considered time window (Luo et al., 2009a). The defending costs are proportional to the efforts of the defender, while the actual damages and the potential damages/costs depend on the success probabilities of the attacks. Contest success function (CSF), introduced in (Skaperdas, 1996; Hausken, 2008), is used to assess these probabilities based on the cumulative efforts of the two players along the realization of the game.

In the PST (τ, T), the cost function of the dynamic system can be determined based on the payoff of the defender. The possible future attacks and defenses are however uncertain, the effort $\tilde{u}_t$ of the defender and the state $\tilde{x}_t$ of the system during time period t are also random. Let $\tilde{L}(\tilde{x}_t, \tilde{u}_t)$ be the possible actual damage and defending cost of the system based on $\tilde{x}_t$ and $\tilde{u}_t$, $\tilde{G}(\tilde{x}_{\tau+T})$ the potential damage/cost of the system after the selected time window. It is assumed that $\tilde{L}(\tilde{x}_t, \tilde{u}_t)$ and $\tilde{G}(\tilde{x}_{\tau+T})$ are independent random variables. As we mentioned earlier, uncertainty in a random objective function $\tilde{X}$ is modeled by replacing the random outcome with its certain equivalent $E(\tilde{X}) + \lambda Var(\tilde{X})$ where the value of $\lambda \geq 0$ represents the willingness of the defender to take risk. In general, $\tau = 0$ is assigned to risk seekers, and $\lambda = \infty$ belongs to risk averters. The certain equivalent of $\tilde{L}(\tilde{x}_t, \tilde{u}_t)$ can be described as:

$$L(\tilde{x}_t, \tilde{u}_t) = E[\tilde{L}(\tilde{x}_t, \tilde{u}_t)] + \lambda Var[\tilde{L}(\tilde{x}_t, \tilde{u}_t)].$$
$$(t = \tau, \tau+1, ..., \tau+T-1) \qquad (4)$$

Similarly, the certain equivalent of $\tilde{G}(\tilde{x}_{\tau+T})$ can be computed as

$$G(\tilde{x}_{\tau+T}) = E[\tilde{G}(\tilde{x}_{\tau+T})] + \lambda Var[\tilde{G}(\tilde{x}_{\tau+T})].$$
$$(5)$$

The cost function $\tilde{V}_t(\tilde{x}_t)$ at time period t includes actual damages and defending costs within the PST (τ, T) and all potential damages/costs beyond it which are uncertain as well. Since $\tilde{L}(\tilde{x}_t, \tilde{u}_t)$ and $\tilde{G}(\tilde{x}_{\tau+T})$ are assumed to be independent, the certain equivalent of $\tilde{V}_t(\tilde{x}_t)$ can be represented as

$$V_t(\tilde{x}_t) = \sum_{t=t}^{\tau+T-1} L(\tilde{x}_t, \tilde{u}_t) + G(\tilde{x}_{\tau+T})$$
$$= \sum_{t=t}^{\tau+T-1} \{E[\tilde{L}(\tilde{x}_t, \tilde{u}_t)] + \lambda Var[\tilde{L}(\tilde{x}_t, \tilde{u}_t)]\}$$
$$+ E[\tilde{G}(\tilde{x}_t)] + \lambda Var[\tilde{G}(\tilde{x}_t)].$$
$$(t = \tau, \tau+1, ..., \tau+T-1) \qquad (6)$$

Dynamic programming seems to be an appropriate approach to find the current optimal defense efforts by moving backward from the end of PST (τ, T) and minimizing the cost at each time period. However, the terms $E^2[\tilde{L}(\tilde{x}_t, \tilde{u}_t)]$ and $E^2[\tilde{G}(\tilde{x}_t)]$ in $Var[\tilde{L}(\tilde{x}_t, \tilde{u}_t)]$ and $Var[\tilde{G}(\tilde{x}_t)]$ are not separable, so $Vt(\tilde{x}_t)$ is not separable as well. We can however overcome this difficulty by using the following approximation:

Proposition 1

Let $\tilde{X}$ be a random objective function with $0 \leq E(\tilde{X}) \leq \frac{1}{2\lambda}$. Then optimizing the certain equivalent $E(\tilde{X}) + \lambda Var(\tilde{X})$ can be approximated by the optimum problem of $E(\tilde{X}) + \alpha E(\tilde{X}^2) + \beta$ with given values of α and β.

Proof:

Notice first that $f(E(\tilde{X})) = E(\tilde{X}) - \lambda E^2(\tilde{X})$ is a concave parabola in $\tilde{X}$. The derivative of $f(E(\tilde{X}))$ with respect to $E(\tilde{X})$ is $1 - 2\lambda E(\tilde{X})$. So the vertex is $E^*(\tilde{X}) = \frac{1}{2\lambda}$. Then in interval $[0, E^*(\tilde{X})]$, we can use the linear approximation $E(\tilde{X}) - \lambda E^2(\tilde{X}) \approx uE(\tilde{X}) + v$.

In order to obtain the best approximation of $f(E(\tilde{X}))$, we need to solve the minimization problem

Minimize

$$M(E(\tilde{X})) = \int_0^{E^*(\tilde{X})} [E(\tilde{X}) - \lambda E^2(\tilde{X}) - (uE(\tilde{X}) + v)]^2 \, dE(\tilde{X})$$

It can be expanded as

$$M(E(\tilde{X})) =$$

$$u^2 \int_0^{E^*(\tilde{X})} E^2(\tilde{X}) dE(\tilde{X}) + v^2 \int_0^{E^*(\tilde{X})} dE(\tilde{X})$$

$$+ 2uv \int_0^{E^*(\tilde{X})} E(\tilde{X}) dE(\tilde{X})$$

$$- 2u \int_0^{E^*(\tilde{X})} (E^2(\tilde{X}) - \lambda E^3(\tilde{X})) dE(\tilde{X})$$

$$- 2v \int_0^{E^*(\tilde{X})} (E(\tilde{X}) - \lambda E^2(\tilde{X})) dE(\tilde{X})$$

$$+ \int_0^{E^*(\tilde{X})} (E(\tilde{X}) - \lambda E^2(\tilde{X}))^2 dE(\tilde{X})$$

The first order conditions have the form

$$\frac{\partial M}{\partial u} = u \int_0^{E^*(\tilde{X})} E^2(\tilde{X}) dE(\tilde{X})$$

$$+ v \int_0^{E^*(\tilde{X})} E(\tilde{X}) dE(\tilde{X})$$

$$- \int_0^{E^*(\tilde{X})} E(\tilde{X})(E(\tilde{X}) - \lambda E^2(\tilde{X})) dE(\tilde{X})$$

$$= 0$$

$$\frac{\partial M}{\partial v} = u \int_0^{E^*(\tilde{X})} E(\tilde{X}) dE(\tilde{X})$$

$$+ v \int_0^{E^*(\tilde{X})} dE(\tilde{X}) - \int_0^{E^*(\tilde{X})} (E(\tilde{X}) - \lambda E^2(\tilde{X})) dE(\tilde{X})$$

$$= 0$$

Solving these Equations for unknowns u and v gives the optimal coefficient values (seen in Box 1).

We can use backward dynamic programming approach to solve this optimal control problem.

However, due to the uncertainty in future attacks, this cost function cannot be used directly. After the possible future attack-defense scenarios are predicted and described on a PST (τ, T), the defender's efforts, the states of the system and the cost function can be obtained based on each realization trajectory.

Let c_t be the unit penalty cost associated with each unit of the defender's efforts at time period t (t = 0, 1, 2, ...), and $L(x_{i_t}, u_{i_t})$ be the actual damage and the defending cost of the system for a possible realization during this time period, then

$$L(x_{i_t}, u_{i_t}) = v \frac{A_{i_t}}{A_{i_{t-1}} + \sum_{k=0}^t w_k^D u_{i_k}} + c_t u_{i_t}$$

$$= v x_{i_{t+1}} + c_t u_{i_t}$$

$$= v \frac{x_{i_t} A_{i_t}}{A_{i_{t-1}} + x_{i_t}(w_t^A a_{i_t} + w_t^D u_{i_t})} + c_t u_{i_t}.$$

$$(i_t = 1, 2, ..., I_t, t = \tau, \tau + 1, ..., \tau + T - 1) \qquad (8)$$

The first two moments and the variance of $\tilde{L}(\tilde{x}_t, \tilde{u}_t)$ can be obtained as

$$E[\tilde{L}(\tilde{x}_t, \tilde{u}_t)] = \sum_{i_t=1}^{I_t} L(x_{i_t}, u_{i_t}) p_{i_t}^{i_{t+1}} = E[L(x_{i_t}, u_{i_t})],$$

$$E[\tilde{L}^2(\tilde{x}_t, \tilde{u}_t)] = \sum_{i_t=1}^{I_t} L^2(x_{i_t}, u_{i_t}) p_{i_t}^{i_{t+1}} = E[L^2(x_{i_t}, u_{i_t})],$$

$$Var[\tilde{L}(\tilde{x}_t, \tilde{u}_t)] = E[L^2(x_{i_t}, u_{i_t})] - E^2[L(x_{i_t}, u_{i_t})].$$

$$(t = \tau, \tau + 1, ..., \tau + T - 1) \qquad (9)$$

Based on Equations (4), (9) and Proposition 1, we have the approximation

$$L(\tilde{x}_t, \tilde{u}_t) \approx E[L(x_{i_t}, u_{i_t})] + \alpha_1 E[L^2(x_{i_t}, u_{i_t})] + \beta_1.$$

$$(t = \tau, \tau + 1, ..., \tau + T - 1) \qquad (10)$$

Let $G(x_{i_{\tau+T}})$ be the potential damage/cost of the system for a possible realization at the end of the PST(τ, T). The probability of this realization is $Q_{i_t} = \prod_{k=\tau}^{t-1} p_{i_k}^{i_{k+1}}$. The first two moments and the variance of the possible damage/cost $\tilde{G}(\tilde{x}_{\tau+T})$ after the selected time window are given as

$$E[\tilde{G}(\tilde{x}_{\tau+T})] = \sum_{i_{\tau+T}=1}^{I_{\tau+T}} G(x_{i_{\tau+T}})Q_{i_{\tau+T}} = E[G(x_{i_{\tau+T}})],$$

$$E[\tilde{G}^2(\tilde{x}_{\tau+T})] = \sum_{i_{t+T}=1}^{I_{\tau+T}} G^2(x_{i_{\tau+T}})Q_{i_{\tau+T}} = E[G^2(x_{i_{\tau+T}})],$$

$$Var[\tilde{G}(\tilde{x}_{\tau+T})] = E[G^2(x_{i_{\tau+T}})] - E^2[G(x_{i_{\tau+T}})].$$

(11)

Considering Equations (5), (11) and Proposition 1, we obtain

$$G(\tilde{x}_{\tau+T}) \approx E[G(x_{i_{\tau+T}})] + \alpha_2 E[G^2(x_{i_{\tau+T}})] + \beta_2.$$

(12)

Based on Equation (7), the total damage and defending cost of the system, $V_{n_t}(x_{i_t})$ starting at a decision node n_t to the end of the PST (τ, T) is presented as follows:

$$V_{n_t}(x_{i_t}) = \sum_{i_t=1}^{I_t}\sum_{i_{t+1}=1}^{I_{t+1}}\cdots\sum_{i_{t+T-1}=1}^{I_{t+T-1}}$$
$$[\sum_{k=t}^{\tau+T-1} L(x_{i_k}, u_{i_k}) + \alpha_1 L^2(x_{i_k}, u_{i_k}) +$$
$$\beta_1 + G(x_{i_{\tau+T}}) + \alpha_2 G^2(x_{i_{\tau+T}}) + \beta_2]Q_{i_t}$$
$$= \sum_{k=t}^{\tau+T-1}\{E[L(x_{i_k}, u_{i_k})]$$
$$+\alpha_1 E[L^2(x_{i_k}, u_{i_k})] + \beta_1\}$$
$$+E[G(x_{i_{\tau+T}})] + \alpha_2 E[G^2(x_{i_{\tau+T}})] + \beta_2.$$

$(n_t=1, 2, ..., N_t, t=\tau, \tau+1, ..., \tau+T-1)$ (13)

Let $V_{i_t}(x_{i_t})$ be the total damage and defending cost starting at an arc i_t to the end of the game. If this arc originates at node n_t, then the relationship between $V_{n_t}(x_{i_t})$ and $V_{i_t}(x_{i_t})$ is

$$V_{n_t}(x_{i_t}) = \sum_{i_t=1}^{I_t} V_{i_t}(x_{i_t})p_{i_t}^{i_{t+1}} = E[V_{i_t}(x_{i_t})]$$

$(n_t=1, 2, ..., N_t, t=\tau, \tau+1, ..., \tau+T-1)$ (14)

Let
$$R(x_{i_t}, u_{i_t}) = L(x_{i_t}, u_{i_t}) + \alpha_1 L^2(x_{i_t}, u_{i_t}) + \beta_1.$$
For any arc i_t connecting nodes n_t and n_{t+1}, we have

$$V_{i_t}(x_{i_t}) = R(x_{i_t}, u_{i_t}) + V_{n_{t+1}}(x_{i_{t+1}})$$

$(i_t=1, 2, ..., I_t, n_{t+1}=1, 2, ..., N_{t+1}, t=\tau, \tau+1, ..., \tau+T-1)$ (15)

where

$$V_{n_{\tau+T}}(x_{i_{\tau+T}}) = E[G(x_{i_{\tau+T}})] + \alpha_2 E[G^2(x_{i_{\tau+T}})] + \beta_2$$

SCENARIO BASED PROACTIVE DEFENSE ALGORITHM (SPD)

Differential Dynamic Programming

In our SPD algorithm, global variations in control (Jacobson and Mayne, 1970) is used to define the defender's efforts and the states of the dynamic system. Let $\bar{u}_{i_t}$ be the nominal efforts of the defender, $\bar{x}_{i_t}$ be the nominal states of the game computed by Equation (3), and $u_{i_t}^*$ be the estimated optimal efforts of the defender for state $\bar{x}_{i_t}$ ($t \in [\tau, \tau+T]$). The efforts u_{i_t} and the states x_{i_t} satisfy the difference Equations

$$u_{i_t} = u_{i_t}^* + \delta u_{i_t}$$

$$x_{i_t} = \bar{x}_{i_t} + \delta x_{i_t},$$

$(i_t=1, 2, ..., I_t, t=\tau, \tau+1, ..., \tau+T)$ (16)

where δu_{i_t} and δx_{i_t} are the effort and state variables, respectively, measured with respect to the nominal state $\bar{x}_{i_t}$ and the optimal defensive effort $u_{i_t}^*$. They are not necessarily small quantities. Under this control policy, x_{i_t} is restricted to the neighborhood of $\bar{x}_{i_t}$. The values of $u_{i_t}^*$ and δu_{i_t} have to be chosen to find u_{i_t}. Large δu_{i_t} is permit-

Box 1.

$$u = \frac{\int_0^{E^*(\tilde{X})} (E(\tilde{X}) - \lambda E^2(\tilde{X})) dE(\tilde{X}) \int_0^{E^*(\tilde{X})} E(\tilde{X}) dE(\tilde{X}) - \int_0^{E^*(\tilde{X})} (E^2(\tilde{X}) - \lambda E^3(\tilde{X})) dE(\tilde{X}) \int_0^{E^*(\tilde{X})} dE(\tilde{X})}{(\int_0^{E^*(\tilde{X})} E(\tilde{X}) dE(\tilde{X}))^2 - \int_0^{E^*(\tilde{X})} E^2(\tilde{X}) dE(\tilde{X}) \int_0^{E^*(\tilde{X})} dE(\tilde{X})}$$

and

$$v = \frac{\int_0^{E^*(\tilde{X})} (E^2(\tilde{X}) - \lambda E^3(\tilde{X})) dE(\tilde{X}) \int_0^{E^*(\tilde{X})} E(\tilde{X}) dE(\tilde{X}) - \int_0^{E^*(\tilde{X})} (E(\tilde{X}) - \lambda E^2(\tilde{X})) dE(\tilde{X}) \int_0^{E^*(\tilde{X})} E^2(\tilde{X}) dE(\tilde{X})}{(\int_0^{E^*(\tilde{X})} E(\tilde{X}) dE(\tilde{X}))^2 - \int_0^{E^*(\tilde{X})} E^2(\tilde{X}) dE(\tilde{X}) \int_0^{E^*(\tilde{X})} dE(\tilde{X})}$$

Therefore

$E(\tilde{X}) + \lambda Var(\tilde{X}) = E(\tilde{X}) + \lambda[E(\tilde{X}^2) - E^2(\tilde{X})] \approx uE(\tilde{X}) + v + \lambda E(\tilde{X}^2)$. Suppose $\alpha = \dfrac{\lambda}{u}$ and

$\beta = \dfrac{v}{u}$, then optimizing $E(\tilde{X}) + \lambda Var(\tilde{X})$ can be approximated by the optimum problem of $E(\tilde{X}) + \alpha E(\tilde{X}^2) + \beta$ in

interval $[0, E^*(\tilde{X})]$.

∇

Based on Proposition 1 and Equation (6), $V_t(\tilde{x}_t)$ can be approximated by the separable function

$$V_t(\tilde{x}_t) = \sum_{t=t}^{\tau+T-1} \{E[\tilde{L}(\tilde{x}_t, \tilde{u}_t)] + \alpha_1 E[\tilde{L}^2(\tilde{x}_t, \tilde{u}_t)] + \beta_1\} + E[\tilde{G}(\tilde{x}_{\tau+T})] + \alpha_2 E[\tilde{G}^2(\tilde{x}_{\tau+T})] + \beta_2$$
$$= L(\tilde{x}_t, \tilde{u}_t) + V_{t+1}(\tilde{x}_{t+1}),$$
$(t = \tau, \tau+1, ..., \tau+T-1)$

(7)

ted when there is the effort of a global change in u_{i_t} to $u_{i_t}^*$.

The goal of the SPD algorithm is to find the defender's best efforts based on the probability distribution of possible future attacks. The values of the optimal efforts $u_{i_t}^*$ can be obtained by minimizing the right hand side of Equation (15) with state $\bar{x}_{i_t}$. However, it is difficult to solve the resulting complex nonlinear optimization problem directly. Therefore, a successive approximation technique based on DDP is employed as follows. At the defender's decision node with a given PST (τ, T), the initial nominal effort trajectories are updated iteratively until the best effort trajectories

are obtained. After each update, the nominal effort trajectories are improved, resulting in the reduced total damage and cost of the system. Each update includes a backward process and a forward process along the possible realizations between the end node and the root of PST (τ, T). At each step of the backward process, we find that $V_{i_t}(x_{i_t})$ is convex based on Equations (8) and (15). Let $V_x^{i_t}(x_{i_t})$ and $V_{xx}^{i_t}(x_{i_t})$ be the first and the second derivative of $V_{i_t}(x_{i_t})$ with respect to x_{i_t}. If $V_{i_t}(x_{i_t})$ is sufficiently smooth then it can be approximated in a sufficiently small neighborhood of $\bar{x}_{i_t}$ by the second order Taylor polynomial

$$V_{i_t}(x_{i_t}) = V_{i_t}(\overline{x}_{i_t} + \delta x_{i_t}) = V_{i_t}(\overline{x}_{i_t})$$

$$+ V_x^{i_t}(\overline{x}_{i_t})\delta x_{i_t} + \frac{1}{2}V_{xx}^{i_t}(\overline{x}_{i_t})\delta x_{i_t}^2 + \ldots$$

$$(i_t = 1, 2, \ldots, I_t, t = \tau, \tau+1, \ldots, \tau+T) \qquad (17)$$

The error of this approximation is third-order in δx_{i_t} if the third derivative of $V_{i_t}(x_{i_t})$ exists and is bounded. Since we require the knowledge of $V_{i_t}(x_{i_t})$ only in the neighborhood of $\overline{x}_{i_t}$, the parameters $V_{i_t}(\overline{x}_{i_t})$, $V_x^{i_t}(\overline{x}_{i_t})$ and $V_{xx}^{i_t}(\overline{x}_{i_t})$ yield good approximations of $V_{i_t}(x_{i_t})$ in this neighborhood. The procedure to obtain these parameters with much less computation is described in the next section.

EFFICIENT PROCEDURE

Considering the global variations in control, Equation (15) can be rewritten as

$$V_{i_t}(\overline{x}_{i_t} + \delta x_{i_t}) = R(\overline{x}_{i_t} + \delta x_{i_t}, u_{i_t}^* + \delta u_{i_t}) + V_{n_{t+1}}(\overline{x}_{i_{t+1}} + \delta x_{i_{t+1}})$$
$$(i_t = 1, 2, \ldots, I_t, t = \tau, \tau+1, \ldots, \tau+T-1) \qquad (18)$$

with

$$\delta x_{i_{t+1}} = x_{i_{t+1}} - \overline{x}_{i_{t+1}} = f(x_{i_t}, u_{i_t}) - f(\overline{x}_{i_t}, \overline{u}_{i_t})$$
$$= f(\overline{x}_{i_t} + \delta x_{i_t}, u_{i_t}^* + \delta u_{i_t}) - f(\overline{x}_{i_t}, \overline{u}_{i_t})$$
$$= f(\overline{x}_{i_t}, u_{i_t}^*) - f(\overline{x}_{i_t}, \overline{u}_{i_t}) + f_x^{i_t}\delta x_{i_t}$$
$$+ f_u^{i_t}\delta u_{i_t} + \frac{1}{2}f_{xx}^{i_t}\delta x_{i_t}^2 + f_{ux}^{i_t}\delta u_{i_t}\delta x_{i_t} + \frac{1}{2}f_{uu}^{i_t}\delta u_{i_t}^2 + \ldots$$
$$(19)$$

based on the second-order Taylor polynomial approximations. In the notation $f_x^{i_t}$, subscript x denotes differentiation with respect to variable x, and superscript it indicates a certain arc in time period t. Similarly, $f_{xx}^{i_t}, f_{ux}^{i_t}$ and $f_{uu}^{i_t}$ are second order partial derivatives.

Let $V_x^{n_{t+1}}(x_{i_{t+1}})$ and $V_{xx}^{n_{t+1}}(x_{i_{t+1}})$ be the first and the second derivative of $V_{n_{t+1}}(x_{i_{t+1}})$ with respect to $x_{i_{t+1}}$ at time period t+1, $R_x^{i_t}, R_u^{i_t}, R_{xx}^{i_t}, R_{ux}^{i_t}, R_{uu}^{i_t}$ be the first and second order derivatives of $R(x_{i_t}, u_{i_t})$. Using the second-order approximation for both sides of Equation (18), it becomes

$$V_{i_t}(\overline{x}_{i_t}) + V_x^{i_t}(\overline{x}_{i_t})\delta x_{i_t} + \frac{1}{2}V_{xx}^{i_t}(\overline{x}_{i_t})\delta x_{i_t}^2 =$$

$$R(\overline{x}_{i_t} + \delta x_{i_t}, u_{i_t}^* + \delta u_{i_t}) + V_{n_{t+1}}(\overline{x}_{i_{t+1}} + \delta x_{i_{t+1}})$$

$$= [R(\overline{x}_{i_t}, u_{i_t}^*) + R_x^{i_t}\delta x_{i_t} + R_u^{i_t}\delta u_{i_t} + \frac{1}{2}R_{xx}^{i_t}\delta x_{i_t}^2 + R_{ux}^{i_t}\delta u_{i_t}\delta x_{i_t} + \frac{1}{2}R_{uu}^{i_t}\delta u_{i_t}^2]$$

$$+ [V_{n_{t+1}}(\overline{x}_{i_{t+1}}) + V_x^{n_{t+1}}(\overline{x}_{i_{t+1}})\delta x_{i_{t+1}} + \frac{1}{2}V_{xx}^{n_{t+1}}(\overline{x}_{i_{t+1}})\delta x_{i_{t+1}}^2] + \ldots$$

$$(i_t = 1, 2, \ldots, I_t, t = \tau, \tau+1, \ldots, \tau+T-1) \qquad (20)$$

Substituting $\delta x_{i_{t+1}}$ of Equation (19) into Equation (20) yields

$$V_{i_t}(\overline{x}_{i_t}) + V_x^{i_t}(\overline{x}_{i_t})\delta x_{i_t} + \frac{1}{2}V_{xx}^{i_t}(\overline{x}_{i_t})\delta x_{i_t}^2 =$$

$$R(\overline{x}_{i_t}, u_{i_t}^*) + V_{n_{t+1}}(\overline{x}_{i_{t+1}}) + V_x^{n_{t+1}}(\overline{x}_{i_{t+1}})[(f(\overline{x}_{i_t}, u_{i_t}^*) - f(\overline{x}_{i_t}, \overline{u}_{i_t})] +$$
$$\frac{1}{2}V_{xx}^{n_{t+1}}(\overline{x}_{i_{t+1}})[f(\overline{x}_{i_t}, u_{i_t}^*) - f(\overline{x}_{i_t}, \overline{u}_{i_t})]^2 + B_{i_t}^I\delta x_{i_t} + B_{i_t}^{II}\delta u_{i_t} +$$
$$\frac{1}{2}B_{i_t}^{III}\delta x_{i_t}^2 + B_{i_t}^{IV}\delta u_{i_t}\delta x_{i_t} + \frac{1}{2}B_{i_t}^V\delta u_{i_t}^2 + e_{i_t},$$
$$(i_t = 1, 2, \ldots, I_t, t = \tau, \tau+1, \ldots, \tau+T-1) \qquad (21)$$

where

$$B_{i_t}^I = R_x(\overline{x}_{i_t}, \overline{u}_{i_t}) + V_x^{n_{t+1}}f_x(\overline{x}_{i_t}, \overline{u}_{i_t})$$
$$+ V_{xx}^{n_{t+1}}[f(\overline{x}_{i_t}, u_{i_t}^*) - f(\overline{x}_{i_t}, \overline{u}_{i_t})]f_x(\overline{x}_{i_t}, \overline{u}_{i_t}),$$

$$B_{i_t}^{II} = R_u(\overline{x}_{i_t}, \overline{u}_{i_t}) + V_x^{n_{t+1}}f_u(\overline{x}_{i_t}, \overline{u}_{i_t})$$
$$+ V_{xx}^{n_{t+1}}[f(\overline{x}_{i_t}, u_{i_t}^*) - f(\overline{x}_{i_t}, \overline{u}_{i_t})]f_u(\overline{x}_{i_t}, \overline{u}_{i_t}),$$

$$B_{i_t}^{III} = R_{xx}(\overline{x}_{i_t}, \overline{u}_{i_t}) + V_x^{n_{t+1}} f_{xx}(\overline{x}_{i_t}, \overline{u}_{i_t})$$
$$+ V_{xx}^{n_{t+1}} \{[f_x(\overline{x}_{i_t}, \overline{u}_{i_t})]^2 + [f(\overline{x}_{i_t}, u_{i_t}^*) - f(\overline{x}_{i_t}, \overline{u}_{i_t})] f_{xx}(\overline{x}_{i_t}, \overline{u}_{i_t})\},$$

$$B_{i_t}^{IV} = R_{ux}(\overline{x}_{i_t}, \overline{u}_{i_t}) + V_x^{n_{t+1}} f_{ux}(\overline{x}_{i_t}, \overline{u}_{i_t})$$
$$+ V_{xx}^{n_{t+1}} \{f_u(\overline{x}_{i_t}, \overline{u}_{i_t}) f_x(\overline{x}_{i_t}, \overline{u}_{i_t}) + [f(\overline{x}_{i_t}, u_{i_t}^*) - f(\overline{x}_{i_t}, \overline{u}_{i_t})] f_{ux}(\overline{x}_{i_t}, \overline{u}_{i_t})\},$$

$$B_{i_t}^{V} = R_{uu}(\overline{x}_{i_t}, \overline{u}_{i_t}) + V_x^{n_{t+1}} f_{uu}(\overline{x}_{i_t}, \overline{u}_{i_t})$$
$$+ V_{xx}^{n_{t+1}} \{[f_u(\overline{x}_{i_t}, \overline{u}_{i_t})]^2 + [f(\overline{x}_{i_t}, u_{i_t}^*) - f(\overline{x}_{i_t}, \overline{u}_{i_t})] f_{uu}(\overline{x}_{i_t}, \overline{u}_{i_t})\}.$$

The values of $V_{n_t}(\overline{x}_{i_t})$, $V_x^{n_t}(\overline{x}_{i_t})$ and $V_{xx}^{n_t}(\overline{x}_{i_t})$ are supposed to be obtained from equating the like coefficients of δx_{i_t} based on Equation (21). However, in addition to δx_{i_t} and $\delta x_{i_t}^2$, the right-hand side of Equation (21) also contains $u_{i_t}^*$, δu_{i_t} and $\delta u_{i_t}^2$. So, we needs to find the relationships between these effort variables and δx_{i_t}.

The estimated optimal control action $u_{i_t}^*$ for state $\overline{x}_{i_t}$ can be found by minimizing $V_{i_t}(\overline{x}_{i_t})$, which is the same as minimizing the right-hand side of Equation (21) with $\delta u_{i_t} = \delta x_{i_t} = e_{i_t} = 0$. That is,

$$u_{i_t}^* = \arg\min_{u_{i_t}} \{$$

$$R(\overline{x}_{i_t}, u_{i_t}) + V_x^{n_{t+1}}(\overline{x}_{i_{t+1}})[f(\overline{x}_{i_t}, u_{i_t}) - f(\overline{x}_{i_t}, \overline{u}_{i_t})] +$$

$$\frac{1}{2} V_{xx}^{n_{t+1}}(\overline{x}_{i_{t+1}})[f(\overline{x}_{i_t}, u_{i_t}) - f(\overline{x}_{i_t}, \overline{u}_{i_t})]^2\}.$$

$$(i_t = 1, 2, ..., I_t, t = \tau, \tau+1, ..., \tau+T-1) \qquad (22)$$

After substituting the obtained values of $u_{i_t}^*$ into Equation (21) and differentiating it with respect to δu_{i_t}, we can find the optimality condition

$$B_{i_t}^{II} + B_{i_t}^{IV} \delta x_{i_t} + B_{i_t}^{V} \delta u_{i_t} = 0.$$

$$(i_t = 1, 2, ..., I_t, t = \tau, \tau+1, ..., \tau+T-1) \qquad (23)$$

Then δu_{i_t} can be represented as a function of δx_{i_t}:

$$\delta u_{i_t} = \pi_{i_t} \delta x_{i_t} + \phi_{i_t}$$

$$(i_t = 1, 2, ..., I_t, t = \tau, \tau+1, ..., \tau+T-1) \qquad (24)$$

with $\pi_{i_t} = -(B_{i_t}^{V})^{-1} B_{i_t}^{IV}$ and $\phi_{i_t} = -(B_{i_t}^{V})^{-1} B_{i_t}^{II}$.

After substituting Equation (24) into Equation (21), neglecting the error term, and equating the like coefficients, we have

$$V_{i_t}(\overline{x}_{i_t}) =$$
$$V_{n_{t+1}}(\overline{x}_{i_{t+1}}) + R(\overline{x}_{i_t}, u_{i_t}^*)$$
$$+ V_x^{n_{t+1}}(\overline{x}_{i_{t+1}})[(f(\overline{x}_{i_t}, u_{i_t}^*) - f(\overline{x}_{i_t}, \overline{u}_{i_t})] +$$
$$\frac{1}{2} V_{xx}^{n_{t+1}}(\overline{x}_{i_{t+1}})[f(\overline{x}_{i_t}, u_{i_t}^*) - f(\overline{x}_{i_t}, \overline{u}_{i_t})]^2,$$

$$V_x^{i_t}(\overline{x}_{i_t}) = B_{i_t}^{I} - (B_{i_t}^{V})^{-1} B_{i_t}^{II} B_{i_t}^{IV} = B_{i_t}^{I} + B_{i_t}^{II} \pi_{i_t},$$

and

$$V_{xx}^{i_t}(\overline{x}_{i_t}) = B_{i_t}^{III} - (B_{i_t}^{V})^{-1}(B_{i_t}^{IV})^2 = B_{i_t}^{III} - B_{i_t}^{V} \pi_{i_t}^2$$

$$(i_t = 1, 2, ..., I_t, t = \tau, \tau+1, ..., \tau+T-1) \qquad (25)$$

with
$$\begin{aligned} V_{i_{\tau+T}}(\overline{x}_{i_{\tau+T}}) &= V_{n_{\tau+T}}(\overline{x}_{i_{\tau+T}}) \\ &= G(x_{i_{\tau+T}}) + \alpha_2 G^2(x_{i_{\tau+T}}) + \beta_2. \end{aligned}$$

Considering the structure of the PST (τ, T), the values of $V_{n_t}(\overline{x}_{i_t})$, $V_x^{n_t}(\overline{x}_{i_t})$ and $V_{xx}^{n_t}(\overline{x}_{i_t})$ can be obtained based on Equation (14) as follows:

$$V_{n_t}(\overline{x}_{i_t}) = \sum_{i_t=1}^{I_t} V_{i_t}(\overline{x}_{i_t}) p_{i_t}^{i_{t+1}}$$

$$V_x^{n_t}(\overline{x}_{i_t}) = \sum_{i_t=1}^{I_t} V_x^{i_t}(\overline{x}_{i_t}) p_{i_t}^{i_{t+1}}$$

$$V_{xx}^{n_t}(\overline{x}_{i_t}) = \sum_{i_t=1}^{I_t} V_{xx}^{i_t}(\overline{x}_{i_t}) p_{i_t}^{i_{t+1}}.$$

$(i_t=1, 2, ..., I_t, t = \tau, \tau+1, ..., \tau +T\text{-}1)$ (26)

BACKWARD AND FORWARD PROCESSES

Suppose the values of $V_{n_{t+1}}(\overline{x}_{i_{t+1}})$, $V_x^{n_{t+1}}(\overline{x}_{i_{t+1}})$ and $V_{xx}^{n_{t+1}}(\overline{x}_{i_{t+1}})$ at the boundary t= τ +T-1are known. The backward process starts from the end points of PST(τ, T) and moves back to its root along the possible realizations. At time period t, $u_{i_t}^*$ and δu_{i_t} can be chosen from Equations (22) and (24) based on the known values of $V_{n_{t+1}}(\overline{x}_{i_{t+1}})$, $V_x^{n_{t+1}}(\overline{x}_{i_{t+1}})$ and $V_{xx}^{n_{t+1}}(\overline{x}_{i_{t+1}})$. The parameters $V_{n_t}(\overline{x}_{i_t})$, $V_x^{n_t}(\overline{x}_{i_t})$ and $V_{xx}^{n_t}(\overline{x}_{i_t})$ at time period t(t> τ) need to be calculated based on Equations (22), (25), (26) in order to find $u_{i_{t-1}}^*$ and $\delta u_{i_{t-1}}$ at time period t-1.

Following a possible realization on PST (τ, T) in the forward process, the state x_{i_t} can be computed from Equation (3), and the defender's effort u_{i_t} can be obtained as

$$u_{i_t} = u_{i_t}^* + \pi_{i_t}(x_{i_t} - \overline{x}_{i_t}) + \phi_{i_t}.$$

$(i_t=1, 2, ..., I_t, t = \tau, \tau +1, ..., \tau +T\text{-}1)$ (27)

where $u_{i_t}^*, \pi_{i_t}$ and ϕ_{i_t} have been already obtained from the backward process. The performance of the improved defensive efforts and the state trajectories can be examined based on the following criteria.

Let $\overline{V}_{n_t}(\overline{x}_{i_t})$ denote the sum of damages and costs based on the nominal conditions $\overline{x}_{i_t}$ and the defender's nominal efforts $\overline{u}_{i_t}$ at a decision node n_t (t = τ, τ + 1, ..., τ +T-1), and let $V_{n_t}(\overline{x}_{n_t})$ represent the total damages and costs based on the nominal conditions $\overline{x}_{i_t}$ and the defender's efforts

u_{i_t} at the decision node. They can be calculated by using Equation (13).

The expected and the actual changes in the total damages and defending costs at the decision node are given respectively as

$$\Delta E V_{n_t} = V_{n_t}(\overline{x}_{i_t}) \text{-} \overline{V}_{n_t}(\overline{x}_{i_t}) \text{ and } \Delta A V_{n_t} = V_{n_t}(x_{i_t})$$
$$\text{-} \overline{V}_{n_t}(\overline{x}_{i_t}), (n_t=1, 2, ..., N_t, t = \tau, \tau +1, ...,$$
$$\tau +T\text{-}1) \quad\quad\quad (28)$$

SPD Algorithm and Its Functions

The SPD algorithm consists of three parts: main algorithm, decision making (DM) function and computing new trajectories (NT). The main algorithm describes the entire structure of the dynamic evolutionary game where the attacker and the defender make their decisions simultaneously at each time period. The DM function is the realization of the defender's decision making processes at time period τ based on the predicted future attack scenarios in the PST(τ, T).

The main algorithm needs to call the DM function at each of the defender's decision nodes. In order to ensure that $\left| u_{i_t} - u_{i_t}^* \right|$ becomes sufficiently small, the DM function employs a step-size adjustment procedure. The basic idea of this procedure is that the new sequence of the defender's efforts is applied over a smaller part of interval $[\tau, \tau + T - 1]$, and this subinterval is reduced until an improved total damage and defending cost is obtained. If no improvement is obtained until the subinterval is reduced to a single time period, then the defender's effort at this period is changed until an improvement is obtained. The DM function needs to call the NT function to find the new trajectories and to check the improved total damages and costs. Since the DM function plays an important role in the SPD algorithm, it is illustrated in Figure 3.

The notations in the SPD algorithm are summarized as follows:

S: the set of discrete time periods in the dynamic game;

t: the index of the time periods, $t \in S$, $t = 0, 1, 2, \ldots$;

τ: the time period when the defender needs to make decision considering future possible attacks, $\tau \in S$;

T: the length of the time window;

ε: the small positive number determined from numerical stability considerations;

$PST(\tau, T)$: the partial scenario tree that illustrates the future possible attacks and the probabilities of their occurrences.

The following notations are defined based on $PST(\tau, T)$ with $t = \tau$, $\tau + 1$, ..., $\tau + T - 1$:

N_t: the total number of nodes starting at time period t;

n_t: the index of nodes starting at time period t, $n_t = 1, 2, \ldots, N_t$;

I_t: the total number of different attack intensity levels at time period t;

i_t: the index of attack intensity levels at time period t, $i_t = 1, 2, \ldots, I_t$;

a_{i_t}: the predicted effort of the attacker with intensity level i_t in time period t;

$p_{i_t}^{i_{t+1}}$: the predicted transition (Markovian) probability of attack intensity levels from i_t to i_{t+1} between adjacent time periods t and t + 1;

u_{i_t}: the defender's defending efforts on arc i_t, which are the decision variables of the defender;

x_{i_t}: the future state of the system representing the success of the attack following a possible realization;

$\bar{u}_{i_t}$: the nominal efforts of the defender;

$\bar{x}_{i_t}$: the nominal states of the dynamic system;

$u_{i_t}^*$: the estimated optimal efforts of the defender for state $\bar{x}_{i_t}$;

δu_{i_t}: the effort variable measured with respect to the nominal state $\bar{x}_{i_t}$;

δx_{i_t}: the state variable measured with respect to the optimal defensive effort $.u_{i_t}^*$;

π_{i_t}, ϕ_{i_t}: terms used to describe the relationship between δu_{i_t} and δx_{i_t};

$\bar{V}_{n_t}(\bar{x}_{i_t})$: the sum of damages and costs based on the nominal conditions $\bar{x}_{i_t}$ and the defender's nominal efforts $\bar{u}_{i_t}$ at a decision node n_t;

$V_{n_t}(\bar{x}_{n_t})$: the sum of damage and costs based on the nominal conditions $\bar{x}_{i_t}$ and the defender's efforts u_{i_t} at a decision node n_t;

ΔEV_{n_t}: the expected changes in the total damage and defending cost at the decision node, which can be obtained from $\Delta EV_{n_t} = V_{n_t}(\bar{x}_{i_t}) - \bar{V}_{n_t}(\bar{x}_{i_t})$;

ΔAV_{n_t}: the actual changes in the total damage and defending cost at the decision node, which can be obtained from $\Delta AV_{n_t} = V_{n_t}(x_{i_t}) - \bar{V}_{n_t}(\bar{x}_{i_t})$.

The SPD algorithm and its functions can be described as follows:

MAIN ALGORITHM

Step 1: Set $t = 0$ and $x_0 = 0$. Choose an arbitrary effort of the defender. Set $t = t + 1$ and go to Step 2.

Step 2: If the defender does not detect any attacks, then STOP. Otherwise, set $\tau = t$, and predict PST (τ, T) with the attacker's future efforts a_{i_t} and their probabilities $p_{i_t}^{i_{t+1}}$ ($i_t = 1, 2, \ldots,$

I_t, $t = \tau$, $\tau + 1$, …, $\tau + T - 1$) based on the updated knowledge about the attacker. Use the **DM function** to find the defender's best effort trajectories u_{i_t} on the PST (τ, T). Then implement the best move at the current decision node, observe the current attack and update the knowledge about the attacker. Set $t = t+1$, and go back to Step 2.

$$\nabla$$

DM Function

Step 1 (Nominal Trajectories)

Initialize the defender's nominal efforts $\bar{u}_{i_t}$ with $t \in [\tau, \ \tau + T - 1]$, and calculate the nominal states $\bar{x}_{i_{t+1}}$ from Equation (3). Then go to Step 2.

Step 2 (New Trajectories and Stopping Rule)

Use the NT function to find the new effort and new state trajectories (u_{i_t} and $x_{i_{t+1}}$) from the nominal effort and state trajectories ($\bar{u}_{i_t}$ and $\bar{x}_{i_{t+1}}$) on the PST(τ, T). Calculate ΔEV_{n_τ}. If $|\Delta EV_{n_\tau}| \leq \varepsilon$, then the optimal effort trajectories of u_{i_t} for $t \in [\tau, \ \tau + T - 1]$ are obtained, and STOP. Otherwise, we have two possibilities:

1. If there is no $t^*(\tau \leq t^* \leq \tau + T - 1)$ such that $\Delta EV_{n_{t^*}} < 0$ and for $t > t^*$, $\Delta EV_{n_t} = 0$ then set the new trajectories as the nominal trajectories and go back to Step 2.

2. If there is such t^*, then calculate u_{i_t} and $x_{i_{t+1}}$ for $t \in [\tau, \ t^*]$ by using the recorded values of π_{i_t}, ϕ_{i_t} and $u_{i_t}^*$, and then calculate u_{i_t} and $x_{i_{t+1}}$ for all $t \in [t^* + 1, \ \tau + T - 1]$ using Equations (27) and (3) based on the

recorded values of π_{i_t}, ϕ_{i_t} and $u_{i_t}^* = 0$. So the new trajectories of effort u_{i_t} and state $x_{i_{t+1}}$ are obtained for $t \in [\tau, \ \tau + T - 1]$. Set k=0, $t_k = 0$, and go to Step 3.

Step 3 (Step-Size Adjustment)

Apply the new effort trajectory over interval $[t_k, t^*]$ and the nominal effort trajectory over intervals $[\tau, t_k - 1]$ (when $t_k \geq 1$) and $[t^* + 1, \tau + T - 1]$ as a new control policy, and then calculate ΔAV_{n_τ} and ΔEV_{n_τ}. If $\Delta AV_{n_\tau} < 0$ and $|\Delta AV_{n_\tau}| \geq \frac{1}{2} |\Delta EV_{n_\tau}|$, then the new policy is the optimal effort u_{i_τ} trajectory for $t \in [\tau, \ \tau + T - 1]$, and STOP. Otherwise, set k = k + 1, and select $t_k = t_{k-1} + \left\lceil \frac{t^* - t_{k-1}}{2} \right\rceil$. If $t_k \neq t^*$, then go back to Step 3. Otherwise, the optimal effort trajectory for $t \in [\tau, \ \tau + T - 1]$ is as follows: $u_{i_t} = \bar{u}_{i_t}$ for $t \in [\tau, \ t_k - 1]$, $u_{i_t} = u_{i_t}^* = u_{i_t} - \varepsilon'(R_u + V_x^{n_{t+1}} f_u)$ for $t = t_k$, where $\varepsilon' > 0$ is prespecified, and $u_{i_t} = \bar{u}_{i_t} + \pi_{i_t}(x_{i_t} - \bar{x}_{i_t}) + \phi_{i_t}$, $x_{i_{t+1}} = f(x_{i_t}, u_{i_t})$, $x_{i_k} = \bar{x}_{i_k}$ and $u_{i_k} = u_{i_k}^*$, for $t \in [t_k + 1, \ \tau + T - 1]$ and then STOP.

NT Function

Step 1 (Initialization)

At time period t=T calculate $V_{n_T}(\bar{x}_{i_T})$, $V_x^{n_T}(\bar{x}_{i_T})$ and $V_{xx}^{n_T}(\bar{x}_{i_T})$ from $G(x_{i_T}) + \alpha_2 G^2(x_{i_T}) + \beta_2$, and set $V_{n_T}(\bar{x}_{i_T}) = V_{i_T}(\bar{x}_{i_T})$, $V_x^{n_T}(\bar{x}_{i_T}) = V_x^{i_T}(\bar{x}_{i_T})$, $V_{xx}^{n_T}(\bar{x}_{i_T}) = V_{xx}^{i_T}(\bar{x}_{i_T})$. Compute $u_{i_{t-1}}^*$, $\pi_{i_{t-1}}$ and $\phi_{i_{t-1}}$ from Equations (22) and (24) and record these values. Then go to Step 2.

Figure 3. Flow chart of the DM function

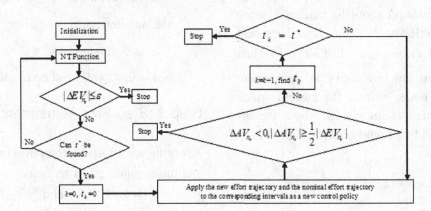

Step 2 (Backward Sweep and Forward Sweep)

Calculate $V_{i_{t-1}}(\overline{x}_{i_{t-1}})$, $V_x^{i_{t-1}}(\overline{x}_{i_{t-1}})$ and $V_{xx}^{i_{t-1}}(\overline{x}_{i_{t-1}})$ from Equation (25). Obtain $V_{n_{t-1}}(\overline{x}_{i_{t-1}})$, $V_x^{n_{t-1}}(\overline{x}_{i_{t-1}})$ and $V_{xx}^{n_{t-1}}(\overline{x}_{i_{t-1}})$ from Equation (26). Compute $u_{i_{t-2}}^*$, $\pi_{i_{t-2}}$ and $\phi_{i_{t-2}}$ based on (22) and (24) and record these values. Set $t=t-1$. If $t<\tau$, then move forward to find the new trajectories of the effort and the state (u_{i_t} and $x_{i_{t+1}}$) on the PST (τ, T) based on Equations (27) and (3), and then STOP. Otherwise, go back to Step 2.

NUMERICAL EXPERIMENT

In this section, we will illustrate the key parts of the SPD algorithm based on a simple example which has been illustrated earlier by Figure 1. This example will show how to improve the trajectories of the state and the defender's effort by iteration and how to find the defender's current best decision based on the PST(τ, T). It is assumed that the attacker and the defender play a multi-stage attack-defense game with $c_t = 10$, $w_t^A = w_t^D = 1$ ($t=0, 1, 2$), v=100, $\alpha_1 = 0.001$, $\alpha_2 = 0.05$, $\beta_1 = 0$, $\beta_2 = 5$, T=2, and the defender needs to find its best effort at the current time period t ($t = 1$) by considering possible future attacks. At this moment, the defender knows that the attacker's effort was 5 during the previous time period ($t = 0$), and its own previous effort was 3. Based on the analysis of network vulnerabilities and the attacker's action, the defender predicts the possible future attacks and describes them as a PST $(1, 2)$ shown in Figure 1. In the meanwhile, the defender realized that he/she underestimated the capacity of the attacker, so a critical damage can be caused by the attacker in two time periods. Then he/she sets a large potential damage as $G(x_{i_3}) = 2.5x_{i_3}^2$. Several iteration steps of improving the trajectory is applied to find the best current decision of the defender. Suppose that the nominal efforts $\overline{u}_{i_1}, \overline{u}_{i_2}$ of the defender in PST $(1, 2)$ are equal to 1. The first iteration step that includes a backward and a forward process is shown in Table 1.

The first row of the table represents the time periods. The second and the third rows describe the decision nodes and arcs in the corresponding time period. The numbers in the fourth row are the indices of the columns which can be used to identify the location of each cell shown in Table 1. The fifth row displays the nominal efforts $\overline{u}_{i_t}$ of the defender (t = 1, 2). The nominal states $\overline{x}_{i_t}$

Table 1. One iteration step of improving trajectory

Time Periods	t=1			t=2						t=3			
Nodes		1			2			3		4	5	6	7
Branches	1-2		1-3	2-4		2-5	3-6		3-7				
Indices	(1)	(2)	(3)	(4)	(5)	(6)	(7)	(8)	(9)	(10)	(11)	(12)	(13)
$\bar{u}_{i_t}$	1		1	1		1	1		1				
$\bar{x}_{i_t}$		0.625			0.75			0.67		0.8	0.76	0.78	0.76
V^{n_t}					246.6			239.44		177.8	159.8	168.7	123.5
$V^{n_t}_x$					263.05			216.51		464	434.9	449.3	372.6
$V^{n_t}_{xx}$					-861.1			-827.6		740	716.6	728.2	668.3
V_{i_t}				264.2		239.1	251.75		190.2				
$V^{i_t}_x$				280.41		255.65	217.67		211.84				
$V^{i_t}_{xx}$				-831.4		-873.8	-808.3		-904.1				
$u^*_{i_t}$	8.84		7.62	4.75		4.85	4.81		4.47				
π_{i_t}	-0.17		-0.23	19.97		20.28	16.74		17.48				
ϕ_{i_t}				2.53		1.98	2.02		1.69				
x_{i_t}		0.625			0.5			0.43		0.586	0.54	0.573	0.443
u_{i_t}	8.67		7.39	2.286		1.76	2.81		1.97				

of the game in the sixth row are calculated by using Equation (3) (t = 1, 2, 3). Since both the states and the payoffs depend on the cumulative efforts of the players, the calculation of the states and the payoffs during time periods $t = 1$, 2 and 3 needs to consider the attacker's and the defender's earlier efforts up to time period t. The parameters in the backward process are given in rows seven to fifteen, and the last two rows indicate the results of the forward process. The backward process starts at the boundary condition (t = 3) of the PST (1, 2). The three parameters V_{n_3}, $V_x^{n_3}$, $V_{xx}^{n_3}$ at each node are calculated from the potential damage $G(\overline{x}_{i_3})$ and are displayed from column (10) to column (13). The optimal effort $u_{i_t}^*$ of the defender with the nominal stage $\overline{x}_{i_t}$ can be calculated as the solution of the minimization problem

$$u_{i_t}^* = \arg\min_{u_{i_t}} [\frac{vA_{i_t}\overline{x}_{i_t}}{A_{i_{t-1}}+\overline{x}_{i_t}(a_{i_t}+u_{i_t})}+c_t u_{i_t}+\alpha_t\left(\frac{vA_{i_t}\overline{x}_{i_t}}{A_{i_t}+\overline{x}_{i_t}(a_{i_t}+u_{i_t})}+c_t u_{i_t}\right)^2 +$$
$$V_z^{n_{t+1}}\frac{A_{i_t}\overline{x}_{i_t}}{A_{i_{t-1}}+\overline{x}_{i_t}(a_{i_t}+u_{i_t})}+\frac{1}{2}V_{zz}^{n_{t+1}}\left(\frac{A_{i_t}\overline{x}_{i_t}}{A_{i_{t-1}}+\overline{x}_{i_t}(a_{i_t}+u_{i_t})}-\frac{A_{i_t}\overline{x}_{i_t}}{A_{i_{t-1}}+\overline{x}_{i_t}(a_{i_t}+\overline{u}_{i_t})}\right)^2].$$

$$(i_t=1, 2, ..., I_t, t = 1, 2) \qquad (29)$$

Equation (29) is derived from (22). Clearly, the objective function is non-convex. Simple differentiation gives the first order condition:

$$\frac{-vA_{i_t}\overline{x}_{i_t}^2}{[A_{i_{t-1}}+\overline{x}_{i_t}(a_{i_t}+u_{i_t})]^2}+c_t+2\alpha_t\left(\frac{vA_{i_t}\overline{x}_{i_t}}{A_{i_t}+\overline{x}_{i_t}(a_{i_t}+u_{i_t})}+c_t u_{i_t}\right)\left(\frac{-vA_{i_t}\overline{x}_{i_t}^2}{[A_{i_{t-1}}+\overline{x}_{i_t}(a_{i_t}+u_{i_t})]^2}+c_t\right)+$$
$$V_z^{n_{t+1}}\frac{-A_{i_t}\overline{x}_{i_t}^2}{[A_{i_{t-1}}+\overline{x}_{i_t}(a_{i_t}+u_{i_t})]^2}+V_{zz}^{n_{t+1}}\left(\frac{A_{i_t}\overline{x}_{i_t}}{A_{i_{t-1}}+\overline{x}_{i_t}(a_{i_t}+u_{i_t})}-\frac{A_{i_t}\overline{x}_{i_t}}{A_{i_{t-1}}+\overline{x}_{i_t}(a_{i_t}+\overline{u}_{i_t})}\right)\frac{-A_{i_t}\overline{x}_{i_t}^2}{[A_{i_{t-1}}+\overline{x}_{i_t}(a_{i_t}+u_{i_t})]^2}=0$$

$$(i_t=1, 2, ..., I_t, t = 1, 2) \qquad (30)$$

Notice that it can be simplified as an aquatic Equation by setting $A_{i_{t-1}}+\overline{x}_{i_t}(a_{i_t}+u_{i_t})=Z_{i_t}$. The four stationary points and the boundary point $u_{i_t}=0$ are the candidates of the optimal solution. Substituting these candidates into the objective function and comparing the function values give

the optimal effort $u_{i_t}^*$ of the defender based on the nominal state $\overline{x}_{i_t}$. The optimal efforts $u_{i_2}^*$ shown in columns (4), (6), (7), (9) can be obtained from this procedure by setting the time period t = 2.

In order to find the improved effort u_{i_2}, in addition to $u_{i_2}^*$, the value of δu_{i_2} is computed from Equation (24) based on the values of π_{i_2} and ϕ_{i_2}.

Table 2 is a complement to Table 1, and shows the details of obtaining π_{i_2} and ϕ_{i_2} based on $u_{i_2}^*$. The values of $B_{i_2}^I$, $B_{i_2}^{II}$, $B_{i_2}^{III}$, $B_{i_2}^{IV}$ and $B_{i_2}^V$ are obtained from Equation (21) for $t = 2$ based on the derivatives found in Box 2.

Table 2 also shows the details of computing the values of $V_{i_2}(\overline{x}_{i_2})$, $V_x^{i_2}(\overline{x}_{i_2})$ and $V_{xx}^{i_2}(\overline{x}_{i_2})$. The coefficients in the last row to approximate the possible payoffs of the defender at time period 2 can be obtained from Equation (25) by using the corresponding coefficients $V_{n_3}(\overline{x}_{i_3})$, $V_x^{n_3}(\overline{x}_{i_3})$ and $V_{xx}^{n_3}(\overline{x}_{i_3})$ at the beginning of time period 3. Then $V_{n_2}(\overline{x}_{i_2})$, $V_x^{n_2}(\overline{x}_{i_2})$ and $V_{xx}^{n_2}(\overline{x}_{i_2})$ (shown in columns (5) and (8) of Table 1) can be computed from $V_{i_2}(\overline{x}_{i_2})$, $V_x^{i_2}(\overline{x}_{i_2})$ and $V_{xx}^{i_2}(\overline{x}_{i_2})$ based on Equation (26). Similarly, we can find $u_{i_1}^*$ (shown in columns (1) and (3) of Table 1) based on Equations (29) and (30) with t = 1. The initial state x_{i_1} of PST (1, 2) is fixed based on the players' previous efforts meaning that $\overline{x}_{i_1} = x_{i_1}$, therefore it is only necessary to compute ϕ_{i_1} from Equation (24) for u_{i_1}. Then the backward process of this iteration terminates. The new trajectories with updated efforts u_{i_t} and states $x_{i_{t+1}}$ (t = 1, 2) in the forward process can be obtained respectively from Equations (27) and (3). Then the values of $V_{n_t}(x_{i_t})$, $V_{n_t}(\overline{x}_{i_t})$ and $\overline{V}_{n_t}(\overline{x}_{i_t})$ with $t \in [1, 2, 3]$ can also be calculated

Table 2. The parameters at time period t = 2

t=2

Time Period Branches	2 - 4	2 - 5	3 - 6	3 - 7
$u_{i_2}^*$	4.75	4.846	4.81	4.47
$B_{i_2}^{I}$	388.66	361.92	297.7	323.37
$B_{i_2}^{II}$	-5.42	-5.24	-4.78	-6.38
$B_{i_2}^{III}$	23.45	212.01	-145.64	247.07
$B_{i_2}^{IV}$	-42.8	-53.54	-39.58	-65.853
$B_{i_2}^{V}$	2.143	2.64	2.364	3.767
π_{i_2}	19.97	20.28	16.74	17.48
ϕ_{i_2}	2.53	1.98	2.02	1.69

Parameters	V_{i_2}	$V_x^{i_2}$	$V_{xx}^{i_2}$	V_{i_2}	$V_x^{i_2}$	$V_{xx}^{i_2}$	V_{i_2}	$V_x^{i_2}$	$V_{xx}^{i_2}$	V_{i_2}	$V_x^{i_2}$	$V_{xx}^{i_2}$
Values	264.2	280.41	-831.4	239.1	255.65	-873.8	251.75	217.67	-808.3	190.2	211.84	-904.1

Box 2.

$$f_u = \frac{-x_{i_t}^2 A_{i_t}}{[A_{i_{t-1}} + x_{i_t}(a_{i_t} + u_{i_t})]^2},$$ (31)

$$f_x = \frac{A_{i_t} A_{i_{t-1}}}{[A_{i_{t-1}} + x_{i_t}(a_{i_t} + u_{i_t})]^2},$$ (32)

$$f_{ux} = \frac{-2x_{i_t} A_{i_t} A_{i_{t-1}}}{[A_{i_{t-1}} + x_{i_t}(a_{i_t} + u_{i_t})]^3},$$ (33)

$$f_{uu} = \frac{2x_{i_t}^3 A_{i_t}}{[A_{i_{t-1}} + x_{i_t}(a_{i_t} + u_{i_t})]^3},$$ (34)

(35)
$$R_u = \frac{-2\alpha_1 v^2 A_{i_t}^2 x_{i_t}^3}{[A_{i_{t-1}} + x_{i_t}(a_{i_t} + u_{i_t})]^3} - \frac{(2\alpha_1 c_t u_{i_t} + 1)v A_{i_t} x_{i_t}^2}{[A_{i_{t-1}} + x_{i_t}(a_{i_t} + u_{i_t})]^2} + \frac{2\alpha_1 c_t v A_{i_t} x_{i_t}}{A_{i_{t-1}} + x_{i_t}(a_{i_t} + u_{i_t})} + 2\alpha_1 c_t^2 u_{i_t} + c_t,$$

(36)
$$R_{ux} = \frac{-6\alpha_1 v^2 A_{i_t}^2 A_{i_{t-1}} x_{i_t}^2}{[A_{i_{t-1}} + x_{i_t}(a_{i_t} + u_{i_t})]^4} - \frac{2(2\alpha_1 c_t u_{i_t} + 1)v A_{i_t} A_{i_{t-1}} x_{i_t}}{[A_{i_{t-1}} + x_{i_t}(a_{i_t} + u_{i_t})]^3} + \frac{2\alpha_1 c_t v A_{i_t} A_{i_{t-1}}}{[A_{i_{t-1}} + x_{i_t}(a_{i_t} + u_{i_t})]^2},$$

(37)
$$R_{uu} = \frac{6\alpha_1 v^2 A_{i_t}^2 x_{i_t}^4}{[A_{i_{t-1}} + x_{i_t}(a_{i_t} + u_{i_t})]^4} - \frac{2\alpha_1 c_t v A_{i_t} A_{i_{t-1}} x_{i_t}^2 + 2(\alpha_1 c_t a_{i_t} - \alpha_1 c_t u_{i_t} - 1)v A_{i_t} x_{i_t}^3}{[A_{i_{t-1}} + x_{i_t}(a_{i_t} + u_{i_t})]^3} - \frac{2\alpha_1 c_t v A_{i_t} x_{i_t}^2}{[A_{i_{t-1}} + x_{i_t}(a_{i_t} + u_{i_t})]^2} + 2\alpha_1 c_t^2.$$

$$f_{xx} = \frac{-2A_{i_t} A_{i_{t-1}}(a_{i_t} + u_{i_t})}{[A_{i_{t-1}} + x_{i_t}(a_{i_t} + u_{i_t})]^3},$$ (38)

$$R_x = \frac{2\alpha_1 v^2 A_{i_t}^2 A_{i_{t-1}} x_{i_t}}{[A_{i_{t-1}} + x_{i_t}(a_{i_t} + u_{i_t})]^3} - \frac{(2\alpha_1 c_t u_{i_t} + 1)v A_{i_t} A_{i_{t-1}}}{[A_{i_{t-1}} + x_{i_t}(a_{i_t} + u_{i_t})]^2},$$ (39)

$$R_{xx} = \frac{2\alpha_1 v^2 A_{i_t}^2 A_{i_{t-1}}^2 - 4\alpha_1 v^2 A_{i_t}^2 A_{i_{t-1}}(a_{i_t} + u_{i_t})x_{i_t}}{[A_{i_{t-1}} + x_{i_t}(a_{i_t} + u_{i_t})]^4} - \frac{2(2\alpha_1 c_t u_{i_t} + 1)v A_{i_t} A_{i_{t-1}}(a_{i_t} + u_{i_t})}{[A_{i_{t-1}} + x_{i_t}(a_{i_t} + u_{i_t})]^3}.$$ (40)

based on Equation (13). They are shown in Table 3.

The values of the actual changes shown in column (4) are all negative, so the new trajectories clearly reduce the total damage and defending cost at the beginning of the time period. Notice that the values of the defender's efforts u_{i_t} in the

Table 3. The results of the first iteration

Values		$V_{n_t}(x_{i_t})$	$V_{n_t}(\overline{x}_{i_t})$	$\overline{V}_{n_t}(\overline{x}_{i_t})$	ΔAV_{n_t}	ΔEV_{n_t}
Indices		(1)	(2)	(3)	(4) = (1) - (3)	(5) = (2) - (3)
Time Periods	$t = 1$	313.6	461.17	327.77	-14.17	133.4
	$t = 2$	168.15	295.37	250.01	-81.86	45.36
	$t = 3$	84.18	162.43	162.43	-78.25	0

new trajectory increase. The expected changes are calculated based on the same nominal state $\overline{x}_{i_t}$. They are all positive as shown in column (5). The cells in Table 1 below the fourth row show the indices which are updated during the next iteration when the new trajectories are placed in the fifth and the sixth rows as the nominal trajectories. Following the same procedures as shown in Table 1, the values of u_{i_t} in the new trajectory of the current iteration can be calculated. They are less than those with the nominal trajectory. There is a $t^*(1 \leq t^* \leq 2)$ such that $\Delta EV_{n_{t^*}} < 0$ and for $t > t^*$, $\Delta EV_{n_t} = 0$. After finding the new policy of the current iteration and applying it to the interval obtained from the step-size adjustment of the DM function, the defender's optimal effort trajectory and its current optimal decision can be obtained.

CONCLUSION AND FUTURE RESEARCH DIRECTIONS

It is assumed that the attacker is rational, so it launches multi-stage attacks to achieve its goal, and the defender seeks to minimize the impact of the attack by its defenses. A dynamic evolutionary game approach is employed to model the interactions between the two players. The contest success function using the accumulative efforts of the attacker and the defender is developed as the fundamental components of the defender's payoff.

Due to the uncertainty in this multi-stage game, the payoffs of the defender at each stage of the game are considered random. Their deterministic equivalents can be obtained based on their first two moments. Instead of solving the resulting complex non-linear programming problem directly, an optimal control problem is developed for the application of a convergent DDP algorithm providing an efficient approach. The optimal trajectories of the future possible states and defensive efforts can be obtained by solving this optimal control problem at each time period of the dynamic game. The defender can also update its knowledge of the attacker for more accurate attacks prediction after each interaction.

This efficient, on-line, proactive response strategy can therefore greatly enhance situational awareness in computer network defense. In our previous work (Szidarovszky and Luo, 2011), we considered only single-stage attacks to multiple targets, and in this chapter we considered multi-stage attacks to a single objective. They are the fundamental building blocks to consider more general and more complicated situations. In our future research we will explore the improvement of situational awareness for such more complex cases.

REFERENCES

Azaiez, M. N., & Bier, V. M. (2007). Optimal resource allocation for security in reliability systems. *European Journal of Operational Research, 181*, 773–786.

Banks, D. L., & Anderson, S. (2006). Combining game theory and risk analysis in counterterrorism: A smallpox example. In Wilson, A. G., Wilson, G. D., & Olwell, D. H. (Eds.), *Statistical methods in counterterrorism* (pp. 9–22). New York, NY: Springer-Verlag.

Bier, V. M., & Azaiez, M. N. (2008). *Game theoretic risk analysis of security threats*. Berlin, Germany: Springer-Verlag.

Bier, V. M., Nagaraja, A., & Abhichandani, V. (2005). Protection of simple series and parallel systems with components of different values. *Reliability Engineering & System Safety, 87*, 315–323.

Carin, L., Cybenko, G., & Hughes, J. (2008). Cybersecurity strategies: The QuERIES methodology. *Computer, 41*(8), 20–26.

Chang, S. C., Chen, H. H., & Fong, I. K. (1990). Hydroelectric generation scheduling with an effective differential dynamic programming algorithm. *IEEE Transactions on Power Systems, 5*(3), 737–743.

Foo, B., Glause, M. W., Howard, G. M., Wu, Y.-S., Bagchi, S., & Spafford, E. H. (2008). Intrusion response systems: A survey. In Qian, Y., Joshi, J., Tipper, D., & Krishnamurthy, P. (Eds.), *Information assurance: Dependability and security in networked systems* (pp. 377–412). Burlington, MA: Morgan Kaufmann.

Foo, B., Wu, Y. S., Mao, Y. C., Bagchi, S., & Spafford, E. (2005, June). *ADEPTS: Adaptive intrusion response using attack graphs in an e-commerce environment*. Paper presented at International Conference on Dependable Systems and Networks, Yokohama, Japan.

Hausken, K. (2002). Probabilistic risk analysis and game theory. *Risk Analysis, 22*(1), 17–27.

Hausken, K. (2008). Strategic defense and attack for series and parallel reliability systems. *European Journal of Operational Research, 186*, 856–881.

Heidari, M. (1970). *Water resources systems analysis by discrete differential dynamic programming*. Department of Civil Engineering, University of Illinois at Urbana-Champaign.

Jacobson, D., & Mayne, D. (1970). *Differential dynamic programming*. New York, NY: Elsevier.

Levitin, G. (2007). Optimal defense strategy against intentional attacks. *IEEE Transactions on Reliability, 56*(1), 148–157.

Li, D., & Ng, W. L. (2000). Optimal dynamic portfolio selection: Multiperiod mean-variance formulation. *Mathematical Finance, 10*(3), 387–406.

Liu, P., & Zang, W. (2003, October). *Incentive-based modeling and inference of attack intent, objectives, and strategies*. Paper presented at the 10th ACM conference on Computer and communications security (CCS'03), Washington, DC.

Luo, Y., Szidarovszky, F., Al-Nashif, Y., & Hariri, S. (2009a, May). *A game theory based risk and impact analysis method for intrusion defense systems*. Paper presented at the Seventh ACS/IEEE International Conference on Computer Systems and Applications (AICCSA 2009), Rabat, Morocco.

Luo, Y., Szidarovszky, F., Al-Nashif, Y., & Hariri, S. (2009b, June). *Game tree based partially observable stochastic game model for intrusion defense systems (IDS)*. Paper presented at IIE Annual Conference and Expo (IERC 2009), Miami, FL.

Luo, Y., Szidarovszky, F., Al-Nashif, Y., & Hariri, S. (2010). Game theory based network security. *Journal of Information Security, 1*, 41–44.

Luo, Y., Szidarovszky, F., & Liu, J. (2011). *Simulation study on the prediction of the attacker's possible moves based on latent social network*. Unpublished working paper, Systems and Industrial Engineering Department, University of Arizona, Tucson.

Lye, K., & Wing, J. (2005). Game strategies in network security. *International Journal of Information Security, 4*, 71–86.

Morimoto, J., Zeglin, G., & Atkeson, C. G. (2003, August). *Minimax differential dynamic programming: Application to a biped walking robot*. Paper presented at *SICE Annual Conference*, Fukui University, Japan.

Murray, D., & Yakowitz, S. (1981). The application of optimal control methodology to nonlinear programming problem. *Mathematical Programming, 21*, 331–347.

Murray, D., & Yakowitz, S. (1979). Constrained differential dynamic programming and its application to multireservoir control. *Water Resources Research, 15*(5), 1017–1027.

Samuelson, P. A. (1970). The fundamental approximation theorem of portfolio analysis in terms of means, variances and higher moments. *The Review of Economic Studies, 37*(4), 537–542.

Shen, D., Chen, G., Blasch, E., & Tadda, G. (2007, October). *Adaptive Markov game theoretic data fusion approach for cyber network defense*. Paper presented at IEEE Military Communications Conference (MILCOM 2007), Orlando, FL.

Siever, W. M., Miller, A., & Tauritz, D. R. (2007, April). *Blueprint for iteratively hardening power grids employing unified power flow controllers*. Paper presented at SoSE' 07 IEEE International Conference on System of Systems Engineering, San Antonio, TX.

Skaperdas, S. (1996). Contest success functions. *Economic Theory, 7*, 283–290.

Stakhanova, N., Basu, S., & Wong, J. (2007). A taxonomy of intrusion response systems. *International Journal of Information and Computer Security, 1*(1/2), 169–184.

Stewart, B. (2010). *Skating on stilts, why we aren't stopping tomorrow's terrorism, No. 591*. Stanford, CA: Hoover Institution Press.

Szidarovszky, F., & Luo, Y. (2011). Optimal protection of computer networks against random attacks. Submitted to *Applied Mathematics and Computation* (Unpublished results).

Toth, T., & Kruegel, C. (2002, December). *Evaluating the impact of automated intrusion response mechanisms*. Paper presented at 18th Annual Computer Security Applications Conference (ACSAC), Las Vegas, NV.

Wood, B. J., Saydjari, O. S., & Stavridou, V. (2000). *A proactive holistic approach to strategic cyber defense*, (p. 2). Menlo Park, CA: SRI International. Retrieved November 3, 2008, from http://www.cyberdefenseagency.com/ publications/A_Proactive_Holistic_Approach_to_Strategic_Cyber_Defense.pdf

Yakowitz, S. (1989). Algorithms and computational techniques in differential dynamic programming. In Leondes, C. T. (Eds.), *Control and dynamical systems: Advances in theory and applications, 31* (pp. 75–91). San Diego, CA: Academic Press, Inc.

Zhang, Z., & Ho, P. (2009). Janus: A dual-purpose analytical model for understanding, characterizing and countermining multi-stage collusive attacks in enterprise networks. *Journal of Network and Computer Applications, 32*(3), 710–720.

Zhuang, J., & Bier, V. M. (2007). Balancing terrorism and natural disasters—Defensive strategy with endogenous attacker effort. *Operations Research, 55*(5), 976–991.

ADDITIONAL READING

Alpcan, T., & Basar, T. T. (2011). *Network security: A decision and game theoretic approach*. New York: Cambridge University Press.

Buttyan, L., & Hubaux, J.-P. (2008). *Security and cooperation in wireless networks*. New York: Cambridge University Press.

Cyert, R. M., & Degroot, M. H. (1987). *Bayesian analysis and uncertainty in economic theory*. Totowa, New Jersey: Rowman & Littlefield.

Filar, J., & Vrieze, K. (1996). *Competitive Markov decision processes*. New York: Springer-Verlag.

Forgo, F., Szep, J., & Szidarovszky, F. (1999). *Introduction to the theory of games*. Dordrecht, The Netherlands: Kluwer Academic Publishers.

Forman, E. H., & Gass, S. I. (2001). The analytic hierarchy process – an exposition. *Operations Research, 49*(4), 469–486.

Fudenberg, D., & Levine, D. K. (1998). *The theory of learning in games*. Cambridge, Massachusetts: MIT Press.

Fudenberg, D., & Tirole, J. (1991). *Game theory*. Cambridge, Massachusetts: MIT Press.

Gintis, H. (2000). *Game theory evolving: A problem-centered introduction to modeling strategic behavior*. Princeton, New Jersey: Princeton University Press.

Szidarovszky, F., Gershon, M., & Duckstein, L. (1986). *Techniques for multiobjective decision making in systems management*. Amsterdam, The Netherlands: Elsevier.

Szidarovszky, F., & Bahill, A. T. (1999). *Linear systems theory* (2nd ed.). Boca Raton, FL: CRC Press.

KEY TERMS AND DEFINITIONS

Decision Making Under Uncertainty: An approach to make decisions in the face of uncertainty.

Dynamic Programming: A method for solving complex multi-stage problems by reducing them into a sequence of simpler one-stage sub-problems.

Game Theory: An appropriate way to model decision making problems with more than one decision maker and conflicting interests.

Network Security: One of the most critical issues in almost every aspect of our society such as administration, business, finance, personal life, etc.

Optimal Control Problem: A problem of finding a control law for a given system such that a certain optimality condition is achieved.

Proactive Intrusion Defense: Acting in anticipation to prevent an incident from taking place.

Chapter 5
An Alternative Framework for Research on Situational Awareness in Computer Network Defense

Eric McMillan
The Pennsylvania State University, USA

Michael Tyworth
The Pennsylvania State University, USA

ABSTRACT

In this chapter the authors present a new framework for the study of situation awareness in computer network defense (cyber-SA). While immensely valuable, the research to date on cyber-SA has overemphasized an algorithmic level of analysis to the exclusion of the human actor. Since situation awareness, and therefore cyber-SA, is a human cognitive process and state, it is essential that future cyber-SA research account for the human-in-the-loop. To that end, the framework in this chapter presents a basis for examining cyber-SA at the cognitive, system, work, and enterprise levels of analysis. In describing the framework, the authors present examples of research that are emblematic of each type of analysis.

INTRODUCTION

In this chapter we propose a theoretical framework of cyber situation awareness (cyber-SA) that attempts to capture cyber-SA as both a process and a state that involves knowledge, action, and the environment. In terms of computer network defense cyber-SA, and situation awareness more broadly, has been generally understood to be the ability to perceive, understand, and project the future status of elements in the environment (Endsley, M. R., 2000). Relying on this definition of cyber-SA, research has been conducted in several contexts over the last twenty-five years, including the military, aviation, air traffic control, and command, control, communication and intelligence (C4i) environments (Salmon, P., Stanton, N., Walker, G., & Green, D., 2006). Despite the proliferation of

DOI: 10.4018/978-1-4666-0104-8.ch005

research in these areas, minimal research has been conducted on SA as it is developed in computer network defense. This is problematic because much of the research on traditional SA may not be as applicable to the highly dynamic and complex environment of computer network defense (Barford, P. et al., 2010; Tadda, G., Salerno, J. J., Boulware, D., Hinman, M., & Gorton, S., 2006; Yen, J. et al., 2010). For example, with cyber-SA there is a greater separation between the user and the physical system due to the inherent virtuality of the environment and this separation presents domain-specific challenges.

Drawing on an alternative theory of SA as both process and state, we argue that the proposed framework should guide research into the study of the internal cognitive processes an analyst employs to make sense of data and information; and how those processes are facilitated by the interfaces and tools analysts employ. Our proposed framework is distinguished from other approaches to understanding cyber-SA in that it moves beyond the artifact and individual cognition and accounts for work-, team-, and enterprise-level factors that impact cyber-SA.

THEORETICAL BACKGROUND

A review of the extant literature reveals that the prior work on situation awareness draws primarily from the work done by Micah Endsley (1995). Endsley theorized SA as consisting of three levels. Level 1 SA represents the perception of cues in the environment salient to the individual's task at hand. Note here, that it is only the perception of cues salient to the task at hand that matters in terms of Level 1 SA. Indeed perception of non-salient cues, or noise, can be understood to degrade SA. Level 2 SA is the comprehension of the perceived cues to include comparison against memory, orientation, and prioritization. Level 3 SA is the projection of future states based on the individual's comprehension. At all three levels

temporality and space play a critical role. Consider the operation of a motor vehicle in traffic. Perceiving that a traffic signal is yellow (Level 1), the operator comprehends that the signal is in a state of change and projects that the light will soon change again to red which means to stop (Level 2) and so he should begin decelerating (Level 3).

The three levels of situation awareness are generally understood to be hierarchical, and implicitly sequential, in nature. That is comprehension is dependent on perception, and projection is dependent on comprehension. Failure to perceive salient cues leads to a lack of comprehension of the current environmental state and an inability to accurately project the future state of the environment. An individual may fail to achieve Level 1 SA or Level 2 SA and still correctly project the future state of the environment through random chance. At the same time, an individual may have perfect SA and still make errors due to insufficient resources (Endsley, M. R., 2000).

Ensdley's model of situational awareness is the most prominent of three models of SA that have been previously theorized in the literature. Two others include SA as a set of cognitive subsystems; and SA as an environmentally driven consciousness – referred to as the 'embedded-interactive' model (Stanton, N. A., Chambers, P. R. G., & Piggott, J., 2001). It is this latter approach that drives this research provides the foundation for our model cognitive process.

The embedded-interactive model of SA conceptualizes SA as spanning the intersection of the human actor and the environment (Smith, K. & Hancock, P. A., 1995). Similar to other sociotechnical theory, in the embedded-interactive model SA is comprised of both internal cognitive processes and external context. In other words, situation awareness is both an internal cognitive process and cognitive state that is directly shaped by the environment in which the human actor resides. Drawing on knowledge about perceived cues from the environment, the human actor takes goal-based actions derived from knowledge and assesses the outcomes, and the assessment produces updates to knowledge.

Consider the following example. A network security analyst looking at network traffic logs becomes aware that the database server has received multiple failed authentication attempts from an IP address that normally does not communicate with the database server [*environment*]. Based on prior experience, the analyst speculates that an intruder is attempting to gain unauthorized access to the server [*knowledge*] and as a result implements a new firewall rule that drops all traffic from the suspicious IP address to his network [*action*]. If the unauthorized attempts cease, the goal of preventing an intrusion into the database is realized and the analyst has situation awareness. If the attempts continue, the analyst does not have situation awareness because he has misunderstood the state of the environment; he adjusts his knowledge based on this new information, and takes additional actions.

One of appeals of this theory of SA is that it speaks to how individuals develop "the big picture" of their environment, something that is a funda-

mental challenge in computer network defense. Understanding how a network analyst forms and maintains an overall understanding of the state of the computer network, the 'big picture,' and the role of situation awareness in those processes is one of the fundamental goals of cyber-SA research.

There is a second element of Smith & Hancock's theory of SA that may prove to be particularly useful to cyber-SA research and that is the concept of risk spaces. A risk space is a two-dimensional (but potentially n-dimensional) matrix of human performance (see Figures 2 and 3 below). The axes of the risk space represent those factors that negatively impact safety (or in the case of computer network defense, the integrity of the network and associated assets). Objects are plotted on the matrix and based on their location and vector, one can determine their priority. Smith & Hancock (1995) demonstrated the concept using the rate of change in distance and lateral distance as their dimensions and plotted the likelihood of aircraft collisions in a specified airspace. In the computer network defense context, one might plot number of clients at risk of infection from

Figure 1. Modified embedded-context model of SA

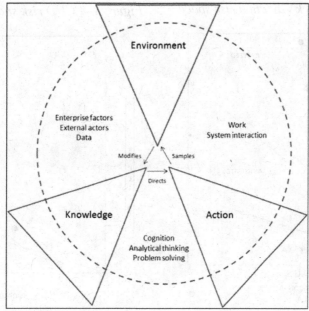

a computer virus, and the speed of the virus' propagation to assess threats.

In the aviation example, the closer the distance and greater the rate of decrease in range between two aircraft the greater the likelihood of a collision. In the computer network defense example, the greater the number of clients at risk and the greater the propagation rate of the infection, the greater the likelihood of catastrophic consequences for the network. This method of assessing risk may prove a useful way for assessing cyber threats and determining courses of action thereby increasing the analyst's SA.

What is Cyber Situation Awareness?

Barford *et al.* (2010) list 7 dimensions of cyber-SA (see Table 1). These dimensions range from awareness of the current situation to awareness of plausible future outcomes. Of the seven dimensions described, the extant research on cyber-SA has focused on dimensions one, six, and seven and largely relied upon the three-level model of SA as a conceptual foundation. Researchers have relied on the three levels of SA described in the

three-level model – perception, comprehension, and projection – to both describe what cyber-SA facilitating tools should do (increase perception and comprehension of salient cues) and to assess the efficacy of such tools (e.g. – how well do tools improve projection accuracy and efficacy?). The alignment of the three-level model of SA with the JDL data fusion process model (Llinas, J. & Hall, D. L., 1998; Tadda, G., et al., 2006) is another reason for its utility in cyber-SA research given the centrality of data fusion to computer network defense. Though the three-level model has been the dominant model employed in cyber-SA research, there are three widely acknowledged differences between cyber-SA and standard SA.

One difference between cyber-SA and standard SA is that the scope of the environment within which cyber-SA occurs is significantly larger than those in which SA has previously been studied such as flying a fighter jet or driving a car. The amount of information generated in real time by sensors monitoring cyberspace – including other human actors, system logs, intrusion detection systems, etc. – can easily overwhelm the human analyst making it virtually impossible to perceive

Figure 2. Smith & Hancock's aviation risk space

Figure 3. A CND risk space

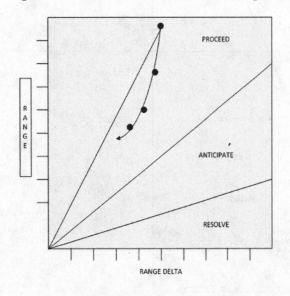

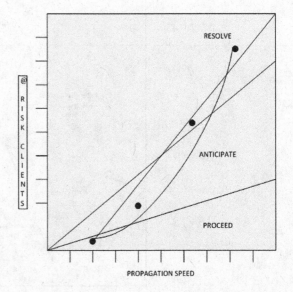

Table 1. Dimensions of cyber-SA

1.	Awareness of current situation
2.	Awareness of impact of attack
3.	Awareness of evolution of situation
4.	Awareness of adversary behavior
5.	Awareness of situational cause
6.	Awareness of information quality and quality of derived decisions
7	Awareness of plausible future outcomes

the salient cues from the environmental noise (Barford, P., et al., 2010; Tadda, G., et al., 2006; Tadda, G. P. & Salerno, J. S., 2010; Yang, S. J., Byers, S., Holsopple, J., Argauer, B., & Fava, D., 2008). The analyst involved in computer network defense must not only process information about attacks on their system (identity and motivation of the attacker, intended outcome of attack, target of attack, likely outcome(s) of the attack) but must also continually evaluate the state of their network (priority, vulnerabilities, current status, etc.). As a result, reducing the cognitive load computer network defense imposes on the human analyst has been the focus on much of the cyber-SA research (c.f., Barford, P., et al., 2010; Bass, T., 2000; Gregoire, M. & Beaudoin, L., 2005; Yen, J., et al., 2010).

A second distinction between cyber-SA and 'standard' SA is the amount of contextual information against which cues can be evaluated. A person driving a car does so in a relatively constrained environment. Contextual cues are omnipresent (the light is red, the road is wet, the other cars are all stopped, etc.). This represents a very different reality from that of the network analyst for which the contextual cues are incomplete and uncertain (Yen, J., et al., 2010). Lack of context can make determining an attacker's intent and capabilities very difficult if not impossible. For example, a system can come under attack but not be the intended target as in the case of the Stuxnet worm which infected multiple systems but had a single (at the

time) undetermined target (Clayton, M., 2010). Similarly, awareness of an attacker's intent may be limited to the intended exploit or the targeted system instead of awareness of the attacker's broader goal of attacking a particular system in a particular manner. For example, even though security experts understand how the Conficker worm works, it is unclear who the attackers are and what they are attempting to achieve (Bowden, M., 2010). Lack of contextual information makes it difficult for analysts to project the appropriate course of action.

The third distinction between cyber-SA and standard SA is the speed at which the environment evolves. Cyberspace is a hyper-dynamic environment in which the environmental state is continually evolving. Humans are incapable of cognitively keeping pace with the rate of change in cyberspace Network analysts can become easily overwhelmed in such an environment and rarely form complete mental models impacting their decision-making processes and the available courses of action (Gregoire, M. & Beaudoin, L., 2005; Yang, S. J., et al., 2008). A rapidly changing information environment requires that analysts be able to identify salient new information and process it against existing knowledge. As a result, the performance speed of SA systems is much higher than that of physical systems (Barford, P., et al., 2010).

A review of the cyber-SA literature reveals that most cyber-SA research has adopted a tool or algorithmic perspective of cyber-SA (Orlikowski, W. J. & Iacono, C. S., 2001); that is, the research has focused primarily on the development of complex computer programs employing probabilistic models to improve cyber-SA. Examples of this research stream include examining how information visualizations can enhance cyber-SA (D'Amico, A. & Kocka, M., 2005; Gregoire, M. & Beaudoin, L., 2005) the development of frameworks for evaluating cyber attacks (Mathew, S., Shah, C., & Upadhyaya, S., 2005; Sudit, M., Stotz,

A., Holender, M., Tagliaferri, W., & Canarelli, K., 2006); and the use of complex programs to project intrusion activity and assess the impacts of cyber attacks (Shen, D., Chen, G., Haynes, L., & Blasch, E., 2007; Yang, S. J., et al., 2008). Two notable exceptions are D'Amico et al.'s (2005) cognitive task analysis of information assurance analysts and Yen et al.'s (2010) development of a hypothesis-reasoning framework using a recognition-primed decision model. While this is important and impactful work, the emphasis on computation and the development of IT artifacts in Cyber-SA research has limited the degree to which the factors that impact cyber-SA and the processes by which cyber-SA is developed and maintained are understood because the human element has largely been omitted from Cyber-SA research.

We argue that the human agent is the most important element in computer network defense and therefore a more holistic approach to Cyber-SA research will contribute to a more thorough understanding of Cyber-SA that is grounded in professional practice. To this end, we propose a new model of cyber-SA that accounts for both human and machine actors as well as enterprise-level factors that can influence cyber-SA.

AN ALTERNATIVE FRAMEWORK FOR CYBER-SA

We propose an alternative framework for cyber-SA for three reasons. One, while the prior work on cyber-SA has been both informative and important, it has focused almost exclusively on developing new technological artifacts to the exclusion of the human actor in computer network defense. As a result, our understanding of cyber-SA has grown but remains incomplete. Through this framework we seek to reintroduce the human element into the human-computer loop.

Two, we argue that to understand how the human analyst makes sense of the cyber-environment in computer network defense, it is critical to understand the broader work context within which cyber-SA is developed. In the literature cyber-SA is understood to be unique because of the uniqueness of the environment within which it is developed. Yet little attention has been paid to the ways in which the cyber environment is actually different from other work contexts. In order to understand the unique cognitive demands presented by cyber environment we must seek to understand how analysts engaged in computer network defense actually work.

Three, we seek to extend theory of situation awareness by focusing attention on intersection of the human agent and the environment. The cyber environment plays a critical role in cyber-SA. The reliance on the three-level model of SA in cyber-SA research implicitly treats SA as a cognitive state. Yet the dynamism of the cyber environment suggests that we may be better served conceptualizing cyber-SA as a process rather than a state.

The Framework

We frame cyber-SA as a domain-specific instance of Smith & Hancock's (1995) model of situation awareness. In this conceptualization, SA is comprised of three dimensions: the environment (or real world), knowledge (or the human's internal cognitive state), and action (interaction with the environment). Each individual dimension is comprised of elements that impact cyber-SA.

Interaction between human actor and the network occurs on the axis linking action and the environment. Assessment of the action's impact on the environment takes place along the axis between the environment and knowledge. Goal setting occurs after the environment has been assessed and the actor's knowledge updated and informs the next action to be taken.

Figure 4. Model of cyber-SA as a process

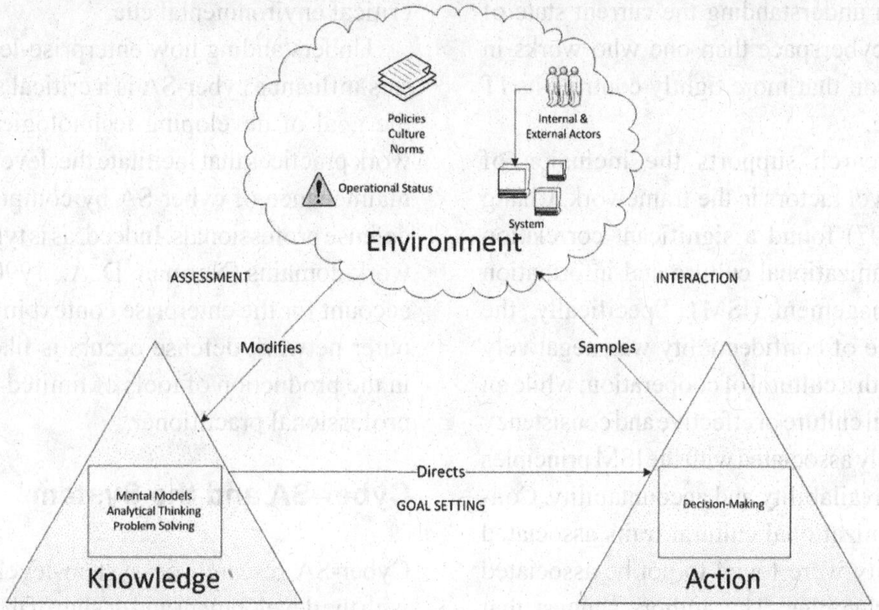

For example, within the *knowledge* dimension we find human cognitive processes such as memory, attention, analytical thinking and problem solving, and mental models. This dimension represents the internal processes and structures by which the analyst draws conclusions about the current state of the environment and informs the setting of task goals (e.g., close a port via firewall rule to prevent unauthorized access). The *action* dimension is where the ends of the human-machine loop connect. Decision-making strategies and processes play a key role in the *action* dimension as it at this point in the SA process that a human determines how to interact with the environment to achieve SA.

Environment

Within the *environment* dimension we find elements such as network operational status (operational, strategic, or critical), enterprise factors such as organizational norms and policies, the computer network system and associated interfaces, and actors both internal and external to the organization.

This list is not exhaustive and more elements are likely to emerge via empirical field-based research. Together these elements comprise the real-world environment within which the network analyst operates. For the purposes of this discussion we will focus on the enterprise factors and system-level issues.

Cyber-SA in the Enterprise

Analysts engaged in computer network defense predominantly do so in an organizational context (public, private, and military), and this context can play a critical role in the analyst's ability to develop and maintain Cyber-SA. Here we are attempting to capture the mediating influence of organizational policies, mode, and culture on the analyst's Cyber-SA. An analyst working in an organization operating in crisis mode is likely to be attending to different environmental cues and have access to different informational resources than analyst working in an organization in normal operating mode. Similarly, an analyst working in an organization that has a permissive culture in regards to employee use of IT faces different challenges in understanding the current state of the internal cyberspace than one who works in an organization that more tightly controls its IT infrastructure.

Prior research supports the inclusion of enterprise-level factors in the framework. Chang and Lin (2007) found a significant correlation between organizational culture and information security management (ISM). Specifically, the ISM principle of confidentiality was negatively correlated with a cultural of cooperation; while an organizational culture of effective and consistency were positively associated with the ISM principles of integrity, availability and accountability. Conversely, organizational cultural traits associated with flexibility were found to not be associated with ISM principles. The authors suggest that a flexible organizational culture is likely to run counter to effective information security management. Based on these findings, from cyber-SA perspective we should expect Cyber-SA is more difficult to develop and maintain in an organization with a flexible culture than one with a control-oriented culture.

Similarly, organizational factors may serve to limit the network security analyst's ability to be cognizant of vulnerabilities in their cyber environment. In a study of computer information security professionals Kraemer, Carayon, & Clem (2009) identified nine organizational areas that can result in vulnerabilities in the computer network defense system. These areas include lack of access to critical computer network defense information, too much policy, an absence or lack of policy documentation, inadequate training, and overburdened security resources. It is easy to how these factors can serve to limit the Cyber-SA of the analyst responsible for maintaining his organization's computer network defense. For example, if the analyst's workload is too high, the amount of attention the analyst can dedicate to any single item is limited, therefore increasing the likelihood

that the analyst will miss (fail to perceive) some critical environmental cue.

Understanding how enterprise-level moderators influence cyber-SA is a critical step towards the goal of developing technological tools and work practices that facilitate the development and maintenance of cyber-SA by computer network defense professionals. Indeed, as is typical in other work domains (Norman, D. A., 1990), failure to account for the enterprise context in which computer network defense occurs is likely to result in the production of tools of limited utility to the professional practitioner.

Cyber-SA and the System

Cyber-SA research on system-level issues deal with the development and design of the technological tools a human analyst uses in computer network defense. One of the challenges of developing SA in the cyber environment is the human actor is decoupled from the physical environment (Stanton, N. A., et al., 2001). Indeed, unlike an automobile or fighter jet, there is no physical environment for the analyst to use senses other than sight to gauge the status of the environment. Everything the computer network defender knows about the state of her network is limited to the feedback displayed on screen (Norman, D.A., 1990). The more automated the computer network defense system is, the more physically- and mentally isolated from the system the analyst becomes (Norman, D. A., 1990). This reality presents numerous challenges to practitioners and designers alike.

One challenge is presenting information in manner that is informative to the analyst. Cues that are too subtle get overlooked. Too many cues overload and distract the analyst. Cues that are too simplistic do not convey enough information to be meaningful and thus useful. Examples of system breakdowns resulting inappropriate or incomplete feedback are manifest and include, the Three Mile Island accident and the crash of American Airlines Flight 191 (Perrow, C., 1999).

As noted previously, the majority of the scholarly work on cyber-SA has been on what we identify as system-level issues. Much of the work has been oriented towards developing better methods of data fusion to improve cyber-SA (c.f., Bass, T., 2000; Mathew, S., et al., 2005; Sudit, M., Stotz, A., & Holender, M., 2005; Sudit, M., et al., 2006). Others have focused on developing methods or tools for projecting intrusion activity and assessing the impact of cyber-attacks (c.f., Shen, D., et al., 2007; Yang, S. J., et al., 2008; Yen, J., et al., 2010). Finally, there is an increasing amount of work being done on developing visualizations of network security data to enhance cyber-SA (c.f., D'Amico, A. & Kocka, M., 2005; D'Amico, A., et al., 2005; Gregoire, M. & Beaudoin, L., 2005). It is likely that much of the work on cyber-SA will continue to be system-level research. The work being done on developing methods for visualizing network data seem particularly promising in terms of reducing the mental-isolation of the human operator engaged in computer network defense.

Knowledge

The second core dimension of our framework represents the knowledge of the human actor about the state of the cyberspace. The knowledge dimension consists of the fundamental cognitive processes that have been associated with situational awareness such as the aforementioned perception, comprehension, and projection, other cognitive constructs such as mental models, and analytical thinking techniques such as structured analysis and problem solving. In this chapter we focus on the last element—analytical and problem-solving techniques.

The Similarity of Computer Network Defense to Intelligence Analysis

For the human operator, the process of defending a computer network from attack similar to that of an intelligence analyst attempting to make sense of a geopolitical situation. Intelligence analysis involves ascertaining meaning through the development of hypotheses and estimates, assessing those hypotheses and estimates, and drawing conclusions about the correct course of action in the future based on the assessments (Clark, R. M., 1996). Like the intelligence analyst, the cyber-security analyst is also forms hypotheses and estimates about the nature of attacks on his network, assesses those hypotheses, and makes decisions about how to proceed based on those assessments. Cyber security analysis and intelligence analysis are similar as well in terms of the errors analysts commonly experience. Most major failures in intelligence analysis take the form of incorrect or incomplete analysis or failure to take the correct action based on the analysis (Clark, R. M., 1996), and we see this with cyber-security analysts as well (Yen, J., et al., 2010). Given the similarities of the two domains, we are likely to find utility in the tools and processes that have developed out of research on intelligence analysts. We find the research on structured analysis to be particularly promising.

Structured Analysis

Structured analysis, or structured problem solving, is an approach to analysis intended to overcome obstacles to analytical thinking such as bias, satisficing, and extrapolation (Jones, M. D., 1995). There are multiple structured analytical techniques ranging from the relatively simple such as a pro/con analysis to the complex such as the utility matrix and advanced utility analysis techniques (see Table 2).

There is a significant opportunity to incorporate prior work on structured analysis into research on cyber-SA for computer network defense. For example, what impact does the use of structured analysis impact human cyber-SA? How can structured analytical techniques be automated to improve both system and human cyber-SA? How do analytical coping strategies such as extrapola-

Table 2. Structured analysis techniques

Problem Restatement
Pros/Cons and Fixes
Divergent/Convergent Thinking
Sorting, chronologies & timelines
Casual flow diagramming
Matrices
Decision/event tree
Weighted ranking
Hypothesis testing
Devil's advocacy
Probability tree
Utility matrix
Advanced utility analysis

tion (Folker Jr., R. D., 2000) serve to impede the development of cyber-SA?

Indeed, much of the algorithmic work on cyber-SA has implicitly incorporated structured analysis techniques. For example, Yen *et al.*'s (2010) work seeks to improve cyber-SA through the use of intelligent agents engaging in hypothesis testing. Research on the development of attack graphs to improve cyber-SA employs Bayesian networks are similar to probability trees (Li, J., Ou, X., & Rajagopalan, R., 2010). D'Amico *et al.*'s (2005) model of threat assessment is, in essence, a deci-

sion/event tree. These examples demonstrate that structured analytical techniques are central to cyber-SA research. In addition to continuing this important work, we advocate for research on the application of structured analysis techniques to include the human operator.

Action

The action dimension of our framework reflects the goals and actions an individual takes to interact with the cyberspace environment based on his understanding of the situation. In the theory underlying our proposed framework, the degree of cyber-SA is measured by the degree to which the individual's chosen action is the correct action in response to environmental cues. When the action is correct, the individual has cyber-SA; when the action is incorrect the analyst does not have cyber-SA.

In computer network defense terminology action could mean responding to an attack, detecting and identifying threats, identifying and addressing vulnerabilities, forensic analysis, and other activities. In many ways, cyber-security actions mimic the OSI network model with actions occurring at different layers – such as the network layer or application layer.

Table 3. Multilayer approach to cyber-security adapted from (Lan, L.-N., Liu, X.-Y., & Yang, T.-H., 2009)

Cyber Security Elements	Description
Information Security	Protection of information assets from unauthorized access, use, disclosure, disruption, modification, perusal, inspection, recording, or destruction (Allen, J. H., 2001)
Application Security	Measures taken throughout an applications' lifecycle to prevent exceptions in the application's security policy or its underlying system through flaws in design, development, deployment or maintenance.
Operating System Security	Measures taken through an operating system's lifecycle to prevent exceptions to the operating system's security policy.
Network Security	The provisions and policies adopted by the network administrator to prevent and monitor unauthorized access, misuse, modification, or denial of service to the network or network-accessible resources.
Physical Security	Physical measures to secure the information resources.

The action component of cyber-SA is perhaps the least researched and most poorly understood aspect of cyber-SA. Some work has been done on action as a component of cyber-SA already. Examples of this work include D'Amico's *et al.*'s (2005) cognitive task analysis investigating how cyber-security analysts form goals, make decisions, and engage in work. Though applied to the assessment of attack threat vectors, the measures proposed by Tadda and Salerno (2010) may also prove useful in assessing the quality of action taken by the human analyst. Other outstanding questions related to action that need to be addressed include: how do analysts choose a specific course of action? What role does experience play in an analysts' ability to correctly choose a course of action? What triage strategy to analysts employ when prioritizing what goals to act on?

FUTURE RESEARCH DIRECTIONS

One of the benefits of the framework proposed in this chapter is its applicability to multiple levels of analysis. The knowledge dimension of the model describes internal cognitive processes and structures. The action component describes the interaction of the actor with the environment. The environment dimension accounts for system, enterprise, and operational factors. In accounting for cyber-SA at these different levels we will develop better knowledge of how cyber-SA is achieved and maintained in practice, while at the same time capitalizing and extending the important scholarly work that has been done in the domain of computer network defense and situation awareness.

This chapter presents a basis for future research in two key directions: the extension and elaboration of extant situation awareness theory; and the expansion of cyber-SA research beyond an algorithmic level of analysis towards a more holistic view. Endsley's (1995) three-level model has proven useful and instructive in cyber-SA research,

particularly as cyber-SA relates to information fusion; but there remain many unanswered questions about cyber-SA that the three-level model may not be adequate to answering. In particular, that the three-level model of SA treats SA as a state rather than a process suggests that it is ill-suited to application in as dynamic and complex an environment as cyberspace.

In describing our framework we have sought to identify exemplar research that is representative of the concepts we are describing. The examples we have cited are by no means exhaustive. There remains much work to be done, particularly in regards to developing empirical knowledge of how cyber-security professionals actually work. We encourage cyber-SA scholars to take up this challenge along with us so that we may all benefit from a better understanding of cyber-SA as it relates to computer network defense.

CONCLUSION

In this chapter we have argued for an alternative, more contextually-grounded framework of cyber-situational awareness that more thoroughly accounts for the interaction of the human agent with the complex cyberspace environment. Our hope is that this framework will serve as a starting point for developing a more thorough knowledge of situation awareness as a cognitive state and process, cyber-security as a practice, and the ways in which information technologies can be designed and enhanced to improve the defenders of computer networks ability to understand the big picture of their cyberspace.

REFERENCES

Allen, J. H. (2001). *The CERT guide to system and network security practices*. Redwood City, CA: Addison-Wesley.

Barford, P., Dacier, M., Dietterich, T. G., Fredrikson, J., Griffin, S., & Jajodia, S. (2010). Cyber SA: Situational awareness for cyber defense - Issues and research. In Jajodia, S., Liu, P., Swarup, V., & Wang, C. (Eds.), *Cyber situational awareness* (pp. 3–14). New York, NY: Springer. doi:10.1007/978-1-4419-0140-8_1

Bass, T. (2000). Intrusion detection systems and multisensor data fusion. *Communications of the ACM, 43*(4), 99–105. doi:10.1145/332051.332079

Bowden, M. (2010, June). The enemy within. *The Atlantic Monthly*. Retrieved from http://www.theatlantic.com/magazine/archive/2010/06/the-enemy-within/8098/

Chang, S. E., & Lin, C. S. (2007). Exploring organizational culture for information security management. *Industrial Management + Data Systems, 107*(3), 438-458.

Clark, R. M. (1996). *Intelligence analysis: Estimation and prediction*. Baltimore, MD: American Literary Press.

Clayton, M. (2010). Stuxnet malware is 'weapon' out to destroy...Iran's Bushehr nuclear plant? *Christian Science Monitor*. Retrieved from http://www.csmonitor.com/USA/2010/0921/Stuxnet-malware-is-weapon-out-to-destroy-Irans-Bushehr-nuclear-plant

D'Amico, A., & Kocka, M. (2005, October 26). *Information assurance visualizations for specific stages of situational awareness and intended uses: lessons learned.* Paper presented at the IEEE Workshop on Visualization for Computer Security (VizSEC 05), Minneapolis, Minnesota.

D'Amico, A., Whitley, K., Tesone, D., O'Brien, B., & Roth, E. (2005, September 26-30). *Achieving cyber defense situational awareness: A cognitive task analysis of information assurance analysts.* Paper presented at the Human Factors and Ergonomics Society 49th Annual Meeting, Orlando, FL.

Endsley, M. R. (1995). Toward a theory of situation awareness in dynamic systems. *Human Factors: The Journal of the Human Factors and Ergonomics Society, 37*(1), 32–64. doi:10.1518/001872095779049543

Endsley, M. R. (2000). Theoretical underpinnings of situation awareness: A critical review. In Endsley, M. R., & Garland, D. J. (Eds.), *Situation awareness analysis and measurement* (pp. 3–30). Mahwah, NJ: Lawrence Earlbaum Associates.

Folker, R. D. Jr. (2000). *Intelligence analysis in theater joint intelligence centers: An experiment in applying structured methods*. Joint Military Intelligence College.

Gregoire, M., & Beaudoin, L. (2005). Visualisation for network situational awareness in computer network defence. *Meeting Proceedings RTO-MP-IST-043*, (pp. 20.21 - 20.26). Retrieved from http://www.rto.nato.int/abstracts.asp

Jones, M. D. (1995). *The thinkers toolkit*. New York, NY: Three Rivers.

Kraemer, S., Carayon, P., & Clem, J. (2009). Human and organizational factors in computer and information security: Pathways to vulnerabilities. *Computers & Security, 28*(7), 509–520. doi:10.1016/j.cose.2009.04.006

Lan, L.-N., Liu, X.-Y., & Yang, T.-H. (2009, 10-11 July 2009). *Multi-layer and multi-aspect design of CA system security.* Paper presented at the International Conference on Information Engineering, 2009 (ICIE '09), Taiyuan, Shanxi, China.

Li, J., Ou, X., & Rajagopalan, R. (2010). Uncertainty and risk management in cyber situational awareness. In Jajodia, S., Liu, P., Swarup, V., & Wang, C. (Eds.), *Cyber situational awareness: Issues and research* (pp. 51–67). New York, NY: Springer. doi:10.1007/978-1-4419-0140-8_4

Llinas, J., & Hall, D. L. (1998, 31 May-3 June). *An introduction to multi-sensor data fusion.* Paper presented at the IEEE International Symposium on Circuits and Systems (ISCAS '98), Monterey, CA.

Mathew, S., Shah, C., & Upadhyaya, S. (2005, 23-24 March 2005). *An alert fusion framework for situation awareness of coordinated multi-stage attacks.* Paper presented at the Third IEEE Workshop on Information Assurance, College Park, Maryland.

Norman, D. A. (1990). The 'problem' with automation: Inappropriate feedback and interaction, not 'over-automation'. *Philosophical Transactions of the Royal Society of London. Series B, Biological Sciences*, *327*(1241), 585–593. doi:10.1098/rstb.1990.0101

Orlikowski, W. J., & Iacono, C. S. (2001). Research commentary: Desperately seeking "IT" in IT research - A call to theorizing the IT artifact. *Information Systems Research*, *12*(2), 121–134. doi:10.1287/isre.12.2.121.9700

Perrow, C. (1999). *Normal accidents: Living with high-risk technologies: with a new afterword and a postscript on the Y2K problem.* Princeton, NJ: Princeton University Press.

Salmon, P., Stanton, N., Walker, G., & Green, D. (2006). Situation awareness measurement: A review of applicability for C4i environments. *Applied Ergonomics*, *37*(2), 225–238. doi:10.1016/j.apergo.2005.02.001

Shen, D., Chen, G., Haynes, L., & Blasch, E. (2007). *Strategies comparison for game theoretic cyber situatational awareness.* Retrieved from http://www.dtic.mil/cgi-bin/GetTRDoc?AD=ADA521036&Location=U2&doc=GetTRDoc.pdf.

Smith, K., & Hancock, P. A. (1995). Situation awareness is adaptive, externally directed conciousness. *Human Factors*, *37*(1), 137–148. doi:10.1518/001872095779049444

Stanton, N. A., Chambers, P. R. G., & Piggott, J. (2001). Situation awareness and safety. *Safety Science*, *39*(3), 189–204. doi:10.1016/S0925-7535(01)00010-8

Sudit, M., Stotz, A., & Holender, M. (2005, March 28). *Situational awareness of a coordinated cyber attack.* Paper presented at the SPIE Conference on Data Mining, Intrusion Detection, Information Assurance, and Data Networks Security, Orlando, FL, USA.

Sudit, M., Stotz, A., Holender, M., Tagliaferri, W., & Canarelli, K. (2006). *Measuring situational awareness and resolving inherent high-level fusion obstacles.* Paper presented at the SPIE Conference on Multisensor, Multisource Information Fusion: Architectures, Algorithms, and Applications, Orlando, FL.

Tadda, G., Salerno, J. J., Boulware, D., Hinman, M., & Gorton, S. (2006, April 19). *Realizing situation awareness within a cyber environment.* Paper presented at the SPIE Conference on Multisensor, Multisource Information Fusion: Architectures, Algorithms, and Applications, Orlando, FL, USA.

Tadda, G. P., & Salerno, J. S. (2010). Overview of cyber situation awareness. In Jajodia, S., Liu, P., Swarup, V., & Wang, C. (Eds.), *Cyber situational awareness* (pp. 15–35). Springer, US. doi:10.1007/978-1-4419-0140-8_2

Yang, S. J., Byers, S., Holsopple, J., Argauer, B., & Fava, D. (2008, June 17-20). *Intrusion activity projection for cyber situational awareness.* Paper presented at the IEEE International Conference on Intelligence and Security Informatics (ISI 2008). Tapei, Taiwan.

Yen, J., McNeese, M. D., Mullen, T., Hall, D. L., Fan, X., & Liu, P. (2010). RPD-based hypothesis reasoning for cyber situation awareness. In Jajodia, S., Liu, P., Swarup, G., & Wang, C. (Eds.), *Cyber situational awareness: Issues and research* (pp. 39–49). New York, NY: Springer. doi:10.1007/978-1-4419-0140-8_3

ADDITIONAL READING

Bostrom, R. P., & Heinen, J. S. (1977). MIS Problems and Failures: A Socio-Technical Perspective. *Management Information Systems Quarterly, 1*(3), 17–32. doi:10.2307/248710

Dennett, P. (1984). Cognitive Wheels: The Frame Problem of A.I. In C. Hookway (Ed.), *Minds, machines, and evolution: philosophical studies* (pp. 129-151). Cambridge [Cambridgeshire]; New York: Cambridge University Press.

Durso, F. T., & Sethumadhavan, A. (2008). Situation Awareness: Understanding Dynamic Environments. *Human Factors: The Journal of the Human Factors and Ergonomics Society, 50*(3), 442–448. doi:10.1518/001872008X288448

Horton, K., Davenport, E., & Wood-Harper, T. (2005). Exploring sociotechnical interaction with Rob Kling: five "big" ideas. *Information Technology & People, 18*(1), 50. doi:10.1108/09593840510584621

Johnson-Laird, P. N. (2001). Mental models and deduction. *Trends in Cognitive Sciences, 5*(10), 434. doi:10.1016/S1364-6613(00)01751-4

Johnson-Laird, P. N., & Savary, F. (1999). Illusory inferences: a novel class of erroneous deductions. *Cognition, 71*(3), 191. doi:10.1016/S0010-0277(99)00015-3

McNeese, M. D., Bautsch, H. S., & Narayanan, S. (1999). A Framework for Cognitive Field Studies. *International Journal of Cognitive Ergonomics, 3*, 307. doi:10.1207/s15327566ijce0304_3

Orlikowski, W. J. (2000). Using technology and constituting structures: A practice lens for studying technology in organizations. *Organization Science, 11*(4), 404–428. doi:10.1287/orsc.11.4.404.14600

Perry, M. (2003). Distributed Cognition. In Carroll, J. M. (Ed.), *HCI Models, Theories, and Frameworks* (pp. 193–223). San Francisco: Morgan Kaufmann Publishers. doi:10.1016/B978-155860808-5/50008-3

Salmon, P. M., Stanton, N. A., Walker, G. H., Baber, C., Jenkins, D. P., & McMaster, R. (2008). What really is going on? Review of situation awareness models for individuals and teams. *Theoretical Issues in Ergonomics Science, 9*(4), 297–323. doi:10.1080/14639220701561775

Sawyer, S., & Chen, T. T. (2002). Conceptualizing Information Technology in the Study of Information Systems: Trends and Issues. In Myers, M. D., Whitley, E., Wynn, E. H., & DeGross, J. I. (Eds.), *Global and Organizational Discourse about Information Technology* (pp. 1–23). London: Kluwer.

Scaachi, W. (2004). Socio-Technical Design. In Bainbridge, W. S. (Ed.), *Berkshire Encyclopedia of Human-Computer Interaction*. Great Barrington, Mass.: Berkshire Pub. Group.

Suchman, L. A. (1987). *Plans and situated actions: the problem of human-machine communication. Cambridge*. New York: Cambridge University Press.

Weick, K. E., Sutcliffe, K. M., & Obstfeld, D. (2005). Organizing and the Process of Sensemaking. *Organization Science, 16*(4), 409. doi:10.1287/orsc.1050.0133

Woods, D. D., & Patterson, E. S. (2000). How unprecedented events produce an escalation of cognitive and coordinative demands. In Hancock, P. A., & Desmond, P. A. (Eds.), *Stress, workload, and fatigue* (pp. 112–136). Mahwah, N.J.: Lawrence Erlbaum Associates, Publishers.

Young, M. F., & McNeese, M. D. (1995). A situated cognition approach to problem solving. In Caird, J., Flach, J., Hancock, P. A., & Vincent, K. (Eds.), *Local applications of the ecological approach to human-machine systems* (pp. 359–391). Hillsdale, N.J.: L. Erlbaum.

KEY TERMS AND DEFINITIONS

Algorithmic Perspective: An analytical perspective technology and the use of technology in which technology is limited to software and hardware and the human-actor is excluded.

Cognition: Mental processes including attention, perception, comprehension, learning, problem-solving, and memory.

Cyber Situation Awareness (Cyber-SA): A form of situation awareness specific to the cyber-security context. Cyber-SA is distinguishable from situation awareness in that it occurs in an entirely virtual hyper-dynamic information-intensive context.

Cyber-Security: The practice of monitoring and security networked computer and information assets to prevent unauthorized access, modification, or service denial.

Risk Space: A n-dimensional matrix in which risk vectors are plotted for the purpose of predicting the degree of risk in a particular setting.

Situation Awareness: The cognitive process by which a human actor perceives and understands environmental cues in relation to a specific task context. A human actor who has correctly comprehended the environmental state and subsequently established the correct task goal has achieved the state of situation awareness.

Structured Analysis: Formal methods of analytical thinking designed to reduce or eliminate the effect of analyst bias and produce more accurate analyses.

Chapter 6
Information Security for Situational Awareness in Computer Network Defense

Uri Blumenthal
MIT Lincoln Laboratory, USA

Joshua Haines
MIT Lincoln Laboratory, USA

William Streilein
MIT Lincoln Laboratory, USA

Gerald O'Leary
MIT Lincoln Laboratory, USA

ABSTRACT

Situational awareness – the perception of "what is going on" – is crucial in every field of human endeavor, especially so in the cyber world where most of the protections afforded by physical time and distance are taken away. Since ancient times, military science emphasized the importance of preserving your awareness of the battlefield and at the same time preventing your adversary from learning the true situation for as long as possible. Today cyber is officially recognized as a contested military domain like air, land, and sea. Therefore situational awareness in computer networks will be under attacks of military strength and will require military-grade protection. This chapter describes the emerging threats for computer SA, and the potential avenues of defense against them.

INTRODUCTION

Hence the saying: If you know the enemy and know yourself, you need not fear the result of a hundred battles. If you know yourself but not the enemy, for every victory gained you will also suffer a defeat. If you know neither the enemy nor yourself, you will succumb in every battle.

Sun Tzu, The Art of War

DOI: 10.4018/978-1-4666-0104-8.ch006

Situational Awareness (SA) is the knowledge or perception of "what is going on" around you in time and space, perception both accurate and timely (definition based on (Endsley, 1995) and (Fracker, 1991)). Having Situational Awareness is crucial in every field or occupation known to mankind. SA is especially important in combat applications, as the payment exacted for lack of awareness is often very severe.

Closely related to the knowledge of what is going on *now* is the ability to determine trends and predict what is likely to happen *in the future*.

Merging of and bridging between Kinetic ("real", "physical") and Cyber ("virtual", "electronic", "computer") worlds that started some time ago, is on the rise. Not only military, but also many critical infrastructures and systems – such as banking, power grid, air traffic control to name a few – are permeated by computers and are interconnected. For example, battlefield in Cyber domain, requires action to defend it with at least as much effort as other domains (Land, Sea, Air and Space) – or even more, because of the ease to launch an attack in Cyber domain and of the difficulty of attribution that makes a response (and deterrence!) much harder.

Traditionally Situational Awareness was a factor for *human* decision-making. Today with the time window available for reaction in Cyber domain being so narrow – we must consider Situational Awareness for automatic systems and algorithms (as humans would not be able to react quickly enough to deal with some computer attacks).

John Boyd (Boyd, 1995) introduced the *OODA loop* (Observe, Orient, Decide and Act) – a concept ruling strategic thinking in both military and business. In a conflict situation the consistency and integrity of the OODA loop will be challenged by the adversary, whose goals are to gain understanding of our intentions while obscuring his own.

This leads to the need to protect our OODA loop – and its SA part in particular – by means of Information Security.

We assume that the "first half" of the OODA loop comprises *detectors* that provide raw data, and *processors* that "digest" the raw information and create CND SA picture for the network operators and/or automatic "first-response" programs, as shown in Figure 1.

Figure 1 shows overlap of SA and the network it monitors. For security reasons it may be beneficial to place the critical components of SA outside of the network it is observing. It would place the SA system out of reach for network-borne direct attacks.

We assume that the components of the network are protected, and individual detectors monitor those components. The components and detectors are assumed to work, but not perfectly. They are subject to both misses and false alarms. The detectors themselves may be attacked by the

Figure 1. Relationship between defended network and SA system

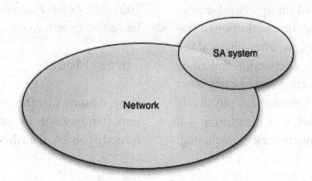

adversary, who can cause them to fail or deliver misleading information.

This chapter describes the security needs of a Situational Awareness system, and mentions the basic techniques that can be applied to achieve these goals and discusses some of the issues. This chapter will discuss advantages and benefits of certain approaches and solutions, and weigh them against the cost of maintaining, difficulty to implementing them or to obtaining the desired degree of reliability. Rather than being a guide for an IT manager or Network Security administrator, this section would serve as a sounding board for a scientist that pushes to expand the boundaries of the Computer Network Defense field, or a designer that evaluates his or her options to decide on the acceptable set of compromises (residual risks) *for the given system*. We hope that the following discourse brings to light what the designer should pay attention to.

JOB OF A SITUATIONAL AWARENESS SYSTEM

The components of the Security Situational Awareness (SA) system are themselves components of the network being protected and therefore require their own protection. A Situational Awareness system comprises sensors, processing nodes, central or decision-point nodes and communications infrastructure joining them all together. This is very much like an ordinary network comprising hosts – clients, servers and peers – with various degrees of hardening and complexity (sensors and processing nodes) and communications infrastructure including routers, switches, physical and virtual circuits, etc. Such a network – and all its elements – requires protection just like any other network! Even if the SA network is physically separate from the network it is monitoring – it still needs protection for many reasons, including:

A. Modern malware demonstrated the ability to "jump the air-gap" and cross from one network to another that is physically separated from it.

B. Advanced Persistent Threat (Barnes, 2008) (Racicot, 2008) (Chen, 2010) (Falliere, 2011) may be present on *all* the networks, including those isolated and dedicated to monitoring and security.

The job of the SA system is as follows, to:

A. Reliably gather the reports from the individual detectors.

B. Process the detections reports and generate a CND SA picture for the operators. It may also suggest or automatically implement certain responses (interacting with the Decide-Act part of the OODA loop).

C. Reliably communicate any decision or instruction back to network operators, or to individual network components.

D. The SA system itself is subject to information assurance (IA) attack and must be protected. *This protection is the main subject of this chapter.*

The second item is the major focus of the rest of this book. This chapter will focus on the remaining issues. One exception to the above is maintaining SA picture for the SA system. Like Internal Affairs in the Police infrastructure (investigators of investigators), is there a need for an SA system for the SA system? As Juvenal (Juvenal, 100) said: *"Quis custodiet ipsos custodes?"*[2] We leave this question open.

Threat Model

If we assume that the system being protected is important enough to warrant the protection afforded by an SA, then this system will be an attractive target to some set of attackers. For instance, consider the presence of motivated attackers with large resources, possessing high level of skills and most sophisticated techniques for exploiting hosts and networks. In such an environment zero-day vulnerability attacks may become routine.

It is possible that such attacks may target all the components of the system in general – and all the components of the SA system in particular such as sensors, the central node itself and communication channels between sensors and the central node.

The attacker may want to "silence" a group of sensors for a period of time, or to subvert them. The attacker may want to cut the communications between the sensors and the central node, or to hijack them.

Finally, the attacker may want to penetrate the central node and either gain control over it or, at least, shutdowns the control center off the rest of the network.

Figure 2 depicts a typical corporate network – such that an SA system may be called on to defend.

Figure 3 shows division of the network nodes into edge devices (hosts and the best examples of those) and infrastructure (switches, routers, and firewalls – devices whose main purpose is carrying traffic on behalf of the edge nodes).

SYSTEM REQUIREMENTS

The basic requirements of the SA system security include all the usual requirements for information security such as authentication, confidentiality, integrity, non-repudiation, timeliness, and the like. In addition, there are additional requirements imposed by the specific SA job. These requirements include supporting the implementation of system-specific policies, gathering information about what constitutes normal network behavior so that deviations can be detected, minimizing the overhead on the network, etc. Further, SA security must be designed in a way that allows it to be incrementally upgraded to adapt to new network components, new threats, and new protective strategies.

Figure 4 shows a schematic view of the SA system and its connection with the network components being protected. In this example, each edge component of the network (hosts – servers, workstations) has embedded sensors that report in-band to the local SA collector and concentrator *Logging Host*. In addition, each local area network (LAN) has a *LAN Probe* device that reports out-of-band on a separate network directly to the Network Operations Center.

Figure 2. An example of a corporate network

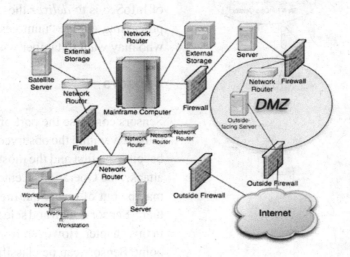

Figure 3. Edge nodes and infrastructure elements

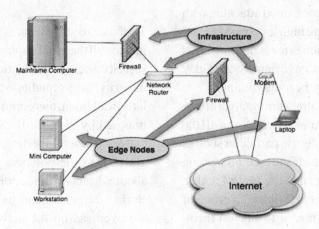

In general, each component of a protected network should be monitored in some way – either by a separate external sensor or by an embedded component that provides data to the SA system, as shown in Figure 4.

Communications system that transmits this information to a control center can be in-band (sharing the bandwidth and channels with the main network) or out-of-band (separate wiring). At the control center the collected data is aggre-

Figure 4. SA overlaying defended network

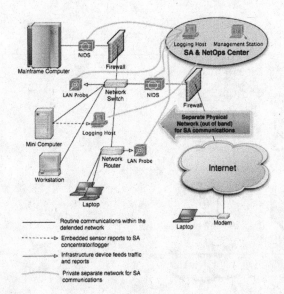

gated, analyzed – and decisions are made to take actions and send control information back to the individual components of the operational network.

GATHERING INFORMATION RELIABLY

The SA information flow starts at the sensors, and unless the decision-making entity can rely with a certain degree of confidence on the data it receives, the rest loses its meaning. The first task of SA Information Security (InfoSec) is to assure that the data SA sensors and probes collect is accurate (this includes authenticity). Second task of InfoSec is to *deliver* the collected data to the processing engine "unmolested" by adversaries who may want to tamper with SA functionality.

Sensors

Sensors comprise the part of the SA system that must stay within the observed network – and thus become the first and the most accessible target to attack. The Operations Center and concentrators may be out of reach, but the sensors are always there. Sensor design and selection are not covered in this chapter. However, from a a security standpoint, Sensors can be classified as:

- Embedded or segregated;
- Hardware- or software-based;
- Communicating back home in-band or out-of-band.

These properties affect how easy it is to subvert a sensor and conversely how difficult it is to protect it against an attack. More on sensors can be found in the section Protection of SA system.

Attackers

There are threats at all levels, including sensors themselves. One goal of an adversary may be to interfere with SA intake data flow. An adversary may want to subvert a group of sensors to make them report, and/or interfere with sensor communications channel – modifying or blocking its traffic. Another possibility is launching a Denial of Service attack by swamping the processing entity with bogus traffic, or traffic from bogus sensors.

Defenses

Complexity of this attack and its likelihood of success depend on the protection of the given sensor.

A software-based sensor that runs on a general-purpose computer is comparatively easy to compromise. Penetrating the host OS would be sufficient for that. The best chance for SA to deal with this class of situations is detecting this attack before it succeeds – thus becoming aware that a given sensor is lost and the data it reports is no longer trusted.

A sensor running on a computer with hardware anchor of trust that includes Measured Boot and stable set of software that runs on the machine would be more difficult to subvert.

Safety in Numbers

This is a difficult subject because if the adversary knows about a sensor, it may be easy to bring it out of commission – by either flooding it with bogus

data (Denial of Service kind of attack), or interrupting its communications with the center. An obvious solution would be to deploy an "army" of sensors so that a loss of some would not eliminate the capabilities. However, an attack that would compromise a particular sensor is likely to have the capability of compromising all other sensors of the same type. Hence, diversity of sensors is also important.

There is a fundamental problem with reliance on multiple sensors. To understand it, compare sensors to policemen guarding a large building against intrusions, each officer assigned a certain small area, with overlap of sectors – so no area is a responsibility of only one guard all the time, and - especially – no area is left without a guard. In this example many officers are needed to guard the building. The intruder on the other hand needs to find only *one* opening, and to subvert only one (or a few at most) guard. It will not matter how many guards perform their mission flawlessly and perfectly – subverting just one is enough for the intrusion to succeed.

Thus – while it is important to place "enough" sensors – one must ensure that sensors in key areas are "sufficiently" protected against determined and directed attacks. The words *enough* and *sufficiently* were put in quotes because each specific installation and SA system require different number of sensors and different level of protection. Once again, one size does *not* fit all.

Communications

Communications with the control center must also be protected. These protections should include best practices for data and user authentication, encryption for data confidentiality, and physical protection to ensure availability. The field of Communications Security is mature enough that we do not need to dive deeply into it. More detailed requirements will be described below in the section Protection of SA system.

WHAT IS SA GOOD FOR?

As mentioned in the introduction to this chapter, Situational Awareness has traditionally been the prerogative of the humans, and the OODA loop is also created with humans in mind. Since in the Computer Network Defense field events are happening with the speed of light (and the irreversible damage can be done before a human has a chance to react) – it may be necessary to create automatic "sentinels" and "responders" that would also be served by Situational Awareness system.

One role of Situational Awareness system is orienting human users to what is happening right now, presenting the picture in an easily digestible way.

Another useful role Situational Awareness system has is detecting and visualizing the trends, indicating to human operators not only what is happening right now – but based on the set of observed events separated by time and space – what is likely to happen next.

Besides orienting humans, SA is a major part of automatic response system. The "deciding" part may be policy-based, but the input from SA is what triggers a policy and therefore a reaction.

What are Risks of SA?

An adversary is likely to want to attack the primary mission. In the process however – just like a burglar tries to disable the alarm system first – the adversary may want to interfere with SA picture and SA system. The SA system, because of its scope and its ability to affect the performance of the system and the outcome of the mission, becomes an attractive target (and potentially a single point of failure) for attackers trying to compromise the system and/or the mission. If the system being protected is handling high-value information, we can reasonably expect that it will become a target for one or more of technically sophisticated, well-funded attacker groups. We must also assume that the attackers will have, or be able to acquire knowledge of how the system, including the SA component, is protected. Given these assumptions, we can expect that the SA system itself would be subject to attack either by blocking the flow of alerts into the system, introducing erroneous information, or blocking protective action. The adversary's purpose could be preventing detection (clandestine), preventing the correct response, or inducing an incorrect response.

There are a number of possible attacks that must be considered:

- Clandestine Implant. This would be an exploit that is embedded in the system without being detected. This exploit can lie dormant until activated either by an external command or by detecting some set of events in the data being sensed.
- Preventing the correct response – e.g. redirecting a return attack, or prevent the system from "closing the gates" and thus allow data exfiltration.
- Inducing an "incorrect response" – that could be exploited in multiple ways. For example, redirecting response against a pre-determined target could (a) hurt adversary's target by our weapons with the adversary having plausible deniability, and (b) damage our image in the world and in the media. This aspect becomes more important as Cyber and Kinetic worlds merge closer.

DIMENSIONS OF SA

SA extends in *Space* and *Time* dimensions, with time axis being used for both the current state and the near future – predicting the likely course of events.

The power of Situational Awareness lies in the ability to correlate multiple events separated by both *time* of their occurrence and *location* (or *space*) of their happening. One individual event may mean much or little. When events are correlated together – a trend can be deduced, and predictions could be made.

Prediction and Response by SA System

An important aspect of a successful SA system its ability to correctly predict the environment it provides awareness of. This prediction is useful in the selection of an appropriate course of action when interpreting the state of the environment. Failure to adequately predict the behavior of the environment suggests that either the SA system is not monitoring the correct features or that the prediction capabilities do not model the environment appropriately.

The evaluation of the predictive power of an SA system must consider several variables, such as the accuracy of the prediction, the relevance of the prediction for the environment predicted and the timeliness of the prediction to enable its use in the decision making process.

To determine the accuracy of the prediction, one must consider units of measurement employed to quantify the variables that are represented in the SA system. In the case of network data, this might be measures of traffic volume, the number of connections or number of users on the network, to name a few. In this case, the accuracy of the predictions of the SA system can be directly measured as the future values of these variables are compared to the predicted values.

By continuously monitoring the discrepancies between predicted and actual values, the predictive power of the SA system can be determined. Moreover, including these error signals in an iterative update process that can be used to improve the predictions, the SA system's ability to model the environment can be made more effective and useful.

When monitoring the environment it is important to choose variables that accurately reflect the important aspects of the environment and that support actions that execute successfully in the environment. Through the use of predictive power assessment described above appropriate variable selection can be made. Appropriate variables may include combinations or derivations from original environment variables if they improve performance of the system.

Automatic Responses by an SA System

If an SA system is successful in predicting the environment, automatic responses can be made by the system and support quicker reaction to a given situation. These responses should be chosen based on the consideration of potential outcomes because of the response. In this way the true value of the predictive power of the SA system can be realized. The SA system is the correct position to consider the effects of responses to given recognized situations because it has been able to accurately predict its environment. As in the case of variable prediction above, the effect of a response can be predicted and compared to its actual impact on the observed environment. Through this process, the response generation aspects of the system can also be improved and optimized for the environment.

It is important evaluate the SA system's responsive capabilities in an evaluation environment before the system is deployed to an operational environment. Accurate replication of the target environment is most important at this point to ensure that automatic responses can be appropriate for the environment.

SA METRICS

Determining the level of resources that should be applied to the SA component itself and to its security is a difficult task. Related to the previous subject is the issue of ROI (Return of Investment),

Figure 5. Illustration of an SA system predicting the future state of the environment based upon observations of the current state

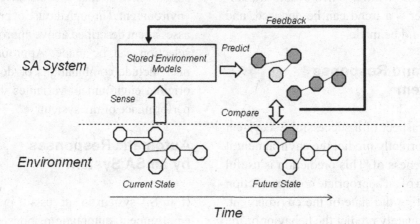

as well as metrics to evaluate an SA system against. What are the latency requirements for SA in CND? Formulating this requirement one must consider the likely latency of adversary's OODA loop. How to measure the confidence of the provided picture? And how much would the system cost? A compromise that offers "enough" confidence within the "acceptable" time frame **and** at the cost affordable to the system/mission owner is the goal here.

Hacking the SA System

Because the SA system is composed of components it is trying to model and predict it is itself subject to attacks similar to those it is trying to protect against. Among the threat aspects that should be tracked in order to characterize the threat are:

1. Who – the actor involved in perpetrating the attack against the system
2. How – the mechanism by which the actor has carried out the attack
3. Why – the goal of the actor in carrying out the attack
4. When – what is the temporal condition of the attack

In most cases, specification of each of these threat attributes will not be possible as the SA system will not have awareness of them. For instance, in a network environment, attribution is very difficult and the 'who' cannot be determined. Indirect methods for determining this must be employed and perhaps only broad, high-level classifications of possible actors can be guessed at based on the observation of many attacks.

Probably the initial aspect of the threat to the SA system is the 'why' or the goal of the actor carrying out the threat. This aspect refers to the target of the attack, such as an active process that is part of the SA system or static component that supports SA system such as a database or other storage. Recognition of the effects of the attack, while not perfect, will most likely be the most recognizable aspect of the threat.

Forensic examination of audit data associated with the SA system components can support the determination of the 'how' and 'when' aspects of the threat event, providing this audit data is of sufficient granularity and reliability.

Given a complete specification of a given threat to an SA system, one can begin to consider the risks associated with the threat. That is, a risk assessment quantifies the potential for a given threat to impact the operation of the SA system.

Risks can be measured given the probabilities that method of the attack matches vulnerabilities of the system.

A final aspect to consider is the effect of countermeasures that can be deployed to protect the SA system, either within the system itself or outside as adjunct capabilities. Countermeasures must not interfere with normal or even exceptional operation of the system but must provide appropriate defensive capabilities. For this reason, the SA system must be well specified and modeled itself to be able consider the effects of countermeasures.

PROTECTION OF SA SYSTEM

This section describes protection methods and mechanisms for an SA system, which include: Authentication, Confidentiality, Detection of malicious behavior, Attribution, etc. Among the existing works on this subject, we recommend Dr. Anderson's book (Anderson, 2008).

Much of the protection can be afforded by Cryptography and cryptographic mechanisms that have been studied for the last fifty years to the point of excellence. For example, a well implemented encryption and key management system can provide a high level of protection to data both in transit and at rest. The weakness is in the anchor of trust that a cryptographic system must rely on. For example it is not sufficient to have an excellent encryption algorithm[3] – the nuances of how one manages and maintains the keys can make or break the security of such system. Likewise, the nuances of the actual implementation can render the best cryptographic algorithm weak. There are several good books dedicated to this subject, including (Schneier, 1996) that covers the practical part of the field, and (Meyer & Matyas, 1982) that was a breakthrough treatise in its time and still provides useful information even though the field has evolved since. Among the cryptographic mechanisms, Public Key Infrastructure (PKI) takes a place of particular importance and is covered in depth in (Adams & LLoyd, 1999).

Embedded Sensors

Sensors have been described in depth elsewhere in this book. Here we will review the sensors from InfoSec point of view.

Figure 6 depicts a host and what it comprises. It also shows possible places where host-embedded SA sensors typically reside.

A typical edge-node (a host) comprises:

- Hardware – difficult to modify and to taper with.
- Hypervisor (when employed) – a relatively thin layer between the hardware and Operating System(s).
- Operating Systems deployed on this host – usually running user software. There has been work however on special-purpose OS dedicated solely to security duties.
- Applications running on the Guest or user operating systems (OS).

Any of these components can (and arguably should) host sensors reporting to SA. Let us now consider advantages and disadvantages of some of these locations. The authors believe that the future of host-based sensors belongs to those invisible to the host they are observing – and that can view or affect any part of the software running on that host. Locating sensors in the hardware (Intel, 2005) is a good example of this approach.

One big issue is authenticity and integrity of the messages coming from the sensors. Providing cryptographic protection is easy – the difficult part is storing the keys in such a place that an attacker cannot reach. For software it is notoriously hard, perhaps impossible. Thus we advocate Public Key Infrastructure (Adams & LLoyd, 1999) combined with *Hardware Root of Trust*. For example, Trusted Platform Module design is a step in the right direction that the industry took (Trusted Computing Group, 2011).

Figure 6. Placement of SA sensors within a host

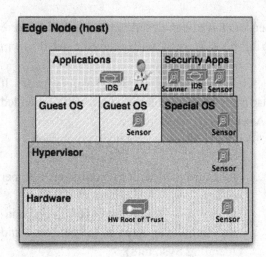

Hardware

A sensor residing in hardware – especially if it is not visible to applications and operating systems – would be the hardest for a remote attacker to compromise. It is difficult to implement – but once it is there it would be hard to compromise. An example of such an approach is early version of Intel iAMT (Intel Active Management Technology (Intel, 2005), (Intel, 2011)): a sensor was implanted in the network card. The main host did not have access to it, while it could examine any memory location and scan or control all the network traffic of the host. This sensor did not have the ability to report on a separate physical channel – but a designer today may include this capability.

Hypervisor

Containing different operations and components within different Virtual Machines can improve the overall security posture. Hypervisor separates OS from one another, and can protect memory regions occupied by sensitive applications even from their OS. A good hypervisor has few interfaces with guest OS and user applications, and thus presents fewer attack surfaces than a guest OS. It can augment hardware root of trust and extent protection to Special OS and sensitive applications running within Special and guest/user OS.

Special OS

Sensors residing in a special OS that is not visible to other OSes but capable of accessing their memory are second best thing. Special OS is not as safe as hardware, as if Hypervisor is compromised it must fall too – but it offers much more flexibility with regard to what sensors are deployed, how they evolve, how they are managed and maintained. Special OS also offers greater capabilities and processing power to the security applications it houses. For example, on a multiprocessor system one can dedicate a CPU or a processor core to Special OS and have user applications running at their normal speed while being supervised better than in the traditional approach (when antivirus runs on the same OS and successfully competes with user applications for CPU time and memory).

Guest OS and User Applications

We treat these two (OS and applications) together because most SA-related applications comprise user-space and OS-space code, i.e. they are not "purely" OS- or application-level entities.

Guest OS is more convenient to deal with than Special OS because it is more common. But since Guest OS usually is the first to fall, a sensor that it houses is not likely to outlive it. The same – only stronger – can be said of applications running under Guest OS. They are the easies to write and deploy – and the easiest to deceive and to disable. A sensor implemented in software running under control of OS on the other hand is not likely to present a significant challenge to a skillful intruder.

Separate Sensors

Sensors can reside outside of the edge nodes (see Figure 4). Usually these sensors are collecting information on the network traffic. Such a sensor can be:

- An independent device passively sitting on the network and collecting traffic.
  - A device that observes traffic.
  - A device that passes the traffic through – and thus has the ability to throttle or filter it if necessary.
- A device that it connected to a router or a switch that feeds it the traffic. Such a device may or may not be able to control the given switch.

If a sensor is not visible on the network – an adversary cannot attack it directly. However an adversary may track it through compromised infrastructure element – if for example a switch is penetrated, its rule set may be analyzed, the "tap" discovered and either disabled or fed deceiving data (modern version of *Funkspiel*[4]). A device that does not rely on infrastructure elements to collect data is not vulnerable to such an attack.

Communications are dealt with in the following section, but it is worth noting that an independent "network observation" device that sends its report via physically separate network is less vulnerable to either discovery or attack than a similar device that reports "in-band".

Communications

For communications between the sensors and the SA control center it suffices to state the obvious:

- Communications must be encrypted so even if they are intercepted, an adversary cannot learn what has been exchanged.
- Communications must be authenticated and integrity-checked (end-points authen-

tication and traffic integrity) so an adversary cannot forge, spoof or otherwise tamper with this traffic. This includes protection against – or detection of – rerouting messages from the intended recipient to another party.

- Communications must be "timely" or "fresh". It is very important to have a mechanism that detects messages that are stale[5] or replayed[6].

Physical

It is the best if SA communications can use a dedicated physical network that is different from the main network being observed. While more expensive, such a solution makes it much more difficult for the adversary to even discover the locations of SA components, let alone tamper with them. Having a separate network does not alleviate the need for cryptographic protection, especially when a well-funded adversary is concerned. But the number of presented attack surfaces is reduced significantly.

Logical

When SA communications must share the network with the routine traffic – cryptographic isolation is the only[7] protection left. The security of the SA traffic then relies on the security of the cryptographic keys stored on the end-points. The main issue here is not how to encrypt or authenticate – today that part is trivial. The difficult question is – where to keep the anchor of trust? How to make sure that if the end-point is compromised, the attacker cannot grab and reuse its keys to further compromise SA system? Like before, the answer we recommend is *hardware*. The key maintenance and management system can be hierarchical – but its anchor of trust must be hardware-based.

Admitting that nothing less than hardware can satisfy the key storage requirements – we must bring up the Supply Chain risks. Even when one designs his SA system properly and securely – there still is a risk of malicious stuff being embedded in the hardware itself! Hard drives arrive with viruses pre-installed at the factory; devices come with counterfeit chips in them… Against such a threat we can only recommend awareness and diligence.

Honeynets

One cannot overemphasize the importance of having a good honeynet (Watson, 2008) deployed. There is only one case when a honeynet is not effective: when an adversary has already mapped your network and knows where the real hosts live.

Operations Center

Protecting SA Operations Center is not different from protecting any other center. One hardens the edge nodes and infrastructure elements comprising it, guards defensive perimeter – both physical and Cyber, filters and validates the incoming and outgoing traffic. As some attacks may go underneath the radar and avoid network-based detection, close attention to system events (usually captured in system logs) is a-must here.

SITUATIONAL AWARENESS IN DIFFERENT ENVIRONMENTS

Different operational environments call for different types of situational awareness. This section compares and contrasts various operational environments and the requirements SA to be effective. SA within an enterprise network requires knowledge of the qualities and characteristics of network components within the domain of the local network, where the goals are maintaining service and security. SA at a network gateway requires knowledge of traffic variables that describe throughput and bandwidth usage; here the goals are maximizing or controlling network usage.

The most difficult part is determining what the baseline is for your environment to then detect deviations from it. In order to address this insurmountable task, it helps to classify network participants and entities with fine "enough" granularity so that behavior patterns of one class do not skew the measured baseline of another. "One size does *not* fit all" should become your daily mantra. Even then the threat would try to exploit the natural variations in the normal patterns to stay underneath the radar…

Tools for SA

This section describes various tools that support the creation and maintenance of situational awareness. Functionality classification follows:

A. Tools that collect data (e.g. capture traffic) for SA.
B. Tools that process and correlate SA data.
C. Tools that visualize processed SA data to present it in the way most conducive for comprehension.
D. Tools that capture the network composition and infrastructure, and model network behavior to help determining potential impact and propagation of various attacks.
E. Specialized tools.

Collecting Data

Meaningful data comprises the actual network traffic and system logs from all the entities that touched that data. The usual approach to collecting network traffic is dedicating an off-the-shelf computer (predominantly running Linux OS) equipped with a good RAID card, a large disk array (whose size depends on the amount of traffic that traverses this network and the length of time this traffic is going to be retained), and a good networking card. Installing software like WireShark (Wireshark) (Orebaugh, 2007) or TCPDUMP

(TCPDUMP, 2011) (TCPDUMP & LibPCAP) completes the preparations. TCPDUMP is a very mature (developed by Van Jacobson at Lawrence Berkeley Laboratory Network Research Group in 1987) command-line packet analyzer. It should be mentioned that WireShark (evolved from the famous Ethereal) packet analyzer in fact presents a complete capture-processing-visualization system and have pretty sophisticated processing and visualization capabilities.

Carnivore (Carnivore (FBI)) project by FBI also deserves being mentioned. Designed to monitor email and electronic communications, it basically was a Windows workstation running a customizable packet sniffer and storing the captured data on a removable drive. Carnivore was implemented in October 1997 and replaced in 2005 with commercial software of which NarusInsight (Narus) is one example.

Processing and Correlating Data

Processing usually narrows down to filtering, culling the benign and irrelevant data, thus reducing the amount of data the "main" analyzer needs to crunch through.

Correlating is hard in general, because of the "*post hoc ergo propter hoc*"[8] fallacy. Still the most obvious and usually unavoidable way to correlate is by aligning timestamps on the events and data packets, and building the sequence chains. It is easier to backtrack from a known incident or intrusion to determine that an attack is in progress by viewing the correlated events chain.

Visualization

Arguably the hardest part of SA is presenting the findings in a form that allows a human being to quickly comprehend the situation. The amount of data involved in SA exacerbates this difficulty. Arguably, WireShark can be listed here in addition to being listed as a data collection and processing tool.

Specialized Tools

NetGlean performs network analysis to catalog and characterize devices on a network.

NetSPA (MIT Lincoln Laboratory, 2008) enables operators and managers to understand how attackers can penetrate their networks so that better protection mechanisms can be deployed.

Ideally all the vulnerabilities should be fixed as soon as they are discovered. In reality there is seldom enough resources to take care of them all at once. This forces administrators to prioritize the issues, deciding what to correct first and what issues could wait. More often than not such decisions are made blindly, without deep understanding of all the consequences of leaving one or another vulnerability unpatched.

Relying on other tools (such as Nessus (Nessus)) for finding vulnerabilities, NetSPA creates attack graphs. These graphs show the administrator how far into his network an attack could reach, given the existing vulnerabilities. Thus one can make an informed decision regarding what vulnerabilities must be patched first, based on their potential impact to the whole network.

NMAT performs network traffic analysis to link the mission to the network and provide information on important infrastructure to protect.

LARIAT (Lincoln Adaptable Real-time Information Assurance Testbed, (Rossey, 2002)) is an extension of the testbed created for DARPA 1998 and 1999 intrusion detection (ID) evaluations that supports real-time, automated and quantitative evaluations of ID systems and other information assurance (IA) technologies. Components of LARIAT generate realistic background user traffic and real network attacks, verify attack success or failure, score ID system performance, and provide a graphical user interface for control and monitoring. Emphasis was placed on making LARIAT easy to adapt, configure, and run without requiring a detailed understanding of the underlying complexity. Among the capabilities LARIAT offers is the ability to quickly stand up a very large network. LARIAT is currently deployed at several production sites and is undergoing continued development and refinement.

TESTING AND EVALUATION

An important component for development of adequate SA is the ability to test and evaluation SA capabilities. This section describes test and evaluation capabilities that permit the investigation of SA production and monitoring technologies in both static and dynamic environments. Realism of the test environment is extremely important, as the tests and evaluations will determine a capabilities readiness for real-world deployment. Among the variables to be tested are the scope and coverage of the SA capability, the processing speed (e.g., ability to keep up with real-time data) and the relationship or inter-relationship to other situational awareness capabilities that integrate into a whole. Among the tools useful for such evaluation are NetGlean and LARIAT.

SUMMARY

Just as there is no perfect information security system, there is no perfect security for an SA system. There are many issues, which will require further study and development. A major challenge will be to find techniques that will perform well against unknown attacks. There is also the question of how much is enough. Even though we do not have a perfect system, the need is immediate and we must make decisions now about what kinds of capabilities we will need to deploy.

REFERENCES

Adams, C., & Lloyd, S. (1999). *Understanding PKI. Concepts, standards, and deployment considerations* (2nd ed.). Addison-Wesley.

Anderson, R. (2008). *Security engineering: A guide to building dependdable distributed systems* (2nd ed.). Indianapolis, IN: Wiley Publishing, Inc.

Barnes, J. E. (2008). Pentagon computer networks attacked. *Los Angeles Times*.

Bloedorn, E. C., Christiansen, A. D., Hill, W., Skorupka, C., Talbot, L. M., & Tivel, J. (2001). *Data mining for network intrusion detection: How to get started.* Retrieved June 15, 2011, from http://citeseerx.ist.psu.edu/viewdoc/download?doi=10.1.1.102.8556.pdf

Boyd, J. R. (1995). *The essence of winning and losing.* Retrieved from http://www.danford.net/boyd/essence.htm

Chen, E. (2010). *W32.Stuxnet dossier (official blog).*

Delarue, J. (1962). *Historie de la gestapo.* Paris, France: Fayard.

Endsley, M. R. (1995). Toward a theory of situation awareness in dynamic systems. *Human Factors*, *37*(1), 32–64. doi:10.1518/001872095779049543

Endsley, M. R., Selcon, S. J., Hardiman, T. D., & Groft, D. G. (1998). *A comparative analysis of SAGAT and SART for evaluations of situation awareness.* 42nd Annual Meeting of the Human Factors & Ergonomics Society. Chicago, IL.

Falliere, N. M. (2011). *W32.Stuxnet dossier.* Retrieved May 11, 2011, from http://www.symantec.com/content/en/us/enterprise/media/security_response/whitepapers/w32_stuxnet_dossier.pdf

Fracker, M. L. (1991). *Measures of situation awareness: Review and future directions.* Armstrong Laboratories, Wright-Patterson Air Force Base, OH.

Intel. (2005). *Intel active management technology quick reference.* Retrieved May 11, 2011, from http://download.intel.com/support/motherboards/desktop/sb/amt_quick_start_guide1.pdf

Intel. (2011). *Intel AMT frequently asked questions.* Retrieved May 11, 2011, from http://software.intel.com/en-us/articles/intel-active-management-technology-frequently-asked-questions/?wapkw=(active+management+technology)

Juvenal. (100). *Satires* (vol. 6). Rome.

Meyer, C. H., & Matyas, S. M. (1982). *Cryptography: A new dimension in computer data security.* John Wiley & Sons.

MIT Lincoln Laboratory. (2008). *Network security: Plugging the right holes. MIT Lincoln Laboratory, Cyber and Systems Technology.* Lexington, MA: MIT Lincoln Laboratory.

Proctor, P. (2001). *Practical intrusion detection handbook.* Upper Saddle River, NJ: Prentice Hall PTR.

Racicot, J. (2008). *U.S Army infected by worm.* Retrieved from http://cyberwarfaremag.wordpress.com/2008/11/20/us-army-infected-by-worm/

Rossey, L. M. (2002). *LARIAT: Lincoln adaptable real-time information assurance testbed.* IEEE Aerospace Conference. Big Sky, MT: IEEE.

Sarter, N. B., & Woods, D. D. (1991). Situation awareness: A critical but ill-defined phenomenon. *The International Journal of Aviation Psychology, 1,* 45–57. doi:10.1207/s15327108ijap0101_4

Schneier, B. (1996). *Applied cryptography* (2nd ed.). John Wiley & Sons.

Trusted Computing Group. (2011). *TPM main part 1 design principles.* (D. Grawrock, Ed.) Retrieved from http://www.trustedcomputinggroup.org/resources/tpm_main_specification

Watson, D. R. (2008). The Honeynet project: Data collection tools, infrastructure, archives and analysis. *Information Security Threats Data Collection and Sharing, 2008* (pp. 24-30). Amsterdam, The Netherlands: WISTDCS '08 (WOMBAT Workshop).

ADDITIONAL READING

Chu, M., Ingols, K., Lippmann, R., Webster, S., & Boyer, S. (2010). Visualizing Attack Graphs, Reachability, and Trust Relationships with NAVIGATOR, VizSec2010, Ottawa, Canada.

Cunningham, R. K., Lippmann, R. P., Fried, D. J., Garfinkel, S. L., Graf, I., Kendall, K. R., et al. (1999) Evaluating Intrusion Detection Systems without Attacking Your Friends: The 1998 DARPA Intrusion Detection Evaluation, *Proceedings of Third Conference and Workshop on Intrusion Detection and Response*, San Diego, California, USA.

Epstein, B., Weinstein, C. J., & Cunningham, R. K. (2003). System Adaptation as a Trust Response in Tactical Ad Hoc Networks. *Proceedings MILCOM, 2003,* 209–214.

Ingols, K., Chu, M., Lippmann, R., & Boyer, S. (2009) Modeling Modern Network Attacks and Countermeasures Using Attack Graphs, ACSAC 2009, Honolulu, HI, Dec. 7, 2009.

Ingols, K., Lippmann, R., & Piwowarski, K. (2006) Practical Attack Graph Generation for Network Defense, *Computer Security Applications Conference*, Miami Beach, Florida.

Ingols, K., Lippmann, R. P., Webster, S. E., Boyer, S., & Chu, M. (2008) Practical Experiences Using SCAP to Aggregate CND Data, *4th Annual IT Security Automation Conference*, Gaithersburg, MD.

Jajodia, S., Liu, P., Swarup, V., & Wang, C. (Eds.). (2009). *Cyber Situational Awareness: Issues and Research.* Springer.

Lippmann, R., & Ingols, K. (2005) An Annotated Review of Past Papers on Attack Graphs - PR-IA-1, *MIT Lincoln laboratory Project Report.* Lexington.

Lippmann, R., & Ingols, K. (2005) Evaluating and Strengthening Enterprise Network Security Using Attack Graphs PR-IA-2, *MIT Lincoln Laboratory Project Report*, Lexington.

Lippmann, R., Ingols, K., Scott, C., Piwowarski, K., Kratkiewicz, K., & Cunningham, R. (2006) Validating and Restoring Defense in Depth using Attack Graphs, *MILCOM 2006*, Washington, DC.

McLain, C. D., Studer, A., & Lippmann, R. P. (2007) Making Network Intrusion Detection Work with IPSEC, *MIT Lincoln Laboratory Technical Report 1121*, Lexington, MA.

Sheyner, O., Jha, S., Haines, J., Lippmann, R. P., & Wing, J. M. (2002) Automated Generation and Analysis of Attack Graphs, in *Proceedings IEEE Symposium on Security and Privacy*.

Streilein, W. W., Kratkiewicz, K., Piwowarski, K., & Webster, S. (2007) PANEMOTO: Network Visualization of Security Situational Awareness through Passive Analysis, *8th Annual IEEE SMC Information Assurance Workshop*, West Point, New York.

Studer, A. McLain, C. D., Lippmann, R. P.,(2007) Tuning Intrusion Detection to Work With a Two Encryption Key Version of IPSEC, *MILCOM 2007*, Orlando, FL.

Weaver, N., Paxson, V., Staniford, S., Cunningham, R. K., (2003) *Large Scale Malicious Code: A Research Agenda*.

Williams, L. C., Lippmann, R. P., & Ingols, K. W. (2007) An Interactive Attack Graph Cascade and Reachability Display, *VIZSEC 2007*, Sacramento, CA.

KEY TERMS AND DEFINITIONS

Attack Graph: A graph depicting how far an adversary can penetrate into your network, given your network map and a set of vulnerabilities that its nodes have. Very useful in prioritizing vulnerabilities fixes.

Baseline: Normal network usage pattern. What kind of traffic in what quantity traverses your network, what are its origination and destination points – and how it varies across (a) time and (b) your entities.

Detection: Discovering malicious activity by observing the traffic (inbound, outbound and local) and tracking down deviation from the baseline, or suspicious event in the log or report.

Deviation: Event or occurrence that breaks the pattern of baseline, e.g. an unusually large amount of traffic going in or out, an unusual type of data exchanged (such as user typically exchanging text emails now sends an encrypted PDF file or receives an executable), etc. One can detect malicious activity by noticing deviations and/or correlating deviations with system event logs.

Hacking SA System: Making your SA system present a picture that your adversary wants you to see, or at least not present what he wants to hide from you.

Honeynet: Multiple – often interconnected and/or interrelated – honeypots on the network. Their presence greatly enhances Intrusion Detection System capabilities. They are most efficient when deployed in a sparse production address space rather than occupying a separate dedicated subnet.

Honeypot: A special entity on the network that pretends to be an ordinary host – the perfect "victim" candidate – which is isolated, heavily instrumented and monitored in order to intruders trap and analyze their behavior and attack tools.

Situational Awareness: Knowing what is going on in and around your network now, what the general situation is (Cyber and Kinetic world at large), and based on it predicting with a reasonably high probability what is likely to happen next in your network.

ENDNOTES

[1] This work was performed under U.S. Air Force contract FA8721-05-C-0002. Opinions, interpretations, conclusions, and recommendations are not necessarily endorsed by the U.S. Government.

[2] Who watches the watchmen?

[3] Today most people can have access to the best products of the cryptographic science, if they choose to.

[4] *Funkspiel* means "radio game" in German and refers to using captured transmitters and "turned" operators to deceive the enemy in counter-intelligence operations (Delarue, 1962).

[5] A *stale* message is authentic. Its content hasn't been tampered with. It may not yet been seen by the intended recipient. However an adversary intercepted, held it for some time – and is releasing it now to aid in his devises. A *stale* message (whose purpose was destroyed by the delay in delivery) is an opposite of *timely* message. For example, a message to alert a garrison that an enemy force is approaching becomes stale and useless after the attack commences.

[6] A *replayed* message is authentic and untampered-with; it may also be still "fresh" aka recent. However its intended recipient has already received it. An adversary is trying to feed this message to the recipient again.

[7] Why not VLAN, etc? These mechanisms are useful and should be employed – but they rely on the infrastructure being intact. If an adversary penetrates it and tampers with a switch – all the traffic separation that the VLAN provided on that switch is gone.

[8] A logical fallacy – "after this, therefore because of this".

Chapter 7
Designing Information Systems and Network Components for Situational Awareness

Cyril Onwubiko
Research Series Limited, UK

ABSTRACT

Operators need situational awareness (SA) of their organisation's computer networks and Information Systems in order to identify threats, estimate impact of attacks, evaluate risks, understand situations, and make sound decisions swiftly and accurately on what to protect against, and how to address incidents that may impact valued assets. Enterprise computer networks are often huge and complex, spanning across several WANs and supporting a number of distributed services. Understanding situations in such dynamic and complex networks is time-consuming and challenging. Operators SA are enhanced through a number of ways, one of which is through the use of situation-aware systems and technology. Designing situation-aware systems for computer network defence (CND) is difficult without understanding basic situational awareness design requirements of network applications and systems. Thus, this chapter investigates pertinent features that are foundation, essential, and beneficial for designing situation-aware systems, software, and network applications for CND.

INTRODUCTION

In the last fifteen years the application of situational awareness has been revolutionary, particularly in Air Traffic Control (ATC), and Defence and Military operation where SA has been extensively researched. ATC operation, for instance, can be compared to CND operation; unfortunately, while the application of situational awareness to computer network defence is still in its embryonic stage, its application to ATC is mainstream (Onwubiko C., 2009).

One of the primary purposes of CND is to ensure that systems and networks are secure, reliable and operational. This includes actions taken via computer networks to protect, monitor, analyse, detect and respond to cyber-attacks, intrusions, disruptions or other perceived unau-

DOI: 10.4018/978-1-4666-0104-8.ch007

thorised actions that could compromise or impact defence information systems and networks. CND is achieved through a collective effort by personnel who monitor, manage and maintain defence systems, networks and infrastructures, such as network operators, security analysts, systems administrators and network engineers. This group of personnel are referred to, in this chapter, as operators, ('human' operators). These personnel are faced with the onerous tasks of coordinating, maintaining, monitoring and ensuring the necessary actions required in keeping defence systems and network infrastructures operational, whilst ensuring that appropriate protection from cyber-attacks is provided on a daily basis.

Cyber-attacks to computer networks are growing and evolving. For example, code-driven attacks, deliberate malicious software attacks, espionage, distributed denial of service attacks, phishing and the recent computer electronics attacks (E.g. Stuxnet). All these contribute in demonstrating the complexity and challenges faced in a CND environment.

Situational awareness is the process of perceiving the elements in the environment, understanding the elements in the environment, and the projection of their status into the near future (Endsley M. R., 2000). SA underscores situation assessment in order to make accurate forecast in dynamic and complex environments. Thus, the underpinning of situational awareness in computer networks is to assist operators to identify adversaries, estimate impact of attacks, evaluate risks, understand situations and make sound decisions on how best to protect valued assets swiftly and accurately (Onwubiko C., 2009). Hence, we believe that the application of SA in CND will yield unprecedented benefits akin to SA for safety and security in aircraft, flight operation and safety controls.

In this chapter we investigate task and system requirements that support situational awareness

in CND. Task requirements are human operator-specific tasks such as risk assessment, protective monitoring and decision making. System requirements are automated system-specific tasks completed by computer systems and network appliances. The elicitation of task and system requirements for CND is the foundation for building CND systems and applications that are situation-aware; and the use of situation-aware systems and applications in a CND environment certainly enhances operator situational awareness.

Situational awareness as a human mental process is enhanced by the use of technology to access, analyse, and present information to have greater understanding of existing situations and how they may change over time (ESRI, 2008). Thus, the aim of this chapter is to investigate situational awareness in computer network security, and to evaluate task and system design requirements (functional and non-functional) that CND systems should possess to enhance operator situational awareness. According to Endsley M. R., and Garland D. J., (2000), the enhancement of operator situation awareness has become a major design goal for those developing operator interfaces, automation concepts and training programs in a wide variety of fields, such as, air traffic control, power plants and advanced manufacturing systems. It is equally important to extend this design assessment to CND infrastructure, systems and applications.

The remainder of this chapter is organised as follows. The first section describes situational awareness in network security. The second section discusses our design requirements framework for developing situation-aware CND systems and applications. Design requirements discussed comprises both functional and non-functional requirements. The third section elaborates on our contribution and outlines benefits of the work, which strengthens the usefulness of the contribution. Finally, the chapter is summarised with a conclusion.

NETWORK SECURITY SITUATIONAL AWARENESS

Situational awareness is described as knowing what is going on around you and within that knowledge of your surroundings, knowing what is important (D'Amico A., and Kocka M., 2005). Situational awareness stems from human factor and cognitive studies. It has been well-studied and applied to several disciplines, including psychology, aviation and military operations, since the seminal work of Endsley M., (1995). SA involves both a person with his cognitive processes, as well as a situation with several information types and statuses (Lambert D. A., et al, 2004). SA is very complex and involves very dynamic states. For example, computer networks with hundreds of network objects (firewalls, IDSes, routers, switches, servers, PADs), maintaining a consistently high situational awareness over these objects can be challenging. The operator through his mental models, experience and training, tries to monitor the network, using a number of mechanisms, technologies and toolkits, each device having a perception of the network being monitored.

Figure 1 is adapted from Endsley's situation awareness reference model (Endsley M., 1995), which presents three levels of situation awareness,

perception, comprehension and *projection*. In addition to McGuinness and Foy's (McGuinness B., and Foy L., 2000) extension of Endsley's SA model that includes *resolution* as the level four situation awareness component.

These terms (*perception, comprehension, projection* and *resolution*) are discussed in this chapter in relation to network security situational awareness. Thus, *perception* deals with evidence gathering of network situations, *comprehension* deals with the analysis of the set of network situation evidence, and also involves with the deduction of exact threat level, identification of attack types, and understanding of associated or interdependent risks. *Projection* deals with predictive measures to address future incidents, while, *resolution* deals with controls to repair, recover and resolve network situations.

To achieve some degree of situational awareness, as shown in Figure 1, we need both Task and systems factors, and individual factors. Task and system factors are system-specific tasks and systems requirements that assist individuals/operators gain situation awareness. For example, systems capability, automation and interface design. Individual factors are human-factor attributes that could enhance or impact operator situational awareness, such as training and experience, or

Figure 1. Network security situation awareness model

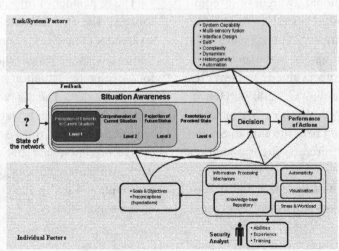

stress and workload. While task and systems factor requirements are discussed in section 0 of this chapter, individual factors are not within the scope of this contribution. This chapter focuses on task and system factor requirements that are essential in designing situation-aware systems and tasks for CND.

Perception, comprehension, projection and *resolution* are core SA components, and each is discussed in details in relation to computer network security, as follows:

1. **Perception (Level 1):** At this level of situational awareness, security analysts are knowledgeable of the elements in the network and are able to gather raw piece of evidence of situations perceived in the network, such as alerts reported by intrusion detection systems, firewall logs, scan reports, as well as the time these pieces of security evidence occurred, and the specific control (source) that reported the alerts or generated the logs. This involves the use of individual and independent toolkits to monitor the network. Whilst these individual and independent toolkits (point solutions) gather raw data about perceived situations, and hence offer a level of protection to computer networks from cyber-attacks; unfortunately, each point solution is directed toward addressing a specific attack. Hence, detection of widespread or enterprise-wide attack situations is still challenging (Onwubiko C., 2008); more so, the way they are deployed, usually localised, makes it extremely difficult to assess enterprise-wide situations, or quantify associated interdependent risks accurately and swiftly. At the *perception* level, information about the status, attributes and dynamics of the relevant elements in the environment are known; and it is also possible to extend the classification of information into meaningful representations that offers

the underlying for comprehension, projection and resolution (Salerno et al., 2004).

2. **Comprehension (Level 2):** At this level of situational awareness, the security analyst uses techniques, methodologies, processes and procedures to analyse, synthesise, correlate and aggregate pieces of evidence data perceived in the network from network elements to gain higher degrees of meaningfulness and understanding than those acquired at Level 1 SA. *Comprehension* also involves a determination of the relevance of the evidence captured to the underlying goal of resolution of the situation (Salerno et al., 2004). Hence, comprehension offers an organised picture of the current situation by determining the significance of the evidence perceived together with the importance of the assets being monitored. And when new set of evidence becomes available the knowledge-base is updated to reflect this change.

3. **Projection (Level 3):** At this level of situational awareness, security analysts now possess the capability to make accurate future prediction or forecast based on the knowledge extracted from the dynamics of the network elements, leveraging on L2 SA. The analyst's ability to make accurate future forecast can be enhanced by the use of powerful monitoring systems and technologies that are able to detect, deduce and predict patterns of occurrence of future events. For example, early warning systems are able to make forecast of future occurrences of weather situations. The use of systems with this capability in CND environment would certainly enhance operator SA, and enable better planning and the use of preventative controls to address potential situations. *Projection* answers the questions, what network attack are possible and what controls may be needed?

4. **Resolution (Level 4):** At this level of situational awareness, security analysts are able to recommend and implement adequate countermeasure controls required to treat risks inherent or interdependent in networks. *Resolution* as part of the core SA was first discussed in situation awareness by McGuinness B., and Foy L., (2000), as an extension of Endsley's SA levels. It is about the necessary actions required to address network situations when they occur.

In many respects, SA is comparable to the OODA (observe, orient, deduce and act) loop. The OODA decision control was first proposed by Boyd J. (1987) used in Command and Control (C2). This means operators need to observe network situations, evaluate the situation, deduce the impact it may have and decide possible mitigation controls to effectively and accurately address the situation. By continually following the OODA loop, an operator or group of operators are able to act in accordance to the situation they are in. The operator may use technology, in this case, protective monitoring, interface, Human Computer Interface (HCI) interactions and all the other requirements mentioned, to enhance situational awareness of the network being monitored, and then decide the best cause of action to be taken.

Whether SA or OODA, the approach for CND are:

- First, the network should be monitored by trained and experienced network security operators;
- Second, these operators through the use of tools and technologies are able to observe, analyse and resolve abnormal situations (faults, errors and attacks) in the network;
- Third, operator SA is enhanced through the use of technologies that are swift and accurate in processing and analysis of perceived situations in networks. Thus, operators gain enhanced situational awareness of the environment by monitoring networks and ensuring network activities (alerts, logs, volumetric statistics and abnormal behaviour) are visualised, whilst using techniques (correlation and fusion techniques) that are able to combine and analyse data from a number of distributed sensors deployed in and around the network;
- Fourth, reliant on operators' mental models (past knowledge of network behaviours, experience and training), they are able to make projections about future network states. For example, due to observed network traffic and volumetric, an experienced operator could make accurate estimation of when the network is under attack from evolving computer worm mutant or variants of a self-propagating malicious code.

DESIGN REQUIREMENTS FRAMEWORK FOR SITUATIONAL AWARENESS IN CND

In this section, task and system design requirements that enable operator situational awareness in computer networks, information security and CND are investigated.

Eliciting and capturing the requirements of a system or an application is one of the first fundamental steps in software and systems engineering. Since designing and implementing an extensible system is complex, as is the case with designing situation-aware systems, we need to clearly establish the requirements, which can be either functional or non-functional.

Figure 2 is our proposed task and system factor design requirements framework for computer network defence. It consists of two main categories, functional and non-functional requirements. Further, requirement attributes are further partitioned in accordance with core SA component requirements, such as global, L1 SA, L2 SA, L3 SA and

L4 SA. *Global requirements* are requirements performed by the system regardless whether they are functional, non-functional, or pertaining to a particular SA level. *L1 SA* are level 1 situational awareness specific requirements. *L2 SA* are level 2 situational awareness specific requirements. *L3 SA* are level 3 situational awareness specific requirements; finally, *L4 SA* is level 4 situational awareness specific requirement.

Functional requirements are concerned with the functions that the system can perform for its users (Emmerich W., 2000). Functional requirements, therefore, are usually localised in the system, and with particular components of the system. For example, human computer interface (HCI) is localised in the systems' interface component, while real-time processing is localised in the memory and processing engine of the system.

Non-functional requirements are concerned with the quality of the system. They are usually difficult to be attributed to any particular component of the system or sub-systems of the system. They are, rather, global system qualities; hence non-functional requirements typically have serious impact on the overall architecture of the chosen system. For example, a distributed system may have serious performance impact if it is not scalable or robust, whereas this for a centralised system does not apply, hence scalability as a non-functional requirement will have an impact on the overall architecture of the system (whether distributed or centralised).

Functional Design Requirements for Situational Awareness in CND

Situation awareness attributes are discussed in relation to functional characteristics of SA in computer network security (CNS) and computer network defence (CND). This list is by no means exhaustive, however, the necessary steps toward understanding the essential attribute to designing and implementing SA in computer network security have been strategically presented, as follows:

1. Automation,
2. Integration,
3. Interface,
4. Usability,
5. Self-*,
6. Real-time processing,
7. Analysis and interpretation,
8. Protective monitoring,
9. Risk Assessment,
10. Multi-sensory data fusion,
11. Visualisation,
12. Decision control,
13. Forecast,
14. Resolution.

Figure 2. Task and system factor situational awareness design requirements

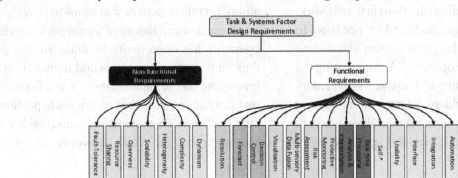

Automation

Human factor researchers in the early 90s believed that automation of *cognitive-aware* systems (systems that performed cognitive tasks) contributed to errors and failures in SA, and often, were metaphors to performance degradation in SA (Wickens C. D., 1992; Endsley M. R., 1996). One would understand their standpoint, especially given the time period when these debates occurred. Their major concern was roles were swapped between *humans* and *machines*. In the past, *humans* performed tasks, but recently, machines are now automated to perform these tasks, while humans now monitor over automated systems.

The advent of very powerful computing systems and the possibility of real-time processing have made automation of technologically-enabled and situation-aware tasks more attractive, appealing and ubiquitous. This is a paradigm shift in the 21st century. The desire to automate every task, (such as, physical, logical, perceptual, and even cognitive) has increased. Furthermore, it is widely believed that automated systems perform better than humans in solving most real world problems, especially those requiring speed, accuracy and reliability. Arguable as it may be, current trends show that automated systems are preferred over humans in performing rigorous numerical, medical and physical tasks. However, automation of cognitive tasks may be different. While the mental models (residual knowledge, experience and training) of the operator are essential to understanding situations in the network, there is certainly a genuine need for operators to leverage on technology and system automation to gain and enhance operator SA. Automating the integration, processing and analysis provided by these systems should go a long way in helping operators gain short term SA over these network probes. Automation of technology is certainly a requirement when designing situation-aware systems and application for CND.

Integration

Computer systems and their components must interact either as autonomous, dependent or interdependent systems. To enable this relationship, computer system components are integrated, often tightly coupled, so that they can interoperate as a self-interacting autonomous system. Using a computer system, for example, separate pieces of components, such as monitor, keyboard, mouse, memory, processor, and storage media are collectively integrated into a single autonomous system referred to as a computer system. Similarly, a network comprising a hub, server and workstation is a collection of autonomous and interdependent systems that collaborate to enable communication. It is pertinent to mention that the possibility to integrate system and system components, a class of powerful systems has evolved, such as the cyber-physical systems (CPS).

Cyber-Physical Systems are embedded systems that integrate computation with physical processes. These class of systems, usually, have embedded computers and network monitors that control the physical processes, and often with feedback loops where physical processes affect computations and vice versa (Lee E. A., 2006). Examples of CPS systems, include communications systems, distributed robotics, defence systems, manufacturing and smart structures. The ability for this class of new systems to provide the much needed collaborative framework provides operators the opportunity to make timely savings on processing, analysis and remediation by leveraging on the capabilities of these to provide real-time or near real-time responses to perceived attack. While CPS systems in themselves are not a requirement for CND, however, integration provides the platform to create multi-functioning systems that assist operators in analysing network probes, events and alerts, which consequently, enable operator gain enhanced SA of the network. Systems integration and application integration are foundation requirements in CND whether it is for the purposes of situational awareness or not.

Interface

Today's information and communications technology (ICT) systems are complex. These systems use a plethora of technologies and software to implement complex business logics, some of which involve a finite number of background processes that are transparent to the operator, and therefore make it challenging for the operator to swiftly identify sequence of erroneous actions or detect fault in the system or spot when an abnormal situation is happening. To assist operators to detect, diagnose and remedy abnormal situations swiftly, complex computer systems should provide interfaces that enable human computer interaction. Operator situational awareness will be enhanced if systems can provide interactive interfaces that enable human interaction, such as graphical user interfaces (GUI), ASCII interface, command line interface, and command and control interface. These interfaces can be used for human computer interaction to enable feedback loop control. Whatever the interface (GUI or command line), systems and system components need to interact (intra and inter communications), integrate and interoperate either as autonomous or interdependent systems. This is one of the reasons why interface design has been acknowledged as a significant factor when assessing SA in systems. Thus, according to Endsley M., and Garland D. J., (2000), one of the primary reasons for measuring SA has been for the purpose of evaluating new system and interface designs.

Human computer interface designs do affect operator performance and system safety. According to Sandom C., (1999), the design of HCI

can have a profound effect on safety assurance, particularly during emergency situations. For example, when emergencies arise and system operators must react swiftly and accurately, the situational awareness of the operator is critical to their ability to make decisions, revise plans and to act purposefully to correct the abnormal situation. This sentiment emphasises the importance of designing HCIs to support situational awareness, especially in complex and dynamically changing environment such as in network monitoring and computer network defence.

We believe that the quality of the interfaces a system offers determines the degree of human interaction possible. Hence, SA designers for CND should ensure that modern network systems are capable of offering a variety of HCI interfaces that aid human interaction.

Usability

Usability (user friendliness) is a design and development construct for testing a system's functionality and how the system interacts with its users. Usability development practices offer a means of quantifying, designing and testing the applicability or fitness of a system. According to Borja A. T. (2003), the application of usability engineering in the product's lifecycle reduces cost over the life of the product's development, by reducing the need to add missed or fix unusable functionality later in the development cycle. Systems that are intuitively easy to use are preferable for operators who are faced with many changes and the complexity of dynamic network activities. So designer should ensure that systems are tested for usability and the use of system to perform work should of minimum easy, that is, it should not require steep learning curve in order to intuitively work out how a system should be used. The difficulty to use system can impose unnecessary constraint and add to the lack of situation awareness by adding to the workload of the operators. It is important that in addition to designing systems that offer the operator with the required information and capabilities, we also ensure that it is provided in a way that is useable cognitively as well as physically (Endsley M. R., 2000; Onwubiko C., 2009).

Self-*

Self-* is the collection of self-oriented attributes such as self-awareness, self-healing, self-reconfiguration, self-autonomous, self-discovery, self-analysis and self-defending that a system performs by itself without human assistance. This list is not exhaustive, but the emphases is that self-* is systems requirements that CND systems could be evaluated against. Whether CND systems should possess self-* is open for discussion, and if asked, modern CND systems should possess a level of self-* attributes, provided it does not replace human intelligence and override human decision control, but should work together synergistically to offer better situational awareness to the operator. The operator will benefits, and invariably gain better awareness of the situation if the system possess a level of self-*, such that they could report internal and on-going situations to the operator, who through the gathering of other external information gain enhanced and complementary SA through the other cues available to them. For example, if a computer system has self-* capabilities to report that its processor cycle is consistently high over a period of time, and that the reason why the cycle is high is because of a new program the user had installed, and that this new program has a register conflict with another software running in background mode. And if the system can report to the operator, without much analysis by the operator, then, the operator would have enough cues to understand better the situation, and therefore, without such reports be able to decide (decision making) on an efficient cause of action, in time and accurately. If every component in the network possesses this level of self-* qualities, then maintaining consistently enhanced situational awareness of the network can

be achievable. If this were to be possible, it will become the underpinning of self-* contribution in computer network defence; and presumably, useful to other areas life such as medical science, military operations and aviation.

Real-Time Processing

In computer network security, as with military defence, aviation and ATC, real-time processing of information, particularly, suspicious traffic, military intelligence or intelligence regarding enemy presence is required. To achieve a higher level of situation awareness, the capability of the computing device used for SA analysis must possess the ability to provide real-time processing of data and information. This is analogous to a person's human cognitive being able to offer instant thoughts about a perceived situation. The absence of real-time processing hinders the possibility to provide swift and instant response to perceived attacks, such that the *'detect, analyse, decide* and *respond'* paradigm in defence becomes less attractive. This will certainly render the application of SA in CND inefficient. Computing systems and their underlying software used for SA to analyse situations must possess the capability to offer real-time processing, spontaneous feedback mechanisms, and real-time responses. Real-time processing is important design functionality for systems and applications, especially, when such systems and application will be used for CND operations. For example, Cisco ASA 5500 series of firewalls can process up to 12Gbps of real world multi-protocol traffic (Cisco System Inc., 2011), while Juniper's latest ISG 2000 integrated security gateways favour of intrusion detection and prevention systems (IDP) can process information at about 3Mbps (Junipers Networks, 2011). This goes to demonstrate the overwhelming importance of real-time or near real-time processing for CND systems and applications.

Analysis and Interpretation

Analysis provided by computer network monitoring systems should be such that it can provide system administrators and network operators a degree of situational awareness to enable them identify and remedy dynamic network situations swiftly. Analysis must be built into networking devices such that a suite of multimedia channels can be utilised. For example, system (or system component) should be able to display alert information (visual), send alert information (as text, email or log messages) and provide audible alerts (alarms). The provision of a variety of alerting channels ensures that operators are provided with the required medium to enable them detect, identify and diagnose swiftly dynamic changes that occur in networks. These changes can be faults, errors, attacks or changes in traffic volumetric. When designing network systems and components for SA, designers should ensure that analysis components of systems are able to provide operators a variety of alerting and reporting channels to enable enhanced situational awareness. In ATC for instance, modern aircrafts are designed to provide both the ATC operators and pilots a variety of alert reporting channels. For example, the aircraft cockpit is designed to display weather information graphically, offer textual information of the same event, and also provide audible (audio) of the changes in the event being reported. For instance, when an aircraft changes altitude, whilst this is displayed on the computer display unit, both text and audio (sound) are provided to ensure that pilot crew are made aware of the changing situation. This has improved pilot's situational awareness as a result of information flow between the pilot and cockpit (Mulgund S., et al. 1997), and this would enhance better interpretation as multiple channels can be correlated.

Multimedia enhancement and support in the analysis is essential so that network warnings, errors faults and changes (situations) can be provided via audio, visual, textual, and pictorial (graphically). This is to ensure that network and security operators are presented with a variety of different channels and facets to enable them detect, diagnose, analyse and interpret dynamic network situations as them occur. Accurate interpretation of information and data is the key to achieving enhanced situational awareness and consequently making timely and accurate decisions. According to Endsley M. R., (2000), in the face of torrent of data, many operators may even be less informed. Hence information must be integrated and interpreted accurately for any operator to stand a chance of providing accurate and timely cause of action to an unknown situation. Situation-aware systems designers for CND operation should consider the provision of rich and wide-ranging analysis and interpretation modules/components for CND systems and applications.

Protective Monitoring

Protective monitoring is a task-specific level 2 SA that helps increase operators' situational awareness in computer network defence (see Figure 1). Protective monitoring is usually an operational task performed by human operators. It involves the use of technology to monitor networks and systems for on-going phenomenon in which data may be continuously changing. These dynamically changing situations are often times normal, and occasionally abnormal. Abnormal situations are suspicious situations that are processed with a view to addressing any situations such as errors, faults or attacks in the platform.

Protective monitoring as a CND requirement provides the provision for adequate accounting, logging and auditing of user and network activities of the platform, such that user interactions, actions and dynamic network activities are monitored, logged and analysed (real-time and retrospectively). User and network activities monitoring help security administrators to identify, detect and resolve abnormal network issues. Protective monitoring is usually achieved through the use of a collection of several protective systems, such as firewalls, intrusion detection systems, identity management systems, log analysis and log integrity management systems to present to network administrators the network health, user interaction, traffic volume and abnormal activities which would be ordinarily impossible from either a sole administrator's or a single sensor perspective.

The benefit is an increased situational awareness of network administrators that offers overall status of the network health, which assists in the detection and identification of abnormal situations in the network or in systems within the network (Onwubiko, C., 2008). Protective monitoring is that aspect of CND that offers security analysts cues in the monitored network; provides the data (network traffic and log) that helps the analyst correlate, analyse and determine the level of perceived threat. And assembling these information, provides the analyst an understanding (comprehension) of perceived status of the network, and enable projection where possible.

Assessment of Risk and Incidents

Risk assessment in network security situation awareness is a level 2 SA, where perceived situations are assessed in order to identify on-going attacks, quantify states and estimate associated risks. Certainly, risk assessment is a very important step of the NSSA. Computer networks are under constant attacks. These attacks result from both attackers with malicious intents, and inadvertently from legitimate users of the system without malicious intents. Cyber-attacks, such as insider attacks, deliberate software attacks, espionage, phishing and denial of service attacks cause harm or predispose assets to harm leading to consequential loss to the organisation (Onwubiko C., 2008). Thus, the risks organisations face are real, evolving, serious and ever-changing, such

that the need to adequately protect their critical and valued assets such as computer networks, computing infrastructures and systems can never be more timely.

Multi-Sensory Data Fusion

Multi-sensory data fusion (MSDF) is a task and system factor requirement, which is provided by the human operator through the use of technology. It is a process carried on multi-source data towards detection, association, correlation, estimation and aggregation (Onwubiko C., 2008). With MSDF data from multiple heterogeneous sources are combined to obtain better and higher degrees accuracy and richer inferences than those obtain from a single source. MSDF encompasses framework, theory, tools and techniques for exploiting the synergy in the data, information or evidence acquired from multiple sources, such as sensors, databases, intelligent sources and humans that helps us better understand a phenomenon and enhance intelligence (Hall D. L., and McMullen S. A. H., 2004).

Multi-source fusion is essential to network security situation awareness, particularly, level 2. It functions on the premise that evidence from multiple sources combined to detect attacks provides better understanding of attacks than a single source. According to Haines J., et al., 2003, "previous results indicate that no single control (for example, IDS) can detect all cyber-attacks. IDS research continues, but researchers have now turned their attention to higher-level correlation systems to gather and combine evidence from many heterogeneous intrusion detection systems and to make use of this broader evidence base for better attack detection".

A significant proposition with situation awareness in computer networks is that it enables security analysts in decision making, and consequently assist them to recommend efficient and adequate countermeasures to address observed situations, and also, to make prediction about future network states. In this respect, the provision of MSDF helps the analyst to identify on-going attacks in the network, comprehend network status and quantify associated risks.

It has been argued that the future of next generation cyberspace intrusion detection systems depends on the fusion of data from myriad heterogeneous distributed network agents to effectively create cyberspace situational awareness (Bass T., 2000). With cyberspace situational awareness network changes, deviation and variations can be easily perceived and analysed. This is beyond the capabilities of current intrusion detection systems. Hence the application of multi-source data fusion is essential to swiftly detecting enterprise-wide situations in computer networks (Onwubiko C., 2008).

Data fusion is a technique to aggregate sets of evidence regarding a perceived situation. The offering is that multi-sensory (multi source) data fusion is better in detecting wide spreading and enterprise-wide situations (network faults, threats and attacks) targeting most networks, and to achieve CND objectives, MSDF becomes pertinent. While MSDF implies the use of multiple sensors to gather and collect piece of evidence about situations perceived in the network, many modern network defence appliance are geared up to 'integrated' suite of products such as the unified threat management solution by Checkpoint, or the integrated security gateway suite by Juniper networks (Juniper Networks, 2011) and Cisco Systems Inc. (Cisco Systems, 2011). These products demonstrate the overwhelming need to design CND products that offer multi-sensory capabilities and support. The trend is also seen with open source products such as Snort IDS that provides the capability to combine several sensors such as Passive Operating System Fingerprint (P0F), Passive Asset Detection System (PADS), and TCP Tracker (TCPTRACK). Designing CND systems and application for SA is a significant contribution, and a factor to consider is ensuring that recent and modern systems and applications

for CND can provide or support multi-sensor operation, integration and analysis.

Visualisation

Patterns of attack or evidence gathered about security attacks need to be visualised to assist security analysts to swiftly spot, detect, decide and respond to attacks. This is also in line with the OODA framework. Security visualisation is the transfer of organised data and information into meaningful patterns or sequence to be visualised. It is part of the comprehension stage of the core situation awareness. Visualisation and user interface need to be selected based on their ability to provide elaborate representation of attacks perceived in the network. Visualisation allows network information to be displayed in such a way that it helps security analysts to detect patterns in traffic, and view large amount of information concisely. Hence, visualisation has proven to be a valuable tool for working more effectively with complex data and maintaining situational awareness in demanding operational domains (D'Amico A. and Kocka M., 2005).

Visualising network activities can be useful to both decision makers and security analysts in identifying patterns of attacks, and in decision making, control selection and cause of action. For example, visual analytics is essential to obtaining enhanced situational awareness in networks (Gregoire M. and Beaudoin L., 2005), understanding host-level netflow traffic in networks (Lakkaraju K., et al., 2004), and monitoring Internet security link-analysis (Yin X., et al., 2008).

There are significant efforts in developing CND visual analytic applications, for example, SIFT (Yurick W., 2005) and SILK (Carnegie Mellon, 2005), that are used to monitor network traffic and system status that assist operators gain better situational awareness of network activities.

Decision Control

Decision making is an operator associated task that involves assessing the situation and then choosing an appropriate cause of action (CoA). According to (US FAA, 1991), decision making is a systematic approach to the mental process used by an operator to consistently determine the best possible course of action in response to a given set of circumstances. Situation assessment involves defining the problem and assessing the levels of risk associated with the situation and the amount of time required to solve the problem and the impact it may have if unresolved.

The fundamental underpinning of cognitive tasks in human factor is concerned with decision making of the various reasoning inputs. This is no different to situation awareness, say in computer network defence, medical operations, ATC, or military defence. All requires a great deal of decision making about a perceived and assessed situation. It requires decision about the level of threat perceived in the network, about the associated risks, it concerns decision about countermeasures required to adequately mitigate the perceived and assessed situation. Particularly in CND, for instance, networks are continuously being monitored and assessed for on-going suspicious traffic, suspicious behaviour or known fingerprints of attacks, and thereafter, decisions are made based on quantifiable risks estimated. Hence, situational awareness is essential for decision makers to efficiently manage their resources, and to greatly improve the rate and quality of human decision making (Gregoire M. and Beaudoin L., 2005).

Forecast

A truly situational awareness toolkit is able to make accurate predictions about future state. The goal of forecasting can be, either to find the likely future state assuming the present progression continues without intervention, or to determine a particular future state based on potential courses of action

(D'Amico A. and Kocka M., 2005). To make accurate future predictions, current states and situations must be accurately assessed, evaluated and responded to. It is difficult to make correct prediction of future states if current situations and states cannot be determined satisfactorily. A forecast is often achieved by comparing baselines, or matching past to current states and situations, provided a reliable model of the system can be obtained. *Projection* provides awareness of how situations may develop over time by predicting or simulating possible scenarios, including the system's own actions and its dynamic effects (Lefebvre J. H., et al. 2005).

Resolution

Resolution of errors in system performance resulting from faults and failures in computer networks and systems infrastructures are important to correct anomalies, repair and restore systems. Errors, faults and failures affect the performance of computing systems and their offered services, such as integrity, confidentiality and availability. And without resolving these abnormalities in systems, their offered services will be rendered unusable, inefficient or unavailable. Resolution encompasses physical and logical restoration of computing infrastructures, network connectivity, and the dissemination of relevant battle-space situation information among cooperating analysts or operators.

Non-Functional Design Requirements for Situational Awareness in CND

Task and system factor in relation to non-functional design requirements to computer network security (CNS) and computer network defence (CND) are discussed. This list is by no means exhaustive, however, the necessary steps toward understanding the essential attribute to designing and implementing SA in computer network security have been strategically presented (see *Figure2*), as follows:

Dynamism

The dynamics of SA was suggested by Endsley M. 1995, but generalised by Garba D. M., and Howard S. K., 1995. They compared SA requirements in aviation to that of anaesthesiology, and found that both fields are similar in characteristics, such as dynamism, complexity, high information load, variable workload and risk (Breton R., and Rousseau R., 2003). This made it possible for SA to be investigated with the same methods in both fields. Interestingly, computer network is analogous to both aviation and anaesthesiology in exhibiting similar characteristics. Computer network is a collection of interdependent systems whose operations are dynamic and often complex. They output huge information (logs), have variable and abrupt workload (traffic) and various associated risks.

1. **Dynamic:** the operation of network objects and computing devices is fast-changing, continuous and dynamic. For instance, network traffic being monitored is abrupt in nature and changes over time due to on-going activities in the network; traffic re-route is dynamic too.
2. **Volumetric information load:** logs and alerts produced by network objects, such as IDS, firewalls, routers, switches and servers are huge, diverse and significant. Often times, these logs are archived and may be required to be kept for several months as stipulated by the prevalent data retention, security compliance standards, archival and retrieval laws. In essence, computer networks are characteristically of high information load, significant logs and carry huge volumes of traffic.
3. **Abrupt in nature and variable workload:** network traffic is abrupt and varied in nature, often within expected baselines and acceptable service level agreements (SLAs).

4. **Risk:** vulnerabilities exist in most computing systems, either in the form of flaws in software or the absence of protection controls, such that threats exploit these vulnerabilities to consequently attack computer systems and networks. Risk may result from faults, failures and errors in computing operations. E.g., errors due to human input, deliberate omission, faults that occur during operations or failures that happen when an adversary perpetuates computing systems.

Dynamic and complex environments were the interest of early work carried out in the field of situation awareness; primarily because, these fields were very susceptible to risks, human errors, faults and failures in systems. As such situation awareness is not applicable or of interest in static, or tightly controlled environments as shown by Anderson H. H. K., and Hauland G., 2000.

It has been suggested that some fields are not SA compliant, for example, results from the nuclear power plant process control was less fruitful. It is believed that operations of nuclear power plant processes were perfectly executed, hence offered no opportunity to make mistakes, and then few opportunities to observe fluctuations in SA (Breton R., and Rousseau R., 2003).

Complexity

By their very nature, some environments are complex. This is particularly true with computer network defence. Computer networks are characteristically complex, some spanning across many distributed wide area networks (WANs) and geography, whilst using technologies to implement complex business logics and engaging in electronic transactions. At a high-level, computer networks will comprise a number of network objects, element managers, and localised and transient computing devices. For example, a computer network may comprise intrusion detection systems, firewalls, anti-malware (anti-virus, anti-SPAM and anti-phising systems), identity management systems, servers, workstations, PCs, switches, routers, PDAs etc. Networks are usually interconnected, with several interconnectivity points; for instance, interconnection with an ISP, partner organisation, vendors and users (telecommuters, and teleworkers). To effectively manage these assets and in addition to managing interdependent risks resulting from in network connectivity (physical, logical, spatial) in time and space is complex and challenging. Hence, it is challenging for administrators to maintain situational awareness over thousands of network objects and events (Gregoire M. and Beaudoin L., 2005).

Heterogeneity

Heterogeneity is the ability of the security analyst to use different heterogeneous sources to observe, gather and detect dynamic changes in the network. E.g., the use of IDS, firewalls, anti-virus systems and security guards to collate security information observed in the network. The idea of using heterogeneous controls assists to create a true situational awareness, since no single control is able to identify all security threats, therefore, it is recommended to use heterogeneous controls in order to detect a wide-range of threats and attacks perceived in the network, which is not possible from a single control perspective. Heterogeneity as a situation awareness attribute was suggested by Lefebvre J. H., et al., 2005; Liu X. 2007; and Gregoire M. and Beaudoin L., 2005 using heterogeneous controls in C2.

Scalability

Scalability is a system requirement, which is used to determine the performance of that system under varying loads, and to deduce how that system would react (handle, perform or degrade) under growing load in future. Scalability denotes the ability to accommodate a growing load in the future (Emmerich W., 2000). This means when designing CND applications, systems and software, including networking infrastructure should be tested to ensure they can cope with the ever-increasing CND demand.

The emphases for systems designers is to ensure that CND systems and architectures are scalable, and support the organisation's mission, and do not contribute to degradation, error or loss of situational awareness. The primary basis for computer network defence is to provide secure, reliable and operational platform for an organisation (Onwubiko C., 2009), by focusing on managing the vulnerabilities and risks inherent in all computer networks (Lefebvre J. H., et al., 2005). Hence, if the sole purpose of the CND is defeated due to performance bottleneck of its own system's or architecture, then it is highly unlikely that operators' situational awareness is enough to support mission critical objectives.

By default, systems and network devices produce high volumes of logs, running significant processes, and analyse huge amount of traffic, handle a significant number of concurrent users, and processing distributed transactions and services, making a computer network defence environment demanding and challenging. Therefore, it is characteristically important that CND systems and infrastructure designs are scalable and distributed to support the dynamic and demanding operational activities of the environment.

Openness

Openness is a non-functional property of a network, system or software when it complies with well-defined and documented standards (a.k.a. open standards). Open systems are systems that can be easily extended and modified either as a whole or component-wise. A key benefit of an open system is that it is built from components that can be readily removed and replaced with multiple-sourced alternatives and so many suppliers can compete for that business (Henderson, P., 2007).

Openness is demanded because the overall architecture needs to be stable even in the presence of changing functional requirements (Emmerich W., 2000). The integration of new components to this system means that they have to be able to communicate with some of the components that already exist in the system. This is the whole essences of having components with well-defined interfaces.

The relationship of openness to CND systems is that CND systems need to be designed with open standards, such as GIS systems, protective monitoring systems, and modern CPS systems such that when a component becomes unavailable, its change or replacement does not put the entire CND environment into unprecedented difficulty, and consequently hinder the operators the capability to respond to ongoing situations in the network.

Resource Sharing

Resource sharing is a typical non-functional requirement of distributed systems such as a computer network defence environment, where multiple users concurrently share the same CND data, hardware or software components. While resource sharing in CND is an essential design requirement, however, access control of shared resource is a concern. Access to shared resource must be controlled, restricted and assessed. The sensitive and criticality of CND operations and dynamic nature of this environment make access control not only for share resources, but also of the entire platform a necessary and essential control requirement.

Fault Tolerance

Network infrastructure, systems and software occasional fail. Some fail because of software error, programming issues, failures in the underlying infrastructure (for example, power failure or air conditioning), abuse by their users, attacks from an

adversary, or just because of ageing hardware. For example, the lifetime of a hard disk lies between two and five years, much less the average lifetime of a distributed system (Emmerich W., 2000).

An essential non-functional requirement that is often demanded from a system is fault-tolerance. That is the ability of a system to continue to operate, even in the presence of faults. This in our opinion is a must-have requirement for computer network defence systems given the important roles they perform, and the business-critical tasks required by missions, institutions and organisations.

Modern computer network defence systems that are designed for situational awareness must not just be fault tolerant; they should also be fail-secure. Fail-secure is a non-functional requirement of a system to close all its channels when it fails. A fail-secure system is one that, in the event of failure, responds in a way that will cause no harm, or at least a minimum of harm, to other devices or dangers to personnel. For example, a fail-secure firewall system is a firewall system that when it fails, does not allow all traffic destined to the network through; rather it denies all traffic. There are variants of fail-secure systems such as fail-close, fail-open, and fail-safe. CND systems should be designed to be both fault-tolerant and fail-secure.

CONCLUSION

Situational awareness as a human factor attribute can be enhanced through a number of ways, such as individual factors (operator abilities, training and experience), workload, stress, goals; and task and system factors, such as the use of technology (interface design, integration, analysis and processing to enrich SA, as shown in Figure 1.

In this chapter, we have investigated task and system design requirements that enables enhance situational awareness in CND. These requirements are decomposed into functional and non-functional design requirements, each area covering both task and system-specific attributes. The contribution of this chapter will underpin the design construct of new and modern computer network defence systems that are able to extend the boundary that already exist, and become foundation for a roadmap that could eventually lead to advances in the CND situational awareness.

There are a good number of contributions in the literature focusing on technical and analytical contributions to computer network defence and situational awareness. Unfortunately, not very many contributions are published that discusses qualitative requirements, especially, system and task related factors pertinent to CND specifically. Existing contributions are in mainstream SA areas such as air traffic control, aviation and warfare. Our contribution is a comprehensive assessment of pertinent factors to be considered when designing modern computer and network systems for situational awareness in a CND environment. We covered a good breadth of both non-functional, and functional system requirements, and also, task-oriented requirements which are partly associated to both human and system.

Our future goal is to investigate human specific design requirements for enhance situational awareness in CND, which should complements this contribution.

REFERENCES

Anderson, H. H. K., & Hauland, G. (2000). Measuring team situation awareness of reactor operators during normal operation: A technical pilot study. *Proceedings of the First Human Performance, Situation Awareness, and Automation Conference*, Savannah, 2000.

Bass, T. (2000). Intrusion detection systems and multisensor data fusion. *Communications of the ACM, 43*(4). doi:10.1145/332051.332079

Borja, A. T. (2003). *Integrating usability engineering in the iterative design process of the land attack combat system (LACS) human computer interface*. San Diego, CA: Space & Naval Warfare Systems Center.

Boyd, J. (Col.). (1987). *Organic design for command and control*. Presentation Slides, May 1987. Retrieved from www.ausairpower.net/JRB/organic_design.ppt

Breton, R., & Rousseau, R. (2003). *Situation awareness: A review of the concept and its measurement*. DREV, TR-2001-220, Defence Research Establishment, 2003.

Carnegie Mellon. (2005). *SILK: System for Internet level knowledge (SILK)*. Carnegie Mellon SEI, CERT NetSA Security Suite, 2005. Retrieved March 29, 2011, from http://tools.netsa.cert.org/silk/

Cisco Systems Inc. (2011). Cisco ASA 5500 series adaptive security appliances. Retrieved from http://www.cisco.com/ en/US/prod/ collateral/ vpndevc/ ps6032/ ps6094/ ps6120/prod _brochure0900aecd80285492.pdf

D'Amico, A., & Kocka, M. (2005). *Information assurance visualisation for specific stages of situational awareness and intended uses: Lessons learned*. Workshop on Visualisation for Computer Security, USA, 2005.

Emmerich, W. (2000). *Engineering distributed objects*. London, UK: John Wiley & Sons, Ltd.

Endsley, M. R. (1995). Toward a theory of situation awareness in dynamic systems. *Human Factors Journal, 37*(1), 32–64. doi:10.1518/001872095779049543

Endsley, M. R. (1996). Automation and situation awareness. *Automation and Human Performance: Theory and Applications*, (pp. 163-181).

Endsley, M. R. (2000). Errors in situation assessment: Implications for system design. In Elzer, P. F., Kluwe, R. H., & Boussoffara, B. (Eds.), *Human Error and System Design and Management, Lecture Notes in Control and Information Sciences* (*Vol. 253*, pp. 15–26). London, UK: Springer-Verlag. doi:10.1007/BFb0110451

Endsley, M. R., & Garland, D. J. (Eds.). (2000). *Situation awareness analysis and measurement.* Mahwah, NJ: Lawrence Erlbaum Associates.

ESRI. (2008). *Public safety and homeland security situational awareness.* An ESRI White Paper, February 2008. Retrieved from www.esri.com

Garba, D. M., & Howard, S. K. (1995). Situation awareness in anaesthesiology. *Human Factors*, *37*(1), 20–31. doi:10.1518/001872095779049435

Gregoire, M., & Beaudoin, L. (2005). Visualisation for network situational awareness in computer network defence. *Proceedings of the Visualisation and the Common Operational Picture*, (pp. 20-1-20-6).

Haines, J., Ryder, D., Tinnel, L., & Taylor, S. (2003). Validation of sensor alert correlators. *IEEE Security & Privacy*, *1*(1), 46–56. doi:10.1109/MSECP.2003.1176995

Hall, D. L., & McMullen, S. A. H. (2004). *Mathematical techniques in multisensor data fusion* (2nd ed.).

Henderson, P. (2007). *On open systems and openness.* University of Southampton, October 30th 2007. Retrieved April 26, 2011, from http://pmhsystems.co.uk/OpenSystems/OpenSystems.pdf

Juniper Networks. (2011). *IGS series integrated security gateway.* Retrieved April 25, 2011, from http://www.juniper.net/us/en/local/pdf/datasheets/1100036-en.pdf#xml=http://kb.juniper.net/index?page=answeropen&type=open&searchid=1255112038522&answerid=16777216&iqaction=6&url=http%3A%2F%2Fwww.juniper.net%2Fus%2Fen%2Flocal%2Fpdf%2Fdatasheets%2F1100036-en.pdf& highlight-info=18875208,1477,1492

Lakkaraju, K., Yurick, W., & Lee, A. J. (2004). *NVisionIP: NetFlow visualizations of system state for security situational awareness.* NVisionIP, VizSEC/DMSEC'04, October 29, 2004, Washington, DC, USA.

Lambert, D. A., Bosse, E., Breton, R., Rousseau, R., Howes, J. R., Hinman, M. L., … White, F. (2004). *Information fusion definitions, concept and models for coalition situation awareness.* (TTCP C31 Group, TR-C31-AG2-1-2004).

Lee, E. A. (2006). *Cyber-physical systems – Are computing foundations adequate?* Department of EECS, UC Berkeley, NSF Workshop on Cyber-Physical Systems: Research Motivation, Techniques and Roadmap, October 16-17, 2006.

Lefebvre, J. H., Gregoire, M., Beaudoin, L., & Froh, M. (2005). *Computer network defence situational awareness information requirements.* Ottawa: Defence R&D Canada.

McGuinness, B., & Foy, L. (2000). A subjective measure of SA: The crew awareness rating scale (CARS). *Proceedings of the First Human Performance, Situation Awareness, and Automation Conference*, Savannah, Georgia, 2000.

Mulgund, S., Rinkus, G., Illgen, C., & Zacharias, G. (1997). *Situation awareness modelling and pilot state estimation for tactical cockpit interfaces.* Presented at HCI International, San Francisco, CA, August 1997.

Onwubiko, C. (2008). Data fusion in security evidence analysis. *Proceeding of the 3rd International Conference on Computer Security and Forensics, 2008.*

Onwubiko, C. (2008). *Security framework for attack detection in computer networks.* VDM Verlag Publisher.

Onwubiko, C. (2009). Functional requirements of situational awareness in computer network security. *Proceeding of the IEEE International Conference on Intelligence and Security Informatics, IEEE ISI 2009,* 8-11, June 2009, Dallas, Texas, USA.

Onwubiko, C. (2011). Modeling situation awareness information and system requirements for the mission using goal-oriented task analysis approach. In Onwubiko, C., & Owens, T. J. (Eds.), *Situational awareness in computer network defense: Principles, methods and applications.*

Salerno, J., Hinman, M., & Boulware, D. (2004). *Building a framework for situation awareness. AFRL/IFEA.* Rome, NY: AF Research Lab.

Sandom, C. (1999). Situational awareness through the interface: Evaluating safety in safety-critical control systems. *IEE Proceedings of People in Control – An International Conference on Human Interfaces in Control Rooms, Cockpits and Command Centres, University of Bath,* UK, 21-23 June 1999.

US FAA. (1991). Aeronautical decision making. U.*S. Federal Aviation Administration (FAA) Advisory Circular (AC),* 60-122.

Wickens, C. D. (1992). *Engineering psychology and human performance* (2nd ed.). New York, NY: Harper Collins.

Yin, X., Yurick, W., & Slagell, A. (2008). *VisFlowConnect-IP: An animated link analysis tool for visualising netflows.* SIFT Research Group, National Centre for Supercomputing Applications, University of Illinois at Urbana-Champaign, 2008.

Yurick, W. (2005). Visualising netflow for security at line speed: The SIFT tool suit. *Proceedings of the 19th Usenix Large Installation System Administration Conference (LISA),* (pp. 169-176).

ADDITIONAL READING

Bares, D. (2010). A Tactical Framework for Cyberspace Situational Awareness (Paper #196). Topic 8: C2 Assessment Metrics and Tools, Air Force Institute of Technology, AFIT/ENG, 2010.

Gruber, D. J. (2000). Computer Networks and Information Warfare – Implication for Military Operations. Occasional Paper No. 17 Center for Strategy and Technology Air War College, Air University Maxwell Air Force Base, 2000.

Juarez-Espinosa, O., & Gonzalez, C. (2004). Situation Awareness of Commanders: A Cognitive Model. Department of Social and Decision Sciences. *Paper, 85,* 2004.

Onwubiko, C. (2008). *Security Framework for Attack Detection in Computer Networks.* Germany: VDM Publishing.

Onwubiko, C. (2011). (in press). Modelling Situation Awareness Information and System Requirements for the Mission using Goal-Oriented Task Analysis Approach. Chapter Contribution in Situational Awareness in Computer Network Defence: Principles, Methods and Applications. *IGI Press.*

KEY TERMS AND DEFINITIONS

Computer Network Defence: CND is the process of protecting computer systems and networks. This includes actions taken via computer networks to protect, monitor, analyse, detect and respond to cyber-attacks, intrusions, disruptions or other perceived unauthorised actions that could compromise or impact defence information systems and networks. CND is achieved through a collective effort by personnel who monitor, manage and maintain defence systems, networks and infrastructures, such as network operators, security analysts, systems administrators and IT support.

Functional Requirements: These are requirements and functions that the system performs for its users such as processing, display, tasks and analysis.

Non-Functional Requirements: Non-functional requirements are concerned with the quality of the system. They are, rather, global system qualities; hence non-functional requirements typically have serious impact on the overall architecture of the chosen system.

Situation Awareness: SA is the process of perceiving the elements in the environment, understanding the elements in the environment, and the projection of their status into the near future (Endsley M. R., 1996).

Section 2
Methods in SA CND

Chapter 8
Cyber Situation Awareness through Instance– Based Learning:
Modeling the Security Analyst in a Cyber–Attack Scenario

Varun Dutt
Carnegie Mellon University, USA

Cleotilde Gonzalez
Carnegie Mellon University, USA

ABSTRACT

In a corporate network, the situation awareness (SA) of a security analyst is of particular interest. The current work describes a cognitive Instance-Based Learning (IBL) model of an analyst's recognition and comprehension processes in a cyber-attack scenario. The IBL model first recognizes network events based upon events' situation attributes and their similarity to past experiences (instances) stored in the model's memory. Then, the model comprehends a sequence of observed events as being a cyber-attack or not, based upon instances retrieved from its memory, similarity mechanism used, and the model's risk-tolerance. The execution of the model generates predictions about the recognition and comprehension processes of an analyst in a cyber-attack. A security analyst's decisions in the model are evaluated based upon two cyber-SA metrics of accuracy and timeliness. The chapter highlights the potential of this research for design of training and decision support tools for security analysts.

INTRODUCTION

With the prevalence of WikiLeaks hacks and other threats to corporate and national cybersecurity, guarding against cyber-attacks today is becoming a significant part of IT governance, especially because most government agencies have moved to online systems (Sideman, 2011). In order to protect national cybersecurity, leaders from the Defense Department, NATO, and the European Union assembled in Brussels recently to discuss a plan to prevent, detect, defend, and recover

DOI: 10.4018/978-1-4666-0104-8.ch008

from cyber-attacks (Sideman, 2011). The leaders there agreed that existing cybersecurity measures were incomplete and decided to fast-track a new plan for cyber-incident response. Similarly, the Department of Homeland Security (DHS) has recently launched a national campaign called, "Stop|Think|Connect," aiming to cultivate a collective sense of cyber–civic duty among personnel in organizations and enterprises that help preserve cybersecurity (Lute & McConnell, 2011). The DHS' message begins with the following wisdom:

Senior management in each and every office, company and department, whether private or public, must take responsibility for the protection of its own systems and information, by fielding up-to-date security technology, training employees to avoid common vulnerabilities, and reporting cybercrime when it occurs. (Lute & McConnell, 2011, p. 1)

As 80%-90% of what individuals and the government do using the Internet today depend upon private corporate networks provided by organizations and enterprises (Sideman, 2011), according to DHS, corporate networks that ensure our cybersecurity have much bigger responsibilities than previously thought (Lute & McConnell, 2011). Thus, meeting the DHS' objectives in a corporate network requires cyber situation-awareness (SA), a three stage process which includes recognition (or the awareness of the current situation in the network); comprehension (or the awareness of malicious behavior in the current situation in the network); and projection (assessment of possible future courses of action resulting from the current situation in the network) (Endsley, 1995; Tadda, Salerno, Boulware, Hinman, & Gorton, 2006).

The ability of a corporate network to protect itself from a cyber-attack using cyber-tools and algorithms without any interventions from human decision-makers is still a distant goal (Jajodia, Liu, Swarup, & Wang, 2010). Thus, the role of human decision-makers in security systems is one that is crucial and indispensible (Gardner, 1987; Johnson-Laird, 2006).

In the absence of perfect cyber-SA tools to recognize, comprehend, and project about cyber-attacks (PSU, 2011), a key role in the cybersecurity process is that of a security analyst. The security analyst is a human decision-maker who is in charge of protecting the online operations of a corporate network (e.g., an online retail company with an external webserver and an internal fileserver) from threats of random or organized cyber-attacks. However, very little is currently known about the role of the cognitive processes of the security analyst (like memory, risk-tolerance, similarity etc.) that might influence the cyber-SA of the analyst and his ability to detect cyber-attacks in corporate networks under different scenarios (Jajodia et al., 2010; PSU, 2011). Also, currently there seems to be a big gap between how security analysts function in the real world according to their cognitive processes and how cyber-SA tools and algorithms function that intend to replace human analysts, sometime in the future (Jajodia et al., 2010; PSU, 2011). Due to these reasons, it becomes important to investigate the influence of cognitive processes of a security analyst on his cyber-SA in popular cyber-attack scenarios.

Past literature shows there has only been one known cognitive attempt, through an expert system called R-CAST, to understand the cognitive decision-making aspects about a security analyst's cyber-SA (Fan & Yen, 2007; Jajodia et al., 2010). The R-CAST is a team-oriented cognitive-agent architecture that is a computational implementation of Klien's Recognition-Primed Decision (RPD) model (Klien, 1989). R-CAST, being a computational implementation of RPD, is a rule-based system which requires *a priori* knowledge base about cyber-attacks in a scenario in which it makes decisions (Fan & Yen, 2007). The *a priori* knowledge base is used during a mental simulation in the RPD. In the mental simulation, the R-CAST applies rules that are constrained by the cyber-attack scenario in which the R-CAST operates to determine the future courses of action (Fan & Yen, 2007). The cognitive approach taken in this chapter (more details below) does not incorporate dependencies about an existing knowledge-base and future courses of action as assumed in the R-CAST.

The main purpose of this chapter is to describe a cognitive model of the recognition and comprehension processes in a security analyst's cyber-SA. The model is based on Instance-Based Learning Theory (IBLT; Gonzalez, Lerch, & Lebiere, 2003). Furthermore, we evaluate the performance of the IBL model of the security analyst using two cyber-SA measures: accuracy and timeliness (Jajodia et al., 2010) on a popular simple cyber-attack scenario about an island-hopping attack (Ou, Boyer, & McQueen, 2006; Xie, Li, Ou, Liu, & Levy, 2010). IBLT is well suited to modeling the security analyst's decisions as the theory provides a generic decision-making process that starts by recognizing and generating experiences through interaction with a changing decision environment, and closes with the reinforcement of experiences that led to good decision outcomes through feedback from the decision environment. Unlike the R-CAST, the IBLT neither assumes a rule-based cognitive process nor needs an existing knowledge-base to choose future courses of action and make decisions; rather, experiences in IBLT are generated overtime as a result of interaction of an IBL model with its decision environment (e.g., a cyber-attack scenario).

In the next section, we describe a popular cyber-attack scenario of an island-hopping attack in a corporate network. Then, we describe a model based upon IBLT that is used to make predictions about the cyber-SA of a security analyst in the scenario. Finally, we discuss the predictions from the IBL model and explain the implication of the model's predictions when designing training and decision support tools for security analysts.

A SIMPLE SCENARIO OF A CYBER ATTACK

The cyber-infrastructure in a corporate network typically consists of a webserver and a fileserver (Ou et al., 2006; Xie et al., 2010) that are protected by two firewalls in the Demilitarized zone (or DMZ) (where the DMZ separates the external network ("Internet") from the company's internal LAN network). The webserver handles customer interactions on a company's webpage. The fileserver is a repository for many workstations that are internal to the company and that allow company employees to do their daily operations. These operations are made possible by enabling workstations to mount executable binaries from the fileserver. An external firewall ('firewall 1' in Figure 1) controls the traffic between the Internet and the DMZ. The firewall 1's rules are configured to allow a bidirectional flow of the incoming "request" traffic and the outgoing "response" traffic between the Internet and company's webserver. Generally, an attacker is identified as a computer on the Internet and thus firewall 1 protects the path between the attacker's computer on the Internet and the company's website hosted by the webserver. Another firewall ('firewall 2' in Figure 1) controls the flow of traffic between the webserver and the fileserver (i.e., company's internal LAN network). Firewall 2 allows a Network File System (NFS) protocol access between the fileserver and webserver. For this cyber-infrastructure, most attackers follow a sequence of an "island-hopping" attack (Jajodia et al., 2010; pp. 30), where the webserver is compromised first, and then the webserver is used to originate attacks on the fileserver (through venerability in the NFS protocol) and other company workstations (by mounting executable binaries from the fileserver).

The security analyst is in charge of overseeing the cyber-infrastructure of the company (consisting on the two firewalls, DMZ, webserver, fileserver, and workstations) from cyber-attacks

Figure 1. A simple scenario of a cyber-attack. The attacker using a computer on the Internet tries to gain access of a company's fileserver indirectly through the company's webserver. Source: Xie et al. (2010).

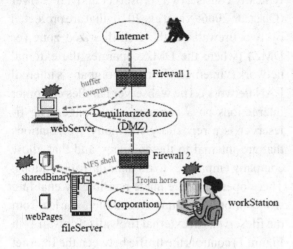

originating from computers on the Internet. Ou et al. (2006) and Xie et al. (2010) defined a simple scenario of an island-hopping cyber-attack within this cyber-infrastructure. In the simple scenario, a security analyst is exposed to a sequence of 25 network events (consisting of both threat and non-threat events), whose nature (threat or non-threat) is not precisely known to a security analyst. Out of the total of 25 events, there are 8 predefined threat events in the sequence that are initiated by an attacker. The attacker, through some of these 8 events, first compromises the webserver by remotely exploiting vulnerability on the webserver and getting local access to the webserver. If the cyber-attack remains undetected by the 8th event, then the attacker gains full access to the webserver. Since typically in a corporate network and in the simple scenario, a webserver is allowed to access the fileserver through only a NFS event, the attacker then modifies data on the fileserver through the vulnerability in the NFS event. If the cyber-attack remains undetected by the security analyst by the 11th event, then the attacker gains full access of the

fileserver. Once the attacker gets access to modify files on the fileserver, he then installs a Trojan-horse program (i.e., a malicious code) in the executable binaries on fileserver that is then downloaded and used by different workstations (event 19th out of 25). The attacker can now wait for an innocent user on workstation to execute the Trojan-horse program and obtain control on the machine (event 21st out of 25).

During the course of this simple scenario, a security analyst is able to observe all 25 events corresponding to file executions and the packets of information transmitted on and between the webserver, fileserver, and different workstations. He is also able to observe alerts that correspond to some network events using an intrusion-detection system (IDS) (Jajodia et al., 2010). The IDS raises an alert for suspicious file executions or suspicious packet transmission events that is generated on the corporate network. Among the alerts generated by the IDS here, there is both a false-positive and a false-negative alert, and one alert that correspond to the 8th event but is received by the analyst after the 13th event in the sequence (i.e., a time-delayed alert). Most importantly, due to the absence of a precise alert corresponding to a potential threat event, the analyst does not have precise information on whether a network event and its corresponding alert (from the IDS) are initiated by an attacker or by an innocent company employee. Even through the analyst lacks this precise information, he needs to decide, as early as possible and most accurately, whether the sequence of events in the simple scenario constitutes a cyber-attack. The earliest possible or proportion of timeliness is determined by subtracting the percentage of events seen by the analyst before he makes a decision to the total number of events (25) in the scenario from 100%. The accuracy of the analyst is determined by whether the analyst's decision was to ignore the sequence of events, or declare a cyber-attack based upon the sequence of observed network events.

BACKGROUND

We believe that a security analyst's accurate and timely classification of a sequence of network events as a cyber-attack or not (or analyst's cyber-SA) is based upon the following three factors:

1. The knowledge level of the analyst in terms of the mix of threat and non-threat experiences stored in analyst's memory.
2. The analyst's risk-tolerance level, i.e., the willingness of an analyst to classify a sequence of events as a cyber-attack.
3. The analyst's similarity model, i.e., the process that the analyst uses to compare network events with prior experiences that are stored in his memory.

Prior literature has shown that the cyber-SA of a security analyst is a function of *a priori* experiences in an analyst's memory about a cyber-attack scenario (Jajodia et al., 2010) and the analyst's risk-tolerance (McCumber, 2004; Salter, Saydjari, Schneier, & Wallner, 1998). Similarly, Dutt, Ahn, & Gonzalez, (2011) and Dutt & Gonzalez, (2011) have provided *a priori* predictions about the cyber-SA of a simulated analyst in an IBL model and demonstrated that these predictions are influenced by the experiences in memory of a simulated analyst and the risk-tolerance of the simulated analyst.

Recent research in judgment and decision making (JDM) has also discussed how our experiences of events in the environment shape our decision choices (Hertwig, Barron, Weber, & Erev, 2004; Lejarraga, Dutt, & Gonzalez, 2011). Typically, having a greater number of bad experiences in memory about an activity (e.g., a cyber-attack) makes a decision-maker (e.g., analyst) avoid the activity; whereas, good experiences with an activity boost the likelihood a decision-maker will underestimate the same activity (Hertwig et al., 2004; Lejarraga et al., in press).

Similarly, past research has found the role of similarity to be critical in problem solving, judgment, decision making, categorization, and cognition (Goldstone, Day, & Son, 2010; Vosniadou & Ortony, 1989). Essentially, two potential and competing models of human similarity judgments have been proposed. These models include the geometric model (Shepard, 1962a, 1962b) and the feature-based model (Tversky, 1977). In the geometric model, similarity between a pair of objects (e.g., a situation event in decision environment and an experience in memory) is taken to be inversely related to the distance between two objects' points in the space. The distance could be either a linear difference (linear-geometric) or a squared difference (squared-geometric) between two objects' points in the space (Shepard, 1962a, 1962b). In contrast, the feature-based similarity model characterizes similarity in terms of a feature-matching process based on weighting common and distinctive features between a pair of objects (Tversky, 1977).

Although there is literature that discusses the role of prior experiences of threats in general and the relevance of risk-tolerance in network security (Jajodia et al., 2010; McCumber, 2004; Salter, et al., 1998), it is difficult to find research that empirically investigates the role of both these factors together on a security analyst's cyber-SA. Similarly, although there is research that applies both models of similarity to human judgments in general (Goldstone, Day, & Son, 2010), research is needed that evaluates the effects of similarity models on the cyber-SA of a security analyst in cyber-attack scenarios.

The above three factors, as well as many other cognitive factors that may limit on enhance the cyber-SA of an analyst, can be studied through computational cognitive modeling. In this chapter, we use IBLT to develop a model of the security analyst, and we assess the effects of the three factors (analyst's knowledge level, risk-tolerance, and similarity model) on the accuracy and timeliness of the analyst to detect a cyber-attack in the simple scenario.

INSTANCE-BASED LEARNING THEORY AND IBL MODEL OF THE SECURITY ANALYST

IBLT is a theory of how people make decisions from experience in dynamic environments (Gonzalez et al., 2003). In the past, computational models based on IBLT have proven to be able to generate *a priori* predictions of human behavior in many dynamic decision making situations like and including those faced by the security analyst (Dutt, Ahn, & Gonzalez, 2011; Dutt, Cassenti, & Gonzalez, 2010; Dutt & Gonzalez, 2011; Gonzalez & Dutt, 2010).

IBLT proposes that people represent every decision making situation as *instances* that are stored in memory. For each decision-making situation, an instance is retrieved from memory and reused depending on the similarity of the current situation's attributes to the attributes of instances stored in memory. An instance in IBLT is composed of three parts: situation (S) (the knowledge of situation attributes in a situation event), decision (D) (the course of action to take for a situation event), and utility (U) (i.e., a measure of the goodness of a decision made for a situation event).

In the case of the decision situations faced by the security analyst, these attributes are those that characterize potential threat events in a corporate network and that needs to be investigated continuously by the analyst. The situation attributes that characterize potential threat events in the simple scenario are the *IP* address of the location (webserver, fileserver, or workstation) where the event took place, the *directory* location in which the event took place, whether the IDS raised an *alert* corresponding to the event, and whether the *operation* carried out as part of the event (e.g., a file execution) by a user of the network succeeded or failed. However, as there are inherent uncertain-

ties present in any scenario, one could think of other attributes that might characterize the simple scenario. Thus, we admit that the list of these four attributes might not be exhaustive and open to inclusion of other attributes or a different set of attributes. However, for the purpose of analysis in this chapter, we assume the above described four attributes to characterize the simple scenario.

In the IBL model of the security analyst, an instance's S slots refers to the situation attributes defined above; the D slot refers to the decision, i.e., whether to classify a sequence of events as constituting a cyber-attack or not; and, the U slot refers to the accuracy of the classification of an situation as a threat. IBLT proposes five mental phases in a closed-loop decision making process: recognition, judgment, choice, execution, and feedback (Figure 2). The five decision phases represent a complete learning cycle where the theory explains how knowledge is acquired, reused, and learnt by human decision-makers. Because the focus of this study is on the recognition and comprehension process in the SA of a security analyst, we will only focus on and discuss the recognition, judgment, choice, and execution phases in the IBLT (for details on the feedback phase refer to Gonzalez and Dutt (2010); and Gonzalez, Lerch, and Lebiere (2003)). In addition to the IBLT's decision-making process, IBLT borrowed some of the proposed statistical-learning mechanisms from a popular cognitive architecture called ACT-R (Anderson & Lebiere, 1998, 2003). Thus, most of the previous cognitive models that have used IBLT were developed for the ACT-R architecture.

The IBLT's process starts in the recognition phase in search for alternatives and classifies the current situation as *typical* or *atypical*. The current situation is typical if there are memories of similar situations (i.e., instances of previous trials that are similar enough to the current situation). If the situation is typical, then the most similar instance is retrieved from memory in the judgment phase and is used to determine the expected utility of the situation being evaluated. In the IBL model,

Figure 2. The five phases of IBL theory (right) and an environment, i.e., a decision task with which a model developed according to the IBLT interacts (left).

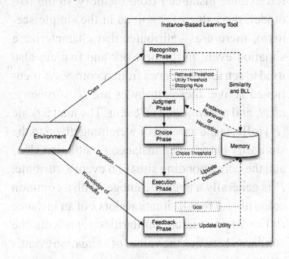

the decision alternatives refer to whether a sequence of events constitutes a cyber-attack or not. The actual determination of the utility is based upon the value in the utility slot of an instance retrieved from memory. The decision to retrieve an instance from memory for a situation event is based upon a comparison of the instance's memory strength, called *activation*. Thus, an instance is retrieved from memory if the instance has the highest activation among all instances in memory.

If the situation event in the network is atypical, then a judgment heuristic rule is applied to determine the utility of a new instance corresponding to a decision alternative. In the IBL model, we prepopulate the memory of a simulated analyst with certain instances to start with. These are assumed to be pre-stored experiences of past situations in the analyst's memory, and thus all situation events are treated by the model as typical.

Next, in the choice phase, a decision alternative is selected based upon the utility determined in the judgment phase (above). Thus, the choice phase in the IBL model consists of whether to classify a set of network events seen up to the scenario's

current event as constituting a cyber-attack, or whether to accumulate more evidence by further observing incoming situation events before such a classification could be made. According to IBLT, this decision is determined in the "necessity level," which represents a satisficing mechanism to stop search of the environment and be "satisfied" with the current evidence (e.g., the *satisficing strategy*, Simon & March, 1958). We will call this parameter in the model, the "risk-tolerance level" (a free parameter) to represent the number of events the model has to classify as threats before the model classifies the scenario as a cyber-attack. For the risk-tolerance level, each time the model classifies a situation event in the network as a threat (based upon retrieval of an instance from memory), a counter increments and signifies an accumulation of evidence in favor of a cyber-attack. If the value of the accumulated evidence (represented by the counter) becomes equal to the analyst's risk-tolerance level, the analyst will classify the scenario as a cyber-attack based upon the sequence of already observed network events; otherwise, the model will decide to continue obtaining more information from the environment and observe the next situation event in the network. We manipulate the risk-tolerance parameter in this study at different number of events: 2, 4, or 6 (more details ahead). Regardless, the main outcome of the choice phase in the model is whether to classify a set of network events as a cyber-attack or not.

The model's choice phase is also based upon a property of the analyst to exhibit "inertia," i.e., simply not to decide to classify a sequence of observed network events as a cyber-attack due to lack of attention and continue to wait for the next situation event. The inertia in the model is governed by a free parameter called *probability of inertia* (Pinertia) (Gonzalez & Dutt, 2010; Gonzalez, Dutt, & Lejarraja, 2011). If the value of a random number derived from a uniform distribution between [0, 1] is less than Pinertia, the model will choose to observe another network event in the scenario and will not classify the sequence of already observed events as a cyber-attack; otherwise, the model will make a decision to classify the observed events based upon the set risk-tolerance level. We assumed a default value of Pinertia at 0.3 (or 30%).

The choice phase is followed by the execution of the best decision alternative. The execution phase for the IBL model means either to classify a sequence of observed events as a cyber-attack and stop online operations in the company, or *not* to classify the sequence of events as a cyber-attack and to let the online operations of the company continue undisrupted.

In IBLT, the activation of an instance i in memory is defined using the ACT-R architecture's activation equation:

$$A_i = B_i + \sum_{l=1}^{k} P_l \times M_{li} + \varepsilon_i \qquad (1)$$

where, i refers to the ith instance that is pre-populated in memory where i = 1,2, ..., Total number of pre-populated instances; and, B_i is the base-level learning parameter and reflects the recency and frequency of the use of the ith instance since the time it was created, which is given by:

$$B_i = \ln \left(\sum_{t_i \in \{1,...,t-1\}} \left(t - t_i \right)^{-d} \right) \qquad (2)$$

The frequency effect is provided by $t-1$, the number of retrievals of the ith instance from memory in the past. The recency effect is provided by $t-t_i$, the event since the tth past retrieval of the ith instance (in Equation 2, t denotes the current event number in the scenario). The d is the decay parameter and has a default value of 0.5 in the ACT-R architecture, and it is the value we assume for the IBL model of the security analyst.

The $\sum_{l=1}^{k} P_l \times M_{li}$ term is the similarity component and represents the mismatch between a situ-

ation event's attributes and the situation (S) slots of an instance i in memory. And k is the total number of a situation's attributes that are used to retrieve the instance i from memory. In the IBL model, the value of $k = 4$, as in the simple scenario, there are 4 attributes that characterize a situation event in the network and that are also used to retrieve instances from memory. As mentioned above, these attributes are *IP*, *directory*, *alert*, and *operation* in an event. The match scale (P_l) reflects the amount of weighting given to the similarity between an instance i's situation slot l and the corresponding situation event's attribute. P_l is generally a negative integer with a common value of -1.0 for all situation slots k of an instance i. The M_{li} or match similarities represents the similarity between the value l of a situation event's attribute that is used to retrieve instances from memory and the value in the corresponding situation slots of an instance i in memory. In this chapter, the $\sum_{l=1}^{k} P_l \times M_{li}$ term has been defined by using both a squared-geometric similarity model and a feature-based similarity model (Shepard, 1962a, 1962b; Tversky, 1977). In the squared-geometric model the $\sum_{l=1}^{k} P_l \times M_{li}$ is defined as:

$$\sum_{l=1}^{k} P_l \times M_{li} = \sum_{l=1}^{4} -1 \times (l_i - l_{event})^2 \qquad (3)$$

However, in the feature-based similarity model, the $\sum_{l=1}^{k} P_l \times M_{li}$ is defined as:

$$\sum_{l=1}^{k} P_l \times M_{li} = \theta \times f(i \cap event) \\ -\alpha \times f(i - event) - \beta \times f(event - i) \qquad (4)$$

The similarity of instance i to situation event is expressed as a linear combination of the measure of the common and distinctive features. The term $f(i \cap event)$ represents the number of features that the four slots of instance *i* and the four attributes in a situation event have in common. The term *f(i−event)* represents the features in the instance *i*'s four slots that are missing from the four attributes in the situation event. The term *f(event−i)* represents the features of the four attributes in the situation event that are missing from the instance *i*'s four slots. Furthermore, θ, α, and β are weights for the common and distinctive components. We assumed default values of the weights and thus, θ=2, α =1, and β =1. The default value assumption is because it balances out the effects of the common features (1st term in Equation 4) and the uncommon features (2nd and 3rd terms in Equation 4). Thus, the default assumption is a safe assumption to make both from literature (Tversky, 1977) and because we make predictions about the working of an analyst where we don't know about the real behavior of an analyst.

In order to find the value of the $\sum_{l=1}^{k} P_l \times M_{li}$ term, the situation events' attributes and the values in the corresponding slots of instances in memory were coded using numeric codes. Table 1 shows the codes assigned to the SDU slots of instances in memory and the situation events' attributes in the simple scenario. The assumption of on these codes is made to yield a nontrivial contribution of the similarity term in the activation equation (Equation 1).

Due to the $\sum_{l=1}^{k} P_l \times M_{li}$ specification, instances that encode a similar situation to the current situation event's attributes, receive a less negative activation (in Equation 1). In contrast, instances that encode a dissimilar situation to the current situation event's attributes receive a more negative activation.

Furthermore , is the noise value that is computed and added to an instance *i*'s activation at the time of its retrieval attempt from memory. The noise value is characterized by a parameter *s*. The noise is defined as,

$$\varepsilon_i = s \times \ln\left(\frac{1 - \eta_i}{\eta_i}\right) \qquad (5)$$

where, η_i is a random draw from a uniform distribution bounded in [0, 1] for an instance *i* in memory. We set the parameter *s* in an IBL model to make it a part of the activation equation (Equation 1). The *s* parameter has a default value of 0.25 in the ACT-R architecture and we assume the default value of *s* in the IBL model of the security analyst.

IMPLEMENTATION AND EXECUTION OF THE IBL MODEL

The IBL model of the security analyst was created using Matlab software. The IBL model goes over a sequence of 25 network events in the simple scenario (Figure 1). The memory of a simulated analyst in the model was pre-populated with instances encoding all possible sequences of network events based upon values of events' attributes. Some of these instances contained a threat value as the utility and some did not (more information below). Unbeknownst to the model (but known to the modeler), out of the 25 events in the scenario (mentioned above), there are 8 pre-defined threat events that are executed by an attacker outside the company (Ou et al., 2006; Xie et al. 2010). For each event in the scenario, the IBL model uses Equations 1, 2, {3 or 4}, and 5 to retrieve an instance that is most similar to the encountered event. Based upon the value of the utility slot of a retrieved instance, the situation event is classified as a threat or not a threat. Depending upon the inertia mechanism and the risk-tolerance level of a simulated analyst in the model, a decision is made to classify a sequence of observed events as a cyber-attack and stop company's online operations, or to let the company continue its online operations (no cyber-attack).

The IBL model was executed for a set of 500 simulated analysts on the same simple scenario

Table 1. The coded values in the slots of an instance in memory and attributes of a situation event

Attributes	Values	Codes
IP (S)	Webserver	1
	Fileserver	2
	Workstation	3
Directory (S)	Missing value	-100
	File X	1
Alert (S)	Present	1
	Absent	0
Operation (S)	Successful	1
	Unsuccessful	0
Decision (D)	Cyber-attack	1
	No Cyber-attack	0
Threat (U)	Yes	1
	No	0

where each simulated analyst encountered 25 or less situation events in the network. For each of the 500 simulated analysts, we manipulated the mix of threat and non-threat instances in memory, i.e., experience of the analyst, the risk-tolerance level of the analyst, and the similarity model used by the analyst.

The mix of threat and non-threat instances in the model's memory could be one of the following three kinds: ambivalent analyst (Ambi): 50% of threat instances and 50% non-threat instances for each situation event in the scenario; an extra-careful analyst (Extra): 75% of threat instances and 25% of non-threat instances for each situation event in the scenario; and a less-careful analyst (Less): 25% of threat instances and 75% of non-threat instances for each situation event in the scenario. The risk-tolerance level of analyst was manipulated on the following three levels: low (2 events out of a possible 25 event need to be classified as threats before the analyst classifies a sequence of observed events as cyber-attack); medium (4 events out of a possible 25 event to be classified as threats before the analyst classifies a sequence of observed events as cyber-attack); and high (6 events out of a possible 25 event to be

classified as threats before the analyst classifies a sequence of observed events as cyber-attack). Please note that the values of 2, 4, and 6 events for the risk-tolerance is a reasonable and balanced manipulation given that there are only 8 total threat events (whose threat identity is unknown to the model) in the scenario. Finally, the similarity model was manipulated at two levels and could be either squared-geometric (Equation 3) or feature-based (Equation 4).

We wanted to derive predictions of the effect of the above manipulations in the model upon the cyber-SA of the analyst. The cyber-SA of a simulated analyst was measured using the accuracy and timeliness of the analyst. The accuracy was evaluated using two different cyber-SA metrics, recall and precision, and the timeliness was evaluated in the model using a single timeliness cyber-SA metric (Jajodia et al., 2010). *Recall* is the percent of events correctly detected as threats out of the total number of known threat events observed by the model before the model stopped in the scenario (Recall is the same as hit rate in Signal Detection Theory; Jajodia et al., 2010). *Precision* is the percentage of events correctly detected as threats out of the total number of threat events detected by the model before it stopped in the scenario. *Timeliness* is 100% minus percentage of events, out of a total 25, after which the model stops in the scenario and classifies the scenario to be a cyber-attack (the timeliness could be defined as the number of events out of 25, but defining it as a percentage allows us to compare it to other two cyber-SA measures). A point to note is that if the model is unable to stop before the 25 events elapse in the scenario, then the denominators of the above cyber-SA metrics equal 25.

For both similarity models, we expected best performance for the IBL model representing an extra-careful analyst with a low risk-tolerance, and the worst performance for the IBL model representing a less-careful analyst with a high risk-tolerance. This fact is because an extra-careful analyst with a low risk-tolerance will be classifying network events more cautiously compared to

Figure 3. The effect of experience (memory) on cyber-SA of an analyst in the squared-geometric similarity model (A) and in the feature-based similarity model (D). The effect of risk-tolerance on cyber-SA of an analyst in the squared-geometric similarity model (B) and in the feature-based similarity model (E). The interaction effect of memory and risk-tolerance on cyber-SA of an analyst in the squared-geometric similarity model (C) and in the feature-based similarity model (F). A greater percentage on all three cyber-SA measures, recall, precision, and timeliness is more desirable as it makes the simulated analyst more efficient.

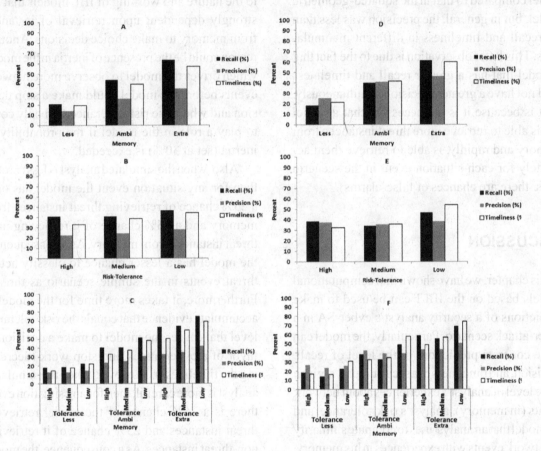

a less-careful analyst with a high risk-tolerance. Also, as both similarity models, squared-geometric and feature-based, aim to search for the most similar instance in memory to a situation event in the simple scenario, we expect a similar performance in the IBL model for both similarity models.

RESULTS

Figure 3 shows the predictions of the cyber-SA measures (recall, precision, and timeliness) of an

average security analyst from the IBL model due to the effects of manipulating the memory, risk-tolerance, and the similarity model used. First, for both similarity models, the effect of memory manipulation on cyber-SA measures (panel A and D) was stronger compared to the risk-tolerance measure (panel B and E). Thus, although there was a pronounced change in the three measures, recall, precision, and timeliness, as a result of the memory manipulation (Less, Ambi, and Extra), the change in the three measures was little due to the risk-tolerance manipulation (High, Medium, and Low). Furthermore, as per our expectation for both similarity models, an extra-careful analyst with a low risk-tolerance did better on all three performance measures compared to a less-careful analyst with a high risk-tolerance (panel C and F). Also, the precision was higher in the feature-based model compared to that in the squared-geometric model, but in general, the precision was less than the recall and timeliness in different manipulations. This latter observation is due to the fact that a model that has a greater recall and timeliness need not have a greater precision simultaneously. That is because it is not necessary that a model that is able to retrieve more threat instances from memory and rapidly, is able to retrieve them accurately for each situation event in the scenario (thus, there are chances of false-alarms).

DISCUSSION

In this chapter, we have shown that computational models based on the IBLT can be used to make predictions of a security analyst's cyber-SA in a cyber-attack scenario. Particularly, the model can make concrete predictions of the level of recall, precision, and timeliness of a security analyst given some level of analyst's experiences about network events (in memory), analyst's risk-tolerance, and the model that an analyst uses to compute similarity of network events with experiences in his memory.

We created an IBL model of the security analyst for a simple scenario of a typical island-hopping cyber-attack. The island-hopping attack portrayed in the simple scenario is one of the most common methods of cyber-attack in the real world (Ou et al., 2006; Xie et al., 2010). Then, using the simple scenario, we evaluated the performance of a simulated analyst on three commonly used measures of cyber-SA. These measures are based upon accuracy of analyst (precision and recall) and the timeliness of the analyst to react to cyber-attacks (timeliness). Our results revealed that both the risk-tolerance level of an analyst and

the mix of experiences of threat and non-threat instances in analyst's memory affect the analyst's cyber-SA; with the effect of the analyst's experiences (in memory) more impacting compared to risk-tolerance. One reason for the lesser impact of the risk-tolerance manipulation could be due to the nature and working of IBL models that are strongly dependent upon retrieval of instances from memory to make choice decisions. Another reason could be the presence of inertia in the model, which drives the model to observe more network events before the model could make a stop decision and where the risk-tolerance will only come to play a role in the model if the probability of inertia (set at 30%) is exceeded.

Also, when the simulated analyst is less careful, then for any situation event the model has only a 25% chance of retrieving threat instances from memory and a 75% chance of it retrieving non-threat instances from memory. As a consequence, the model has a lesser chance to classify actual threat events in the simple scenario as threats. Furthermore, it takes more time for the model to accumulate evidence that equals the risk-tolerance level that causes the model to make a decision in favor of a cyber-attack and stop work (decreasing the timeliness). However, when the simulated analyst is more careful, then for any situation event there is a 75% chance of the model retrieving threat instances and 25% chance of it retrieving non-threat instances. As a consequence, the model has a greater chance to classify actual threats in the simple scenario as threats and also takes less time to accumulate evidence that is equal to the risk-tolerance level (increasing the Timeliness).

The most important aspect of the model is the fact that although the recall and timeliness increase as a direct function of the model's ability to retrieve threat instances from the memory and its risk-tolerance, there is not a substantial increase in its precision when either of the two manipulations (memory and risk-tolerance) is favorable (Figure 3). The slow increase in precision is expected because a model that is able to retrieve more threat instances from memory and is less risk-tolerant might not necessarily be more precise in its actions. However, there is still an increase in precision with a manipulation of both memory and risk-tolerance and this suggests that making a security analyst less risk-tolerant as well as extra-careful might help increase his job efficiency. Because the IBL model is a process model that observes events, and makes decisions by retrieving experiences from memory, these are only some of the many predictions that the IBL model can make regarding the cyber-SA of human analysts.

Furthermore, although the current model is able to make *a priori* predictions, these need to be actually validated with human data. We plan to run laboratory studies in the near future to assess human behavior in this simple scenario. An experimental approach will allow us to validate our model's predictions and improve the relevance of the model and the assumptions made in it on its free parameters. In these experimental studies, we believe that some of the interesting factors to manipulate would include the experiences of the human analyst (stored in memory). One method we are currently considering is to make participants read or watch examples of more and less threatening scenarios before they participate in the act of detecting cyber-attacks in the simple scenario (i.e., priming the memory of the model with more or less threat instances as we did in the IBL model). Also, we plan to record the risk-seeking and risk-averse behavior of participants using popular measures involving gambles to control for the risk-tolerance factor (typically a risk-seeking person is more risk-tolerant compared to a risk-averse person). Also, once we calibrate the current predictions of the model with an empirical study data (that we plan to collect in the future), we can evaluate the efficacy of different similarity models. Thus, our next goal will be to validate the predictions from the IBL model.

IMPLICATIONS FOR TRAINING AND DECISION SUPPORT OF SECURITY ANALYSTS

If our model is able to represent the cyber-SA of human analysts accurately, this model would have significant potential to contribute towards the design of training and decision support tools for security analysts. Based upon our current predictions, it might be better to devise analyst training and decision support that primes them to have experienced more threat rather than non-threat network events. The analyst's cyber-SA is also impacted by how tolerant he/she is to cyber-attacks. Thus, companies recruiting security analysts for network monitoring operations could measure the risk-seeking/risk-aversion character of a potential analyst (by using different risk-orientation measures that use gambles). Doing so would help evaluate a humans fit for the security analyst's position. Furthermore, although risk-orientation is a characteristic of a person (like his personality) that comes about as a result of his day-to-day experience and education, but there might be training interventions that could make analysts conscious of their risk-orientation or alter their risk-orientation. Based upon our results, making analysts less risk-tolerant (or more risk-averse) would help in increasing their efficiency in their job. Finally, based upon our results, training security analysts about the similar and dissimilar features between threats and non-threats in different cyber-attacks will benefit making analyst more precise on their job.

CONCLUSION

Due to the growing threat to our cyber infrastructure and the heightened need to implement cybersecurity, it becomes important to evaluate the cyber situation awareness (cyber-SA) of security analysts in different cyber-attack scenarios. In this chapter, we suggest a memory-based account, based upon instance-based learning theory, of the decisions of a security analyst who is put in a popular cyber-attack scenario of an island-hopping attack. Our results indicate that the cyber-SA of an analyst is a function of his memory of threat and non-threat events, his risk-tolerance, and the similarity methods he uses to compare network events to prior experiences of events in his memory. Based upon our predictions, it might be helpful to devise analyst job training that makes analysts cautious about the possibility of cyber threats, less risk-tolerant, and that enable them to look for features in attributes of network events that communicate the indication of potential threats.

ACKNOWLEDGMENT

This research was a part of a Multidisciplinary University Research Initiative Award (MURI; # W911NF-09-1-0525) from Army Research Office for a research project on Cyber Situation Awareness. We would like to thank Dynamic Decision Making Laboratory for providing the computing support for this chapter. Furthermore, we would like to thank Young-Suk Ahn, Dynamic Decision Making Laboratory for helping with compiling some of the results reported in this chapter and providing helpful comments. Finally, we are grateful to Hau-yu Wong, Dynamic Decision Making Laboratory for providing her editorial comments on this chapter.

REFERENCES

Anderson, J. R., & Lebiere, C. (1998). *The atomic components of thought*. Hillsdale, NJ: Lawrence Erlbaum Associates.

Anderson, J. R., & Lebiere, C. (2003). The Newell test for a theory of mind. *The Behavioral and Brain Sciences*, *26*(5), 587–639. doi:10.1017/S0140525X0300013X

Dutt, V., Ahn, Y., & Gonzalez, C. (2011). *Cyber situation awareness: Modeling the security analyst in a cyber-attack scenario through instance-based learning*. Manuscript submitted for publication.

Dutt, V., Cassenti, D. N., & Gonzalez, C. (2010). Modeling a robotics operator manager in a tactical battlefield. In *Proceedings of the IEEE Conference on Cognitive Methods in Situation Awareness and Decision Support* (p. xx). Miami Beach, FL.

Dutt, V., & Gonzalez, C. (2011). Cyber situation awareness: Modeling the security analyst in a cyber attack scenario through instance-based learning. In *Proceedings of the 20th Behavior Representation in Modeling & Simulation (BRIMS) Conference*. Sundance, Utah, USA.

Endsley, M. R. (1995). Toward a theory of situation awareness in dynamic systems. *Human Factors Journal*, *37*(1), 32–64. doi:10.1518/001872095779049543

Fan, X., & Yen, J. (2007). R-CAST: Integrating team intelligence for human-centered teamwork. In

Gardner, H. (1987). *The mind's new science: A history of the cognitive revolution*. New York, NY: Basic Books.

Goldstone, R. L., Day, S., & Son, J. Y. (2010). Comparison. In B. Glatzeder, V. Goel, & A. von Müller (Eds.), *On thinking: Volume II, towards a theory of thinking* (pp. 103-122). Heidelberg, Germany: Springer Verlag.

Gonzalez, C., & Dutt, V. (2010). Instance-based learning: Integrating decisions from experience in sampling and repeated choice paradigms. *Psychological Review*, *118*(4).

Gonzalez, C., Dutt, V., & Lejarraja, T. (2011). *How did an IBL model become the runners-up in the market entry competition?* Manuscript in preparation.

Gonzalez, C., Lerch, J. F., & Lebiere, C. (2003). Instance-based learning in dynamic decision making. *Cognitive Science, 27*(4), 591–635. doi:10.1207/s15516709cog2704_2

Hertwig, R., Barron, G., Weber, E. U., & Erev, I. (2004). Decisions from experience and the effect of rare events in risky choice. *Psychological Science, 15*(8), 534–539. doi:10.1111/j.0956-7976.2004.00715.x

In *Proceedings of the2010IEEE/IFIP International Conference on Dependable Systems and Networks (DSN)* (pp. 211 - 220). Hong Kong, China: IEEE Press.

Jajodia, S., Liu, P., Swarup, V., & Wang, C. (2010). *Cyber situational awareness*. New York, NY: Springer.

Johnson-Laird, P. (2006). *How we reason*. London, UK: Oxford University Press.

Klein, G. A. (1989). Recognition-primed decisions. In Rouse, W. B. (Ed.), *Advances in man-machine system research* (*Vol. 5*, pp. 47–92). Greenwich, CT: JAI Press.

Lejarraga, T., Dutt, V., & Gonzalez, C. (in press). Instance-based learning: A general model of decisions from experience in repeated binary choice. *Journal of Behavioral Decision Making*.

Lute, J. H., & McConnell, B. (2011). *A civil perspective on cybersecurity*. Retrieved February 28, 2011, from http://www.wired.com/threat-level/2011/02/dhs-op-ed/

McCumber, J. (2004). *Assessing and managing security risk in IT systems: A structured methodology*. Boca Raton, FL: Auerbach Publications. doi:10.1201/9780203490426

Ou, X., Boyer, W. F., & McQueen, M. A. (2006). A scalable approach to attack graph generation. In

Proceedings of the 13th ACM Conference on Computer and Communications Security (pp. 336–345). Alexandria, VA: ACM.

Proceedings of Twenty-Second AAAI Conference on Artificial Intelligence (pp. 1535 – 1541). Vancouver, British Columbia, Canada.

PSU. (2011). *Center for cyber-security, Information Privacy, and Trust*. Retrieved March 1, 2011, from http://cybersecurity.ist.psu.edu/research.php.

Salter, C., Saydjari, O., Schneier, B., & Wallner, J. (1998). Toward a secure system engineering methodology. In *Proceedings of New Security Paradigms Workshop* (pp. 2-10). Charlottesville, VA: ACM.

Shepard, R. N. (1962a). The analysis of proximities: multidimensional scaling with an unknown distance function: Part I. *Psychometrika, 27*, 125–140. doi:10.1007/BF02289630

Shepard, R. N. (1962b). The analysis of proximities: Multidimensional scaling with an unknown distance function: Part II. *Psychometrika, 27*, 219–246. doi:10.1007/BF02289621

Sideman, A. (2011). *Agencies must determine computer security teams in face of potential federal shutdown*. Retrieved March 1, 2011, from http://fcw.com/articles/2011/02/23/agencies-must-determine-computer-security-teams-in-face-of-shutdown.aspx

Simon, H. A., & March, J. G. (1958). *Organizations*. New York, NY: Wiley.

Tadda, G., Salerno, J. J., Boulware, D., Hinman, M., & Gorton, S. (2006). Realizing situation awareness within a cyber environment. In *Proceedings of SPIE Vol. 6242* (pp. 624204). Orlando, FL: SPIE.

Tversky, A. (1977). Features of similarity. *Psychological Review, 84*, 327–352. doi:10.1037/0033-295X.84.4.327

Vosniadou, S., & Ortony, A. (1989). *Similarity and analogical reasoning*. New York, NY: Cambridge University Press. doi:10.1017/CBO9780511529863

Xie, P., Li, J. H., Ou X., Liu, P., & Levy, R. (2010). Using Bayesian networks for cyber security analysis.

ADDITIONAL READING

Busemeyer, J. R., & Diederich, A. (2009). *Cognitive modeling*. New York, NY: Sage.

Endsley, M. R. (2004). Situation awareness: Progress and directions. In Banbury, S., & Tremblay, S. (Eds.), *A cognitive approach to situation awareness: Theory, measurement and application* (pp. 317–341). Aldershot, UK: Ashgate Publishing.

Endsley, M. R., & Garland, D. J. (Eds.). (2000). *Situation awareness analysis and measurement*. Mahwah, NJ: Lawrence Erlbaum Associates.

Gonzalez, C., & Dutt, V. (2010). Instance-based learning models of training. In *Proceedings of the 54th AnnualMeeting of the Human Factors and Ergonomics Society (pp. 2319-2323)*. San Francisco, CA: Human Factors and Ergonomics Society.

Li, J., Ou, X., & Rajagopalan, R. (2009). Uncertainty and risk management in cyber situational awareness. Retrieved February 28, 2011, from http://www.hpl.hp.com/techreports/2009/HPL-2009-174.html

KEY TERMS AND DEFINITIONS

Cyber-Attack: Also known as cyber-warfare and is the use of computers and the Internet in conducting warfare in cyberspace.

Cyber-Situation Awareness: When a security accident occurs, the top three questions security administrators would ask are in essence: What has happened? Why did it happen? What should I do? Answers to these questions form the "core" of Cyber Situational Awareness.

Dynamic Decision-Making: The interdependent decision making that takes place in an environment that changes over time either due to the previous actions of the decision maker, or due to events that are outside of the control of the decision maker.

Instance-Based Learning Theory: A theory of how humans make decisions in dynamic tasks. According to the theory, individuals rely on their accumulated experience to make decisions by retrieving past solutions to similar situations stored in memory. Thus, decision accuracy can only improve gradually and through interaction with similar situations.

Intrusion-Detection System: A device or software application that monitors network and/or system activities for malicious activities or policy violations and produces reports to a security analyst.

Network Events: Events that take place over a network like opening of a file by a user on a workstation that resides on a remote server. These events could be further classified as threats (executed by a cyber-attacker) or non-threats (executed by a normal user of the network without any malicious intensions).

Security Analyst: A decision-maker who is in charge of observing the online operations of a corporate network (e.g., an online retail company with an external webserver and an internal fileserver) from threats of random or organized cyber-attacks.

Chapter 9
Information Data Fusion and Computer Network Defense

Mark Ballora
The Pennsylvania State University, USA

Nicklaus A. Giacobe
The Pennsylvania State University, USA

Michael McNeese
The Pennsylvania State University, USA

David L. Hall
The Pennsylvania State University, USA

ABSTRACT

Computer networks no longer simply enable military and civilian operations, but have become vital infrastructures for all types of operations ranging from sensing and command/control to logistics, power distribution, and many other functions. Consequently, network attacks have become weapons of choice for adversaries engaged in asymmetric warfare. Traditionally, data and information fusion techniques were developed to improve situational awareness and threat assessment by combining data from diverse sources, and have recently been extended to include both physical ("hard") sensors and human observers (acting as "soft" sensors). This chapter provides an introduction to traditional data fusion models and adapts them to the domain of cyber security. Recent advances in hard and soft information fusion are summarized and applied to the cyber security domain. Research on the use of sound for human-in-the-loop pattern recognition (sonification) is also introduced. Finally, perspectives are provided on the future for data fusion in cyber security research.

INTRODUCTION

Historically, an enormous amount of research and development on information fusion has been conducted in support of military operations (e.g., fusion of multi-sensor data for target tracking, identification, and threat assessment and situation awareness) (Hall and McMullen, 2004) (Liggins et al., 2008). The research has included development of process models, creation of algorithms for signal and image processing, pattern recognition, state estimation, automated reasoning, and dynamic resource allocation.

DOI: 10.4018/978-1-4666-0104-8.ch009

This chapter adapts these models to the domain of cyber security. This is a field in which data fusion techniques and terminology are becoming increasingly relevant, given the complex tasks of maintaining overall awareness of a network's current status, projecting future actions of adversaries, and making timely adjustments. Following a discussion of hard and soft information fusion and their relevance to the cyber security domain, we propose a novel means of situational awareness involving an auditory representation (sonification) of network traffic.

The Organization of this Chapter

This chapter is organized as follows. We begin by exploring of some of the background research in three areas of interest – use of humans as soft sensors, data fusion technologies in cyber security, and sonification. The first content area of human-centric information fusion outlines the use of humans as "soft" sensors. The second content area presents the general data fusion framework (the JDL model) as it applies to the cyber security context. The third main content area, sonification, is construed as a cognitive refinement. The chapter concludes with a discussion of future research directions in cyber situational awareness.

BACKGROUND

The Changing Landscape: Humans as Observers

It is clear that for a variety of applications—ranging from asymmetric warfare to emergency crisis management to business applications—a need exists to characterize and understand the human landscape. In understanding and addressing natural disasters such as Hurricane Katrina in New Orleans (Palser, 2005), it is clearly insufficient to observe and predict weather patterns, model the interaction between high winds, buildings, and other structures. While these are clearly factors to be considered, we must also address information such as population locations and demographics. We must understand how people of different ages, socio-economic backgrounds, cultures and experiences might react to a major disaster and to each other. Information and models are needed that address attitudes, reaction patterns, reactions to outside aid agencies and people, and ways that the news media affect the dynamics of the interactions—to list just a few factors. In regards to the cyber-security domain, we will need an understanding of the adversaries who plan and effect network attacks (e.g., their strategies, weaknesses, rules of engagement, and cultural imperatives) if we ever seek to become predictive, rather than simply reactive, to cyber attacks.

The Data Fusion Process Model and Cyber Security

Historically, data fusion research has focused primarily on utilizing physical sensors to observe and characterize the physical landscape. The Joint Directors of Laboratories (JDL) Data Fusion Process Model (Kessler et al., 1991) has become a standard model to describe the process of receiving multi-sensor data, annotating it, and fusing common threads in order to create predictive capabilities. The process is broken down into a series of levels, each of which adds a layer of intelligence and inference.

The data fusion process for military applications can be leveraged to characterize the cyber "landscape." The chapter summarizes the JDL model, illustrates its relevance to cyber security, and describes new trends in human-centered information fusion (Hall and Jordan, 2010) that impact cyber security (viz., the utilization of human observers to augment physical sensors, use of human pattern recognition and semantic level reasoning for improved inferencing, and collaborative decision-making).

Bass (2000) proposed the use of multi-sensor data fusion for intrusion detection. Since that time, a number of researchers have implemented multi-sensor data fusion techniques in cyber security, especially in intrusion detection. Because intrusion detection sensors (IDSs) are plagued with high false-positive rates and often low correct detection rates, they are likely candidates for improvement through data fusion. Thomas and Balakrishnan (2008) proposed a system based on a neural network-based fusion algorithm to increase the true positive detection rate of three IDSs (28%, 32% and 51% for PHAD, ALAD and SnortIDS respectively) to a net gain of 68% true detection rate. Other researchers have proposed using neural networks (Liang, et al., 2007) (Wang, et al., 2007), support vector machines (Liu, et al., 2007), and D-S evidence theory (Tian, et al., 2005) to address the IDS false positive rate. However, these researchers do not extend their recommendation for data fusion beyond increasing efficiency in detection rates of IDS.

Possibilities of Sonification

Extensive work has been performed in developing two- and three-dimensional displays to visualize a computer network and its current condition. Examples of such displays can be found at http://www.slideshare.net/amiable_indian/network-security-data-visualization. By contrast, little research has been conducted on the translation of network data into sound (sonification) to allow analysts to perform aural pattern recognition and anomaly detection. Sonification is an emerging form of representation that capitalizes on the strengths of the auditory system. Besides the fact that a sound representation keeps the eyes free for other tasks, the auditory system is particularly sensitive to dynamic changes and patterns.

Types of Sonification

The simplest functional type of auditory display is *simple triggering*, wherein a recording or simple synthesized sound is played when certain conditions occur. This is effective for a limited number of known conditions, but is too coarse for study of data for unknown conditions. Simple triggering of audio files lacks variety. For more detailed study, small variations in the data should create corresponding subtle variations in the character of the sound that is created.

Increased nuance can be achieved with *parameter-based* sonifications (Kramer, 1994), sometimes called an "auditory scatter plot," whereby the data values are mapped to synthesizer sound characteristics such as oscillator frequency, filter cutoff frequency, volume, or stereo panning. A multi-dimensional data set is sonified as a multi-instrumental synthesizer ensemble. An effective design creates the possibility of auditory gestalts (Bregman, 1990), wherein characteristics of the sound combine to create unexpected synergies.

We instinctively recognize subtle changes in our sound environments. Hermann (2002) makes the distinction between two listening types. The first is *musical listening*, which concerns itself with tracking acoustic properties such as pitch and timbre, and is the type of listening employed in parameter-based sonification work. In contrast, *analytical everyday listening* concerns itself with identifying sources of sounds. This complex process of making judgments as to object's characteristics is largely instinctive (unlearned). Our auditory system routinely makes accurate and quick ascertainments of the source and characteristics of objects. When hearing the sound of a rolling ball, for example, we can make generally correct estimations of the size, speed, and material of the ball, based on a complex interplay of auditory parameters.

Extrapolating on Herrmann's argument, we recognize that this type of analytical listening, while unlearned, certainly benefits from further learning efforts. This is seen in professionals such as seasoned auto mechanics and sonar operators, who gain insights from practiced, focused listening for subtle changes in the sound of a system.

Herrmann proposes *model-based* sonification, which involves mapping data values to resonances and/or mechanics of a *physical model* (Smith, 1992). A physical model is a computer synthesis technique based on wave equations describing vibrating objects.

Earlier Sonifications of Network Activity

Gilfix and Crouch (2000) described the Peep Network Auralizer System, which played various natural recordings to reflect network conditions such as incoming and outgoing email, load average and number of users logged in. Through various sound libraries listeners could be placed in a variety of listening environments such as a rainforest or desert. For example, the amount of rain might represent load average while the flow of a waterfall might represent email traffic. The creation of nature-inspired soundscapes was an effective design choice, as it resulted in a pleasant and unobtrusive listening environment that could be heard in the background over extended periods of time. The basis of the display in simple triggering, however, limits its utility in other types of implementations, where a higher degree of subtlety is required.

Everyday analytical listening was employed by Chafe and Leistikow (2001), who created a physical model of a plucked string, which was "plucked" by ping commands, and whose timbral character reflected the message tracerout quality. The virtual string was responsive to various frequency and timbral parameters, and responses to factors such as pluck placement and strength.

Their instrument was the basis of an art installation, in which visitors listened to the melody, rhythm, and timbral changes of the ping.

Our present work in this area is just one thread in the evolving arena of data fusion, which is summarized in the next section.

PERSPECTIVES ON HUMAN CENTRIC INFORMATION FUSION

Data fusion is concerned not just with information collected from physical sensors, but also with insights into the human behavior that is represented with sensor information. While traditional data fusion systems focus primarily on observing of physical targets by physical sensors, evolving applications are moving towards characterization of non-physical targets such as small groups, organizations, or cyber-attackers. This expanded focus involves the use of physical and non-physical sensors to observe a given landscape—individuals, groups, populations, organizations and their interactions. Figure 1 shows these emerging concepts, including: (1) use of an ad hoc community of observers as a dynamic network of "soft" sensors to gather information about an emerging situation or activity, (2) use of human analysts in a joint cognitive system in which the human's visual and aural pattern recognition skills and semantic reasoning capabilities are effectively engaged by the information fusion system to assist in the overall situation assessment and decision-making, and (3) use of a dynamic ad hoc community of analysts (e.g., analytical crowdsourcing) to collaboratively analyze a situation or threat—the interaction may be mediated by a virtual world environment such as Second Life or Protosphere.

On one hand, extensive tools and displays exist to characterize the physical landscape via displays of terrain, weather phenomena, political boundaries, man-made features, and a wide variety of other characteristics. From the rapidly

Figure 1. Concept of new roles for humans in data fusion systems

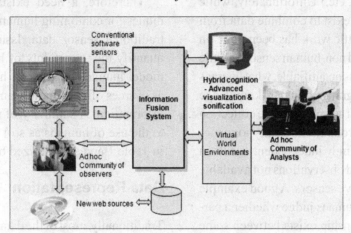

evolving *Google Earth*™, which includes purchased imagery from the GeoEye-1 satellite, to resources such as Accuweather (http://www.accuweather.com/), we are nowhere at a loss for physically-based information. In contrast, similar data is not so readily available for analyzing the human landscape. Many of the geo-spatial, geo-temporal aspects of a situation can be integrated with human intentions, interaction, and movement to improve situation awareness. At a global and national level, resources exist to provide information about populations, large organizations and long-term trends. Examples of such sources include:

- Opinion data collected by the Gallup organization via their world data base project (http://www.gallup.com/consulting/worldpoll/24046/about.aspx), which collects extensive polling from 140 different countries;
- Data collected by the United Nations (http://data.un.org/, http://www.fao.org/);
- Data from the U.S. State Department (http://www.state.gov/);
- The CIA fact book (https://www.cia.gov/library/publications/the-world-factbook/);
- And numerous news organizations throughout the world.

The information collected about the human landscape varies from large-scale, long-term information in the form of facts, population statistics, political information, and minute-by-minute news reports from the news media, web-based metadata, and web sociometrics (computational sociology). Simultaneously, information is collected *ad hoc* by independent individuals acting as reporters, bloggers, amateur photographers, and analysts.

Human as Soft Sensor: Use of Pattern Recognition/ Context Reasoning

The rapid growth of cell phone dissemination and continually improving cellular communications bandwidth provides the opportunity to create a dynamic observation resource: in effect, allowing humans to act as "soft" sensors, providing data via direct reports and information from open source information on the Internet. This information can be valuable and significantly augment data obtained from traditional software sensors, which monitor a network system. Individual analysts can provide information about the context of a network operation (e.g., interpretation of anomalies, patterns of use as a function of time, special conditions or workloads, new trends in cyber attacks, information about current political affairs that might trigger attacks, etc.) Unfortunately, while extensive techniques exist to combine data from traditional sensors, little work has been done on combining human and non-human sensors. While the human "data" is less quantifiable, what humans can provide are the cognitive basis and knowledge to interpret the context surrounding the collection of data (the sense surround), the ability to inductively combine seemingly independent events in a meaningful way, and observations not available from standard objective sensors. A good example is the case in which humans judge whether a particular type of relationship exists between some entities. Virtually no hard sensor provides *prima facia* evidence of the existence of a relationship, since hard sensors are designed primarily to measure attributes and features of entities.

Therefore, a need exists to develop techniques for combining human-supplied data with traditional sensor data. Issues include how to quantify the uncertainty of human data, how to model humans as sensors, how to task humans as sources of information, and even how to elicit information. A summary of some issues related to the use of humans as soft sensors is provided in Table 1 and summarized below.

Data Representation

Traditionally, most of the data reported by humans is in the form of language constructs (sentences, phrases, identifications and judgments), although, with the use of cell phones with cameras and geo-tagged locations and the use UAVs, video and still imagery are now associated with typical language

Table 1. Issues related to use of humans as soft sensors

Issue	Description	Comments
Data representation	How should data and information be characterized or reported by a user?	• Humans tend to report information in a self-referential mode (e.g., the automobile is in front of me), and using fuzzy terminology (terms such as "near", "far").
Uncertainty Representation	How to characterize the reports provided by a human as a "soft" sensor; what are the characteristics and performance of human sensors; how are these affected by fatigue, emotion, expectations, training, etc? In particular, how to provide metrics for reporting uncertainty and second order uncertainty	• Human observers are affected by traditional factors that affect hard sensors (observing conditions, terrain, weather) and also by personal characteristics such as level of training, attention, fatigue
Tasking	How can or should we task humans for information (e.g., via requests communicated over a cell phone; use of standard data input forms; encouragement of free texting via systems such as Twitter, etc.)	• Unlike physical sensors, humans do not respond to demands for information and are generally an uncontrolled source; • Tasking may involve a priori agreements and training for selected observers or involve ad hoc reporting such as reporting of emergencies or general "gossip"
Knowledge Elicitation	What are the specific mechanisms and methods to elicit information from humans; how can one address common biases without "leading" an observer; what is the role of human aided knowledge elicitation (e.g., a 911 emergency operator) versus computer aided elicitation via structure forms or guided questions?	• Knowledge elicitation is a well studied area for developing the knowledge base for expert systems; however, issues in dynamic, ad hoc knowledge elicitation require further study
Fusion with hard sensor data	How can we effectively combine data from traditional physics based sensors with human reports?	• Challenges exist in data association and correlation • Fusion of hard and soft data requires accurate characterization of the sources (1st and 2nd order uncertainties)

constructs to formulate the basis of mental models that are richer in representation than previous practices. Antony (2008) provides examples of human reports of physical targets and illustrates how the reporting involves fuzzy descriptions and mixed Boolean and fuzzy logic reasoning. He develops some initial models to convert these descriptions into quantitative expressions of target location, characteristics and identification. Because the data are generally text-based information, fusion processing of such data requires functions such as text parsing, fuzzy decomposition, use of ontological and thesaurus relationships, and semantic level processing. Perusich & McNeese (2006) have also used fuzzy cognitive maps and fuzzy edges to translate human language into contextual understanding and mental models. While humans have a very rich language capability (Pinker, 1999), the automated interpretation of this language by computer processing remains a challenge. Issues in data representation are coupled with how the data/knowledge are elicited (e.g., via natural language "stream of conscious" input versus use of structured input templates and restricted vocabularies).

Hybrid Cognition: Humans as Collaborative Decision-Makers

A *joint cognitive system* refers to the use of human visual/aural pattern recognition along with semantic reasoning in collaboration with automated processing performed by a computer. One might consider a human (or multiple human)/computer team working together in a dynamic way to understand an evolving situation or threat. Humans employ higher-level cognition where deep semantic processing and pattern differentiation can lead to the use of analogy, metaphorical understanding, and other symbolic reasoning to comprehend complex situations. Pinker (1999) notes that humans have two powerful natural cognitive abilities:

1. The ability to recognize and reason with language;
2. The ability to recognize patterns and reason using a kind of visual physics.

For example, while sitting in a room, it is easy for a human to identify all of the containers that could hold a liquid—despite the fact that these may include water glasses, coffee cups, pots for plants, a kitchen sink, or a bottle. But this would be a daunting task for an automated computer process. Even using sophisticated pattern recognition techniques, the variety of possible containers and even the notion of a container would be difficult to encode into a pattern recognition algorithm. Similarly, we can express situations via sentences, descriptions or even stories about an event, activity, groups of humans, or collection of entities. Again, despite significant advances in automated reasoning via rules, frames, scripts, logical templates, Bayesian Belief Nets or other methods, it is challenging for a computer to match the semantic abilities of even the most naïve, untrained human.

In contrast, computers are excellent at prodigious numerical calculations such as those associated with differential equations of motion, fluid flow, statistical estimation, or physics-based modeling. Hence, computers can perform calculations and predictions that are not possible for humans. Clearly, information fusion systems should strive to combine the capabilities of humans and computers to create hybrid reasoning systems capable of performing better than either alone (McNeese, 1986).

THE JDL DATA FUSION PROCESS MODEL IN CYBER SECURITY TERMS

Here, we summarize attempts to apply an old model to a new problem. The JDL Data Fusion Process Model (Kessler et al., 1991) is a general-purpose reference model that describes the overall process of combining data from varied sources for purposes of gaining a better understanding of the situation being observed (Steinberg et al., 1999). The fusion process is hierarchical, with different tasks being carried out at various levels. At each level of the fusion process, algorithms combine the data and make inferences about the meaning of the data in context. This multi-level breakdown is meant to identify types of processing functions rather than identify a sequential flow. Thus, it is not necessary to first perform level 0 processing prior to level 1 processing, before level 2 processing, and so on. In actual system implementation the levels of processing are often interleaved and iterative rather than forming a linear progression from level 0 through level 5. Inferencing capability is key to the fusion process, giving the data fusion system its power. At each level, the answers to specific questions improve situational awareness. Here, the JDL Data Fusion Process Model is fitted to the context of cyber security.

This description continues an inquiry suggested by Bass (2000), when he proposed that data fusion techniques are well suited for enhancing situational awareness in network security events. We hope our description here will be useful to future researchers as means of modeling new data fusion-driven cyber security tools. It is important to note that individual fusion applications do not have to address the JDL model in its entirety. For example, a given fusion application may focus on identification, while another might address future impacts (Hall and McMullen, 2004) (Liggins et al., 2008) (Kessler et al., 1991). However, the entire scope of topics presented here will be relevant to the development of security components.

Figure 2 shows the relationship of the basic components and levels of the fusion process in cyber security terms. Each step in the process, from sensing through Levels 0 to 5, will be discussed separately below.

Sensors and Information Sources

Sensors in a fusion system are devices that provide information about a domain of interest. In the area of cyber security, the domain of interest consists of the characteristics and operation of a computer network (or networks). Examples of relevant sensors include intrusion detection systems (IDSs), firewall logs and host-based security logs. Network based IDS (NIDS) are commonly-

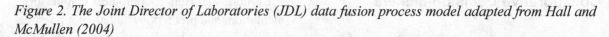

Figure 2. The Joint Director of Laboratories (JDL) data fusion process model adapted from Hall and McMullen (2004)

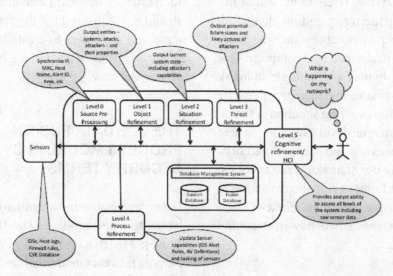

used sensing devices, but they are not the only source of observations. Host-based IDSs are often overlooked or are deprecated in terms of output due to the likelihood that the system's software could be compromised and unable to provide unbiased data. However, this does not mean that host-based sensors should be eliminated as viable sensors. On the contrary, host log file data, system locations, operating systems installed, patches installed, system configuration and other routine information technology (IT) support data are all essential to understanding the current landscape of the network being defended.

Enterprise antivirus software applications can provide centralized logging and management of virus activities on hosts. Other enterprise management applications can be helpful as well in providing information about account login attempts, software (and versions) installed, as well as other information that is critical for understanding the specific details about individual hosts on a network. While network devices are generally thought to be passive, they can provide specific information about which computing devices are connected or disconnected, and can also provide volume and characterization data of the traffic emanating from a given host.

Essential components of any network can be monitored, and the information provided can feed into the current understanding of the network's state. For example, switches and routers can provide data about IP addresses currently in use by given hosts by matching them to Media Access Control (MAC) addresses. Firewalls can provide specific details about connections between hosts and the rest of the Internet, especially if configured to report on specific actions of interest taken by hosts.

In the near future it is entirely possible that additional sensors might take the form of centralized knowledge bases. These could provide data about the availability of patches for the operating system, the list of known attacks and vulnerabilities, known tools and methods in use by attackers and other universally applicable data. Use of these

data sources situated in different parts of the fusion system can provide a characterization of defended hosts, attacks, attack methods and possible future states. A community of practice among security analysts may also provide valuable contextual information about current attack types.

Primary Fusion Levels – 0 to 3

This section describes the primary data fusion levels. Each of these levels provides a certain level of inference capability. Level 0/1 provides a capability to identify individual entities in the environment being observed. Level 2 provides a comprehension of the current situation. Level 3 provides the ability to project into the near future for possibilities and likelihoods of future states. The levels are cumulative, with each building on information from lower-numbered levels. Often, data fusion systems use various fusion algorithms to combine the data. The selection of data sources somewhat drives the choice of algorithm. The most important considerations are the inferencing capabilities desired – or, more simply, questions intended to be answered by the system.

Level 0/1 Data Alignment/ Object Refinement

Levels 0 and 1 are low level fusion processes that identify, detect and characterize individual entities (Hall and McMullen, 2004). Level 0 parses and synchronizes data from various sources and addresses the problems of unique key matching. In the context of cyber-security, one example of this matching would be host name to Internet Protocol (IP) address, chronometer differences, differences in reporting output formats, etc.

The Level 1 fusion process combines Level 0 data to identify individual security events as they are inferred from multiple sensors. The players on the field are identified, from the host itself, to various data flows via normal socket connections, to attackers and the particular brand of intrusion being attempted. Examples of entities could be individual computers, adversaries, physical network connections, or flows of data between hosts. Individual computers are described with source data (obtained at the Sensing level), such as information about the system's physical location, as well as other features such as its operating system, hardware, patches, installed software, CPU utilization, security log, etc. Intrusions may be inferred via source data such as intrusion alert data from a NIDS such as Snort or Cisco, or host-based IDS information such as security logs or anti-malware software. Adversaries may be described as known or unknown, or in terms of characteristics such as source location or attack methods used. Table 2 lists examples of entities and source data.

The output of a Level 1 fusion system is a list of entities and their properties. The implementation of a specific fusion system may have a limited scope or focus. For instance, a fusion system might combine all of the known intrusion detection data from multiple IDS reports and report a single intrusion (or attack) as being compromised of multiple IDS alerts. Such a correlation might aid the human analyst in being able to manage a limited number of attacks.

Combining sensor data to provide entity identification can involve a wide variety of algorithm types (Hall and McMullen, 2004). In the area of cyber security, the algorithms typically involve matching hostnames, IP addresses, and other similarly known data, because different systems may report their findings based on different key factors. However, some cyber security systems provide data that is not 100% confirmed. For example, IDSs provide alert data that is plagued by high false positive rates and with lower successful detection rates. Because some IDSs have different capabilities—including pattern matching and anomaly detection methods—outputs from multiple IDSs may be fused to provide higher levels of reliability and lower false positive rates. Rapid pattern matching/data mining techniques such as

Table 2. Examples of entities and source data

Entity	Source Data Examples
Defended Host	• Physical Location • Hardware Details • Operating System • List of Patches Applied • Application Level Software Installed • CPU and Memory Utilization • Applications Currently Running • End-User Account Access Data • Security Log Data • Classification of Data Stored on the System
Intrusion	• IDS Type and Location • Source Address • Destination Address • Attack Method • Time of Attack
Attacker	• Source Address(es) • Methods of Attack
Flows of Data	• Source and Destination Addresses • Type of Traffic (Protocols Used) • Traffic Volume • Encryption Used

neural networks and support vector machines can be used to classify similar types of data from different classifying engines. These rapid, automated techniques can be helpful in fusing high volume, low reliability data from multiple different systems to provide a better, more reliable output. Figure 3 provides an example of such a system.

Level 2 Situation Refinement: Awareness

Level 2 summarizes the current system state based on the active entities. Processing at this level involves developing a contextual understanding of Level 1 information. The goal is to combine multiple individual entities to provide a perspective of the system's current state. Entities are typically complex and have many features, and sensors can only detect individual features. The Level 1 process potentially combines the multiple features of an individual entity. It is at Level 2

Figure 3. A Level 1/Object Refinement example of multiple IDSs monitoring same network traffic

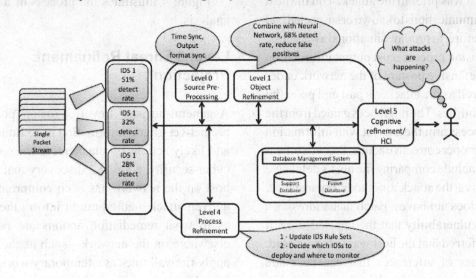

that entities are combined into a comprehensive picture of the current situation.

In the context of cyber security, an estimation of the system's overall health and ability for self defense, if attacked with a certain attack method, may be obtained by combining a number of system health indicators such as operating system patches installed, antivirus software definition set being used, or a list of processes running on the system. Representing all of this data for all systems (computers, servers, firewalls, VPN appliances, etc.) in a defended network can provide the analyst with an improved awareness of the current system state.

The algorithms that apply to Level 2 fusion involve pattern matching and automated reasoning (Hall and McMullen, 2004). As reports from a system on its own health (patch level, antivirus definitions, and so on) are matched against a known, desired state, systems that do not match the desired state can be flagged as being out of date, running undesired software or versions, or exhibiting undesired behaviors (high CPU load, low available drive space, high overall network traffic, etc).

The network's defensive posture may be assessed via the combined information about its specific devices. For example, each host on a network has its particular condition, which may be described in terms of its specific location, its network address, what specific version of an operating system it is running, what specific patches are installed, what the set of AV definitions are the basis of an antivirus program, or what specific application software is installed. Similar descriptors may also apply to other network devices, such as routers and firewalls. However, an entire network security state is not only the sum of its own parts. As the terrain includes "us and them," a complete description of a network's security state must also include a description of attackers' potential capabilities. An attacker's capability set and the known state of the network's defensive posture combine to create an awareness of the current system security level.

Assessing an attacker's capability involves taking into consideration attacks that have occurred and assessing the success level of those attacks. Inferences about whether or not the attacks were successful may be developed based on further investigation of the attacked host. For example: Are there new processes running since the attack? Does the host's security log provide additional relevant details? Is the host's configuration different than it was prior to the attack? Did the host initiate communications to known or suspected bad sites? Therefore, to provide situational awareness, a Level 2 fusion process must output information about the defensive posture of the network under attack, as well as the attacker's past and potential future capabilities. The inferences gained from the Level 2 process arm the analyst with information needed for proper corrective action. Proactive measures may include comparing the host's defensive capabilities vs. the attack's methods. For instance, if the host does not have a patch that addresses a particular vulnerability that the attacker uses, it could be inferred that the host was compromised.

The types of inferences that can be made depend on the lowest level in the process: the types of sensors in place. For instance, Data Leak Protection (DLP) sensors could be used to identify whether an intruder has attempted to access or send sensitive data from the protected host. If a host has been compromised, the analyst may decide to remove the host from the network and perform some kind of forensic analysis. Or if a given host has not received or applied updates, this could be an indicator of a management system failure, indicating policy- or workflow-related issues that require attention.

Figure 4 illustrates the process of a Level 2 analysis.

Level 3 Threat Refinement: Projection

A general-purpose Level 3 fusion process is predictive, giving information as to future states and likely actions of attackers. In the context of cyber-security, a Level 2 discovery that a single host on the network has been compromised by a given attack method might inform the analyst as to what remediation actions are necessary elsewhere on the network—such as the need to apply firewall rules as a temporary work-around to address a zero-day exploit until patches can be rolled out. But a predictive, Level 3 understanding of an attacker's possible capabilities (knowing that a specific zero-day exploit is a possibility) could trigger the same action preemptively, before the exploit occurs.

A repository like the Common Vulnerabilities and Exposures (CVE) Database (http://cve.mitre. org) may provide insights into the attacker's options. However, data from these systems need to be coordinated with the defensive posture of the defended network. The simple knowledge of

Figure 4. A Cyber Security Level 2/Awareness Fusion System Example

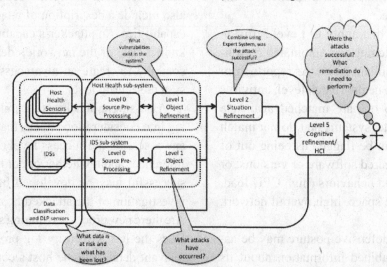

a potential attack option is of little use without knowledge of what is likely to result should that attack be used on a given network with its particular set of defensive capabilities (patches, firewalls, IDS/IPS actions, etc). Additionally the data from the CVE database is so vast and changes so quickly that human attempts to process it manually would be unfeasible. An automated fusion process would combine an understanding of an attack, referenced in the CVE database, with the current set of hosts in the network and their "health." From this combination, a list of exploits to which the network is vulnerable could be inferred. From that list of vulnerabilities, additional defensive system capabilities could be evaluated to determine whether an attacker would likely be successful with a particular attack method. Based on this determination, the analyst could decide whether additional actions need to be taken—which could take the form patches to apply, firewall rules to configure, IDS/IPS actions to take, etc. A prioritized decision of which actions to take could be informed by understanding what data that is at risk (from data classification sensors) on given hosts.

It is also helpful to understand an attacker's capabilities from a "tool perspective": what tools are at the attacker's disposal and how those tools may be updated. Knowledge of the tools and methods of attackers, and how those tools integrate new exploits as they become available, are all invaluable in understanding the capabilities of an attacker.

A Level 0/1 assessment of attack options available to the attacker could provide an understanding of what the attacker is likely to do next. While a novice attacker might simply use every attack option available, a more sophisticated attacker might try rudimentary attacks and then choose new attack methods based on the feedback received from initial attempts. A Level 3 projection system is illustrated in Figure 5.

Supporting Processes: Fusion Levels 4, 5

Levels 4 and 5 of the JDL Model can be considered supporting levels. In terms of the fusion process, they do not add any inferencing capabilities. However, they are extremely important to the overall functioning of the system. Level 4 is process

Figure 5. A cyber security level 3/projection fusion system example

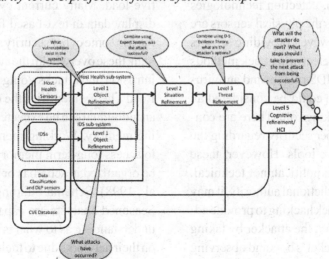

refinement, characterized by the management and update of sensor capabilities – giving sensors new detection capabilities, tuning sensors to detect specific situations, or placement and management of sensors. Level 5 is cognitive refinement, characterized by the ability to interface with the human analyst. Specific refinements can aid or detract from the analyst's ability to understand the information presented by the system.

Level 4 Process Refinement: Sensor Management and Selection

In a general purpose fusion system, Level 4 addresses the system's capability to task sensors and maintain their health. Here, adjustments are made based on the predictive inferences gained in Level 3, allowing the analyst to narrow the terrain and zoom in on certain activities. Hall and McMullen (2004) describe this level as a meta-process that is tasked with observing the fusion system and that takes input from outside of that system. In military fusion contexts, the decision of where to "look" and which sensors to use may be dictated by the mission objectives. The use of certain technologies in a military application (radar, sonar, etc.) may be contraindicated in certain missions or parts of the mission (where stealth is a mission requirement, for example).

In the cyber domain, detection technologies are not as controllable as the physical sensors are in military contexts. However, providing sensors with the capabilities to detect new attack methods (through updates to the IDS rule set and antivirus definition, for example) could be considered an example of a sensor tasking role. There are constraints in defensive cyber security regarding the use of passive vs. active tools. However, these constraints are legal and political, not technical. Under proper legal jurisdictional authority, it may be possible to employ back hacking to provide additional information about the attacker by taking control of one of the attacker's bots and observing its command and control functions.

Even in a purely defensive operational mode, the selection of which tools to use and what activities to monitor represents a Level 4 function with a human-in-the-loop providing mission requirements. An example of this would be monitoring for specific types of traffic (for example, the presence of IRC traffic, or connections to servers/hosts in foreign countries) as an indicator of compromised hosts on the network. If a host on the network starts opening a number of connections to computers on the Internet on Port 25, a border monitoring service could alert an analyst of a possible spam-bot infection on that host. As new compromise methods are found, specific monitoring tools can be deployed by the analyst to observe evidence of those compromises. In cyber security (as of this writing), these Level 4 processes are generally manual and therefore slow to deploy.

Level 5 Cognitive Refinement and HCI

Level 5 is the interface between the human analyst and the data fusion system. Compared to data fusion in other domains, in the domain of network security, analysts are burdened with two confounding issues.

The first is that high data rates increase cognitive load. Many current cyber security systems display data in text-based formats. As false alert rates in some cyber security systems are extremely high, these overwhelm the analyst and result in real intrusion and attacks going unnoticed. Cognitive Load Theory identifies the quantity of items that an individual can be expected to maintain in working memory. Working memory is, in turn, used to access long-term memory, which is thought to be organized in schemas or structures (Sweller et al., 1998). Schema building is time consuming. Seasoned analysts are capable of high levels of understanding as to what is normal and abnormal on their networks due to their experience, and their ability to match current scenarios to previously-built schemas (D'Amico and Whitley, 2007).

In the 1999 revision of the JDL Data Fusion Process Model diagrams, the HCI part of the system appears to accept inputs from the highest level of the fusion process (Liggins, et al., 2008). However, the description of the Level 5 fusion process has been clarified to indicate that the HCI interface should provide access to and human control at each level of the fusion process (Blasch and Plano, 2002). The design mantra of "Overview, Filter/Zoom and Details-on-Demand" provides a suggestion for how to organize and display data in an information visualization system (Schneiderman, 1996). Following this mantra, HCI for a network security data fusion system should present the security analyst with an overview of the defended system's current state. The analyst should have the ability to zoom into a specific region of the defended network (even to the level of an individual host), select specific details from the raw data, and filter them to select specific details. This level of detail capability is an important sense-making feature for the analyst's cognitive schema creation and maintenance processes, and addresses relevant forensic and legal reporting requirements.

This brings to light the second issue in Level 5 in cyber security: the lack of a shared mental model of the problem space. Because the "terrain" is virtual, a given analyst may have a different mental picture of what the defended network "looks like" than the data fusion system designer, or even other security analysts. While a representation of the defended network may take the form of the physical terrain, there really is no physical space constraint. Often, logical topologies are more suitable to representing the workspace. It should be noted that a single, optimal representation is unlikely to be created. The goal of Level 5 should be to present the data in such a way as to leverage the analyst's understanding of the cyber workspace and allow the analyst to access security information at all levels of the system.

The next section explores a specific type of cognitive refinement, the presentation of information through an auditory display (sonification).

SONIFICATION

Earlier Work in Pattern Recognition and Cyber Security

Earlier work in the area of pattern recognition and cyber security has dealt with entropy as applied to aggregates of activity. Evans and Barnett (2002) demonstrate that the Kolmogorov Complexity, which is a measure of a text string's predictability, or its "noisiness," is a factor in detecting FTP attacks. Complexity was estimated by using the utility tcpdump (http://tcpdump.org/) to convert packets to ASCII strings, which were then compressed. Packets that included various intrusions were compressed to smaller sizes, indicating that the presence of intrusions can be found in patterns that are not present in the "noise" of normal network activity.

Gu et al. (2005) describe using maximum entropy in the detection of everyday network traffic anomalies such as worms, port scans, and denial of service attacks. They create a multi-dimensional classification system for packets according to destination port numbers and protocol (TCP, UDP, TCP SYN, or TCP RST). A baseline distribution was determined showing normal distribution of packet traffic. If traffic differed from the baseline by a certain amount, an alarm was raised. Eiland and Liebrock (2006) also show differences in Kolmogorov Complexity when packets are concatenated into equal time windows and compressed. Packets containing intrusions attempts are more compressible, again implying that reduced complexity implies likely presence of an intrusion attempt.

Justification for Auditory Display

Lowered entropy levels in the presence of intrusion of attempts suggests that sonification may be an appropriate means to explore enhanced situational awareness. Normal server traffic is random; in contrast, intrusion attempts, being more compressible, suggest a greater level of repetitiveness in the traffic. This quality plays into the benefits of sonifications, which exploit the auditory system's high sensitivity to periodicity, temporal changes, and pattern recognition. Therefore, an effective sonification of network activity could be expected to sound different during intrusion attempts. Normal traffic would presumably sound random and "noisy," while traffic containing intrusion attempts would sound more "regular," producing pattern-based renderings with noticeable rhythms or melodies.

Our sonification approach represents an attempt to capitalize on both musical and everyday listening (described in the Background section) by creating a familiar sound that is capable of subtle yet easily perceptible changes. Our goal is to build enough layers of potential subtlety that experienced listeners can gain increased levels of understanding. While certain conditions must be readily apparent, our hope is that continued listening can yield insights beyond those that are immediately obvious.

There are, as yet, no standardized software tools for sonification work. Researchers typically make custom applications of some type of software sound synthesis (SWSS) program. Such programs, the basis of computer music (Roads, 1996), have existed since the 1950s. We sonify the data with the SWSS program SuperCollider (http://supercollider.sourceforge.net/), a specialized programming language designed for real-time audio applications. SuperCollider displays exceptional versatility, with capabilities including real time signal processing, algorithmic composition and inter-machine remote control. SuperCollider is well suited to our sonification model because of its computational efficiency, its array and list processing capability, its methodology for generating musical events (Streams) according to a programmer's instructions, and its interactive potential through the use of custom-designed graphical user interfaces (GUIs).

Our interface is a mixing board-like onscreen control surface. Its functionality follows the design of our earlier work in cardiac data sonification (Ballora et al., 2004). Users can start, pause, and reset playback via buttons; speed up or slow the rate at which the dataset is traversed; or scrub the dataset so that playback may start from any arbitrary point, with the timestamp of the current position displayed visually; and separate volume sliders for the rumble and sizzle components.

Sonification Strategies

A gong is an instrument possessing a high degree of subtlety. Stockhausen (1965) created an entire musical work based on instructions on how to play a gong. It is notable for the various types of strikers it calls for—besides mallets and drumsticks, the score calls for paper clips, erasers, and other everyday objects used to elicit unique sounds from the instrument. The score also contains detailed directions on where microphones should be placed to capture the various sound subtleties, and how the sound should be processed with a variety of filters and modulators. The performing ensemble consists of gong players, microphone operators, and filter operators.

The sound of a gong is commonly described in two stages, informally called the "rumble" and the "sizzle." By studying spectrograms of gongs, we have created a synthesized gong-like sound, which is based on eight frequency values (some of which are duplicated and multiplied by non-integer values to create the inharmonic sound inherent in gongs). A force factor between 0 and 1 also affects the amplitude of the frequencies and the timing and relative amplitude of the sizzle, so that higher force values produce the sound of a gong being hit with greater strength.

Our dataset consists of simulated traffic dumps that have become standard reference documents in the area of intrusion detection (Lippmann et al., 2000). Each data point is an array consisting of information about a packet received by the network server. We work with information about the socket connections each packet exchange reflect; the array representing each data point includes the date and time of the exchange, the sender's IP address and port number, and the receiver's IP address and port number.

We map each socket exchange to a strike of the gong, with the type and placement of the strike based on the packets' source and destination IP octets. The rumble's timbre is based on the values of the sending IP octet, and the sizzle's timbre is created from the four values of the receiving octet.

Each strike's force value is derived from how often identical IP values are connected. We keep a running list of packets previously received, with the length being adjustable. With each packet, the list is scanned for the same socket values. A higher percentage of these values in the list indicates an ongoing "conversation," and produces a stronger force value for the gong.

The panning of each strike is more abstract. While we would like to create a stereo pan position based on the geographic locations of the sender, so that packets received from Asia would appear at a very different pan position than packets received from South America, for example, obtaining geographic information on an IP address is not an automatic process, and requires querying external registries. As an alternative, we simply create a unique pan position based on the sender-receiver IP values, so that each combination of IP octets is mapped to a unique stereo pan position between -1 for extreme left and 1 for extreme right.

This design is meant to incorporate a great deal of frequency, timbre, and panning subtlety of the instrument. Given the range of IP values, we have a large amount of resolution in these sound parameters, producing changes that are very much microscopic in nature. This produces a subtle control source that is often difficult to obtain with other, more standard synthesis techniques. The changes in each parameter are unlikely to be terribly informative in and of themselves. Hearing small changes in pan position, for example, would likely be impossible, but in combination with the other pitch and timbral changes that might accompany it, the panning might add a useful layer of discrimination. By assigning characteristics of the data to as many parameters of the sound as possible, we leave the door open for unexpected auditory gestalts to emerge, which may enable analytical everyday listening in unforeseen ways.

In using a gong timbre, we are hoping to create an implicit step from a Level 1 fusion to Level 2. The individual packets represent raw, de-contextualized data. They are analogous to individual pixels from an image or video. Randomly distributed packets received should sound like a low rumble appearing throughout the stereo field. The presence of distinct entities, in the form of ongoing connections, will produce more forceful gong strikes, giving an immediate indication of their presence. This is akin to being able to recognize figures from a video from the aggregate of pixels. The gong model is meant to bring out aggregates in the data, implicitly identifying discrete entities.

The receiving port numbers are used in the creation of other types of "sound effects." Common ports (0-1023) are mapped to a plucked string sound, a generalization of the model used by Chafe and Leistikow (2001), with each port number producing a distinct pitch within a range of four octaves. Port scans can be readily perceived as melodic runs up or down. If no port number is included, indicating that the message protocol is ICMP rather than the more common TCP or UDP, the sound of two stones clicking together is produced. A series of ICMP messages produces a motor-like sequence of cracking sounds, which is recognizable to even the most untrained ears.

Figure 6. Overview of MURI research approach

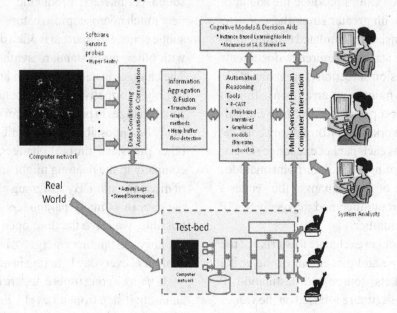

FUTURE DIRECTIONS FOR CYBER SITUATION AWARENESS

The work of implementing data fusion capabilities in the cyber security domain is still in its infancy. At Penn State University multiple researchers are collaborating to address the area of cyber situation awareness and information fusion, funded by an Army Research Office (ARO) Multidisciplinary University Research Initiative (MURI) grant. The MURI research involves a multi-university team. Figure 6 provides a top-level view of the research activities, including work on the data input/sensing area, information aggregation and correlation, automated data fusion, cognitive models to assist analyst decision making, and multi-sensory (e.g., visualization and sonification) techniques to support analyst pattern recognition and anomaly detection. In addition, work is underway to develop a test bed to support analysis of tools for improved individual, team, and hybrid cognition.

This chapter describes the theoretical model in terms that cyber security researchers will find familiar, but is incomplete. This explanation of the model will need additional revision to include

other areas of cyber security that are not addressed in this paper. This work is predicated on the organizational level of the problem space, but different individuals and small networks have their own needs that are not addressed in this paper. However, even in this organizational level assessment, more work needs to be done in several areas of development including sensors, algorithms and Human Computer Interaction (HCI).

Sensor Development

Additional sensors need to be developed to provide evidence of cyber security status. Sensors could be simple, ad-hoc software tools on each system in a defended network. They could take on the form of complex intrusion detection and prevention systems. However, a number of already existing systems in the enterprise environment could be leveraged as sensors. The most obvious include antivirus systems, centralized management systems (Microsoft SMS, for example), patch management systems, centralized authentication systems (Active Directory, OpenLDAP, among others), host log files, and other similar tools that exist in the enterprise, but remain untapped for fused cyber security systems.

Algorithm Development

Algorithms need to be developed at all levels of the JDL model. The hints as to which algorithms might be most fruitful in specific situations should be taken from other data fusion domains. It is not so much that new algorithms need to be invented; rather, existing algorithms need to be selected and applied to the problem space of cyber security. The high data rate of elements in cyber security might pose unique problems and limitations, but algorithm choice for lower vs. higher levels of fusion could be guided by successes in other domains.

Human Computer Interaction

The human-computer interaction aspect of the fusion process is the level that needs the most attention. The analyst needs access to all levels of the fusion process, not simply the highest level available. Awareness of the individual entities active in the current situation, and their properties, requires that the analyst have the ability to access the system from the highest representation down to the lowest data element available. These qualities are also vital components of the analyst's ability to respond to legal requirements and requests for forensic analyses and details. However, the analyst has only a limited (human) capacity to observe and interpret these details. New HCI development needs to take the analyst's cognitive capabilities into consideration in order to reduce fatigue and support attention to the important details of the security situation.

Sonification

Much remains to be discovered about the nature of the sonification described here. Its specific implementations may vary, depending on the needs of the analyst. One use would be to have it running at all times, as an unobtrusive background sound. Our hearing is part of the situational awareness of everyday living. Anecdotal examples include sudden changes in the ambient sound of our house or workplace. These environments contain a variety of ambient sounds, from the electrical and plumbing systems, to ventilation, and the sounds created by devices such as refrigerators, copiers, or outdoor traffic. Changes in the normal behavior in any of these areas can alert our attention instantly to a situational difference of some kind.

Another use would be as a means of quickly reviewing the activity of a period of time when no analysts are on duty. An analyst beginning a day's work might start by listening to what occurred during the night over the span of a few minutes, getting a quick overview of whether or not anything unusual happened.

However, our purpose here is not so much to present a full solution, but rather to make a convincing case for our intuition that the auditory system cannot be ignored as new forms of rendering information are developed. As sources of information become increasingly intricate and dense, it seems unrealistic to expect that only one sense, the visual, will be able to find meaning in it. Use of sound as a complement to a visual display, or as an option in a flexible multi-modal display, seems inevitable. Sonification software for astrophysical datasets developed for use by blind researchers (Candey, et. al., 2005) is often preferred by sighted colleagues, who find that they are better able to discern patterns by listening to the data, rather than studying visual plots.

Our design goal is to maximize realization through frequency, timbre, and panning, to gain subtlety in the sound of the instrument. As discussed earlier, applying IPv6's possible range of 2^{128} addresses to discrete pan positions between a left and right speaker may at first seem simply absurd. Minute changes in stereo positioning will occur, well below what is easily perceptible. On the other hand, it does no harm to add this dimension to the realization. Many factors of hearing, such as timbre perception or loudness, are termed *emergent properties* to describe a combination that is more than the sum of its parts (acoustically, they are difficult to describe through objective measurements). These emergent gestalts may enable analytical everyday listening in unforeseen ways, as stereo position, frequency, timbral and other parameters combine to create additional layers of discrimination via their cumulative effects.

While further synthesis processes will be developed, another avenue of exploration could be that of machine learning, and adopting principles described by Rowe (2001), which are principles of artificial intelligence applied to automated analysis of music. Just as a computer can be taught to "listen" to a performer and improvise a duet, which the computer creates based on past information received from the performer, so too might these principles of pattern recognition be used to identify patterns in the network traffic flow, and used to create recognizable musical signatures.

HUMAN CENTRIC INFORMATION FUSION FOR CYBER SECURITY

Human centric information in the cyber security realm involves contextualizing the information provided by the cyber security system. New data available from the trade press about new viruses and worms are only a beginning. As new malware activities emerge, current practice is to share that information with other cyber defenders, generally on closed-membership lists and mechanisms. This information in its raw form may be found in blog entries and electronic mail communications on specific types of network behavior.

However, context can also come from the organization hosting the network. If the network security apparatus is carefully watching access to specific files on the file server, for instance, then new employee assignments or organizational structure changes might well provide context to interpret the file access logs. Help desk reports can be used at a high level as potential indicators of malware as well as general system performance issues.

In a grander focus on network security, depending on the organization's overall mission, news reports of geopolitical actions might give context to the current cyber security data. For instance, if the organization has international interests in China, then current political situations in China might provide context for understanding cyber actions attributable to Chinese national interests.

This soft data may come from a variety of sources, including online resources such as blogs or email lists, textual reports from other analysts and end-users, or even refined news reports. Fusion of this soft data with IDS alerts, firewall logs, traffic flow data and other similar hard data is complex. However, it offers the potential for higher levels of inference and improved true situational awareness.

CONCLUSION

We anticipate that this challenging research area will require multi-disciplinary efforts and seek to work on multiple areas including:

1. algorithms and techniques to address the "inside the machine" problem (viz. new software sensors, improved data mining, automated alert techniques, reactive immune-type cyber systems that are resilient to attacks, smart data that "knows" who should be allowed access, etc.); and

2. "outside the machine" techniques to improve the ability of analysts to understand (a) an evolving cyber situation, (b) identify and predict threats, and (c) develop collaborative decision making methods.

We believe that success in this domain will require simultaneously addressing both areas, from both directions: starting at the attack and data end and moving towards the user/analyst, and starting at the human cognition process and moving towards the data. Ultimately the efforts will need to model and illuminate not only the cyber-space environment but also the human landscape to address the cyber attacks.

ACKNOWLEDGMENT

Research described in this chapter was supported in part by a Multidisciplinary University Research Initiative (MURI) grant from the Army Research Office (ARO) under the direction of Dr. Cliff Wang.

REFERENCES

Antony, R. (2008). Data management support to tactical data fusion. In Liggins, M. E., Hall, D. L., & Llinas, J. (Eds.), *Handbook of multi-sensor data fusion: Theory and practice* (2nd ed., pp. 619–653). Boca Raton, FL: CRC Press. doi:10.1201/9781420053098.ch24

Ballora, M. Pennycook, B., Ivanov, P. Ch., Glass, L., & Goldberger, A. L. (2004). Heart rate sonification: A new approach to medical diagnosis. *Leonardo, 37*, 41–46. doi:10.1162/002409404772828094

Bass, T. (2000). Intrusion detection systems and multisensor data fusion. *Communications of the ACM, 43*(4), 99–105. doi:10.1145/332051.332079

Blasch, E. P., & Plano, S. (2002). JDL level 5 fusion model: User refinement issues and applications in group tracking. [SPIE]. *Proceedings - Society of Photo-Optical Instrumentation Engineers, 4729*, 270–279.

Bregman, A. (1990). *Auditory scene analysis: The perceptual organization of sound*. Cambridge, MA: MIT Press.

Candey, R. M., Schertenleib, A. M., & Diaz Merced, W. L. (2005, December). *Sonification prototype for space physics*. Presentation at American Geophysical Union, Fall Meeting 2005, abstract #ED43B-0850, San Francisco, CA.

Chafe, C., & Leistikow, R. (2001, July). *Levels of temporal resolution in sonification of network performance*. Paper presented at the 2001 International Conference on Auditory Display, Helsinki University of Technology, Espoo, Finland.

D'Amico, A., & Whitley, K. (2007, October). *The real work of computer network defense analysts*. Paper presented at the Workshop on Visualization for Computer Security (VizSEC 2007), Sacramento, CA.

Eiland, E. E., & Liebrock, L. M. (2006). An application of information theory to intrusion detection. *Proceedings of the Fourth IEEE International Workshop on Information Assurance (IWIA '06)* (pp. 119-134). Washington, DC: IEEE Computer Society Washington.

Evans, S. C., & Barnett, B. (2002, October). *Network security through conservation of complexity*. Paper presented at IEEE Military Communications Conference (MILCOM) 2002, Anaheim, CA.

Gilfix, M., & Couch, A. (2000, December). *Peep (the network auralizer): Monitoring your network with sound*. Paper presented at the 14th Systems Administration Conference (2000 LISA XIV), New Orleans, LA.

Gu, Y., McCallum, A., & Towsley, D. (2005). Detecting anomalies in network traffic using maximum entropy estimation. *ICM '05 Proceedings of the 5th ACM SIGCOMM Conference on Internet Measurement*, (pp. 345-350). Berkeley, CA: USENIX Association.

Hall, D., & McMullen, S. (2004). *Mathematical techniques in multisensor data fusion*. Norwood, MA: Artech House.

Hall, D. L., & Jordan, J. (2010). *Human centered information fusion*. Norwood, MA: Artech House.

Hermann, T. (2002). *Sonification for exploratory data analysis*. Unpublished doctoral dissertation, Bielefeld University, Germany.

Kessler, O., Askin, K., Beck, N., Lynch, J., White, F., & Buede, D. (1991). *Functional description of the data fusion process*. Warminster, PA: Office of Naval Technology, Naval Air Development Center.

Kramer, G. (Ed.). (1994). *Auditory display: Sonification, audification, and auditory interfaces. Santa Fe Institute Studies in the Sciences of Complexity (Vol. 18)*. Reading, MA: Addison Wesley.

Liang, Y., Wang, H., & Lai, J. (2007, August). *Quantification of network security situational awareness based on evolutionary neural network*. Paper presented at 2007 International Conference on Machine Learning and Cybernetics, Hong Kong, China.

Liggins, M. E., Hall, D. L., & Llinas, J. (Eds.). (2008). *Handbook of multisensor data fusion: Theory and practice* (2nd ed.). Boca Raton, FL: CRC Press.

Lippmann, R. P., Fried, D. J., Graf, I., Haines, J. W., Kendall, K. R., & McClung, D. … Zissman, M. A. (2000). Evaluating intrusion detection systems: The 1998 DARPA off-line intrusion detection evaluation. *Proceedings of the 2000 DARPA Information Survivability Conference and Exposition (DISCEX)*, vol. 2 (pp. 12-26). Los Alamitos, CA: IEEE Computer Society Press.

Liu, X., Wang, H., Lai, J., & Liang, Y. (2007, November). *Network security situation awareness model based on heterogeneous multi-sensor data fusion*. Paper presented at 22nd International Symposium on Computer and Inormation Sciences, Ankara, Turkey.

McNeese, M. D. (1986). Humane intelligence: A human factors perspective for developing intelligent cockpits. *IEEE Aerospace and Electronic Systems Magazine, 1*(9), 6–12. doi:10.1109/MAES.1986.5005199

Palser, B. (2005). *Hurricane Katrina: Aftermath of disaster*. Bloomington, IN: Compass Point Books.

Perusich, K. A., & McNeese, M. D. (2006). Using fuzzy cognitive maps for knowledge management in a conflict environment. *IEEE Systems. Man and Cybernetics, 36*(6), 810–821.

Pinker, S. (1999). *How the mind works*. New York, NY: W.W. Norton & Company.

Roads, C. (1996). *The computer music tutorial*. Cambridge, MA: MIT Press.

Rowe, R. (2001). *Machine musicianship*. Cambridge, MA: MIT Press.

Schummer, T., & Lukosch, S. (2007). *Patterns for computer mediated interaction*. Hoboken, NJ: Wiley.

Shneiderman, B. (1996, September). *The eyes have it: A task by data type taxonomy for information visualizations*. Paper presented at the 1996 IEEE Symposium on Visual Languages, Boulder, CO.

Smith, J. O. (1992). Physical modeling using digital waveguides. *Computer Music Journal, 16*(2), 74–91. doi:10.2307/3680470

Steinberg, A. N., Bowman, C. L., & White, F. E. (1999). Revisions to the JDL data fusion model. In B. V. Dasarathy (Ed.), *Sensor Fusion, Architectures, Algorithms and Applications III, Proceedings of the Society of Photo-Optic Instrumentation Engineers (SPIE), 3719,* (pp. 430-441). Bellingham, WA: SPIE Publications.

Stockhausen, K. (1965). *Mikrophonie I, no. 15, for tam-tam, 2 microphones, 2 filters and potentiometers.* Vienna, Austria: Universal Edition.

Sweller, J., Van Merrienboer, J., & Paas, F. (1998). Cognitive architecture and instructional design. *Educational Psychology Review, 10*(3), 251–296. doi:10.1023/A:1022193728205

Thomas, C., & Balakrishnan, N. (2008, July). *Performance enhancement of intrusion detection systems using advances in sensor fusion.* Paper presented at the 11th International Conference on Information Fusion, Cologne, Germany.

Tian, J., Zhao, W., Du, R., & Zhang, Z. (2005, December). *D-S evidence theory and its data fusion application in intrusion detection.* Paper presented at Sixth International Conference on Parallel and Distributed Computing, Applications and Technologies, Dalian, China.

Wang, H., Lai, J., & Liu, X. (2007, August). *Network security situational awareness based on heterogeneous multi-sensor data fusion and neural network.* Paper presented at Second International Multi-Symposiums on Computer and Computational Sciences (IMSCCS), Iowa City, IA.

ADDITIONAL READING

Ballora, M. (2000). *Data Analysis through Auditory Display: Applications in Heart Rate Variability.* Unpublished doctoral dissertation, McGill University, Montreal.

Barrass, S. (1997). *Auditory Information Design.* Unpublished doctoral dissertation, Australian National University.

Ben-tal, O., & Berger, J. (2004). Creative Aspects of Sonification. *Leonardo, 37*(3), 229–233. doi:10.1162/0024094041139427

Collins, N. (2010). *Introduction to Computer Music.* Hoboken, NJ: Wiley Books.

De Campo, A. (2009). *Science by Ear. An Interdisciplinary Approach to Sonifying Scientific Data.* Unpublished doctoral dissertation, Institute of Electronic Music and Acoustics – IEM, University for Music and Dramatic Arts Graz.

Dean, R. T. (Ed.). (1999). *The Oxford Handbook of Computer Music.* New York, NY: Oxford University Press.

Dodge, C., & Jerse, T. A. (1997). *Computer Music.* New York, NY: Schirmer Books.

Gogins, M. (1991). Iterated Functions Systems Music. *Computer Music Journal, 15*(1), 40–48. doi:10.2307/3680385

Handel, S. (1989). *Listening: An Introduction to the Perception of Auditory Events.* Cambridge, MA: MIT Press.

Hermmann, T., & Hunt, A. (Eds.). (2005). Interactive Sonification (Human Interaction with Auditory Displays) - Special issue. *IEEE MultiMedia, 12*(2).

Howe, J. (2008). *Crowdsourcing: Why the Power of the Crowd is Driving the Future of Business*. New York, NY: Crown Business.

International Community for Auditory Display. (www.icad.org). Web site has downloadable conferences proceedings dating back to its inception in 1992.

Jajodia, S., Liu, P., Swarup, V., & Wang, C. (2009). *Cyber Situational Awareness: Issues and Research* (1st ed.). New York, NY: Springer Publishing Company, Inc.

Moore, B. C. J. (1989). *An Introduction to the Psychology of Hearing* (3rd ed.). London: Harcourt Brace Jovanovich.

Moore, F. R. (1990). *Elements of Computer Music*. Englewood Cliffs, NJ: PTR Prentice Hall.

Pierce, J. R. (1983). *The Science of Musical Sound*. New York: Scientific American Books.

QCD-Audio. (http://qcd-audio.at/), a sonification research consortium of several Austrian universities.

Rossing, T. D. (1990). *The Science of Sound* (2nd ed.). Reading, MA: Addison-Wesley Publishing Company.

Sawyer, K. (2007). *Group Genius: The Creative Power of Collaboration*. New York, NY: Basic Books.

Wilson, S., Cottle, D., & Collins, N. (Eds.). (2011). *The SuperCollider Book*. Cambridge, MA: MIT Press.

Xenakis, I. (1971). *Formalized Music*. Indiana University Press: Bloomington Indiana. (Originally published 1963 as *Musique formelles*, Paris La Revue Musicale).

KEY TERMS AND DEFINITIONS

Data Fusion: Fusion of multi-sensor data for target tracking, identification, and threat assessment and situation awareness.

"Hard" Sensors: Physical sensors.

HCI: Human-Computer Interaction.

Hybrid Cognition: Human pattern recognition and reasoning with automated processing functions.

IDS: Intrusion Detection System.

JDL Data Fusion Process Model: A general-purpose reference model that describes the overall process of combining data from varied sources.

"Soft" Sensors: Human observers.

Sonification: The use of non-speech audio for purposes of conveying information.

Chapter 10
Usefulness of Sensor Fusion for Security Incident Analysis

Ciza Thomas
College of Engineering, India

N. Balakrishnan
Indian Institute of Science, India

ABSTRACT

Intrusion Detection Systems form an important component of network defense. Because of the heterogeneity of the attacks, it has not been possible to make a single Intrusion Detection System that is capable of detecting all types of attacks with acceptable levels of accuracy. In this chapter, the distinct advantage of sensor fusion over individual IDSs is proved. The detection rate and the false positive rate quantify the performance benefit obtained through the fixing of threshold bounds. Also, the more independent and distinct the attack space is for the individual IDSs, the better the fusion of Intrusion Detection Systems performs. A simple theoretical model is initially illustrated and later supplemented with experimental evaluation. The chapter demonstrates that the proposed fusion technique is more flexible and also outperforms other existing fusion techniques such as OR, AND, SVM, and ANN, using the real-world network traffic embedded with attacks.

INTRODUCTION

The probability of intrusion detection in a corporate environment protected by an Intrusion Detection Systems (IDS) is low because of various issues. The network IDSs have to operate on encrypted traffic packets where analysis of the packets is complicated. The high false alarm rate is generally cited as the main drawback of IDSs.

For IDSs that use machine learning technique for attack detection, the entire scope of the behavior of an information system may not be covered during the learning phase. Additionally, the behavior can change over time, introducing the need for periodic online retraining of the behavior profile. The information system can undergo attacks at the same time the intrusion detection system is learning the behavior. As a result, the behavior profile

DOI: 10.4018/978-1-4666-0104-8.ch010

contains intrusive behavior, which is not detected as anomalous. In the case of signature-based IDSs, one of the biggest problems is maintaining state information for signatures in which the intrusive activity encompasses multiple discrete events (i.e., the complete attack signature occurs in multiple packets on the network). Another drawback is that the misuse detection system must have a signature defined for all possible attacks that an attacker may launch against the network. This leads to the necessity for frequent signature updates to keep the signature database of the misuse detection system up-to-date.

Many of the IDS technologies are complement to each other, since for different kind of environments some approaches perform better than others. The processes followed by IDS operations for detecting intrusions are mainly by monitoring and analyzing the network activities, by finding vulnerable parts in a network, or by integrity testing of sensitive and important data. If a single IDS is to monitor all these activities, the complexity of the IDS becomes unacceptably large. If we look at the present day information system security, a network intrusion detection system would be considered the best choice to protect the machines from Denial of Service (DoS) attacks. At the same time, a host intrusion detection system would be the right choice to protect the systems from internal users. In order to protect against Trojans on systems, a file integrity checker might be more appropriate. To protect the servers from attackers, an intrusion prevention system could be the best bet. This shows that the sensors available in literature show distinct preference for detecting a certain attack with improved accuracy and that none of them shows good detection rate for all types of attacks or a complete intrusion detection coverage. Since an information system has to be protected from all types of attacks, it is most likely that we will actually need a combination of all these methods or sensors. This argument is ascertained in this chapter by looking at the usefulness of sensor fusion in intrusion detection systems.

In this chapter, the distinct advantage of sensor fusion over individual IDSs is proved. All the related work in the field of sensor fusion has been carried out mainly with one of the methods like probability theory, evidence theory, voting fusion theory, fuzzy logic theory or neural network in order to aggregate information. The Bayesian theory is the classical method for statistical inference problems. The fusion rule is expressed for a system of independent learners, with the distribution of hypotheses known a priori. The Dempster-Shafer decision theory is considered a generalized Bayesian theory. It does not require a priori knowledge or probability distribution on the possible system states like the Bayesian approach and it is mostly useful when modeling of the system is difficult or impossible (Wu, Seigel, Stiefelhagen, & Yang, 2002). An attempt to prove the distinct advantages of sensor fusion over individual IDSs is done in this chapter using the Chebyshev inequality. Threshold bounds of fusion unit are derived using the principle of Chebyshev inequality using the false positive rates and detection rates of the IDSs. The goal is to achieve best fusion performance with the least amount of model knowledge, in a computationally inexpensive way. Threshold bounds instead of a single threshold give more freedom in steering system properties. Any threshold within the bounds can be chosen depending on the preferred level of trade-off between detection and false alarms.

Simple theoretical model is initially illustrated in this chapter for the purpose of showing the improved performance of fusion IDS. The detection rate and the false positive rate quantify the performance benefit obtained through the fixing of threshold bounds. Also, the more independent and distinct the attack space is for the individual IDSs, the better the fusion IDS performs. The theoretical proof was supplemented with experimental evaluation, and the detection rates, false positive rates, and F-score were measured. In order to understand the importance of threshold, the anomaly-based IDSs, Packet Header Anomaly Detector (PHAD) and Application Layer Anomaly Detector (ALAD) have been individually analyzed. Preliminary experimental results prove the correctness of the theoretical proof. The chapter demonstrates that proposed fusion technique is more flexible and also outperforms other existing fusion techniques such as OR, AND, Support Vector Machine (SVM), and Artificial Neural Network (ANN) using the real-world network traffic embedded with attacks.

This chapter is organized as follows. Sensor fusion algorithms are initially discussed followed by the related work in this area. The analysis of detection error assuming traffic distribution is undertaken in this chapter. The paper also includes a complete modeling of the fusion IDS by defining proper threshold bounds. The validation of the theoretical model with the fusion of IDSs within the threshold bounds is demonstrated in this chapter. The chapter also includes a discussion on the practical impact of the proposed method. The conclusion of the chapter is finally drawn.

SENSOR FUSION ALGORITHMS

In this section, we provide state-of-the-art review in the area of intrusion detection based on sensor fusion approaches. Several approaches have been proposed for sensor fusion such as weighted average, fuzzy logic, neural networks, Bayesian Inference and probability techniques, Dempster-Shafer evidence theory and Kalman filters. Intrusion detection using machine learning algorithms has the advantage in identifying new or unknown data or signal that a machine learning system is not aware of during training.

MACHINE LEARNING FOR INTRUSION DETECTION

The most prominent works on data mining for intrusion detection have been conducted in University of New Mexico (S. Forrest and S. A Hofmeyr),

Purdue University (T. Lane and C. E. Brodley), Reliable Software Technologies (A. K. Ghosh, A. Schwartzbard, and M. Schatz), University of Minnesota (V. Kumar, P. Dokas, L. Ertoz, and A. Lazarevic), Columbia University (S. Stolfo and E. Eskin), North Carolina State University (W. Lee), Florida Institute of Technology (P. Chan and M. Mahoney), George Mason University (S. Jajodia, D. Barbara, and N. Wu), Arizona State University (Nong Ye). Of course, this list is not exhaustive. Different machine learning algorithms for sensor fusion include the statistical approaches, Artificial Neural Networks (ANN), Radial Basis Functions (RBF), Support Vector Machines (SVM) and Naive Bayes (NB) trees.

Statistical approaches are mostly based on modeling the data based on its statistical properties and using this information to estimate whether a test samples comes from the same distribution or not. The simplest approach can be based on constructing a density function for data of a known class, and then assuming that data is normal computing the probability of a test sample of belonging to that class. The probability estimate can be threshold to signal the intrusion. Two main approaches exist to the estimation of the probability density function, parametric and non-parametric methods. The parametric approach assumes that the data comes from a family of known distributions, such as the normal distribution and certain parameters are calculated to fit this distribution. However, in most real world situations, the underlying distribution of the data is not known and hence such techniques have little practical importance. In non-parametric methods the overall form of the density function is derived from the data as well as the parameters of the model. As a result non-parametric methods give greater flexibility in general systems.

A subjective view supports the use of artificial neural network for sensor fusion in order to achieve novelty detection in intrusion detection applications. The artificial neural networks gain experience by training the system to correctly identify the preselected examples of the problem. The computational complexity of neural networks has always been an important consideration for practical applications. One important consideration with neural networks is that they cannot be as easily retrained as statistical models. Retraining is done when new class data is to be added to the training set or when the training data no longer reflects the environmental conditions.

The support vector machine (SVM) is a supervised classification system that minimizes an upper bound on its expected error. It attempts to find the hyperplane separating two classes of data that will generalize best to future data. Such a hyperplane is the so called maximum margin hyperplane, which maximizes the distance to the closest points from each class. Generally, they work well when the number of features is magnitudes higher than the available training data. They also avoid the two problems of dimensionality; they generalize well to unseen data and they are efficient as they avoid explicit use of higher order dimensional spaces.

Bayes estimator is an estimator or decision rule that maximizes the posterior expected value of a utility function or minimizes the posterior expected value of a loss function. The estimator which minimizes the posterior expected loss also minimizes the Bayes risk like the mean square error and therefore is a Bayes estimator.

Decision trees (D-trees) dominate SVMs which in turn dominate NB in both the precision and recall values. However, D-trees show a much larger fluctuation in accuracy in the initial stages. This is to be expected because decision trees are known to be unstable classifiers. SVMs are better in the initial stages of active learning when the training data is small but they loose out later. SVMs are known to excel on accuracy but the uncertainty value measured as the distance from SVM separator is perhaps not too meaningful. D-trees turn out to be better in the combined metric. The complementary behavior of NB and the D-trees has given rise to their hybrid which outperforms most of the earlier methods for intrusion detection application.

RELATED WORK

Hall and McMullen (Hall, & McMullen, 2004) state that if the tactical rules of detection require that a particular certainty threshold must be exceeded for attack detection, then the fused decision result provides an added detection up to 25% greater than the detection at which any individual IDS alone exceeds the threshold. This added detection equates to increased tactical options and to an improved probability of true negatives (Hall, & McMullen, 2004). Another attempt to illustrate the quantitative benefit of sensor fusion is provided by Nahin and Pokoski (Nahin, & Pokoski, 1980). Their work demonstrates the benefits of multisensor fusion and their results also provide some conceptual rules of thumb. Aalo and Viswanathan (Aalo, & Viswanathan, 1989) perform numerical simulations of the correlation problems to study the effect of error correlation on the performance of a distributed detection systems. The system performance is shown to deteriorate when the correlation between the sensor errors is positive and increasing, while the performance improves considerably when the correlation is negative and increasing. Drakopoulos and Lee (Drakopoulos, & Lee, 1991) derive an optimum fusion rule for the Neyman-Pearson criterion, and use simulation to study its performance for a specific type of correlation matrix. Kam et al. (Kam, Zhu, & Gray, 1992) consider the case in which the class-conditioned sensor-to-sensor correlation coefficient are known, and expresses the result in compact form. Their approach is a generalization of the method adopted by Chair and Varshney (Chair, & Varshney, 1986) for solving the data fusion problem for fixed binary local detectors with statistically independent decisions. Kam et al. (Kam, Zhu, & Gray, 1992) use Bahadur-Lazarsfeld expansion of the probability density functions. Blum and Kassam (Blum, Kassam, & Poor) study the problem of locally most powerful detection for correlated local decisions.

ANALYSIS OF DETECTION ERROR ASSUMING TRAFFIC DISTRIBUTION

In this chapter, the Gaussian distribution is assumed for both the normal and the attack traffic due to its acceptability in practice. Often, the data available in databases is only an approximation of the true data.

When the information about the goodness of the approximation is recorded, the results obtained from the database can be interpreted more reliably. Any database is associated with a degree of accuracy, which is denoted with a probability density function, whose mean is the value itself. Formally, each database value is indeed a random variable; the mean of this variable becomes the stored value, and is interpreted as an approximation of the true value; the standard deviation of this variable is a measure of the level of accuracy of the stored value.

Assuming the attack connection and normal connection scores to have the mean values $y_i^{j=1} = \mu_1$ and $y_i^{j=0} = \mu_0$ respectively, $\mu_1 > \mu_0$ without loss of generality. Let σ_1 and σ_0 be the standard deviation of the attack connection and normal connection scores. The two types of errors committed by IDSs are often measured by False Positive rate (FP_{rate}) and False Negative rate (FN_{rate}). FP_{rate} is calculated by integrating the attack score distribution from a given threshold T in the score space to ∞, while FN_{rate} is calculated by integrating the normal distribution from $-\infty$ to the given threshold T.

$$FP_{rate} = \int_T^\infty \left(p^{k=0} \right) dy \qquad (1)$$

$$FN_{rate} = \int_{-\infty}^T \left(p^{k=1} \right) dy \qquad (2)$$

The threshold T is an unique point where the error is minimized, i.e., the difference between FP_{rate} and FN_{rate} is minimized by the following criterion:

$$T = \arg\min(FP_{rate} - FN_{rate}) \qquad (3)$$

At this threshold the resultant error due to FP_{rate} and FN_{rate} is a minimum. This is because the FN_{rate} is an increasing function (a cumulative density function, *cdf*) and FP_{rate} is a decreasing function (1 - *cdf*). T is the point where these two functions intersect. Decreasing the error introduced by the FP_{rate} and the FN_{rate} implies an improvement in the performance of the system. The fusion algorithm accepts decisions from many IDSs, where a minority of the decisions is false positives or false negatives. A good sensor fusion system is expected to give a result that accurately represents the decision from the correctly performing individual sensors, while minimizing the decisions from erroneous IDSs. Approximate agreement emphasizes precision, even when this conflicts with system accuracy. However, sensor fusion is concerned solely with the accuracy of the readings, which is appropriate for sensor applications. This is true despite the fact that increased precision within known accuracy bounds would be beneficial in most of the cases. Hence the following strategy is being adopted:

- The false alarm rate FP_{rate} can be fixed at an acceptable value α_0 and then the detection rate can be maximized. Based on the above criteria a lower bound on accuracy can be derived.
- The detection rate is always higher than the false alarm rate for every IDS, an assumption that is trivially satisfied by any reasonably functional sensor.
- Determine whether the accuracy of the IDS after fusion is indeed better than the accuracy of the individual IDSs in order to support the performance enhancement of fusion IDS.
- To discover the weights on the individual IDSs that gives the best fusion.

Given the desired false alarm rate which is acceptable, $FP_{rate} = \alpha_0$, the threshold (T) that maximizes the TP_{rate} and thus minimizes the FN_{rate};

$$TP_{rate} = \Pr[alert \, / \, attack] = \Pr[\sum_{i=1}^{n} w_i s_i \geq T \, | \, attack]$$

$$\tag{4}$$

$$FP_{rate} = \Pr[alert \, / \, normal] = \Pr[\sum_{i=1}^{n} w_i s_i \geq T \, | \, normal] = \alpha_0$$

$$\tag{5}$$

The fusion of IDSs becomes meaningful only when $FP \leq FP_i \forall i$ and $TP > TP_i > \forall i$. In order to satisfy these conditions, an adaptive or dynamic weighting of IDSs is the only possible alternative. Model of the fusion output is given as:

$$S = \sum_{i=1}^{n} w_i s_i$$

and

$$TP_i = \Pr[s_i = 1 | attack], FP_i = \Pr[s_i = 1 | normal]$$

where TP_i and FP_i are the detection rate and the false positive rate of an individual IDS indexed *i*. It is required to provide low value of weight to any individual sensor that is unreliable, hence meeting the constraint on false alarm as given in Equation 5. Similarly the fusion improves the TP_{rate} as the detectors get appropriately weighted according to their performance. One justification for this evaluation metric is that when searching large databases like the network traffic, it is more reasonable to have the results to be most relevant (precision), without caring whether all the relevant examples are seen (recall) or not. We choose the number α_0 depending on the proportion of attacks in the normal traffic (base-rate). This threshold is of course adjustable and one may vary the scale of the measured performance numbers by adjusting it. It also happens that these features' precision-

at-α_0 scores are quite distinct from one another, facilitating meaningful comparison.

Fusion of the decisions from various IDSs is expected to produce a single decision that is more informative and accurate than any of the decisions from the individual IDSs. Then the question arises as to whether it is optimal. Towards that end, a lower bound on variance for the fusion problem of independent sensors is presented in this work.

MODELING THE FUSION IDS BY DEFINING PROPER THRESHOLD BOUNDS

Every IDS participating in the fusion has its own detection rate D_i, and also positive rate F_i, due to the preferred heterogeneity of the sensors in the fusion process. Each IDS indexed *i* provided an alert or no-alert indicated by s_i taking a value of one or zero respectively. The fusion center collected these local decisions and formed a binomial distribution s, as given by $s = \sum_{i=1}^{n} s_i$, where *n* is the total number of IDSs taking part in the fusion.

Let D and F denote the unanimous detection rate and the false positive rate respectively. The mean and variance of s in case of attack and no-attack, are given by the following equations:

$$E[s|alert] = \sum_{i=1}^{n} D_i,$$

$$Var[s|alert] = \sum_{i=1}^{n} D_i(1 - D_i);$$

in case of attack

$$E[s|alert] = \sum_{i=1}^{n} F_i,$$

$$Var[s|alert] = \sum_{i=1}^{n} F_i(1 - F_i);$$

in case of no - attack

The fusion IDS is required to give a high detection rate and a low false positive rate. Hence the threshold T has to be chosen well above the mean of the false alerts and well below the mean of the true alerts. The threshold T is chosen at the point of overlap of the two parametric curves for normal and attack traffics. Consequently, the threshold bounds are given as:

$$\sum_{i=1}^{n} F_i < T < \sum_{i=1}^{n} D_i.$$

The detection rate and the false positive rate of the fusion IDS is desired to surpass the corresponding weighted averages and hence:

$$D > \frac{\sum_{i=1}^{n} D_i^2}{\sum_{i=1}^{n} D_i} \tag{6}$$

$$F < \frac{\sum_{i=1}^{n} (1 - F_i) F_i}{\sum_{i=1}^{n} (1 - F_i)} \tag{7}$$

Now, using simple range comparison,

$$D = \Pr\{s \geq T | attack\} = \Pr\{|s - \sum_{i-1}^{n} D_i \leq (\sum_{i=1}^{n} D_i - T)|attack\}$$

Using Chebyshev inequality on the random variable s, with $Mean = E[s] = \sum_{i=1}^{n} D_i$ and

$$Variance = Var[s] = \sum_{i=1}^{n} D_i(1 - D_i)$$

$$\Pr\{|s - E(s)| \geq k\} \leq \frac{Var(s)}{k^2}$$

With the assumption that the threshold T is greater than the mean of normal activity,

$$\Pr\{|s - \sum_{i-1}^{n} D_i \leq (\sum_{i=1}^{n} D_i - T)|attack\} \geq 1 - \frac{\sum_{i=1}^{n} D_i(1 - D_i)}{(\sum_{i=1}^{n} D_i - T)^2}.$$

From equation 6 it follows that

$$1 - \frac{\sum_{i=1}^{n} D_i(1 - D_i)}{(\sum_{i=1}^{n} D_i - T)^2} \geq \frac{\sum_{i=1}^{n} D_i^2}{\sum_{i=1}^{n} D_i}.$$

The upper bound of T is derived from the above equation as:

$$T \leq \sum_{i=1}^{n} D_i - \sqrt{\sum_{i=1}^{n} D_i}$$

Similarly, for the false positive rate, $F = \Pr\{s \geq T | no - attack\}$ in order to derive the lower bound of T,

From Equation 7 it follows that

$$\frac{\sum_{i=1}^{n} F_i(1 - F_i)}{(T - \sum_{i=1}^{n} F_i)^2} \leq \frac{\sum_{i=1}^{n} F_i(1 - F_i)}{\sum_{i=1}^{n} (1 - F_i)}.$$

The lower bound of T is derived from the above equation as:

$$T \geq \sum_{i=1}^{n} F_i + \sqrt{\sum_{i=1}^{n} (1 - F_i)}$$

The threshold bounds for the fusion IDS is:

$$[\sum_{i=1}^{n} F_i + \sqrt{\sum_{i=1}^{n} (1 - F_i)}, \sum_{i=1}^{n} D_i - \sqrt{\sum_{i=1}^{n} D_i}]$$

Since the threshold T is assumed to be greater than the mean of normal activity, the upper bound of false positive rate F can be obtained from the Chebyshev inequality as:

$$F \le \frac{Var[s]}{(T - E[s])^2} \qquad (8)$$

In a statistical intrusion detection system, a false positive is caused due to the variance of network traffic during normal operations. Hence, to reduce the false positive rate, it is important to reduce the variance of the normal traffic. In the ideal case, with normal traffic the variance is zero. The Equation 8 shows that as the variance of the normal traffic approaches zero, the false positive rate should also approach zero. Also, since the threshold T is assumed to be less than the mean of the intrusive activity, the lower bound of the detection rate D can be obtained from the Chebyshev inequality as:

$$D \le 1 - \frac{Var[s]}{(E[s] - T)^2} \qquad (9)$$

For an intrusive traffic, the factor $D_i (1 - D_i)$ remains almost steady and hence the variance given as:

$$Variance = \sum_{i=1}^{n} D_i(1 - D_i), \text{ is an appreciable}$$

value. Since the variance of the attack traffic is above a certain detectable minimum, from Equation 9, it is seen that the correct detection rate can approach an appreciably high value. Similarly the true negatives will also approach a high value since the false positive rate is reduced with IDS fusion.

It has been proved above that with IDS fusion, the variance of the normal traffic is clearly dropping down to zero and the variance of the intrusive traffic stays above a detectable minimum. This additionally supports the proof that the fusion IDS gives better detection rate and a tremendously low false positive rate.

RESULTS AND DISCUSSION

Choice and Modification of the Individual IDS

Taking into account the fact that the acceptable false alarm rate is extremely low, almost as low as the prior probability (Thomas & Balakrishnan, 2008b), the two IDSs PHAD (Mahoney, & Chan, 2001) and ALAD (Mahoney, & Chan, 2002), which give extremely low false alarm rate of the order of 0.00002 are considered in this work. For PHAD and ALAD, the Bayesian detection rate is of the order of 35% and 38% respectively. Thus one of the primary reasons for choosing the IDSs PHAD and ALAD was the requirement of acceptability in terms of the number of false alerts that does not overload a system administrator.

The other reason for the choice of PHAD and ALAD was that most of the existing IDS algorithms neglect the minority attack types, R2L and U2R in comparison to the majority attack types, Probes and DoS. ALAD is highly successful in detecting these rare attack types.

The detection performance of the anomaly detectors PHAD and ALAD can be improved further by training them on additional normal traffic other than the traffic of weeks one and three of the DARPA 1999 data set. To improve the performance of the IDSs PHAD and ALAD, more data has been incorporated in their training. Normal data was collected from an University internal network and this has been randomly divided into two parts. PHAD is trained on week three of the data set and one portion of the internal network traffic data, and ALAD is trained on week one of the data set and the other portion of the internal network traffic data. Hence the two anomaly-based IDSs PHAD and ALAD are trained on disjoint set of training data. The correlation among the classifiers is lowered due to factors like more training data and that too disjoint, and also more training time. All the Intrusion Detection Systems that form part of the fusion IDS were separately evaluated with the DARPA data set as well as real-world network traffic. The usefulness of the DRAPA 1999 data set for IDS evaluation is given in the work of Thomas and Balakrishnan (Thomas & Balakrishnan, 2008a).

METRICS FOR PERFORMANCE EVALUATION

This section introduces the metrics for IDS performance evaluation undertaken in this work.

Detection Rate and False Alarm Rate

Let true positives (TP) be the number of attacks that are correctly detected, false negatives (FN) be the number of attacks that are not detected, TN be the number of normal traffic packet/connections that are correctly classified, and FP be the number of normal traffic packet/connections that are incorrectly detected as attack. In the case of an IDS, there are both the security requirements and the usability requirements. The security requirement is determined by the TP_{rate} and the usability requirement is decided by the number of FPs.

Precision

Precision (P) is a measure of what fraction of test data detected as attack is actually from the attack class.

$P = TP / (TP+FP)$

Recall

Recall (R) is a measure of what fraction of attack class is correctly detected.

$R = TP / (TP+FN)$

There is a trade-off between the two metrics precision and recall. As the number of detections increase by lowering of the threshold, the recall will increase, while precision is expected to decrease.

F-Score

F-score scores the balance between precision and recall. The F-score is a measure of the accuracy of a test. The F-score can be considered as the harmonic mean of recall and precision, and is given as:

$F\text{-}score = 2*P*R / (P+R)$

EXPERIMENTAL EVALUATION

The fusion IDS and all the IDSs that form part of the fusion IDS were separately evaluated with the same two data sets, namely, i) the real-world network traffic and ii) the DARPA 1999 data set. The real traffic within a protected University campus network was collected during the working hours of a day. This traffic of around two million packets was divided into two halves, one for training the anomaly IDSs, and the other for testing. The test data was injected with 45 HTTP attack packets using the HTTP attack traffic generator tool called libwhisker (rfp@wiretrip.net/libwhisker). The test data set was introduced with a base rate of 0.0000225, which is relatively realistic. The test data of the DARPA data set consisted of 190 instances of 57 attacks which included 37 probes, 63 DoS attacks, 53 R2L attacks and 37 U2R/Data attacks with details on attack types given in Table 1.

The large observational data set were analyzed to find unsuspected relationships and was summarized in novel ways that were both understandable and useful for the detector evaluation. There are many types of attacks in the test set, many of

Table 1. Various attack types in DARPA 1999 data set (Kendall, 1999)

Attack Type	Solaris	SunOS	WinNT	Linux	All
Probe	Portsweep queso	Portsweep queso	Ntinfoscan portsweep	Isdomain mscan queso Portsweep satan	illegal sniffer ipsweep ports-weep
DoS	Neptune pod processtable smurf syslogd tcpreset warezclient	arppoison land, pod neptune mail-bomb processtable	Arppoisonb crashiis dosnuke smurf tcpreset	apache2, back arppoison mailbomb neptune pod processtable smurf tcpreset teardop upstorm	
R2L	Dict, ftpwrite guest httptunnel xlock xsnoop	Dict xsnoop	dict framespoof netbus netcat ppmacro	dict, imap, named ncftp phfsendmail, sshtrojan xlock, xsnoop	snmpget
U2R	eject, ps fdformat ffbconflig	loadmodule	casesen ntfsdos nukepw sechole, yaga	perl, xterm sqlattack	
Data	Secret		ntfsdos ppmacro	Secret sqlattack	

them not present in the training set. Hence, the selected data also challenged the ability to detect the unknown intrusions. When a discrete IDS was applied to a test set, it yields a single confusion matrix. Thus, a discrete IDS produced only a single point in the Receiver Operating Characteristics (ROC) space, whereas scoring IDSs can be used with a threshold to produce different points in the ROC space. The fusion IDS was initially evaluated with the DARPA 1999 data set. The individual IDSs chosen in this work are PHAD and ALAD, two research IDSs that are anomaly-based and having extremely low false alarm rate of the order of 0.00002. The other reason for the choice of PHAD and ALAD was that the two are almost complementary in attack detection. This helps in achieving the best results from the fusion process. The analysis of PHAD and ALAD has

resulted in a clear understanding of the individual IDSs expected to succeed or fail under a particular attack. On combining the two sensor alerts and removing the duplicates, an improved rate of detection is achieved as shown in Table 4.

The performance in terms of F-score of PHAD, ALAD and the combination of PHAD and ALAD is shown in the Table 5, Table 6, and Table 7, respectively for various values of false positives by setting the threshold appropriately. The improved performance of the combination of the alarms from each system can be observed in Table 7, corresponding to the false positives between 100 and 200, by fixing the threshold bounds appropriately. Thus the combination works best above a false positive of 100 and much below a false positive of 200. In each of the individual IDSs, the number of detections were observed at

Table 2. Types of attacks detected by PHAD at 0.00002 FP rate (100 FPs)

Attack type	Total attacks	Attacks detected	% detection
Probe	37	26	70%
DOS	63	27	43%
R2L	53	6	11%
U2R/Data	37	4	11%
Total	*190*	*63*	*33%*

Table 3. Types of attacks detected by ALAD at 0.00002 FP rate (100 FPs)

Attack type	Total attacks	Attacks detected	% detection
Probe	37	9	24%
DOS	63	23	37%
R2L	53	31	59%
U2R/Data	37	15	31%
Total	190	78	41%

Table 4. Types of attacks detected by the combination of ALAD and PHAD at 0.00004 FP rate (200 FPs)

Attack type	Total attacks	Attacks detected	% detection
Probe	37	29	78%
DOS	63	42	67%
R2L	53	33	62%
U2R/Data	37	17	46%
Total	190	121	64%

false positives of 50, 100, 200 and 500, when trained on inside week 3 and tested on weeks 4 and 5. Figure 1, Figure 2, and Figure 3 are drawn for the selected thresholds for the false positives of 50, 100, 200 and 500. The fusion IDS has improved performance than single IDSs for all the threshold values. The performance is seen to be optimized within the bounds of 100 to 200 false positives. The improved performance of the fusion IDS over some of the fusion alternatives using the real-world network traffic is shown in Table 8.

Table 8 demonstrates that the DD fusion method outperforms other existing fusion techniques such as OR, AND, SVM, and ANN using the real-world network traffic.

DISCUSSION ON THE PRACTICAL IMPACT OF THE PROPOSED METHOD

Consider a typical case of the fingerprinting attack in order to discuss the practical impact of the proposed method. Fingerprinting a server or host provides critical information to the attacker by knowing the version and the type of a target. This information can be derived by sending specific commands and analyzing the output. This information allows an attacker to easily determine known vulnerabilities and the appropriate exploits. Typically, information leakage issues center around a few specific HTTP standard and proprietary header fields. This attack can be identified only by the PHAD, and not by ALAD.

Improper File Extension Handling easily determines which technologies, languages, or plug-ins must be used to complete the web request. Although consistent with RFCs, standard file extensions can provide useful information to an attacker about the underlying technologies used by a web application during service and operating system fingerprinting activities, which can simplify the process of determining further exploits. This attack can be identified only by the ALAD, and not by PHAD.

The proposed fusion method will detect both these attacks, thereby outperforming any of the individual IDSs involved in the fusion process. Although the work discussed in this chapter has thus far focused on the two IDSs, namely, PHAD and ALAD, the method works well with any IDS. The proposed system provides great benefit to a security analyst. The computational complexity introduced by the proposed method can be justified by the possible gains which are illustrated. The proposed method results in a detector that is better than the best of the individual detectors that take part in the fusion process.

Table 5. F-score of PHAD for different choice of false positives

FP	TP	Precision	Recall	Accuracy	F-score
50	38	0.43	0.20	0.99	0.27
100	63	0.39	0.33	0.99	0.36
200	66	0.25	0.35	0.99	0.29
500	66	0.12	0.35	0.99	0.18

Table 6. F-score of ALAD for different choice of false positives

FP	TP	Precision	Recall	Accuracy	F-score
50	50	0.5	0.26	0.99	0.34
100	78	0.44	0.41	0.99	0.42
200	85	0.3	0.45	0.99	0.36
500	89	0.15	0.47	0.99	0.23

Table 7. F-score of fused IDS for different choice of false positives

FP	TP	Precision	Recall	Accuracy	F-score
50	52	0.51	0.27	0.99	0.35
100	121	0.55	0.64	0.99	0.59
200	140	0.41	0.74	0.99	0.53
500	144	0.22	0.76	0.99	0.34

SUMMARY

The network situational awareness is to develop engineering solutions and research approaches for analyzing broad network activity. The goal of this chapter is to quantitatively detect threats and targeted intruder activity using sensor fusion. Simple theoretical model is initially illustrated in this chapter for the purpose of showing the improved performance of fusion IDS. The detection rate and the false positive rate quantify the performance benefit obtained through the fixing of threshold bounds. Also, the more independent and distinct the attack space is for the individual IDSs, the better the fusion IDS performs. The theoretical proof was supplemented with experimental evaluation, and the detection rates, false positive rates, and F-score were measured. In order to understand the importance of thresholding, the anomaly-based IDSs, PHAD and ALAD have been individually analyzed. Preliminary experimental results prove the correctness of the theoretical proof. The unconditional combination of alarms avoiding duplicates as shown in Table 4 results in a detection rate of 64% at 100 false positives, and F-score of 0.59 in comparison to the individual IDSs with detection rates of 33% and 41% at 100 false positive. The chapter also demonstrates that our technique is more flexible

Figure 1. Detection rate vs Threshold for all the IDSs

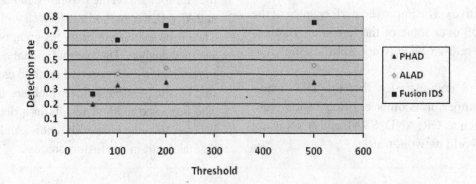

Figure 2. Precision vs threshold for all the IDSs

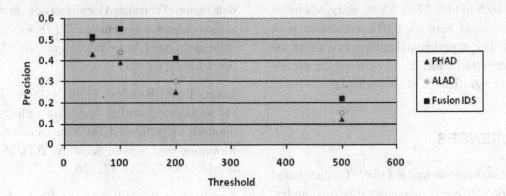

Figure 3. F-score vs Threshold for all the IDSs

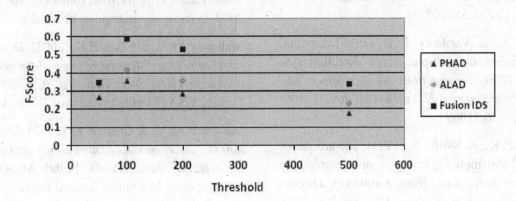

Table 8. Comparison of the evaluated IDSs using the real-world network traffic

Detector/ Fusion type	Total Attacks	True Positives	False Positives	Precision	Recall	F-score
PHAD	45	10	45	0.18	0.22	0.2
ALAD	45	18	45	0.29	0.4	0.34
OR	45	22	77	0.22	0.49	0.3
AND	45	9	29	0.24	0.2	0.22
SVM	45	19	49	0.3	0.42	0.35
ANN	45	19	68	0.22	0.42	0.29
Fusion IDS	45	26	37	0.41	0.58	0.48

and also outperforms other existing fusion techniques such as OR, AND, SVM, and ANN using the real-world network traffic embedded with attacks. The experimental comparison using the real-world traffic has thus confirmed the usefulness and significance of the method.

REFERENCES

Aalo, V., & Viswanathan, R. (1989). On distributed detection with correlated sensors: Two examples. *IEEE Transactions on Aerospace and Electronic Systems, 25*, 414–421. doi:10.1109/7.30797

Blum, R., Kassam, S., & Poor, H. (1997). Distributed detection with multiple sensors- Part II: Advanced topics. *Proceedings of the IEEE*, 64–79. doi:10.1109/5.554209

Chair, Z., & Varshney, P. K. (1986). Optimal data fusion in multiple sensor detection systems. *IEEE Transactions on Aerospace and Electronic Systems, 22*(1), 98–101. doi:10.1109/TAES.1986.310699

Chan, P. K., & Stolfo, S. (1993). Toward parallel and distributed learning by metalearning. In *Working Notes AAAI Work, Knowledge Discovery in Databases,* Portland, OR, (pp. 227-240). AAAI Press.

Drakopoulos, E., & Lee, C. C. (1991). Optimum multisensor fusion of correlated local. *IEEE Transactions on Aerospace and Electronic Systems, 27*, 593–606. doi:10.1109/7.85032

Forrest, S., Hofmeyr, S. A., & Somayaji, A. (1997). Computer immunology. *Communications of the ACM, 40*(10), 88–96. doi:10.1145/262793.262811

Hall, D. H., & McMullen, S. A. H. (2004). *Mathematical techniques in multi-sensor data fusion* (2nd ed.). Artech House.

Kam, M., Zhu, Q., & Gray, W. (1992). Optimal data fusion of correlated local decisions in multiple sensor detection systems. *IEEE Transactions on Aerospace and Electronic Systems, 28*, 916–920. doi:10.1109/7.256317

Lane, T., & Brodley, C. E. (1999). Temporal sequence learning and data reduction for anomaly detection. *ACM Transactions on Information and System Security, 2*(3), 295–331. doi:10.1145/322510.322526

Lee, W., Fan, W., Miller, M., Stolfo, S., & Zadok, E. (2000). *Toward cost-sensitive modeling for intrusion detection and response. Tech. Rep. No. (CUCS-002-00). Computer Science.* Columbia University.

Libwhisker. (n.d.). *Website*. Retrieved March 16, 2009, from rfp@wiretrip.net/libwhisker

Mahoney, M. V., & Chan, P. K. (2001). *Detecting novel attacks by identifying anomalous network packet headers. Tech. Rep. No. (CS- 2001-2).* Florida, USA: Florida Institute of Technology.

Mahoney, M. V., & Chan, P. K. (2002). *Learning non stationary models of normal network traffic for detecting novel attacks.* Eighth Association of Computing Machinery Special Interest Group Knowledge Discovery and Data Mining International Conference on Knowledge Discovery and Data Mining.

Nahin, P. J., & Pokoski, J. L. (1980). NCTR plus sensor fusion equals IFFN or can two plus two equal five? *IEEE Transactions on Aerospace and Electronic Systems, AES-16*(3), 320–337. doi:10.1109/TAES.1980.308902

Thomas, C., & Balakrishnan, N. (2008b). Improvement in minority attack detection with skewness in network traffic. In V. Dasarathy (Ed.), *Defense and Security Symposium: Vol. 6973 (23), Proceedings of the SPIE* (pp. 242-253).

Thomas, C., Sharma, V., & Balakrishnan, N. (2008a).Usefulness of DARPA data set for intrusion detection systems evaluation. In V. Dasarathy (Ed.), *Defense and security symposium: Vol. 6973 (15), Proceedings of the SPIE* (pp. 137-150).

Wu, H., Seigel, M., Stiefelhagen, R., & Yang, J. (2002). Sensor fusion using Dempster-Shafer theory. *IEEE Instrumentation and Measurement Technology Conference* (pp. 21-23).

ADDITIONAL READING

Anderson, J. P. (1980). *Computer Security Threat Monitoring and Surveillance. (Tech. Rep. No.).* Fort Washington, PA: James P. Anderson Co.

Anderson, R., & Khattak, A. (1998). *The Use of Information Retrieval Techniques for Intrusion Detection, RAID '98.* Belgium: Louvain-la-Neuve.

Axelsson, S. (2000). *Intrusion Detection Systems: A Survey and Taxonomy.* Chalmers University. (Tech. Rep.No. 99-15) http://citeseer.nj.nec.com/axelsson00intrusion.html

Chair, Z., & Varshney, P. K. (1986). Optimal data fusion in multiple sensor detection systems. *IEEE Transactions on Aerospace and Electronic Systems, 22*(1), 98–101. doi:10.1109/TAES.1986.310699

Chan, P. K., & Stolfo, S. (1993). Toward parallel and distributed learning by metalearning. In Working Notes AAAI Workshop in Knowledge Discovery in Databases, Portland, OR, (pp. 227-240), AAAI Press.

Dasarathy, B. V. (1997). Sensor fusion potential exploitation-innovative architectures and illustrative applications. *Proceedings of the IEEE, 85*(1), 24–38. doi:10.1109/5.554206

Deba, H., Dacier, M., & Wespi, A. (1999). Toward a taxonomy of Intrusion Detection Systems. *Computer Networks, 31,* 805–822. doi:10.1016/S1389-1286(98)00017-6

Denning, D. E. (1987). An Intrusion-Detection Model. *IEEE Transactions on Software Engineering, SE-13,* 222–232. doi:10.1109/TSE.1987.232894

Denning, D. E. (1999). *Information Warfare and Security.* Addison Wesley.

Iyengar, S. S., & Brooks, R. R. (1998). *Multi-Sensor Fusion: Fundamentals and Applications with Software.* Prentice Hall.

Lee, W., & Stolfo, S. J. (1998). Data mining approaches for intrusion detection. *Seventh USENIX Security Symposium,* San Antonio, TX. USENIX.

Lee, W., Stolfo, S. J., Chan, P. K., Eskin, E., Fan, W., Miller, M., et al. (2001). Real time data mining-based intrusion detection. *Second DARPA Information Survivability Conference and Exposition,* IEEE Computer Society, (pp. 85-100).

Northcutt, S., & Novak, J. (2003). *Network Intrusion Detection.* Indianapolis, IN: New Riders/Pearson.

Skoudis, E. (2002). *Counter Hack: A step-by-step guide to computer attacks and effective defenses.* Prentice Hall. CERT report of vulnerabilities. Retrieved February 13, 2011, http://www.cert.org/stats/cert stats.htm/#vulnerabilities

Thomas, C. (2009). *Performance Enhancement of Intrusion Detection Systems using Advances in Sensor Fusion.* Unpublished doctoral dissertation. Supercomputer Education and Research Centre, Indian Institute of Science, India.

Thomas, C., & Balakrishnan, N. (2008). Advanced Sensor Fusion Technique for Enhanced Intrusion Detection. *IEEE International Conference on Intelligence and Security Informatics,* 1-4244-2415, (pp. 173-178).

Thomas, C., & Balakrishnan, N. (2008). Modified Evidence Theory for Performance Enhancement of Intrusion Detection Systems. *International Conference on Information Fusion*, 4883, 2, (pp. 1751-1758).

Thomas, C., & Balakrishnan, N. (2009). Mathematical Analysis of Sensor Fusion for Intrusion Detection Systems. *International Conference on Communications and Networking*, 97, (pp. 51-58).

KEY TERMS AND DEFINITIONS

Chebyshev Inequality: Chebyshev's inequality ensures that in any data sample or probability distribution, nearly all values are close to the mean.

F-Score: F-score scores a balance between precision and recall and can be simply defined as the harmonic mean of precision and recall.

Intrusion Detection Systems: Intrusion Detection Systems detect unauthorized use of a system, or attacks on a system or network.

Precision: Precision of an Intrusion Detection System refers to the fraction of intrusions detected from the total alerts generated.

Recall: Recall of an Intrusion Detection System refers to the fraction of intrusions detected from the actual intrusions.

Sensor Fusion: Sensor fusion of Intrusion Detection Systems is to meet the requirements of a better than the best detection by a refinement of the combined response of different detectors with largely varying detection coverage.

Chapter 11
GCD:
A Global Collaborative Defense Approach to Thwart Internet Attacks

Subrata Acharya
Towson University, USA

ABSTRACT

With the tremendous growth in the dependence of services on the Internet, service disruption has become less and less tolerable. The greatest threat to service availability is the rapid growth in the complexity and frequency of large-scale distributed attacks. These attacks cause economic losses due to unavailability of services and potentially serious security concerns by the incapacitation of critical infrastructures. Despite the tremendous attention by the research community to find distributed attack countermeasures, a practical and comprehensive solution is yet to see the light of the day. In this research, the authors present a research direction aimed at finding a solution to the above problem.

INTRODUCTION

It is well understood that it is difficult to eliminate all distributed attacks, as it would require securing all machines on the Internet against misuse, which is not a economically feasible solution. A possible practical approach is to design defense mechanism that will detect the attack and respond to it by dropping the excessive malicious traffic. These mechanisms will incorporate tools and mechanisms to comprehend the situational awareness information for such network systems. Generally, it is very easy to detect the distributed

DOI: 10.4018/978-1-4666-0104-8.ch011

attack near the *destination*; however this is too late in attack detection. In the ideal case, the attack should be mitigated as close to the source as possible, but with the distributed nature of the attack it is not possible to decipher such attack with the little information available near the source of the attack. Additionally, the attack source is distributed in nature. Thus, a realistic solution should move away from single-point and local solutions towards a global and collaborative approach of attack detection and subsequent attack mitigation. To this effect this research presents the *Global Collaborative Defense* approach to detect and mitigate Internet attacks.

Distributed attacks are a serious threat to establishing and maintaining the stability and reliability of the Internet. To be specific, a *DoS* attack (Denial of Service Attack 2011) is an explicit attempt to interrupt an online service by generating a high volume of malicious traffic. These attacks consume all available network resources, thus rendering legitimate users to face service disruptions. The impact of the attack can vary from minor inconvenience to the users of a website, to serious financial loss to companies that rely on their on-line availability to do business (Mirkovic et al 2002), (Papadopoulos et al 2003).

Recent massive Internet worm outbreaks such as *Slammer* (Moore et al 2003), *Blaster* (Symantec Security Response 2003) or *Sasser* (Symantec Security Response 2004) have shown that a large number of hosts (Lemos 2004) are patched lazily or are operated by security unaware users. Such hosts can be compromised within a short time to run arbitrary and potentially malicious attack code transported in a worm or virus or injected through installed back-doors. *DDoS* (Distributed Denial of Service 2011) use such poorly secured hosts as attack platform and cause degradation and interruption of Internet services, which result in major financial loss, especially if commercial servers are affected (Dubendorfer et al 2004).

Keeping a commercial server available round the clock is a tough task; while attackers are able to exploit the processing and bandwidth resources and the flexibility of a huge number of compromised hosts to construct new attack tools and variants; operators of Internet servers are left without appropriate means to counteract attacks. Widespread availability of attack tools makes it trivial for naive users to carry out large-scale attacks. As a consequence, new attacks appear frequently, while defense strategies lag far behind. We believe that current security technologies and concepts that focus on end-system and access-networks are not able to cope with the growing number and the increasing intensity of these Internet attacks. Hence, it is evident that large-scale attacks can only be efficiently handled by providing increased security within the core network.

This motivates the need for robust, scalable and effective approaches for detecting and mitigating such attacks. Any effective and realistic solution should not add significant complexity in the core routers and should exhibit characteristics that allow it to scale to large network sizes and to handle large-scale distributed attacks. Also, the attack defense infrastructure should possess mechanisms to aid collaborative operation and be able to easily adapt to the traffic dynamics of the network. Most importantly such a solution should enable ease of security policy enforcement while maintaining and preserving the semantic integrity of the policy set. Finally, the proposed solution should not require considerable changes in the existing infrastructure in order to ease deployment in such large-scale networks. Thus, in this research we focus on a *clean-slate approach* and argue for a separate security plane to detect and mitigate distributed attacks. The decision logic for the security mechanisms is distributed in a small set of active security guards (*Active sentinels*), each responsible for a set of core routers. The *Active sentinels* collaborate both by proactive and reactive mechanisms to mitigate attacks. In *section 3* we present although discussion of the proposed collaborative defense model aimed at limiting distributed attacks.

BACKGROUND AND MOTIVATION

The phenomenal success of the Internet is primarily attributed to the *end-to-end* principle (Saltzer et al 1984) and the notion of core routers as dumb transmission systems, which enables *fast transmission* and *best-effort* delivery. Unfortunately, the success also encompasses the inborn limitations of the Internet, *i.e. Security (policing)* and *QoS (reliability, rate control)*.

The inventors of the Internet had designed the networked system for communication where everyone was a friend of the other (*Figure 1*) and had estimated a very limited scale and volume of use of the designed communication system. But with the exponential growth and popularity of Internet use (*Figure 2*), in the past 40 years there has been rapid proliferation of attacks, that has caused stringent demands and forced placement of strong restrictions for the use of such networked system. This has further lead to significant obstacles to any enterprise's mission of providing open collaboration through these communication systems.

With the growth in the social dependence on networked information systems there has been a similar growth in threats against the security of the networked infrastructure and services. Traffic anomalies and attacks are commonplace in today's information infrastructure and networks. Attacks span the spectrum from computer worms and individual, localized intrusions aimed at gaining access to information and system's resources, to coordinated and distributed attacks aimed at disrupting services and disabling critical infrastructure.

Furthermore, the number and frequency of these attacks has been increasing noticeably (Symantec Internet Security Report 2011), (Symantec Internet Threat Report 2010) as the knowledge and tools required for carrying out devastating attacks are readily available on the Internet. Ironically, attackers have used the enormous power and ubiquity of the networked information systems and services to bolster the magnitude, scope and sophistication of their attacks and increase the harm these attacks may cause to critical information infrastructure. As these attacks proliferate and grow in scope and sophistication, different institutions find themselves under growing pressure to place *significant restrictions* on open Internet access in the form of firewalls, selective applications deployment, and mandatory proxies. These restrictions are often antithetical to the institution

mission and form significant obstacles to open collaboration.

We believe there are ways to deal with attacks and security threats, while sustaining open access policy to foster and enable collaboration among geographically dispersed institutions. Recent years have seen the emergence of several intrusion detection/prevention systems as powerful tools to help institutions deal with security threats. These systems are typically classified as host or network-based. Host-based systems execute specific programs on individual computers to monitor system activities. The shortcoming of a host-based intrusion detection system is its inability to efficiently detect an attack before the end-system is compromised. Network-based intrusion detection systems aim at detecting intrusions in the network, providing the ability to deal with attacks before they infiltrate the end-systems.

Two general approaches, namely *misuse detection* and *anomaly detection,* are typically used to achieve this goal (Amoroso 1999). Misuse detection relies on the signatures of known attacks to detect intrusion using simple rule-based detection. Alarms are raised when incoming activity signatures match those of a known attacks. Although simple to implement, misuse detection relies on maintaining an up-to-date database of

Figure 1. Internet 1969

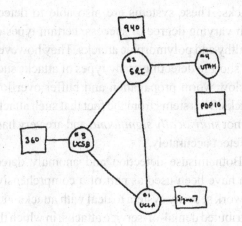

Figure 2. Internet 2010

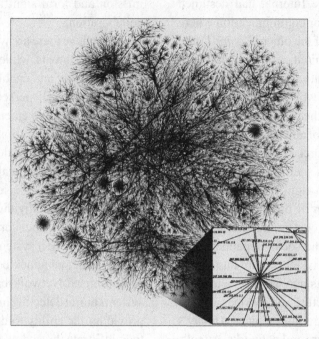

rules/attack characteristics that may require substantial overhead and enormous administrative expenditure. Anomaly detection uses the specification of *normal behavior* to detect suspicious activities. Activities, which deviate substantially from normal behavior, are labeled intrusive or *abnormal*. This is achieved using data mining and machine learning techniques to develop a model of normal behavior. Unlike misuse detection, which requires known characteristics of specific attacks, anomaly detection systems have the ability to deal with previously unseen or modified attacks. These systems are also able to detect, with varying degree of success, certain types of stealthy and polymorphic attacks. They however, fall short in detecting many types of attacks such as slow worm propagation and buffer overflow attacks. This stems from the fact that such attacks are not *statistically significant*, and are very hard to detect accurately.

Both misuse detection and anomaly detection have been used as part of a comprehensive network security system to deal with attacks such distributed denial-of-service attacks, in which the victim is subjected to high volume of traffic with the intent to overload its resources and render it incapable of performing normal operations. Several commercial products, *Cisco NetRanger* and *Asta*, have been developed to support intrusion detection and mitigation against known *Denial-of Service (DoS)* attacks. A limited number of products (Mazu Networks Inc. 2011), (Riverhead Networks Inc. 2011) have the capability to support adaptive, statistics based, packet filtering methods to further improve intrusion detection and accuracy.

While intrusion detection systems have seen a great deal of commercialization in recent years, these products are not geared towards extremely challenging environments, which require support for high performance applications and open access policy for collaboration. Many of the existing intrusion detection systems are *reactive*, and as such, are not practical in dynamically changing environments. To overcome this shortcoming, most of the Internet service providers still rely on *off-line* traffic analysis and manual detection to deal with security threats and *DoS* attacks. Once an attack is reported by a customer; usually in the form of an incident report; traffic is subjected to fine-grained analysis by an expert in order to identify, characterize and classify attack packets. The analysis typically leads to the deployment in the routers of new filtering rules and access control lists to block these attacks. This process has poor response time, which may lead to severe performance degradation and hamper collaboration between different parties.

A second limitation of existing intrusion detection systems is their lack of flexibility to deal with the ever-evolving characteristics of the attacks, in terms of diversity and intensity. Current intrusion detection systems rely on pre-configured filtering rules and access lists in all routers to control access to network resources. The expressiveness of these filtering rules is limited and rigid with an inability to deal with attacks unseen before. This shortcoming considerably limits the effectiveness in detecting intrusions in highly diverse environments. While the use of machine learning based approaches holds promise, the schemes remain offline in nature, with potentially prohibitive high overhead.

Another critical point is that commercially available intrusion detection systems target mainstream networking applications, such as e-mail and Web access. Applications in high-performance collaborative environments are very diverse, with possible extreme performance requirements. Consequently, effective strategies to detect attacks in these environments strongly depend on how closely the underlying intrusion detection mechanisms reflect the "specifics" of the application. Attackers typically rely heavily on quantity, rather than content, to inflict damage on their targets. They use source address spoofing to hide the identity of the source of the attack and make attack packets appear to be similar to legitimate traffic.

Since attacks alter the traffic dynamics, *application driven intrusion detection*, as opposed to detection based solely on the network traffic characteristics, can improve detecting the types and severity of the intrusions directed against the services provided by the application. The fundamental challenge here is to model the process underlying the application traffic data, in terms of parameters and structure, and not the traffic pattern alone.

Finally, intrusion detection systems for high-performance collaborative environments must be able to detect in *real-time* that an attack has occurred or is underway. The major challenges lie in the variability and scale of the threat. The capability of today's commercial products to support general intrusion detection does not go beyond *2 Gbps* access links. Recent advances in the development of new hardware architectures for ultra-high speed intrusion detection will undoubtedly result in improved performance of current systems (Kruegel et al 2002), (Sekar et al 1999), (Mölsä 2005). Cost considerations, however, will limit large-scale deployment of these devices. Intrusion detection systems for high-performance collaborative environments must be designed with dynamically evolving defense strategies and mechanisms, whereby resources are gradually *mobilized* to deal with attacks as they develop and intensify. However, it is not easy to determine where and how the resources must be mobilized. It is equally difficult to determine how collaboration between intrusion detection systems must be achieved to encounter attacks as they evolve.

In order to demonstrate the problem we present a motivational case scenario from a *Tier-1* Internet backbone network as illustrated in *Figure 3*. The Internet backbone consists of various core routers-which are process the packets, and edge routers-which filter malicious flows. Due to the scale of the current core backbone network; the variety of applications that are operational in the network; and the highly complex nature of the Internet operations; there is a huge challenge for the edge routers to detect and subsequently mitigate anomalous behavior accurately and also in a very short time. Moreover, the placement of the filtering routers at the edges also inhibits the real-time detection of ongoing attack cases in the core routing nodes. Additionally, any anomalous activity in a localized Internet domain is not communicated over the global backbone to aid information exchange and to provide accurate situational awareness, which in turn makes the task of the attackers easier and aids them to easily launch similar attacks, at the same time over different parts of the Internet. Finally, the lack of correlation and detection mechanisms of *self-similar* attacks over the entire network domain causes inaccuracy of detection and subsequent unavailability of network information systems.

Thus the only approach to understand, detect and address these real-time anomalies is to provide mechanisms to 1) Place information gathering and policing entities (Sentinels) at the core of the Internet (*core dynamic monitoring*); 2) Share information amongst various distributed local Internet domains (*global monitoring*) and finally, 3) Correlate network traffic information amongst all flows in the Internet (*collaborative detection*). In the next section we will discuss the design of such a *Global, Collaborative Defense* approach for the detection and mitigation of Internet attacks.

GLOBAL COLLABORATIVE DEFENSE MODEL

Defending against large-scale cyber attacks is challenging, with large changes to the network core or end-hosts often suggested. Any practical solution must provide incentives for deployment. Furthermore, as link speeds increases, there is mounting pressure on routers to perform forwarding at link speed. With the increased complexity of the control, management and data planes, it is important that a solution does not add further complexity to the core routers. To this effect the salient features of the proposed *Global Collaborative Defense* infrastructure are the following:

- There are no changes required to the core routers or in the end-hosts. This implies that the proposed architecture can be easily deployed.
- There is no change in the computational overhead on core routers.
- The proposed architecture adds no complexity to management, control or data plane.

Figure 3. Case scenario – Internet backbone network

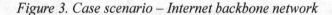

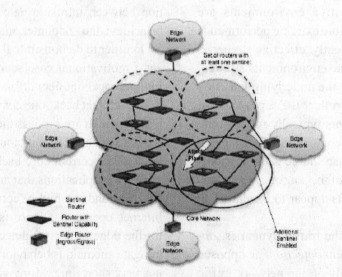

- There is better detection capability against a variety of attacks, which aids in proving effective on-time situational awareness. The strength of the proposed architecture is its ability to handle distributed *DoS* attacks by the coordination of Active sentinels, which cannot be achieved by simple edge-to-edge filtering, &
- Attack detection is possible both from in-network and out-of-network attacks.

Mechanism for Global Collaborative Defense

The task of the proposed *Active sentinels is* to act as policing agents and actively probe packets sent probabilistically by the core routers in the network. Upon the detection of an attack the *Active sentinels* send messages to the *Edge firewall nodes* to filter the attack traffic. The *Active sentinels* can also direct the core routers to increase *p*, the sampling rate. The *Global Collaborative Defense (GCD) architecture* is illustrated in *Figure 4*. The collaborative action is achieved *via* two mechanisms,

namely, *Intrusion Detection and Response* and *Packet Filtering and Traffic Monitoring*.

Intrusion Detection and Response

Intrusion detection and response consists of a network of peers, which dynamically and collaboratively defend against intrusions and denial of service attacks. The thrust of this task is the design of resource efficient algorithm for probabilistic sampling and inspection of packets to detect attacks, and the development of algorithms and methods for a collaborative Sentinel deployment, which guarantees *optimal* network coverage and a scalable response to attacks.

Packet Filtering and Traffic Monitoring

Pack filtering and traffic monitoring are critical components of the *Intrusion Detection System* for the proposed collaborative defense architecture. Upon detection of an attack, a security policy, consisting of a set of rules and their corresponding actions, must be present to drop attack pack-

Figure 4. Global collaborative defense architecture

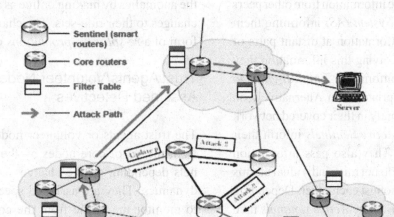

ets before they infiltrate the systems. With the dramatic advances in link speed, packet filtering must be constantly optimized to cope with traffic demands and attacks. This problem is even more critical when application level filtering is used. In this task, we investigate and develop efficient, yet easy to implement, collaborative packet filtering techniques. The focus is on dynamic, collaborative solutions, which use the network traffic statistics to reduce the overhead. We propose to import architectures and algorithms designed in the area of firewall optimization from prior research work in order to achieve the above goal.

Types of Nodes in GCD Approach

There are three basic node types in the *GCD* approach as discussed in the following:

Active Sentinels/Dominating Nodes/Smart Detectives

Active sentinels are smart nodes, which are responsible for monitoring the core nodes in their coverage. These nodes are responsible for taking decisions about traffic anomalies and inform the *Firewall-enabled routers* for changes in the rule-set to mitigate the upcoming anomaly. *Active Sentinels* also receive information from other peers in the *Autonomous System (AS)* informing them of local anomaly information at distant parts of the network. On receiving this information they take a decision to inform the *Firewall-enabled routers* to take appropriate action. Alternatively, on detection of an anomaly in their covered network of core nodes, the *Active Sentinels* inform their peers of the same. They also pass information about flows, which do not raise individual alarms probabilistically amongst each other. Depending on a specified criterion the *Active sentinels* then aggregate the values periodically (*during online operation*) to check if the defined threshold is exceeded. If the aggregate behavior of a flow is unexpected, the *Active sentinels* inform the filtering agents to take necessary action to prevent distributed attacks. This is a collaborative process and helps to mitigate distributed attacks.

Passive Sentinels/ Covered Nodes/ Core Routers

The *Passive sentinels* are the core router nodes, which are covered by the *Active sentinels*. The *r* criteria or *redundancy* criteria determines the number of *Active Sentinels* that are responsible for these nodes. Their function is to perform normal router operation and also to forward the packet to the enquiring *Active sentinel* at the desired rate set by *p* (assigned by the *Active sentinel*). It is to be noted that the core router node is not deviated from its normal operation and hence would not inhibit its normal routing capabilities.

Firewall Enabled Routers

These nodes are the filtering agents pre-assigned by the *Autonomous System (AS)* administrator. We model them to include the various firewall optimizations as discussed in the prior research to the *GCD* model. These routers receive messages from the *Active sentinels* and incorporate the anomalies by making online as well as offline changes to their rule-sets. The change can in the form of a *re-splits*, *re-promotions* or *reorders*.

Trust Agents/Volunteer Nodes/ Assigned Detectives

The trust agents or volunteer nodes are chosen from the set of core nodes by the Active sentinels depending on the changes in the network dynamics. They are assigned special privileges to monitor the traffic from the core nodes and perform functionalities similar to that of the Active Sentinels. The trust nodes are an optional architectural component of the *GCD* model.

Types of Communication in GCD Approach

The communication amongst the various nodes in the collaborative defense infrastructure is detailed in *Figure 5*. These interactions help to achieve the mitigation of anomalies in the network. Due to the scale of the network system the *GCD* approach uses the asynchronous method of message passing. The messages are passed between the *Active sentinel* and the *Agents/Routers* in a given *Autonomous System* or are passed between groups of *Active sentinels*.

There are five basic types of communication as described in the following subsections. There are three basic message types, *Activate*, *Update* and *Create*. The *Activate* message is sent by the *Active Sentinels* to their respective core nodes specifying them to forward the packet at a probability "*p*". The *Update* message is invoked when the traffic characteristics of a packet filter(s) exceeds the previous assigned threshold. The *Create* message is a variant of the *Update* message that helps to set a different threshold.

Active Sentinel ←→ Passive Sentinel

This communication is from the Active sentinel to the Passive sentinel informing it to increase/decrease *p*, the sampling rate to forward packets to the *Active sentinel*.

Figure 5. Basic message in GCD approach

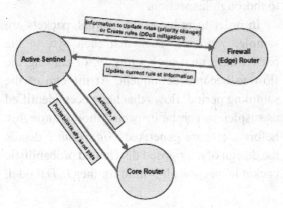

Passive Sentinel ←→ Active Sentinel

The Passive sentinel samples packets at the assigned rate *p* and then sends the sampled information to the *Active sentinel*. It also receives messages from the *Active sentinels* to update *p* periodically.

Active Sentinel ←→ Firewall Enabled Router

In this communication the *Active sentinel* sends a list of rules whose priority is to be updated to the *Firewall enabled router*.

Firewall Enabled Router ←→ Active Sentinel

The *Firewall enabled router* receives the update message from *Active sentinels* and accordingly modifies its rule-set. The rules are either reordered or new rules are added in the form of default deny rules.

Active Sentinel ←→ Active Sentinel

The communication between the *Active sentinels* helps to propagate local traffic information to the peering nodes. This is the basis for performing collaborative defense operation.

GLOBAL COLLABORATIVE DEFENSE OPERATION

Optimal Sentinel Placement

In its most general form, the *Optimal Sentinel Placement* (*OSP*) problem seeks to determine a minimum number of sentinels, *S*, such that any core node, *i*, is *covered* by at least one node in *S*. This is necessary to ensure that all traffic entering the network is ultimately inspected by at least one Active sentinel. To illustrate this, consider the case where core routers *A* and *B* use adjacent router *C* to forward traffic to its destination. It is clear that activating router C to forward probabilistically selected traffic to the covering active sentinel is sufficient to cover router A and C. The minimum cardinality of the dominating set S is denoted by C', and is called the domination number. The *OSP* problem is closely related to the *Dominating Set (DS)* problem, where coverage represents adjacency to a sentinel in S. The *DS* problem can be formally described as follows:

Given a graph $G = (V, E)$, where V represents the set of vertices and E the set of edges, the *DS* process divides V into a collection of subsets V_1, $V_2 ..... V_n$, such that $V = U\ i = 1...n\ V_i$ and each subset V_i induces a connected sub-graph of G. Notice that subsets need not be disjoint. Furthermore, if the graph induced by S is connected, it is called a connected dominating set. The computation of a *DS* of minimum cardinality for arbitrary graphs is known to be NP-complete (Barey et al 1978). Several heuristics have been proposed to produce a near-optimal solution for a variety of problems (Chen et al 2002). These heuristics, however, fall short in addressing the major requirements of proposed defense system.

The vulnerability of sentinels to attacks, coupled with potential sentinel failures or network disconnection, imposes a variety of conditions that must be satisfied in order to produce a resilient, secure and fault-tolerant IDS defense. In order to ensure a high level of redundancy and resiliency against attacks directed at the defense system, we ensure that each core node in $V - S$ be dominated by at least r sentinels in S, for a fixed positive integer r.

Furthermore, in order to ensure that the communication delay between core routers and sentinels is bound, we require that each core node $V - S$ be within distance d of at least r vertex in S, for a fixed positive integer d. We refer to this problem as the $(r, d) - OSP$ problem (Jariyakul et al April, 2005), (Jariyakul et al December, 2005). The problem of computing $(r, d) - OSP$ of minimum cardinality for arbitrary graphs is *NP-Complete*.

There have been several heuristics designed to compute an approximate solution to this problem via experimental analysis on various topology and Tier-1 ISP network traffic. In the following we discuss one of the most salient heuristic solutions for sentinel placement in accordance with the Collaborative Defense Model. For our design we have developed a heuristic to compute an approximate solution as discussed in *Algorithm 1*.

Algorithm 1 is applicable to a general graph. Recent measurements of various Internet domain networks have shown that connectivity in these networks follow a distinct pattern, that most nodes are connected to a few, but a few are connected to many. This distinguishing feature is referred to as the *power-law*. Power-law connectivity affords economy of deployment and high protection for the proposed *GCD* approach.

Probabilistic Packet Inspection

The probabilistic packet inspection approach designed builds on the observation that effective intrusion detection can be achieved based on a reduced amount of packet sampling and logging. The proposed technique uses random sampling to inspect packets. To illustrate this process, the following simple, and traffic sampling model is used as discussed. Assume that a flow is considered suspicious if its bandwidth usage exceeds a threshold percentage, $t\%$ (t is specified by the network administrator) of the link capacity. These flows are labeled as delinquent and become subjected to thorough inspection.

In order to reduce false alarms, packets are sampled randomly such that each byte of the packet has equal probability, p, of causing the flow to become delinquent. At the end of the sampling period, flows that have been identified as suspicious can be inspected more thoroughly before alerts are generated. *Algorithm 2* details the design of a proposed distributed probabilistic packet inspection algorithm for the *GCD* model.

Dynamic Collaborative Packet Filtering

The prior research work leading to the design of the *GCD* approach has successfully developed effective, traffic-aware optimizations to improve the operational cost of firewalls (Acharya et al 2005), (Acharya et al April 2006), (Acharya et al 2006) for both centralized (Acharya et al June 2006) and de-centralized firewall operation (Acharya et al March, 2007).

The proposed technique adapts rule-set configurations to the dynamically changing network traffic characteristics, while maintaining policy integration across the different networks. A unique feature of the approach is its adaptive anomaly detection and countermeasure mechanism, used to dynamically alter the firewall rule-set to improve performance.

The strong motivation to the online dynamic packet filtering approach is the observation that the major portion of the network traffic matches only a subset of the field values in the security policy rules. This is known as the 80–20 rule, which states that 80% of the traffic is filtered by 20% of the rules. One of the important traffic characteristics commonly observed in our analysis of large number of Internet traces is the *skewness* of the traffic matching in the policy, which reveals that the majority of inbound or outbound packet is matched against a small subset of filtering field values which exists in the security policy implemented by the firewalls. What is important of this property is that the traffic *skewness* property is unlikely to change over a short period of time, and the total number of different *skewness* property is unlikely to be large in a firewall policy. The goal of this research is aimed at embedding the adaptive dynamic packet optimization technique developed to the *Collaborative Defense* infrastructure. The architectures and algorithms are imported to the Firewall Enabled edge routers to perform efficient traffic-aware filtering and attack mitigation.

These approaches mitigate *out-of-network* or *denial-of-service (DoS)* attacks. In order to handle distributed in-network attacks (DDoS) the firewall routers depend upon the collaborative action taken by the smart router nodes. In this research we discuss the various techniques and approaches to apply traffic characteristic information to determine distributed attacks for such dynamic network systems.

The basic operation of an *Active sentinel* and the steps of the collaborative defense action are depicted in *Figure 6*. In the first step of the defense operation we aim at developing a novel node placement algorithm in the proposed separate security plane. In the second step we aim at the design and implementation of a simple probabilistic packet inspection mechanism amongst the smart defense node in the separate security plane. The probabilistic approach in packet inspection is due to the large volume of the network traffic and the fast link speed operations of *Tier-1 ISPs*. The third step imports all the traffic aware optimizations from prior research work into the edge firewall nodes to enable fast and traffic-aware packet filtering and attack mitigation. The implementation of these approaches help to mitigate *out-of-network* and *denial of service* anomalies/attacks. This step however does not answer to the *in-network* attacks. In the last step our goal is the design of efficient but simple techniques to recognize the presence of *in-network (stealth)* anomalies in the distributed collaborative framework.

The proposed approach is based on distributed statistical inference of traffic characteristics amongst the smart defense nodes. The smart nodes would aggregate the information received from one another and monitor (check) to detect any possible threshold violations. The threshold information is best determined if specified by the network administrator. If a violation of threshold is detected, the smart nodes immediately inform the edge firewall (filtering) nodes to take appropriate action, either to *promote* the filter or *create* a new filter corresponding to the misbehaving

Algorithm 1. Optimal sentinel placement algorithm

Algorithm 2. Probabilistic packet inspection algorithm

```
Algorithm 1 Sentinel Placement Algorithm
  G(V,E) = Graph G, with V vertices and E edges; S, set
  of dominating nodes; n = (V − S) initially set of non-
  dominating nodes, at the end of the algorithm run set of
  covered nodes; r = redundancy level in the number of S
  for a covered node; d = delay level for a covered node
  specifies that r dominating nodes for i should be <= d
  distance from the node; D, C, N marking for dominating,
  covered and non-dominating node; d_vᵢ for any node i is
  defined as the total number of nodes in S which are at a
  distance <= d from node; r_dᵢ for any node i is defined as
  number of nodes required to ensure that i is dominated
  by at least r sentinels in S; r_dᵢ=r - d_vᵢ, initially equals
  to r; d_pᵢ is the benefit of making the node dominating
  one; d_pᵢ =sum of all node i = 1...n_d, where n_d = number
  of nodes where r_dᵢ <= d
  Require: G(V,E); r; i = 0; S = emptyset; n = |V|; high =
  0; mark all nodes in n as N and set r_dᵢ as r
  Compute dominating and covered nodes
  while n != 0 () do
     for i = 1 to n do
        Compute d_pᵢ for node i
        if d_pᵢ > high then
           high == i
        end if
        i + +
     end for
     mark i as D, include to set S, remove marking N for
     i; n − −; i = 0
     for i = 1 to n do
        Compute r_dᵢ
        if r_dᵢ == 0 then
           mark i as C, remove marking N for i
        end if
     end for
  end while
  Ensure: Computed nodes D and C, and C are (r, d) covered
  by those in S
```

```
Algorithm 2 Probabilistic Packet Inspection Algorithm
  G(V, E) graph G, with V vertices and E edges; S = set
  of dominating nodes, C = V − S = set of covered nodes;
  Sᵢ, represents the iₜₕ sentinel; Cᵢⱼ, represents the jₜₕ
  covered node for the iᵗʰ sentinel; flowᵢⱼ, flow of covered
  node j by Sᵢ; packetᵢⱼ, packet of covered node j by Sᵢ;
  RANDOM(), randomization function; p = probability of
  random sampling of bytes in packetᵢⱼ; BW_Cᵢⱼ, bandwidth
  of covered node j in Sᵢ; Initialize all Suspicious level of
  all flows to be 0
  Require: Sᵢ, Cᵢⱼ, x, Link_Capacity, BW_Cᵢⱼ, counter
     Threshold = 0.0x * Link_Capacity
     for i = 1 to Sᵢ do
        counter = 0
        for j = 1 to Cᵢⱼ do
           if BW_Cᵢⱼ > Threshold then
              Suspiciousᵢⱼ = 1
              counter + +
           end if
           j + +
        end for
        check = 0
        for j = 1 to Cᵢⱼ do
           if Suspiciousᵢⱼ == 1 then
              check = value of RANDOM(packetᵢⱼ)
              if check > Threshold then
                 Alarm_ij = 1
                 Send anomaly alarm to Firewall edge router and
                 other Sentinels
              end if
           end if
        end for
        i + +
     end for
  Ensure: Computes probabilistic packet sampling
```

packet and thus limit or mitigate the developing anomaly. This consequently helps to limit the distributed attack.

EVALUATION

In order to evaluate the proposed *GCD* approach we have designed an experimental evaluation setup as shown in *Figure 7*. The data used for the experiments are emulated rule-set and traffic traces generated from a large *Tier–1 ISP* and the firewall used is the open source *Linux* firewall (Linux IPChains 2011). A strong proactive traffic based anomaly based detection scheme (Roughan et al 2002) is included as part of the proposed *GCD* model in order to provide both the short-term and long-term anomaly detection and inference for the distributed attacks. This mechanism includes perform periodic profiling of the traffic to revel anomalies and alert the system. This in turn prompts the *edge firewall enabled routers* to enable (selectively) *dynamically profiling* and *dynamic rate limiting* of the traffic as necessary to thwart the anomalies.

The basic evaluation test-bed consists of a network with ten *core nodes*. There are three *Active Sentinels, which* cover these core nodes. The OSP algorithm described in *Algorithm 1* determines the coverage. The core nodes are assigned probabilities by the *Active sentinels*, in order to forward packets to them. We inject a distributed malicious attack into the network, which follows three distinct paths, *P1, P2* and *P3*. The attack maintains the threshold limitations in all three paths and hence is appears as legitimate flows. The three attack flows pass through distinct paths in the *Autonomous System (AS)*. All these flows are intended to reach the destination server, *D*.

By the design proposed by the *GCD* approach we have every core node covered by at least one *Active sentinel* and hence we can monitor these flows *via* the respective *Active sentinels*. We establish as threshold value, *t*, to define the permissible value of any flow. The threshold is usually set by the network administrator and can be set on any characteristics of the traffic flow. Threshold monitoring is performed per interval determined *via* experimentation. We have determined two primary metrics for evaluation: the *response time* to attack (**security metric**) and the *throughput while attack* at the destination server (**availability metric**).

The traffic characteristic for our evaluation is *traffic hit-count* information. As the *Active sen-*

tinels monitor the traffic probabilistically, they exchange information about the top hit flows. In a given time interval, if the aggregate hit-count of any given flow exceeds the threshold, the *Active sentinels* immediately inform their respective *Edge routers* by raising an alarm message. The *Edge routers* take action to drop the misbehaving stream by either reordering the rule (if it is already present in their rule-set) or by adding a default deny rule for it (if it is not present in the rule-set). This above collaboration aids to limit the extent of the anomaly before leads to a full-fledged attack on the destination server. We present the results of the evaluation in the following subsections.

Response Time to Attack (Security Metric)

The strength of *GCD* depends on the ability of the approach to limit distributed attacks. This is achieved by evaluating the response time to the detection and mitigation of attacks. The *Response time* is measured by varying the intensity of the attack beyond the pre-set threshold *t*. We evaluate the *response time* to a distributed attack with and without the proposed *GCD* infrastructure. The threshold *t* for our evaluation is set to *20%* of attack intensity. The threshold is to be determined experimentally. Results in *Figure 8* demonstrate the potential of the proposed approach. Due to

Figure 6. Basic active sentinel operation

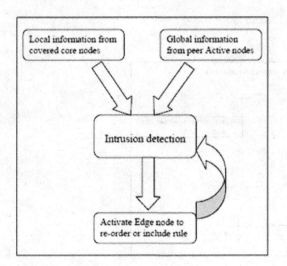

Figure 7. Evaluation setup

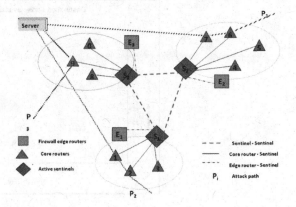

Figure 8. Response time

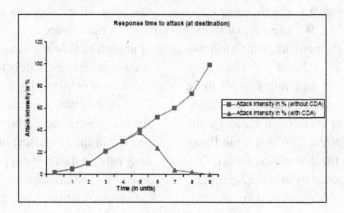

the collaborative action of the *Active nodes*, the distributed attack is detected early and appropriate actions are invoked by the Edge nodes to filter the malicious flow and hence proactively prevent distributed network attacks.

Throughput while Attack (Availability Metric)

The experimental setup compares the availability of the destination server, *D*, under attack condition with and without the proposed *Global Collaborative Defense* infrastructure. The *availability* is very slightly affected during the attack

detection and mitigation phase, after which full server availability is established.

The approach was able to recognize the flow and limit its damage intensity at the destination. As depicted in *Figure 9*, without *Global Collaborative Defense* approach, the server, *D*, will very rapidly be unavailable for any service and lead to service disruption of legitimate traffic over the Internet.

APPLICATION

The goal of this research is the design of architectures and algorithms towards *secure*, *trustworthy*, *privacy-aware* & *situationally aware*-networked

Figure 9. Destination server availability

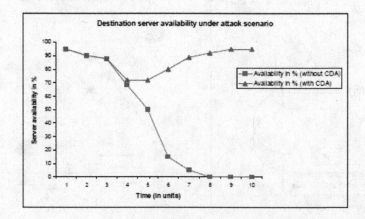

systems. In this regard the global, collaborative, adversarial approaches presented play a vital role to detect and defend against innumerable anomalies and lead to a system, which is both–*secure* and *usable*. In order to emphasize this further we will discuss the mapping of the proposed *GCD* approach onto five relevant real-world applications as follows – *Tier-1 ISP*, *Distributed Anti-Virus*, *Peer-to-Peer Network*, *Healthcare Information Security* and *Data-Stream Management* application.

Tier-1 Internet Service Provider (ISP) Application

To demonstrate a real-world application of the *GCD* approach we have evaluated and implemented it on a well-known Tier-1 ISP application (Acharya et al 2009). The firewall used by the Tier-1 ISP backbone is the *Checkpoint* firewall (Checkpoint NGX firewall 2011). The system flow diagram of the implementation is demonstrated in *Figure 10*. The implementation is in the *network layer* of the Tier-1 ISP data communication. The evaluation by the corporate branch at the Tier-1 ISP organization demonstrated improvement in the security, availability and reliability of network data communication.

Distributed Anti-Virus Application

We evaluated the proposed *GCD* approach on a well-known application from a Anti-Virus corporation. The implementation was at the application layer for the anti-virus software. The problem also consisted of large distributed database of files with real time queries for the reliable use (upload, download, operation) of the application. A similar collaborative approach was applied to classify and manage the files. Additionally, the information from the local and global entities was included as *reputations (wisdom from the crowds)* for the decision system. The goal is to improve the efficiency of operation of the distributed anti-virus application. Preliminary evaluations indicate the immense potential of the approach in improving the efficiency and reliability of the anti-virus application.

Peer-to-Peer Network Application

The Internet's numerous benefits have been coupled with the realization of several vices that are often referred to as cyber crime. Internet fraud is a common cyber crime that has manifested itself in various forms including fake websites, spam emails, and auction fraud. In addition to immediate monetary losses, such Internet fraud

Figure 10. System flow diagram for Tier-1 ISP application

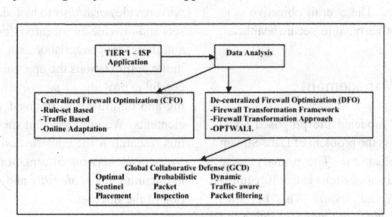

has long-term trust-related implications for users that can result in a reluctance to engage in future online transactions. In this application of the *GCD* approach we address the above shortcomings by the development of novel algorithms and metrics to incorporate peer-to-peer application features with a focus on designing a cross-layer mechanism to detect cyber deviants and integrate this situational aware information over various Internet layers in order to identify cyber-deviance patterns. This approach is aimed at the development of features and techniques to accurately identify fraudulent activities and subsequently mitigate them in order to establish trust over such peer-to-peer applications (eBay, Amazon, *etc.*).

Healthcare Information Security Application

Healthcare Information Security has emerged as one of the primary Internet applications of today's networked systems. The critical nature of the information combined with the scalable and distributed nature of the healthcare dataset mandates security providers to design approaches to provide real-time access; along with security and reliable operation and interaction of healthcare data among distributed service providers. In this regard we have conducted a preliminary evaluation and implementation of the *GCD* approach to provide a platform for review and assessment of the application and the various information technology entities. The overall objective is to design a collaborative, reliable, secure healthcare security system.

Data-Stream Management

Finally, we have modeled the proposed *GCD* approach to address the problem of Data-Stream management applications. The primary issue with stream-based applications is that it requires *fast search* and *quick update*. This becomes more challenging due to the *highly scalable* and *distributed* nature of the stream database. Additionally, *security* and *reliability* of the searches and updates becomes a critical concern to the database administrator. In this regard we have applied the proposed approach to the data stream management applications to improve the overall operation cost for the dynamic, distributed data-stream application. Our preliminary evaluations have demonstrated the improvement in the efficiency as well as security of these applications.

FUTURE RESEARCH DIRECTIONS

The future goal of this research is to implement and deploy the proposed approach in every possible real network environment in order to study the strength of proposed research. As detailed in the previous section the proposed approach have being applied to real world applications and have demonstrated strong security and efficiency capabilities. Additionally, we believe the approach can be successfully used in the modeling of Internet Security and Privacy towards the design of a secure *Socio-economic* model or an efficient *Incentive* model for the Internet. Further the exploration and inclusion of *cross layer features* can further promote defense against such cyber attacks.

Furthermore, the proposed *GCD* approach can act as a building block and be easily integrated with other *source-based* as well as *destination based* defense models. We believe the approach will provide *portability* to include other ISPs data sets and provide an incentive for ISPs to deploy and allow for open collaboration. As demonstrated in the optimizations the approach would be successful in providing a *platform* for policy modeling and optimization amongst various network elements. We envision that the overall goal of this research is the construction of *survival* and *trustworthy* network information systems, while maintaining the *scalability* and *real-time* operation of the Internet.

CONCLUSION

This research presents the design of a dynamic collaborative defense infrastructure to detect and limit distributed attacks. The *GCD* approach introduces the design of a separate security plane to manage and collaborate information between the various network elements. The design and evaluation study confirms that a global coordinated approach would be real-time and cost-effective with very minimal changes to the current network infrastructure. Moreover it would also addresses scalability and promises ease of deployment. Along with the collaborative defense approach, the proposed approach also benefits from the dynamic optimized packet filtering approaches proposed in our previous research. The approach also contributes resource efficient algorithms and simple packet inspection mechanisms to detect distributed attacks and provide situational awareness in the core network elements. To conclude, the *GCD* approach aids in limiting the extent of malicious traffic and improves security, reliability and availability over the Internet.

REFERENCES

Acharya, S., & Ablitz, M. Mills., B., Znati, T., Wang, J., Ge, Z., & Greenberg, A. (March, 2007). OPTWALL: A hierarchical traffic-aware Firewall. In *Proceedings of 14th Annual Network & Distributed System Security Symposium.*

Acharya, S., Ge, Z., Greenberg, A., & Wang, J. (2006). *Methods and apparatus for optimizing firewalls.* (US Patent Docket Number: 2005-0520).

Acharya, S., Wang, J., Ge, Z., Greenberg, A., & Znati, T. (April, 2006). Simulation study of firewalls to improve performance. In *the 39th Annual Simulation Symposium,* Alabama, USA.

Acharya, S., Wang, J., Ge, Z., Znati, T., & Greenberg, A. (September, 2005). Traffic-aware framework & optimization strategies for large-scale enterprise networks. *Technical Report, University of Pittsburgh,* (pp. 1-20).

Acharya, S., Wang, J., Ge, Z., Znati, T., & Greenberg, A. (June, 2006). *Traffic-aware Firewall optimization strategies.* In IEEE International Conference on Communications, Istanbul, Turkey.

Acharya, S., & Znati, T. (May, 2009). *Dynamic traffic driven architectueres and algorithms to secure networks.* Security Technology Response, Symantec Corporation.

Amoroso, E. (1999). *Intrusion detection.* Intrusion.net Books, New Jersey.

Barey, M., & Johnson, D. (1978). *Computer and intractability.* San Francisco, CA: Freeman.

Checkpoint. (2011). *NGX firewall.* Retrieved May, 2011, from http://www.checkpoint.com

Chen, G., Nocetti, F., Gonzalez, J., & Stojmenovic, I. (2002). Connectivity based k-hop clustering in wireless networks. *Proceedings of the 35th Annual Hawaii International Conference on System Sciences (HICSS).* IEEE Computer Society.

Denial of Service Attack. (2011). *Website.* Retrieved May, 2011, from http://en.wikipedia.org/wiki/Denial-of-service_attack

Distributed Denial of Service. (2011). *Website.* Retrieved May, 2011, from https://www.cert.org/homeusers/ddos.html

Dubendorfer, T., Wagner, A., & Plattner, B. (2004). An economic damage model for large-scale Internet attacks. In *Proceedings of the 13th International Workshop on Enabling Technologies.*

Jariyakul, N., & Znati, T. (April, 2005). On the Internet delay-based clustering. *Proceedings of the 38th Annual Simulation Symposium.*

Jariyakul, N., & Znati, T. (December, 2005). A clustering-based selective probing framework to support Internet quality of service routing. *Distributed Computing - IWDC, Proceedings of the 7th International Workshop,* Kharagpur, India.

Kruegel, C., Toth, T., & Kirda, E. (March, 2002). Service specific anomaly detection for network intrusion detection. In *Proceedings of the Symposium on Applied Computing (SAC).* ACM Press. Spain.

Lemos, R. (2004). *Msblast epidemic far larger than believed.* Retrieved May, 2011, from http://news.com/msblast

Linux IPChains. (2011). *Website.* Retrieved May, 2011, from http://people.netfilter.org/rusty/ipchains

Mazu Networks Inc. (2011). *Website.* Retrieved May, 2011, from http://www.mazunetworks.com

Mirkovic, J., Prier, G., & Reiher, P. (November, 2002). Attacking DDoS at the source. *Proceedings of ICNP.*

Mölsä, J. (2005). Mitigating denial of service attacks: A tutorial. *Journal of Computer Security, 13,* 807–837.

Moore, D., Paxson, V., Savage, S., Shannon, C., Staniford, S., & Weaver, N. (2003). *Inside the Slammer Worm.* IEEE Security and Privacy.

Papadopoulos, C., Lindell, R., Mehringer, J., Hussain, A., & Govindan, R. (2003). *Cossack: Coordinated suppression of simultaneous attacks.* DARPA Information Survivability Conference and Exposition, Washington, DC.

Riverhead Networks Inc. (2011). *Website.* Retrieved May, 2011, from http://www.riverhead-networks.com

Roughan, M., Greenberg, A., Kalmanek, C., Rumsewicz, M., Yates, J., & Zhang, Y. (2002). Experience in measuring backbone traffic variability: Models, metrics, measurements and meaning. In *Proceedings of the 2nd ACM SIGCOMM Workshop on Internet Measurement,* (pp. 91–92). New York, NY: ACM Press.

Saltzer, J., Reed, D., & Clark, D. (1984, November). End-to-end arguments in system design. *ACM Transactions on Computer Systems, 2*(4). doi:10.1145/357401.357402

Sekar, R., Guang, Y., Verma, S., & Shanbang, T. (1999). A high-performance network intrusion detection system. In *Proceedings of the 6th ACM Conference on Computer and Communications Security.*

Symantec. (2010). *Internet threat report.* Retrieved May, 2011, from http://symantec.com

Symantec. (2011). *Internet security report.* Retrieved May, 2011, from https://eval.symantec.com

Symantec Security Response. (2003). *w32.blaster.worm.* Retrieved May, 2011, from https://securityresponse.symantec.com/avcenter/venc/data/w32.blaster.worm.html

Symantec Security Response. (2004). *w32.sasser.worm.* Retrieved May, 2011, from https://securityresponse.symantec.com/avcenter/venc/data/w32.sasser.worm.html

ADDITIONAL READING

Al-Shaer, E., & Hamed, H. (March, 2004). Discovery of Policy Anomalies in Distributed Firewalls. *IEEE INFOCOM.*

Aslam, T. (August, 1995). A Taxonomy of Security Faults in the Unix Operating System. *Master's Thesis, Department of Computer Sciences, Purdue University, Purdue, USA.*

Avizienis, A., Laprie, J., Randell, B., & Landwehr, C. (2004, January – March). Basic concepts and taxonomy of dependable and secure computing. *IEEE Transactions on Dependable and Secure Computing, Volume, 1*(Issue: 1), 11–33. doi:10.1109/TDSC.2004.2

Axelsson, S. (March, 2000). Intrusion detection systems: A survey and taxonomy. *In Technical Report 99-15-Chalmers University-Department of Computer Engineering, Goteburg, Sweden.*

Bishop, M. (May, 1995). A Taxonomy of Unix System and Network Vulnerabilities. *Technical Report CSE-9510, Department of Computer Science, University of California at Davis.*

Brucker, P. (1997). On the complexity of clustering problems. In *Optimization and Operations Research* (pp. 45–54). Springer-Verlag.

Charikar, M., Guha, S., Tardos, E., & Shmoys, D. (1999). A constant-factor approximation algorithm for the k-median problem. *In ACM Symposium on Theory of Computing.*

Cisco Systems. (October, 2004). NetFlow Services Solutions Guide. Accessed May, 2011, from http://www.cisco.com/en/US/docs/ios/solutions_docs/netflow/nfwhite.html

Cuppens, F., & Miège, A. (May, 2002). Alert Correlation in a Cooperative Intrusion Detection Framework. *In Proceedings of the IEEE Symposium on Security and Privacy.*

Ellison, R., Fisher, D., Linger, R., Lipson, H., Longstaff, T., & Mead, N. (November, 1997). Survivable Network Systems: An Emerging Discipline. *Technical Report CMU/SEI-97-TR-013 Software Engineering Institute, Carnegie Mellon University.*

Estan, C., & Varghese, G. (2001). New directions in traffic measurement and accounting. *In ACM SIGCOMM Internet Measurement Workshop.*

Garfinkel, T., & Rosenblum, M. (2003). A Virtual Machine Introspection Based Architecture for Intrusion Detection. *In Proceedings of the Internet Society's Symposium on Network and Distributed System Security.*

Hochbaum, D. (1982). Approximation algorithms for the set covering and vertex cover problems. *SIAM Journal on Computing*, 555–556. doi:10.1137/0211045

Johnson, D. (1973). Approximation algorithms for combinatorial problems. *STOC: Proceedings of the fifth annual ACM symposium on Theory of computing, pp.38-49.*

Keromytis, A., Parekh, J., Gross, P., Kaiser, G., Misra, V., Nieh, J., et al. (October, 2003). A Holistic Approach to Service Survivability. *In Proceedings of the ACM workshop on Survivable and self-regenerative systems: in association with 10th ACM Conference on Computer and Communications Security.*

Lakshman, T., & Stidialis, D. (1998). High speed policy-based packet forwarding using efficient multi-dimensional range matching. *In Proceedings of SIGCOMM. ACM Press.*

Noonan, W., & Dubrawsky, I. (June, 2006). Firewall Fundamentals: An introduction to network and computer firewall security.

Sangpachatanaruk, C., Khattab, S., Znati, T., Melhem, R., & Mosse', D. (March, 2003). A Simulation Study of the Proactive Server Roaming for Mitigating Denial of Service Attacks. *In Proceedings of the 36th Annual Simulation Symposium.*

Xiang, Y., & Zhou, W. (October, 2005). Intelligent DDoS packet filtering in high-speed networks. *Lecture Notes in Computer Science, Springer Berlin / Heidelberg.*

Zhao, X., & Sun, J. (November, 2003). A parallel scheme for IDS. *In Proceedings of the Second International Conference on Machine Learning and Cybernetics.*

KEY TERMS AND DEFINITIONS

Clean-Slate Design Approach: Complete re-design approach.

Firewall-Enabled Routers: Routers with firewall functionalities.

Hierarchical: In a tiered/staged level ordered manner (example a tree).

Network Information Systems (NIS): An information system for managing networks.

Network Security: Consists of the provisions and polices adopted by the network administrators to prevent and monitor unauthorized access, misuse, modification, or denial of the computer network and network-accessible resources.

Operational-Cost: Cost of operating a given data set (policy set) in a given firewall over a given period of time.

Privacy-Aware: Ability of an individual or group or system to seclude themselves or information about themselves and thereby reveal themselves selectively and be aware of the challenges and consequences.

Sentinels: Smart Routers with policing capabilities.

Situational Awareness: The perception of environmental elements with respect to time and/or space, the comprehension of their meaning, and the projection of their status after some variable has changed, such as time (e.g. change in network dynamics over the Internet).

Trustworthy System: A system of component whose security will not fail.

Chapter 12
DNSSEC vs. DNSCurve:
A Side-by-Side Comparison

Marios Anagnostopoulos
University of the Aegean, Greece

Georgios Kambourakis
University of the Aegean, Greece

Elisavet Konstantinou
University of the Aegean, Greece

Stefanos Gritzalis
University of the Aegean, Greece

ABSTRACT

Without a doubt, Domain Name System (DNS) security is a complicated topic of growing concern. In fact, it can be argued that the whole Internet infrastructure depends on the smooth operation of the DNS service. Despite this fact, the original DNS design concentrated on availability, not security, and thus included no authentication. Nowadays, this security gap has been addressed by two cryptographic mechanisms: DNSSEC and DNSCurve. They both utilize public key cryptography and extend the core DNS protocol. Although the second mechanism is still in its infancy while the first is well-standardized, they are both promising and are quite likely to compete with each other in the near future to gain acceptance. This work aims to provide a comprehensive and constructive comparison between the aforementioned security mechanisms. Towards this direction, the authors theoretically cross-evaluate and assess the benefits and the drawbacks of each particular mechanism based on several distinct criteria. This is necessary in order to decide which mechanism is the best fit for each particular deployment.

INTRODUCTION

The Domain Name System (DNS) (Mockapetris, 1987a; Mockapetris, 1987b) is probably the most critical service in the Internet as it translates domain names into the numerical IP address of any network host. One can say that DNS is found virtually everywhere in the Internet. Today, an apparent example where DNS plays a vital role is cloud computing. In fact, cloud computing has been with us for many years. It is the provision of computational resources on demand over a

DOI: 10.4018/978-1-4666-0104-8.ch012

network which up until now has usually been a corporate local area network. However, the advent of the widespread availability of cheap broadband connections to the Internet is set to change our experience of the cloud. The computational resources accessed do not need to exist on a local area network and may exist on the network of a service provider accessed over an Internet connection. This gives rise to dramatically different business models for the provision of computing resources at the corporate level and to the home. In particular, the maintenance tasks associated with making an application available can be outsourced. The potential implications of this are currently the subject of much discussion within the popular media. For network professionals, more significant is the fact that taking cloud computing outside of the corporate network potentially allows company staff to access applications that are not feasible on the corporate network for reasons of cost or deployment complexity. This has major implications for situational awareness. Network professionals will need to more extensively monitor the use of cloud resources over the Internet by company staff. However, the starting point for all discussions associated with the outsourcing of business critical information services over the Internet is availability. Setting aside issues that may arise with the service provider, if business critical computational resources can only be accessed over the Internet then the availability of Internet connection to those resources is a fundamental consideration. Internet connection depends on the smooth operation of the DNS service. Moreover, since any other popular service, i.e. web, mail, ftp etc relies on smooth DNS operation, its potential vulnerabilities could set at risk the secure usage of any other Internet application that depends on the proper operation of the DNS service. Of course, DNS security is complicated and of widespread concern.

Despite its crucial significance, DNS still suffers from the same vulnerabilities that it had at the beginning of its deployment. Potential attackers aim to exploit the lack of protection mechanisms and corrupt or undermine the integrity of the authoritative responses. For instance, DNS does not provide origin authentication of DNS data leaving the system open to Denial of Service (DoS) attacks. Although the motivation for DNS-oriented attacks varies, the ultimate goal of any aggressor is to provide misleading or bogus data to the end-user. Usually, however, the attackers aim to be gain financially, e.g. by identity theft, or cause DoS. In such an attack incident, called DNS cache poisoning, the attacker tries to deceive the resolvers of the service into accepting and storing forged DNS data in their cache. Consequently, the end-users based on these resolvers are redirected to fake sites instead of what they requested. As already mentioned, the consequences could be identity theft, malware infection, DoS and other similar risks. Eventually, successful cache poisonings could change the way end-users experience the Internet and expose them to a variety of serious threats.

In order to make cache poisoning and other similar attacks very difficult to perform, two long-term security mechanisms are proposed, namely DNS Security Extensions (DNSSEC) and DNS-Curve that utilize public key cryptography and extend the core DNS protocol. The first mechanism was initially proposed in 1997 with RFC 2065 (Eastlake, Kaufman, 1997). Since then, several modifications have been introduced that lead to the current version of the protocol, known also as DNSSEC-bis. This new version is described mainly in RFC 4033 (Arends et al., 2005a), RFC 4034 (Arends et al., 2005b) and RFC 4035 (Arends et al., 2005c). On the other hand, DNSCurve was recently proposed (Bernstein, 2009b; Bernstein, 2009c) by Daniel J. Bernstein and is part of a major project to deploy public key cryptography, and specifically Elliptic Curve Cryptography (ECC), in every Internet packet. The purpose of this effort is to protect the confidentiality and the integrity of all transactions for each protocol used in the Internet. Unfortunately, so far DNSCurve has not been documented in detailed or implemented by any vendor. Therefore, its effectiveness cannot be examined in practice but only theoretically. Until now, only one internet draft has been published that provides a general overview of the DNSCurve (Dempsky, 2009).

The main contribution of this work is to provide a comprehensive and constructive comparison of these two security mechanisms (extensions). To do so, we theoretically evaluate and assess the benefits and the drawbacks of each method based on several distinct criteria. This gives a clear idea of which solution is optimal for each particular case. To the best of our knowledge, this is the first work in the DNS literature that provides an extensive side-by-side comparison of these protocols.

BACKGROUND

DNS

The Domain Name System (DNS) is the service that translates a domain name, for instance www.example.com, into the numerical IP address of the corresponding host. The DNS protocol is based on the client-server architecture. The server part of the service constitutes a distributed database that utilizes a hierarchical tree structure to organize the domain name space. While a client, called recursive resolver, locates the authoritative name server in the tree structure, which is responsible for the zone containing the domain name in question and requests from it the corresponding IP address or other related data. Then, the recursive resolver provides the received response to the end-user which triggered the resolution process and caches the data to fulfill similar subsequent requests from other end-users.

Each time a user types a domain name in his browser or wants to access a network resource via its domain name it triggers the domain name resolution. The stub-resolver of the computer undertakes to forward the request to the configured

DNS recursive resolver and then to provide the answer to the requesting application. Usually, the recursive server is assigned to the local computer, when the computer is plugged to the network. Therefore, the recursive resolver is determined from the connected network and the user relies on its smooth operation to securely access the Internet and other network resources.

DNSSEC

DNSSEC constitutes a set of specifications aiming to protect certain aspects of the core DNS protocol. The proposed mechanisms require the introduction of four new Resource Records (RR) types, namely the DNS public key (DNSKEY), the Resource Record Signature (RRSIG), the Delegation Signer (DS) and the Next Secure (NSEC) (or the more advanced NSEC3). These new RR types are described in RFC 4034 (Arends et al., 2005b). DNSSEC also requires the support of the Extension mechanisms for DNS (EDNS0) in order to support larger DNS messages resulting from the use of the DNSSEC-related records. Finally, it needs new DNS header flags that are used to specify the support for DNSSEC (DNSSEC OK (DO)) (Conrad, 2001) and the mode of verification of DNSSEC messages (AD, CD) (Arends et al., 2005c). The latest version of the protocol, known also as DNSSEC-bis, is defined mainly in RFC 4033 (Arends et al., 2005a), RFC 4034 (Arends et al., 2005b) and RFC 4035 (Arends et al., 2005c).

Every DNSSEC enabled zone has a public and private key pair. The public key of the zone is advertised with the DNSKEY record. This key must be used for the verification of the signed data within the zone. On the other hand, the private key of the zone is used to generate a digital signature for each authoritative RR set of the zone. This signature is contained in a RRSIG record. Also, the RRSIG determines a validity period for the signature, which means that this record should not be used for authentication prior to the inception and after the expiration of this time period. Certainly, before using the public key of a zone one has to verify that it truly belongs to the specific zone. This is achieved with the use of the DS record. The latter holds the digest of the DNSKEY of a zone and is placed in the parent zone. Every DS record is accompanied with a RRSIG record generated by the parent's private key. This creates a chain of trust from higher towards lower authorities which is able to authenticate DNSKEY records of zones. Finally, the Next Secure (NSEC/NSEC3 (Laurie, 2008)) record type is used to provide authenticated denial of existence of records. Specifically, this kind of record is returned when originally a NXDOMAIN response would be returned, and in conjunction with the corresponding RRSIG, is used by the receiver to prove the nonexistence of the requested record.

DNSCurve

DNSCurve constitutes an alternative method to introduce public key cryptography to the DNS protocol. This method is based on Elliptic Curve Cryptography (ECC), having appealing characteristics like the short key-length and the high speed of the encryption and decryption process. Essentially, DNSCurve creates a secure link between the Name Server (NS) and the client.

Initially, every DNSCurve-compliant server and client generates a 32-byte private key (s and c respectively) (Bernstein, 2009a). The corresponding public keys are calculated with the use of the Curve25519 function, namely the Curve25519(s) and Curve25519(c). The public key of each name server is published as part of the domain name of the authoritative name server. This NS RR is located in the parent's zone file. Therefore, whenever a recursive DNS resolver desires to query a server, firstly it examines if the authoritative's domain name contains a valid DNSCurve public key. Then, it can produce a shared key k from its secret key and the server's public key. The server is able to produce the same shared key from its own secret key and the client's public key. This

key is the Curve25519(sc). The same shared key is used for subsequent transactions between these two entities and for this reason could be stored by them locally in order to increase performance (Bernstein, 2009b;) (Bernstein, 2009a).

After that, the client selects the format of the packet that it will send to the NS. The possible options are the "streamlined" and the "TXT" expanded DNS query packet (Bernstein, 2009b). The first one is simpler, smaller and exposes less information, as it carries a cryptographic box containing the original DNS query and response. The latter has actually the same format as a typical DNS TXT query and reply. By doing so, the encipherment of the original query is carried on the queried domain name, whereas the initial response is encoded in the answer's TXT record. Consequently, TXT packets are not blocked from firewalls that impose rigid format constraints on DNS packets. The client expects that the server would respond back using the same format (Bernstein, 2009b).

Thereafter, the client selects a 12-byte nonce and assigns it to the packet (Bernstein, 2009b). Then it uses the shared key k to expand the nonce into a long stream key with the usage of the Salsa20 stream cipher function (Bernstein, 2007). The input nonce to the stream cipher is a 24-byte long string, which consists of the 12-bytes chosen from the client and 12 zeroed bytes. This stream is then used for the encryption and authentication of the packet (Bernstein, 2009b).

At this point the client uses the first part of the previously computed keystream to create the authenticator of the message. In this calculation the client utilizes the Poly1305-AES message-authentication code function (Bernstein, 2005). Then, it encrypts the initial query by XORing it with the remaining part of the key stream. The final encipherment is comprised of the authenticator followed by the ciphertext itself. Now the client is ready to create and send the query packet to the NS. This packet will contain in cleartext the client's DNSCurve public key and the packet specific 12-byte nonce, followed by the cryptographic box that encodes the original query packet (Bernstein, 2009b). The use of the cryptographic box provides origin authenticity and confidentiality for the original packet.

Upon reception, the NS extracts the sender's public key and the nonce for the specific packet and generates the shared stream keys. Then, it calculates and validates the authentication code of the received packet in order to make sure that the sender truly possesses the private key corresponding to the public key located in the packet. Then, the NS decrypts the box and extracts the query. If any of the previous process fails, then the server should handle the packet as unprotected. Otherwise, it should create the corresponding response and send it encrypted to the client (Bernstein, 2009b).

As noted, the steps for the construction of the answer are similar to the steps followed by the client. The only difference is that the input to the Salsa20 function is a 24-byte long string, of which the 12-bytes are the nonce chosen by the client and the remaining are the nonce chosen by the server. This 12-bytes string is attached in cleartext to the answer. Therefore, the response packet, which is in the same format as the query, includes the 12-byte nonce of the server in cleartext

and the cryptographic box containing the original response. The box is created with the usage of the server's private key, the client's public key and the 24-byte nonce. The client verifies and decrypts the box to extract the desired response. If this process fails, it means that the packet is forged. Therefore, the client should silently reject it and continue to wait for a legitimate one.

It is important to notice, that the client and server should generate and use a different nonce for each DNSCurve packet encrypted with the same shared key. This requirement is cryptographically crucial and applies during the period that the same shared key is utilized.

Attack Vector

The resolution process of a DNS query can be divided into two phases. First, the end-user inquires recursively the recursive NS. Next, the recursive NS traverses iteratively the DNS hierarchy aiming to locate the suitable authoritative server. These two phases are based on the following processes (steps) shown in Figure 1, which represent the internal data flow in the DNS infrastructure (Antonakakis et al., 2010; Manning, 2003).

The information about a zone is contained in the corresponding zone file. This file is kept, and

Figure 1. DNS attack vector

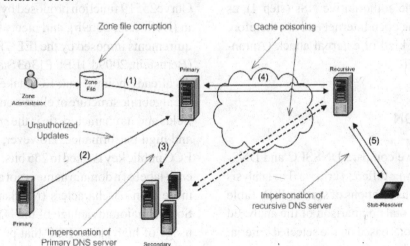

modified by the administrator whenever needed, in the primary NS of the zone (step 1). At the same time, data are added dynamically from various external sources (step 2). The contents of the zone file are transferred to the secondary NSs, during a zone transfer. Thus, these servers can act as authoritative servers of the zone (step 3). On the other hand, the recursive DNS server requests information about the resources of the zone on behalf of the end-user. Note that this server cannot differentiate whether it contacts the primary or the secondary NS (step 4). Finally, it provides the requested information to the end-user who was responsible for the initiation of the resolution process (step 5).

Several threats are identified that aim to exploit each aforementioned process of data transfer and inject bogus records. First off, an attacker could corrupt the zone file if he succeeds in compromising the NS (step 1). Then, the attacker could trick the primary NS and maliciously perform a dynamic update of false records (step 2). Also, the attacker may impersonate the primary NS to any secondary and change their zone file (step 3). Another effort to pass bogus data could target the connection in step 5, where an attacker could forge the reply provided by the recursive DNS server, or impersonate the recursive server to the stub resolver. However, the most common target of poisoning attacks is the connection between the recursive and the authoritative NSs (step 4), as they reside in the open Internet and are therefore exposed to any kind of external attack (Antonakakis et al., 2010).

COMPARISON

In this section we compare DNSSEC and DNSCurve based on nine different criteria. The analysis is based on the observations of section II.D. Table 1 provides a pivotal comparison of the analyzed security extensions based on the selected criteria. In the rest of this section, these criteria are ex-

plained and the two methods are compared based on them. Using this approach, a clear view of the advantages and disadvantages of each method is provided. At the end of the section a discussion of the findings is furnished.

Cryptography

DNSSEC utilizes mainly RSA Public Key Cryptography (PKC) and permits the usage of various key lengths. The use of ECC is compatible, but is not standardized yet. It is recommended that a zone should have two separate pairs of keys, a Zone Signing Key (ZSK) and a Key Signing Key (KSK). The private pair of the ZSK key pair is used for signing the records contained in the zone, including the DNSKEY records. On the other hand, the private key of KSK key pair is used to create only the signatures of the zones' keys, for both the ZSK and KSK. This key is used for the creation of the DS record. It is observed that the KSK is used for the certification of the DNSKEY records and therefore its role is more critical than that of ZSK. For this reason, larger key sizes are suggested in order to be more resistant and require less often a rollover (longer key effectivity period). Therefore, a 1200-bits key size is proposed for the KSK and 1024-bits for the ZSK (Kolkman & Gieben, 2006).

On the other hand, DNSCurve is based on the Curve25519 function proposed by D. J. Bernstein in (Bernstein, 2009b), and meets the security requirements imposed by the IEEE P1363 standard (Bernstein, 2009d; IEEE P1363 Standards, 2009). As already pointed out, ECC takes advantage of the algebraic structure of elliptic curves over finite fields and its characteristic is the small key length and high performance. However, the size of the ECC public key is fixed to 255 bits. This is because each label of a domain name is not allowed to have more than 63 characters (Mockapetris, 1987b). So, the major advantage of the DNSCurve is the usage of high speed ECC that provides a strong level of security with significantly smaller key

Table 1. DNSSEC vs. DNSCurve

Criterion	Sub-criterion	DNS	DNSSEC	DNSCurve
Impact	Documentation	Yes	Yes	Limited
	Implementation	Yes	Yes	No
Cryptography	Performance	-	Low speed (PKC)	High speed (ECC)
	Security	-	80-bit	128-bit
	Key length	-	1024-bit (variable)	255-bit (fixed)
Security	Protection	-	End-to-end	Link-level
	Confidentiality of Transaction	-	No	Yes
	Confidentiality of zone (Zone walking)	Yes	No (NSEC/NSEC3)	Yes
	Integrity & Origin Authentication	-	Yes, in the general case. Not provided for delegating, not expired, localized records	Yes
	Authenticated Denial of existence	-	Yes (NSEC/NSEC3)	Yes
Attacks	Amplification	-	Yes	No
Performance	Size of Zone File	-	x 5-7 times	Same
	Packet size	-	Support of EDNS0	The original packet size is limited to 512 bytes, the domain name of the NS is increased by 54 bytes
	DNS traffic	-	Increased (queries for DNSKEY and DS)	None
	Total query-response time	-	Increased	Same
Modification	Change of SW	-	Yes	Yes
	Message format	-	Same	Different
	New RR types	-	4	0
Administration	Modification of the zone	-	Requires resign	None
	Absolute time synchronization	No	Yes	No
Key management	Private Key storage	-	Offline	Online
	Key Rollover	-	Often, complex, lengthy, scheduled process, no revocation mechanism has been predicted	Seldom

length. According to NIST recommendations, the typical 1024-bit RSA algorithm provides equivalent security to 80 bits of symmetric keys, while 255-bit ECC is equivalent to 128 bits of symmetric keys (ECRYPT II, 2009).

In addition to the Curve25519 function, DNSCurve utilizes the Salsa20 stream cipher and the Poly1305 message authentication code.

Both functions are proposals of D.J.Bernstein. Salsa20 is a stream cipher that maps a 256-bit key, a 64-bit nonce, and a 64-bit stream position to a 512-bit output (Bernstein, 2007). It was selected as a member of the final portfolio of the eSTREAM project, part of a European Union research directive (eSTREAM, 2008). On the other hand, Poly1305 is a MAC that can compute a 128-bit authenticator of a variable-length message (Bernstein, 2005).

Integrity and Origin Authentication

The designers of DNSSEC primarily aim to offer means such that the clients, both resolvers and end-users, are able to validate the integrity and the origin of DNS responses (either positives or negatives). This is achieved with the pre-computation of RRSIG for each authoritative RRset. The private key of the zone is used during the signing process while the rest of the time it is stored in a safe place offline. This way only whoever controls the private key can generate valid records.

However, there are some cases where DNSSEC is not capable of protecting the integrity of the responding resource records. First, a zone does not sign the delegating records, namely the NS record of a child zone with the corresponding A records. This is because these records do not belong to the parent's zone and a zone creates only a signature for its own authoritative data (Yang, et al. 2010). Therefore, when a resolver receives a DNSSEC response containing delegating records for a child zone it cannot verify if these specific records have been forged. However, the response could contain other records in the authoritative section with valid signatures and for this reason the packet seems valid and unmodified.

Another related flaw of DNSSEC is the case when some data are administratively changed and the zone's file is resigned but the signatures of the old records have not yet expired (Osterweil, et al. 2008; Osterweil, et al. 2007). In such situation, an attacker could store the preceding records with the accompanying valid signatures and use them until their expiration time as part of a replay attack. In such a situation the aggressor is able to redirect the victim to a malicious site or just cause DoS (also referred to as freshness attack). Up to the time the signatures become obsolete the victim cannot differentiate which of the received data are valid. Unfortunately, this expiration time could be lengthy as the RRSIG records are pre-computed

and not created on-the-fly, so they are generated with a high validity period (usually 30 days) for performance reasons. So far, the only proposed countermeasure against this flaw is (Yan, et al. 2008), which utilizes hash chains in an effort to prove that the records are fresh and to limit down the replay window. However, this method is rather incompatible requiring changes to both the RRSIG type's format and the functionality of the servers and resolvers.

DoS could also be caused due to the manipulation of localized services' RRs. Many companies install multiple copies of their resources in different network areas in order to offer specific services to individual local area groups. An eavesdropper could capture records with their appropriate signatures from a particular area and replay it to users of a different area. Consequently, even though these users are able to verify the authenticity of the records, they are not able to access the content they request. So, by replaying valid RR, the attacker is able to cause DoS to the unsuspecting users (Bernstein, 2009b).

Summarizing, there are some occasions when the end-user may be deceived by "legitimate" DNSSEC responses and redirected to malicious site or experience DoS. Moreover, as stated in (Osterweil, et al. 2008), cryptographic verification does not always mean validation, meaning that verifiable RR could still contain false data and not what the zone administrator intended to provide in the first place.

In contrast, DNSCurve performs its cryptographic operations online. Therefore, the private key of the zone is stored in the server and is used for the encryption and authentication of the original response upon the reception of the query. Each response packet is created independently from other responses and is unique. Consequently, authenticated answers can only be created by whoever controls the (primary or secondary) authoritative server.

Confidentiality

Generally, the DNS protocol does not concern itself with the confidentiality of the DNS messages or the zone's contents. This is because the zone functions as a public directory of the contained hosts. Therefore, DNSSEC does not propose any mechanism to protect the confidentiality of the packet in transit. However, the introduction of the NSEC record (Arends et al., 2005b), which is used for the authenticated denial of existence, creates a new security vulnerability, namely zone enumeration (also known as zone walking).

Using the traditional DNS protocol a user must know the domain name of the host in order to request the respective record. Therefore, an attacker has to exhaustively search the possible names, aiming to find out the host names within a zone and the corresponding types of RRs. However, with the deployment of DNSSEC and the usage of the NSEC record such discovery is almost straightforward. A NSEC record links two consecutive names (in the canonical sorting) in order to prove that intermediate domain names do not exist. Consequently, the attacker only has to follow the chain created with this kind of records to eventually retrieve the zone's data. This way, an attacker acquires valuable information about the structure of a targeted network (referred to as reconnaissance attack). This enumeration is not considered as an attack against the DNS protocol itself, but rather is a threat against the privacy of the zone's data (Arends et al., 2005a).

The response to this flaw was the proposition of a new extension called DNSSEC Hashed Authenticated Denial of Existence specified in RFC 5155 (Laurie, 2008). With this extension the DNSSEC-enabled NSs respond with an NSEC3 record, instead of a NSEC, whenever a requested record does not exist. This record also provides authenticated denial of existence for DNS RRsets, but does not permit zone enumeration. The main difference of the NSEC3 record is that it links two consecutive hash values of domain names in order to prove that domain names with intermediate hash values do not exist.

Nevertheless, even with the usage of the NSEC3 record zone enumeration is still possible and indeed it is more effective than in the case of the original DNS protocol. When an attacker wants to determine the hosts and their respective attributes inside a zone implementing the DNS protocol, the only thing he has to do is to exhaustively query for any possible combination of domain names. However, this requires sending a vast amount of packets towards the authoritative servers of the zone. Therefore, such an attack does not remain unnoticed by the administrator of the server and could be easily blocked during the execution. Nevertheless, in the case of DNSSEC, the attacker could silently obtain the NSEC3 records through few interactions with the NS, and then offline test the hash values in order to figure out the initial domain names. This could be achieved by performing a dictionary attack i.e., calculating the hash value of likely possible domain names. Such attack is noiseless and the administrator of the server will not suspect anything (Bernstein, 2009d).

On the other hand, DNSCurve calculates a different keystream for each DNS packet and encrypts it. This way, DNSCurve protects the contents (query and response) of the transaction from a passive Man-in-the-Middle attack. Certainly, the eavesdropper is able to determine the zone inquired but he is not able to see the exact domain name and resource type in question. Also, concerning the confidentiality of the zone, DNSCurve behaves as the original DNS protocol. Therefore, an attacker should exhaustively query the DNSCurve-enabled name server in order to find out the contents of the zone.

Authenticated Denial of Existence

Due to performance reasons, the DNSSEC cryptographic signing operations on the zone's data are performed prior to their publication. Therefore, to provide proof of nonexistence a NS sends back a Next Secure (NSEC/NSEC3) record rather than a simple NXDOMAIN response. Unfortunately, this kind of records leak sensitive information about the hosts within the zone.

DNSCurve operations are on-the-fly and therefore the responses (either positives or negatives) are encrypted and authenticated upon the reception of the DNS query. By doing so, the NXDOMAIN response is encrypted and authenticated with the combination of the client's private key, server's public key and the nonce of the session. Therefore, this negative response is unique for the specific transaction.

Amplification Attacks

During an amplification attack, the aggressor tries to force multiple authoritative NSs to produce large responses when processing corresponding queries. In these queries, the attacker advertises the usage of a large size UDP buffer. Also, the queries seem to originate from the victim system, as the attacker forges the source IP address of the query packet. Therefore, the authoritative servers unconsciously flood the targeted system with large UDP packets and they cause denial of service (Damas & Neves, 2008; Vaughn & Evron, 2006).

Unfortunately, the size of DNS packets among transacting DNSSEC-enabled entities is increased significantly, as the response packets in this case carry a signature for every contained records set. Even worse, the remaining DNSSEC related records have extensive size as well. Hence, these entities should support the EDNS0 extension. This way, DNSSEC facilitates successful reflection attacks against the targeted systems since it increases the size of the responses and thus augments the amplification ratio of the attack even more.

Contrariwise to DNSSEC, DNSCurve does not augment the size of the messages, as it restricts the size of the initial (prior to execution of any cryptographic function) DNS responses to a maximum of 512 bytes. Whenever the initial response exceeds this limit, the server sends the reply as a truncated packet, which is also protected by DNSCurve. Possibly, after encryption, a DNSCurve packet would exceed the 512 bytes threshold; these extra bytes are generated because of the cryptographic operations. Moreover, DNSCurve lengthens the name of each NS by 54 bytes, causing extensive glue records compared to the original DNS. However, the overall amplification ratio is low and at the same level as that of traditional DNS. Consequently, DNSCurve does not provide to attackers the means to launch an amplification attack (Bernstein, 2009b).

Modification of the DNS Infrastructure

Certainly, both DNSSEC and DNSCurve require major modifications to the DNS functionality and infrastructure, which hampers the wider adoption of cryptographic solutions to DNS protocol vulnerabilities. Obviously, both the DNS network entities, the server and client, need to change their software and perform cryptographic operations so they are capable of carrying out the necessary functions.

Furthermore, as already pointed out, DNSSEC utilizes four new RR types. Also, it uses the DNSSEC OK (DO) EDNS0 header bit (Conrad, 2001) to advertise the ability of the client to handle DNSSEC records. Finally, it adds two new DNS header flags, the Authenticated Data (AD) and the Checking Disabled (CD) bit (Arends et al., 2005c). These flags are used in the communication between a stub-resolver and a recursive NS, that both support DNSSEC. A recursive sets the AD bit in the responses when it successfully verifies the authenticity of all the contained RRsets, including the NSEC records. Also, a resolver sets the CD bit, when it wants to perform the validation of the RRSIG records by itself according to its local security policy. This way, it forces the recursive to not validate the signatures of the response.

On the other hand, DNSCurve also requires means to carry the encoded message between the client and the server. Towards this direction, the two introduced message formats are the streamlined and TXT expanded DNS packet. Additionally, it modifies the domain name of the NS in order to announce the public key of the zone.

Zone Administration

Considering DNSSEC, the zone file should be re-signed whenever new records are inserted on the zone. This is because the signatures for the new records and the NSEC/NSEC3 records have to be regenerated (re-adjustment of the gaps). In the case, the new records are not covered by their related signatures, the zone cannot ensure their authenticity. This process is very computational intensive and time consuming and for this reason the use of DNSSEC is recommended for static zones alone that do not change frequently. A re-signing process is also necessary before the expiration of the old signatures. Otherwise, if the RRSIG records expire, then the zone data will not be validated by the clients and the domain will be invisible.

Another disadvantage of DNSSEC is that it imposes time synchronization between the transacting entities. Since every signature is valid for a particular time-duration with specific time of inception and expiration, the resolver should have the same concept of absolute time as the NS so that it is able to figure out if the signatures are still valid or they have expired. Unfortunately, an attacker could fool a user into trusting expired signatures or rejecting still valid records by manipulating the client's perception of time. Similarly, an attacker could also drive the NS to generate signatures with validity period different than the current time.

DNSCurve only changes the way the servers and clients communicate. Besides this, it does not imply modifications to the core DNS protocol. Therefore, the DNS entities continue to behave like they did previously. In fact, they just send encrypted the initial message. Thus, DNSCurve is appropriate for dynamically changing zones, since its zone file is not affected by the insertion or removal of RRs.

Consequently, the administration of a DNSCurve compliant server or client requires only the initial installation and configuration of the suitable software. After that, the system is able to automatically handle messages of DNSCurve format without further intervention.

Key Management

Another important issue that applies to both methods is the storage of the zone's private key. Because DNSSEC pre-computes the signatures prior to their publication, the key is preserved offline. This restricts the capability to update the zone dynamically, as there is no way to create the RRSIG records for the new resources in real-time. Therefore, dynamically updated records in DNSSEC would be either unavailable or unprotected until the next scheduled signing process (Ariyapperuma & Mitchell, 2007).

Concerning the key management, DNSSEC requires the frequent replacement of the asymmetric key and particular the Zone Signing Key (ZSK). As this key is used often for the signing of the records, an attacker could collect enough plaintext and ciphertext samples to launch a known-plaintext attack. Also, for performance reasons, the ZSK length is smaller than the rarely-used Key Signing Key (KSK). So, it is essential for it not to be used for long periods of time. However, this rollover process is complex, lengthy and needs to be scheduled somehow. In case the rollover is not successful, the DNSSEC clients are not able to obtain the proper public key in time, and therefore cannot validate the signatures of the records they receive.

Additionally, no mechanism exists that would automatically revoke a compromised DNSKEY (Garrancho, et al. 2009). Consequently, when an attacker manages to find out the private key of a zone, the attacker is able to create valid signatures for malicious data during the time the compromised key resides in the cache of the resolvers. This time period is determined by the TTL value and usually it is long enough for the purpose of such an attack.

Contrarily, DNSCurve-enabled name servers store the private key online, as they use it in every DNSCurve transaction. Naturally, this raises the risk that in case a server is compromised the intruder would be in position to entirely control the DNS transactions for this server.

Moreover, the key rollover for DNSCurve should not necessarily take place so often. In addition, when the process of the replacement happens, it only affects the domain name of the authoritative server, which should be added in the parent zone's file. The propagation of the new public key to the clients would happen within the TTL value of the NS record. However, it is not clear which of the two public key the server should use during that time and how it should handle queries produced with the revoked key. Finally, in case a malicious user discovers the private key of the zone, they would be able to masquerade as the authoritative server for the duration of the TTL.

Performance

In order to perceive the actual performance of the mechanisms, we have to analyze the actions taken by each of the DNSSEC and DNSCurve enabled servers, when they receive a query. In this analysis we assume that the client has located the authoritative name server of the parent zone of the inquired domain name. In the case of DNS-SEC, we also assume that the client has created a chain of trust towards the parent zone and thus has authenticated the DNSKEY of this zone. This is depicted in Figure 2, where the client starting from the root zone has authenticated the public key of the com zone, which in turn is used to authenticate the public key of the example.com zone.

We have to mention at this point that the actual behavior of the security-aware server and client may vary from that of the following analysis, as it depends solely on the implementation. However, we present here the common case.

Firstly, the client queries the parent zone for the NS record of the child (step 1 of Figure 3). The answer (step 2) contains the authoritative server of the child zone and the appropriate glue records. In the reply of the delegating records is also included the DS record containing the fingerprint of the public key of the child zone (Ager, et al. 2005).

Figure 2. An example of a DNSSEC chain of trust

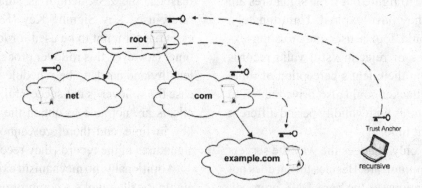

Figure 3. An example of a DNSSEC transaction

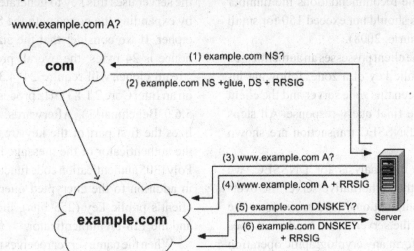

The inclusion of the DS record augments the size of the reply by 36 bytes (Ager, et al. 2005). The latter record is accompanying by its corresponding RRSIG generated by using the private key of the parent zone. Each RRSIG record adds an overhead of 46 bytes plus the key size and the length of the zone name (Ager, et al. 2005).

Afterwards, the client requests from the authoritative server of the child zone the desired resource record (step 3). The response contains this record, with its RRSIG calculated by using the private key of the inquired zone (step 4). In addition this packet could carry more RRSIG records in the authority and additional section for each authoritative RRset that the server includes in the response (Ager, et al. 2005). In order to verify the authenticity of the response the client needs an authenticated copy of the DNSKEY record of the zone. It is possible however that the DNSKEY record does not fit into the previous reply (Arends et al., 2005a). This is due to the extensive volume this record might have. So, the client would again ask the authoritative explicitly about its DNSKEY records (step 5).

This final reply (step 6) is increased by 18 bytes in addition to the size of the key for each DNSKEY record plus the size of the corresponding RRSIGs (Ager, et al. 2005). It is recommended that low-value zones should have a KSK of 1200 bit size and a ZSK of 1024 bit size (Kolkman & Gieben, 2006; Ager, et al. 2005). There are two accompanying RRSIGs, one generated with the KSK's private key and one with the ZSK's. Upon reception of this final response the client can authenticate the public key of the zone and then the desired records.

In the case the desired resource record does not exist, the DNSSEC-enabled server should respond with a NSEC/NSEC3 RRset to provide authenticated denial of existence with the corresponding signatures. In the most cases the response is comprised of two NSEC/NSEC3 records, one that authenticates the non-existence of the exact name and one that authenticates the non-existence of an applicable wildcard record that can expand to the desired domain name (Arends et al., 2005c). The size overhead for each NSEC record is 23 bytes plus the length of the domain name and the length of the label (Ager, et al. 2005). If the server supports the NSEC3 record type, it should first calculate the hash value of the requested domain name before sending the response. This would introduce a computational overhead that depends on the number of the iterations of the hash function.

According to the recommendations the number of the iterations should not exceed 150 for small length ZSK (Laurie, 2008).

As long as the client possesses an authenticated copy of the public key of a zone, following interactions between this zone server and the client require only the final query-response. All steps of a complete DNSSEC transaction are shown in Figure 3.

Concluding the analysis for DNSSEC, we notice that for the authoritative server the overhead for the computational load arises from the larger data that the server has to send, as it does not have to perform any cryptographic operation (Ager, et al. 2005). Therefore, the computational load cannot be estimated theoretically, but only in practice.

In the case of DNSCurve, the client requests the NS record of the authoritative server (step1 of Figure 4). The domain name contains the public key of the zone, and therefore the reply (step 2) is 54 bytes greater than the simple case. Next, the client calculates the shared key from its private and server's public key with the usage of the Curve25519 function. The process of creating the shared key will not take more than 957904 cycles on a Pentium 4 processor (Bernstein, 2006). Then,

the server uses this key to generate the keystream by expanding the nonce with the Salsa20 stream cipher. If we consider that the size of the input nonce is 24 bytes, the overall procedure of the stream cipher will require 24*4.3=103.2 cycles on an Intel Core 2 1.83 GHz processor (Crypto++ 5.6.0 Benchmarks). Afterwards, the client utilizes the first part of the keystream to generate the authenticator of the message by using of the Poly1305 authentication code function. The packet in addition to the encrypted query contains the client's public key (255 bits), the 96-bit nonce and the 128-bit authenticator.

When the name server receives the packet (step 3), it calculates similarly the shared key from its private key and the client's public key and generates the keystream. Then it verifies the authenticator of the message and decrypts the query. Afterwards, it calculates the answer with a new nonce and keystream. The response (step 4) is comprised of the requested record encrypted, the 96-bit nonce and the 128-bit authenticator. Finally, the client upon reception generates the new keystream and authenticates and verifies the response. Subsequent interactions between the same client and server do not request the calculation of the shared key. The above procedure is the same

Figure 4. An example of a DNSCurve transaction

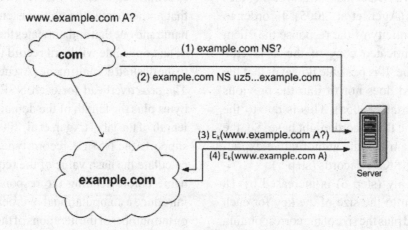

for positive and negatives responses. An example of the way the DNSCurve client interacts with the authoritative DNSCurve server is given in Figure 4.

Taking into account the performance of the proposed mechanisms, it seems that DNSCurve is supposed to behave better than DNSSEC. First of all, DNSSEC uses the RSA algorithm (Arends et al., 2005b) for the cryptographic procedures. The RSA algorithm requires large key length and thus has low performance. For this reason and in order to reduce its computational load to the minimum possible a DNSSEC enabled server pre-computes the signatures for every record set of the zone. Therefore, the load is not affected by the volume of the requests. However, a DNSSEC server should make hash calculations in the case it utilizes NSEC3 records, whenever a non-existent domain name or type is inquired. If we consider that for such response the server should iterate many times the hash function (the upper limit is 150 iterations for small ZSK (Laurie, 2008)) and the significant percentage of queries for non-existent resource records toward the authoritative server, the computational load of the server is considerably increased. Overall, the computational overhead because of the cryptographic operations peaks during the signing process, while in normal operation it depends on the utilization of NSEC3. Secondly, due to the new introduced RR the size of a signed zone is considerably augmented (by a factor of 5 to 7 times) (Ariyapperuma & Mitchell, 2007). This occurs because for every RR set two large records are added: the RRSIG and NSEC/NSEC3. As a consequence, the computational load on the server because of the larger size of the database is heavily aggravated.

Moreover, the size of DNS packets among transacting DNSSEC-enabled entities is increased notably, as the packet in this case carries a signature for every contained records set. The remaining DNSSEC-related records are sizeable enough. Thus, the limit of 512 bytes per DNS packet is no longer applicable and thereby the deployment of the EDNS0 mechanism is necessary. The increased size of DNS packets augments the network traffic between the server and the client and consumes valuable bandwidth. Overall, the total amount of bandwidth is estimated to increase by a factor of 2 or 3 (Bernstein, 2009c).

Another disadvantage of DNSSEC is that it increases the amount of the messages that a resolver sends towards a DNSSEC enabled NS (Ager, et al. 2005). In order to locate and verify the authenticity of a zone's public key the resolver must first consult the zone about its DS and DNSKEY records. This way, the client approximately sends two new queries for every new zone in question.

As a result, the total bandwidth allocated for DNS traffic is increased. Furthermore the overhead of the authoritative server is augmented. This is because it has a larger size zone and serves more queries. Also, the signature validation process increments the workload of the client (Ariyapperuma & Mitchell, 2007). All these factors affect substantially the overall time of a transaction to complete. Ultimately, these overheads are reflected in the way that the end-users experience access to the Internet and other related network resources and services.

On the contrary, as already noted, DNSCurve is based on ECC, which is characterized by short key lengths and the high speed of cryptographic operations. The computational load because of the cryptographic operations depends on the queries as the server encrypts/decrypts each response/request. However, the average overhead is expected to be tolerable, because of the ECC characteristics. Furthermore, DNSCurve does not imply extensive modifications to the zone file of a domain. It only requires the modification of the NS's domain name of the zone in question. This record provides the public key of the zone and is stored in the NS parent and the queried zone file, so a client is able to obtain the public key by requesting the specific record. The extra size for each NS record/public key is 54 bytes, which is negligible compared to the size of a zone file.

Additionally, DNSCurve does not increase notably the size of the packet. It always keeps the original DNS response smaller than 512 bytes. The extra bytes exceeding this 512 bytes threshold are generated because of the cryptographic operations and the carried nonces. In such a case, the DNSCurve server is allowed to send the expanded response packet through UDP. Also, as already pointed out, DNSCurve lengthens the name of each NS by 54 bytes, causing extensive glue records compared to the original DNS (Bernstein, 2009b).

Finally, since the public key is embedded in the domain name of the server, the client does not need additional queries to acquire it, as in the case of DNSSEC. Therefore, the volume of DNS messages exchanged among DNS entities remains the same.

CONCLUSION

DNS constitutes one of the most critical services of the Internet infrastructure, since many other protocols base their undisturbed operation on it. Therefore, any DNS security breach could cause severe problems to affected network domains and in the worst case to the Internet as a whole. Potential attackers could take advantage of the design and implementation flaws of the DNS service and provide the end-users with forged data. By acting this way, they may be able to redirect the end-users to network locations controlled by them instead of what was requested in the first place. The impact of such attack could be identity theft, commercial and financial loss, malware infection to mention just a few. Ultimately, successful cache poisoning attacks change the way the users experience Internet.

DNSSEC and DNSCurve compete to be the secure replacement of the DNS protocol. It is true that so far DNSSEC leads the way having several of its features standardized. Both protocols utilize public key cryptography and aim to protect the DNS transaction between authoritative servers and clients. Based on the cryptographic operations the proposed mechanisms are able to protect the integrity of the DNS messages and ensure that cache poisoning attacks is very difficult to achieve, if not infeasible.

Based on the previous discussion, we can conclude that DNSCurve offers stronger security against active and passive man-in-the-middle attacks, while it keeps the computational load of the NSs low. However, DNSCurve only protects the communication between the authoritative server and the recursive resolver by creating an encrypted link amongst them (see step 4 of Figure 1). Therefore, it fails to offer end-to-end security. The DNSCurve-enabled recursive resolver does not have the means to notify the stub-resolver about the validity of the response and thus the stub-resolver should trust it blindly. In addition, DNSCurve differentiates itself from the core DNS protocol and in an effort to offer enhanced security obscures some of the core DNS protocol characteristics, making it less "open". For instance, a firewall may block a DNSCurve packet because it is impossible to process it and identify that it comprises part of a DNS transaction. Certainly, we have to wait until an implementation for DNSCurve is announced in order to estimate its behavior in actual scenarios.

On the other hand, DNSSEC covers all the DNS transactions and thus end-users can fully benefit from its deployment. It aims to protect the integrity of the authoritative data against active actions. However, there are some cases where it fails to accomplish this purpose. Another disadvantage of DNSSEC is that it increases the workload of the NSs and imposes a significant penalization in the DNS traffic. As a result, DNSSEC increases the overall time for the involved entities to respond and loads the network with additional traffic. Nevertheless, DNSSEC appears to comply better with the core DNS protocol and be the cryptographic descendant of it.

Taking all the above into account a mechanism that combines the advantages of both methods, would be highly appreciated. Such a new mechanism should utilize ECC cryptography, which is characterized by the high speed of the encryption and decryption process. Also, it should guarantee both the integrity and confidentiality of the transmitted messages. On the other hand, it should protect all the aspects of a DNS transaction, not only the communication link between the NS and the client. This way, the end-users would obtain secure, reliable and smooth DNS services. Unfortunately, this is impractical for the moment. The main reason is that it would impose significant changes to the current DNS infrastructure and severe modifications to the DNS protocol messages format. It is also obvious that such changes would not be backward compatible. Another issue is that the usage of ECC is not standardized yet for use in the DNSSEC protocol.

REFERENCES

Ager, B., Dreger, H., & Feldmann, A. (2005). *Exploring the overhead of DNSSEC*. Retrieved September 2010 from http://www2.net.informatik.tu-muenchen.de/ ~anja/ feldmann/ papers/ dnssec06.pdf

Antonakakis, M., Dagon, D., Luo, X., & Lee, W. (2010). *Anax: A monitoring infrastructure of improving DNS security*. International Symposium on Recent Advances in Intrusion Detection, (RAID). Berlin, Germany: Springer Verlag.

Arends, R., Austein, R., Larson, M., Massey, D., & Rose, S. (2005a). *DNS security introduction and requirements*. IETF RFC 4033.

Arends, R., Austein, R., Larson, M., Massey, D., & Rose, S. (2005b). *Protocol modifications for the DNS security extensions*. IETF RFC 4035.

Arends, R., Austein, R., Larson, M., Massey, D., & Rose, S. (2005c). *Resource records for the DNS security extensions*. IETF RFC 4034.

Ariyapperuma, S., & Mitchell, C. J. (2007). Security vulnerabilities in DNS and DNSSEC. *Second International Conference on Availability, Reliability and Security*, (pp. 335-342).

Bernstein, D. J. (2005). *A state-of-the-art message-authentication code*. Retrieved September 2010 http://cr.yp.to/mac.html

Bernstein, D. J. (2006). Curve25519: New Diffie-Hellman speed records. *Ninth International Conference Theory and Practice of Public Key Cryptography*, (pp. 229-240).

Bernstein, D. J. (2007). *Snuffle 2005: The Salsa20 encryption function*. Retrieved September 2010 from http://cr.yp.to/snuffle.html

Bernstein, D. J. (2009a). *Cryptography in NaCl*. Retrieved September 2010 from http://cr.yp.to/highspeed/naclcrypto-20090310.pdf

Bernstein, D. J. (2009b). *DNSCurve*. Retrieved September 2010 from http://dnscurve.org.

Bernstein, D. J. (2009c). *DNSCurve: Usable security for DNS*. Retrieved September 2010 from http://cr.yp.to/talks/2008.08.22/slides.pdf

Bernstein, D. J. (2009d). *High-speed cryptography and DNSCurve*. Retrieved September 2010 from http://cr.yp.to/talks/2009.06.27/slides.pdf

Conrad, D. (2001). *Indicating resolver support of DNSSEC*. IETF RFC 3225. Crypto++ 5.6.0 Benchmarks. (2009). *Speed comparison of popular crypto algorithms*. Retrieved October 2010 from http://www.cryptopp.com/benchmarks.html

Damas, J., & Neves, F. (2008). *Preventing use of recursive nameservers in reflector attacks*. IETF RFC 5338.

Dempsky, M. (2009). *DNSCurve: Link-level security for the Domain Name System*, draft-dempsky-dnscurve-01.

Eastlake, D., & Kaufman, C. (1997). *Domain name system security extensions*. RFC 2065. eSTREAM. (2008). *The ECRYPT stream cipher project*. Retrieved September 2010 from www.ecrypt.eu.org/stream/salsa20.html

European Network of Excellence in Cryptology II (ECRYPT II.) (2009). *D.SPA.7: ECRYPT2 yearly report on algorithms and keysizes* (2008-2009).

Garrancho, B., Pinto, E., Sousa, L., & Loureiro, N. (2009). *Vanishing point: Resilient DNSSEC key repository*. Retrieved September 2010 from http://dev.sig9.net/files/ResearchProject.pdf

IEEE P1363 Standards. (2009). *Standard specifications for public-key cryptography*.

Kolkman, O., & Gieben, R. (2006). *DNSSEC operational practices*. IETF RFC 4641.

Kolkman, O. M. (2005). *Measuring the resource requirements of DNSSEC*. Technical report, RIPE NCC / NLnet Lab. Retrieved September 2010 from http://www.ripe.net/docs/ripe-352.html

Laurie, B., Sisson, G., Arends, R., & Blacka, D. (2008). *DNS security (DNSSEC) hashed authenticated denial of existence*. IETF RFC 5155.

Manning, B. (2003). *DNSSEC & operations*. Retrieved September 2010 from http://www.nordunet2003.is/smasidur/presentations/Manning.pps

Mockapetris, P. (1987a). *Domain names – Concepts and facilities*. IETF RFC 1034.

Mockapetris, P. (1987b). *Domain names – Implementations and specification*. IETF RFC 1035.

Osterweil, E., Massey, D., & Zhang, L. (2007). *Observations from the DNSSEC Deployment*. 3rd Workshop on Secure Network Protocols (NPSec).

Osterweil, E., Ryan, M., Massey, D., & Zhang, L. (2008). Quantifying the operational status of the DNSSEC deployment. *In Internet Measurement Conference '08: Proceedings of the 8th ACM SIGCOMM Conference on Internet Measurement*, (pp. 231–242).

Vaughn, R., & Evron, G. (2006). *DNS amplification attacks*. ISOTF, Tech.

Yan, H., Osterweil, E., Hajdu, J., Acres, J., & Massey, D. (2008). *Limiting replay vulnerabilities in DNSSEC*. 4th IEEE ICNP Workshop on Secure Network Protocols (NPSec).

Yang, H., Osterweil, E., Massey, D., & Zhang, L. (2010). Deploying cryptography in Internet-scale systems: A case study on DNSSEC. *IEEE Transactions on Dependable and Secure Computing*, 7(2).

ADDITIONAL READING

Aitchison, R. (2011). *Pro DNS and BIND*. Berkeley, CA: Apress. doi:10.1007/978-1-4302-3049-6

Antonakakis, M., Perdisci, R., Dagon, D., Lee, W., & Feamster, N. (2010). Building a dynamic reputation system for DNS. *USENIX Security '10 Proceedings of the 19th USENIX conference on Security*. Berkeley: USENIX Association.

Bau, J., & Mitchell, J. C. (2010). A Security Evaluation of DNSSEC with NSEC3. *Network and Distributed System Security Symposium (NDSS 2010)*.

Chandramouli, R., & Rose, S. (2009). Open Issues in Secure DNS Deployment. *Security & Privacy, IEEE*, 7(5), 29–35. doi:10.1109/MSP.2009.129

Dagon, D., Antonakakis, M., Day, K., Luo, X., Lee, C., & Lee, W. (2009). Recursive DNS Architectures and Vulnerability Implications. *Network and Distributed System Security Symposium (NDSS 2009)*.

Dagon, D., Antonakakis, M., Vixie, P., Jinmei, T., & Lee, W. (2008). Increased DNS Forgery Resistance Through 0x20-Bit Encoding. *15th ACM Computer and Communications Security Conference.*

Dagon, D., Provos, N., Lee, C. L., & Lee, W. (2008). Corrupted DNS Resolution Paths: The Rise of a Malicious Resolution Authority. *Network and Distributed System Security Symposium (NDSS 2008).*

Dostalek, L., & Kabelova, A. (2006). *DNS in Action*. Birmingham, UK: Packt Publishing.

Frienlander, A., Mankin, A., & Maughan, W. D. (2007). DNSSEC a protocol toward securing the internet infrastructure. *Magazine Communications of the ACM - Smart business networks,* Vol 50(n. 6) 44-50

Jackson, C., Barth, A., Bortz, A., Shao, W., & Boneh, D. (2009). Protecting browsers from DNS rebinding attacks. *Journal ACM Transactions on the Web, 3*(1), 2–26.

Karrenberg D. (2010). DNSSEC: Securing the global infrastructure of the Internet. *Elsevier Network Security* 2010(6) 4-6

Krishnaswam, S., Hardaker, W., & Mundy, R. (2009). DNSSEC in Practice: Using DNSSEC-Tools to Deploy DNSSEC. *Conference for Homeland Security Cybersecurity Applications & Technology(CATCH '09)*, 3-15

Liu, C., & Albitz, P. (2006). *DNS and Bind* (5th ed.). Sebastopol, CA: O'Reilly.

Massey, D., & Denning, D. E. (2009). Guest Editors' Introduction: Securing the Domain Name System. *IEEE Security & Privacy, 7*(5), 11–13. doi:10.1109/MSP.2009.121

Pappas, V., Wessels, D., Massey, D., Lu, S., Terzis, A., & Zhang, L. (2009). Impact of Configuration Errors on DNS Robustness. *IEEE Journal on Selected Areas in Communications, 27*(3), 275–290. doi:10.1109/JSAC.2009.090404

Rose, S., Chandramouli, R., & Nakassis, A. (2009). Information Leakage through the Domain Name System. *Conference for Homeland Security Cybersecurity Applications & Technology(CATCH '09)*, 16-21

Son, S., & Shmatikov, V. (2010). The Hitchhiker's Guide to DNS Cache Poisoning. *Security and Privacy in Communication Networks, 50*(9), 466–483. doi:10.1007/978-3-642-16161-2_27

Vixie P. (2007). DNS Complexity. *Magazine Queue – DNS,* 5(3) 24-29

Vixie P. (2009). What DNS Is Not. *Magazine Queue – DNS,* 7(10) 1-6

Yang H., Osterweil E., Massey D., Lu S., Zhang L. (2010). Deploying Cryptography in Internet-Scale Systems: A Case Study on DNSSEC. *IEEE Transactions on Dependable and Secure Computing.*

KEY TERMS AND DEFINITIONS

DNS Zone: A group of hosts with a common parent authoritative Name Server. This server is responsible to provide answers regarding to this hosts.

DNSCurve: Constitutes an alternative method to introduce public key cryptography to the DNS protocol. This method is based on Elliptic Curve Cryptography (ECC), having appealing characteristics like the short key-length and the high speed of the encryption and decryption process. DNSCurve is aiming to offer confidentiality of the exchanged packets and integrity of the responses.

Domain Name System (DNS): The service that translates a domain name, for instance www. example.com, into the numerical IP address of the corresponding host. Servers in the network are assigned with a domain name corresponding to a unique IP. Whenever a user wishes to access a network resource, he translates first the host name into its unique IP address with the usage of DNS. The utilization of DNS is more convenient for the users, since they only have to remember the domain name of a host rather the 32-bit number of its IP.

Domain Name System Security Extensions (DNSSEC): Constitutes a set of specifications aiming to guarantee the data origin authentication and data integrity of the DNS messages. This is accomplished with the utilization of public-key cryptography and digital signatures. DNSSEC requires modifications to the current DNS infrastructure and specifications. Moreover, it enforces the introduction of four new resource records types, namely the DNS public key (DNSKEY), the Resource Record Signature (RRSIG), the Delegation Signer (DS) and the Next Secure (NSEC) (or the more advanced NSEC3).

Elliptic Curve Cryptography (ECC): A branch of public public-key cryptography based on the algebraic structure of elliptic curves. ECC offers strong security with small key length. Therefore, the time required for the encryption and decryption process is significant smaller than that of the traditional public-key algorithms, such as RSA.

IPsec: IPsec (IP security) is a suite of protocols for securing Internet Protocol communications by encrypting and/or authenticating each IP packet in a data stream. IPsec also includes protocols for cryptographic key establishment.

Name Server (NS): A Name Server accepts DNS queries and provides the corresponding answer. In the case, the NS is authoritative for the specific domain zone it can provide the full answer. Otherwise it designates which NS is more authoritative to give the correct answer.

Public-Key Cryptography a.k.a Asymmetric Cryptography: Has the property that the communicating parties do not use a single key, but rather a key pair. The public part of the pair is used for the encryption process, while the corresponding private key is used for the decryption. The most significant feature of the public-key cryptography is that none of the key pair can be deduced from the other.

Recursive Name Server: A Recursive Name Server is a special case of Name Server. It is not authoritative for any zone. Instead, its role is to accept queries from the end-users and provides back the complete answer. In order to resolve the query, it traverses the tree hierarchy from the root to the authoritative name server of the domain name in question. Also, to increase performance, the recursive server caches the acquired answers for a specific time to fulfill subsequent questions.

Resource Record (RR): The basic data element in the domain name system. Each RR connects a domain name with specific data according to the RR's type. The answers provided by the NS are in the form of RRs.

Zone Singing Key (ZSK) and Key Singing Key (KSK): Each DNSSEC enabled zone, should have two pairs of public-private key. The private pair of the ZSK key pair is used for signing the records contained in the zone, including the DNSKEY ones. On the other hand, the private key of KSK key pair is used to create only the signatures of the zones' keys, for both the ZSK and KSK. This key is used for the creation of the DS record. It is observed that the KSK is used for the certification of the DNSKEY records and therefore its role is more critical than that of ZSK.

Chapter 13
IEEE802.21 Assisted
Fast Re-Authentication
Scheme over GSABA

Qazi Bouland Mussabbir
Brunel University, UK

Thomas John Owens
Brunel University, UK

ABSTRACT

To satisfy customer demand for a high performance "global" mobility service, network operators are facing the need to evolve to a converged "all-IP" centric heterogeneous access infrastructure. However, the integration of such heterogeneous access networks brings major mobility issues. Dynamic service bootstrapping and authorization mechanisms must be in place to efficiently deploy a mobility service, which will allow only legitimate users to access the service. Authentication, access, and accounting based authentication mechanisms like Extensible Authentication Protocol (EAP) incur signalling over-heads due to large Round Trip Times (RTTs). As a result, overall handover latency also increases. A fast re-authentication scheme is presented in this chapter, which utilizes IEEE802.21 Media Independent Handover (MIH) services to minimize the EAP authentication process delays and reduce the overall handover latency. In this way, it is shown that the demands mobility places on availability can broadly be met, leaving only the generic issues of Internet availability.

INTRODUCTION

In order to satisfy the demand for high bit rate services to be available in real-time in mobility and globally, network operators (Internet Service Providers (ISPs), carriers, mobile operators, etc.) are facing the need to evolve to a converged "all-IP" centric heterogeneous access infrastructure generally referred to as a Next Generation Network

(NGN). For network professionals, NGNs will potentially allow company staff to access corporate network or outsourced real-time applications away from the office while mobile. This has major implications for situational awareness. Network professionals would need to monitor the use of such resources in real-time by company staff who are out of the office and on the move. However, the starting point for all discussions associated

DOI: 10.4018/978-1-4666-0104-8.ch013

with business critical information services over the Internet is availability. In the context of NGNs use of real-time applications in mobility is critically dependent on stringent QoS requirements being met. Roaming often implies a temporary service disruption due to handover from one Point of Attachment (PoA) to another. Authentication, Access and Accounting (AAA) based authentication mechanisms like Extensible Authentication Protocol (EAP) incur signalling overheads due to large Round Trip Times (RTTs) and as a result overall handover latency also increases. Such disruption is unacceptable for potentially business critical applications such as Voice over IP (VoIP), video conferencing, streaming media, etc. In this chapter a fast re-authentication scheme is presented in which utilizes IEEE802.21 Media Independent Handover (MIH) services to minimize the EAP authentication process delays and as a result reduce the overall handover latency. Therefore, it is shown that the demands mobility places on availability can broadly be met leaving only the generic issues of Internet availability. For situational awareness authentication of all users of the network is an absolute requirement. For users accessing company provided resources out of the office on a NGN there will be two steps to authenticating users, first the user must be authenticated by the NGN, then the corporate network must authenticate users of resources it provides who are accessing those resources over a NGN.

In presenting a fast re-authentication scheme this chapter shows that the overall handover procedure across integrated IP-based access networks is a very complicated process, which occurs at almost every layer of the protocol stack. In order to perform an intelligent and optimized handover, it is essential to exchange and utilize cross-layer information between different layers of the protocol stack. Even when intelligent and optimised handover is enabled the complexity of the process will raise major challenges for situational awareness. For NGN operators the first challenge will be the need to educate their own

analysts as to the nature of, and the risks posed by, the process. For corporate network professionals the challenge will be to find ways of working with NGN operators to obtain the assurances they need to make their resources available in real-time to company employees who away from the office and on the move. These assurances could include the provision of information related to company employees' use of the network.

Mobile IPv6 (MIPv6) and Fast Mobile IPv6 (FMIPv6) have been specified by the Internet Engineering Task Force (IETF) as mobility standards to tackle the issues associated with handover latencies at the IP (i.e. Layer 3 (L3)) layer. Similarly, there are media specific mechanisms intended to improve the Layer 2 (L2) handover, such as, the handover optimization in 802.16e and the fast Base Station (BS) transition in 802.11r (Goldman 2008). Also, the IEEE802.21 Working Group (WG) has developed a standard for cross-layer interactions to enable handover and interoperability between heterogeneous network types including both 802 and non 802 networks.

Wireless handover between PoAs (Access Points (APs), Base Stations (BSs)) is typically an intrinsic process that involves several layers of protocol execution, which results in long latencies causing undesirable service disruptions. It must be noted that additional latencies are incurred for networks, or a mesh of integrated networks, due to AAA services. EAP based solutions will play a fundamental role in NGNs by providing a generic authentication framework. However, such solutions are responsible for contributing significantly to the overall handover latency. This is due to the fact that, existing EAP implementations run a full EAP method (a very time-consuming process) when a Mobile Node (MN) encounters a new authenticator (i.e. PoA), irrespective of whether it has been authenticated to the network domain recently and has unexpired keying material. Additionally, the home domain is contacted each time the MN is authenticated and this may introduce long delays when the home domain is far away (e.g. inter-continental). The home domain is expected to send keys to the access devices (e.g. APs, Access Routers (ARs)) within the visited domain for establishing security associations.

Within the IETF, several alternatives have been proposed to reduce the handover delay when EAP authentication is required. The Protocol for Carrying Authentication for Network Access (PANA) WG has proposed mechanisms to pre-authenticate users to a new domain while connected to their current PoA (Izguierdo et al 2008). On the other hand, the Handover Key (HOKEY) WG has been responsible for developing solutions (Nakhjiri 2007; Ohba and Das 2007; Arkko and Haverinen 2008; and Narayanan and Dondeti 2007) for providing fast re-authentication mechanisms without re-executing a full EAP method and re-using EAP derived keying material for handovers. However, such solutions either method specific or method independent, suffer from issues such as high signalling overheads and require major changes to the EAP protocol.

The IEEE802.21 WG formed a task group (TG), known as IEEE802.21a to investigate the potential of applying MIH services to reduce latency caused by authentication and key establishment during handovers between heterogeneous access networks. However, IEEE802.21a is in its infancy at the moment and there is a lack of clearly defined solutions to the question of how to use existing 802.21 MIH services to aid in the optimized re-authentication process.

Concurrently, the 802.21a TG has also undertaken the responsibility to provide solutions for data integrity, replay protection, confidentiality and data origin authentication for the IEEE 802.21 MIH protocol exchanges and enable authorization for MIH services. At the moment, no such solution has been specified by the 802.21a TG. As a result there is great need to define mechanisms for 802.21 service authorization, and also for Security Associations (SAs) to be established, so that IEEE802.21 MIH protocol messages are securely exchanged between end-points.

The fast re-authentication scheme presented in this chapter is a novel IEEE802.21 assisted EAP based Re-Authentication scheme over a Generic Service Authorization and Bootstrapping Architecture (i.e. GSABA). An explanation of the GSABA concept is provided elsewhere (Mussabbir 2010; ENABLE 2006). The purpose of the proposed scheme is to reduce the signalling latency during the EAP re-authentication process, and as a result reduce the overall handover delay. Moreover, the proposed scheme would enable 802.21 service authorization and allow for SAs to be established between the MN and Information Server (IS) for securely provisioning MIH Information Services (MIIS). It will be shown through analysis of the signalling process that the overall handover latency for mobility protocols will be reduced by the proposed scheme.

PROBLEM STATEMENT

The issues associated with fast re-authentication are:

Further Optimization Required for Existing Solutions

There are many solutions that have been defined by the IETF to provide re-authentication solutions based on EAP. As mentioned earlier, the solutions either provide method specific or method independent re-authentication mechanisms. Examples have been provided of method specific re-authentication mechanisms which are not suitable for NGNs (Haverinen and Salowey 2006; Clancy and Tschofenig 2008). This is due to the fact that NGNs will comprise of heterogeneous access networks and will require re-authentication support for any (not just a few) EAP method. On the other hand, the IETF has proposed a few method independent EAP re-authentication mechanisms (Nakhjiri 2007; Ohba and Das 2007; and Narayanan and Dondeti 2007. However, such solutions (Nakhjiri 2007; Ohba and Das 2007; Narayanan and Dondeti 2007) have issues, such as high signalling (i.e. RTTs) overhead or require major changes to EAP state machines and message flows. Moreover, EAP is originally based on a 2-party trust model between the peer and the authentication server. This imposes certain issues (Harkins et al 2007) described later in this section. As a result, there is great need to clearly specify a 3-party re-authentication infrastructure. Even though an existing proposed solution (Clancy and Tschofenig 2008) is essentially motivated by the 3-party approach it is still a rough "straw man".

Need for a 3-Party EAP Re-Authentication Model

Existing EAP methods perform authentication using a two-party approach, where only two parties perform the EAP authentication, namely the EAP peer and the EAP server. However, from a key distribution standpoint, three parties are involved and the two-party model proposed for EAP is not valid for a secure key distribution. In the fast re-authentication scenarios, a key must be sent from a server to the EAP authenticator (i.e. target PoA) which the EAP peer (i.e. MN) has recently attached to (or will attach to) in order to establish a SA between the EAP peer and the EAP authenticator through a *security association protocol*. In other words, the authenticator is another party involved in the key distribution process since it receives a key from a trusted server.

Problems with using a two-party trust model have been noted (Harkins et al 2007) and are generally referred to as a problem with "Channel Binding". Basically the MN infers the identity of the authenticator but has no direct indication of the identity of the authenticator to which the authentication server transmitted the keying material. In other words, in an unintended situation where a Network Access Server (NAS) is impersonating another NAS, the peer and the authentication server may have two different views of the NAS identity.

As a result a 3-party model seems the right approach for key distribution in mobile scenarios to provide channel binding procedures in order to avoid a compromised intermediate authenticator providing unverified and conflicting service information to both the peer and the EAP server.

Need for IEEE802.21 MIH Services to Assist Re-authentication

As mentioned earlier, recently, the IEEE802.21 WG established a TG (802.21a) to investigate ways to use the IEEE802.21 MIH services, namely the Media Independent Information Service (MIIS), to optimize authentication/re-authentication and key establishment mechanisms during handovers. Additionally, 802.21a will define solutions for securely exchanging MIH protocol messages by providing data integrity, replay protection, confidentiality and data origin authentication for IEEE 802.21 MIH services.

The 802.21a TG has liaised with IETF HOKEY WG to define solutions that utilize the MIIS to discover candidate PoAs with which the MN intends to start the fast re-authentication process with. Discovering only the candidate PoAs that offer the re-authentication capabilities will reduce the overall signalling overheads; i.e. target PoAs that do not support re-authentication will not be considered and contacted for handovers. However, at the moment there is a lack of clearly defined mechanisms that specify how the IEEE802.21 MIH Services (i.e. MIIS) could be integrated and deployed in an EAP based infrastructure.

Integration of IEEE802.21 MIH Services with an AAA based Service Bootstrapping and Authorization Framework

IEEE802.21 MIH can be used to drastically reduce the overall handover latency in heterogeneous access networks. Like any promising solution that can contribute significantly to the revenue stream, the IEEE802.21 functionalities will be considered as a "*payable*" service, since they will be used to assist in optimizing the overall handover process, which includes the authentication procedure. As a result, users need be authorized to be granted access to the 802.21 MIH services. Therefore, it is essential, to integrate the components of the IEEE802.21 MIH entities and services with a service authorization and bootstrapping framework (GSABA), for the purpose of efficient service authorization and bootstrapping.

It was mentioned earlier in this section, that the IEEE802.21 MIH protocol messages must be securely exchanged between end-points. The 802.21 Media Independent Handover Function (MIHF) infrastructure is vulnerable to many security threats. For example, information sent by the IS to the MN can be tampered with in transit by an attacker which could result in malformed unreliable information being received, which could possibly lead to denial of service or the MN being redirected to a wrong network (e.g. where price of accessing the network is more expensive).

A detailed description of all the known security threats to 802.21 MIH services has been provided (Saha, S and Lagutin 2009). To date, there has been no solution defined by the IEEE802.21a TG which allows IEEE802.21 MIH messages to be securely transmitted. However, the integration of IEEE802.21 with the GSABA will allow for dynamic SAs (i.e. keys derived) to be established between the MNs and the IS. It will be shown later in section 4.3, how the derived keys can be used to secure the MIIS signalling.

ARCHITECTURAL OVERVIEW

An architectural overview of the proposed mechanism is illustrated in Figure 1. Before delving into the specifics of the proposed mechanism, it is important to understand the impact of integrating IEEE 802.21 with the GSABA framework. Specifically, for the MIIS provisioning, it is essential to investigate the IS deployment strategies and scenarios.

Deploying an Information Server for MIIS Provisioning

The IS is the main logical network entity that provides MIIS as defined in the 802.21 specification. However, the 802.21 formal specification does not provide an explicit definition of the IS nor the mechanism for maintaining and accessing it. As a result, the IEEE 802.21 specification provides flexibility in real IS deployments and implementations, with respect to how to store, collect and provide the information from the neighbouring access networks.

The information at the IS could be stored in the following ways:

1. Pre-configured and stored locally in the MN.
2. Stored in a distributed fashion across the network by multiple network nodes, which provide the information to the MN.
3. The information is stored, and provided by a separate network entity, i.e. the IS.

Although the first option (i.e. pre-configure the information on the MN) is the easiest to implement, it is definitely the least flexible, since the information to be provided will be static in nature and composed of only a small subset of the all required network information for an optimized handover. On the other hand, storing the information in a distributed manner will lead to significant transmission overhead and complicated discovery and maintenance mechanisms. Also, information

Figure 1. Overview of the proposed architecture

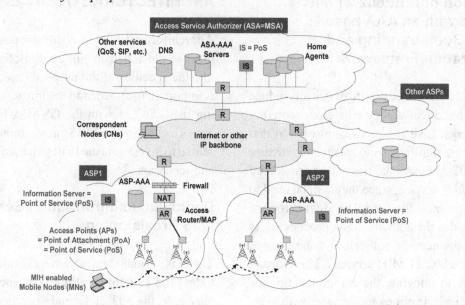

synchronization will become an issue. It is therefore preferable to store all the desired information in a centralized manner (i.e. IS) or hierarchically by connecting individual ISs.

Relationships between Business Entities and the IS

Since the IS will be a new network entity that will be introduced into the NGN architectural models (e.g. GSABA), it is only natural to ask: who is going to deploy this entity and how it is going to fit in with existing business models for NGNs. The relationship that the IS will form with business entities such as the Access Service Authoriser (ASA), Access Service Provider (ASP), Mobility Service Authorizer (MSA) and Mobility Service Provider (MSP) needs to be analyzed. As explained earlier, the IS will be the entity storing the information of neighbouring access networks within a geographic area inside a local domain (i.e. an operator's domain). It is thus reasonable to consider the IS as a part of the ASP network rather than the mobility infrastructure even though theoretically a third party MSP could also deploy

ISs. Considering the sensitive nature of the information (e.g. billing/pricing, Point of Attachment (PoA) capabilities, etc.) that could be involved, it is highly unlikely that the ASPs or MSPs belonging to different administrative domains (i.e. different operators) would wish to share much information (even if roaming agreements are in place).

Therefore, in answer to the question at the beginning of this sub-section: It is ideal for the IS to be deployed by the ASP. The deployment of the IS and, furthermore, the maintenance of all the 802.21 MIH services will be the responsibility of the ASPs of an administrative domain. Even though, the introduction of 802.21 MIH services will bring new business opportunities, it doesn't necessarily require any change to the established business relationships between the ASP, ASP, MSP, and MSA as shown in Figure 1.

Considered Network Scenarios

There are two possible network scenarios which arise from integrating IEEE 802.21 to assist in optimizing handover (i.e. re-authentication in this case):

1. S1: (Intra-domain, intra-technology) handover between the same type of access network provided by ASPs and authorized by the same administrative domain.
2. S2: (Intra-domain, inter-technology) handover between different types of access networks provided by ASPs and authorized by the same ASA-AAA (i.e. same administrative domains).

Of these two scenarios, S2 is a realistic option since re-authentication in NGNs will comprise of inter-technology handovers. Technology specific solutions for handovers and re-authentication (as in S1) already exist (IEEE Standard 802.11r 2008; IEEE Standard 802.16e 2005). An emphasis is placed on the scenario S2 in using ISs for handling inter-technology (vertical) handovers, particularly, when a MN is roaming in a visitor/foreign network within the domain. It must be noted that inter-domain (i.e. between different operators) handover scenarios are not considered because, as explained earlier, the IS is part of the local access network (ASP). It will be unlikely that the ISs deployed in the home domain of a particular operator can provide any useful information to a MN about the access networks in a visited domain, belonging to a different operator. In that situation, the MN should try to access the local ISs provided by the

ASP in the visited domain. Figure 1 provides a reference architecture (IEEE802.21 integrated with GSABA) where there are ISs in the ASPs and another IS in the ASA network.

IS Deployment Strategy

In this section, a IS deployment scheme is investigated and analyzed. In the scheme shown in Figure 2, the IS is deployed outside the MN's subnet, serving several subnets. It is possible to deploy only one IS within a single domain that will serve all the access networks, or a hierarchy/chain of ISs could be deployed to provide information to different blocks (home/visiting) of the administrative domain. The latter approach has the advantage of tackling redundancy issues (in case one of the IS fails, other ISs could still provide information). The MN will discover the IS through Dynamic Host Control Protocol v6 (DHCPv6) (IEEE802.21 Draft P802.21/D00.05 2006) and access it directly through a L3 transport protocol.

In must be noted that other deployment schemes can be derived, such as:

1. An IS is deployed in each subnet and co-located with the AR/NAS.

Figure 2. IS deployment in the ASP

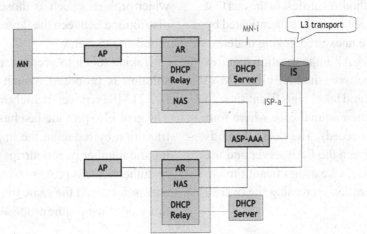

2.   IS or IS-Proxies are deployed in each subnet (co-located with the AR/NAS) and connected in a hierarchical manner.

However, such schemes suffer from scalability problems. To deploy and maintain an IS or an IS-proxy at each subnet in an access network requires a significant amount of work and effort by the ASPs since the Access Router (AR) needs to be heavily modified. Operators are likely to favour a solution that involves minimal changes to the network infrastructure to support 802.21 MIH (MIIS in this case) services. The deployment scheme presented in Figure 2 is potentially the most attractive one for ASPs because of its simplicity. Only one new network element will be introduced to the existing network, and only one new interface needs to be introduced to the MN at the IP layer. There is no need to modify each subnet in the access network.

AN OVERVIEW OF THE IEEE802.21 ASSISED EAP BASED RE-AUTHENTICATION MECHANISM OVER GSABA

As mentioned earlier, authentication in wireless networks (e.g. 802.11a/b/g, 802.16e etc.) is usually based on EAP; this could be a problem when the MN moves to a new PoA (i.e. authenticator), since it runs a full EAP method, regardless of the fact that the MN may have been recently authenticated by the domain and have unexpired keying material. The process of a full EAP authentication requires several roundtrips between the EAP client (MN) and the EAP server and takes significant time to complete (even in the minimal case where four EAP messages are needed). The delay depends on the distance between the EAP server and the MN. As a result, it can take a significant time to perform re-authentication increasing the overall handover latency.

In the subsequent sections, an EAP re-authentication mechanism is defined which is integrated with the IEEE802.21 infrastructure over GSABA to reduce the handover latency due to re-authentication.

The 3-Party Approach

The HOKEY WG is working to specify a solution to reduce the latency introduced by EAP authentication during handover. The issues that have been described in section 2 present some drawbacks which triggered the investigation of a new solution based on the extension to EAP Re-Authentication Protocol (ERP) (Narayanan and Dondeti 2008) defined by the IETF HOKEY WG. The ERP provides a fast re-authentication process between the MN and the server in a single roundtrip at the cost of modifications to existing EAP deployments. The basic idea consists of securely distributing specific keys between the MN and the PoA from a trusted server without incurring the delays associated with lengthy full EAP authentications. The distributed keying material will eventually serve for the establishment of SAs between the MN and the PoA.

However, the ERP follows the traditional EAP two-party model for key distribution. As explained in section 2 of this chapter, this solution has inherited the EAP model for key distribution, that is, a two-party model which is inefficient and open to wider problems such as those related to the key distribution between the three parties involved in mobile handover.

Taking this into account, a 3-Party approach solution is proposed, which utilizes the IEEE 802.21 MIH services (namely MIIS) over GSABA. The goal is to provide fast handover and smooth transition by reducing the impact (i.e. minimizing the number of roundtrips) of the EAP based re-authentication process when the MN changes authenticator. At the same time, the key distribution mechanism of the proposed solution provides proper channel binding of the key to the parties that will use it. Taking into account the problem of handover keying, the proposed solution must meet the requirements listed below:

- Confidentiality - disclosure of the keying materials to passive and active attackers must not be possible.
- Integrity protection – alteration of a network access credential must be detected.
- Validation of credential source - the recipient of a network access credential must validate from which entity it came from and for what context the credential was delivered.
- Verification of identity - The three parties involved must confirm the identities of each other.
- Agreement by all parties – Upon successful completion of the protocol, all three parties must agree on the keying material being disclosed and the identity of the entity to which the keying material was disclosed.
- Peer consent – the credential should not be distributed without the consent of the client.
- Replay protection - replay attacks must not affect the key distribution protocol.
- Transport independent - The 3-party protocol must be independent of the transport protocol used for carrying the 3-party protocol messages.

Keying Hierarchy to be Used

The proposed mechanism of the 3-party model for re-authentication over GSABA utilizes the EAP keying hierarchy (Aboba and Simon 2008; Narayanan and Giaretta 2007). Upon successful completion of the EAP authentication method, the EAP server generates the EAP Extended Master Session Key (EMSK) as defined by the executed EAP method. From the EMSK, a Usage Specific Root Key (USRK) and further

keys may then be derived for various purposes, including, handover keys, encryption, integrity protection, entity authentication/re-authentication. The keys to establish SAs between the MN and IS to secure the MIIS signalling will be derived from the USRK key. The USRK key is referred to as the GSABA key (Mussabbir 2010). The GSABA key could also be called the Root Master Key (RMK). Specification of the generation of USRKs is in progress (Narayanan and Giaretta 2007) but it is expected that since the EAP layer does not export the EMSK, the GSABA Proxy server needs to request derivation of the GSABA Key (i.e. the RMK) from the EAP server after authorization has been provided. The EMSK root key hierarchy is used to derive keys for efficient EAP re-authentication and IS SA establishment (Narayanan and Giaretta 2007).

Detailed Explanation of the Proposed Mechanism

To start with, there is an assumption that there exists a SA between the MN and GSABA server. The GSABA Proxy and GSABA Server have another SA. Also, another assumption is that the EAP peer (i.e. the MN) has already completed a successful full EAP authentication with the EAP server (i.e. GSABA Server) through the currently attached EAP authenticator (i.e. the PoA). This allows the MN and the GSABA server to share a fresh EMSK. From the EMSK, a key hierarchy is derived for supporting the proposed 3-party re-authentication mechanism. This step is only performed once while the EMSK lifetime is still valid.

When the MN senses (e.g. through L2 triggers) that it is losing connectivity with the currently attached PoA as a result of signal degradation, it immediately sends a MIH message that carries the '*MIH_Get_ Information*' request TLV (Type Length Value) as its payload to the IS. The IS can be discovered by using DHCP. The purpose of sending the *MIH_Get_ Information*' request message is to discover neighbouring candidate PoAs/authenticators that support the proposed EAP re-authentication mechanism. Such security related information is crucial to make a handover decision and to prepare a fast handover using fast authentication options (e.g. pre-authentication, re-authentication, etc) supported by the network which the candidate PoA is associated with.

As explained earlier, there is a substantial delay due to re-transmissions of EAP-Initiate/ Re-auth messages before the MN realizes that a particular candidate PoA does not support EAP re-authentication. As a result, there will be significant signalling overhead and resource wastage if there are many candidate PoAs that need to be contacted before the actual handover. Moreover, using the information provided by the IS, the L2 scanning phase will be eliminated. This will drastically reduce the overall handover delay.

On receiving the '*MIH_Get_ Information*' request, the IS responds with a '*MIH_Get_ Information*' reply message which contains the requested information as an Information Element (IE) container. A container named '*SEC_CON-TAINER*' has been defined for this purpose. The '*SEC_CONTAINER*' will include information about the PoA Medium Access Control (MAC) address, the PoA IPv4/6 address, the supported EAP methods, and EAP re-authentication support etc. The contents of the '*SEC_CONTAINER*' are presented in Table 1.

However, it must be noted that prior to the '*MIH_Get_ Information*' request/reply message exchange, the IS and the MN must establish SAs to secure the MIIS signalling. In the following subsection, the SA establishment with the IS is explained.

SA Establishment between the MN and the IS

After the MN has been successfully authenticated for initial network access, the GSABA Server delivers the GSABA key to the GSABA proxy.

Table 1. SEC_CONTAINER

Type = TYPE_IE_ HNI_REPORT	Length = Variable
SEC_CONTAINER #1	
Open Authentication Support (Information Element) IE	
Password Support IE	
Certificate Authority IE	
Authentication Protocol Type IE	
Supported EAP Methods IE	
Re-authentication Support IE	
Pre-authentication Support IE	
Roaming Partners IE	
PoA MAC address	
PoA IPv4/6 address	
SEC_CONTAINER #2	
... ...	

Since the IEEE802.21 functionalities will be considered as *premium* services, which would enable optimized handovers across heterogeneous networks, it is essential to authorize and bootstrap the offered 802.21 MIH services. As a result, the MN sends an Authorization and Bootstrapping Information Response (ABIRES) message to the GSABA Proxy. It is assumed here that the MN profile (i.e. statement that gives the authorization for services for the MN) is delivered in advance to the GSABA Proxy during the initial EAP full-authentication phase. This is an enhanced case, since the GSABA Proxy will be free to generate authorization decisions locally instead of having to contact the home AAA server (i.e. GSABA server) every time a service is requested.

The MN secures the Authorization and Boot-strapping Information Request (ABIREQ) message with the Bootstrapping Configuration Agent (BCA) key which is derived from the GSABA Key. The minimum set of parameters in the ABIREQ message is the Bootstrapping Client Identifier (BCID), Service Request Identifier (SRID) (i.e. the ID of the IEEE802.21 service in this case), and the corresponding identifier intended to be used on the Sp interface. In response, the GSABA Proxy sends an ABIRES message containing the needed parameters. The BCA key protects the ABIREQ/ABIRES message by providing data confidentiality and integrity.

Immediately after the initial network authentication and service authorization, the MN will use the HOKEY protocol to create SAs (i.e. keys) to protect the MIIS signalling between the MN and the MIIS. The HOKEY protocol assumes that the MN shares a key, called the Information Master Key (IMK), with the GSABA Server. The IMK can be thought of as a GSABA key or a USRK which is derived from the EMSK.

A Message Integrity Key (MIK) is derived from IMK at the MN and the GSABA proxy. The MIK is used to provide data integrity for messages exchanged between the MN and the GSABA Proxy and is in fact the BCA Key. The Information Key (IK) which is used to protect the signalling exchange between the MN and the IS is also derived from the IMK, as shown in Figure 3.

Prior to sending the '*MIH_Get_Information*' request, the MN sends a Handover Key Request (HKReq) message to the IS in order to start the HOKEY process. The integrity of the HKReq message is protected by the use of a MIK. The IS forwards the content of the HKReq message via an Service Request (SIREQ) message to the GSABA Proxy, as only the GSABA Proxy can verify the message and generate a new Information Key (IK). The GSABA Proxy Server authenticates the MN and checks whether the MN is authorized for IEEE802.21 MIH Services (namely MIIS). If so, the GSABA Proxy derives the IK. The GSABA Proxy delivers the IK and the AAA nonce N2 as well as the IK lifetime and PRF (Preferences) which denotes the encryption algorithm chosen by the MN. Thereby; it is assumed that the IS and the Handover Key Server (HKS) share a security association protecting the AAA messages. On receiving the SIRES, the IS sends a Handover Key Response (HKResp) message to the MN, containing, beside other parameters, N2 and MN-AR_MAC, which is protected using the IK. Using the contents of the HKResp, the MN is able to derive the IK. As a result, a SA is established between the MN and the IS, which enables MIIS signalling (i.e. '*MIH_Get_ Information*' request/reply) to be protected.

Details of the Proposed Re-Authentication Process during Handover

The re-authentication during the handover phase is presented in Figure 4. As mentioned earlier, this chapter presents an EAP Re-authentication

Figure 3. SA establishment between the MN and IS

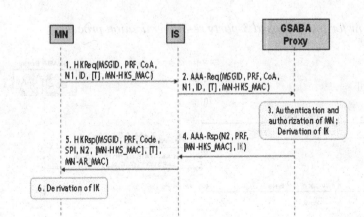

based on a 3-party approach over GSABA (EN-ABLE 2007). Using an EAP based model is the ideal option due to the fact that many devices implement EAP. Extension of the EAP messages *EAP Response Id* and *EAP Success* is required. However such extensions have minimal impact on the *EAP state machine,* compared to others solutions (Narayanan and Dondeti 2008).

In this phase the goal is to achieve the installation of a key in the new authenticator. It must be noted that if the MN needs to be authorized by the ASP as part of the proposed re-authentication process, then there needs to be an ABIREQ/ABI-RES message exchange between the MN and the GSABA Proxy. The process of obtaining such authorization from the GSABA is identical to the process described in section 4.2.1 of this chapter.

The message flow depicted in Figure 5 shows the movement of the MN when it wants to attach to another authenticator. The new authenticator sends an EAP Request Identity message in order to authenticate the MN (step 1). The EAP Request Identity message is integrity protected using a key denoted by rIK which is derived from the GSABA key. As has been explained earlier, the GSABA Key is derived from either the EMSK or a DSRK. For the purpose of GSABA key derivation, this chapter specifies the derivation of a USRK or a Domain-Specific USRK (DSUSRK) for re-authentication (Aboba, and Simon 2008). The USRK designated for re-authentication is the re-authentication root

key (the GSABA Key). Next, the MN responds with an EAP Response Identity message and this message is modified to allow the insertion of the additional information needed to perform the proposed 3-Party Protocol (step 2).

The proposed model provides a protected facility to carry channel binding (CB) information to tackle the issues describe in section 2 (Saha and Lagutin 2009). The TLV type range of 128-191 is reserved to carry CB information in the EAP-Response Id. Examples of CB information such as Called-Station-Id will be included in the EAP-Response Id message sent to the authenticator, as shown in Figure 4.

The EAP Response Identity message sent by the MN to the authenticator is forwarded by the authenticator to the GSABA Proxy, where the authenticator adds additional information (i.e. a NAS-Identifier as CB information) in the AAA message in order to be authenticated by the GSABA Proxy (step 3). At this point, both parties are authenticated by the GSABA Proxy and the key that it is going to be installed in the authenticator is derived by the GSABA Proxy. This key is known as the rMK and is derived from the GSABA key. A message which is a modified EAP Success message and the rMK is sent to the authenticator (step 4). The authenticator installs the key sent by the GSABA Proxy. With this key the authenticator and the MN establish a SA. Then, the authenticator sends a modified EAP Success

Figure 4. Message flow for the proposed 3-party re-authentication process

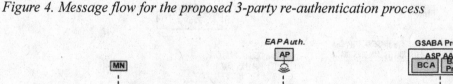
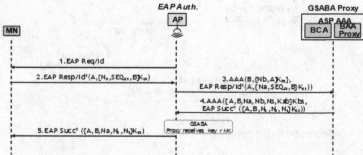

Figure 5. Overall handover delay for FMIPv6

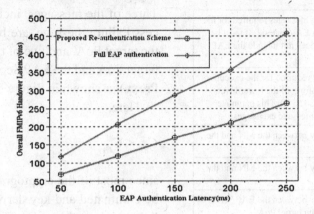

message to transport the necessary information to derive the same key that was installed in the authenticator (step 5). Finally to finish, the MN receives the modified EAP Success message. The MN is now authenticated by the network and derives the same rMk that was derived by the authenticator in order to establish a SA for the re-authentication mechanism.

PERFORMANCE EVALUATION

In this section, the overall latency due to the security signalling of the proposed EAP based re-authentication scheme is analyzed, and compared to the un-optimized (i.e. full) EAP re-authentication mechanism. The performance of the two schemes is evaluated using the authentication signalling and the EAP method latency metrics. The authentication signalling latency D_{SA} is defined as the time elapsed between the sending of the first authentication message (i.e. L2 SA such as the 4-way handshake in 802.11) until the Acknowledgment of the last authentication message is received by the MN. On the other hand, the EAP method latency, D_{EAP}, is defined as the time elapsed between the sending of the first EAP message and the reception of either an EAP SUCCESS or EAP FAILURE message.

The notation used to express the parameters and variables of the authentication signalling latency is provided in Table 2.

Full Authentication

The latency incurred by a full EAP method authentication exchange is expressed as:

$$D_{EAP} = 2d_{MT} + (d_{MT} + d_{ST}) \cdot S_{EAP} + d_{ST} + C_{FA}$$

(1)

where, $2d_{MT}$ is the delay caused by the initial two EAP messages. It is the delay incurred at the very beginning, when the authenticator sends an EAP-Request message, which contains a Type field, requesting a MN's Identity. In response to a valid request, the MN sends its identity in a Response message. Here, $(d_{MT} + d_{ST}) \cdot S_{EAP}$ is the time taken to complete a full authentication. The delay introduced by the key distribution procedure is represented by d_{ST}.

After a successful EAP authentication, media dependent SA protocol exchanges take place. For example, in 802.11 the MN undergoes a 4-way handshake to establish unicast and multicast SAs for protecting the signalling between the MN and the PoA (i.e. the authenticator). The delay

Table 2. Notation used in expressing the security latencies

S_{EAP}	Total number of signalling messages required for the successful execution of an EAP method. It must be noted that this parameter does not include the EAP Start message
S_{Auth}	Total number of messages required for the execution of the authentication signalling of the lower layers (e.g. 4-way handshake in 802.11i). This parameter does not include the EAP message exchanges.
d_{MC}	Average propagation delay between the MN and the currently attached PoA.
d_{MT}	Average propagation delay between the MN and the target PoA.
d_{ST}	Average propagation delay between the EAP Server (i.e. GSABA Proxy) and the target PoA.
C_{FA}	Time required for the involved parties to perform all the cryptographic operations, including key derivations, for a full EAP authentication.
C_{RA}	Time required for the involved parties to perform all the cryptographic operations, including key derivations, needed by the proposed re-authentication mechanism.

introduced by the media dependent SA protocol exchange is shown in (2).

$$DSA = dMT \times SAuth \qquad (2)$$

where, D_{SA} is the latency incurred by exchanging media specific authentication messages. The total latency for the overall authentication phase is expressed as:

$$D_{Total} = D_{EAP} + D_{SA} \qquad (3)$$

Proposed Re-authentication Scheme

The EAP latency for the proposed re-authentication mechanism is expressed in (4) below.

$$DPr\text{-}reauth = 2dMT + DRe\text{-}auth + CRA \qquad (4)$$

where

$$DRe\text{-}auth = 3d_{MT} + 2d_{ST} \qquad (5)$$

In (5), the EAP re-authentication method exchange is composed of a total of five messages. Three of the messages, including the EAP Success/Failure message, are between the MN and the target PoA, and two of them are between the target PoA and the EAP Server (i.e., the GSABA Proxy) as shown in Figure 5.

Here,

$$C_{RA} < C_{FA}$$

since most of the cryptographic operations will be eliminated and key derivation is much more lightweight and simpler. The overall authentication latency for the proposed scheme is, therefore, expressed as:

$$D_{Total} = D_{Pr\text{-}reauth} + D_{SA} \qquad (6)$$

where

$$DPr\text{-}reauth < D_{EAP}$$

System Modelling

With reference to the system model (Li Wang, Mei Song and Jun-de Song 2008) the GSABA Proxy in the proposed mechanism presented in section 4 of this chapter can manage a number of ARs in its management domain. The GSABA Server is in the home domain and other layers containing the GSABA Proxy disperse from it. It is assumed that the distance from a GSABA Server to a GSABA Proxy follows a Poisson distribution with a parameter value of μ. It is also assumed that a MN needs to move its PoA m times until it leaves the domain of the GSABA Proxy, which means that there are m-1 intra-domain authentications and the mth one is the inter-domain (i.e. inter GSABA Proxy) authentication. The probability that a MN moves out of a PoA's coverage area (i.e. intra domain) is:

Exhibit 1.

$$C_{org} = \frac{((1 - \sum_{N=0}^{K}(\frac{\mu N e_\mu}{N!})) \cdot \sum_{N=0}^{K}(\frac{\mu N e_\mu}{N!})m - 1(DEAP + DSA) + (m-1)(\frac{\mu N e_\mu}{N!})(DEAP + DSA).}{T}$$

(12)

where

$$C_{each} = C_{first}$$

(13)

$$\alpha = \frac{\mu N e_\mu}{N!}.$$

(7)

Where N is the number cells visited by the MN in a given domain.

The probability of a MN moving out of the GSABA Proxy's domain is expressed as (Li Wang, Mei Song and Jun-de Song 2008):

$$\beta = \left(1 - \sum_{N=0}^{K}\left(\frac{\mu N e_\mu}{N!}\right)\right) \cdot \sum_{N=0}^{K}\left(\frac{\mu N e_\mu}{N!}\right)m - 1,$$

(8)

where $1 \leq m \leq \infty$ and K is the radius of a GSABA Proxy's domain.

Based on (7) and (8), the total authentication cost C_{total} can be derived as:

$$C_{total} = \frac{(\beta).Cj + (\alpha).Ci}{T},$$

(9)

where T is the total time, Cj and Ci are the cost of inter (i.e. mobility from a GSABA server to a GSABA Proxy) and intra domain (mobility within a GSABA Proxy's domain) authentication respectively.

The total cost of the full EAP based authentication solution C_{org} (i.e. C_{total} for the full authentication) is:

$$C_{org} = \frac{Cfirst(\beta) + (m-1).Ceach(\alpha)}{T}$$

(10)

Where,

$$C_{first} = DEAP$$

(11)

C_{first} is the authentication cost incurred when the MN moves to the GSABA's Proxy's domain for the first time. C_{each} is the authentication cost every single time the MN moves to a new authenticator's (i.e. PoA) link. In the case of the un-optimized EAP mechanism (i.e. C_{org}), C_j would be equal to C_{first}, since the home domain (i.e. GSABA server) will be contacted every time the MN moves to a new GSABA Proxy's domain. In essence, C_{first} is a case of an inter-domain authentication (i.e. $C_j = C_{first}$). In Equation (10), C_{each} can be considered as the cost of the intra-domain authentication (C_j), since the MN moves within the boundary of a GSABA proxy. However, the total authentication cost for the full EAP authentication, C_{org} in Equation (10) can be derived as: (see Exhibit 1).

Based on Equation (9), the total cost of the proposed scheme, C_{pr} can be derived as:

Exhibit 2.

$$C_{pr} = \frac{((1 - \sum_{N=0}^{K}(\frac{\mu N e_\mu}{N!})) \cdot \sum_{N=0}^{K}(\frac{\mu N e_\mu}{N!})m - 1(DEAP + DSA) + (m-1)(\frac{\mu N e_\mu}{N!})(D\Pr - reauth + DSA).}{T}$$

(16)

$$C_{pr} = \frac{Cfirst(\beta) + (m-1).Cother(\alpha)}{T} \qquad (14)$$

where

$$C_{other} = D_{Pr\text{-}reauth} + D_{SA} \qquad (15)$$

C_{other} is the cost of the re-authentication mechanism. As mentioned earlier, it can be inferred that:

$$C_{pr} < C_{org}$$

since

Cother < Ceach

The cost of the proposed re-authentication scheme (i.e. C_{total}) is expressed as: (see Exhibit 2)

In Equation (16), C_j is equal to C_{other} due to the fact that C_{other} is the cost for an intra-domain handover (i.e. C_j).

Results Analysis

The results presented in this sub-section have been derived using provided parameters (Li Wang, Mei Song and Jun-de Song 2008) and from the simulation and experimental results (Mussabbir 2010). From the analytical results presented in Figures 6 and 7, it is clear that the proposed IEEE802.21 assisted re-authentication scheme outperforms the original (i.e. full EAP authentication) solution in terms of the reducing the overall handover latency for both FMIPv6 and MIPv6. The results suggest that the overall handover latency can be reduced by roughly 70% by using the proposed mechanism. This is due to the fact that the proposed mechanism reduces the total EAP authentication signalling (i.e.

Figure 6. Overall handover delay for MIPv6

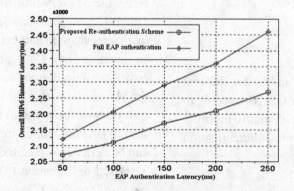

Figure 7. Impact on EAP latency of end-to-end delay

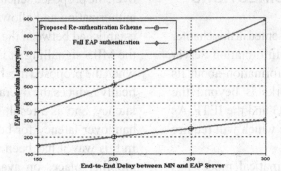

$D_{Pr\text{-}reauth}$) and the required cryptographic operations (i.e. $C_{RA} < C_{FA}$). Also, by using the IEEE802.21 MIIS, the scanning phase of the L2 handover is eliminated which drastically reduces the overall handover latency.

The results of Figures 5 and 6 support the findings where the total cost (i.e. handover and authentication latency) increases as the Average Residence Time (AVR) decreases (Li Wang, Mei Song and Jun-de Song 2008). The AVR is defined as the average time a MN stays within the coverage of a PoA. Even though the results in Figure 6 compare the overall handover latency with the EAP authentication delays as opposed to the total cost versus AVR (Li Wang, Mei Song and Jun-de Song 2008), the results on total cost versus AVR (Li Wang, Mei Song and Jun-de Song 2008) still support the concepts of the proposed scheme presented in section 4 of this chapter and the results shown in Figure 6. For instance, a decrease in the AVR means that the MN stays within an authentication server's domain for a shorter period of time, which will lead to an increase in the rate of handover and authentication signalling. An increase in the total authentication signalling leads to an increase in the authentication cost. Since authentication is a fundamental component of a NGN handover, an increase in the authentication signalling/cost will lead an increase in the handover latency.

The results in Figure 6 which take into account the total cost (i.e. Authentication signalling cost) presented in Equations (12) and (16) of this chapter are a testament to the fact that an increase in the total cost due to an increase in the authentication signalling will result in an incremental increase in the overall handover latency.

The impact of the distance between the MN and the EAP server (the GSABA Proxy/Server in this case) on the overall handover latency is illustrated in Figure 6. In Figure 6, the distance is directly proportional to the end-to-end delay between the MN and the GSABA Proxy/Server. Unsurprisingly, the overall handover latency increases with the end-to-end (i.e. distance) delay between the MN and the GSABA server. If the GSABA Proxy is far away from the MN, then the packet transmission cost for the EAP authentication signalling is also increased.

The results in Figure 7 support findings (Li Wang, Mei Song and Jun-de Song 2008) where an increase in the distance between the MN and the AAA server (i.e. GSABA and GSABA Proxy) would result in an increase in the overall handover latency. The findings hold true to the conventional wisdom for end-to-end latency which depends on many factors such as processing delays at intermediate routers due to queuing, the number of hops between the MN and the EAP server, transmission delays, bottlenecks at public exchanges, etc.

FUTURE RESEARCH DIRECTIONS

The proposed mechanism presented in this chapter is heavily dependent on the Information Server (IS). How the IS collects information about its neighbouring access networks is beyond the scope of the IEEE802.21 WG and the IETF. As a result, this is an open issue which will require active research.

In this chapter, a mathematical model has been presented to evaluate the performance of the IEEE802.21 fast EAP re-authentication mechanism. Due to the lack of security tools available in network simulator (ns-3) a simulation has not been possible. In order to provide a more detailed analysis, simulation results are required.

Lastly, this chapter has considered most of the existing access technologies (both IEEE and non-IEEE, such as UMTS). However, it does not consider the upcoming uni-directional broadcast technologies, such as DVB-H (ETSI standard EN 302 304 2004). Very recently, the IEEE802.21b TG has taken the initiative to define mechanisms to support optimized handovers between these technologies and other technologies already supported by IEEE 802.21. Currently, there is no standard which specifies such handovers. Therefore, much research is required in this field.

CONCLUSION

In this chapter, a mechanism has been proposed which optimizes the EAP re-authentication procedure with the assistance of IEEE802.21 MIH services over a GSABA infrastructure. To do this, the MIIS has been exploited to provide information about discovered target PoAs in neighbouring networks that support the re-authentication mechanism. A new Information Container, the '*SEC_CONTAINER*', has been defined for this purpose. Also, using the MIIS eliminates the need to perform a L2 scanning process which dramatically reduces the overall handover delays. More-over, the proposed scheme enables 802.21 service authorization and allows for dynamic SAs to be established between the MN and the IS to secure the MIIS signalling. It is shown analytically that when the proposed mechanism is applied, it drastically reduces the overall EAP re-authentication latency, and as a result, also reduces the overall handover latency for both MIPv6 and FMIPv6. In this way it has been shown that the demands mobility places on availability can broadly be met leaving only the generic issues of Internet availability.

For corporate network professionals the challenge will be to find ways of working with NGN operators to obtain the assurances they need to make their resources available in real-time to company employees who away from the office and on the move. These assurances could include the provision of information related to company employees' use of the network.

REFERENCES

Aboba, B., & Simon, D. (2008). *Extensible authentication protocol (EAP) key management framework*. RFC 5247, IETF, August.

Arkko, J., & Haverinen, H. (2008). *Extensible authentication protocol method for 3rd generation authentication and key agreement (EAP-AKA)*. RFC 4182, IETF, January.

Clancy T., & Tschofenig, H. (2008). *EAP generalized pre-shared key*. RFC 5433, IETF, November 19.

ENABLE. (2006). *Requirements, scenarios and initial architecture. Deliverable D1.1*. Project IST ENABLE.

ENABLE. (2007). *Service authorization and control for fast/smart handover*. Project IST ENABLE Deliverable D4.3, December.

ETSI Standard EN 302 304. (2004)., *ETSI standard*, November.

Goldman, J. (2008). *Introducing IEEE802.11r* [Online]. Retrieved from http://www.wi-fiplanet.com/news/article.php/3776351

Harkins, D., Ohba, Y., Nakhjiri, M., & Lopez, R. (2007). *Problem statement and requirements on a 3-party distribution protocol for handover keying*. Internet Draft (work in progress), IETF, March.

Haverinen, H., & Salowey, J. (2006). *Extensible authentication protocol method for global system for mobile communications (GSM) subscriber identity modules (EAP-SIM)*. RFC 4186, IETF, January.

IEEE802.21 Draft P802.21/D00.05. (2006). *Standard and metropolitan area networks: Media independent handover services*. IEEE, March.

Izguierdo, A., Hoeper, K., Golmie, N., & Chen, L. (2008). Using the EAP framework for fast media independent handover authentication. *Proceedings of the 4th Annual International Conference on Wireless Internet*, Maui, Hawaii, (pp. 1-8).

Li, W., Mei, S., & Jun-de, S. (2008). An efficient hierarchical authentication scheme in mobile IPv6 networks. *Journal of China Universities of Posts and Telecommunications, 15*(1), 9–13.

Mussabbir, Q. B. (2010). *Mobility management across converged IP-based heterogeneous access networks*. Unpublished doctoral thesis, Brunel University.

Nakhjiri, M. (2007). *Keying and signaling for wireless access and handover using EAP (EAP-HR)*. Internet Draft (work in progress), IETF, April.

Narayanan, V., & Dondeti, L. (2007). *EAP extensions for efficient re-authentication*. Internet Draft (work in progress), IETF, January.

Narayanan, V. and Dondeti, L., (2008). *EAP extensions for reauthentication protocol*. RFC 5296, IETF, March 29.

Narayanan V., & Giaretta, G. (2007). *EAP-based keying for IP mobility protocols*. Internet Draft (work in progress), IETF, November 16.

Ohba, Y., & Das, S. (2007). *An EAP method for EAP extension*. Internet Draft (work in progress) July.

Saha, S., & Lagutin, D. (2009). *PLA-MIH: A secure MIH transport signaling scheme*. IEEE International Conference on Wireless and Mobile Computing, Networking and Communications, WIMOB 2009.

IEEE Standard 802.16e. (2005). *IEEE standard and metropolitan area networks: Part16: Air interface for fixed and mobile broadband wireless access systems*. IEEE, December 7.

IEEE Standard 802.11r. (2008). *Information Technology - Telecommunications and information exchange between systems - Local and metropolitan area networks - Specific requirements – Part 11: Wireless LAN Medium Access Control (MAC) and Physical Layer (PHY) specifications - Amendment 2: Fast BSS Transition*. IEEE, January.

ADDITIONAL READING

Aboba, B., et al. (2004). Extensible Authentication Protocol (EAP), *RFC 3748, IETF, June Avispa Project*, (2010). from http://avispa-project.org/

Bajko, G. (2009). Locating IEEE 802.21 Mobility Servers using DNS, *RFC 5679, IETF, December*

Bound, J., et al., (2003). Dynamic Host Configuration Protocol for IPv6 (DHCPv6), *RFC 3315, IETF, July*.

Calhoun, P., (2010) Diameter Base Protocol, *RFC 3588, IETF, April*

CALM –Medium and Long Range, High Speed, Air Interfaces parameters and protocols for broadcast, point to point, vehicle to vehicle, and vehicle to point communication in the ITS sector – Networking Protocol – Complementary Element, (2005). *ISO draft ISO/WD 2121 (works in progress), ISO, Technical committee* 204, WG16, *Decem*Devarapali, V. et al., (2005). Network Mobility (NEMO) Basic Support Protocol, *RFC 3963, IETF, January*

Chowdhury, K., & Yegin, A. (2008). *MIP6-bootstrapping via DHCPv6 for the Integrated Scenario, Internet Draft (work in progress)*. IETF April.

Deering, S., et al, (1998). Internet Protocolv6 Specification, *RFC 791, IETF, December*

Devarapalli, V., et al. (2007). Mobile IPv6 Bootstrapping for the Authentication Option Protocol, *Internet Draft (work in progress), IETF March fmipv6.org – Source code for FMIPv6, (2010).,* from www.fmipv6.org

Funk, P., & Blake-Wilson, S. (2008). Extensible Authentication Protocol Tunneled Transport Layer Security Authentication Protocol Version 0(EAP-TTLSv0), *RFC 5281, IETF, August Generic Authentication Architecture (GAA); Generic bootstrapping architecture, (2010).* from http://www.3gpp.org/ftp/Specs/html-info/33220.html

Giaretta, G., et al., (2006). MIPv6 Authorization and Configuration based on EAP, *Internet Draft (work in progress), IETF, October*

Giaretta, G., et al., (2007). Mobile IPv6 bootstrapping in split scenario, *IETF, RFC 5026, October*

Gundavelli, S. et al., (2008). Proxy Mobile IPv6, *RFC 5213, IETF, August*

Hannes, T., et al., (2005) Enriching Bootstrapping with Authorization Information, *Internet Draft (work in progress), IETF October* 22

Jayaraman, P. (2008). *Protocol for Carrying Authentication for Network Access (PANA) Framework, RFC 5193.* IETF.

Johnson, D. et al., (2004). Mobility Support in IPv6, *RFC 3775, IETF, June*

Kempf, J., et al.,(2005). SEcure Neighbor Discovery (SEND), *RFC 3971, IETF, March*

Koodli, R., et al., (2005). Fast Handovers for Mobile IPv6, *RFC 4068, IETF, July*

Melia, T. et al., (2008). Mobility Services Transport: Problem Statement, *RFC 5164, IETF, March*

Moskowitz, R. et al., (2008). Host Identity Protocol, *RFC 5201, IETF, April*

Narayanan, V., et al., (2007). Establishing Handover Keys using Shared Keys, *Internet Draft (work in progress), IETF, March* 6

NIST Project- Seamless and Secure Mobility tool suits, (2010). from http://www.antd.nist.gov/seamlessandsecure/pubtool.shtml#tools

Palekar, A., et al., (2007). Protected EAP Protocol (PEAP) Version 2, *Internet Draft (work in progress), IETF, October* 15

Patel A. and Giaretta, G., (2006). Problem Statement for Bootstrapping Mobile IPv6 (MIPv6), *RFC 4640, IETF, September*

Rey, M, (1981). Internet Protocol Specification, *RFC 2460, IETF, September*

Rigney, C., et al., (2006). Remote Authentication Dial In User Service (RADIUS), *RFC 3971, IETF, June*

Rosenberg, J. et al., (2002). SIP: Session Initiation Protocol, *RFC 3261, IETF, June*

Salowey, J, et al., (2008). Specification for the Derivation of Root Keys from an Extended Master Session Key (EMSK), *RFC 5295, IETF, June* 23

Schulzrinne, H. et al., (2003), RTP: A Transport Protocol for Real-Time Applications, *RFC 3550, IETF, July*

Simon, D., et al., (2008). The EAP-TLS Authentication Protocol, *RFC 5216, IETF, March*

Socolofsky, T. and Kale, C., (1991). TCP/IP tutorial, *RFC 1180, IETF,* January

Soliman, H., et al., (2005). Hierarchical Mobile IPv6 Mobility Management (HMIPv6), *RFC 4140, IETF, August*

Sreemanthula,S. et al., (2006). Requirement For Handover Information Services, *Internet Draft (work in progress), IETF, March*

Tschofenig, H., et al., (2008). The Extensible Authentication Protocol-Internet Key Exchange Protocol version 2 (EAP-IKEv2) Method, *RFC 5281, IETF, August*

KEY TERMS AND DEFINITIONS

Authentication, Authorization and Accounting (AAA): AAA refers to the process of providing network security through Authentication, Authorization and Accounting mechanisms.

Access Point (AP): A wireless access point, identified by a Medium Access Control address, providing service to the wired network for wireless nodes.

Access Router (AR): The entity interconnecting the access network to the Internet or other IP-based networks; The AR provides connectivity between hosts on the access network at different customer premises. It is also used to provide security filtering, policing, and accounting of customer traffic.

Access Service Authorizer (ASA): A network operator that authenticates a mobile node and establishes the mobile node's authorization to receive Internet service.

Access Service Provider (ASP): A network operator that provides direct IP packet forwarding to and from the end host.

Bootstrapping Configuration Agent (BCA): The BCA is a functional component that is responsible for providing necessary bootstrapping information to the mobile node (e.g. Home Agent address, the security association and the Home address).

Base Station (BS): A wireless station, providing services to the wired network for wireless nodes.

Extensible Authentication Protocol (EAP): EAP is an authentication framework which is frequently used in wireless networks and point-to-point connections to provide authentication services.

Home Address (HoA): A unicast routable address assigned to a mobile node, used as the permanent address of the mobile node. This address is within the mobile node's home link. Standard IP routing mechanisms will deliver packets destined for a mobile node's home address to its home link. Mobile nodes can have multiple home addresses, for instance when there are multiple home prefixes on the home link.

Home Agent (HA): A router on a mobile node's home link with which the mobile node has registered its current care-of address. While the mobile node is away from home, the home agent intercepts packets on the home link destined to the mobile node's home address, encapsulates them, and tunnels them to the mobile node's registered care-of address.

Internet Engineering Task Force (IETF): The IETF develops and promotes Internet standards for the TCP/IP and Internet Protocol suite, by cooperating with other standards bodies such as the World Wide Web Consortium (W3C) and

International Organization for Standardization (ISO).

Internet Service Provider (ISP): A company that offers Internet access to its customers using technologies such dial-up, Digital Subscriber Line, cable modem etc.

Internet Protocol (IP): A protocol used to identify an end-device in the Internet and used for communicating data and routing packets across a packet-switched internetwork.

Medium Access Control (MAC): The MAC layer is a sub-layer of the Data Link Layer of the TCP/IP protocol suite. It provides addressing and channel access control mechanisms that allow for multi-point network communication.

Mobile Node (MN): A node that can change its point of attachment from one link to another, while still being reachable via its home address.

Mobility Service Authorizer (MSA): A service provider that authorizes Mobile IPv6 service.

Mobility Service Provider (MSP): A service provider that provides Mobile IPv6 service. In order to obtain such service, the mobile node must be authenticated and be authorized to obtain the service.

Network Access Server (NAS): A server that provides access to a network.

Point-of-Attachment (PoA): The PoA is a device with which a mobile device has wireless connectivity such as an Access Point or Base Station.

Quality of Service (QoS): Quality of Service refers to resource reservation control mechanisms rather than the achieved service quality. Examples of QoS metrics are delay, jitter, packet dropping probability, etc.

Round-Trip Delay Time (RTT): Is the time taken for a segment to be sent and the time it takes to receive an acknowledgment of that segment.

Universal Mobile Telecommunications System (UMTS): UMTS is a next generation network for mobile communication. UMTS is a 3G network (3rd generation) and is the successor of the 2nd generation GSM.

Voice Over Internet Protocol (VoIP): Is a general term for an umbrella of transmission technologies for transmitting voice data over the Internet. VoIP systems employ session control protocols to control the set-up and termination of calls as well as audio codecs which encode the voice data.

APPENDIX: ACRONYMS USED

AAA Authentication, Authorization and Accounting

ABIREQ Authorization and Bootstrapping Information Request

ABIRES Authorization and Bootstrapping Information Response

AP Access Points

AR Access Router

ASA Access Service Authoriser

ASP Access Service Provider

AVR Average Residence Time

BCA Bootstrapping Configuration Agent

BCID Bootstrapping Client Identifier

BS Base Station

CB Channel Binding

DHCPv6 Dynamic Host Control Protocol v6

DSUSRK Domain-Specific Usage Specific Root Key

EAP Extensible Authentication Protocol

EMSK EAP Extended Master Session Key

ERP EAP Re-Authentication Protocol

FMIPv6 Fast Mobile IPv6

GSABA Generic Service Authorization and Bootstrapping Architecture

HKReq Handover Key Request message

HKResp Handover Key Response

HKS Handover Key Server

IETF Internet Engineering Task Force

IE Information Element

IK Information key

IMK Information Master Key

IS Information Server

ISP Internet Service Provider

MAC Medium Access Control

MIH Media Independent Handover

MIHF Media Independent Handover Function

MIIS Media Independent Handover Information Services

MIPv6 Mobile IPv6

MIK Message Integrity Key

MN Mobile Node

MSA Mobility Service Authorizer

MSP Mobility Service Provider

NAS Network Access Server

PANA Protocol for Carrying Authentication for Network Access

PoA Point of Attachment

RMK Root Master Key

SA Security Association

SIREQ Service Request message

SRID Service Request Identifier

TLV Type Length Value

QoS Quality of Service

USRK Usage Specific Root Key

VoIP Voice over IP

Section 3
SA CND Applications

Chapter 14
Modelling Situation Awareness Information and System Requirements for the Mission using Goal-Oriented Task Analysis Approach

Cyril Onwubiko
Research Series Limited, UK

ABSTRACT

This chapter describes work on modelling situational awareness information and system requirements for the mission. Developing this model based on Goal-Oriented Task Analysis representation of the mission using an Agent Oriented Software Engineering methodology advances current information requirement models because it provides valuable insight on how to effectively achieve the mission's requirements (information, systems, networks, and IT infrastructure), and offers enhanced situational awareness within the Computer Network Defence environment. Further, the modelling approach using Secure Tropos is described, and model validation using a security test scenario is discussed.

INTRODUCTION

This chapter describes an approach to modelling, which is used to model mission information technology (IT) services requirements, and network services required by the mission to support network-centric operations (NCO) and enhance situational awareness (SA) for computer network defence (CND). In this chapter, a *Mis-*

sion is a military organisation or an agency. A *Force Command* is military or agency personnel responsible for the mission's computer network defence comprising network-centric operations, network services and IT support. Network-centric operations are concerned with exploiting information to maximise combat power, and the ability to protect the mission's information systems and to respond to enemy attacks swiftly. According to

DOI: 10.4018/978-1-4666-0104-8.ch014

Endsley M. R. (Endsley 2000), situation awareness is the process of perceiving the elements in the environment, understanding the elements in the environment, and the projection of their status into the near future.

To maximise the exploitation of network-centric operations for computer network defence, enhanced situational awareness is required of the mission's computer networks and IT services. IT infrastructure, systems and networks have to develop to collect data and information from disparate sources, process the data into logical outputs, and push it to the Force Command to make better and informed decisions, make calculated judgements on perceived incidents, determine and authorise appropriate cause of actions (CoA).

Situation awareness over the mission's computer networks and IT services requires understanding of the mission's operational capability requirements. Given these requirements, IT services requirements of the mission can be modelled, and IT services required by the Force Command can be modelled and validated. The premise is that operational capability requirements of the mission must be decided and outlined (see Section 2.2). And until these are known, it is impossible to model accurately the services requirements of the mission.

There are a good number of significant research contributions in situational awareness for CND and network security as demonstrated by the following: Tadda G. P. and Salerno J. S., 2009, Grégoire, M. and Beaudoin, L., 2005, Bass T., 2000, Juarez-Espinosa O. and Gonzalez C. 2004, Blais C. L. 2005, Jones R.E.T. et al., 2010, Bell, M. I., and Bates, E. A., 2005, Onwubiko C., 2009, Lefebvre J. H. et al 2005, Jajodia S. et al. 2009 and Onwubiko, C., 2011b.

Majority of the CND SA contributions focus on addressing low-level network events, D'Amico and Whitley, 2008, Wang L., et al 2007; while these contributions on their own help to shape the situation awareness in CND discipline; unfortunately, it is still ever so challenging to achieve a

mission's objectives without a clear description of a mission's information and system operational capability requirements. According to Lefebvre J. H. et al 2005, "research into CND situation awareness (SA) lacks a clear semantics for describing network missions, and an effective tool for modelling IT Services and network resources. Once these missing pieces are defined, and then the existing CND SA research on managing low-level network events becomes meaningful."

We identified whilst going through these contributions (Grégoire, M. and Beaudoin, L., 2005, ESRI, 2008, Lefebvre J. H. et al 2005) that:

1. Information Technology (IT) Services required by the mission to support operations need to be investigated (Juarez-Espinosa O. and Gonzalez C., 2004, Lefebvre J. H. et al 2005, Bell M. I., and Bates E. A., 2005).
2. A comprehensive system modelling tool is needed which can model mission requirement IT services definitions (Lefebvre J. H. et al 2005, Endsley M. R. 20001, and Jajodia S. et al. 2009, Bares D., 2010).

The aim of this chapter is to address these two SA in CND essential issues. That is, IT service definition and modelling of Mission network and IT services requirements. It is pertinent to note that military operations for warfare (MOFW), military operations other than war (MOOTW), network centric warfare (NCW), counterterrorism (CT), antiterrorism (AT) or computer network attack (CNA) is beyond the scope this chapter. The scope of this chapter is modelling of situational awareness of network and IT services requirements for the mission in a CND environment. According to Lefebvre J. H. et al 2005, a CND environment is one that focuses on managing the vulnerabilities and risks inherent in all computer networks.

The significance of our contribution is underpinned on the provision of a modelling approach that utilises the mission statement as the primary driving force for effective and enhanced situational awareness in a CND environment to drive network-centric operations towards information superiority.

The chapter is organised as follows. The first section describes goal-oriented task analysis, and the reasons why it is used in this study. The second section discusses the security modelling of the agent oriented software engineering (AOSA) application utilised to model CND SA requirements. The third section demonstrates CND SA requirements modelling; each component of the proposed model is discussed and shown how it can be used to achieve both the high-level mission objectives and the low-level tasks that enable these goals to be accomplished. The fourth section provides discussion around model validation by presenting an attack scenario which was tested with results. This helps to strengthen the contribution in the chapter. Finally, the chapter is summarised with a conclusion.

GOAL-ORIENTED TASK ANALYSIS

This section presents a list of requirements for the Goal-Oriented Task Analysis (GOTA) model that represents the mission's CND systems and information requirements. Although it is almost impossible to model the full spectrum of GOTA processes that can be required in a CND environment, we present a comprehensive high-level semantic model needed in a CND environment that enables network-centric operations and enhanced situational awareness.

Goal-oriented task analysis is a modelling approach that combines both goal-oriented and task-oriented models. Goal-oriented methods provide specific support for coping with high-level users' and stakeholders' goals that facilitate the exploration of design alternatives and the definition of requirements at a suitable level of abstraction (Bolchini, D., and Mylopoulos, J., 2003). Goal-oriented methodology is most suited for modelling high-level strategic objectives that

are elusive, passive and intangible. As such, goal-based techniques are appropriate for the early stages of requirements analysis.

Task models focus on fine-grained and precisely defined user needs, thereby risking a commitment to premature design decisions. Moreover, since task analysis focuses on users doing things with the system, tasks do not capture the goals of other stakeholders who are not users. Task models can be used for later stages, such as detailed interaction design and usability evaluation. According to Richardson J. et al 1998, task analysis is a methodology that can be used to analyse system functionality in terms of the human user's goals and sub-goals inherent in performing the task.

Goal-oriented task analysis is most suited for modelling CND SA requirements because it captures both the high-level mission objectives (modelled using goal-oriented models) of the Mission and Force Command, while low-level actionable tasks rendered by Network Commands, Network Analysts and IT Support personnel are represented by the task-oriented models. GOTA provides the structures to facilitate the exploration of strategic definition requirements, and also the mechanism to decompose goals into tasks which can be precisely modelled using the task-oriented aspects methodology. For example, the United States of America, Department of Defence, Joint Vision 2020 strategic aim is 'preparing for tomorrow' (DoD Joint Vision 2000). To model this initiative with either the goal-oriented method or task-oriented method would be extremely challenging, because neither the high-level mission statement, nor the low-level task-based activities could be reasonably and comprehensively modelled. For this reason, it is appropriate to utilise goal-oriented task analysis modelling that combines both the high-level mission statement using goal-oriented models and low-level actionable task using task-oriented models.

The use of goal-oriented task analysis paradigm to model CND SA requirements is one of the most significant strengths of our contribution.

MISSION'S MISSION STATEMENT

The mission's mission statement is to have information superiority over its adversaries (enemies) by having the capability to acquire, exploit and disseminate an uninterrupted flow of information while possessing the capability to impact an adversary's ability to do same (DoD Joint Vision 2000, Lefebvre J. H. et al 2005). This mission goal is decomposed into reducible actionable goals (hard and soft sub-goals). While modelling the high-level strategic goals, most of the reducible sub-goals are transparent.

The mission's objective is stated in the mission's mission statement. The mission provides the mission statement, and ensures that resources are made available to the Force Command. The Force Command ensures that mission objectives are accomplished. The Force Command is also responsible for engaging external intelligence, coordinating and sharing intelligence, and making sure that pertinent threat actors are identified (see Figure 1). Between the *Mission* actor and the *Force Command* actor, the Mission depends (shown by the D-line from Mission actor) on the Force Command to accomplish its mission objectives. Whereas the Force Command depends on the Mission to define its mission statement (shown by the D-line relations from Force Command), and also provide the resources required to accomplish its mission objectives (see Figure 1).

Figure 1 is our proposed GOTA security enhanced actor diagram (SEAD) for the mission. It shows actors, goals, plans and security constraints. Details of each actor, goal, security constraint and plan are explained in Section 4.

Mission Operational Capability Requirements

The mission statement is decomposed to reducible operational capability requirements provided through the Force Command. These requirements are modelled as goals using the Goal-Oriented Tasks Analysis methodology, as follows:

1. To ensure that impacts due to network incidents are assessed and addressed, and the impact of potential events can be estimated (forecast of impact of potential incidents);
2. To provide risk management of the mission's computer networks and IT services such as quality of protection (QoP) services – availability, confidentiality, integrity and privacy are achieved and maintained;

Figure 1. Mission security enhanced actor diagram

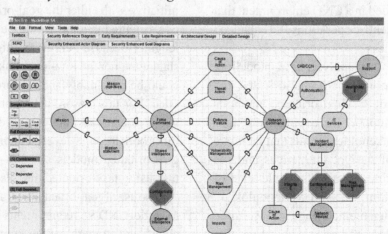

3. To provide vulnerability management such that vulnerabilities that may exist in all computer networks and IT systems are identified and addressed;

4. To provide information about the posture of the network, which can be used to assess the level of threats, and to decide when to heighten security postures due to perceived risks;

5. To detect intrusions, interceptions and interruptions, and to ensure that capabilities exist to identify threats and threat actors who may want exploit vulnerabilities in mission systems;

6. To provide reliable information about all possible threat actors that may be interested in exploiting the network, or gaining unauthorised access, or limiting the mission's operational capability;

7. To deduce cause of action (CoA) for all incidents swiftly and reliably;

8. To provide secure, reliable and 'passive' information about adversaries through collaborative, shared and point of interest external intelligence;

9. To ensure the mission has the capability to carry out post incident analysis, investigation and possesses forensic readiness capability;

10. To ensure reliable, stable and secure network and IT services for the mission.

These requirements (goals) together help to accomplish the mission's objectives (see Section 2.1); and each goal can be decomposed into sub-goals, which could be secure goals, hard goals or soft goals (see Section 3.1). The benefit of goal-oriented task analysis is that it mimics the human cognitive model, such that human actions (in real world) can be modelled exactly as if they were executed by the person, including attributing cognitive mental models. Goals are assigned as tasks to actors, and each actor has some dependent relationships.

For example, using Figure 1, the Force Command depends on the Network Command to do the following:

1. Assess impacts of incidents on the network and the mission in general;

2. Carryout risk management of the network for the mission;

3. Conduct vulnerability management of the entire network and IT services systems for the mission;

4. Provide information about current and forecasted defence posture of the network states and status.

These goals of the Network Command are decomposed to sub-goals and sub-tasks for the Network Analyst and IP Support; hence the dependence is passed further down the reporting chain. For example, the Network Command depends on the IT Support to plan change control notifications (CCN), organise a change advisory board (CAB), and ensure IT Services availability; while the IT Support depends on the Network Command for authorisation or approval of all change management requests (see Figure 1).

Conversely, the Network Command depends on the Force Command to:

1. provide information about threat actors that the Mission must be aware of, and;

2. decide courses of action, and be responsible for decision making.

Sections 4.1, 4.2 and 4.3 provide a detailed description of each actor's objectives and their relationships, goals and tasks, including decomposed actionable goals and tasks (sub-goals and sub-tasks).

THE MODELLING ENVIRONMENT

Secure Tropos

Secure Tropos is a requirements engineering (RE) methodology based on the agent-oriented software engineering (AOSE) paradigm (Giorgini P. et al, 2005, Mouratidis H. and Giorgini P., 2007a). It is an extension of the Tropos methodology (Giorgini P. et al, 2005b, Castro J. et al, 2002, Mouratidis H. et al 2003), and used for modelling and analysing of functional and non-functional security requirements.

Secure Tropos is used in this chapter to model CND SA requirements because it presents an appropriate modelling paradigm, the goal-oriented task analysis, for modelling CND SA requirements that comprises both high-level mission objectives that require goal-oriented methods, and low-level situational awareness tasks, such performed by Network Analysts and IT Support personnel that require task-oriented modelling. While there exist a plethora of modelling tools such as, UML, i*, KAOS, AOSE, etc, Tropos not only combines most of the principles presented by these well-known methods, but also extends them by offering security requirements methods (Giorgini P, 2010). Secure Tropos is an extension of the Tropos methodology that incorporates security requirements naturalistically. It has been used to model security and dependability requirements of information services (Asnar Y., and Giorgini P., 2010); develop an electronic single assessment system (eSAP), an agent-based health and social care system for the effective care of older people (Mouratidis H., 2004); and model risk management activities (Matulevičius R., et al, 2008).

Our objective is to utilise an appropriate method to model CND SA requirements, hence we encourage readers who may be interested in a comparative study of modelling tools, especially, Secure Tropos and other agent-oriented software engineering methods to make reference to these contributions (Yu, E., 1995, Mouratidis, H. and Giorgini, P., 2007, Giorgini, P. 2010, Evans, R. et al, 2001) for further reading.

Secure Tropos is extended and built to describe both the system-to-be (reference diagram, as shown in Figure 3) and its organisational environment starting from the early phases of the system development process. The main advantages of this approach is that one can capture not only the *what* or the *how*, but also the *why* of when a security mechanism should be included in the system design (Bryl V. et al, 2006). It uses the concept of actor, agent, role, position, goal, plan, resource, secure elements (security constraint, secure goal, secure plan and secure resource), social and secure relationships. Social relations are used for defining entitlements, capabilities and responsibilities of actors; while secure relations are used to impose restrictions on actors and the system, and it allows developers to perform an analysis by introducing relationships between the security constraints or a security constraint and its context (Mouratidis H. and Giorgini P., 2007a).

An *actor* is an intentional entity that performs actions to achieve goals. An *actor* can be an *agent* (human or software) that occupies a *position* and performs a *role*. For example, Cyril is a Person. Cyril occupies the position of Commander. The position commander covers the roles of army advisor and analyst. A *goal* represents an objective of an actor, which can be a *hard goal*, which is an actor's strategic interest or a *soft goal*, which is a goal without clear criteria to determine whether it is satisfied or not. A *task* specifies a particular sequence of actions that should be executed for satisfying a goal. A *resource* represents a physical or an informational entity. In a *Social dependency* between two actors, one actor (the *Depender*) depends on another actor (the *Dependee*) to accomplish a goal, execute a task, or deliver a resource. A *security constraint* is a restriction related to security issues, such as privacy, integrity and availability imposed by an actor. A *secure goal* represents a strategic interest of an actor with respect to security. A *secure plan*

Figure 2. Secure Tropos modelling concept

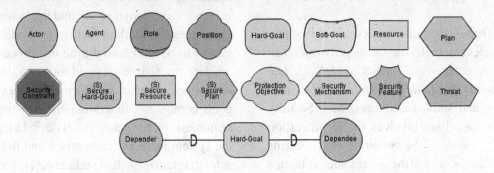

is a plan that represents a particular way of satisfying a secure goal (see Figure 2). Secure entities modelling involves, the analysis of the secure goals, tasks and resources identified in a multiagent system and is considered to be complementary to the security constraints modelling.

Security Constraints Modelling

Security constraint modelling involves the modelling of the security constraints imposed on the actors and the system, and it allows developers to perform an analysis by introducing relationships between the security constraints or a security constraint and its context. For example, the *Force Command* actor can impose a security constraint on the *External Intelligence* actor to shared intelligence only in an encrypted form. This is why confidentiality is modelled as a security constraint between the Force Command and External Intelligence (see Figure 1). Security constraint modelling is divided into a number of smaller modelling activities such as security constraint delegation, security constraint assignment, and security constraint analysis.

Figure 3. CND SA reference diagram

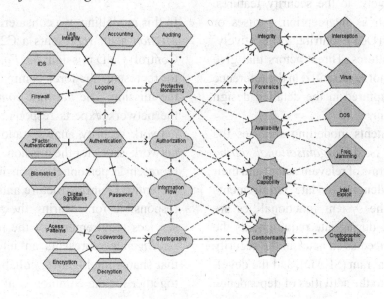

Secure Tropos Modelling Process

Secure Tropos methodology covers five main software development stages: *security reference modelling, early requirements modelling, late requirements modelling, architectural design modelling,* and *detailed design modelling.* Security reference modelling involves the identification of security needs of the system-to-be, problems related to the security of the system, such as threats and vulnerabilities, and possible solutions to the security problems. During the security reference modelling activity, a security reference diagram is constructed (see Figure 3).

Figure 3 is only a part of the CND SA reference diagram. The main security features of the CND SA platform represented in the security reference diagram are integrity, forensics, availability, intelligence capability and confidentiality. Security mechanisms, such as logging, authentication, and codewords, are implemented to achieve protection objectives such as protective monitoring, authorisation and cryptography. Security mechanisms decompose into security sub-mechanisms. For example, authentication can be achieved using 2-factor authentication, biometrics, digital signatures or password. Protection objectives, accomplished through security mechanisms, contribute 'positively' to the security features, while threats such as interception, viruses or denial of service (DoS) contribute 'negatively' to the security features. Threat actors that give rise to threats are not represented in the reference model, but are captured in the detailed design phase of the system.

Early requirements modelling analyses the environment that is, the *organisational setting* and models it in terms of relevant actors and their respective dependencies. A late requirements phase is where the system functionalities are identified. Hence, during late requirements the '*system*' is introduced as an actor in the security enhanced actor diagram (SEAD), and the developer can proceed to the activities of dependency modelling and security constraint modelling between the external actors and the system. Late requirement modelling focuses on modelling the *system* to be built; and during this process goals are decomposed; *means-end* and *contribution* relationships analysis is performed on the system's goals comprising functional and non-functional requirements. At architectural design modelling, the system actor is decomposed and the system actor diagram refined to include new actors due to delegation of sub-goals upon goal analysis; inclusion of new actors due to specific design patterns to fulfil some non-functional requirements, and possible transition from actors to agents. During architectural design modelling, security attack testing, security attack scenarios, a capability diagram and an agent interaction diagram are generated. Detailed design modelling involves specification of the agent's micro level interaction taking into account the implementation of the platform. It covers modelling capabilities, plans and agents interaction. During this process, a security attack scenario template, plain, capability, and agent interaction diagrams are generated.

MODELLING CND SA REQUIREMENTS

In this modelling, we considered six actors. The *Mission* actor represents a C2 (Command and Control) CND mission; the *Force Command* actor represents the force commander in charge of the mission. The *network command* represents the network experts responsible for managing network security analysts and coordinating all network issues for the mission. *IT Support* actors represent IT personnel responsible for supporting the entire IT infrastructure and estate. They are responsible for ensuring the availability of IT services requirements of the mission. *External Intelligence* represents an intelligence agency that shares intelligence, collaborates and works together for the common goal of protecting the nation or world. The *Network Analyst* actor represents the network security analyst responsible for managing, maintaining, supporting and resolving network issues, security incidents, and taking instructions from the network command, to ensure that the network is available, protected and secure (see Figure 1).

The Force Command Goal-Oriented Task Analysis

The Force Command is the most senior responsible officer for the mission. Force Command is responsible for ensuring that the mission's objectives are accomplished, and is responsible for all the other personnel within this mission, such as the Network Command, Network Analysts, External Intelligence and IT Support. Force Command also responsible for ensuring that all personnel receive security awareness training appropriate for them to carry out their duties and responsibilities.

The security enhanced actor diagram models a number of the goals that enhances the Force Command situational awareness and aids his

Figure 4. Force command security enhanced actor diagram

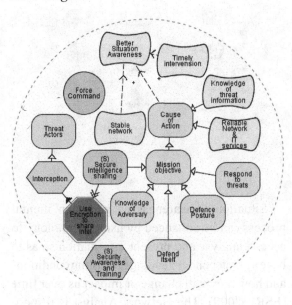

decision making. These goals are decomposed to sub-goals, tasks and plans, including security constraints imposed by the Mission. The Force Command ensures that the mission's objectives are accomplished. This is achieved by responding to threats perceived in the CND SA platform, knowing the security and defensive posture of the mission, having knowledge of adversaries, and possessing the capability to defend itself (see Figure 4).

The sensitive surrounding intelligence data, its sharing is imposed some security constraints – the use of encryption and codewords, which restrict attacks such as interception from threat actors. CoA is determined from the collective assessment of the knowledge of threat information, defensive posture and reliability of network and IT services. Overall, the Force Command's situational awareness is enhanced, which contributes to the provision of timely interventions to nullify adversary attacks, in invariably offers much more stable network.

The Network Command Goal-Oriented Task Analysis

The Network Command is the Mission's network controller who takes responsibility for ensuring the stability, availability, protection of the network, system and IT infrastructure, and provision of security resource required by both the Network Analyst and IT Support. The Network Command is responsible for both the Network Analyst and IT Support; and therefore provides the cause of action, authorisation and decision making.

The Network Command must assess the impacts situations, security incidents and threat actors (adversaries) may have on the platform and the wider mission platform. Hence, Network Command determines the defensive posture, and risk level of the CND SA platform. Based on the GOTA analysis, both the defensive posture and risk level are escalated to the Force Command to make the overall tactical and strategic decisions of the overall CoA for the mission. Defensive posture is very challenging to assess and quantify because it is achieved from the collective analysis of the goals, tasks, plans and any security constraints imposed by *depender* actors (such as the Mission and Force Command). Risk management, vulnerability management, impacts analysis, authorisation and cause of action are hard goals of the Network Command. Sensor fusion as a security constraint uses secure intelligence sharing and secure monitoring to offer situational awareness to the Network Command. These collectively contribute to increased mean-time to repair (MTTR) and swift coordination, which ultimately influences the situational awareness of the Network Command (see Figure 5).

Each goal of the Network Command in the SEAD (see Figure 5) is decomposed into smaller actionable sub-goals and tasks. For example, vulnerability management encompasses vulnerability assessment, scanning, network profiling, enumeration and attempted exploitation. These sub-goals are not represented at the SEAD because they are transparent at this level of the modelling process, but elaborated at the detailed design phase.

The Network Analyst Goal-Oriented Task Analysis

To achieve the overarching goal of the mission, every actor must accomplish its own goals and perform its tasks and undertake responsibilities. The Force Command is responsible for strategic objectives, the Network Command performs tactical objectives, while the Network Analyst is responsible for operational tasks, and carrying out low-level goals (some of which are sub-goals to high-level goals) that assist in fulfilling the overall mission objectives. In this section, we discuss how the Network Analyst' goal-oriented task analysis assists the mission to accomplish its set goals using the Network Analyst Security Enhanced Actor Diagram (see Figure 6).

Figure 5. Network command security enhanced actor diagram

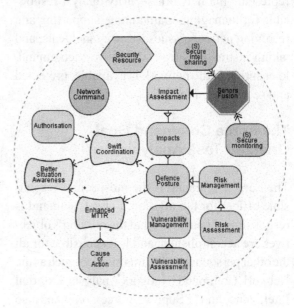

Figure 6. Network analyst security enhanced actor diagram

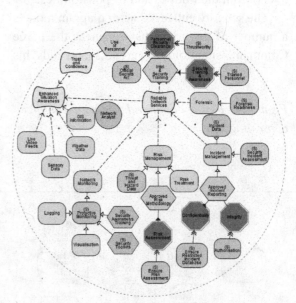

Situational awareness as a human mental process can be enhanced by using technology to access, analyse and present information so as to have a greater understanding of existing conditions and how they will change or impact us over time (ESRI, 2008). The Network Analyst is responsible for incident management, risk management, protective monitoring, visualisation, logging, live video feeds analysis, GIS information integration, weather data analysis, sensory data analysis, and network monitoring as their top-level goals. These goals together contribute to enhancing the situational awareness of the Network Analyst, which invariable contributes towards achieving the mission's statement, by enabling the Network Analyst to offer to the Network Command a well managed and maintained CND. Incident management, risk management and network monitoring all contribute to achieving reliable network services (a software goal of the Network Analyst). The use of Network Analysts who have or are willing to undergo personnel security clearance instils trust and confidence in the CNO operations because the trustworthiness of these personnel is established, and an obligation is imposed on them through the official secrets act. The provision of intelligence and information security training and awareness makes personnel more adept in recognising dynamic changes associated with networks (physical and logical). Each of the top-level goals is briefly described to demonstrate how it assists in providing enhanced situational awareness to the Network Analyst.

Incident management contributes towards providing reliable network services. It ensures that security incidents are detected, reported and contained. Security incident assessments are conducted and incident data are protected and access to these data is restricted. All security incidents are logged onto a database that is secured and restricted to ensure its confidentiality and access to this data are granted and authorised to ensure that the integrity of the data is maintained, and the reporting must use an approved incident reporting method. These are security constraints imposed by the Network Command. Managing incidents in a dynamic and ever-changing CND environment can be challenging. While it is the aim of the mission to ensure it detects and stops potential security incidents, unfortunately this may not be realistic, and in such situations, forensic readi-

ness capabilities are exploited. Forensic analysis is utilised to ensure that the mission is aware what happened and is able to associate security incidents with their adversaries and lessons can be learned from traceback analysis and forensic investigations (see Figure 6).

Visualisation is another essential aspect of the CND activity that assists in providing better situational awareness to the Network Analyst. For example, having the ability to predict or model and visualise how the circumstances of a pending or evolving incident may change over specific times allows Network Analysts to allocate resources to priority issues in the network before further damage or loss of critical infrastructures occur. According to ESRI 2008, having comprehensive information relevant to the specific location of an incident and related surrounding areas, as well as the location of public safety resources and personnel, is an example of how dynamic and spatial data are combined to create better situational awareness.

Situational awareness is achieved by integrating a myriad of technologies to provide the Network Analyst with access to information about the enemy and the mission environment based on the circumstances. For example, integration of live video feeds of monitoring of critical national infrastructures, sensory data from traffic analysis of various data sources and weather data can help the Analyst observe, detect and spot common attack profiles, pattern and spot of concentration of crime swiftly. The use of GIS enhances the current state of CND situational awareness because it provides the capability for data to be geo-referenced, enhancing the Analyst's ability to understand, react, and make decisions based on a set of circumstances presented in a geographic context (ESRI 2008). The use of security analysts who are information security, military intelligence and situation awareness trained and have undergone personnel security clearance can be invaluable.

All the top-level goals together contribute to enhanced situational awareness of the Network Analyst. For example, weather or terrain data, geospatial data and live video feeds contribute to environmental awareness, sensory data provides awareness of both communications-level and physical-level awareness, while network monitoring offers communication and data awareness of the adversary; together an enhanced situational awareness is achieved. According to Onwubiko, C. 2009, the underpinning of situational awareness in CND is to identify adversaries, estimate impact of attacks, evaluate risks, understand situations and make sound decisions on how to protect valued assets swiftly and accurately.

The IT Support Goal-Oriented Task Analysis

The *IT Support* is responsible for providing the resources for carrying out change control notification and a change advisory board. They also ensure the availability of IT services to the mission. Availability of the IT services is represented as a security requirement, and an availability restriction is imposed by the Network Command on IT Support. This involves the use of mission recommended controls, processes and procedures to monitor and protect critical national infrastructures and mission business-critical systems, whilst limiting an adversary's ability to impact the mission's objectives. *IT Support* depends on the *Network Command* to authorise and approve all change controls through the change advisory board, and provide cause of action decision making.

The External Intelligence Goal-Oriented Task Analysis

The *External Intelligence* is responsible for gathering intelligence about the mission's adversaries, and ensures that shared intelligence data are securely protected. Sharing of intelligence is something that is done in a much secured manner, and in this model, confidentiality of the shared intelligence is a requirement imposed by the Force Command to the External Intelligence to ensure

that an adversary could not intercept, relay or participate in intelligence dissemination, notifications and also, could not gain unauthorised access to the mission's intelligence database.

DISCUSSION

Situation awareness being a human attribute can be challenging to demonstrate from a technology standpoint. Hence, modelling CND SA requirements (information, system and infrastructure) can be extremely challenging. For example, when is SA achieved, enhanced or lost? Situational awareness can be attained through a number of different ways, such as personnel training, GIS geo-referencing, multisensory fusion etc, modelling information and systems requirements that encompasses these features is not straightforward. Throughout this chapter, we have shown that a number of goals must be accomplished, which consequently enable mission personnel achieve enhanced SA in CND. According to Bares D., 2010, operators (Force Command, Network Command, Network Analysts and IT Support) all need to maintain an appropriate level of situational awareness in cyberspace in order to achieve the mission objectives. This we have demonstrated by representing each stakeholder's security enhanced actor diagram, such as Force Command, Network Command, Network Analyst and IT Support, showing how they gained or enhanced situational awareness of the CND.

To validate our proposed CND SA model, a security test scenario was constructed, as shown in Figure 8. The scenario shows an attacker who tries to intercept intelligence notification and attempts to gain unauthorised access to the mission's platform. By simulating this attack, we observed how the goal-oriented task analysis model catered to the system by providing mechanisms that protected the systems, detecting the attack, and limiting the adversary's capability. The platform's actors (Force Command and External intelligence) pos-

Figure 7. Security attack scenario

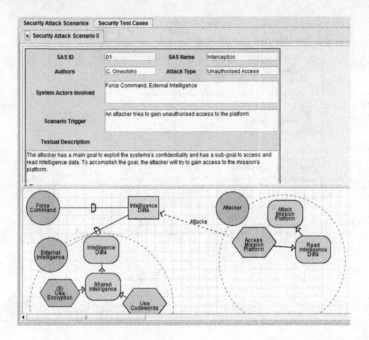

sessed the capability to detect intrusion, prevent unauthorised access to restricted intelligence data as shown in Figure 4, and demonstrated by the result (see Figure 7).

Security Attack Scenario

Figure 7 shows a security attack scenario modelling of an attacker who tries to gain unauthorised access to the mission's intelligence data. This is just one example of a number of security attack scenarios that can be constructed to validate the model. For example, one may be interested in modelling an attack scenario were an adversary may want to limit the capability of the mission by launching a denial of service attack, or carrying out cryptographic attacks as represented using the CND SA reference diagram, shown in Figure 3.

Security Test Case

Figure 8 shows the outcome of the simulated security attack scenario launched on the CND SA representation platform. It was observed that the

platform had the capability to detect, prevent and repel the attack. Security test cases are vital for model validation, because they are used to reveal if, and when, the proposed system caters for a number of different conceptual attack scenarios.

CONCLUSION

We have shown that our goal-oriented task analysis modelling paradigm is an appealing approach to representing and modelling CND SA system and information requirements. Our methodology offers a comprehensive semantic approach comprising both goal-oriented (high-level) and task-oriented (low-level) aspects, which makes it pertinent to modelling situational awareness for the mission, whose activities are disparate, dynamic and challenging.

The security enhanced actor diagram used to model the mission's security operational capability requirements represents each stakeholder's objectives and demonstrates how these objectives can be modelled to achieve enhanced situational

Figure 8. Security test case - Model validation

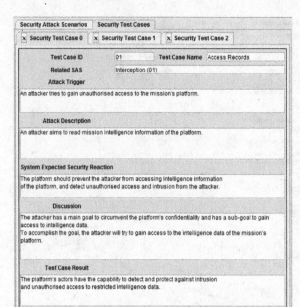

awareness for each stakeholder in the CND environment, such as the Force Command, Network Command, Network Analysts and IT Support. These personnel collectively ensure that the mission's objectives are accomplished.

A reference diagram of the CND SA is represented. This diagram shows threats such as interception, viruses, intelligence exploits, and frequency jamming that can make negative contributions to security features such as integrity, availability or confidentiality. While security mechanisms such as authentication, logging, encryption are implemented that contribute to achieving protection properties such as protective monitoring, authorisation and cryptography.

Model validation shows how the proposed system was evaluated using security attack scenario testing. It was demonstrated to show how a simulated attack can be assessed using the proposed model. The outcome of the security scenario testing is a security test case (see Figure 8), which showed that the model had the capability to detect and dispel the type of attacked launched. This goes to highlight the significance of the proposed model and supports its completeness.

Our proposed model can be used to achieve a number of capability-based network centric warfare (NCW) elements, even when they are beyond the scope of the work presented. For example, our proposed model can be used for communications and data networks, and intelligence, surveillance and reconnaissance (Bell M. I., and Bates E. A., 2005), similar to those evaluated against FORCEnet, the U.S. Navy and Marine Corps approach to NCW (Clark V., and Hagee M. W., 2005).

Overall, we have demonstrated that network and IT services required by the mission to support its operations can be clearly outlined and articulated; and CND SA system and information requirements of the mission can be modelled.

REFERENCES

Asnar, Y., & Giorgini, P. (2010). Multi-dimensional uncertainty analysis in secure and dependable domain. *International Conference on Availability, Reliability and Security,* (pp. 148-155).

Bares, D. (2010). *A tactical framework for cyberspace situational awareness.* 15th ICCRTS, The Evolution of C2, C2 Assessment Metrics and Tools, Paper #196, Air Force Institute of Technology, 2010.

Bass, T. (2000). Cyberspace situational awareness demands mimic tradition command requirements. *AFCEA Signal Magazine*, 2000.

Bell, M. I., & Bates, E. A. (2005). Analysis for network centric warfare in the navy. In *Analytical Support to Defence Transformation Meeting Proceedings*, (pp. 19-1-19-14). RTO-MP-SAS-055, Paper 19, Neuilly-sur-Seine, France, 2005.

Blais, C. L. (2005). Modelling and simulation for military operations other than war, naval postgraduate school. *Proceedings of the Interservice and Industry Training, Simulation and Education Conference (I/ITSEC)*, 2005.

Bolchini, D., & Mylopoulos, J. (2003). *From task-oriented to goal-oriented Web requirements analysis.* Fourth International Conference on Web Information Systems Engineering (WISE'03), Roma, Italy, 10-12 December 2003.

Bryl, V., Massacci, F., Mylopoulos, J., & Zannone, N. (2006). Designing security requirements models through planning. *Proceedings of the CAiSE 2006, LNCS 4001, (*pp. 33-47). Springer-Verlag, 2006.

Castro, J., Kolp, M., & Mylopoulos, J. (2002). Towards requirements-driven Information Systems engineering: The Tropos project. [Amsterdam, The Netherlands: Elsevier.]. *Information Systems, 27*, 365–389. doi:10.1016/S0306-4379(02)00012-1

Clark, V., & Hagee, M. W. (2005). FORCEnet: A functional concept for the 21st century. Retrieved March 28, 2011, from http://forcenet.navy.mil/concepts/fn-concept-final.pdf

D'Amico, A., & Whitley, K. (2007). *The real work of computer network defense analysts: The analysis roles and processes that transform network data into security situation awareness. VizSEC 2007* (pp. 19–37). Mathematics and Visualization.

Department of Defense (DoD). (2000). *Joint vision 2020. America's Military - Preparing for tomorrow.* Washington, DC, Summer 2000. Retrieved March 25, 2011, from http://www.dtic.mil/doctrine/jel/jfq_pubs/1225.pdf

Endsley, M. R. (2000). Errors in situation assessment: Implications for system design. In Elzer, P. F. (Eds.), *Human Error and System Design and Management: Lecture Notes in Control and Information Sciences- (Vol. 253*, pp. 15–26). London, UK: Springer-Verlag. doi:10.1007/BFb0110451

ESRI. (2008). *Public safety and homeland security situational awareness.* ESRI White Paper, February 2008.

Evans, R., Kearney, P., Stark, J., Caire, G., Carijo, F. L., Gomez, J., … Massonet, P. (2001). *MESSAGE: Methodology for engineering systems of software agents.* AgentLink Publication, September 2001.

Giorgini, P. (2010). *Tropos: Basic, agent oriented software engineering course. Laurea Specialistica in Informatica, Dipartimento Ingegneria e Scienza* (pp. 2009–2010). Italy: University of Trento.

Giorgini, P., Massacci, F., Mylopoulos, J., & Zannone, N. (2005). *Modelling security requirements through ownership, permission and delegation. Proceeding of Requirements Engineering (RE'05)* (pp. 167–176). IEEE Press.

Giorgini, P., Massacci, F., Mylopoulos, J., & Zannone, N. (2005b). *Modelling social and individual trust in requirements engineering methodologies. Proceedings of iTrust'05, LNCS 3477* (pp. 161–176). Springer-Verlag.

Grégoire, M., & Beaudoin, L. (2005). Visualisation for network situational awareness in computer network defence. In *Visualisation and the Common Operational Picture Meeting Proceedings* (pp. 20-1 – 20-6). RTO-MP-IST-043, Paper 20; Neuilly-sur-Seine, France, RTO, 2005.

Jajodia, S., Liu, P., Swarup, V., & Wang, C. (Eds.). (2009). *Cyber situational awareness: Issues and research (Advances in Information Security)*. Springer.

Jones, R. E. T., Connors, E. S., Mossey, M. E., Hyatt, J. R., Hansen, N. J., & Endsley, M. R. (2010). Modelling situation awareness for army infantry platoon leaders using fuzzy cognitive mapping techniques. *Proceedings of the 19th Conference on Behaviour Representation in Modelling and Simulation*, Charleston, SC, 21 - 24 March 2010.

Juarez-Espinosa, O., & Gonzalez, C. (2004). *Situation awareness of commanders: A cognitive model.* Carnegie Mellon University, Department of Social and Decision Sciences, Papers 85. Retrieved from http://repository.cmu.edu/sds/85

Lefebvre, J. H., Grégoire, M., Beaudoin, L., & Froh, M. (2005). *Computer network defence situational awareness information requirements.* Defence R&D Canada – Ottawa, Technical Memorandum, DRDC Ottawa TM 2005-254, December 2005.

Matulevičius, R., Mayer, N., Mouratidis, H., Dubois, E., Heymans, P., & Genon, N. (2008). Lecture Notes in Computer Science: *Vol. 5074. Adapting Secure Tropos for security risk management in the early phases of Information Systems development. Advanced Information Systems Engineering* (pp. 541–555).

Mouratidis, H. (2004). *A security oriented approach in the development of multiagent system: Applied to the management of the health and social care needs of older people in England/* PhD Thesis, University of Sheffield, 2004.

Mouratidis, H., & Giorgini, P. (2007a). Secure Tropos: A security-oriented extension of the Tropos methodology. *International Journal of Software Engineering and Knowledge Engineering, 17*(2), 285–309. doi:10.1142/S0218194007003240

Mouratidis, H., Giorgini, P., & Manson, G. (2003). An ontology for modeling security: The Tropos approach. In *the Proceedings of the 7th International Conference on Knowledge-Based Intelligent Information & Engineering Systems (KES 2003),* 2003.

Onwubiko, C. (2009). Functional requirements of situational awareness in computer network security. *IEEE International Conference on Intelligence and Security Informatics*, ISI '09, Dallas, TX, USA, 8-11 June 2009.

Onwubiko, C. (2011b). Designing Information Systems and network components for situational awareness. In Onwubiko, C., & Owens, T. J. (Eds.), *Situational awareness in computer network defense: Principles, methods and applications.*

Richardson, J., Ormerod, T. C., & Shepherd, A. (1998). The role of task analysis in capturing requirements for interface design. [Elsevier.]. *Interacting with Computers, 9,* 367–384. doi:10.1016/S0953-5438(97)00036-2

Tadda, G. P., & Salerno, J. S. (2009). Overview of cyber situation awareness. In Jajodia, S. (Eds.), *Cyber situational awareness: Issues and research (Advances in Information Security).* Springer.

Wang, H., Liu, X., Lai, J., & Liang, Y. (2007). Network security situation awareness based on heterogeneous multi-sensor data fusion and neural network. *Second International Multi-Symposiums on Computer and Computational Sciences. IMSCCS, 2007,* 352–359.

Yu, E. (1995). *Modelling strategic relationships for process reengineering.* PhD Thesis, Department of Computer Science, University of Toronto, Canada, 1995.

ADDITIONAL READING

Anderson, H. H. K., & Hauland, G. (2000), "Measuring Team Situation Awareness of Reactor Operators during Normal Operation: A Technical Pilot Study", Proc. of the first Human Performance, Situation Awareness, and Automation Conference, Savannah, 2000.

Bass, T. (2000). Intrusion Detection Systems and Multi-sensor Data Fusion. *Communications of the ACM, 43*(4), 2000. doi:10.1145/332051.332079

Borja, A. T. (2003), "Integrating Usability Engineering in the Iterative Design Process of the Land Attack Combat System (LACS) Human Computer Interface", Space & Naval Warfare Systems Center, San Diego, CA 92152-5001, USA, 2003.

Boyd, J. (Col.), (1987), "Organic Design for Command and Control", Presentation Slides, May 1987 [Accessible from] www.ausairpower.net/JRB/organic_design.ppt

Breton R., and Rousseau R., (2003), "Situation Awareness: A Review of the Concept and its Measurement", DREV, TR-2001-220, Defence Research Establishment, 2003.

Emmerich, W. (2000). *Engineering Distributed Objects*. England, UK: John Wiley & Sons, Ltd.

Endsley, M. R. (1995), "Toward a Theory of Situation Awareness in Dynamic Systems", *Human Factors Journal, Vol. 37, No. 1, pp. 32-64, 1995*.

Endsley, M. R. (1996), "Automation and Situation Awareness", Automation and Human Performance: Theory and Applications, pp. 163-181, NJ, 1996.

Endsley, M. R., & Garland, D. J. (Eds.). (2000). *Situation Awareness Analysis and Measurement*. Mahwah, NJ: Lawrence Erlbaum Associates.

Garba, D. M., & Howard, S. K. (1995). Situation Awareness in Anaesthesiology. *Human Factors, 37*(Issue 1), 20–31. doi:10.1518/001872095779049435

Gregoire, M., & Beaudoin, L. (2005), "Visualisation for Network Situational Awareness in Computer Network Defence", Proceedings of the *Visualisation and the Common Operational Picture, pp. 20-1-20-6, RTO-MP-IST-043*, 2005.

Haines, J., Ryder, D., Tinnel, L., & Taylor, S. (2003, Jan-Feb.). Validation of Sensor Alert Correlators. *IEEE Security & Privacy, 1*(1), 46–56. doi:10.1109/MSECP.2003.1176995

Hall, D. L., & McMullen, S. A. H. (2004). *Mathematical Techniques in Multisensor Data Fusion* (2nd ed.).

Lakkaraju K., Yurick W., and Lee A. J., (2004), "NVisionIP: NetFlow Visualizations of System State for Security Situational Awareness", NVisionIP, *VizSEC/DMSEC '04*, October 29, 2004.

Lambert D. A., Bosse E., Breton R., Rousseau R., Howes J. R., Hinman M. L., Karakowski M., Owen M., and White F., (2004), "Information Fusion Definitions, Concept and Models for Coalition Situation Awareness", *TTCP C31 Group, TR-C31-AG2-1-2004*, 2004.

Lee, E. A. (2006), "Cyber-Physical Systems – Are Computing Foundations Adequate?", Department of EECS, UC Berkeley, NSF Workshop on Cyber-Physical Systems: Research Motivation, Techniques and Roadmap, October 16-17, 2006

McGuinness, B., & Foy, L. (2000), "A Subjective Measure of SA: The Crew Awareness Rating Scale (CARS)", *Proc. of the First Human Performance, Situation Awareness, and Automation Conference, Savannah, Georgia, 2000*.

Mulgund, S., Rinkus, G., Illgen, C., & Zacharias, G. (1997), "Situation Awareness Modelling and Pilot State Estimation for Tactical Cockpit Interfaces", *Presented at HCI International, San Francisco, CA, August 1997*

Onwubiko, C. (2008), "Data Fusion in Security Evidence Analysis"; Proceeding of the 3rd International Conference on Computer Security and Forensics, 2008.

Onwubiko, C. (2008). *Security Framework for Attack Detection in Computer Networks*. VDM Verlag Publisher.

Salerno, J., Hinman, M., & Boulware, D. (2004), "Building a Framework for Situation Awareness", AFRL/IFEA, AF Research Lab., Rome, NY 13441-4114, USA, 2004.

Sandom, C. (1999), "Situational Awareness through the Interface: Evaluating Safety in Safety-Critical Control Systems", *IEE Proceedings of People in Control – An International Conference on Human Interfaces in Control Rooms, Cockpits and Command Centres, University of Bath*, UK, 21-23 June 1999.

Wickens, C. D. (1992). *Engineering Psychology and Human Performance* (2nd ed.). New York: Harper Collins.

Yin X., Yurick W., and Slagell A., (2008), "VisFlowConnect-IP: An Animated Link Analysis Tool for Visualising Netflows", SIFT Research Group, National Centre for Supercomputing Applications, University of Illinois at Urbana-Champaign, 2008.

Yurick, W. (2005), "Visualising Netflow for Security at Line Speed: the SIFT tool suit", *Proc. of the 19th Usenix Large Installation System Administration Conference (LISA), pp. 169-176, 2005.*

KEY TERMS AND DEFINITIONS

Computer Network Defence (CND): CND is the process of protecting computer systems and networks. This includes actions taken via computer networks to protect, monitor, analyse, detect and respond to cyber-attacks, intrusions, disruptions or other perceived unauthorised actions that could compromise or impact defence information systems and networks. CND is achieved through a collective effort by personnel who monitor, manage and maintain defence systems, networks and infrastructures, such as network operators, security analysts, systems administrators and IT support (Onwubiko, C. 2011b).

Goal-Oriented Task Analysis (GOTA): A modelling approach that combines both goal-oriented and task-oriented models. Goal-oriented methods provide specific support for coping with high-level users' and stakeholders' goals that facilitate the exploration of design alternatives and the definition of requirements at a suitable level of abstraction.

Situational Awareness: As the state of being aware of circumstances that exist around us, especially those that are particularly relevant to us and which we are interested about (Onwubiko C. and Owens J.T., 2011).

Chapter 15
On Situational Aware En-Route Filtering against Injected False Data in Cyber Physical Systems

Xinyu Yang
Xi'an Jiaotong University, P. R. China

Xinwen Fu
University of Massachusetts Lowell, USA

Jie Lin
Xi'an Jiaotong University, P. R. China

Genshe Chen
Independent Consultant Professional, USA

Wei Yu
Towson University, USA

Erik P. Blasch
Air Force Research Laboratory, USA

ABSTRACT

Cyber-physical systems (CPS) are systems with a tight coupling of the cyber aspects of computing and communications with the physical aspects of dynamics and engineering that abide by the laws of physics. The real-time monitoring provided by wireless sensor networks (WSNs) is essential for CPS, as it provides rich and pertinent information on the condition of physical systems. In WSNs, the attackers could inject false measurements to the controller through compromised sensor nodes, which not only threaten the security of the system, but also consume significant network resources and pose serious threats to the lifetime of sensor networks. To mitigate false data injection (FDI) measurement attacks, a number of situation aware en-route filtering schemes to filter false data inside the networks have been developed. In this book chapter, the authors first review those existing situation aware en-route filter mechanisms such as: Statistical En-route Filtering (SEF), Location-Based Resilient Secrecy (LBRS), Location-ware End-to-end Data Security (LEDS), and Dynamic En-route Filtering Scheme (DEFS). The authors then compare the performance of those schemes via both the theoretical analysis and simulation study. These extensive simulations validate findings that most of the schemes can filter out false data within few hops, and the filtering efficiency increases as the number of hops increases and the filtering efficiency of most schemes decreases rapidly as the number of compromised nodes increases.

DOI: 10.4018/978-1-4666-0104-8.ch015

INTRODUCTION

Monitoring and controlling physical systems through geographically distributed sensors and actuators have become an important task in numerous environment and infrastructure applications. These applications have received a renewed attention because of the advances in sensor network technologies and new development in cyber-physical systems (CPS) (*CPSweek*, 2010). To monitor and control the physical systems, a typical CPS integrates sensor nodes, actuators, controllers, and networks. In a CPS system, sensor nodes obtain the measurement from the physical components, process the measurements, and send measured data to the controller through computer networks. According to these measurements, the controller estimates the states of physical systems and sends feedback commands to the actuators, which control the operation of physical systems. Thus, the real-time monitoring provided by wireless sensor networks (WSN) is essential for CPS, as it provides rich and pertinent information on the condition of physical systems.

WSNs are important components in CPS and are formed by a set of resource-constrained sensor nodes communicated through an ad hoc fashion. In WSNs, sensor nodes usually are deployed in unattended or even harsh environments (e.g., battlefield) and the lack of tamper-resistance hardware increases the possibility of nodes to be compromised by attackers. Once nodes are compromised, the secret information stored in nodes becomes visible to the attackers. Even worse, the attackers could launch false data injection attacks via compromised nodes, consuming significant network resources and posing serious threats to the lifetime of sensor networks (Ye, 2004; Chen, 2009). In particular, the false data injected by compromised nodes can lead to false events and affect the decisions made at the sink of WSNs. Because a large amount of false data injected by compromised nodes are transmitted to the sink via multiple-hop routes, the false data increases the

communication overhead of energy-limited nodes and ultimately shortens the lifetime of WSNs.

To mitigate the false data injection (FDI) type of attacks, we shall develop the situation aware filtering schemes to filter out false injected data inside the network before arriving at the sink of WSNs (or the key controller of CPS). Note that situational awareness (SA) is commonly described as *knowing what is going on around the system and within that knowledge of surroundings and being able to identify which events in those surroundings are important* (Shen 2007, Shen 2009). Hence, we shall continue to monitor system performance and threats and develop techniques for accurate analysis, fast detection and response against threats. Following this design principle, a number of the situations aware en-route filtering schemes to filter false data injected from the compromised nodes have been developed.

The basic idea of situation aware en-route filtering is based on *T-authentication*. That is, a legitimate data report must carry at least T valid message authentication codes (MACs) generated by different nodes within the network. T is a threshold and predefined before WSN is deployed. Generally speaking, MAC is a small fixed-size block of data generated based on the message M and a shared authentication key K, and used to be attached in message M and allow the receiver to authenticate the integrity of message M. The formula of MAC generation is denoted as $MAC = F(M, K)$, where $F(.)$ is the MAC generation function. Various MAC generation approaches have been studied in the past, including Cipher Block Chaining (CBC-MAC), One-key (OMAC), and Hash-based (HMAC) and others. The detailed description of MAC generations approach is beyond the scope of this book chapter, and readers can find more details in (Block, 2002; T. Iwara, 2002; H. Krawczyk, 1997). In terms of the false date en-route filtering schemes studied in this chapter, when a report is transmitted to the sink along the route, each forwarding node determines whether T valid MACs are attached to the report.

If not, the report will be determined as false data and will be dropped. Otherwise, the report will be forwarded to the next node. Using the forwarding node to process the MAC validity ensures false data will be filtered out along the route as quickly as possible before arriving at the sink.

As shown in Figure 1, node u_1, u_2, and u_3 generate the MACs of event E and send these MACs to u_4, respectively. After receiving these MACs, Node u_4 integrates them into an integrated report R of the event E, and sends R to the sink. Forwarding nodes v, s, w, and m determine the correctness of MACs via the authentication keys shared with u_1, u_2 and u_3. As long as at least one MAC included in the report is false, the report will be dropped inside the network; otherwise, the report will be forwarded to the sink. Note that, forwarding nodes could verify the correctness of the MAC only if they have the authentication keys. Otherwise, the forwarding nodes will consider that the MAC is correct one and forwards the report to the sink. As we can see from Figure 1, u_1, u_2 and u_3 generate the MAC_1, MAC_2 and MAC_3 of event E and send them to u_4, respectively. Node u_4 generates the integrated report R, which consists of MAC_1, MAC_2, MAC_3 and E and sends R to the sink. Assume that v, s, and m share the authentication keys with u_1, u_2 and u_3, respectively, and m has no authentication key shared with u_1, u_2 and u_3.

Then v, s and m could verify the correctness of MAC_1, MAC_2 and MAC_3, respectively, while w only could forward R to m and could not verify MACs included in R. Following this basic idea, a number of en-route filtering schemes to filter false data inside the networks have been developed in the past (Ye, 2004; Yang, 2005; Yu, 2009; Ren, 2008; Zhu, 2004; Yang, 2004; Yu, 2010; Chen, 2010).

In this chapter, we first review the existing situation aware en-route filter techniques, including *Statistical En-route Filtering* (SEF), *Location-Based Resilient Secrecy* (LBRS), *Location-ware End-to-end Data Security* (LEDS), and *Dynamic En-route Filtering Scheme* (DEFS). We find that although these schemes can filter false data effectively, they have different kinds of limitations. For example, SEF (Ye, 2004) have the T-threshold limitation (i.e., if more than T partitions are compromised, which can generate T different valid MACs for report, the whole area will be compromised). LBRS (Yang, 2005) and LEDS (Ren, 2008) resolve the T-threshold limitation through the cell-based report generation and location-ware key generation techniques. However, because of using node localization and node association, these schemes are only effective to the network using the fixed sink and special route protocol and these schemes take a quite long time and consume a large amount of energy. Although

Figure 1. Example of en-route filtering

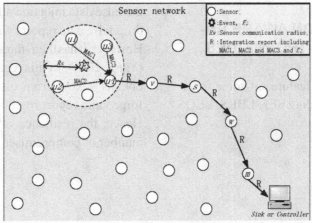

DEFS (Yu, 2010) do not rely on special routes, they have a low resilience to the growing number of compromised nodes. In addition, most of these schemes have no resilience to the selective forwarding attack (Karlof, 2003) and report disruption attack (Yang, 2005).

We compare the above methods by conducting a theoretical analysis and then deriving a set of closed formulae for the schemes we compared. We also carry out simulations to validate our findings. With the same forwarding hops, the filtering efficiency of deterministic schemes for key sharing (e.g., LEDS (Ren, 2008) and DEFS (Yu, 2010)) is higher than that of statistical schemes for key sharing (e.g., SEF (Ye, 2004) and LBRS (Yang, 2005)). Most of the schemes can filter out false data within few hops, and the filtering efficiency increases as the number of hops increases and the filtering efficiency of most schemes decreases rapidly as the number of compromised nodes increases. We also find that only LEDS and LBRS can deal with the growing number of compromised nodes effectively. We also evaluate the *compromised area ratio* defined as the percentage of compromised area in the terrain and find that the schemes without location-ware authentication keys (e.g., SEF (Ye, 2004) and DEFS (Yu, 2010)) have a larger compromised area ratio than the schemes using the location-ware authentication keys and data dissemination protocol (e.g., LEDS (Ren, 2008) and LBRS (Yang, 2005)).

EXISTING SITUATION AWARE EN-ROUTE FILTERING TECHNIQUES

We now review the key features of some representative schemes, including SEF, LBRS, LEDS and DEFS.

Statistical En-Route Filtering

Statistical En-route Filtering (SEF) (Ye, 2004) is the earliest en-route filtering strategy for WSN. In SEF, there is a globe key pool, which is divided into n non-overlapping partitions. Before deployment, each node stores a small number of authentication keys randomly selected from one partition of globe key pool. Nodes with keys from same partition are considered as the same group. In this way, all nodes are divided into n groups via non-overlapping key partitions. The SEF scheme adopts T-authentication, that is, the legitimate report must carry T MACs generated by T nodes from different groups. Each of these T nodes generates MAC with one of authentication keys it stored. Forwarding node, which is in the same group as any of these nodes generating the MACs, knows the key of the node used to generate MAC. It can determine whether the corresponding MACs carried in report are correct. If not, forwarding node will not forward the report and drop it directly. As we can see, the filtering efficiency of single forwarding node is low and the filtering efficiency of SEF will achieve a greater level as the forwarded hops increases. This is caused by the accumulative effect of filtering efficiency from multiple forwarding nodes. In addition, SEF can be combined with Bloom filter (Bloom, 1970), say SEF-B, to reduce the size of MACs carried in the report in order to reduce the communication overhead. SEF is the first scheme that can mitigate the false data injection attack, and can detect and drop false data reports within few hops en-route. However, it has the T-threshold limitation problem (Yang, 2005). In this regard, when the adversary obtains T keys from distinct partitions, he can forge valid report freely at an arbitrary location. Hence, the resilience of SEF to the increasing number of compromised nodes is low.

Location-Based Resilient Secrecy

Location-Based Resilient Secrecy (LBRS) (Yang, 2005) has a major improvement over SEF, and mitigates T-threshold limitation problem in SEF by location-ware authentication key. LBRS adopts the cell-based report generation methodology and divides the terrain into multiple cells. In LBRS, there are two novel techniques: location-binding key generation and location-guided key selection. LBRS generates multiple authentication keys for a cell with different parameters, and all these keys are bound with the location of the cell. The nodes which can sense events within this cell store one of these keys. LBRS is also based on T-authentication, i.e., a legitimate report generated from a cell must carry T MACs generated with T authentication keys bound with the location of the cell. Forwarding nodes share the authentication keys of a cell via location-guided key selection, which relies on beam model. For a cell, only nodes, which are in the downstream beam region of the cell and are close to the sink, can store one of the keys of the cell with the probability d/D_{max}, where d is the node's distance to the sink, and D_{max} is the max distance from the terrain edge to the sink. In LBRS, a forwarding node verifies the received reports and filters out false ones in the same way as SEF. Based on these above two techniques and the filtering approach as in SEF, LBRS can en-route filter false data with high possibility and mitigate the T-threshold limitation problem. However, in LBRS, a forwarding node can only verify the reports generated from the cells, which are in the upstream beam region of the node, and thus LBRS relies on the fixed sink and special routing protocols (i.e., beam model). Thus, LBRS cannot work effectively in the networks with mobile sink and various routing protocols.

Location-Ware end-to-end Data Security

Location-ware End-to-end Data Security (LEDS) (Ren, 2008) is an end-to-end data security strategy. The LEDS approach adopts the several key techniques, including the interleaved cell-by-cell authentication, the cell-based report generation, and location-ware key generation as it tends to tackle the T-threshold limitation problems. LEDS needs an association discovery phase to select the downstream authentication cells for each node. Authentication cells of a node denote the cells in the report forwarding route. The downstream authentication cell of a node in event cell is the one x cells away from the event cell, where x is a random integer belonging to $[1, T+1]$. The randomly chosen x ensure that each cell less than $T+1$ cells away from the event cell could be the downstream authentication cell of at least one node in the event cell. The downstream authentication cell of a forwarding node is the one $T+1$ cells closer to the sink, and if the forwarding node is less than $T+1$ cells away from the sink, then the sink is chosen. Each node shares the authentication key with all nodes in its downstream authentication cell, and the key is bound with the locations of these two cells. A legitimate report generated from the event cell must carry $T+1$ MACs generated by T nodes in the event cell with the use of shared authentication keys stored in them. Note that, there is one node in event that can generate two different MACs to attach to the report. The selected T nodes should have different downstream authentication cells from each other. Thus, a forwarding node u can verify the MAC carried in the report and generated by node v while u is the member of v's downstream authentication cell. If the MAC is correct, u generates a new MAC by the authentication key shared with its downstream authentication cell to replace the old MAC, and forwards the report; otherwise, it replaces the old MAC with '0' and forwards the report. In order to mitigate selective forwarding attack, LEDS uses a one-to-many data forwarding approach. In addition, to mitigate report disruption attack, LEDS also adopts (t, T) threshold linear secret sharing scheme (LSSS), in which only if forwarding nodes detect that less than t nonzero MACs are included in the report, R, the report will be treated as the false one and be filtered out. Because of the abovementioned techniques, LEDS can effectively mitigate T-threshold problem and achieve high filtering efficiency and high attack resilience. Nevertheless, the node localization and cell association limits LEDS to work effectively in the network with fixed sink and limited dynamic topology.

Dynamic En-Route Filtering Scheme

Dynamic En-route Filtering Scheme (DEFS) (Yu, 2010) is the scheme to address both false report injection and denial-of-service (DoS) attacks. Nodes in DEFS are organized into clusters, where cluster sensing nodes generate sensing reports, and the cluster-head integrates these sensing reports to an integration report and sends the integration report to the sink. In DEFS, authentication keys are generated by hash chain, which could improve the resilience to keys disclosing. In addition, DEFS adopts the *Hill Climbing* approach to ensure nodes far from the sink hold more authentication keys than nodes closer to the sink do. DEFS defines two keys: y-key and z-key. The first one is used to verify MACs of the report, and the second one is used to verify the authentication message. DEFS can be divided into three phases: (i) key pre-distribution phase, (ii) key dissemination phase, and (iii) report forwarding phase. In key pre-distribution phase, each node generates a hash chain of authentication keys, and stores l y-keys and one z-key. The z-key is selected from a globe z-key pool. For l y-keys, DEFS divides all y-keys in globe y-key pool into l hash chain, and node

selects one y-key from each hash chain. In key dissemination phase, the cluster-head disseminates authentication message, including each node's first authentication key. Each key has $l+1$ copies encrypted by l y-keys and one z-key, respectively. Forwarding nodes, which receives the authentication message, verifies whether T different z-keys are included. If not, the message will be dropped. Otherwise, it decrypts the sensing node's authentication key only if the index of y-key that it holds is larger than that sensing node can hold. Next, the forwarding node encrypts the sensing node's authentication key with its larger index y-key, and replaces the sensing node's authentication key encrypted by the smaller index y-key with new one. Only forwarding nodes decrypting the authentication key of the sensing node can verify the MAC generated by this sensing node. In the report forwarding phase, each forwarding node verifies the disclosed authentication keys by disseminated ones, and verifies the report with decrypted disclosed authentication keys. Although DEFS does not need node localization and association, it involves a large number of extra control messages, incurring not only the long transmission delay of report, but also the large energy consumption of forwarding nodes.

ANALYSIS

We now conduct theoretical analysis and derive a set of closed formulate to evaluate the performance of schemes discussed above.

Metrics

For the effectiveness of en-route filtering schemes, we consider the following three key metrics:

- *False data filtering efficiency* is defined as the probability of false data to be filtered within a number of hops. It measures the effectiveness of false data filtering schemes.

- *Energy consumption* is defined as the communication overhead of the nodes where a certain number of false data are injected into the network. Because the computation overhead of the nodes is far less than the communication overhead, the computation overhead will be ignored when energy consumption is analyzed. Because one of important goals of false data injection attack is to consume the energy of forwarding nodes caused by forwarding a large number of false data, the en-route filtering scheme must achieve energy saving in comparison with the scenario, where no en-route filtering scheme is used. Obviously, the scheme with lower energy consumption has a better energy consumption performance.

- *Compromised area ratio* is defined as the percentage of compromised area in the terrain. In the compromised area, the attacker can forge false data and bypass the en-route filtering. Hence, it measures the effectiveness of filtering resilience to the growing number of compromised nodes. If the compromised area ratio slowly increases with the number of compromised nodes increases, we can determine that the filtering scheme has good resilience to the growing number of compromised nodes.

Analytical Results

The existing schemes discussed in Section II use different preconditions. To fairly compare them, we now derive a set of closed formulae for those schemes in a uniformed setting. All notations are defined in Table 1. In the following, the false data filtering efficiency P_h is defined as the probability of filtering false data within h hops, compromised area ratio P_s is defined as the ratio of area, where attackers can successfully forge false data without being detected, and energy consumption EC is defined as the total communication overhead for different schemes. When we analyze EC, the

false data forwarded hops $E(h)$ is introduced, which is defined as the number of hops a false report is forwarded before it is filtered, Note that SEF-B represents the SEF with Bloom filter technology. The detailed derivations of formulae of these schemes are shown below. Note that we assume that all schemes discussed are under the random node capture attack and each node has equal probability to be compromised by attackers. The derivation of formulae of each scheme is shown below.

SEF and SEF-B

As mentioned in (Ye, 2004), we can obtain the filtering efficiency of single forwarding node of SEF

$$f_j = \frac{T-j}{n} \cdot \frac{k}{m},$$ (1)

where j is the number of key partitions that attackers obtain, and T, n, m, k are defined in Table 1.

If attackers obtain the keys in partition i, we can say partition i is compromised. When N_c nodes are compromised, the compromised probability of each node becomes N_c/N, and the probability of partition i being compromised is

$$p' = 1 - (1 - \frac{1}{n})^{N_c}.$$ (2)

Hence, with N_c compromised nodes, the probability of j partitions being compromised becomes

$$p_{\{j\}} = \binom{n}{j} p'^j (1 - p')^{n-j},$$ (3)

and the filtering efficiency of SEF with j compromised partitions becomes

$$p'' p_{\{j\}} (1 - (1 - f_j)^h).$$ (4)

Table 1. Notations

N	The size of network
n	The number of nodes within one cell
N_c	The number of compromised nodes
R	Terrain radius
R_c	Node communication radius
T	The number of MACs in a legitimate report
h	Data forwarding hops for false report
H	Data forwarding hops for legitimate report
m	The number of keys in one partition in SEF
m_H	The size of MACs under Bloom filter
L_H	The length of hash chain used in Bloom filter
t	t of LSSS(t, T) in LEDS – nodes
T	T of LSSS(t, T) in LEDS – cell
k	The number of keys stored by a node in SEF
C	The side length of a cell in LBRS
L	The number of key types of a cell in LBRS
b	The width of the bean model in LBRS
w	The number of z keys in DEFS
v	The number of y keys in DEFS
l	The number of y keys stored by a node in DEFS
β	The ratio of false data traffic to legitimate traffic
e	The communication overhead of a node with receiving and sending a bit.

Note that if more than T partitions are compromised, SEF loses the entire situation aware en-route filtering capability. Hence, we just consider the case, where less than T partitions are compromised and there are at most N_c compromised nodes, and the filtering efficiency of SEF within h forwarded hops is

$$P_h = \sum_{j=0}^{T-1} p'' = \sum_{j=0}^{T-1} p_{\{j\}}\left(1 - (1 - f_j)^h\right) \quad (5)$$

The false data forwarded hops of SEF is

$$E(h) = \sum_{i=1}^{H_{max}} i(1 - P_{i-1})f_j = \sum_{i-1}^{H_{max}}\left(\sum_{j=0}^{T-1} p_{\{j\}}(1 - f_j)^{i-1} f_j\right). \quad (6)$$

SEF has T-threshold limitation: if more than T partitions are compromised, which can generate T different valid MACs for report in any place of the whole area, the whole area will be compromised. Hence, with N_c compromised nodes, the compromised area ratio of SEF is the same as the probability of more than T partitions being compromised and we have

$$P_s = \sum_{j=T}^{n} p_{\{j\}} = 1 - \sum_{j=0}^{T-1} p_{\{j\}}. \quad (7)$$

In SEF, a legitimate report consists of an event, T key IDs and T MACs. Let the size of an event, a key index and a MAC be L_r, L_k, and L_{MAC}, respectively, and the amount of legitimate report and false report be 1 and β, respectively. According to SEF, a legitimate report should be forwarded H hops, where H is the average forwarding hops, and a false report should be forwarded $E(h)$ hops, where we use H for legitimate, and h for false report to clarify the difference. Thus, the energy consumption of the network with SEF is

$$EC = (L_r + TL_k + TL_{MAC})(H + \beta E(h))e, \quad (8)$$

where H, β, and e are defined in Table 1.

SEF-B improves SEF using the Bloom filter technology. SEF-B reduces the size of MAC attached in a report, but increases the false negative rate of forwarding nodes. As mentioned in (Ye, 2004), we can obtain the filtering efficiency of single forwarding node of SEF-B,

$$f_j = \frac{T-j}{n} \cdot \frac{k}{m}\left(1 - \left(\frac{L_H T}{m_H}\right)^{L_H}\right), \quad (9)$$

where j is the number of key partition that attackers obtain, and T, k, m_H, n, L_H are defined in Table 1. The other parameters, such as p', $p_{\{j\}}$, P_h, $E(h)$ and P_s, can be derived in the same way as in SEF.

Due to use of Bloom filter technology, SEF-B reduces the size of MAC attached in the report to m_H. Hence, the energy consumption of the network with SEF-B is

$$EC=(L_r+TL_k+m_H)(H+\beta E(h))e, \qquad (10)$$

where m_H is defined in Table 1.

LBRS

As mentioned in (Yang, 2005), LBRS depends on beam model, and the forwarding node only can verify the report generated from the cell, which is the upstream region of the forwarding node. The forwarding node verify the report of a cell in its upstream region (i.e., have the authentication key of the cell) with the probability of $\frac{R-iR_c}{R}$ where R is the maximum distance between the network edge and the sink, and $(R-iR_c)$ is the forwarding node's distance to the sink, i.e., the forwarding nodes is i hops away from the source cell. Because LBRS selects the upstream region of a forwarding node based on beam model, based on our analysis, the forwarding nodes, which are i hops away from the source cell, can verify the report of the source cell with a probability of $\frac{R-iR_c}{R}$ only if these forwarding nodes locate in the special region with the area of $(2b-C)C$, where the definitions of b and C can be found in Table 1. That is, the forwarding nodes, which are $(R-iR_c)$ away from the sink and locate in the special region with the area of $(2b-C)C\frac{R-iR_c}{R}$, have authentication keys of the source cell. In addition, as mentioned in (Yang, 2005), if the source cell locates in the sensing range of a node, the node should have one authentication key of the cell. Hence, nodes in the special region with area of $\pi R_c^2 + 4R_c C + C^2$ have authentication keys of the source cell. Hence, the ratio of the

special area, where nodes have the authentication keys of the source cell, is

$$p_n = \frac{(2b-C)C}{\pi R^2}\sum_{i=1}^{\frac{R}{R_c}-1}\left(\frac{(R-iR_c)}{R}+\frac{\pi R_c^2 + 4R_c C + C^2}{\pi R^2}\right). \qquad (11)$$

Note that, we assume that the whole region is circular area with radius being R. Then the number of nodes, which have the authentication keys of the source cell is $\lfloor Np_n \rfloor$, because nodes are located evenly within the whole area.

When attackers compromised N_c nodes, the probability that j nodes that have authentication keys of the source cell are compromised is

$$p^j = \frac{\binom{\lfloor Np_n \rfloor}{j}\binom{N-\lfloor Np_n \rfloor}{N_c - j}}{\binom{N}{N_c}}. \qquad (12)$$

The probability that attackers obtain one authentication key of the source cell is

$$p' = 1-\left(1-\frac{1}{L}\right)^j. \qquad (13)$$

Then the probability that attackers obtain k authentication keys of the source cell is

$$p_{\{k\}} = \sum_{j=k}^{\min(x,\lfloor Np_n \rfloor)}\left(\binom{L}{k}p'^k(1-p')^{L-k}\right)p^j. \qquad (14)$$

As mentioned in (Yang, 2005), when k authentication keys of the source cell is revealed to attackers, a forwarding node i hops away from the source cell verifies the report of the source cell with probability, determined by

$$f_{k,i} = \frac{(T-k)(R-iR_c)}{RL}. \tag{15}$$

When T or more keys are revealed to attackers, the forwarding nodes could not filter false reports generated from the cell. Hence, we only study the filtering efficiency of LBRS while less than T keys are revealed. The filtering efficiency of LBRS within h hops can be determined by,

$$P_h = \sum_{k=0}^{T-1} p_{\{k\}} \left[1 - \prod_{i=1}^{h} (1-f_{k,i}) \right]. \tag{16}$$

The false date forwarded hops is

$$E(h) = \sum_{i=1}^{H_{max}} i(1-P_{i-1})f_{k,i} = \sum_{i=1}^{H_{max}} i \left(\sum_{k=0}^{T-1} p_{\{k\}} f_{k,i} \prod_{j=1}^{i-1} (1-f_{k,j}) \right). \tag{17}$$

If a cell contains T or more compromised nodes, the cell is considered as compromised cell. Hence, the probability of a cell being compromised (i.e., compromised area ratio) is

$$P_s = \sum_{j=T}^{L} p_{\{j\}} = 1 - \sum_{j=0}^{T-1} p_{\{j\}}. \tag{18}$$

In LBRS, a legitimate report consists of an event, a cell ID, T key IDs and T MACs, and the size of these components is L_r, L_{cell}, L_k and L_{MAC}, respectively. In the same way as in SEF, the energy consumption of the network with LBRS is

$$EC = (L_r + L_{cell} + TL_k + TL_{MAC})(H + \beta E(h))e. \tag{19}$$

LEDS

As mentioned in (Ren, 2008), by using the location-ware key generation and cell-based report generation, LEDS reveals the authentication key of a

cell to attackers only if one or more nodes in the cell are compromised by attackers. Let $p_{\{i\}}$ be the probability that exactly i nodes are compromised in one cell, LEDS defines

$$p_{\{i\}} = \frac{\binom{n}{i}\binom{N-n}{N_c - i}}{\binom{N}{N_c}}. \tag{20}$$

LEDS uses LSSS(T, t) to deal with the report disruption attack, which indicates that a cell could be compromised only if at least t nodes are compromised in the cell T. Thus, we only evaluate the filtering efficiency of LEDS with less than t compromised nodes in a cell. In addition, LEDS adopts a one-to-many data forwarding approach to deal with the selective forwarding attack, but it causes that the forwarding cell with at least one compromised node will lose their filtering capacity, i.e., it could forward the forged report to next cell. The probability that a forwarding cell with at least one compromised node can be represented as $(1 - p_{\{0\}})$. The cell with at least one compromised nodes is defined the affected cell.

LEDS adopts the interleaved cell-by-cell authentication, and if i nodes are compromised in a cell, i forwarding cells will be assigned the compromised nodes, and these forwarding cells will lose filtering capacity. As mentioned in (Ren, 2008), a valid report contains $T+1$ MACs, and only if more than $t+1$ MACs are invalid, the report could be detected as forged one. In addition, the effected forwarding cell also can forward a forged report without detection. Hence, within h forwarded cells, only if ($h-(i+T+1-(t+1))$) effected forwarding cells are included in the routing path, a forged report could not be filtered out. Note that, with the use of interleaved cell-by-cell authentication, LEDS could become effective within first $T+1$ forwarding cells, i.e., when the number of forwarded cells is more than $T+1$, filtering efficiency of LEDS could maintain constant. Hence, with N_c compromised nodes in the whole area, the filtering efficiency of LEDS within h forwarded hops is

$$
P_h = \begin{cases} \sum_{i=0}^{t-1} p_{\{i\}}\left(1-(1-p_{\{0\}})^{(h-(i+T-t))}\right) & (h \leq T) \\ \sum_{i=0}^{t-1} p_{\{i\}}\left(1-(1-p_{\{0\}})^{(t-i)}\right) & (h > T) \end{cases}
$$

(21)

Note that, if t or more compromised nodes are in a cell, all forwarding cells cannot detect the forged report of this cell, and thus we only consider the filtering efficiency of LEDS with less than t compromised nodes in a cell.

$$
E(h) = H_{max} \sum_{i=0}^{t-1} p_{\{i\}}(1-p_{\{0\}})^{t-i} + \frac{T}{2}\left(1-\sum_{i=0}^{t-1} p_{\{i\}}(1-p_{\{0\}})^{t-i}\right).
$$

(22)

If a cell contains t or more compromised nodes, the cell is considered as a compromised cell. Hence, the probability of a cell being compromised becomes

$$
P_s = 1 - \sum_{j=0}^{t-1} p_{\{j\}}.
$$

(23)

As mentioned in LEDS, a legitimate consists of T shares of events, which are computed via predefined (t, T) LSSS, T node IDs, $T+1$ MACs and a cell ID, and the size (e.g. data length) of one of them can be represented as L_{sr}, L_{ID}, L_{MAC} and L_{cell}. In the same way used for computing the energy consumption of the network with SEF, the energy consumption for LEDS is

$$
EC = (TL_{sr} + L_{cell} + TL_k + (T+1)L_{MAC})(H+\beta E(h))e
$$

(24)

DEFS

Recall that DEFS defines two keys: y-key and z-key. The first one is used to verify MACs of the report, and the second one is used to verify the authentication message. As mentioned in (Yu, 2010), only if the authentication message contains T different z-keys, the message could be considered as a valid one. Hence, to forge a valid report, the attacker must have enough different z-keys. With N_c compromised nodes, the probability of one z-key that is revealed to the attacker is

$$
p' = 1 - \left(1 - \frac{1}{w}\right)^{N_c},
$$

(25)

where w is the number of z-keys in key pool. Then, the probability of j different z-keys that are revealed to the attacker is

$$
p_{\{j\}} = \binom{w}{j} p'^j (1-p')^{w-j}.
$$

(26)

DEFS adopts the *Hill Climbing* technology, which can reduce the storage overhead of forwarding nodes and ensure that the nodes closer to data source have a stronger filtering capacity. In addition, using the *Hill Climbing* eliminates the redundant decryptions and verifications because if an authentication key has been decrypted by an upstream node, any downstream node no longer needs to decrypt the key (or use it to verify reports). As mentioned in (Yu, 2010), by using the *Hill Climbing*, the filtering efficiency of a single forwarding node that is i hops away from the source cluster is

$$
f_{j,i} = 1 - \left(1 - (\frac{1}{2})^i\right)^{l(T-j)},
$$

(27)

where j is the number of compromised z-keys. Then, with N_c compromised nodes, the filtering efficiency of DEFS within h forwarded hops is

$$P_h = \sum_{j=0}^{T-1} p_{\{j\}} \left[1 - \prod_{i=1}^{h} (1 - f_{j,i}) \right], \qquad (28)$$

where $p_{\{j\}}$ represents the probability that j different z-keys are compromised with N_c compromised nodes in the whole area. The false data forwarded hop $E(h)$ and compromised area ratio P_s can be derived in the way used in DEFS, and can be represented by

$$E(h) = \sum_{i=1}^{H_{max}} i(1 - P_{i-1}) f_{j,i} = \sum_{i=1}^{H_{max}} i \left(\sum_{j=0}^{T-1} p_{\{j\}} f_{j,i} \prod_{k=1}^{i-1} (1 - f_{j,k}) \right). \qquad (29)$$

$$P_s = 1 - \sum_{j=0}^{T-1} p_{\{j\}}. \qquad (30)$$

As mentioned in DEFS, there are three phases in DEFS. First, the source cluster-head node sends the authentication message $K(n)$, denoted as

$$K(n) = \{Auth(u_1), Auth(u_2), ..., Auth(u_n)\}, \qquad (31)$$

where $Auth(u_i)$ is the Auth message of cluster node u_i, and it can be denoted as

$$Auth(u_i) = \begin{bmatrix} u_i, j_i, id(y_1^{u_i}), \{id(y_1^{u_i}), k_{j_i}^{u_i}\}_{y_i^{u_i}} \\ ..., id(y_l^{u_i}), \{id(y_l^{u_i}), k_{j_i}^{u_i}\}_{y_l^{u_i}}, id(z^{u_i}), \{id(z^{u_i}), k_{j_i}^{u_i}\}_{z^{u_i}} \end{bmatrix}, \qquad (32)$$

where u_i is the node ID, j_i is the key index of its current authentication key, $id(.)$ represents the key index, and $\{.\}_y$ means an encryption operation using key y. Second, source cluster-head sends multiple event reports, each of which consists of event E, T MACs, T node ID and T key index, to the sink. Only if a forwarding node receives the OK message from upstream forwarding node, it can forward the reports to the downstream forward-ing node along the routing path. Lastly, the source cluster-head disseminates the authentication keys of T nodes using $K(T)$. The forwarding nodes de-crypts the authentication keys of the reports from $K(T)$, and uses them to verify the reports. If the reports are valid, forwarding nodes sends an OK message to the downstream forwarding nodes. Assuming that γ and δ is the ratio for $K(t)$ and $K(n)$, respectively over all nodes. As mentioned in (Yu, 2010), the energy consumption for DEFS becomes

$$EC = (L_r + T(L_{ID} + L_K + L_{MAC}) + \gamma(LK_{(T)} + L_{OK}) + \delta L_{K(n)}) (H + \beta E(h))e, \qquad (33)$$

$$L_{K(i)} = i(L_{ID} + L_K + (l+1)L_k + (L_k + L_{key})), \qquad (34)$$

where L_r, L_{ID}, L_k, L_{MAC}, L_{key} are the size of event E, a node ID, a key index, a MAC, and an authen-tication key, respectively. H, e, and l are defined in Table 1.

Performance Evaluations

We now evaluate the performance of those schemes discussed in previous sections. In our simulation, we consider a 1km x 1km area, where 1000 sensor nodes are randomly deployed, and evaluate the schemes investigated in Sections II and III. To meet the requirements of cell-based schemes, we divide the whole square region into small square cells with the side length of $50m$, and the number of nodes deployed in one cell is 10. In our simulation, we assume that the rate of authentication keys in statistical schemes, the node communication radius, and the number of MACs in a legitimate report are 0.5, $50m$, and 5, respectively.

Filtering Efficiency

The data in Figures 2 and 3 show the filtering efficiency of schemes vs. forwarded hops and conclude that the filtering efficiency increases as the number of hops increases in all schemes.

The simulations in terms of filtering efficiency are conducted in the scenarios, where 1 and 9 nodes are compromised in the network. We can see that with the same forwarded hops, the filtering efficiency of deterministic schemes is higher than that of statistical schemes. This is because the probability of authentication keys shared among the forwarding nodes in statistical schemes is less than "1" while the probability in deterministic schemes is "1".

In comparison Figure 2 with Figure 3, we can see that the filtering efficiency reduces as the number of compromised nodes grows. This is because that the attacker can obtain more authentication keys from the compromised nodes. As a result, the filtering efficiency of SEF, SEF-B, and DEFS decrease rapidly with the larger number of compromised nodes due to the T-threshold limitation. Because of the characteristics of interleaved authentication, the filtering efficiency of LEDS will remain a constant while the number of forwarding hops is larger than $T+1$. The filtering efficiency of DEFS will remain constant after a few forwarded hops. This can be explained, using the *Hill Climbing* technique makes the authentication keys not being decrypted by the nodes close

to the sink and the reports cannot be verified by these nodes. As we can see, the most of existing schemes can maintain a high value of filtering efficiency, and the filtering efficiency of them increases as the number of hops grows.

Compromised Area Ratio

Note that in existing schemes, if the attacker has T the authentication keys that can generate T valid MACs attached to the report in any place of the area, that area will be totally compromised. Since SEF-B has the same resilience as SEF, we do not show the curves of SEF-B in Figure 4 and 5. In Figure 4, because of the T-threshold limitation, the compromised area ratios of SEF and DEFS increase to "1" while the number of compromised nodes approaches 15 (i.e. 1.5% of whole network), which means that the attackers can forge false reports that "appear" in anywhere of the whole area. The compromised area ratios of other schemes maintain low values as shown in Figure 5. From Figure 5, when the number of compromised nodes reaches 300 (i.e., 30% of whole network), the compromised area ratio of LBRS approaches "1", and when the number of compro-

Figure 2. Filtering efficiency vs. forwarded hops (1 compromised node)

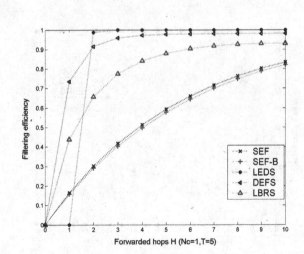

Figure 3. Filtering efficiency vs. forwarded hops (9 compromised nodes)

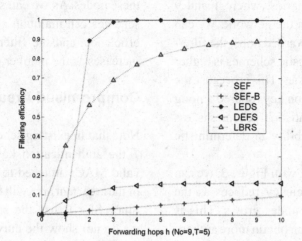

mised nodes reaches 500 (50% of whole network), the compromised area ratios of LEDS approaches "0.8". Our simulation data also validates that the schemes without location-ware authentication keys (e.g., SEF and DEFS) have low resilience to the growing number of compromised nodes, and the schemes with location-ware authentication keys and special data dissemination protocol (e.g., LEDS and LBRS) have a better resilience to the growing number of compromised nodes.

Energy Consumption

Before comparing the energy consumption of the network with these schemes, we investigate the energy consumption of the network where no en-route filtering scheme is used. Obviously, without en-route filtering, all legitimate reports and false reports could reach the sink. Hence, the energy consumption in the network without any en-route filtering scheme becomes,

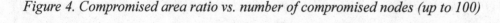

Figure 4. Compromised area ratio vs. number of compromised nodes (up to 100)

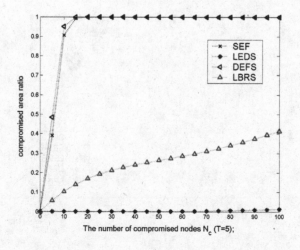

Figure 5. Compromised area ratio vs. number of compromised nodes (up to 500)

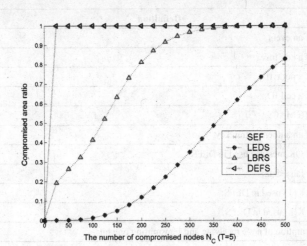

$$EC=(1+\beta)L_r He, \tag{35}$$

where L_r is the length of event, and other parameters are defined in Table 1.

For the evaluation of energy consumption, we define the length of all parameters in Table 2, which are typical values used in (Ye, 2004; Yang, 2005; Ren, 2008; Yu, 2010).

In Figure 6, we show the Energy consumption vs. Ratio of injected false data and Number of compromised nodes. E_{DEFS}, E_{SEF}, E_{LBRS}, E_{SEF-B}, E_{LEDS} represent the energy consumption of the network with DEFS, SEF, LBRS, SEF-B, LEDS, respectively. E_{none} represents the energy consumption of the network without any scheme being used. As shown in Figure 8, with the increase of the ratio of injected false data, the energy consumption increase no matter what schemes are used or not. As the number of compromised nodes increases, the energy consumption also increases. This is caused by the reduction of filtering efficiency. When the number of compromised nodes is less than 40 (i.e., 4% of whole size), the energy consumption of the network with DEFS, SEF and SEF-B increases rapidly, when the number are more than 40, the energy consumption maintains

a constant with a certain ratio of injected false data. This can be explained that DEFS, SEF and SEF-B have low resilience to the number of compromised nodes, and these schemes will lose en-route filtering capacity when the number of compromised nodes is more than 40.

Because of the extra control message, DEFS achieves the highest energy consumption, and LEDS achieves the smallest due to the greatest filtering capacity. Because of using Bloom Filter, SEF-B reduces the size of MACs attached in the report, and has lower energy consumption than SEF does.

In addition, when the number of compromised nodes is less than 15 (i.e., 1.5% of whole size), all schemes can save energy. However, when it is more than 15, DEFS, SEF and SEF-B will consume more energy than the scenario where no en-route filtering scheme is used. When the number of compromised nodes is more than 25 (i.e., 2.5% of whole size) and 80 (i.e., 8% of whole size), LBRS and LEDS could not save energy, respectively. Hence, we can see that all schemes can achieve energy saving when few nodes are compromised. As the number of compromised nodes increases, all schemes will lose the capability of energy saving

Table 2. Length of parameters used in evaluation of energy consumption

Parameter	Definition	Length
L_r	The length of an event;	24*8bits
L_k	The length of a key index;	10bits
L_{ID}	The length of a node ID;	8bits
L_{cell}	The length of a cell ID;	8bits
L_{mac}	The length of a MAC;	64bits
L_{key}	The length of an authentication key;	64bits
L_{OK}	The length of OK message used in DEFS;	8bits
β	The radio for false data;	10
γ	The radio for K(T) used in DEFS;	0.1
δ	The radio for K(n) used in DEFS;	0.01
e	Energy consumption of node receiving and transmitting one bit;	1

Figure 6. Energy consumption vs. ratio of injected false data and number of compromised nodes

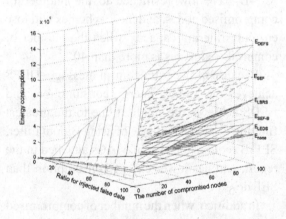

ultimately because of the limitation of en-route filtering capacity. Although LBRS and LEDS achieve better energy saving than other schemes, those schemes require the localization phase and node association phase, which will consume extra energy. Since the energy consumption for LBRS and LEDS depends on the frequency of node localization and node association, we cannot say that LBRS and LEDS achieve a better performance with the consideration of energy consumption.

Relationships among These Schemes

After analyzing and comparing the performance of SEF, LBRS, LEDS and DEFS, we now list the relationships between them. To this end, Figure 7 shows the relationships of those schemes. In Figure 7, the circle represents the specific scheme, and the number in the circle represents the year that the scheme was developed. The context in the rectangular represents the pros that the arrow referring scheme regarding to arrow embarking scheme. For example, the context in rectangular 1 shows the pros of LBRS vs. SEF. That is, in comparison with SEF, LBRS adopts the cell-based report generation and location-ware key generation, and mitigates the *T*-threshold problem appeared in SEF. Meanwhile, the context in rectangular 2 shows the pros of SEF vs. LBRS. That is, SEF does not rely on node localization and special routing protocols (i.e., beam model). This makes SEF more suitable for a dynamic environment than LBRS does.

DISCUSSION

Besides the performance metrics, including the false data filtering efficiency, false data filtering hops, compromised area ratio, and energy consumption; which we discussed above, the applicability of these schemes need to be considered. As an excellent en-route filtering schemes, it shall achieve not only a reasonable performance, but also a desired applicability. However, the existing schemes cannot achieve good performance and applicability simultaneously. For example, in comparison with LBRS and LEDS, SEF and DEFS achieve a worse performance, including worse filtering capacity, worse attack resilience and worse energy saving. SEF and DEFS achieve a great applicability, i.e., having no dependency on fixed sink and special routing protocols. In contrast, LBRS and LEDS achieve greater performance while depending on the fixed sink and special routing protocols. Hence, developing en-route schemes to address both the performance and applicability is still an open issue in the field.

To design a robust scheme for FDI mitigation, the filtering capacity and attack resilience must be considered. To achieve high attack resilience, the effect of compromised nodes should be limited to a local area, and one of the effective approaches is to organize nodes into clusters. Assigning different authentication information for different clusters can achieve the optimal security condition: only if more than a certain number of nodes in a local area are compromised, the local area will be compromised. In terms of applicability, the en-route filtering scheme should avoid node localization (location-ware authentication key generation) and node association, which is dependent on the fixed sink and special routing protocols. Hence, authentication information stored in nodes should not be bound with node location and should be stored in node before nodes are deployed.

According to the analysis above, the *polynomial-based* authentication information and the polynomial-based authentication is a promising option to achieve both the performance and applicability simultaneously. Different primitive polynomials will be used in different clusters.

Figure 7. Relationships among SEF, LBRS, LEDS, and DEFS

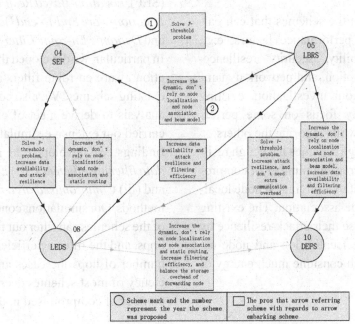

Nodes in one cluster store the authentication polynomial derived by their primitive polynomial and their node index, and nodes outside the cluster store the check polynomial of the cluster, which is also derived by primitive polynomial of the cluster and different from the derived authentication polynomials, with a certain probability. The authentication polynomial stored in each node is used to endorse the report of local component measurement while the check polynomial is used to validate the received reports. In the polynomial-based approach, different authentication information will be assigned for different clusters, and authentication information is stored in a node before nodes are being deployed. Using the clusters for authentication ensures that the designed scheme achieves not only a robust performance, but also a general applicability.

FUTURE RESEARCH DIRECTIONS

Our research summarizes the state-of-art research and can lay out future directions of situation aware en-route filtering mechanisms. Here, we list our future directions of:

- Develop design the schemes that can balance multiple performance factors, e.g., filtering capability, security resilience, energy consumption, and network dynamics. Based on our investigation, existing schemes mainly focus on some performance factors while ignoring the others.
- Ensure the design schemes have high resilience to the increasing number of compromised nodes without relying on node localization and node association. The existing schemes increase their attack-resilience by using the node localization and node association, which consume much energy of nodes.

- Reduce the design schemes reliance on the static sink and data dissemination protocols with static routes.
- Apply the design schemes to mobile networks with mobile nodes. Most of existing schemes are based on the association between nodes and locations. The entering, exit, and movement of nodes in the network will increase the time of initialization and incur much energy consumption.
- Utilize resilient insider attacks. Besides the false data injection attack, there are other insider attacks, including the selective forwarding attack and report disruption attack. Hence, the situation aware en-route filtering scheme shall not only filter out false data effectively, but also be able to mitigate other insider attacks.

CONCLUSION

To mitigate the false data injection attacks in WSNs, a number of situation aware en-route filtering schemes have been proposed, tested, and compared; namely *Statistical En-route Filtering* (SEF), *Location-Based Resilient Secrecy* (LBRS), *Location-ware End-to-end Data Security* (LEDS), and *Dynamic En-route Filtering Scheme* (DEFS). In particular, we developed the taxonomy of situation aware en-route filters and categorized the existing schemes. We also conducted theoretical analysis to derive a set of closed formulae and carried out extensive simulations to validate our findings. We developed the metrics of (i) *False data filtering efficiency*, (ii) *Energy consumption*, and (iii) *Compromised area ratio* to compare the methods. Our simulations concluded that that most of the schemes can filter out false data within few hops, and the filtering efficiency increases as the number of hops increases and the filtering efficiency of most schemes decreases rapidly as the number of compromised nodes increases.

REFERENCES

Block, J., & Rogaway, P. (2002). A block-cipher mode of operation for parallelizable message authentication. *Advance in Cryptology—EUROCHRYPT 2002. LNCS, 2332*, 384–397.

Bloom, B. (1970). Space/time trade-offs in hash coding with allowable errors. *Communications of the ACM, 7*(13), 422–426. doi:10.1145/362686.362692

Cardenas, A., Amin, S., & Sastry, S. S. (2008). Secure control: Towards survivable cyber-physical systems. In *Proceedings of 28th International Conference on Distributed Computing Systems (ICDCS)*, (pp. 495–500).

Cardenas, A. A., Amin, S., & Sastry, S. (2008, July). Research challenges for the security of control systems. In *Proceedings of 3rd USENIX workshop on Hot Topics in Security* (HotSec). USENIX Association Berkeley, CA, USA

Cardenas, A. A., Amin, S., Sinopoli, B., Giani, A., Perrig, A., & Sastry, S. S. (2009, July). Challenges for securing cyber physical systems. In *Proceedings of Workshop on Future Directions in Cyber-Physical Systems Security*.

Chen, G., Shen, D., Kwan, C., Cruz, J. B. Jr, Kruger, M., & Blasch, E. (2008). Game theoretic approach to threat prediction and situation awareness. *Journal of Advances in Information Fusion, 2*(1), 35–48.

Chen, X., Makki, K., & Pissinou, N. (2009). Sensor network security: A survey. *IEEE Communications Surveys & Tutorials, 2*(11), 52–73. doi:10.1109/SURV.2009.090205

Chen, Y.-S., & Lei, C.-L. (2010). Filtering false messages en-route in wireless multi-hop networks. *IEEE Wireless Communications and Networking Conference (WCNC)*, Sydney, Australia, (pp. 1-6).

CPS Week. (2010). Retrieved from http://www.cpsweek2010.se/

Iwata, T., & Kurosawa, K. (2002). OMAC: One-key CBC MAC. *Pre-proceedings of Fast Software Encryption. FSE, 2003*, 137–161.

Karlof, C., & Wagner, D. (2003). Sensor network protocols and applications. *Proceedings of the First IEEE Secure Routing in Wireless Sensor Networks: Attacks and Countermeasures*, (pp. 113-127).

Krawczyk, H., Bellare, M., & Canetti, R. (February, 1997). *HMAC-keyed-hashing for message authentication.* Internet Engineering Task Force, Request for Comments (RFC) 2104.

Ren, K., & Zhang, Y. (2008). LEDS: Providing location-aware end-to-end data security in wireless sensor networks. *IEEE Transactions on Mobile Computing, 5*(7), 585–598. doi:10.1109/TMC.2007.70753

Shen, D., Chen, G., Cruz, J. B. Jr, Blasch, E., & Pham, K. (2009). An adaptive Markov game model for cyber threat intent inference. In Er, M. J., & Zhou, Y. (Eds.), *Theory and novel applications of machine learning* (pp. 317–334).

Shen, D., Chen, G., Cruz, J. B., Jr., Haynes, L., Kruger, M., & Blasch, E. (2007). A Markov game theoretic data fusion approach for cyber situational awareness. *Proceedings of SPIE*, vol. 6571.

Yang, H., & Lu, S. (2004). Commutative cipher based en-route filtering in wireless sensor networks. In *Proceedings of 60th IEEE Vehicular Technology Conference Fall* Los Angeles, CA, vol. 2, (pp. 1223-1227).

Yang, H., Ye, F., & Arbaugh, W. (2005). Toward resilient security in wireless sensor networks. *In Proceedings of The Sixth ACM International Symposium on Mobile Ad Hoc Networking and Computing* (MobiHoc), Urbana-Champaign, Illinois, USA, (pp. 34-45).

Ye, F., Luo, H., & Zhang, L. (2004). Statistical en-route filtering of injected false data in sensor networks. In *Proceedings of the 23th IEEE International Conference on Computer Communications,* Hong Kong, China, (pp. 2446-2457).

Yu, L., & Li, J. (2009). Grouping-based resilient statistical en-route filtering for sensor networks. *In Proceedings of the 28th IEEE International Conference on Computer Communications*, Rio de Janeiro, Brazil, (pp. 1782-1790).

Yu, Z., & Guan, Y. (2010). A dynamic en-route filtering scheme for data reporting in wireless sensor networks. *IEEE/ACM Transactions on Networking, 18,* 150–163. doi:10.1109/TNET.2009.2026901

Zhu, S., & Setia, S. (2004). An interleaved hop-by-hop authentication scheme for filtering of injection false data in sensor networks. *IEEE Symposium on Security and Privacy*, Berkeley, CA, USA, (pp. 259-271).

ADDITIONAL READING

Akyilidz, (2002). Wireless sensor networks: a survey. *Computer Networks, 38*(3), 393–424. doi:10.1016/S1389-1286(01)00302-4

Al-Karaki, J. N., & Kamal, A. E. (2004, December). Routing Techniques in wireless sensor network: a survey. *IEEE Wireless Communications, 11*(6), 6–28. doi:10.1109/MWC.2004.1368893

Balfanz, D., Smetters, D. K., Stewart, P., & Wong, H. C. (2002, February). Talking to Strangers: Authentication in Ad-Hoc Wireless Networks. *in Proceedings of 2002 Symposium on Network and Distributed Systems Security* (NDSS).

Banerjee, S., & Bhattacharjee, B. (2001, Novermber). Scalable Secure Group Communication over IP Mulitcast. *In Proceedings of International Conference on Network Protocols,* (pp. 261-269).

Blum, J. J. (2004, December). Challenges of inter-vehicle ad hoc networks. *IEEE Transactions on Intelligent Transportation Systems, 5*(4), 347–351. doi:10.1109/TITS.2004.838218

Capkun, S., Rasmussen, K. B., Cagalj, M., & Srivastava, M. (2008, April). Secure Location Verification With Hidden and Mobile Base Stations. *IEEE Transactions on Mobile Computing, 7*(4), 470–483. doi:10.1109/TMC.2007.70782

Chan, H., Perrig, A., & Song, D. (2003, May). Random Key Predistribution Schemes for Sensor Networks. *in Proceedings of IEEE Symposium on Research in Security and Privacy,* (pp. 197-213).

Chan, H., Perrig, A., & Song, D. (2006, November). Secure Hierarchical In-Network Aggregation in Sensor Networks. *In Proceedings of the 13th ACM Conference on Computer and Communications Security* (CCS), (pp, 278-287).

Du, W., Deng, J., Han, Y. S., Chen, S., & Varshney, P. (2004, April). A Key Management Scheme for Wireless Sensor Networks Using Deployment Knowledge. *In Proceedings of 28th IEEE International Conference on Computer Communications,* (Vol.1).

Gnawali, O., Fonseca, R., Jamieson, K., Moss, D., & Levis, P. (2009). Collection Tree Protocol. *In Proceedings of the 7th ACM Conference on Embedded Networked Sensor Systems* (SenSys), (pp. 1-14).

Gu, Y., & He, T. (2007). Data Forwarding in Extremely Low Duty-Cycle Sensor Networks with Unreliable Communication Links. *in Proceedings of ACM Conference On Embedded Networked Sensor Systems,* (pp. 321-334).

Guo, S., Gu, Y., Jiang, B., & He, T. (2009, September). Opportunistic Flooding in Low-Duty-Cycle Wireless Sensor Networks with Unreliable Links. *In the Proceedings of 15th Annual International Conference on Mobile Computing and Networking* (MobiCom), (pp. 133-144).

Intanagonwiwat, C., Govindan, R., Estrin, E., Heidemann, J. and Silva, F. (2003). Directed Diffusion for Wireless Sensor Networking. *IEE/ACM Transactions on Networking*, 11(1), 2-16.

Karlof, C., Sastry, N., Li, Y., Perrig, A., & Tygar, J. D. (2004, February). Distillation Codes and Applications to DoS Resistant Multicast Authentication. *In Proceedings of the 11th Annual Network and Distributed System Security Symposium* (NDSS), (pp. 37-65).

Liu, D., & Ning, P. (2003, October). Location-Based Pairwise Key Establishments for Static Sensor Networks. *in 2003 ACM Workshop on Security in Ad Hoc and Sensor Networks* (SASN), (pp. 72-82).

Misic, J., & Misic, V. B. (2007, January). Implementation of security policy for clinical information systems over wireless sensor networks. *Ad Hoc Networks*, 5(1), 134–144. doi:10.1016/j.adhoc.2006.05.008

Parno, B., Luk, M., Gaustad, E., & Perrig, A. (2006, December). Secure Sensor Network Routing: A Clean-Slate Approach. *In Proceedings of the 2nd Conference on Future Networking Technologies* (CoNEXT 2006), (No. 11).

Perrig, A., Szewczyk, R., Wen, V., Culler, D., & Tygar, J. D. (2001). Security protocols for sensor networks. In *Proceedings of (MOBICOM)*. SPINS.

Sun, K., Ning, P., Wang, C., Liu, A., & Zhou, Y. (2006, October/November). TinySeRSync: Secure and Resilient Time Synchronization in Wireless Sensor Networks. *in Proceedings of the 13th ACM Conference on Computer and Communications Security* (CCS), (pp. 264-277).

Zhu, S., Setia, S., & Jajodia, S. (2006, November). LEAP+: Efficient Security Mechanisms for Large-scale Distributed Sensor Networks. *ACM Trans. on Sensor Networks*, 2(4), 500–528. doi:10.1145/1218556.1218559

Zhu, S., Setia, S., Jajodia, S., & Ning, P. (2004, May). An Interleaved Hop-by-Hop Authentication Scheme for Filtering False Data in Sensor Networks. *To appear in the Proceedings of IEEE Symposium on Security and Privacy,* (Berkeley, CA, USA, pp. 259-271).

Zhu, T., Zhong, Z., He, T., & Zhang, Z.-L. (2010). Exploring Link Correlation for Efficient Flooding in Wireless Sensor Networks. *in the Proceedings of Networked System Design and Implementation,* (pp.4-4).

KEY TERMS AND DEFINITIONS

Attack Resilience: The resistance of attack damage which the scheme can achieve.

Compromised Area Ratio: The percentage of compromised area in the terrain.

En-Route Filtering: Filtering out the false data while being forwarded along the forwarding route.

False Data: The measurement data forged by the attacker.

False Data Filtering Efficiency: The probability of false data to be filtered within a number of hops. It measures the effectiveness of false data filtering schemes.

False Data Forwarded Hops: The average hops that false data will be forwarded before being filtered.

False Data Injection Attack: The attack in which false data is injected to the network via the compromised nodes.

T-**Threshold Problem:** If more than T partitions are compromised, which can generate T different valid MACs for report, the whole area will be compromised.

Chapter 16
Attack Graphs and Scenario Driven Wireless Computer Network Defense

Peter J. Hawrylak
The University of Tulsa, USA

George Louthan IV
The University of Tulsa, USA

Jeremy Daily
The University of Tulsa, USA

John Hale
The University of Tulsa, USA

Mauricio Papa
The University of Tulsa, USA

ABSTRACT

This chapter describes how to use attack graphs to evaluate the security vulnerabilities of an embedded computer network and provides example cases of this technique. Attack graphs are powerful tools available to system administrators to identify and manage vulnerabilities. Attack graphs describe the steps an adversary could take to reach a desired goal and can be analyzed to quantify risk. The systems investigated in this chapter are embedded systems that span hardware, software, and network communication. The example cases studied will be (1) radio frequency identification (RFID), (2) vehicle networks, and (3) the Smart Grid (the next generation power and distribution network in the USA).

INTRODUCTION

Embedded systems are systems composed of a microprocessor embedded within a larger product other than a typical desktop or laptop computer and are becoming pervasive. Embedded systems include sensors and actuators, which are controlled and monitored by microprocessors. Some examples of embedded systems are the engine control module found in vehicles, a washing machine, a cell phone, and a thermostat. Often an embedded system includes some form of network connec-

DOI: 10.4018/978-1-4666-0104-8.ch016

tion (e.g. RS-232, USB, CAN, RFID, or Wi-Fi) to connect to other devices. With the proliferation and networking of embedded systems, the security of these systems is of critical concern.

For embedded systems, security is addressed component by component in isolation. The goal is to secure a given component and then to do this for all components in a system. This technique may have worked in the past when most embedded systems were designed entirely from scratch or in-house components. However, today's embedded systems often incorporate third party intellectual property (IP) blocks that cannot always be verified or modified to fix security issues. The system-on-a-chip (SOC) design philosophy (Keating & Bricaud, 2002), built around reuse of IP blocks, requires a new approach to securing an embedded system.

Many embedded systems blend the physical (or continuous) world and the digital (or discrete) worlds. Such systems are often termed *cyber-physical systems*. The electronics in an automobile is one example of this blending of physical processes. For example, oxygen sensors provide analog signals to a digital control system that adjusts fuel mixture in a way that reduces hydrocarbon emissions. Because of this cyber-physical linkage, an attack may now be introduced into the system through both physical and cyber (software, hardware, and communications network) components. One example of such an attack is the Stuxnet worm, which targeted nuclear centrifuges using the motor to cause a catastrophic failure (centrifuge will break apart) (Broad & Sanger, 2010). Another example of cyber-physical attack is exploiting the electronic communication bus present on all modern automobiles to take control of physical variables or components (e.g. speed or door locks) (Koscher, *et. al.*, 2010). These kinds of blended attacks force a sea-change in the approach adopted by conventional IT security tools and methods. Security must be evaluated from the software, hardware, network, and physical viewpoints.

Attack graphs are one method to model and describe attacks. This chapter will describe how to use attack graphs to evaluate the security vulnerabilities of an embedded computer network and provide example cases of this technique. The systems investigated in this chapter are embedded systems that span hardware, software, and network communication domains. The example cases studied will be (1) radio frequency identification (RFID), (2) vehicle networking, and (3) the smart grid (the next generation power and distribution network in the USA). First, a definition and explanation of attack graphs will be provided. Then, the methods of using these attack graphs to identify vulnerabilities and improve system security will be presented. Finally, the three example cases will be presented in separate sections. Each example case will be defined and attack graphs will be generated to enumerate vulnerabilities in that system.

BACKGROUND

Definition of Attack Graphs

An attack graph denotes one of any number of closely related formalisms that utilize graph theory to represent the state space of attacks on systems. Vertices of the graph represent individual network or system states, and edges represent state transitions generally due to the actions of an adversary. The term attack graph first appeared in the literature in 1998 (Philips & Swiler, 1998) including three features that continue to comprise the formalism: "attack templates," or generalized attacks to be employed in state transitions; configurations of individual network elements; and the topology of the network. The original formalism also included some features that are only sometimes present in modern incarnations of attack graphs such as a separate *attacker profile*, which represents a particular attacker's capabilities; and edge weights representing a *probability-*

of-success measure (Philips & Swiler, 1998). Similar structures such as attack trees (Schneier 1999) and privilege graphs (Dacier, Deswarte & Kaâniche, 1996) were introduced independently around the same time.

Chaining together exploits over matching preconditions and postconditions yields a network of attack vectors approachable by an adversary. Systematic analysis of attack graphs can reveal likely paths of attack, the global impact of a vulnerability on a system's security posture, and critical remediation points in a system.

The major research pathways under investigation in relation to attack graphs include and frequently combine the following: determining the level of security of a given network, e.g. as a topology-aware network vulnerability analysis tool (Ammann, Wijesekera, & Kaushik, 2002); specification of formal languages to represent attack graphs (Templeton & Levitt, 2001); intrusion detection system integration (Tidwell, Larson, Fitch & Hale, 2001; Noel & Jajodia, 2009); delivery of security recommendations from attack graph analysis (Wang, Noel & Jajodia, 2006); improving scalability of attack graph generation (Ingols, Lippmann & Piwowarski, 2006; Ammann, Wijesekera & Kaushik, 2002); and reachability analysis over individual network states (i.e. between hosts) (Ingols, Chu, Lippmann, Webster & Boyer, 2009; Lippmann & Ingols, 2005).

Attack Graph Structure

A central issue in attack graphs is the structure and scope of the underlying system model used to describe network state. Most approaches share the application of qualities to individual elements and of topologies among them, and since their explicit introduction (Templeton & Levitt, 2002) the notion of modeling exploits using preconditions and postconditions has also become common (Lippman & Ingols, 2005).

Network state may be specified in a highly general fashion with arbitrary keywords serving as named qualities of, and topologies among, network objects. This chapter explores this method, which is also used in attack graph research originating at George Mason University (Ammann, Wijesekera, & Kaushik, 2002; Wang, Noel & Jajodia, 2006). The specification may also be constrained to certain sets of terms to impose common computer networking semantics (Templeton & Levitt, 2001), and therefore facilitate reachability analysis (Ingols, Chu, Lippmann, Webster & Boyer, 2009). This approach is favored in the work from, among others, MIT Lincoln Laboratory and University of California, Davis.

An advantage of the more liberal method of specification is that it enables the straightforward introduction of the continuous domain into the formalism. This novel application of attack graphs onto hybrid systems requires little adaptation of our specification syntax but allows the inclusion of continuous domain topologies such as distance, signal strength, or latency, and qualities such as temperature, velocity, battery level, and system load. These extensions permit more holistic analysis of cyber-physical systems such as those addressed in this chapter.

Generation of Attack Graphs

Attack graph generation is done in several ways, but they share a common general architecture, as illustrated in Figure 1 in which a generation engine combines network state and exploit preconditions as input and applies exploit postconditions to generate new network states as output.

Attack generation is the process of chaining exploits interpreted as functional vulnerability models within a specific system context to enumerate the full attack space (Campbell, *et.al.*, 2003; Philips & Swiler, 1998; Sheyner, Haines, Jha, Lippmann & Wing, 2002). The flexibility of attack generation makes possible modeling attack

Figure 1. Automatic generation of attack graphs

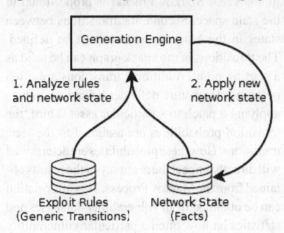

vectors that incorporate non-cyber elements such as social engineering (e.g. insider attacks) or kinetic exploits (e.g. applying a force to a strain sensor). The principal challenges to attack graph generation are computational and cognitive scalability.

The central issue in attack graph generation is the scope and granularity of the underlying system model. The richness and composability of the system modeling substrate defines the variety and depth of attack vectors to be found in a generated attack graph, and also impacts the inherent scalability of the generation process itself. A sparse modeling system may unduly limit the generated attack space, while an overly rich and expressive system may prohibit exhaustive graph generation due to time and storage space constraints. One practical matter that must be addressed in attack graph and network modeling is the adoption of a standard lexicon for system elements and attributes. Attack graph generation demands symbolic precision in terminology to match exploit conditions with network state characteristics. The potential for modeling vulnerabilities and exploits in the continuous domain also presents a serious challenge, both in modeling and generation of attack graphs.

To address computational scalability, heuristic approaches that dynamically limit the complexity of an attack graph based on some metric, e.g., likelihood of attack, or make simplifying assumptions about the nature of an exploit chain, e.g., functional monotonicity, are often employed (Amman, Wijesekera & Kaushik, 2002; Artz, 2002; Ingols, Lippmann, & Piwowarski, 2006). Cognitive scalability issues present themselves when an analyst is tasked to make sense of highly complex attack graphs. Research in this area focuses on aggregation and visualization techniques to reduce the logical or visual complexity of the generated graph as presented to the analyst (Homer, Varikuti, Ou & McQueen, 2008; Noel & Jajodia, 2004).

Analysis of Attack Graphs

The generation of comprehensive attack graphs is predicated on the idea that useful analytical techniques can be applied to them. The objective is to derive actionable security intelligence and provide a sound basis for decisions regarding system defense and incident response. Of direct importance is the feature space for decision-making. As a consequence, the nature of the modeling scheme heavily influences the potential for analysis.

Standard strategies for analyzing graphs can be applied, including reachability analysis and model checking (Clark, Tyree, Dawkins, & Hale, 2004; Ritchey & Ammann, 2000). Fault tree analysis provides a baseline set of methods for attack graph analysis. Nodes and edges can be weighted with quantitative values to reflect elements of risk, fundamentally characterizing likelihood and/or impact as means of computing the risk associated with specific attack vectors or the criticality of specific vulnerabilities. Techniques such as Markov Processes and those steeped in game theory can be leveraged once numeric weights are systematically and soundly applied to an attack graph. These approaches rely on suitable scoring schemes that address relevant system and adversary attributes.

Risk assessment and threat modeling methodologies can be of use in evaluating the criticality of attack vectors revealed in attack graphs (Clark, Tyree, Lee & Hale, 2007). The Microsoft STRIDE and DREAD methodologies are designed to help security analysts and engineers enumerate and measure system vulnerabilities (Howard & Leblanc, 2003). When combined with attack graphs, they afford the opportunity to identify abstract patterns of adversary behavior, reveal systemic weaknesses, and compute risk metrics over multistage attacks. One challenge in this space is the seemingly arbitrary and subjective nature of quantitative values placed on core risk attributes.

Attack graphs and Markov Processes have a similar structure and provide a computationally efficient mechanism to evaluate parameters in systems, such as energy consumption of a sensor or RFID network (Hawrylak, 2006; Hawrylak, Cain & Mickle, 2007; Hawrylak, Cain, & Mickle, 2009). Thus, it is possible to translate the structure of the attack graph into a Markov Process (Zhang, Fan, Xue, & Xu, 2008). However, a Markov Process requires that the transitions between states (vertices) depend only on the present input and the current state (Howard, 1971). If these two properties do not hold, the well understood and computationally efficient methods for analyzing the Markov Process cannot be applied. The Markov requirement may require the state space to be slightly modified to account for conditions in the attack graph that cannot be represented as a Markov Process.

The four steps to convert an attack graph into a Markov Process are illustrated in Figure 2. First, the state space of the Markov Process must be defined. The vertices in the attack graph can be converted into states in the Markov Process and then additional states are added as needed to capture the behavior of the attack graph. It is important to keep the state space of the Markov Process to a minimum because the time required

to analyze a Markov Process is proportional to the state space. Second, the transitions between states in the Markov Process must be defined. The transitions in the attack graph can be used as a starting point. Additional transitions are often necessary to capture defender behavior, such as applying a patch to a particular asset. Third, the transition probabilities are assigned to the state transitions. How these probabilities are determined will directly impact the accuracy of the results obtained from the Markov Process. This information can be obtained from vulnerability databases and statistics on how often a particular vulnerability has been exploited. Currently, information of this type exists for viruses and new databases would need to be created to this record information for vulnerabilities. Existing databases record definitions and descriptions of vulnerabilities but any statistics relating to how often the vulnerability is exploited are not publicly available. Fourth, a reward can be defined for each state transition or for each state. The reward represents a profit (gain) or loss for taking a transition or being in a particular state (Howard, 1971). Rewards can represent a number of quantities such as benefit to the attacker in reaching a goal or monetary cost to the defender since the attack began. Finally, the Markov Process can be analyzed to investigate and quantify risk to a particular system.

THE APPLICATION OF ATTACK GRAPHS TO SYSTEM DEFENSE

Attack graphs represent a powerful analytical tool in four major phases of system security engineering and operations. As a risk assessment tool, attack graphs can be used early in the system development life cycle to prioritize threat mitigating and vulnerability remediation controls. Where risk assessment is practiced as part of a periodic review process for a fielded system, attack graphs permit a deeper and more meaningful inspection of prevailing threats. For systems that are operational,

Figure 2. Conversion of an attack graph into a Markov process

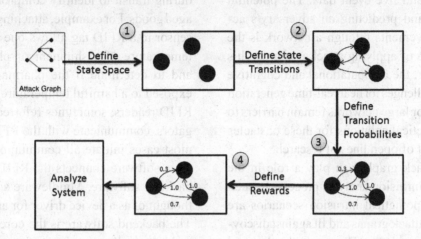

attack graphs support predictive analysis in near real-time, illuminating likely attack vectors over compound exposures. Such analysis is predicated on static and dynamic network topology and system state information. Attack graphs are also useful for establishing situational awareness in the face of an on-going attack or anomalous event. Lastly, attack graphs can be used to reconstruct an intrusion – filling in gaps or focusing discovery efforts – to unearth the path an attacker took in penetrating a system.

The fundamental objective of risk assessment is sound decision making in the development of risk reducing activities. For cyber security this entails prioritizing threats and evaluating the effectiveness of controls. Increasingly, attacks on information systems are composite, the result of chaining exploits over a web of vulnerabilities. While most risk assessment processes emphasize a comprehensive enumeration of the system vulnerability space, a process that integrates attack graphs places vulnerabilities in greater context. An attack graph identifies potential pathways attackers can take to strike their targets. A subsequent analysis of an attack graph may reveal vulnerabilities that, ostensibly benign when evaluated out of context, underpin a cluster of high impact multi-stage attack vectors. Depending on the modeling scheme

adopted, attack graph generation and analysis can be pursued at various stages of a security engineering process – from architecture and design to implementation and testing.

The benefits and process for attack graph generation in predictive analysis of fielded systems are nearly identical to those for risk assessment in the security engineering life cycle. The principal difference is the availability of system state data. Effective use of attack graph analysis in this context requires the integration of detailed network models backed by practical monitoring and logging solutions. The fusion of these models and information creates a rich knowledge base upon which to build accurate network models and correspondingly thorough attack graphs. By stringing together a series of low-level attacks, a hacker may be able to achieve a serious compromise while evading system defenses that only target the *home run* attack. The attack graphs generated in this phase of security management operations reveal latent paths previously undiscovered and illuminate effective counter measures. In this regard, they can be used to calibrate security monitoring elements in a network defense to watch for events that might otherwise fly under the radar.

Situational awareness combines static model and dynamic system state information with real traffic flows and live event data. The potential for tracking and predicting an adversary's actions and movements through a network is the primary allure of applying attack graphs in this way. However, the computational and cognitive scalability challenges for near real-time generation and analysis for large networks remain barriers to adoption. Practical solutions for these obstacles are the subject of open lines of research.

Lastly, attack graphs can play a role in the post-mortem intrusion analysis process. In such a process, hypothetical intrusion scenarios are generated by attack graphs and fit against discovered intrusion evidence. The result may be used to help an investigative team determine the origin and path of an attack vector, and ultimately lead to the discovery of additional evidence.

ILLUSTRATIVE EXAMPLE CASES OF ATTACK GRAPHS

Modern embedded cyber-physical systems can be divided into four domains: (1) physical systems involving mechanical components, (2) hardware used for semiconductors and integrated circuits (ICs), (3) logic implemented with software, and (4) communications over a distributed network. Modern security threats extend between two or more of these domains. Three illustrative cases are presented each describing a potential threat. For each case, attack graphs are generated to illustrate and then analyze the threat.

Radio Frequency Identification (RFID) Example Case

RFID technology is used to identify assets wirelessly. RFID systems are broken down into four major components (1) RFID tags, (2) RFID readers, (3) middleware software, and (4) backend software. RFID tags are attached to assets and some include sensors. Such sensor-equipped tags enable the user to monitor the condition of assets during transit to identify compromised or damaged goods. For example, attaching a temperature sensor to a RFID tag allows one to monitor the temperature of a shipment of pharmaceuticals and to determine if the pharmaceuticals were exposed to a harmful temperature during transit. RFID readers, sometimes referred to as interrogators, communicate with the RFID tags, and in most cases initiate all communication. Middleware software connects the RFID reader to the backend software. Middleware software can be thought of as a device driver for an RFID reader. The backend software is the core of the system and is typically some form of enterprise resource planning (ERP) system.

One flavor of RFID tag is the *active tag*. An active tag is powered by a battery, is able to communicate over long distances, and supports sensors. Active tags are used to track and secure cargo containers. Because active tags are battery powered, they must conserve their battery reserve to extend their lifetime. To do this they are equipped with an operating mode termed *sleep mode*. When in sleep mode the active tag has most of its functionality turned off to conserve its battery. A special command termed the *wake-up signal* is used to trigger the tag to enter its active (high power consuming) mode. In sleep mode the active tag is sampling for an incoming wake-up command very infrequently. Rapidly entering and leaving sleep mode and remaining in active mode for prolonged periods of time will rapidly deplete the active tag's battery and must be avoided.

One type of active tag is based on the ISO 18000-7 standard used by the US Department of Defense (DoD) to track and monitor shipments, and by the US Department of Energy (DOE) to monitor containers of spent nuclear fuel (Chen, Tsai, Fabian, Liu & Shuler, 2009; Tsai, *et. al.*, 2008). The DOE implementation allows them to reduce the number of times that a human must enter the radioactive storage area to take measurements of spent nuclear fuel containers. This reduces the dose of radiation the worker receives and has significant health benefits. This system also monitors the attachment of the container lid and issues an alert if the lid is starting to loosen or is removed. This is very useful for both security and safety during transportation of the containers, and can be used to monitor the health of containers in storage.

One potential threat is termed an *energy draining attack* (Raymond, Marchany, Brownfield & Midkiff, 2009). The purpose of an energy draining attack is to deplete the wireless device's battery to the point where it can no longer function. In the case of the DOE application an energy draining attack could have severe consequences. It is critical that the active tags used in this system must last as long as possible because replacing the active tags or their batteries early will expose the worker to an additional and unneeded dose of radiation.

ISO 18000-7 defines that a tag will return to sleep mode after not hearing a valid command or the wake-up signal for 30 seconds. An energy draining attack on ISO 18000-7 can be carried out in two ways. First, a rogue reader could be used to transmit the wake-up signal periodically to keep the tags awake longer than normal. The second option is to issue commands to the tags to continuously reset the 30-second counters maintained by the tags. In both cases, the tags would not return to sleep mode, but would remain in the high power active mode, quickly draining their batteries. Such an attack is difficult to detect because the additional traffic would appear at first glance to be normal traffic on the network. Both methods of attack use normal commands or signals associated with ISO 18000-7.

An energy draining attack can be carried out if one of two conditions is met. Both conditions provide the attacker with a reader they can control or influence to carry out the energy draining attack. The first method for an attacker to acquire the use of a reader is for the attacker to place the reader within range of the tags they wish to expose to an energy draining attack. This attack is known as a physical attack and is a manual

process. Good physical security around the site can prevent a physical attack. The second option is for the attacker to hack into an existing reader and use that reader to carry out the energy draining attack. This is a cyber attack and can be conducted by exploiting a network or software vulnerability in the RFID system. This is only possible if the readers are connected to the Internet or if the attacker can gain access to the private network, to which the readers are attached. Once the attacker has a reader within range of the tags he can carry out the energy draining attack by issuing wake-up signals and/or commands to keep the tags awake. The resulting attack graph is illustrated in Figure 3.

The above attack graph depicts the steps that an adversary can take to carry out an energy draining attack on an RFID tag. The adversary starts from the top vertex, labeled "Normal operation" and has two options, a cyber attack or a physical attack, to gain use of a reader to launch the energy draining attack. The adversary then moves to one of the two states where they have use of a reader represented by the "Spoof messages" (result of a successful physical attack) vertex or the "Elevation of privilege" (result of a successful cyber attack) vertex. Once, they have use of a reader within range of the tag the adversary can transmit either the wake-up signal or any valid ISO 18000-7 command to keep the tag awake. These options are shown as the two edges emanating from either reader vertex and leading to the "Energy drain" vertex. These edges represent the energy draining attack on the tag. These edges are repeatedly traveled to drain the tag's battery.

Starting at the initial stages of the attack, the top of the graph illustrated in Figure 3, the attack graph provides a means to identify defensive actions and their effectiveness in thwarting the attacker's goal. First, defenses such as hardened security of existing readers or increased physical security (e.g. a fence around the parameter) can be effective against preventing the attack. Due to the distributed nature of an RFID system physical security is difficult to maintain and its long range

Figure 3. Attack graph for the energy draining attack

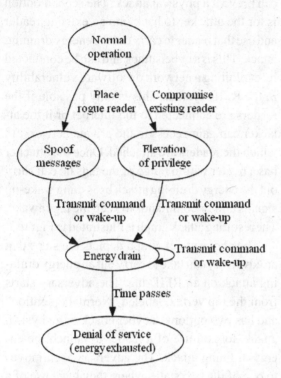

Vehicle Networking Case

As vehicle technology advances, integration and networking of various systems is the mainstay of the modern vehicle. From "info-tainment" systems to basic drivetrain functions, in-vehicle networks are ubiquitous. Furthermore, electric cars and hybrid/electric cars may contain telematics systems to interconnect with the entire transportation network. The networking of vehicles and vehicle sub-systems provide opportunities for functional enhancement, but also introduces new opportunities for attacks. Proprietary systems, such as GM's OnStar, have the ability to send vehicle network commands to diagnose and even disable vehicles (anti-theft system) through wireless communication.

The Controller Area Network (CAN) bus is the common network infrastructure used to connect the electronic components together in a vehicle. The CAN bus is designed to ensure communication between components in the harsh vehicle environment. The CAN bus was developed in the mid-1990s when security was not the major concern that it is today. Steps must be taken to secure the CAN bus to prevent attacks on vehicles similar to the attack described in this section.

Examining every possible attack vector is daunting. This discussion is limited to intrusion points that do not require physical destruction of the vehicle system. Exposed network connections like those found on a commercial vehicle and wireless systems like remote tire pressure monitoring systems (TPMS) can benefit from the concept of attack graphs for vehicle systems.

An example attack could be to prevent someone from opening their door by sending remote door locking commands at a rate faster than someone can operate the mechanical lock. There are different strategies to accomplish this attack. One could decrypt the key fob commands and set up a remote transmitter to repeat the lock command. Protection against this is in the form of strong encryption of the key fob. Another strategy is to

(several hundred meters) these options may not be very effective in preventing an energy draining attack. The STRIDE and DREAD methods can be used to analyze the effectiveness of such hardening operations in preventing a successful attack. This analysis can provide the necessary input to perform a fault tree analysis or use Markov processes to quantify the risk. Another approach is to monitor for an energy draining attack and intervene when one is detected. As shown in the graph the key step in the attack is to repeatedly transmit the wake-up signal or a command to keep the tag awake and drain its battery. The normal amount of RFID reader messages is known or can be determined by observation. Monitors can be setup to monitor the wireless communication and can raise alerts when traffic is above normal without reason. This is a reactive defense to an energy draining attack and proactive methods must be developed to defend against such attacks as the use of wireless battery powered devices increases.

install a rogue device on the vehicle network. This would require access to the vehicle network and may be prevented through physically securing the vehicle. However, some vehicles are prone to this attack since network communication wires can be accessed from underneath the vehicle. Finally, the attacker could gain access to the vehicle network through a telemetry system and issue the commands remotely. In any case, the unsuspecting operator would be caught off-guard.

The manifestation of the above example is illustrated as an attack graph in Figure 4. The adversary starts at the top and gains access to the door lock controller in one of three different ways. For example, the adversary could modify an RF key fob or an RF signal generator, e.g. a modified cell phone, to transmit the proper identification code to the vehicle to send the lock door command. Once the wireless communication link is established the adversary needs to determine the proper messages to send to the vehicle to issue a valid lock door command. Other methods such as installing a remote device in the vehicle's network could inject the lock door command (Albrady & Mahmud, 2005; Francillon, Danev & Capkun, 2010). Once the adversary gains access to the network, they must be able to issue the correct commands to complete the attack. Other such attack graphs could be generated for other vehicle subsystems, e.g. engine throttle control, and help security engineers discover unnecessary risk in modern vehicles.

This attack graph identifies three ways that an attacker can gain access to the vehicle's electronic control system: a stolen key fob, compromising a telemetry device, or by installing a rogue device. Countermeasures to address these threats include increasing physical security by limiting the access points to the vehicle's network and limiting wireless connectivity to critical systems. Guarding one's key fob from theft and employing a robust authentication scheme between key fob and vehicle will mitigate this threat.

Once the attacker has access to the network through a compromised device, they simply inject commands into the network. Without spoofing commands there is little that the attacker can do to achieve the denial of service attack of repeated locking the doors. The network is another critical point that must be hardened against attack. Using robust authentication between devices on the vehicle network will eliminate the rogue device. Enforcing strict access control requirements between network devices to limit the capabilities of each to their specific area, e.g. a GPS navigation system can only give directions, but not control the windshield wipers, will limit the range of systems a compromised device can corrupt. However, the impact on system availability and cost of the secure system must be balanced against such a threat. These options may be implemented on a subset of devices that are critical to the vehicle operation and occupant safety, e.g. headlights, engine control system, or the door locks.

Smart Grid Example Case

The Smart Grid refers to the national initiative to modernize the U.S. electrical grid and make it more reliable, efficient and secure in an environmentally friendly manner. It is a digitalized and more intelligent version of the traditional power grid and therefore, it supports the functionality of the present grid while adding new characteristics that include new communication and networking features. The electric grid comprises four major elements: generation, transmission, distribution, and consumers.

Electric substations are part of the distribution component and are also being modernized. In particular, Stage 4 Substation Automation (Idaho National Laboratory, 2009; Newton-Evans Research Company, 2008) efforts incorporate integrated IEDs (Intelligent Electronic) using LAN (Local Area Network) communications. In this type of substation, automation software

Figure 4. Attack graph for the vehicle door lock attack

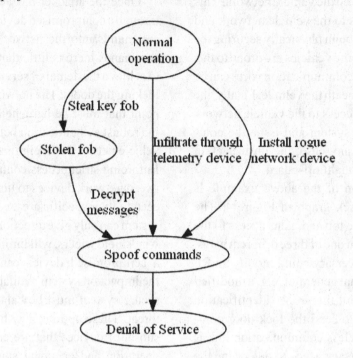

runs at the substation level while full control is possible from a central control room. This scenario applies to this type of substation. Consider the network topology for a Stage 4 substation as shown in Figure 5.

The network is partitioned into three zones protected by firewalls: Substation, DMZ and Corporate. The substation employs two IEDs (labeled PLC1 and PLC2 in Figure 5) and a gateway device used to communicate with a Historian Server and the Corporate Zone. Assume an adversary who has obtained limited access to the Corporate network and his/her goal is to gain access to the Substation LAN to inject commands into the IEDs to disrupt operation. One possible mechanism to reach the goal would be to follow the following steps:

1. Scan the corporate network using a passive sniffer to avoid detection. During this phase, the host running the Client historian is identified.

2. Compromise the Client historian and monitor DMZ/Corporate traffic to find open ports in the firewall to scan the DMZ.

3. The previous scan reveals the existence of a Historian server in the DMZ. Port probing and OS (operating system) fingerprinting reveal a vulnerable service. The attacker gains access to the Historian server by exploiting this vulnerability.

4. The attacker installs, in the Historian server, scanning, redirection and exploitation software to gain further access.

5. Using the installed tools, the attacker monitors DMZ/Substation traffic. Open ports in the second firewall, additional hosts as well as the existence of a trust relationship between the Historian server and the gateway device are discovered.

6. Using the trust relationship the intruder gains access to the gateway in the Substation network by exploiting a vulnerable service and then gaining privileged access.

Figure 5. Example Smart Grid network topology

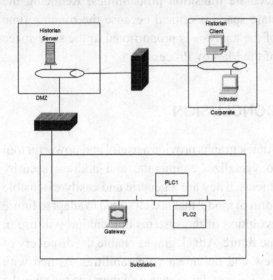

Figure 6. Attack graph of the substation attack

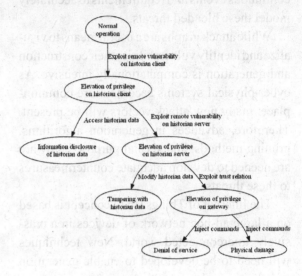

7. The attacker uploads and installs network intrusion tools to the compromised gateway.

8. The intruder proceeds to scan the Substation network to identify the IEDs and then uses a packet injection tool to insert commands, using a protocol such as DNP3, to negatively affect the automation functions.

This multi-stage attack is represented by the attack graph shown in Figure 6.

The attack graph illustrated in Figure 6 identifies the historian server as the first critical link in the attack and, therefore, it also helps identify the place where a first line of defense should be deployed. Preventing the attacker from gaining elevated privileges on the historian server will eliminate the possibility of all four goals: disclosure of information, tampering with data, denial of service, and physical damage. However, the hardening of the historian server must be balanced against the need for the historian server to be accessible to authorized personnel. Analysis methods such as fault tree analysis or Markov processes can be used to evaluate this tradeoff. Hardening the gateway will prevent the denial of service and physical attacks but this may be the better option depending on the reduction in availability of the historian server resulting from hardening it against attacks. Also, the elevating privilege on the gateway is required for the attacks that cause immediate damage.

While the attack graph highlights the value of protecting the client and server side of the historian, it also identifies an additional point of interest in the SCADA gateway. The defense in depth principle dictates that multiple layers of security be deployed to minimize impact should a layer fail. In other words, protecting the SCADA gateway will not only add a security layer that helps prevent injection attacks at the field level but it will also strengthen the global security posture by following a sound layered security approach.

FUTURE RESEARCH DIRECTIONS

Attack graphs are a powerful tool to visualize security threats to systems. As cyber-physical systems become more pervasive, the need to investigate both the continuous (physical) and discrete (computer) domains will become critical. Such threats are termed *blended threats*. Attack graphs will need to be modified to incorporate continuous events and requirements to accurately model these blended threats.

While attack graphs are a useful means to visualize and identify vulnerabilities their construction and generation is computationally intensive. As cyber-physical systems become more commonplace, many new attack vectors will be present. Therefore, advances in generation algorithms, pruning methods, and special purpose hardware are needed to develop adequate countermeasures to these threats.

The Internet of Things (IoT) concept is based on a large ad-hoc network of devices in a massively interconnected world. New techniques will need to be developed to enable generation of attack graphs for the large interconnected systems envisioned in the IoT environment. The ad-hoc nature of the IoT requires modification to the attack graph structure and analysis methods to account for devices entering or leaving the network. Thus, existing security measures may not be feasible for such devices and new defenses must be developed.

Currently most work in attack graphs focuses on development of the attack graph and not on the analysis of the resulting attack graph. Analysis techniques must be developed to quantify security properties about a system or subsystem. Many probabilistic analysis techniques, such as Markov modeling, have similar structure to an attack graph. These analysis tools are well understood and are applied in a number of different fields. However, research is required to determine how to generate the probabilities required for the probabilistic components and to keep the state space to a reasonable level. The quality of the probabilistic models is based on the quality of the data from which the model parameters are derived. Therefore, more data on attacks and vulnerabilities must be collected and made available to enable the security analyst to derive more accurate transition probabilities. Reducing the state space is critical because the running time of the analysis is proportional to the state space of the Markov Process.

CONCLUSION

Attack graphs provide a useful and powerful tool to visualize, enumerate, and address security threats. They are a generic and easily extensible form of model that is well suited to adapt to future evolution of the systems humankind will use in the future. Attack graphs enable the discovery of new and unknown vulnerabilities. Armed with this information system designers can redesign the system to address and remove these vulnerabilities. System administrators can use this information to apply patches and other defensive measures to secure existing or deployed systems. Analysis methods that are both accurate and computationally efficient must be developed and formalized. Markov Processes offer one such analysis vehicle but more research is needed in the attack graph to Markov Process conversion, on the generation of transition probabilities and reward values, and on defining the parameters to analyze.

ACKNOWLEDGMENT

This material is based on research sponsored by DARPA under agreement number FA8750-09-1-0208. The U.S. Government is authorized to reproduce and distribute reprints for Governmental purposes notwithstanding any copyright notation therein. The views and conclusions contained herein are those of the authors and should not be interpreted as necessarily representing the official policies or endorsements, either expressed or implied by DARPA or the U.S. Government.

REFERENCES

Alrabady, A., & Mahmud, S. (2005). Analysis of attacks against the security of keyless-entry systems for vehicles and suggestions for improved designs. *IEEE Transactions on Vehicular Technology, 54*(1), 41–50. doi:10.1109/TVT.2004.838829

Ammann, P., Wijesekera, D., & Kaushik, S. (2002). Scalable, graph-based network vulnerability analysis. In *Proceedings of the 9th ACM Conference on Computer and Communications Security* (pp. 217-224).

Artz, M. L. (2002). *NetSPA: A network security planning architecture*. Unpublished M.S. thesis, Massachusetts Institute of Technology, Cambridge, MA.

Broad, W. J., & Sanger, D. E. (November 18, 2010). Worm was perfect for sabotaging centrifuges. *New York Times*. Retrieved Nov. 19, 2010, from http://www.nytimes.com/2010/11/19/world/middleeast/19stuxnet.html?_r=1

Campbell, C., Dawkins, J., Pollet, B., Fitch, K., Hale, J., & Papa, M. (2003). On modeling computer networks for vulnerability analysis. In Gudes, E., & Shenoi, S. (Eds.), *Research directions in data and applications security* (pp. 233–244). Boston, MA: Kluwer Academic Publishers.

Chen, K., Tsai, H. C., Fabian, B., Liu, Y., & Shuler, J. (2009 July). A radiofrequency identification (RFID) temperature-monitoring system for extended maintenance of nuclear materials packaging. *Proceedings of the 2009 ASME Pressure Vessels and Piping Division Conference* (pp. 109-115). ASME.

Clark, K., Tyree, S., Dawkins, J., & Hale, J. (2004, June). Quantitative and qualitative analytical techniques for network security assessment. *Proceedings of the 2004 IEEE Workshop on Information Assurance and Security* (pp. 321-328). IEEE.

Clark, K., Tyree, S., Lee, C., & Hale, J. (2007, June). Guiding threat analysis with threat source models. *Proceedings of the 2007 IEEE Workshop on Information Assurance* (pp. 262-269). IEEE.

Francillon, A., Danev, B., & Capkun, S. (2010). *Relay attacks on passive keyless entry and start systems in modern cars* (Rapport technique). Cryptology ePrint Archive, Report 2010/332.

Hawrylak, P. J. (2006). *Analysis and development of a mathematical structure to describe energy consumption of sensor networks*. Unpublished doctoral dissertation, University of Pittsburgh, Pittsburgh, PA.

Hawrylak, P. J., Cain, J. T., & Mickle, M. H. (2007). Analytic modeling methodology for analysis of energy consumption for ISO 18000-7 RFID Networks. *International Journal of Radio Frequency Identification Technology and Applications, 1*(4), 371–400. doi:10.1504/IJRFITA.2007.017748

Hawrylak, P. J., Cain, J. T., & Mickle, M. H. (2009). Analysis methods for sensor networks. In Misra, S., Woungang, I., & Misra, S. C. (Eds.), *Guide to wireless sensor networks* (pp. 635–658). New York, NY: Springer. doi:10.1007/978-1-84882-218-4_25

Homer, J., Varikuti, A., Ou, X., & McQueen, M. A. (2008). Improving attack graph visualization through data reduction and attack grouping. *Proceedings of the 5th International Workshop on Visualization for Computer Security* (pp. 68-79). ACM.

Howard, M., & Leblanc, D. (2003). *Writing secure code*. Redmond, WA: Microsoft Press.

Howard, R. A. (1971). Dynamic probablistic systems: *Vol. I. Markov models*. New York, NY: John Wiley & Sons, Inc.

Idaho National Laboratory. (2009, October). *National SCADA testbed substation automation report*.

Ingols, K., Chu, M., Lippmann, R., Webster, S., & Boyer, S. (2009). Modeling modern network at-tacks and countermeasures using attack graphs. In *2009 Annual Computer Security Applications Conference* (pp. 117--126).

Ingols, K., Lippmann, R., & Piwowarski, K. (2006, December). Practical attack graph generation for network defense. *Proceedings of the 22nd Annual Computer Security Applications Conference* (pp. 121–130). IEEE.

Jajodia, S., Noel, S., & OBerry, B. (2005). Topological analysis of network attack vulnerability. *Managing Cyber Threats*, (pp. 247-266).

Keating, M., & Bricaud, P. (2002). *Reuse methodology manual for system-on-a-chip designs.* Boston, MA: Kluwer Academic Publishers.

Koscher, K., Czeskis, A., Roesner, F., Patel, S., Kohno, T., & Checkoway, S. … Savage, S. (2010, May). *Experimental security analysis of a modern automobile.* Paper presented at the 2010 IEEE Symposium on Security and Privacy, Oakland, CA.

Lippmann, R., Ingols, K., & Lincoln Lab, M. I. T. (2005). *An annotated review of past papers on attack graphs.* Massachusetts Institute of Technology, Lincoln Laboratory.

Newton-Evans Research Company. (2008). *Substation automation report.*

Noel, S., & Jajodia, S. (2004, October). Managing attack graph complexity through visual hierarchical aggregation. *Proceedings of the 2004 ACM Workshop on Visualization and Data Mining for Computer Security* (pp. 109-118). ACM.

Philips, C., & Swiler, L. P. (1998). A graph-based system for network-vulnerability analysis. *Procedings of the 1998 Workshop on New Security Paradigms* (pp. 71-79). ACM.

Raymond, D. R., Marchany, R. C., Brownfield, M. I., & Midkiff, S. F. (2009, January). Effects of denial-of-sleep attacks on wireless sensor network MAC protocols. *IEEE Transactions on Vehicular Technology, 58*(1), 367–380. doi:10.1109/TVT.2008.921621

Ritchey, R., & Ammann, P. (2000). Using model checking to analyze network vulnerabilities. *Proceedings of the 2000 IEEE Symposium on Research on Security and Privacy* (pp. 156–165). IEEE Computer Society.

Schneier, B. (1999, December). Attack trees: Modeling security threats. *Dr. Dobb's Journal*, December, 21–29.

Sheyner, O., Haines, J., Jha, S., Lippmann, R., & Wing, J. M. (2002). Automated generation and analysis of attack graphs. *Proceedings of the 2002 IEEE Symposium on Security and Privacy* (pp. 273–284). IEEE Computer Society.

Templeton, S., & Levitt, K. (2001). A requires/provides model for computer attacks. In *Proceedings of the 2000 Workshop on New Security Paradigms* (pp. 31--38).

Tidwell, T., Larson, R., Fitch, K., & Hale, J. (2001). Modeling internet attacks. In *Proceedings of the 2001 IEEE Workshop on Information Assurance and Security* (vol. 59).

Tsai, H. C., Chen, K., Liu, Y., Norair, J. P., Bellamy, S., & Shuler, J. (2008). Applying RFID technology in nuclear materials management *Packaging, Transport. Storage and Security of Radioactive Material, 19*(1), 41–46. doi:10.1179/174651008X279000

Wang, L., Noel, S., & Jajodia, S. (2006). Minimum-cost network hardening using attack graphs. *Computer Communications, 29*(18), 3812–3824. doi:10.1016/j.comcom.2006.06.018

Zhang, Y., Fan, X., Xue, Z., & Xu, H. (2008, November). Two stochastic models for security evaluation based on attack graph. In *The 9th International Conference for Young Computer Scientists*, (pp. 2198-2203). Washington, DC: IEEE Computer Society.

ADDITIONAL READING

Butler, M., Pollet, B., & Hale, J. (2006, March). *Dynamic Policy Enforcement in a Network Environment*. Paper presented at the 2006 Security Enhanced Linux Symposium, Baltimore, Maryland.

Butts, J., Kleinhans, H., Chandia, R., Papa, M., & Shenoi, S. (2009). Providing Situational Awareness for Pipeline Control Operations. In Palmer, C., & Shenoi, S. (Eds.), *Critical Infrastructure Protection III* (pp. 97–111). New York, NY: Springer. doi:10.1007/978-3-642-04798-5_7

Chandia, R., Gonzalez, J., Kilpatrick, T., Papa, M., & Shenoi, S. (2007). Security strategies for SCADA networks. In Goetz, E., & Shenoi, S. (Eds.), *Critical Infrastructure Protection* (pp. 117–131). New York, NY: Springer. doi:10.1007/978-0-387-75462-8_9

Clark, K., Dawkins, J., & Hale, J. (2005, June). Security Risk Metrics: Fusing Enterprise Objectives and Vulnerabilities. In *Proceedings of the 2005 IEEE Workshop on Information Assurance and Security* (pp. 388-393). IEEE.

Clark, K., Singleton, E., Tyree, S., & Hale, J. (2008, October). Strata-Gem: Risk assessment through mission modeling. In *Proceedings of the Fourth ACM workshop on Quality of Protection* (pp. 51-58). New York, NY: ACM.

Cole, E., Krutz, R. L., & Conley, J. W. (2009). *Network Security Bible*. Indianapolis, IN: Wiley Publishing, Inc.

East, S., Butts, J., Papa, M., & Shenoi, S. (2009). A Taxonomy of Attacks on the DNP3 Protocol. In Palmer, C., & Shenoi, S. (Eds.), *Critical Infrastructure Protection III* (pp. 67–82). New York, NY: Springer. doi:10.1007/978-3-642-04798-5_5

Edmonds, J., Papa, M., & Shenoi, S. (2007). Security analysis of multilayer SCADA protocols: A Modbus TCP case study. In Goetz, E., & Shenoi, S. (Eds.), *Critical Infrastructure Protection* (pp. 205–221). New York, NY: Springer. doi:10.1007/978-0-387-75462-8_15

Garfinkel, S. L., Juels, A., & Pappu, R. (2005, May-June). RFID privacy: an overview of problems and proposed solutions. *IEEE Security & Privacy, 3*(3), 34–43. doi:10.1109/MSP.2005.78

Gonzalez, J., & Papa, M. (2007). Passive scanning in Modbus networks. In Goetz, E., & Shenoi, S. (Eds.), *Critical Infrastructure Protection* (pp. 175–187). New York, NY: Springer. doi:10.1007/978-0-387-75462-8_13

Hawrylak, P. J., Cain, J. T., & Mickle, M. H. (2008). RFID Tags. In Yan, L., Zhang, Y., Yang, L. T., & Ning, H. (Eds.), *The Internet of Things: from RFID to Pervasive Networked Systems* (pp. 1–32). Boca Raton, Florida: Auerbach Publications, Taylor & Francis Group. doi:10.1201/9781420052824.ch1

Hawrylak, P. J., Mats, L., Cain, J. T., Jones, A. K., Tung, S., & Mickle, M. H. (2006, July). Ultra Low-Power Computing Systems for Wireless Devices. *International Review on Computers and Software, 1*(1), 1–10.

Hawrylak, P. J., & Mickle, M. H. (2009) EPC Gen-2 Standard for RFID. In Y. Zhang, L. T. Yang and J. Chen (Eds.) *RFID and Sensor Networks: Architectures, Protocols, Security and Integrations* (pp. 97-124), Boca Raton, Florida: Taylor & Francis Group, CRC Press.

Huitsing, P., Chandia, R., Papa, M., & Shenoi, S. (2008). Attack taxonomies for the Modbus protocols. *International Journal of Critical Infrastructure Protection*, *1*, 37–44. doi:10.1016/j.ijcip.2008.08.003

Ingols, K., Chu, M., Lippmann, R., Webster, S., & Boyer, S. (2009). Modeling modern network attacks and countermeasures using attack graphs. In *2009 Annual Computer Security Applications Conference* (pp. 117-126).

Juels, A. (2006, February). RFID Security and Privacy: A Research Survey. *IEEE Journal on Selected Areas in Communications*, *24*(2), •••. doi:10.1109/JSAC.2005.861395

Kilpatrick, T., Gonzalez, J., Chandia, R., Papa, M., & Shenoi, S. (2006). An architecture for SCADA network forensics. In Olivier, M., & Shenoi, S. (Eds.), *Advances in Digital Forensics II* (pp. 273–285). New York, NY: Springer.

Kilpatrick, T., Gonzalez, J., Chandia, R., Papa, M., and Shenoi, S. (2008) Forensic analysis of SCADA systems and networks. *International Journal of Security and Networks - Special Issue on Network Forensics*, vol. 3, no. 2, pp. 95-102.

Kissinger, A., & Hale, J. (2006, March). *Lopol: A Deductive Database Approach to Policy Analysis and Rewriting*. Paper presented at the 2006 Security Enhanced Linux Symposium (pp. 388-393), Baltimore, Maryland.

Krutz, R. L., & Vines, R. D. (2003). *The CISSP® Prep Guide: Gold Edition*. Indianapolis, IN: Wiley Publishing, Inc.

Lee, E. (2006). Cyber-physical systems-are computing foundations adequate. In *Position paper for NSF workshop on cyber-physical systems: Research motivation, techniques and roadmap*.

Liu, A. X., & Bailey, L. A. (2008). RFID Authentication and Privacy. In Yan, L., Zhang, Y., Yang, L. T., & Ning, H. (Eds.), *The Internet of Things: from RFID to Pervasive Networked Systems*. Boca Raton, Florida: Auerbach Publications, Taylor & Francis Group.

Maguire, S. (1993). *Writing Solid Code*. Redmond, WA: Microsoft Press.

Mickle, M. H., Mats, L., & Hawrylak, P. J. (2008). Resolution and integration of HF and UHF. In Miles, S. B., Sarma, S. E., & Williams, J. R. (Eds.), *RFID Technology and Applications* (pp. 47–60). New York, New York: Cambridge University Press. doi:10.1017/CBO9780511541155.005

Noel, S., & Jajodia, S. (2005). Understanding complex network attack graphs through clustered adjacency matrices, In *Proceedings of the 21st Annual Computer Security Applications Conference* (pp. 160-169).

Roberts, W., Johnson, C., & Hale, J. (2010). Transparent Emergency Data Destruction. In E. Armistead (Ed.), *Proceedings of the 5th International Conference on Information-Warfare & Security* (pp. 271-278). Academic Conferences Limited.

Sabbah, E., & Kang, K.-D. (2009). Security in Wireless Sensor Networks. In Misra, S., Woungang, I., & Misra, S. C. (Eds.), *Guide to Wireless Sensor Networks* (pp. 491–512). New York, NY: Springer. doi:10.1007/978-1-84882-218-4_19

Shayto, R., Porter, B., Chandia, R., Papa, M., & Shenoi, S. (2008). Assessing the Integrity of Field Devices in Modbus Networks. In Papa, M., & Shenoi, S. (Eds.), *Critical Infrastructure Protection II* (pp. 115–128). New York, NY: Springer. doi:10.1007/978-0-387-88523-0_9

Sklavos, N., & Agarwal, V. (2008). RFID Security: Threats and Solutions. In Yan, L., Zhang, Y., Yang, L. T., & Ning, H. (Eds.), *The Internet of Things: from RFID to Pervasive Networked Systems*. Boca Raton, Florida: Auerbach Publications, Taylor & Francis Group. doi:10.1201/9781420052824.ch5

Trček, D., & Jäppinen, P. (2008). RFID Security. In Yan, L., Zhang, Y., Yang, L. T., & Ning, H. (Eds.), *The Internet of Things: from RFID to Pervasive Networked Systems* (pp. 107–125). Boca Raton, Florida: Auerbach Publications, Taylor & Francis Group.

Wang, L., Anoop, S., & Jajodia, S. (2007). Toward measuring network security using attack graphs. In *Proceedings of the 2007 ACM workshop on Quality of protection* (pp. 49-54). ACM, New York, NY, USA.

Xiao, Y., Shen, X., Sun, B., & Cai, L. (2006, April). Security and privacy in RFID and applications in telemedicine. *IEEE Communications Magazine, 44*(4), 64–72. doi:10.1109/MCOM.2006.1632651

KEY TERMS AND DEFINITIONS

Attack Graph: A graphical representation of the various steps an adversary can take to achieve their goal of compromising a system.

CAN: The Controller Area Network (CAN) is a wired communication network that is designed to be resistant to interference and hardware failures. CAN networks are used in automobiles to connect sensors, actuators, and controller modules together.

Cyber Physical System: A system that includes both the continuous and discrete domains. Modern control systems are examples of cyber physical systems. A thermostat controlling a heater is one example of a cyber physical system with the temperature being the continuous element and the heater control logic being the discrete element.

Markov Process: Markov Processes are a probabilistic way to represent and analyze a system. Markov Processes decompose a system into a set of system states and defines the transitions between those states based only on the current state and present input values. Markov Processes can be used to analyze a wide range of systems from engineering, computer science, software, and business.

Multi-Stage Attacks: An attack where the primary goal is achieved using a series of smaller attacks. Often these smaller attacks are not noticed by the defender. Attack graphs provide a means to identify which of the smaller attacks is of particular concern.

RFID: Radio Frequency Identification (RFID) is a wireless communication technology often employed to identify assets and people.

Smart Grid: The next generation power grid and distribution network. The Smart Grid will include digital meters to monitor electricity use in order to optimize generation and usage to conserve resources.

Chapter 17
Advanced Security Incident Analysis with Sensor Correlation

Ciza Thomas
College of Engineering, India

N. Balakrishnan
Indian Institute of Science, India

ABSTRACT

This chapter explores the general problem of the poorly detected attacks with Intrusion Detection Systems. The poorly detected attacks reveal the fact that they are characterized by features that do not discriminate them much. The poor performance of the detectors has been improved by discriminative training of anomaly detectors and incorporating additional rules into the misuse detector. This chapter proposes a new approach of machine learning method where corresponding learning problem is characterized by a number of features. This chapter discusses the improved performance of multiple Intrusion Detection Systems using Data-dependent Decision fusion. The Data-dependent Decision fusion approach gathers an in-depth understanding about the input traffic and also the behavior of the individual Intrusion Detection Systems by means of a neural network learner unit. This information is used to fine-tune the fusion unit since the fusion depends on the input feature vector. Thus fusion implements a function that is local to each region in the feature space. It is well-known that the effectiveness of sensor fusion improves when the individual IDSs are uncorrelated. The training methodology adopted in this work takes note of this fact. For illustrative purposes, the DARPA 1999 data set as has been used. The Data-dependent Decision fusion shows a significantly better performance with respect to the performance of individual Intrusion Detection Systems.

INTRODUCTION

The threat of attacks on the Internet is quite real and frequent and this has led to an increased need for securing any network on the Internet. An Intrusion Detection System (IDS) provides an additional layer of security to network's perimeter defense, which is usually implemented using a firewall. The goal of an IDS is to collect information from a variety of systems and network sources, and then analyze the information for signs of intrusion and misuse. IDSs are implemented in hardware, software, or a combination of both.

DOI: 10.4018/978-1-4666-0104-8.ch017

The network traffic is made up of attack or anomalous traffic, and normal traffic. The real-world traffic is predominantly made up of normal traffic rather than attack traffic. Even in the attack traffic, some attacks are rarer. Rarer attacks may also cause significant damage. The IDSs are normally characterized by the overall accuracy. Though an IDS can give very high overall accuracy, its performance for the class of rarer attacks has been found to be less than acceptable as illustrated in the next section. Basic domain knowledge about network intrusions makes us understand that User to Remote (U2R) and Remote to Local (R2L) attacks are intrinsically rare. The problem of designing IDSs to work effectively and yield higher accuracies for minority attacks like R2L and U2R even in the mix of data skewness has been receiving serious attention in recent times.

The imbalance in data degrades the prediction accuracy. In most of the available literature this is overcome by resampling the training distribution. The resampling is done either by oversampling of the minority class or by undersampling of the majority class (Breiman, Friedman, & Olshen, 1984, Kubat, Holte, & Matwin, 1997, Chawla, Bowyer, Hall, & Kegelmeyer, 2002). The other commonly used approaches for overcoming data imbalance include the cost-sensitive learning (McCarthy, Zabar, & Weiss, 2005, Chan, & Stolfo, 1998), the two-phase rule induction method (Joshi, Agarwal, & Kumar, 2001), and rule based classification algorithms like RIPPER (Cohen, 1995) and C4.5 rules (Quinlan, 1993). However, none of these attempts have shown any significant contribution in overcoming the data skewness problems. Hence, in spite of all the earlier attempts, there is still room for a significant improvement in the detection of rare attacks.

There is an increased demand for effective monitoring of information systems. The importance of network situational awareness by developing engineering solutions and research approaches for analyzing broad network activity is beyond doubt. Since there is no perfect Intrusion Detection Systems (IDS), it is only natural to combine IDSs such that the weakness of one is compensated by the strength of another. Sensor fusion refers to a process that integrates and correlates heterogeneous data. It is the process of combining information from various suboptimal sources in order to obtain a more accurate and optimal result. The utility of sensor fusion for improved sensitivity and reduced false alarm rate of intrusion detection has been demonstrated in the literature (Bass, 1999). In view of enormous computing power available in present day processors, the trend to deploy multiple IDSs in the same network to obtain best-of-breed solutions has been attempted for enhancing the performance of attack detection. The goal of this chapter is to quantitatively detect threats and targeted intruder activity using a fusion architecture taking into account the correlation of the individual detectors. This chapter presents a method of combining the decisions of multiple IDSs using Data-dependent Decision fusion (DD fusion) technique. For illustrative purposes the DARPA 1999 dataset has been used. The performance of the data-dependent decision fusion IDS has been shown to be better than those reported so far for the minority attacks along with the improved performance for the majority attacks.

This chapter is organized as follows. The limitation of single IDSs and the need for sensor fusion is initially exemplified. This is done with reference to the DARPA dataset and with three IDSs, namely, Snort, Packet Header Anomaly Detector (PHAD), and Application Layer Anomaly Detector (ALAD). The chapter reviews the existing approaches followed by the discussion on the motivation behind the present study and the details of the presented approach. The data-dependent decision fusion architecture has been discussed. The chapter covers the implementation, discussion of the results and also the support proof for the use of DARPA dataset for IDS evaluation. The conclusion of the chapter is finally drawn after a discussion on the findings of this study.

LIMITATION OF SINGLE IDSS AND THE NEED FOR SENSOR FUSION

The utility of sensor fusion for improved sensitivity and reduced false alarm rate of intrusion detection has been demonstrated in the literature. In this chapter we have further explored the general problem of the poorly detected attacks with Intrusion Detection Systems (IDS). The poorly detected attacks reveal the fact that they are characterized by features that do not discriminate them much. For illustrative purpose we have incorporated three IDSs namely, snort (Snort, 2009), PHAD (Mahoney & Chan, 2001), and ALAD (Mahoney & Chan, 2002) using the DARPA 1999 data set (DARPA, 1999).

Data Set

The data set consists of weeks one, two and three of training data and weeks four and five of test data. In training data, the weeks one and three consist of normal traffic and week two consists of labeled attacks. The DARPA 1999 test data consisted of 190 instances of 57 attacks which included 37 Probes, 63 DoS (Denial of Service) attacks, 53 R2L attacks, 37 U2R/Data attacks with details on attack types given in Table 1.

Classification of Attacks

The classification of the various attacks found in the network traffic is explained in detail in the thesis work of Kendall (Kendall, 1999), with respect to DARPA Intrusion Detection Evaluation dataset (DARPA) and is discussed here in brief. The various attacks found in the DARPA 1999 dataset are given in the Table 1. The probe or scan attacks automatically scan a network of computers or a DNS server to find valid IP addresses (ipsweep, lsdomain, mscan), active ports (portsweep, mscan), host operating system types (queso, mscan) and known vulnerabilities (satan). The DoS attacks are designed to disrupt a host or

Table 1. Various attack types in DARPA 1999 data set (Kendall, 1999)

Attack Class	Attack Type
Probe	portsweep, ipsweep, lsdomain, ntinfoscan, mscan, illegal-sniffer, queso, satan
DoS	apache2, smurf, neptune, dosnuke, land,pod, back, teardrop, tcpreset, syslogd, crashiis, arppoison, mailbomb, selfping, processtable, udpstorm, warezclient
R2L	dict, netcat, sendmail, imap, ncftp, xlock, xsnoop, sshtrojan, framespoof, ppmacro, guest, netbus, snmpget, ftpwrite, httptunnel, phf, named
U2R	sechole, xterm, eject, ntfsdos, nukepw, secret, perl, ps, yaga, fdformat, ppmacro ffbconfig, casesen, loadmodule, sqlattack

network service. These include crash the Solaris operating system (selfping), actively terminate all TCP connections to a specific host (tcpreset), corrupt ARP cache entries for a victim not in others' caches (arppoison), crash the Microsoft Windows NT web server (crashiis) and crash Windows NT (dosnuke).

In R2L attacks, an attacker who does not have an account on a victim machine gains local access to the machine (e.g., guest, dict), exfiltrates files from the machine (e.g., ppmacro) or modifies data in transit to the machine (e.g., framespoof). New R2L attacks include an NT PowerPoint macro attack (ppmacro), a man-in-the middle web browser attack (framespoof), an NT trojan-installed remote-administration tool (netbus), a Linux trojan SSH server (sshtrojan) and a version of a Linux FTP file access-utility with a bug that allows remote commands to run on a local machine (ncftp). In U2R attacks, a local user on a machine is able to obtain privileges normally reserved for the UNIX super user or the Windows NT administrator. The Data attack is to exfiltrate special files, which the security policy specifies should remain on the victim hosts. These include secret attacks, where the user who is allowed to access the special files exfiltrates them via common applications such as mail or FTP, and other attacks where privilege to access the special files is obtained using a U2R attack (ntfsdos, sqlattack). An attack could be labeled as both U2R and Data if one of the U2R attacks was used to obtain access to the special files. The Data category thus specifies the goal of an attack rather than the attack mechanism (Kendall, 1999).

Attack Behavior

A discussion on the various attack types in the network traffic has resulted in certain inferences that are listed below.

Probing attacks are expected to show limited variance as it involves making connections to a large number of hosts or ports in a given time frame. Likewise, the outcome of all U2R attacks is that a root shell is obtained without legitimate means, e.g., login as root, su to root, etc. Thus, for these two categories of attacks, given some representative instances in the training data, any learning algorithm was able to learn the general behavior of these attacks. As a result, the IDSs detect a high percentage of old and new Probing and U2R attacks. On the other hand, DoS and R2L have a wide variety of behavior because they exploit the weaknesses of a large number of different network or system services. The features constructed based on the available attack instances are very specialized to the known attack types. Hence most of the trivial IDS models missed a large number of new DoS and R2L attacks. It is understood that the misuse detection models fail in the case of novel attacks. Even the anomaly detection models do not work well when there is large variance in user behavior since the algorithm tries to model the normal behavior and the attack behavior shows a large variance many times overlapping with the normal behavior. Hence it turns out to be difficult to guard against the new and diversified attacks. The same is the case with the network traffic with a relatively small number

of intrusion only patterns; normal network traffic can have a large number of variations.

It is observed from most of the previous studies that there was no attempt to consider the correlation information in the input network traffic for improving the detection effectiveness. The network traffic can be characterized in terms of sequences of discrete data with temporal dependency (Lane, & Brodley, 1999, Thottan, & Ji, 2003, Jin, & Yeung, 2004). It is observed in (Jina, Yeunga, & XizhaoWangb, 2007) that different network intrusions have different correlation statistics which can be directly utilized in the co-variance feature space to distinguish multiple and various network intrusions effectively. By constructing a covariance feature space, a detection approach can thus utilize the correlation differences of sequential samples to identify multiple network attacks. It is also pointed out that the covariance based detection will succeed in distinguishing multiple classes with near or equal means while any traditional mean based classification approach will fail. Even the best intrusion detection systems for the DARPA evaluation (*DARPA)* shows that less than 10% of new R2L intrusion attempts have been detected. Therefore the numbers for the new attacks are more significant in determining the quality of IDSs.

Usefulness of DARPA Data Set for IDS Evaluation

Usefulness of DARPA data set for IDS evaluation (Thomas, Sharma, & Balakrishnan, 2008a)

The DARPA's sponsorship, the AFRL's evaluation and the MIT Lincoln Laboratory's support in security tools have resulted in a world class IDS evaluation setup that can be considered as a ground breaking intrusion detection research. With the increase in the network traffic and the introduction of new applications and attacks over time, continuous improvement is required to make the IDS evaluation data set a key element to keep it valuable for researchers. The user behavior also shows great unpredictability and changes over time. Modeling the network traffic is an immensely challenging undertaking because of the complexity and intricacy of human behaviors. The DARPA data set models the synthetic traffic from a session level. Evaluating the proposed IDS with DARPA 1999 data set may not be representative of the performance with more recent attacks or with other attacks against different types of machines, routers, firewalls or other network infrastructure. All these reasons have caused a lot of criticisms against this IDS evaluation data set (McHugh, Christie, & Allen, 2000). The DARPA data has certainly been useful in the development of the system proposed in this work. The details of the usefulness of the DARPA data set are included in the work of Thomas, Sharma and Balakrishnan (2008a). The DARPA evaluation data set has the required potential in modeling the attacks that are commonly found in the network traffic. Hence we conclude by commenting that it can be used to evaluate the IDSs in the present scenario, even though any effort to make the data set more "real" and therefore fairer for IDS evaluation is to be welcomed. If a system is evaluated on the DARPA data set, then it cannot claim anything more in terms of its performance on the real network traffic. Hence this data set can be considered as the base line of any research.

Choice and Modification of the Individual IDSs

In the case of IDSs, there are both the security requirements and the acceptability requirements. The security requirement is determined by the rate of true positives and the acceptability requirement is decided by the number of false positives because of the low base rate in the case of the network traffic. Taking into account the fact that the acceptable false alarm rate is extremely low (Thomas & Balakrishnan, 2008b), almost as low as the prior probability, the two IDSs, PHAD and

ALAD, which give extremely low false alarm rate of the order of 0.00002 and a third IDS which is the popularly used open source IDS, the Snort (Snort, 2009) are considered in this work. With the first two IDSs, the Bayesian detection rate is of the order of 35% and 38% respectively. Thus one of the primary reasons for choosing the IDSs, PHAD and ALAD was the requirement of acceptability in terms of the number of false alerts that does not overload a system administrator.

The other reason for the choice of PHAD and ALAD was that most of the existing IDS algorithms neglect the minority attack types, R2L and U2R in comparison to the majority attack types, Probes and DoS. ALAD is highly successful in detecting these rare attack types. Also Snort detects the U2R/Data attacks exceptionally well.

The detection performance of the anomaly detectors PHAD and ALAD can be improved further by training them on additional normal traffic other than the traffic of weeks one and three of the DARPA 1999 data set. Also the focus is on improving the misuse-based IDS Snort by modifying the snort rules. When trying to incorporate the rules, care has been taken not to overfit or to make it very generic. This avoids false negatives and false positives to the maximum extent possible. For example when the signature is "connection type=ftp", the misclassification should not happen because it can be due to DoS also in the flooding attempt. Hence rule R2L has to be refined for the absence of DoS attacks (Joshi, 2002). The rules may thus incorporate more conditions for refinement and thus avoid misclassification and hence the misclassification cost also.

To improve the performance of the IDSs PHAD and ALAD, more data has been incorporated in their training. Normal data was collected from an University internal network and this has been randomly divided into two parts. PHAD is trained on week three of the data set and one portion of the internal network traffic data, and ALAD is trained on week one of the data set and the other portion of the internal network traffic data. Hence the two anomaly-based IDSs PHAD and ALAD are trained on disjoint set of training data. The correlation among the classifiers is lowered due to factors like more training data, which is disjoint and also more time for training.

Snort: Improvements by Adding new Rules

Snort has been identified to have a lot of rules that are named differently from that in the DARPA 99 data set. For example the "land" attack which comes under the DoS attack class is found in the bad traffic rules folder of Snort and not in the DoS rules. The attack "warezclient" which downloads illegal copies of software has been identified by Snort with a rule that looks for the executable code on the FTP port. Also, many of the rules are very generic and hence the chances of false positive were very high. However, it was identified that it requires tremendous effort to modify those generic rules and we have succeeded only to a very small extent. We seek for a higher recall objective in the first phase and the fusion is expected to reduce the false alarms to some extent. Snort rules were modified for the DoS attacks like land, dosnuke and selfping. The rules may thus incorporate more conditions for refinement and thus avoid misclassification and hence the misclassification cost also. This has increased the Snort detection of DoS.

PHAD/ALAD

PHAD was highly reliable in detecting all the probes except for the stealthy slow scans which have been included in the DARPA'99 data set. The stealthy probes which PHAD missed are ipsweep, lsdomain, portsweep and resetscan. However, Snort was effective in identifying those stealthy ones by waiting for longer that one minute between the successive network transmissions. PHAD has the disadvantage that it classifies attacks based on a single packet. We have improved PHAD by examining a session and detecting the anomalies in the connection rather than only at the packet level. A connection (record) is a sequence of TCP packets starting and ending at some well-defined times, between which data flows from the source IP address to the target IP address under some well-defined protocol. PHAD was trained on week three of the data set and one portion of the internal network traffic data, and ALAD is trained on week one of the data set and the other portion of the internal network traffic data. Hence, the two anomaly-based IDSs PHAD and ALAD are trained on disjoint sets of the training data. The correlation among the classifiers is lowered by incorporating more of training time and that too being disjoint. The disjoint data sets given to PHAD and ALAD for training have also helped to an extent in feature selection and also in reducing the correlation between the two IDSs. Both PHAD and ALAD look into almost disjoint features of the traffic. PHAD detects anomaly based on the intrinsic features of the Transmission Control Protocol (TCP), User Datagram Protocol (UDP), Internet Protocol (IP), Internet Control Message Protocol (ICMP) and the Ethernet headers. ALAD detects anomaly based on almost disjoint features of the traffic by looking at the inbound TCP stream connection to well-known server ports.

Experimental Evaluation of the IDSs

The Snort is designed as a network IDS; extremely good at detecting distributed port scans and also fragmented attacks which hide malicious packets by fragmentation. The pre-processor of Snort is highly capable of defragmenting the packets. Matching the alert produced by Snort with the packets in the data set by means of timestamp might sometimes cause missing the attacks. This is mainly because of the time gap within ±10seconds between the two.

In a study made by Sommers et al. (Sommers, Yegneswaran, & Barford, 2001) after comparing the two IDSs Snort and Bro (Paxson & Vern, 1999), they comment that Snort's drop rates seem to degrade less intensely with volume for the DARPA data set. They have also concluded in the paper that Snort's signature set has been tuned to detect DARPA attacks.

Preprocessing of the DARPA data set is required before applying to any machine learning algorithm. With the anomaly based IDSs, PHAD and ALAD, we tried to train them by mixing the normal data from an isolated network along with the week 1 and week 3 respectively of the training data set. Even then, the algorithms produce less than 50% detection and around 100 false alarms for the entire DARPA test data set. The usual reasoning for the poor performance of the anomaly detectors is that the training and the test data are not correlated. The normal user behavior changes so drastically from what the algorithm has been trained with, and hence we expect the machine learning algorithms to be extremely sophisticated and learn the changing behavior.

The main reasons for the poor performance of the IDSs with the DARPA 1999 IDS evaluation data set are the following:

- The training and test data sets are not correlated for R2L and U2R attacks and hence most of the pattern recognition and machine learning algorithms except for the anomaly detectors that learn only from the normal data, will perform badly while detecting the R2L and the U2R attacks.
- The normal traffic patterns in real networks and also in the data set are not correlated and hence the trainable algorithms are expected to generate a lot of false alarms.
- None of the network based systems did very well against host based, U2R attacks (Kubat, Holte, & Matwin, 1997).
- Several of the surveillance attacks probe the network and retrieve significant information, and they go undetected, by limiting the speed and scope of probes (Kubat, Holte, & Matwin, 1997).

- The data set provides a large sample of computer attacks embedded in normal background traffic.
- Many threats and thereby the exploits that are available on the computer systems and networks are undefined and open-ended.
- The DoS and the R2L attacks have a very low variance and hence difficult to detect with a unique signature by a signature-based IDS or to observe as an anomaly by an anomaly detector (Lee, Stolfo, Chan, Eskin, Fan, Miller, Hershkop, & Zhang, 2000).
- There are a number of DoS as well as R2L attacks that are difficult to get detected since they exploit a large number of different network or system services. There is no regular pattern for such attacks for detection by misuse detection systems. The anomaly detection systems are also unable to detect them since they may look like normal traffic because of the attacker evading some trusted hosts and using them for an attack. These attacks are highly sophisticated and need a thorough analysis by a specialized detector.
- There is an observable imbalanced intrusion results due to DoS having more connections than any other attack. Most of the IDSs will try to minimize the overall error rate, but this leads to increase in the error rate of rare classes.

Hence, more efforts should be made to improve the detection rate of the rare classes. This section has highlighted that even with an effort to improve the available IDSs PHAD, ALAD and Snort, these IDSs still remain suboptimum with detection rates less than 60%.

The above limitations have to be overcome by sophisticated detection techniques for an improved and acceptable IDS performance. We have also seen that Snort performs exceptionally well in detecting the U2R attacks and DoS attacks, PHAD performs well in detecting the probes and ALAD performs well in detecting the R2L attacks. This clearly shows that each IDS is designed to focus on a limited region of the attack domain rather than the entire attack domain. Hence IDSs are limited in their performance at the design stage itself. Multi-sensor fusion meets the requirements of a better than the best detection by a refinement of the combined response of different IDSs with largely varying accuracy. The motivation for applying sensor fusion in enhancing the performance of intrusion detection systems is that a better analysis of existing data gathered by various individual IDSs can detect many attacks that currently go undetected.

PROPOSED APPROACH

Various IDSs reported in the literature as well as the three IDSs as illustrated in Tables 2, 3, and 4, have shown distinct preferences for detecting a certain class of attacks with improved accuracy, while performing moderately on the other classes. With advances in sensor fusion it has become possible to obtain more reliable and accurate decisions for a wider class of attacks by combining the decisions of multiple IDSs. This will provide optimal overall performance with potentially suboptimal individual solutions. An

architecture that considers a method of improving the detection rate of the minority class types without increasing the false positive rate has been used in this work. A neural network learner is used to gather an in-depth understanding about the input traffic and also the behavior of the individual IDSs. This helps in automatically learning the individual weight for the combination when the IDSs are heterogeneous and shows difference in performance. Also it provides higher weighting to local experts, and is relatively insensitive to the poor performing IDSs. Hence the problem is approached making use of the availability of the observational data, which can be analyzed to find unsuspected relationships. This helps in summarizing the data in novel ways that are helpful in the analysis rather than distorting the data.

Data-Dependent Decision Fusion Scheme

An architecture, which introduces the data dependence in the fusion technique, is introduced in this work. The idea of this architecture is to properly analyze the data and understand when the individual IDSs fail. The fusion unit should incorporate this learning from the input as well as from the output of detectors, to make an appropriate decision. This chapter discusses the improved performance of multiple IDSs using Data-dependent Decision fusion. The Data-

Table 2. Attacks detected by Snort from the DARPA 1999 data set

Attacks detected by Snort	**Probe:** portsweep, satan, imap, ntinfoscan, ls **DoS:** teardrop, dosnuke, land, tcpreset, selfping, dosnuke, crashiis, neptune, udpstorm **R2L:** sshtrojan, ftpwrite, phf, netcat, nc-setup, nc-breakin, ncftp, guessftp, httptunnel, xlock, xsnoop, named **U2R:** sechole, yaga, secret, sqlattack, loadmodule, ppmacro
Attacks not detected by Snort	**Probe:** portsweep, queso **DoS:** crashiis, pod, crashiis, apache2, warez, arppoison, mailbomb, processtable, smurf, ntfsdos, arppoison, syslogd, land **R2L:** sendmail, netcat, sshtrojan, ftpwrite, back,guesspop, xsnoop, snmpget, dict, guesstelnet, guestftp, httptunnel, named, netbus **U2R:** ps, nfsdos, eject, sqlattack, sechole, fdformat, loadmodule, ffbconfig, secret, xterm, casesen

Table 3. Attacks detected by PHAD from the DARPA 1999 data set

Attacks detected by PHAD	**Probe:** portsweep, satan **DoS:** teardrop, dosnuke, land, neptune **R2L:** phf **U2R:** fdformat
Attacks not detected by PHAD	**Probe:** lsdomain, ntinfoscan, mscan, illegal-sniffer **DoS:** arppoison, land, mailbomb, processtable, arppoison, crashiis, smurf, warez, ntfsdos, nfsdos **R2L:** named, httptunnel, xlock, xsnoop, sendmail, netbus, snmpget, guesstelnet, guestftp, anypw, sshtrojan, guesspop **U2R:** ffbconfig, secret, loadmodule, sqlattack, eject, perl, ps, sechole, ppmacro, fdformat, casesen

dependent Decision fusion approach gathers an in-depth understanding about the input traffic and also the behavior of the individual IDSs by means of a neural network learner unit. This information is used to fine-tune the fusion unit since the fusion depends on the input feature vector. Thus fusion implements a function that is local to each region in the feature space. It is well-known that the effectiveness of sensor fusion improves when the individual IDSs are uncorrelated. The training methodology adopted in this work takes note of this fact. For illustrative purposes two different data sets, namely the DARPA 1999 data set as well as the real-world network traffic embedded with attacks, have been used. The architecture is shown in Figure 1.

The data-dependent decision fusion architecture is a three-stage architecture, with optimizing the individual IDSs as the first stage, the Neural Network learner determining the weights of the individual IDSs as the second stage, and the fusion unit doing the weighted aggregation as the final stage. The Neural Network learner can be con-

sidered as a pre-processing stage to the fusion unit. The neural network is most appropriate for weight determination as it is difficult to define the rules clearly, mainly when more IDSs are added to the fusion unit. When a record is correctly classified by one or more detectors, the neural network will accumulate this knowledge as a weight and with more iterations, the weight gets stabilized. The architecture is independent of the data set and the structures employed, and can be used with any real valued data set. Thus, it is reasonable to make use of Neural Network learner unit to understand the performance and assign weights to various individual IDSs for a large data set. The weight assigned to any IDS, not only depends on the output of that IDS, but also on the input traffic which causes this output. A neural network unit is fed with the output of the IDSs along with the respective input for an in depth understanding of the reliability estimation of the IDSs. The alarm produced by the different IDSs when they are presented with a certain attack clearly tells which sensor generated the more

Table 4. Attacks detected by ALAD from the DARPA 1999 data set

Attacks detected by ALAD	**DoS:** crashiis **R2L:** phf, ncftp, guessftp **U2R:** casesen, eject, fdformat, ffbconfig, sechole, xterm, yaga, ps
Attacks not detected by ALAD	**Probe:** portsweep, ipsweep, lsdomain, ntinfoscan, mscan, illegal-sniffer, queso, satan **DoS:** warez, arppoison, land, mailbomb, processtable, smurf, nfsdos **R2L:** ppmacro, named, xlock, uesspop, xsnoop, snmpget, httptunnel, anypw, sendmail, sshtrojan, netbus **U2R:** sqlattack, sechole, perl, loadmodule, secret, loadmodule

Figure 1. Data-dependent decision fusion method

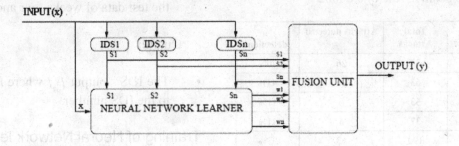

precise result and what attacks are actually occurring on the network traffic. The output of the neural network unit corresponds to the weights which are assigned to each one of the individual IDSs. With the improved weight factor, the IDSs can be fused to produce an improved resultant output.

Thus the data-dependent decision fusion architecture refers to a collection of diverse IDSs that respond to input traffic and the weighted combination of their predictions. The weights are learned by looking at the response of the individual sensors for all input traffic. The fusion output can be represented as:

$$y = F_j \left(w_j^i \left(x, S_j^i \right), S_j^i \right)$$

where the weights w_j^i are dependent on both the input x as well as individual IDS's output S_j^i, the suffix j refers to the class label and the prefix i refers to the IDS index. The Data-dependent Decision fusion architecture incorporates a neural network unit to generate the weight factor depending on the input as well as the IDSs' outputs. The correlation enables any learning algorithm to learn the weight of a particular sensor while performing sensor fusion, thus selecting the best sensor for that particular class of attack. This justifies the use of neural networks for learning the weights of the individual IDSs. The proposed method has successfully demonstrated that the neural network learner encapsulates expert knowledge for the

weighted fusion of individual detector decisions. This creates an adaptable algorithm that can substantially outperform state-of-the-art methods for minority class type detection in both coverage and precision. This has resulted in a more accurate and precise detection for a wider class of attacks. If the individual sensors were complementary and looked at different regions of the attack domain, then this Data-dependent Decision fusion enriches the analysis of the incoming traffic to detect attacks with appreciably low false alarms. The individual IDSs that are components of this architecture in this particular work were PHAD, ALAD and Snort with detection rates 0.33, 0.41 and 0.61 respectively after modifications to these IDSs as shown in Tables 5, 6, and 7.

Data-Dependent Decision Fusion Algorithm

Training of IDSs

Input:

- The DARPA 1999 training dataset $\{(x_n, y_n)\}$ where n refers to the number of the record in the dataset.
- The two anomaly IDSs are trained with ALAD on week one and PHAD on week three.

Table 5. Attacks of each type detected by PHAD at a false positive rate of 0.00002

Attack Type	Total Attacks	Attacks detected	% detection
Probe	37	26	70%
Dos	63	27	43%
R2L	53	6	11%
U2R/ Data	37	4	11%
Total	190	63	33%

Table 6. Attacks of each type detected by ALAD at a false positive rate of 0.00002

Attack Type	Total Attacks	Attacks detected	% detection
Probe	37	9	24%
Dos	63	23	37%
R2L	53	31	59%
U2R/ Data	37	15	31%
Total	190	78	41%

Table 7. Attacks of each type detected by Snort at a false positive rate of 0.0002

Attack Type	Total Attacks	Attacks detected	% detection
Probe	37	15	41%
Dos	63	35	56%
R2L	53	30	57%
U2R/ Data	37	34	92%
Total	190	115	61%

Testing of IDSs

Input:

- The DARPA 1999 test dataset $\{(x_j)\}$ where j refers to the number of the record in the dataset.

- The testing of the three IDSs are done on the test data of weeks four and five.

Output:

- The IDS's output $\{s_i\}$ where i corresponds to the IDS number.

Training of Neural Network learner

Input:

- The IDS's output $\{s_i\}$ where i corresponds to the IDS index.
- The DARPA training dataset $\{(x_n, y_n)\}$ where n refers to the number of the record in the dataset.

The IDS outputs as well as the training class labels are such that $s_i \in C_k$ where C_k are the 58 class labels, and k varies from 1 to 58. With the IDSs used in this experiment, it was simplified as a binary detector with class labels either zero or one depending on the anomaly score of the anomaly detectors or the severity of the Snort alert.

Training:

- MATLAB Neural Network tool box is used.
- Algorithm: Feed Forward Back Propagation
  : Four input neurons
  : One hidden layer with 25 sigmoidal units
  : Output layer of three neurons

The three inputs correspond to the outputs of the three constituent IDSs and the fourth input neuron is a vector which corresponds to a single record of the DARPA dataset where all values of the vector are run.

Testing of the Neural Network learner

Input:

- The IDS's output $\{s_i\}$ where i corresponds to the index of IDSs.
- The DARPA test dataset $\{(x_j)\}$ where j refers to the number of the record in the dataset.

The IDS outputs are such that $s_i \in C_k$ where C_k are the 58 class labels, and k varies from 1 to 58. With the IDSs used in this experiment, it was simplified as a binary detector with class labels either zero or one depending on the anomaly score of the anomaly detectors or the severity of the Snort alert.

Testing:

- MATLAB Neural Network tool box was used.
- Algorithm: Feed Forward Network
  : Four input neurons
  : One hidden layer with 25 sigmoidal units
  : Output layer of three neurons

Output:

- $\{w_j\}$ is the output of the NN learner which is expected to give a measure of the reliability of each of the IDS, i depending on the observed data class type j.

Fusion Unit

Input:

- The IDS's output $\{s_i\}$ where i corresponds to the index of IDSs.
- The weight factor for the fusion process, $\{w_j\}$ which is the output of the NN learner which is expected to give a measure of the reliability of each of the IDS, i depending on the observed data class type j.

Output:

Binary fusion output is one if the weighted linear aggregation of the output from all the IDSs is greater than zero and zero otherwise.

$y = 1$, if $\sum w_i^j s_i > 0$
0, otherwise

The fusion unit performed the weighted aggregation of the IDSs' outputs. The weights are directly proportional to the reliability of the particular IDS in detecting a particular attack. The fusion unit used binary fusion by giving an output value of 1 or 0 depending on the value of the weighted aggregation of the decisions from the IDSs. The packets were identified by their timestamp on aggregation. A value of 1 at the output of the fusion unit indicated the record to be under attack and a 0 indicated the absence of an attack.

EXPERIMENTAL EVALUATION

All the IDSs that take part in fusion were modified and separately evaluated with the same data set, and then the empirical evaluation of the proposed data-dependent decision fusion method was also presented. It can be observed from the Tables 5, 6, and 7 that the attacks detected by different IDSs were not necessarily the same and also that no single IDS was able to provide acceptable values of all the performance measures.

Correlation between the Individual IDSs

A quantitative analysis provides the correlation coefficient among the different sensors as follows:

Correlation coefficient of PHAD and ALAD: -0.36
Correlation coefficient of PHAD and snort: -0.42
Correlation coefficient of ALAD and snort: 0.59

It is well-known that the effectiveness of sensor fusion improves when the individual IDSs are uncorrelated. The training methodology adopted in this work takes note of this fact.

Table 8 provides the correlation coefficient of the detectors as well as the correlation coefficient of the detections with the actual attacks for all the attack types. It has been demonstrated in Table 8 that for probes the attack predictions of PHAD are highly correlated to the actual attacks with a correlation coefficient of 0.97. The correlation enables any learning algorithm to learn the weight of a particular sensor while performing sensor fusion, thus selecting the best for that particular class of attack. Table 8 also justifies why R2L attacks become difficult to detect. The correlation coefficient of the detections with the actual attacks for all the attack types has been calculated.

The result in table 9 shows that the DD fusion performs significantly better than any of the individual IDSs. In real world network environments, the rare attacks like U2R and R2L are more dangerous than probe and DoS attacks. Hence, it is essential to improve the detection performance of these rare classes of attacks while maintaining a reasonable overall detection rate. The results presented in Table 9 and figure 2 and 3 indicate that the proposed method performs significantly better for rare attack types. The claim that the data-dependent decision fusion method performs better is supported by a statement from Kubat et al. (Kubat, Holte, & Matwin, 1997), which states that "a classifier that labels all regions as major-

ity class will achieve an accuracy of 96%. A system achieving 94% on the minority class and 94% on the majority class will have worse accuracy yet be deemed highly successful". The evaluations show the strength and ability of the proposed approach to perform very well with 64% detection for R2L attacks and 92% detection for U2R attacks with an overall false positive rate of 0.002% at an overall detection rate of 70%.

Discussion

Most of the U2R attacks like loadmodule, perl and sqlattack are made stealthy by running the attack over multiple sessions. These attacks are detected by Snort but at the expense of a higher false positive rate. Snort was comparably better in the detection of all the new attacks like queso, arppoison, dosnuke, selfping, tcpreset, ncftp, netbus, netcat, sshtrojan, ntfsdos, and sechole for which Snort had the signatures available. Snort identifies the attack warezclient which downloads illegal copies of software by an addition of the rule of looking for executable codes on the FTP port. Thus each rule in the rule set uses the most discriminating feature values for classifying a data item into one of the class types.

Although the research discussed in this chapter has thus far focused on the three IDSs, namely, PHAD, ALAD and Snort, the algorithm works well with any IDS. The proposed system provides great benefit to a security analyst. Snort was comparably better in the detection of all the new attacks for

Table 8. Correlation coefficient of the detections with actual attacks

Attack Type	Correlation Coefficient					
	PHAD & ALAD	PHAD & Snort	ALAD & Snort	PHAD & Actual	ALAD & Actual	Snort & Actual
Probe	-0.18	0.95	-0.1	0.97	-0.18	0.9
DoS	0.02	0.65	0.5	0.1	0.46	0.65
R2L	-0.01	0.35	0.75	-0.2	0.3	0.4
U2R	0.17	0.2	0.74	0.04	0.61	0.67

Table 9. Types of attacks detected by DD fusion IDS at a false positive rate of 0.00002 (100 FPs)

Attack Type	Total Attacks	Attacks detected	% detection
Probe	37	28	76%
Dos	63	40	64%
R2L	53	34	64%
U2R/Data	37	34	92%
Total	190	136	70%

Figure 2. Semilog ROC curve of single and DD fusion IDSs

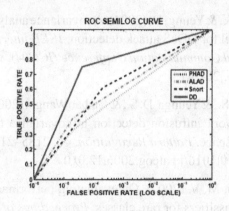

Figure 3. Performance of evaluated systems

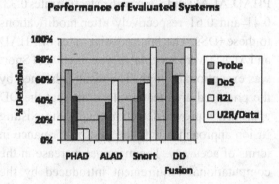

which the signatures were available with Snort. The computational complexity introduced by the proposed method can be justified by the possible gains which are illustrated.

The result of the Data-dependent Decision Fusion method is better than what has been predicted by the Lincoln Laboratory after the DARPA IDS evaluation. With the fusion architecture proposed in this chapter, an improved intrusion detection of 70% with a false positive of as low as 0.002% was achieved.

SUMMARY

The data skewness in the network traffic demands an extremely low false positive rate of the order of the prior probability of attack for an acceptable value of the Bayesian attack detection rate

(Thomas & Balakrishnan, 2008b). The research and development efforts in the field of IDS, and the state-of-the-art IDSs, all are still with marginal detection rates and high false positive rates, especially in the case of stealthy, novel and R2L attacks. The poor performance of the detectors has been improved by discriminative training of anomaly detectors and incorporating additional rules into the misuse detector.

We have adapted and extended notions from the field of multi-sensor data fusion for the Data-dependent Decision Fusion. The extensions are principally in the area of generalizing feature similarity functions to comprehend observations in the intrusion detection domain. The approach has the ability to fuse decisions from multiple, heterogeneous and sub-optimal IDSs. In the proposed data-dependent decision fusion architecture, a neural network unit was used to generate a weight factor depending on the input as well as the IDSs' outputs. The method applies appropriate weights to the outputs of various individual IDSs that take part in fusion. This results in a more accurate and precise detection for a wider class of attacks. If the individual sensors were complementary and looked at different regions of the attack domain, then this DD fusion enriches the analysis of the incoming traffic to detect attacks with appreciably low false alarms.

The individual IDSs that are components of this architecture in this particular work were PHAD, ALAD and Snort with detection rates 0.33, 0.41 and 0.61 respectively after modifications to these IDSs. The false positive rates of PHAD and ALAD were acceptable whereas that of Snort was exceptionally high. The results obtained by the proposed architecture illustrate that the DD approach improved detection beyond the existing fusion approaches with the best performance in terms of accuracy. The marginal increase in the computational requirement introduced by the data-dependency can be justified by the acceptable ranges of false alarms and an overall detection rate of 0.7, which have resulted with an exceptionally large data set and suboptimal constituent IDSs.

REFERENCES

Agarwal, R., & Joshi, M. V. (2000). *PN rule: A new framework for learning classifier models in data mining (a case-study in network intrusion detection). (Tech. Rep. RC 21719), IBM Research report*. Computer Science/Mathematics.

Bass, T. (1999). Multisensor data fusion for next generation distributed intrusion detection systems. *IRIS National Symposium on Sensor and Data Fusion* (pp. 24-27).

Breiman, L., Friedman, J. H., Olshen, R. A., & Stone, C. J. (1984). *Classification and regression trees*. Belmont, CA: Wadsworth.

Chawla, N. V., Bowyer, K. W., Hall, L. O., & Kegelmeyer, W. P. (2002). Smote: Synthetic minority over-sampling technique. *Journal of Artificial Intelligence Research, 16*, 321–357.

Cohen, W. W. (1995). Fast effective rule induction. *Proceedings of 12th International Conference on Machine Learning*, (pp. 115—123).

DARPA. (2009). *Intrusion detection evaluation dataset*. Retrieved October 16, 2009, from http://www.ll.mit.edu/IST/ideval/data/data_index.html

Jin, S., & Yeung, D. (2004). A covariance analysis model for DDoS attack detection. *IEEE International Communication Conference (ICC04)*, vol. 4 (pp. 20-24).

Jina, S., & Yeunga, D. S., & Xizhao Wangb. (2007). Network intrusion detection in covariance feature space. *Pattern Recognition, 40*, 2185–2197. doi:10.1016/j.patcog.2006.12.010

Joshi, M. V. (2002). On evaluating performance of classifiers for rare classes. *Proceedings of the 2002 IEEE International Conference on Data Mining* (pp. 641-644).

Joshi, M. V., Agarwal, R. C., & Kumar, V. (2001). Mining needles in a haystack: Classifying rare classes via two-phase rule induction, *Association for Computing Machinery Special Interest Group on Management of Data, 30*(2).

Kendall, K. (1999). *A database of computer attacks for the evaluation of intrusion detection systems*. Unpublished dissertation, Massachusetts Institute of Technology, USA.

Kubat, M., Holte, R. C., & Matwin, S. (1997). Learning when negative examples abound: One sided selection. *Proceedings of the Ninth European Conference on Machine Learning* (pp. 146-153).

Lane, T., & Brodley, C. E. (1999). Temporal sequence learning and data reduction for anomaly detection. *ACM Transactions on Information and System Security, 2*(3). doi:10.1145/322510.322526

Lee, W., Stolfo, S. J., Chan, P. K., Eskin, E., Fan, W., Miller, M., et al. (2000). Real time data mining-based intrusion detection. *Second DARPA Information Survivability Conference and Exposition, IEEE Computer Society*, (pp. 85-100).

Mahoney, M. V., & Chan, P. K. (2001). *Detecting novel attacks by identifying anomalous network packet headers*. Florida Institute of Technology. (Tech. Rep. No. CS- 2001-2).

Mahoney, M. V., & Chan, P. K. (2002). *Learning non stationary models of normal network traffic for detecting novel attacks*. The Eighth Association of Computing Machinery Special Interest Group Knowledge Discovery and Data Mining International Conference on Knowledge Discovery and Data Mining.

McCarthy, K., Zabar, B., & Weiss, G. (2005). Does cost-sensitive learning beat sampling for classifying rare classes? *First International Workshop on Utility-Based Data Mining* (pp. 69-77).

McHugh, J., Christie, A., & Allen, J. (2000, Sep/Oct.). Defending yourself: The role of intrusion detection systems. *IEEE Software*, *17*(5). doi:10.1109/52.877859

Paxson, V. (1999). Bro: A system for detecting network intruders in real-time. *Computer Networks*, *31*(23), 2435–2463. doi:10.1016/S1389-1286(99)00112-7

Quinlan, J. R. (1993). *C4.5: Programs for machine learning*. Morgan Kaufmann.

Snort. (2009) *Snort manual*. Retrieved October 16, 2009, from www.snort.org/docs/snort_htmanuals/htmanual_260

Sommers, J., Yegneswaran, V., & Barford, P. (2001). *Toward comprehensive traffic generation for online IDS evaluation. Tech. Report*. Department of Computer Science, University of Wisconsin.

Thomas, C., & Balakrishnan, N. (2008b). Improvement in minority attack detection with skewness in network traffic. In V. Dasarathy (Ed.), *Proceedings of the SPIE Defense and Security Symposium: Vol. 6973* (pp. 242-253).

Thomas, C., Sharma, V., & Balakrishnan, N. (2008a). Usefulness of DARPA data set for intrusion detection systems evaluation. In V. Dasarathy (Ed.), *Proceedings of the SPIE Defense and Security Symposium: Vol. 6973*, (pp. 137-150).

Thottan, M., & Ji, C. (2003). Anomaly detection in IP networks. *IEEE Transactions on Signal Processing*, *51*(8), 2191–2204. doi:10.1109/TSP.2003.814797

ADDITIONAL READING

Aalo, V., & Viswanathan, R. (1989). On distributed detection with correlated sensors: Two examples. *IEEE Transactions on Aerospace and Electronic Systems*, *25*, 414–421. doi:10.1109/7.30797

Anderson, J. P. (1980). *Computer Security Threat Monitoring and Surveillance. Tech. Report*. Fort Washington, PA: James P. Anderson Co.

Anderson, R., & Khattak, A. (1998). *The Use of Information Retrieval Techniques for Intrusion Detection, RAID '98*. Belgium: Louvain-la-Neuve.

Andersson, D., Fong, M., & Valdes, A. (2002). Heterogeneous Sensor Correlation: A Case Study of Live Traffic Analysis. *IEEE Information Assurance Workshop*.

Axelsson, S. (2000). *Intrusion Detection Systems: A Survey and Taxonomy*. Chalmers University. (Tech. Rep. No. 99-15) http://citeseer.nj.nec.com/axelsson00intrusion.html

Chair, Z., & Varshney, P. K. (1986). Optimal data fusion in multiple sensor detection systems. *IEEE Transactions on Aerospace and Electronic Systems*, *22*(1), 98–101. doi:10.1109/TAES.1986.310699

Chan, P. K., & Stolfo, S. (1993). Toward parallel and distributed learning by metalearning. In *Working Notes AAAI Work, Knowledge Discovery in Databases* (pp. 227–240). Portland, OR: AAAI Press.

Dasarathy, B. V. (1997). Sensor fusion potential exploitation-innovative architectures and illustrative applications. *Proceedings of the IEEE, 85*(1), 24–38. doi:10.1109/5.554206

Deba, H., Dacier, M., & Wespi, A. (1999). Toward a taxonomy of Intrusion Detection Systems. *Computer Networks, 31*, 805–822. doi:10.1016/S1389-1286(98)00017-6

Debar, H., & Wespi, A. (2001). Aggregation and Correlation of Intrusion-Detection Alerts, *Fourth International Symposium on the Recent Advances in Intrusion Detection (RAID)*. Springer-Verlag LNCS.

Denning, D. E. (1987). An Intrusion-Detection Model. *IEEE Transactions on Software Engineering, SE-13*, 222–232. doi:10.1109/TSE.1987.232894

Denning, D. E. (1999). *Information Warfare and Security*. Addison Wesley.

Drakopoulos, E., & Lee, C. C. (1991). Optimum multisensor fusion of correlated local. *IEEE Transactions on Aerospace and Electronic Systems, 27*, 593–606. doi:10.1109/7.85032

Hall, D. H., & McMullen, S. A. H. (2004). *Mathematical Techniques in Multi-Sensor Data Fusion* (2nd ed.). Artech House.

Iyengar, S. S., & Brooks, R. R. (1998). *Multi-Sensor Fusion: Fundamentals and Applications with Software*. Prentice Hall.

Kam, M., Zhu, Q., & Gray, W. (1992). Optimal data fusion of correlated local decisions in multiple sensor detection systems. *IEEE Transactions on Aerospace and Electronic Systems, 28*, 916–920. doi:10.1109/7.256317

Lee, W., & Stolfo, S. J. (1998). Data mining approaches for intrusion detection, *Seventh USENIX Security Symposium*, San Antonio, TX: USENIX.

Lee, W., Stolfo, S. J., Chan, P. K., Eskin, E., Fan, W., Miller, M., et al. (2001). Real time data mining-based intrusion detection. *Second DARPA Information Survivability Conference and Exposition*, IEEE Computer Society, (pp. 85-100).

Northcutt, S., & Novak, J. (2003). *Network Intrusion Detection*. Indianapolis, IN: New Riders/Pearson.

Thomas, C. (2009). *Performance Enhancement of Intrusion Detection Systems using Advances in Sensor Fusion*. Unpublished doctoral dissertation. Supercomputer Education and Research Centre, Indian Institute of Science, India. CERT report of vulnerabilities. Retrieved February 13, 2011, http://www.cert.org/stats/cert stats.htm/#vulnerabilities

Thomas, C., & Balakrishnan, N. (2008). Advanced Sensor Fusion Technique for Enhanced Intrusion Detection. *IEEE International Conference on Intelligence and Security Informatics*, 1-4244-2415, (pp. 173-178).

Thomas, C., & Balakrishnan, N. (2008). Modified Evidence Theory for Performance Enhancement of Intrusion Detection Systems. *International Conference on Information Fusion*, 4883, 2, (pp. 1751-1758).

Thomas, C., & Balakrishnan, N. (2009). Mathematical Analysis of Sensor Fusion for Intrusion Detection Systems. *International Conference on Communications and Networking*, 97, (pp. 51-58).

Valdes, A., & Skinner, K. (2001). *Probabilistic alert correlation*. Springer Verlag Lecture notes in Computer Science.

KEY TERMS AND DEFINITIONS

Data-Dependent Decision Fusion: The Data-dependent Decision Fusion approach gathers an in-depth understanding about the input and also the behavior of the individual detectors by means of a learner unit, which help to fine-tune the fusion unit.

Intrusion Detection Systems: Intrusion Detection Systems detect unauthorized use of a system, or attacks on a system or network.

Sensor Fusion: Sensor fusion of Intrusion Detection Systems is to meet the requirements of a better than the best detection by a refinement of the combined response of different detectors with largely varying detection coverage.

Chapter 18
PITWALL:
Tools, Techniques and Metrics for the Optimization of Enterprise Network Defense Systems

Subrata Acharya
Towson University, USA

ABSTRACT

The continuous growth in the Internet's size, the amount of data traffic, and the complexity of processing this traffic give rise to new challenges in building high performance network devices. Such an exponential growth, coupled with the increasing sophistication of attacks, is placing stringent demands on the performance of network Information Systems. These challenges require new designs, architecture, and algorithms for raising situational awareness, and hence, providing performance improvements on current network devices and cyber systems. In this research, the author focuses on the design of architecture and algorithms for optimization of network defense systems, specifically firewalls, to aid not only adaptive and real-time packet filtering but also fast content based routing (differentiated services) for today's data-driven networks.

INTRODUCTION

The conventional security of the Internet has been *static, perimeter based* and is *oblivious* to traffic dynamics in the network. The above model causes the lack of knowledge to identify, address and prevent anomalous behavior and maintain the desired operation of current network defense systems. In recent years, there has been tremendous effort towards the design and development of several techniques and strategies to deal with the above shortcomings. Unfortunately, the current solutions have been able to address only some aspects of security. This is primarily due to the lack of adaptation and dynamics in the design of such solutions.

To this effect, this research presents various algorithmic and architectural techniques that aims to address the shortcomings in terms of *adaptation, speed of operation* (under attack or heavily

DOI: 10.4018/978-1-4666-0104-8.ch018

loaded conditions), and *overall operational cost-effectiveness* of such network defense systems. The dynamic network behavior and events in such networks can be measured and analyzed to aid the design of efficient systems. The proposed research presents approaches for *Tier-I ISP* networks and filtering routers to correlate the dynamic metrics and achieve situational awareness required to protect critical network infrastructure and data driven operations over the Internet. Thus, the overall goal is the design of reliable and survival network defense systems. The tools proposed also aim to offer the flexibility to include new approaches, and provide the ability to migrate or deploy additional entities for attack detection and defense.

Data communication networks have become an indispensable infrastructure for most industrial and academic institutions. Today's Internet has undoubtedly become the largest public data network, enabling and facilitating both personal and business communications worldwide. The volume of traffic moving over the Internet, including all corporate networks, is expanding exponentially every day. As social dependence on such information systems continues to grow exponentially, a similar growth in threats is concurrently taking place. Traffic anomalies and attacks are commonplace in today's network information systems. Attacks span the spectrum from computer worms and individual, localized intrusions aimed at gaining access to information and system resources, to coordinated and distributed attacks aimed at disrupting services and disabling critical infrastructure.

Furthermore, the number and frequency of these attacks has been increasing dramatically (Symantec Internet Security Report 2011), as the knowledge and tools required to carryout these devastating attacks are readily available on the Internet. As these attacks proliferate and grow in scope and sophistication, different institutions find themselves under growing pressure to place significant restrictions on open Internet access

and collaboration. In this regard, institutions and organizations rely heavily on Intrusion Detection Systems (*IDSs*) for most network defense operations.

While such network defense systems have been designed, they are not geared towards extremely challenging network environments, which require support for high performance applications and open access policy for collaboration. Furthermore, these systems lack the critical *on-time* network aware information to identify and address the highly dynamic network environment while ensuring reliable, guaranteed and efficient network operation. Additionally, many of the existing intrusion detection systems are *reactive* in nature, and as such, are not practical in these dynamically changing environments. To overcome the above shortcoming, most of the Internet service providers still rely on *offline* traffic analysis and manual detection to deal with the various security threats and attacks. Current *Tier-1* network defense systems are also limited by their lack of flexibility to deal with the ever-evolving characteristics of the attacks, in terms of diversity and intensity. While the use of machine learning based approaches holds promise, the schemes remain offline in nature, with potentially prohibitive high overhead in providing the real-time and situational significant knowledge for the efficient functioning of these network devices (Xiang et al 2005, Zhao et al 2003).

A comprehensive solution towards ensuring a practical defense against intrusions and attacks for such high-performance collaborative environments (*i.e. Internet*) must include a *proactive*, *real-time*, and *adaptive* solution aimed at the design of efficient and survival network systems. The necessary design goals that the design must meet are as follows:

- *Accurate attack detection in real-time with minimal false alarms,*

- *Dynamic, collaborative, and resource efficient defense to counter and mitigate attacks, and*
- *Reliable delivery of legitimate traffic even under attack conditions*

These goals can be achieved using a *dynamic*, *proactive*, and *data-driven* approach for providing security and efficient of such network information systems. In this regard the primary focus of this research is to provide *real-time* and *efficient* network defense system operation and optimization to achieve the above goals. Furthermore, the proposed design framework also aims to offer flexibility to include new approaches, and would aid the ability of various networked systems to migrate or deploy additional entities for detection of the various dynamic network situations and providing mechanisms for their real-time defense. To summarize, this research presents a novel idea of dynamic packet filtering firewall optimization to increase efficiency and security of current network systems. The dynamic design aspects presented in the automated tool (*PITWALL*) aids to inform administrators of the current network situation and hence helps maintain the security of the *Tier-1 ISP* network.

BACKGROUND AND RELATED WORK

Intrusion Detection Systems are becoming ubiquitous and indispensable to the efficient operation and survival of network information systems. Analysis of real configuration data has shown that current enterprise network systems are often enforcing policies that are incoherent and violate the established security guidelines. Furthermore, due the huge volume of traffic and the scalability and complexity of the current *Internet* there is a need to deal with large set of diverse security policies, which in turn imposes additional burden on *IDSs*, thereby rendering the performance of these

network devices highly critical to enforcing the efficiency, reliability and security of these systems. In this context, the *protection* that these devices provide becomes as good as, not only the policies it is configured to implement, but also equally importantly the *speed* at which it enforces these policies. Under attack or heavy load conditions, these subsequently become the bottleneck for the operation of such network information systems.

As the network size, bandwidth, and processing power of networked hosts continue to increase; there is a high demand for optimizing network defense system operations for improved performance. The efficiency of these systems in protecting the infrastructure, however, depends not only on the integrity and coherence of the security policies they are configured to implement, but equally importantly on the speed at which these policies are enforced. In this regard, the *optimization* of these systems, however, remains a challenge for enterprise network designers and system administrators.

Due to the enormous impact of *IDSs* on network security, there has been a significant amount of research work on how to *optimize* these systems. Recent researchers in both industry and academia have focused extensively on the problem of packet classification and optimization, though it still remains an evolving problem. With the growth and changing needs of security threats and services, the security policies are larger and more and more complex. This increased complexity and size impose challenges to hardware-based solutions and drive the design of software solutions. Current packet classification solutions aimed at improving the matching time of filters include *hardware based, geometric based, specialized data structure based* or other *heuristics* and *statistical* solutions.

Hardware-based packet classification solutions using the concept of *Context Addressable Memory (CAM)* exploit the notion of parallelism in hardware to speed of the rate of packet matching. These solutions are limited to small sized policy sets due to cost, power and size limitations of the

CAMs. There are other hardware-based solutions described in (McAulay et al 1993), but all of the solutions are limited to number of policies. The policy structures the rules as a *trie*, with the classification time as $O(B)$, where B is the total number of bits in all dimensions. The value of B can be very large as the bits and dimensions in the *tuples* increase.

The *Aggregated Bit Vector (ABV)* approach (Baboescu et al 2001) helps to solve the problem with d independent lookups on one dimension followed by a merging phase. Lookups are performed for each dimension and then the final rule list is computed by finding rules with highest priority. The memory consumed for storing the rules is extremely large and hence a compressed bit vector is used instead. The approach presented in (Srinivasan et al 1999) builds a table of all possible field value combinations and pre-computes the earliest rule matching each cross product. Search is conducted by separate lookups on each field. The results are then combined into a cross-product table followed by indexing into the table. The limitation of this approach is that the cross-product table grows significantly with the number of rules. There have been other similar hardware based solutions over the years but all of them lack the ability to handle (with real time guarantees) large policy sets (~1,000,000) due to memory size, power and cost limitations.

Another research direction to address the above problem is to search for a geometric based solution. The authors in (Feldmann et al 2000) proposed a geometric based solution and introduced a data structure called *Fat Inverted Segment (FIS) Tree*. *FIS* partitions the first dimension with the endpoints of the projection of the rules on that dimension. Each of the segments is then partitioned, according to the remaining dimensions of the rules covering each segment, into a number of d dimensional regions. To curb the storage requirement of such a structure, d dimensional regions are linked in a *FIS Tree* of bounded depth, and the common partitions of the regions are pushed up in

the tree. The proposed solution scales better than others, but still cannot meet the *tuple* sizes for large Tier-1 ISPs. Another geometrical based solution, the Decision-tree based algorithm was introduced by (Woo et al 2000), (Gupta et al August, 1999), (Gupta et al October, 1999) builds a decision tree using local optimizations at each intermediate node to choose the next bit to test. Additionally, (Woo et al 2000) uses multiple decision trees that help to reduce storage with increase in search time. Similarly, (Gupta et al August, 1999) uses range checks instead of bit checks at each node of the decision tree to advance the search for a packet match.

Researchers have also proposed various specialized data structures to enable fast packet classification. The authors in (Srinivasan et al 1999) build a table of all possible field value combinations and pre-compute the earliest rule matching each of them. Performing separate lookups on each field and then combining the results into a combination table followed by indexing into the table accelerates the search. However, the approach does not scale to large number of rules. Furthermore, numerous heuristic approaches have also been researched to aid fast packet classification. The *Recursive Flow Classification (RFC)* (Gupta et al 2001) approach pipelines various packet-matching stages to achieve high throughput for hardware-based implementations. Although all the above research contributes to fast packet filtering, they only focus on improving the worst-case (not the average case) matching time for packet filters. In addition, they exhibit high space complexity, which limits their practical deployment in large Tier-1 ISPs.

In (Gupta et al 2000) the authors introduced a statistical data structures in optimizing packet filtering. They used depth-constrained alphabetic trees to reduce lookup time of destination IP addresses of packets against entries in the routing table. The authors demonstrate that statistical data structures can be used to improve the average-case lookup time for packet filters. The work focuses on only single dimensional filters and does not consider any traffic dynamics in rule-set building or real time operation of packet filters. The work in (Qian et al 2001) presents algorithms to optimize filtering policies by aggregating adjacent rules and eliminating redundant ones to reduce the size of the rule list. However, the work did not consider traffic information in its optimization approach.

Most of the current research in IDS optimization has been in the area of firewall policy modeling and optimization (Gupta et al August, 1999, Gupta et al October, 1999, Fulp 2005, Fulp 2006, Qui et al 2001, Singh et al 2003, Eronen et al 2001, Hinrichs 2005, Tarsa et al 2005). Very few attempts have been made to achieve multi-dimensional firewall (Firewall Computing 2011) optimization. In (Al-Shaer et al 2004), a tool to model firewall policies and detect conflicts is described. In this work, the authors focus mainly on single attribute rules. Similarly, (Eronen et al 2001) describes a constraint logic-programming (CLP) framework to analyze rule-sets. In recent years various tools to model firewall policies and detect conflicts have been introduced. Though these related studies offer a good insight in how to model and analyze rule-sets, none of these approaches, however, considers optimizing a multi-dimensional rule-set.

The approach proposed in (Fulp 2005) optimizes the firewall rule-set using *Directed Acyclic Graphs (DAGs)* to describe rule dependencies. However, it does not provide a methodology to build the DAG, specifically for complex graph structures. The approach proposed in this research removes all the dependencies and hence it becomes possible to achieve optimum rule ordering. In (Qian et al 2001), a framework to analyze and optimize policy sets is described. However, the authors do not provide specific details on how optimization can be achieved within the proposed framework. Furthermore, this work does not consider the traffic characteristics in its optimization approach. In this research we design tools and approaches to optimize IDS policy sets that differs

from literature, in its unique approach to consider network traffic characteristics in optimizing the security policy sets and hence provide awareness to the relevant network information systems.

Recently there has been great attention to address traffic-aware IDS optimization. Some efforts in rule reordering using traffic specifications as in (El-Atawy et al 2007), (Hamed et al March 2006), (Hamed et al April, 2006) have been proposed. But these approaches consider a very small firewall policy set (~200) in comparison to realistic *Tier-1* ISP firewall policy sets (~1,000,000 policies). The current approaches also lack complete rule reordering due to existing dependencies in the policy sets. Furthermore, in these approaches all traffic characterizations are not considered for firewall optimization. All these previous efforts suggest the lack of and need for dynamic, global optimization tools and approaches towards achieving next generation Internet security.

The design and deployment of the decentralized packet-filtering framework requires the understanding of the various types of distributed attacks in the current networked systems. In the following we present a brief background of attacks (CERT 2011), (Mirkovic et al 2004), (Douligeris et al 2004). The primary reason behind such attacks over the Internet is its design solely for functionality and not security. Security, especially in today's data driven networks is a highly interdependent concept; the resources are limited and the intelligence is not collocated. Additionally the distributed nature and the absence of common policies over the *Internet* make it susceptible to various kinds of attacks. A typical distributed attack starts when the attacker *recruits* multiple slave machines by infecting them with attack code. These slave machines typically launch attacks on behalf of the attacker with a spoofed source address. The goal of attacker is to inflict damage on the victim either for personal reasons, material gain or for popularity.

Distributed attacks are classified either based on the means used to prepare and perform the attack, the characteristics of the attack itself, and the effect it has on the victim. In the classification based on the *Degree of Automation* the attacker needs to locate prospective agent machines and infect them with the attack code. These attacks are classified as *manual, semi-automatic* or *automatic attacks*. Current distributed attacks are either *semi-automatic* or *automatic*. In the *semi-automatic* attacks the nodes are infected using automated scripts but then the attacker manually issues commands for the actual attack (with direct and indirect communication *e.g.* usage of IRC channels for agent/handler communication) and automatic attacks. Attack phase is also automated, thus avoiding the need for communication between the attacker and the agent machines. *Automatic* distributed attacks automate the attack phase. They avoid communication between the attacker and the agent machines. All operations of the attack are preprogrammed in the attack code.

The agent machines in the *semi-automatic* and *automatic* attacks deploy various scanning and propagation techniques. The scanning can be *random scanning* (e.g. *Code Red*), *hit list scanning*, *topological scanning*, *permutation scanning*, and *local subnet scanning*. In *random scanning* the compromised host probes random addresses in the IP address space, using a different speed. The scanning in *hotlist scanning* is performed based on an externally provide list. This technique is very powerful as there are no collisions during the scanning phase. *Topological scanning* employs information on the compromised host to select new targets. Email worms follow topological scanning technique. In *Permutation scanning* all the compromised machines share a common pseudo-random permutation of the IP address space, where each IP address is mapped to an index in this permutation. *Local subnet scanning* preferentially scans for targets that reside on the same subnet as of the compromised host. *Code Red II* and *Nimda Worm* are examples of *Local subnet scanning* attacks.

Another classification of distributed attacks is based on the target of vulnerability during the attack. These attack classifications of *Exploited Vulnerability* include those that are *Protocol* and the *Brute-force attacks*. Protocol attacks exploit a single or multiple feature of any protocol. *TCP SYN attack, CGI request attack* and *Authentication server attack* are examples of *Protocol attacks*. *Brute-force attacks* are achieved by initiating a vast amount of seemingly legitimate transactions. This exhausts the victims network resources. *Brute-force attacks* are classified as either *Filterable* or *Non-filterable* attacks. Attacks that employ packets for non-critical services of the victim's operation and can be filtered by a firewall belong to the category of *Filterable attacks*. *UDP flood attack* and *ICMP request flood attack* on a Web server are *Filterable attacks*. Attacks requesting legitimate services from the victim constitute *Non-filterable attacks*. Example of *Non-filterable attacks* is a *HTTP request flood* targeting a Web server or a DNS request flood targeting a name server.

One other classification of distributed attack is based on the *Attack Rate Dynamics*. The attacks in this classification include those that are either *Continuous rate attacks* or *Variable rate attacks*. Most attacks employ continuous rate mechanisms. The rate of change of attacks can be either *increasing rate* or *fluctuating rate*. The final category of classification of distributed attacks is based on the impact of the attack. *Impact attacks* can be classified either as *Disruptive attacks* or *Degrading attacks*. In the *Disruptive attack* case the attacker completely denies the victim's service to its clients. Most distributed attacks are disruptive in nature. *Degradation attacks* as the name implies attack only a portion of the victim's resources. Due to its extent of disruption there attacks remain undetected for a significant period of time.

To counter these attacks there are various defense mechanism proposed in the current literature. The distributed defense mechanisms are classified either based on the *activity level* or on the location of deployment. Activity level defense mechanisms are either *Preventive* or *Reactive* in nature. *Preventive* mechanisms work by either mitigating the attack while maintaining desired availability to the legitimate clients or by completely eliminating the attack. These include resource accounting and resource multiplication mechanisms. *Preventive attacks* are classified as *attack prevention* and *denial of service prevention* mechanisms.

In *attack prevention* the system configuration is modified to eliminate the possibility of attack. In *denial of service* prevention the victim endures the attack while servicing the legitimate clients. Contrary to *Preventive* mechanisms, *Reactive* mechanisms include mechanisms where the goal is to detect as quickly as possible and have a low degree of false positives. *Reactive* mechanisms are classified based on their attack detection strategy to those of *Pattern detection, Anomaly detection* and *Hybrid detection*. In *Pattern detection* the known attack signatures are stored in a database. Periodic comparison against a normal behavior model is the basis of *Anomaly detection*. Challenges in this detection strategy include threshold setting and model update. *Hybrid detection* uses a combination of the above two defense mechanisms.

Defense mechanisms of *location of deployment* are categorized based on the location as *Victim-Network, Intermediate-Network* or *Source-Network mechanisms*. *Victim-Network* mechanisms protect the victim against distributed attacks. *Intermediate-Network* mechanisms provide support mechanisms and service numerous Internet hosts. In the *Source-Network* mechanism, clients using the network monitor the source network to prevent service abuse. These attack and defense classification helps to understand the impact of distributed attacks and provide motivation towards the design of dynamic defense network systems.

We have discussed the background and related research in the area of packet classification and optimization. The large size of the policy sets and the complexity due to the varied services imposes tough challenges to non-linear multi-dimensional firewall optimization. The current solutions lack in providing a realistic solution for large security policy sets, as in large *Tier-1* enterprise networks. Our goal is the design of *dynamic* and *adaptive* optimization techniques that detect and mitigate attacks in *real-time*. To this effect this research proposes fundamental approaches and tools aimed at network security policy optimization and mitigation of anomalies to provide security and efficiency of network information systems.

PROBLEM AND CHALLENGES

The constantly changing nature, scale and scope of information technology environments, coupled with the increasing number and complexity of security threats, is forcing *Tier-1* enterprise networks to resort to increasingly complex security policies and mechanisms. In this regard, *Tier-1* ISP networks employ *IDSs* as network defense systems to monitor and regulate traffic. The efficiency of such network systems in protecting the infrastructure, however, depends not only on the integrity and coherence of the security policies they are configured to implement, but equally importantly on the speed at which these policies are enforced. With the dynamic change in the network load, topology, and bandwidth demand, these network defense systems are becoming a bottleneck to the operation and efficient functioning of these information systems. All these factors create a demand for more efficient, highly available, and reliable network defense mechanism and approaches. Optimization of such network defense systems, however, remains a challenge for network designers and administrators.

Conventional network defense technology of the Internet is *static*, *perimeter based* and *oblivious* to traffic dynamics in the network. With the advent of gigabyte and terabyte networks, the above model of security has been a major hindrance to providing security and performance of such networked systems. Hence, as a whole security in such network defense systems remains a major issue primarily due to the:

- *Lack of dynamics in the design of these network detection and mitigation systems,*
- *Lack of adaptation of such network defense systems, &*
- *Classical perimeter based model towards intrusion detection and mitigation*

Thus, the objective of this research is to address the above shortcomings and develop a sound and effective framework to accelerate the operations of such network defense systems and *adapt* its performance to the dynamically changing network traffic characteristics. This enables network administrators to obtain an *real-time* view of the traffic and react appropriately to the dynamism and complexity of these network information systems.

Achieving this goal however is challenging, primarily due to the large number of security policies enforced by the *Tier-1* enterprise networks. In addition, there is a need for maintaining high policy integration. This is further compounded by the limited resources of such network defense systems relative to the increased ability of the network to process and forward traffic at extremely high speed. Thus, the complexity of packet filtering along with providing content-based services for such scalable network systems, under the constantly changing and evolving network dynamics makes network defense system optimization a challenging problem. Along with this, maintaining the availability of these network defense agents (core routers or firewall servers), while meeting real time requirements, is a daunting task. This research proposes to address these challenges by presenting an improved way to search, update and filter a large set of data based on specific policies to optimize and provide better strategies to defend against Internet attacks.

The goal is the design of an *adaptive* (*traffic-aware*) and *scalable, global* defense framework to provide network security. This research offers significant contribution in terms of *adaptation, speed of operation* (under attack/heavily loaded conditions) and overall *operational cost-effectiveness* of such network systems. The tool and approaches proposed also aims to offer the flexibility to include new approaches, and provide the ability to migrate or deploy additional entities for attack detection and defense.

The research addresses the problem of network defense system optimization by focusing both on *policy (rule-set) based*, as well as *network traffic based* optimizations and discuss mechanisms to integrate it into a novel accelerating automated toolkit, *PITWALL*. We also introduce a novel adaptive anomaly detection/countermeasure mechanism to deal with short term and long-term anomalies for such network systems. The basic tenet of this framework is that the design of next generation IDSs must leverage their packet inspection capabilities with traffic awareness in order to optimize the operational cost they incur in defending against intrusions and attacks. The performance of the firewall optimization approaches both for worst case and normal operation of the firewall is studied. Evaluation study demonstrates that the proposed toolset leads to reduce operational cost of a typical *Tier-1* ISP enterprise network. The research findings will significantly impact the design, operation and management of secure and reliable *Next-Generation* network information systems.

PITWALL

This section introduces the network defense optimization toolset: *PITWALL*. The research aims at understanding the problem and challenges towards firewall optimization via an in-depth study of IDS policy sets (packet filtering firewall rule sets) and daily traffic logs obtained from a large *Tier-1 ISP network*. The analysis helps to understand the problem of network defense system optimization and lays the foundation towards the design of efficient approaches for managing and optimizing these network defense systems. We first discuss the policy representation and data set from the representative *Tier-1* ISP network and present details on *list-based* firewall representation. We then introduce the optimization tool: *PITWALL*, present the cost metrics and finally discuss the evaluation results from the *Tier-1* ISP network data set.

Firewall Policy Representation

To motivate the importance of considering traffic characteristics in firewall optimization, we have analyzed the firewall data set and traffic log information from a real world scenario (Acharya et al April 2006). The data set used in the study is obtained from list-based firewalls managed by a large *Tier-1 ISP* for its partner networks. The *Tier-1 ISP* provides secure access to and from about *300* business partners. The data set consists of two parts; the firewall policy-sets and the traffic logs. We have obtained firewall data from six firewalls of the *Tier-1 ISP*. The analysis is conducted on all six firewalls. All the other five firewalls follow the similar trends.

Firewall security policies for an organization are expressed in the form of a policy representation set. This representation governs the manner in which rules are invoked during firewall operation. There are various policy representations, namely- *trie-based*, *tree-based*, *direct-acyclic graph (DAG) based*, and *list-based*. The *trie-based* policy representation is structured as an *n-ary* (where *n* is the number of rules in the security policy set) retrieval tree with *k* levels, also referred to as the *trie*. Each level corresponds to a network attribute and the nodes in the *trie* store the actual value of the security policy. In the *tree-based* policy representa-

tion the rules are structured as a single rooted tree. Each node of the tree represents a network field, and each branch at this node represents a possible value of the associated field. A tree path starting at the root and ending at the leaf node defines a rule. Rules that have similar network field value at any given node share the same branch representing that value. As the name suggests in the *DAG* based policy representation the rule-set is modeled as a *DAG*, in which the vertices are firewall rules and edges indicate precedence relationships. A rule is modeled as an ordered *tuple* of sets; the order is necessary to maintain the predefined semantic order of the original policy set. In the *list-based* policy representation the security policies are in the form of a list and the network packets for filtering traverse sequentially through the list. The focus of this research is the list-based firewall representation (most of the ISPs at its core are list-based representations).

Firewall Data

The *Tier-1 ISP* firewall data consists of *firewall rule-set* and *firewall traffic log* information. The ISP provides service to 300 customer or business partner networks. Partner network services are disjoint from one another. The security policies detailing a partner network security requirements are represented in the form of a *block*. The firewall rule-set consists of a number of *blocks*, each *block* corresponding to a customer network, as depicted in *Figure 1*. The security policies within *blocks* are disjoint from one another. Each *block* consists of a set of multi-dimensional security policies called the *rules,* as illustrated in *Figure 2*. A typical block consists of several thousand rules. Each rule is a multi-dimensional structure of *tuples*. A typical rule on average consists of more than a million *tuples*. The numbers of tuples indicate the strength of the data set under consideration.

Figure 3 shows an instance of a rule structure. The multidimensional structure of the rule include the source address: *src*, the destination address:

Figure 1. Firewall structure

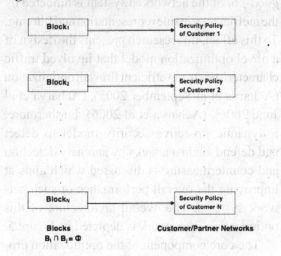

Figure 2. Block structure

Figure 3. Rule structure

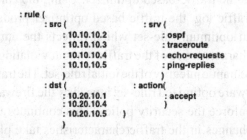

dst, the service type: *srv*, and the *action* field. The *action* can take values as *accept*, *drop* or *forward*. It is important to note that each dimension contains multiple values. Each such instance of the firewall rule is a *tuple*. We define *tuple* as the fundamental unit of packet filtering of the firewall. A typical *tuple* instance of a rule is represented as the following:

<src:10.10.10.2; dst: 10.20.10.1; srv: ospf; action: accept>.

The *Tier-1 ISP* firewall data also consists of the *firewall traffic log* information. *Figure 4* depicts an entry of the firewall traffic log. The firewall traffic log information is reported on every action of the firewall. Rule traffic is logged once per entry for every action per session of firewall operation. *Firewall traffic log* includes various packet log information such as the date and time the packet was filtered by the firewall rule, the *action* taken on the packet (either *accept*, *drop* or *forward*), the source and destination *ip address*, *protocol type*, *service type*, *port number*, *etc*. We conduct detailed analysis on the firewall rule-set and traffic log to understand the manageability and performance of the Tier-1 ISP firewall. The goal of all data analysis and optimizations is aimed at improving the *operational cost* (*average processing time*) of the *tuples* for the given firewall rule-set.

List Based Firewalls

This research concentrates on "*List based*" firewalls, one of the widely used firewalls for most large *Tier-1 ISPs*. *List-based* firewall structures rules and policies in a *priority* list. The list contains the security policies that govern the network packet filtering process in the operation of the firewall. The set of rules in the firewall set are referred to as the firewall *rule-set*. The priority of a rule or a policy in the firewall *rule-set* is based on its position in the list. Earlier occurring rules have higher priority than later ones and are enforced first. Subsequently, the packet is filtered by the earliest rule or policy that matches the filter definition – this is referred to as the *first hit principle*. In the following we present the *list-based* policy representation, which is the focus of this research work.

A firewall security is typically defined by a set of rules or filters. A firewall rule is a multidimensional structure, where each dimension is either a set of network fields or an action field. A network field can be *source address*, a *destination*

Figure 4. Traffic log instance

```
num;date;time;orig;type;action;alert;i/f_name;i/f_dir;
product;src;dst;s_port;service;proto;....................

1;27Jul2005;23:59:04;10.10.10.1;log;accept;;qfe1;
inbound;X;10.30.10.1;10.20.10.1;53480;161;udp;;;
```

address, a *service type*, a *protocol number* or a *port number*. An action field can be either *accept* or *deny*, or *others* (e.g. redirect to a server that perform further processes etc). Formally, a rule R can be represented as $R=[\Phi^1, \Phi^2,..., \Phi^k; \Sigma]$ where Φ^j represents network fields and $\sum$ is an action field. In an Internet environment, a typical rule can be represented as follows:

$$<src=\{s_1,s_2,...,s_n\};dst=\{d_1,d_2,...,d_m\};$$

$$srv=\{\sigma_1, \sigma_2,..., \sigma_l\}; action=\{drop\}>,$$

where s_i represents a source IP address, d_i represents the destination IP address, and σ_i a service type. In list-based firewalls, rules describing the network security policies form a *"priority"* list. The priority of a rule, also referred to as its *rank*, is based on its position within the list. Earlier occurring rules have higher rank than later ones. *List-based firewalls* work by logically examining the rules in sequential order. For each packet, the first matching rule determines the action taken by the firewall.

Firewall Optimization Model

Firewall policies of an actively managed enterprise network may often change in response to new services, new threats or when the underlying network changes. The intrinsic complexity of the firewall policies makes it difficult to track down these changes. As a consequence, inefficiency, such as redundancies between rules, and suboptimal representations of rule-sets and fields within a rule, arise. Furthermore, the *availability* and

good-put of the networked system is hindered by the inefficiency in rule representation and filtering. To this effect, this research presents the design of a novel optimization model that involved traffic characteristics to aid efficient firewall optimization (Acharya et al September 2005), (Acharya et al June 2006), (Acharya et al 2006). Furthermore, a dynamic proactive security model to detect and defend against attacks by anomaly detection and countermeasure is discussed which aims at improving the overall performance of such network systems. The overall architecture of this optimization framework is depicted in *Figure 5*.

The core component of the optimization process uses a *"rule-set based"* optimizer and a *"traffic based"* optimizer. Both optimizers cooperate to adaptively optimize the rule-set in response to dynamically changing traffic characteristics. This cooperation is achieved through a dynamic feedback mechanism.

The rule-set based optimizer takes as input the pre-optimized rule-set and produces a rule-set based optimized set of rules. This set is then fed to the traffic-based optimizer. Using the current traffic log, the traffic based optimizer produces an optimum rule-set which reflects the current characteristics of the traffic without violating the semantic integrity of the initial rule-set. The traffic-aware optimized rule-set is used by the firewall to enforce the security policy. This continues until changes in the traffic characteristics take place. In response to these changes, the adaptive optimization process is re-invoked using the current rule-set and a new traffic-aware optimized rule-set is produced. This process continues iteratively, until the enterprise network security administrator changes the rule-set. When this occurs, the new rule-set is pre-optimized before the rule-based and traffic-based optimizers are invoked.

Figure 5. Firewall optimization framework

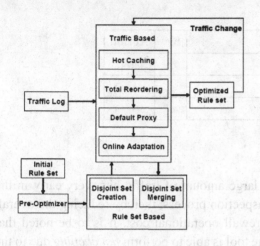

STAGE 1: PRE-OPTIMIZATION

The process starts with the *Pre-optimization* phase. The main objective of this phase is to remove all redundancies in the rule-set. At the end of this phase, all internal and external redundancies in the rule-set are removed. The details of rule redundancies with examples from firewall rule filters.

STAGE 2: RULE-SET BASED OPTIMIZATION

The rule-set based optimizer operates exclusively on the rule-set, with no additional consideration of other factors impacting network or traffic behavior. The optimizer continuously seeks to create new definitions in order to make rules in the current rule-set disjoint. This, in turn, provides the traffic-based optimizer with full flexibility to reorder rules based on traffic characteristics.

The rule-set based optimizer is composed of two basic components, namely the *Disjoint Set Creator (DSC)* and the *Disjoint Set Merger (DSM)*. These two components are typically executed sequentially. Initially *DSC* detects and removes dependencies from the current rule-set. Then it creates new rule definitions in order to make the

entire rule-set disjoint. It is to be noted that this phase may lead to an increase in the rule-set size. This is due to the fact that more rules may be needed to define each set of dependent rules. It is typical that there is only a small portion of rules that are dependent on other rules. In the analyzed firewall data set, this ratio is around $1/15^{th}$ of the total number of rules.

The main task of *DSM* is to merge the rules of the disjoint rule-set produced by *DSC* in order to optimize the rule-set representation. The merging process iteratively selects one rule and tries to merge it with other rules. Merging occurs between rules with same action field, to preserve semantic integrity. Merging between two rules, with respect to a specific different field, occurs when the other corresponding field values are same in the field space. Upon completion of this optimization step, the rule-set size is reduced to its most concise representation.

Notice that it is possible to reduce the rule-set based optimization strategy to rule merging only, without the creation of disjoint rules. Such an approach still results in improved rule-set representation, while minimizing the processing overhead. Combining disjoint set creation and merging, however, enables the optimizer to effectively capture the dynamics of the traffic characteristics, thereby resulting in an optimized rule-set representation. It is important to note that *DSC* enables full flexibility of rule reordering during online adaptation based on the dynamics nature of the incoming traffic to the firewall. As we will discuss in later making the rules disjoint from one another also aids de-centralized firewall optimization. To illustrate the process of creation of disjoint rules out of an initial pre-optimized set of rules, and merge the resulting disjoint rules into a concise rule-set representation, consider the example of a pre-optimized rule-set, S_I, as shown in *Table 1*.

Notice that R_2 is dependent on R_1, since the source and destination fields of R_2 intersect with the corresponding fields of R_1, while the action

Table 1. Pre-optimized rule-set: S_I

Rule	Src	Dst	Srv	Action
R_1	s_1, s_2, s_3	d_1, d_2, d_3	σ_1	drop
R_2	s_2, s_3, s_4	d_2, d_3, d_4	σ_1	accept
R_3	s_5	d_4	σ_1	accept

fields of the two rules are different. These rules can be made disjoint, without violating semantic integrity. This is achieved by keeping R_1 unchanged and forking R_2 into two new rules, R^1_2 and R^2_2, resulting in the disjoint rule-set, S_D, as shown in *Table 2*. As observed from the above example, creating new disjoint rule-set increases the size of the original rule-set. The new set size can be further optimized by merging rule R^2_2 and R_3 into R_4, to produce the final rule-set, S_F, as shown in *Table 3*.

STAGE 3: TRAFFIC BASED OPTIMIZATION

The traffic-based optimizer operates on the rule-set produced by the rule-set based optimizer. The optimizer uses current traffic characteristics to determine the order in which rules in the rule-set are to be invoked to optimize the operational cost of the firewall. To achieve this goal, we have designed four schemes, namely *hot caching*, *total reordering*, *default proxy*, and *online adaptation*.

Hot Caching

Hot caching revolves around the concept of a *hot rule-set*. A rule is said to be *hot* if it experiences a large number of traffic hits. The basic idea of this approach is to identify a small set of very heavily used or *hot* rules, relative to the original rule-set, and cache these rules at the top of the rule-set. Such a strategy results in dealing with

a large amount of traffic hits, very early in the inspection process, thereby reducing the overall firewall operational cost. It is to be noted that the tool is able to perform *hot caching* due to the removal of dependencies amongst the rules during *Disjoint Set Creator*. This scheme is supported by the fact that in such network systems 80% of the traffic is filtered by 20% of the rules.

Total Reordering

Contrary to the first scheme which focuses only on a small set of rules, the *total reordering* scheme takes a more aggressive approach and performs a total reordering of the rule-set based on the current traffic characteristics. This *reordering* is achieved based on a priority assignment, which takes into consideration, not only the frequency at which the rule is invoked, but equally importantly the rule size. More specifically, the priority of rule, R_i, can be expressed as: $Pr(R_i) = hit\ count(R_i) / size(R_i)$. Notice that ordering firewall rules based on the above priority assignment achieves the lowest expected cost.

Default Proxy

The *default proxy* is the third scheme and is based on the observation that, during traffic inspection, the default deny action is heavily invoked, in comparison to actions resulting from other rules. In a list-based firewall, the default deny action is "enforced" when a packet fails to match any of the rules within a rule-set. Relatively high hit ratios

Table 2. Disjoint rule-set: S_D

Rule	Src	Dst	Srv	Action
R_1	s_1, s_2, s_3	d_1, d_2, d_3	σ_1	drop
R_2^1	s_4	d_2, d_3, d_4	σ_1	accept
R_2^2	s_2, s_3	d_4	σ_1	accept
R_3	s_5	d_4	σ_1	accept

of the default deny action is, therefore, bound to increase considerably the overall operational cost of the firewall. The main reason for this increase is that, before a default deny action is enforced and the packet is dropped, all rules in a rule-set have to be examined. This is mainly caused by the absence of any representation of the default deny action in the rule-set. This, in turn, suggests that the addition of drop rules may alleviate the problem. Adding drop rules, however, brings about several issues, including how may rules must be created, what values should be associated with these new reject rules and what should be their priorities. The *default proxy* scheme addresses these issues by creating a set of reject rules. The field values of these rules are derived from the corresponding fields of the packets dropped by the default deny action. Initially, the fields of a reject rule are set to *any*, except for the action field, which is set to *drop*. The reject rule can be represented as:

$$<\Phi^1 : any; \ \Phi^2 : any; \ \cdots, \Phi_n : any; \ action = drop>$$

As packets are dropped by default deny rule, the values of the reject rule are set to the values of corresponding fields of the dropped packets. This corresponds to the hit rate of the reject rule. The priority of each newly created reject rule is computed based on its hit rate and size similar to the process as in total reordering.

Online Adaptation

This optimization is a proactive security measure to improve the availability of firewalls under dynamically changing network environment. The *online adaptation* scheme encompasses two basic mechanisms: *profile based reordering* and *anomaly detection and countermeasure. Profile based reordering* uses traffic characteristics to build a long-term rule hit profile during offline operation. The approach used to build this profile

Table 3. Final rule-set: S_F

Rule	Src	Dst	Srv	Action
R_1	s_1, s_2, s_3	d_1, d_2, d_3	σ_1	drop
R_2^1	s_4	d_2, d_3, d_4	σ_1	accept
R_4	s_2, s_3, s_5	d_4	σ_1	accept

exploits traffic variability. The resulting rule hit profile is then used to detect long and short-term anomalies and adapt the rule-set accordingly during online operation of the firewall. The basic idea of *Anomaly detection and countermeasure* is to compare the short-term traffic pattern with a long-term established traffic profile. The later is used to optimize the firewall rules. If a significant discrepancy exists between the short-term traffic pattern and long term profile, and this discrepancy can result in bad predicted performance, the rules are adjusted as a countermeasure against anomalies. Adjusting the rules entails rule reordering and adding explicit reject rules.

Note that anomalies can be either *transient* or *long-lived*. If the anomaly analysis reveals a potential performance hazard, a temporary reordering of rules is performed. If a given anomaly occurs consistently then it is absorbed into the long-term offline profile. The same anomaly detection and countermeasure procedure is also applied to the default deny rule. Depending on any potential performance hazard created by a default deny rule, a temporary default deny rule is added to the short-term profile. If the pattern is repetitive then the new default deny rule is added to the rule-set based on its priority and hence absorbed into the long-term profile.

THEORY: RULE SIZE AND COST METRIC

The main factor that affects the performance of a firewall is the processing overhead due to packet inspection. The metric calculation is performed for a rule and can easily be applied to tuples within a rule.

We define two metrics to capture the overhead cost incurred by a firewall to process a rule and enforce the security policy. The first metric, denoted as *rule size()*, measures the size of a given rule in terms of the number of bits necessary to determine unambiguously a match between the rule definition and the corresponding fields of a packet under inspection. The assumption underlying the *rule size()* metric stems from the fact that the complexity of a matching operation is proportional to the size of the rule. Formally, given a rule r, rule size(r) can be defined as:

$$rule\_size(r) = \begin{cases} \Sigma s_p, \mathcal{D}_p \{\alpha_1 \times \|s_p\| + \alpha_2 \times \|d_p\|\} \\ + \beta \times N_s \times (\|Pr_r\| + \|Po_r\|), \end{cases}$$

Where α_1, α_2 and β *are* weight parameters, S_p and D_p are respectively the set of source and destination prefixes which occur within the definition of the rule, s_p and d_p are the bit representation of the source and destination prefixes, respectively, N_S is the number of services defined within the rule, and Pr_r and Po_r are the bit representation of the protocol and port identifiers, respectively. The second metric used in our experimentation is the cost of operating a given rule-set. This cost depends on the rule's rank and size, and on how often the rule is invoked by the firewall.

Formally, given a set of rules $r_1, r_2, \ldots, r_k$, the cost of a given rule, r_i, cost(r_i), is defined as follows:

$$cost(r_i) = hit\_count(r_i) \times \Sigma_{\forall r_k \in Pr_i} \|r_k\|$$

where, Pr_i is the set of r_i's predecessors in the list-based set of rules.

Using the above metrics, the aim of optimization is to reduce the rule-set size and consequently the processing time of the rule-set. This in turn reduces the overall firewall operational cost. The resources that affect are the CPU utilization and the memory usage of the firewall machine. In the following subsection we present the proof of the optimality of the metric *via* contradiction.

Theorem 1.1. *Firewall rules in a list-based ordering based on priority achieves the lowest expected cost.*

Proof. Assuming a rule-set in the order of r_1, $r_2, \ldots, r_n$ achieves the lowest expected cost and priority $(r_i) <$ *priority* (r_i+1), the total cost associated with this rule order is

$$Cost = \sum_{t=1}^{n} cost(r_t) = \sum_{t=1}^{n} f(r_t)\sum_{k=1}^{t} \| r_k \|$$

By swapping r_i and r_i+1, the new rule order has a lower cost. The function $f()$ defines the rule-hit frequency. This is proportional to the hit count of the rule. The rule-hit frequency is denoted by the function $f()$.

The total cost associated with the new rule order is

$$
\begin{aligned}
Cost' &= \sum_{t=1}^{i-1} cost(r_t) + cost(r_{i+1}) \\
&\quad + cost(r_i) + \sum_{t=i+2}^{n} cost(r_t) \\
&= \sum_{t=1}^{i-1} cost(r_t) + f(r_{i+1})(\sum_{k=1}^{i-1} \| r_k \| + \| r_{i+1} \|) \\
&\quad + f(r_i)(\sum_{k=1}^{i} \| r_k \| + \| r_{i+1} \|) + \sum_{t=i+2}^{n} cost(r_t) \\
&= Cost + f(r_i) \| r_{i+1} \| - f(r_{i+1}) \| r_i \|
\end{aligned}
$$

Since *priority* $(r_i) <$ *priority* (r_i+1), we have

$$\frac{f(r_i)}{\| r_i \|} < \frac{f(r_{i+1})}{\| r_{i+1} \|}$$
$$f(r_i) \| r_{i+1} \| < f(r_{i+1}) \| r_i \|$$
$$f(r_i) \| r_{i+1} \| - f(r_{i+1}) \| r_i \| < 0$$

Now the *Cost'* $<$ *Cost*, thus the new rule order has a lower cost than the earlier rule order. This contradicts our assumption that the first order is optimal. Since this is a contradiction, the theorem is hence proved.

EVALUATION

In this section we discuss the performance of *PIT-WALL* and the results of the evaluation study. The details of the metrics designed for the evaluation are presented in the following sections. In order to evaluate the impact of the various optimization strategies on the firewall performance, an experimental simulation-based study is conducted. The evaluation is performed on a large *Tier-1* ISP network on a *SunOS 5.8* over a *Sun-Fire-15000*. Results show that the optimization strategies lead to considerable network defense system performance improvement.

RULE-SET BASED OPTIMIZATION

The results depicted in *Figure 6* shows that the final rule-set size after optimization is similar to the size of the initial rule-set, but most importantly, the rules in the resulting rule-set are all *disjoint* from each other. Rule-set disjoincy helps to provide the network system administrator full flexibility to reorder the rules based on traffic characteristics, as is necessary to respond to the traffic dynamics in such network systems.

TRAFFIC BASED OPTIMIZATION

In this experiment, traffic based optimization are applied to the firewall rule-set. Results in *Figure 7* demonstrate a significant decrease in the number of rules. More specifically, the results show that nearly *20%* of initial operational rules are eliminated.

The final experiment is aimed at evaluating the impact of the various optimization strategies on the operational cost of firewalls. The results depicted in *Figure 8* indicate that the optimization strategies, applied to the pre-processed dataset, result in reducing the initial operational cost to around *6.3%*. The evaluation study clearly indicates that the proposed traffic-aware optimization strategies have great potential to significantly improve the performance of firewalls and reduce their operational cost. A more extensive analysis of the schemes and experimental results can be found.

Figure 6. Rule set based optimization: Size based

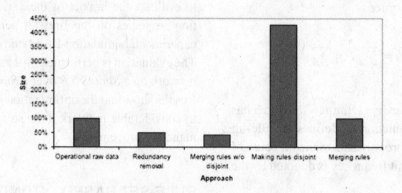

Furthermore, the study also confirms the importance of integrating traffic characteristics into the optimization process. Finally, it should be noted that adaptive anomaly detection is crucial in preventing and eliminating attacks, and avoiding bottlenecked firewalls. The proposed approaches help to maintain availability of network defense systems during critical conditions *(overload/attack)* to ensure the design of secure networks.

ONLINE ADAPTATION

In this section we detail the evaluation of the online adaptation module for the proposed Firewall Optimization approach.

Benefit/Cost Evaluation

It is important to estimate the *Benefit/Cost* ratio for invoking the online optimization module in *PITWALL*. This experiment evaluates the ratio for the *emulated* (*average*) case scenario. The firewall used for the experiment is open source *Linux* firewall (Linux IPChains 2011). The rule-set and traffic load for the evaluation is emulated rule-set and traffic log information from a large

Figure 7. Traffic based optimization: Size based

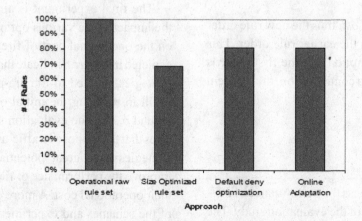

Figure 8. Traffic based optimization: Cost based

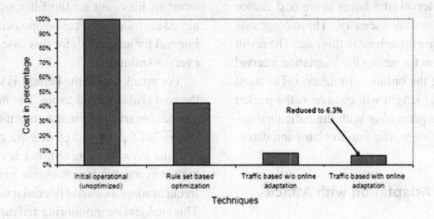

Tier-1 ISP. It is to be noted that this evaluation is workload dependent. The traffic load is at the rate of *7000* packets/sec. The results are validated over *20* runs of the experiment.

The results depicted in *Figure 9* demonstrate that an adaptation interval of *75* minutes is the most optimal (taking into account the benefit-cost ratio) for a typical packet filter set with the typical traffic load. If the network administrator wishes they could have a slightly higher cost and perform adaptation at fewer intervals (3 hours). Results will vary with the variation of filter sets and traffic characteristics. The evaluation acts as feedback to the network designer to prevent over

engineering the adaptation interval beyond the point of diminishing returns.

Determining Best Adaptation Interval

This evaluation is for the *emulated (average)* case scenario. The firewall used for the experiment is open source *Linux* firewall. The rule-set and traffic load for the evaluation is emulated rule-set and traffic log information from a large *Tier-1 ISP*. The traffic load is at the rate of *7000* packets/sec. The results are validated over *20* runs of the experiment. The result for the best adaptation interval depends on the workload under evaluation.

Figure 9. Online adaptation benefit/cost curve

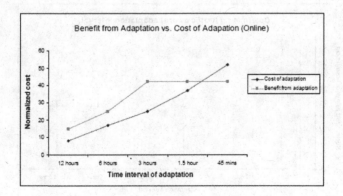

The results depicted in *Figure 10* show that an adaptation interval of *3* hours is the best choice for the above test case scenario. The average rule processing time is the least in this case. The result is an indication for setting the adaptation interval for executing the online optimization. The most suited interval length will change as the packet filter set changes and/or with dramatic changes in the in-coming traffic into the intrusion detection system.

Benefit of Adaptation with Attack Traffic

This evaluation is for the worst-case scenario of firewall operation. The firewall used for the experiment is the open source *Linux* firewall (Linux IPChains 2011). The rule-set considered for evaluation is the worst-case filter set. The traffic load is at the rate of *2000* packets/sec. The results are validated over *20* runs of the experiment. It is to be noted that the result depends on the workload under consideration.

For this evaluation an attack scenario on a single filter was designed by increasing its hit count step by step following an exponential path. The rule-set is also designed to fit the worst-case evaluations. The attack duration is *2* hours. The attack increased in intensity from *0-100-0* percent during the observed time period. The attack; in terms of hit count on the filter which attack is aimed at; followed a bell shaped curve. The best interval for adaptation for this case is a period of every *30* minutes.

For attack traffic the benefit is very high, but the cost is also considerable. The main aim in an attack scenario is to make sure there is *"availability"* of the networked defense system. In this case the network administrator is ready to pay a higher average rule-processing price by having frequent adaptations and finer adaptation intervals. This enables fine monitoring and rule switching in the rule-set to discard attack traffic at the earliest possible time. The evaluation study demonstrates for typical attack traffic the gain in rule processing time by performing the adaptations (including the cost of performing such adaptations) is more than *4* folds in comparison to the optimizer with no online adaptation. Along with this the firewall remains available and fully functional during the attack (in contrast to the firewall getting unavailable due to the attack).

Proportionality of Rule Processing Cost

The final evaluation is to study the variation of CPU utilization with the change in the network

Figure 10. Determining best adaptation interval

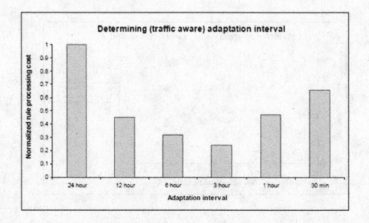

Figure 11. CPU utilization versus number of rules

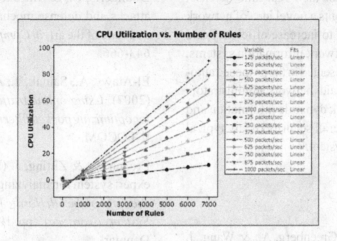

traffic load or changes in the number of rules in the firewall rule-set. This study helps to establish the relationship between the above stated entities. The firewall rule-set is from a large *Tier-1 ISP* and the traffic is emulated from traffic traces obtained from the *Tier-1 ISP*. The firewall used for our experimental study is the open source *Linux* firewall (Linux IPChains 2011). Results in *Figure 11* and *Figure 12* depict the proportionality relationship between CPU utilization verses number of rules or variation in traffic load. This evaluation concludes that the cost of rule processing is linearly proportional to the number of rules in the firewall rule-set.

Figure 12. CPU utilization versus load

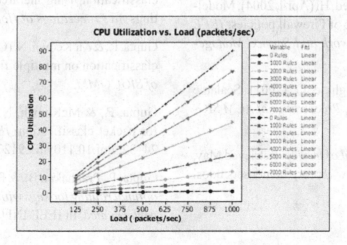

CONCLUSION

These goals this research is to present a *dynamic*, *proactive*, and *data-driven* approach for providing security and efficient of such network information systems. In this regard the primary focus is to provide *real-time* and *efficient* network defense system operation and optimization for today's data driven networks. The tool and proposed framework aims to offer flexibility to include new approaches as well as support legacy systems, and aids the ability of various networked systems to migrate and/or install additional entities for detection of the various dynamic network situations and providing mechanisms for their real-time defense. In summary, we presents a novel idea of network defense optimization to increase efficiency and security of current network information systems. The design aspects presented in the proposed automated tool: *PITWALL* aids network administrators gain *real-time* network dynamic information and hence ensures the overall security of any typical enterprise network system.

REFERENCES

Acharya, S., Ge, Z., Greenberg, A., & Wang, J. (2006). *Methods and apparatus for optimizing Firewalls*. US Patent Docket Number: 2005-0520.

Acharya, S., Wang, J., Ge, Z., Greenberg, A., & Znati, T. (April, 2006). *Simulation study of firewalls to improve performance*. In 39th Annual Simulation Symposium, Alabama, USA.

Acharya, S., Wang, J., Ge, Z., Znati, T., & Greenberg, A. (September, 2005). *Traffic-aware framework and optimization strategies for large-scale enterprise networks*, (pp. 1-20). Technical Report, University of Pittsburgh.

Acharya, S., Wang, J., Ge, Z., Znati, T., & Greenberg, A. (June, 2006). *Traffic-aware Firewall optimization strategies*. In IEEE International Conference on Communications, Istanbul, Turkey.

Al-Shaer, E., & Hamed, H. (April, 2004). Modeling and management of Firewall policies. *IEEE Transactions in Network and Service Management, 1*(1).

Baboescu, F., & Varghese, G. (2001). Scalable packet classification, *Proceedings of ACM SIGCOMM.*

CERT. (2011). *Denial of service*. Retrieved May, 2011, from http://www.cert.org/homeusers/ddos. html

Douligeris, C., & Mitrokotsa, A. (2004). DDoS attacks and defense mechanisms: Classification and state of the art, *in Computer Networks, 44*(5), 643-666.

El-Atawy, A., Samak, T., Al-Shaer, E., & Li, H. (2007). *Using online traffic statistical matching for optimizing packet-filtering performance*. IEEE INFOCOM.

Eronen, P., & Zitting, J. (November, 2001). An expert system for analyzing firewall rules. In *Proceedings of the 6th Nordic Workshop on Secure IT Systems (NordSec),* (pp. 100–107). Copenhagen, Denmark.

Feldmann, A., & Muthukrishnan, S. (March, 2000). *Tradeoffs of packet classification*. In IEEE INFOCOM.

Firewall Computing. (2011). *Wikipedia*. Retrieved May, 2011, from http://en.wikipedia.org/wiki/Firewall_computing

Fulp, E. (2005). Optimization of network firewalls policies using directed acyclic graphs. In *Proceedings of the IEEE Internet Management Conference.*

Fulp, E. (2006). *Parallel firewall designs for high-speed networks*. In IEEE INFOCOM High Speed Networking Workshop.

Gupta, P., & McKeown, N. (August, 1999). Packet classification using hierarchical intelligent cuttings. In *Proceedings of Hot Interconnects.*

Gupta, P., & McKeown, N. (October, 1999). Packet classification on multiple fields. In *Proceedings of SIGCOMM.*

Gupta, P., & McKeown, N. (2001). Algorithms for packet classification. *IEEE Network, 15*(2), 24–32. doi:10.1109/65.912717

Gupta, P., Prabhakar, B., & Boyd, S. (2000). *Near optimal routing lookups with bounded worst-case performance*. In IEEE INFOCOM.

Hamed, H., & Al-Shaer, E. (March, 2006). *Dynamic rule-ordering optimization for high-speed firewall filtering*. In ASIACCS.

Hamed, H., El-Atawy, A., & Al-Shaer, E. (April, 2006). *Adaptive statistical optimization techniques for firewall packet filtering*. In IEEE INFOCOM.

Hinrichs, S. (2005). Integrating changes to a hierarchical policy model. In *Proceedings of 9th IFIP/IEEE International Symposium on Integrated Network Management*, Nice, France.

Linux. (2011). *IPChains*. Retrieved May, 2011, from http://people.netfilter.org/rusty/ipchains

McAulay, A., & Francis, P. (1993). Fast routing tables lookup using cams. *Proceedings IEEE INFOCOM.*

Mirkovic, J., & Reiher, P. (2004). A taxonomy of DDoS attack and DDoS defense mechanisms. *Computer Communication Review, 34*(2), 39–52. doi:10.1145/997150.997156

Qian, J., Hinrichs, S., & Nahrstedt, K. (2001). ACLA: A framework for access control list (ACL) analysis and optimization. In *Proceedings of IFIP Conference on Communications and Multimedia Security.*

Qiu, L., Varghese, G., & Suri, S. (2001). Fast firewall implementations for software based and hardware-based routers. In *Proceedings of the ACM SIGMETRICS International Conference on Measurement and Modeling of Computer Systems*, (pp. 344–345). New York, NY: ACM Press.

Singh, S., Baboescu, F., Varghese, G., & Wang, J. (2003). *Packet classification using multidimensional cutting*. In ACM SIGCOMM.

Srinivasan, V., Suri, S., & Varghese, G. (1999). Packet classification using tuple space search. *In Proceedings of SIGCOMM*. ACM Press.

Srinivasan, V., & Varghese, G. (1999). Fast address lookups using controlled prefix expansion. *ACM Transactions on Computer Systems, 17*(1). doi:10.1145/296502.296503

Symantec. (2011). *Internet security report*. Retrieved May, 2011, from http://eval.symantec.com

Tarsa, S., & Fulp, E. (2005). Trie-based policy representations for network firewalls. In *Proceedings of the IEEE International Symposium on Computer Communications.*

Woo, T. (March, 2000). A modular approach to packet classification: Algorithms and results. *In Proceedings of IEEE INFOCOM.*

Xiang, Y., & Zhou, W. (October, 2005). Intelligent DDoS packet filtering in high-speed networks. *Lecture Notes in Computer Science,* vol. 3758. Berlin, Germany: Springer.

Zhao, X., & Sun, J. (November, 2003). A parallel scheme for IDS. *Proceedings of the Second Internatonal Conference on Machine Learning and Cybernetics.*

ADDITIONAL READING

Avizienis, A., Laprie, J., Randell, B., & Landwehr, C. (2004, January – March). Basic concepts and taxonomy of dependable and secure computing. *IEEE Transactions on Dependable and Secure Computing, Volume, 1*(Issue: 1), 11–33. doi:10.1109/TDSC.2004.2

Axelsson. S. (March, 2000). Intrusion detection systems: A survey and taxonomy. *In Technical Report 99-15-Chalmers University-Department of Computer Engineering, Goteburg, Sweden.*

Barey, M., & Johnson, D. (1978). *Computer and Intractability*. San Francisco: Freeman.

Brucker, P. (1997). On the complexity of clustering problems. In *Optimization and Operations Research* (pp. 45–54). Springer-Verlag.

Charikar, M., Guha, S., Tardos, E., & Shmoys, D. (1999). A constant-factor approximation algorithm for the k-median problem. *ACM Symposium on Theory of Computing.*

Checkpoint NGX firewall (2011). Accessed May, 2011, from http://www.checkpoint.com.

Chen, G., Nocetti, F., Gonzalez, J., & Stojmenovic, I. (2002). Connectivity-based-k-hop clustering in wireless networks. *In Proceedings of the 35th Annual Hawaii International Conference on System Sciences (HICSS 02), IEEE Computer Society.*

Dubendorfer, T., Wagner, A., & Plattner, B. (June, 2004). An economic damage model for large scale Internet attacks. *In Proceedings of the 13th International Workshop on Enabling Technologies.*

Estan, C., & Varghese, G. (2001). New directions in traffic measurement and accounting. *In ACM SIGCOMM Internet Measurement Workshop.*

Jariyakul, N., & Znati, T. (April, 2005). On the Internet delay-based clustering. *In Proceedings of the 38th Annual Simulation Symposium.*

Jariyakul, N., & Znati, T. (December, 2005). A clustering-based selective probing framework to support Internet quality of service routing. *Distributed Computing - IWDC, In Proceedings of the 7th International Workshop, Kharagpur, India.*

Lakshman, T., & Stidialis, D. (1998). High speed policy-based packet forwarding using efficient multi-dimensional range matching. *In Proceedings of SIGCOMM. ACM Press.*

Lemos, R. (2004). Msblast epidemic far larger than believed. Accessed May, 2011, from http://news.com/msblast.

Mirkovic, J., Prier, G., & Reiher, P. (November, 2002). Attacking DDoS at the source. *In Proceedings of ICNP.*

Moore, D., Paxson, V., Savage, S., Shannon, C., Staniford, S., & Weaver, N. (July, 2003). Inside the slammer worm. *In IEEE Security and Privacy.*

Noonan, W. & Dubrawsky, I. (June, 2006). Firewall Fundamentals: An introduction to network and computer firewall security.

Papadopoulos, C., Lindell, R., Mehringer, J., Hussain, A., & Govindan, R. (2003). Cossack: Coordinated suppression of simultaneous attacks. *In DARPA Information Survivability Conference and Exposition, Washington, DC.*

Roughan, M., Greenberg, A., Kalmanek, C., Rumsewicz, M., Yates, J., & Zhang, Y. (2002). Experience in measuring backbone traffic variability: Models, metrics, measurements and meaning. *In Proceedings of the 2nd ACM SIGCOMM Workshop on Internet Measurement, pages 91–92, New York, NY, USA. ACM Press.*

Symantec security response (2003). w32.blaster.worm. Accessed May, 2011, from http://security-response.symantec.com/avcenter/venc/data/w32.blaster.worm.html.

Symantec security response (2004). w32.sasser.worm. Accessed May, 2011, from http://security-response.symantec.com/avcenter/venc/data/w32.sasser.worm.html.

KEY TERMS AND DEFINITIONS

Firewalls: A technological barrier designed to prevent unauthorized or unwanted communications between computer networks or hosts.

Network Information Systems (NIS): An information system for managing networks.

Network Security: Consists of the provisions and polices adopted by the network administrators to prevent and monitor unauthorized access, misuse, modification, or denial of the computer network and network-accessible resources.

Operational-Cost: The cost in terms of resources (*e.g.* processing time) for execution or operation.

Optimization: Refers to the selection of a best element from some set of available alternatives.

Rule-Set: A set or group of firewall/IDS policies or filters.

Security Policy: Defines constraints on functions and flow among them, constraints on access by external systems and adversaries including programs and access to data.

Situational Awareness: The perception of environmental elements with respect to time and/or space, the comprehension of their meaning, and the projection of their status after some variable has changed, such as time (*e.g.* change in network dynamics over the Internet).

Survival Systems: Refers to systems those are able to remain in operation or exist in the event of failure.

Chapter 19
Forensic Investigative Process for Situational Awareness in Information Security

Khidir Mohamed Ali
Jubail University College, Saudi Arabia

Thomas John Owens
Brunel University, UK

ABSTRACT

As a starting point for the development of a common visualization of the forensics process by the members of an investigating team, this chapter provides algorithms that provide guidance and step by step instructions on how to deal with computer forensics and the investigations they carry out. A general introductory overview of computer forensics is provided, and the framework of a forensic investigation is summarized. On the basis of this framework, three algorithms are provided, one for each phase of a forensic investigation, which cover the different aspects of computer forensics and address key elements to be considered when attacked systems are investigated.

INTRODUCTION

Essential security features of Computer Network Defense Situational Awareness (SA) are integrity, forensics, availability, intelligence capability and confidentiality. One of the core objectives of Cyber-SA is to ensure the mission has the capability to carry out post incident analysis, investigation, and possesses forensic readiness capability. The aim of the mission to ensure it detects and stops potential security incidents, however, incidents do succeed and in such situations forensic readiness capabilities are required for situational awareness. Forensic analysis can ensure that the investigative team is aware of the nature of an incident. Lessons learned from analyzing the parts of the path of the attack vector can inform the strengthening of mission security (Onwubiko 2011). In seeking to discover additional evidence the investigative team may generate hypothetical

DOI: 10.4018/978-1-4666-0104-8.ch019

intrusion scenarios and try to fit them against discovered intrusion evidence. The results can be used to help the investigative team determine the origin and complete path of an attack vector, and ultimately lead to the discovery of additional evidence (Hawrylak et al 2011).

Visualization and collaboration are key enablers in the overall Cyber-SA command and control process (Ruiz and Redmond 2011). Therefore, they are essential for the effective working of an investigating team. However, a major issue in cyber security is the lack of shared mental models of the elements of the problem space of Cyber-SA. Different analysts often have different mental models of a problem because the "terrain" is virtual and because they possess different expertise. The defended network can be represented as the physical interconnection of devices but the possibility of attackers getting access to the physical devices means that there is in reality no physical space constraint. Consequently, logical topologies are more suitable to representing a workspace (Ballora et al 2011).

As a starting point for the development of a common visualization of the forensics process by the members of an investigating team this chapter provides algorithms which give guidance and step by step instructions on how to deal with computer forensics and the investigations they carry out. These algorithms cover different aspects of computer forensics and address key elements to be considered when attacked systems are investigated. Algorithms are unlikely to be created that provide a complete model of the forensics process but they are a starting point from which additional guidance can be provided to analysts on the basis of their particular expertise that leverages their existing understanding of the workspace.

Computer and information crimes can be looked at as the result of the growing trend of society depending upon and improving its use of technology.

As e-commerce and online business become part of today's business world, computer attacks and cybercrimes are continually on rise. The legal system, law enforcement, computer forensics and investigations seem to be behind in their efforts to track down criminals and successfully to prosecute them.

Computer forensics is a new discipline in computer science. It is concerned with the gathering, retrieving and evaluating of electronic data, for the purpose of stopping and preventing computer fraud, or gather and preserve digital evidence for a criminal investigation, or to recover data accidentally lost or deleted.

Computer forensics requires detailed and comprehensive knowledge in all aspects of computing such as computer architecture, hardware design, programming, and operating systems.

This chapter addresses some of the most important elements of computer forensics and evidence including issues that deals with investigations and enforcement. The emphasis of this chapter is on creating and developing a computer forensics investigation framework.

Computer forensics is an approach or method used by investigators to identify the source of an attack on computer and data-related resources and systems. Investigations should be conducted in a predefined and structured manner that enables the information and data collected to be used as evidence in a court of law during criminal prosecution of the attacker. We can conclude from what was stated above the primary goals of computer forensics as follows:

- Identification of undesirable events and activities that occurred.
- Gathering, processing, storing and preserving evidence to be introduced in the court of law.
- To use that knowledge to prevent future occurrences. (ISACA 2011).

This chapter will start by introducing basic concepts of computer forensics and investigations:

1. **Computer Attacks:** Computer attacks are any kind of unauthorized activity targeted against computer resources; examples include but are not limited to data alteration, denial of service attacks, computer viruses, etc.

2. **Evidence:** is any physical or electronic information that is collected during computer forensic investigation. Evidence includes but is not limited to log files or any other computer generated files.

Gathered evidence is used to identify the source of the attack, recover from damage caused by the attack and most importantly to introduce the evidence as testimony in a court of law during a prosecution of the attacker. In order to support prosecution, the evidence must be admissible in the court and be able to withstand challenges as to its authenticity. In order to achieve that, investigators need to follow specific instructions and to adhere to certain regulations and requirements as will be explained later.

BACKGROUND

Investigators, while conducting computer forensic gathering and analysis need to understand some issues before undertaking investigation processes.

In a cyber crime, a computer can play one of the following roles:

1. A computer can be the target of the crime.
2. A computer can be the instrument of the crime.
3. A computer can serve as an evidence repository storing critical and important information about the crime.

4. In some cases a computer can play multiple roles, for instance a computer can be the target of the crime and can store critical evidence about the crime. (Carroll and Brannon 2008).

Investigators and forensic experts when investigating a case must know what roles the computer (under investigation) played in the crime. Knowing that role will narrow down the whole investigation process and will make it much easier in terms of the effort needed as well as the time needed for investigations. In addition to that, using and applying information about how the computer was used in the crime is critical in the search for evidence and in narrowing down the evidence collection process.

For example if a computer was used as a tool to break into another system and steal passwords, the investigator will know where to search for evidence, they have to look for password cracking software and password files.

As was stated earlier the objective in computer forensics is to recover, analyze and present computer based material as admissible evidence in a court of law. Therefore the main concern of computer forensics is absolute accuracy, in other words the emphasis must be on evidential integrity and security and this can only be achieved if every forensic investigator adheres to specific forensic and investigation guidelines. These guidelines, also known as the forensic analysis framework will be explained in detail in next sections.

The first question an organization must answer is whether to prosecute the attacker. In case the organization decided to prosecute the attacker, considerable time and effort will be added to the forensic analysis and investigation processes. The reason behind this added time and effort is that precautions must be taken to adequately preserve computer data and images so that they can later be admitted as admissible evidence in a court of law. Obviously if the intention is not to prosecute the attacker some considerations for managing and handling the information gathered during the forensic investigation might not be needed. However in all cases organizations must treat all gathered information as though it might be used as evidence in a court of law. Therefore the manner in which evidence was collected and analyzed is critical (Vacca 2009).

When collecting evidence, investigators need to demonstrate and prove that the evidence is authentic and that it was generated from the attacked system and accurately represents the state of the system at a specific point of time. Authenticity means the evidence is what it is claimed to be. Authenticity of the gathered evidence to great extent depends on the reliability of the computer system that was attacked. If the system under investigation proved to be reliable and uncorrupted, then records (evidence) produced by that system are considered to be reliable as well, which means they should be considered authentic and admissible as evidence in the court of law.

Investigators and computer forensic experts who are performing forensics on a system in question must maintain and document in detail the history of investigation. This document must include the collection, handling and preservation of evidence along with a record of anyone who came into contact with this evidence. The process of documenting the history of investigation is known as chain of custody.

Due to the fact that electronic evidence can be easily modified, a clear defined chain of custody demonstrates that the evidence is trustworthy. The chain of custody must adhere to specific requirements, which are:

- The chain of custody must show that the evidence was collected from the system under investigation.
- The evidence was stored and managed without alteration.

- The chain of custody should document data that cannot be recovered, backed up or is known to be missing. (Harris 2010).

One of the most important and decisive steps in a computer forensic investigation is to safely make two precise and intact copies of the disk image and memory dump. One copy along with original data is submitted as evidence, while the other is used for analysis. Investigations must not be performed on the original data or on the copy that was prepared to be used for evidence. Investigators failure to comply with this requirement will leave them without a legal case.

To ensure the authenticity of the original data while performing investigations on the copy of the data, different hardware devices with the capability to disable the ability to write or modify existing data are used.

The use of cryptographic signatures and hashes of the original system image is widely practiced and strongly recommended since it will prove that the image was not modified. The cryptographic signing of the data should be performed in such a way that it prevents the signature itself becoming part of the evidence. (Weise and Powell 2005)

In addition to the above discussed points there many other points and factors to be carefully considered by investigators when performing computer forensic investigations. These points and factors are:

- **Shutdown the system:** The system under investigation must be shut down or powered down as quickly as possible. Depending on the computer operating system this process might involve pulling the plug or shutting down a networked computer using relevant operating systems commands.
- **Documentation of the computer hardware configuration:** It is very crucial to document all the system hardware components, where they were located and how they were connected. This can be done by

taking pictures from different angles and labeling all wires and system components and devices so that the original configuration of the system can be restored when needed.

- **Securing the computer system:** the computer under question and all hardware, software and all other resources that belong to the system under investigation should be treated as evidence, therefore it should be stored out of reach of all outsiders and not left unattended. (A. Agarwal, M. Gupta, S. Gupta and S. Gupta, 2011).

- **Backup all storage devices:** The system should not be used or operated and no evidence can be processed until at least two bit stream backup (exact copies) have been made on all disk drives and other storages devices. The original evidence should not be touched at all. It can only be introduced in a court of law in the form of admissible evidence. Preservation of evidence is the most important and crucial factor to consider. All evidence processing should be performed on one copy of the data while the other copy is kept to be presented in the court of law along with the original data. As it is known that computer material related evidence is very fragile and can easily be destroyed or altered and knowing that without preserving it security and integrity such evidence will not be acceptable in a court of law. Extra measures should be taken when dealing with evidence.

- **Authentication of the data on all storage devices:** Investigators need to prove that collected evidence is not altered or changed by any means. Such proof can be provided by authenticating the data with high level accuracy that is beyond question. Many data authentication programs and software tools for this purpose are available for free.

- **System date and time:** from an evidence standpoint, the accuracy of data and the times associated with data files are very important. If the computer clock is wrong or not accurate the data file timestamps will reflect the wrong time. To address these problems it is crucial to document the system date and time settings at the time when the system is taken for investigation. Different software programs such as GetTime are used for this purpose.

- **Develop a list of search words:** Due to the fact that modern data storage devices are so voluminous, it is impossible to perform a manual viewing and evaluation of all data files on system data storage devices. High technology and modern automated forensic text search tools are used to find relevant evidence. One such tool is TextSearch NT which is certified by the U.S. Department of Defense. It is important to develop a list of relevant key words which can be used to search all data storage devices. Such list can be developed by gathering information from individuals familiar with the case.

- **Evaluation of file slack:** File slack is a data storage which is beyond the reach or view of computer users and operators. File slack is a source of significant security leads. In order to view and evaluate file slack, special forensic tools are required. File slack can provide wealth of information and investigative leads such as relevant search key words.

- **Erased files:** As is well known the delete command or function in most of operating systems does not permanently erase file names or content, the storage space associated with such files becomes unallocated and available to be overwritten by new files. This unallocated space can be a source of significant leads because it contains erased files and file slack associated with erased files. Information obtained from unallocated space can help provide relevant key words that can be added to the investigator's list of key words which will be used in searching data storage devices for possible evidence.

- **Search for key words:** The list of relevant key words indentified in previous steps is used to search all relevant system storage devices for potential evidence. Several forensic text tools and utilities are available in the market. The outcome of the search utility must be reviewed. When relevant evidence or leads are identified, the fact must be noted and identified data should be documented. If new key words are identified in the searching process, then they should be added to the list and a new search should be conducted using the search utility and updated search list.

- **File attributes:** It is very important to document all file attributes such as file names, creation dates, last modified, etc. From file attributes, with the help of special forensic tools, a time line of computer usage can be obtained which is crucial from an evidence standpoint. In addition to that it is important to take electronic snapshot of relevant files along with relevant file attributes. These snapshots can be used to document evidence related to specific files.

- **Identification of data and data storage types:** In case data stored in storage devices are encrypted, compressed or stored in graphic files, text search programs cannot identify these types of files. As a result investigators need to perform manual evaluations of these files, not only that but in the case of encrypted files much more technical work is required. There are some software tools that can easily identify such files. In order to ensure the reliability and integrity of the findings investigators need to use certified tools. For most operating systems, it is vital to search and evaluate the recycle bin. The fact that files have

been selected for deletion may have some relevance to the investigation.

- **Program functionality:** Forensic experts need to investigate all installed software programs, applications and tools. Investigators need to identify the purpose of all installed software. This can be achieved by running and executing these programs.

- **Documentation of findings:** As was stated earlier, it is essential to treat all findings as evidence. Therefore, investigators need to document all their findings along with date, time, software programs and tools used in investigations.

- **Elements of the Computer Forensic Process:** A complete definition of computer forensics is as follows: "The use of scientifically derived and proven methods toward the preservation, collection, validation, identification, analysis, interpretation, documentation and presentation of digital evidence derived from digital sources for the purpose of facilitating or furthering the reconstruction of events found to be criminal". (Carroll and Brannon 2008).

Based on the above mentioned definition, the key elements of computer forensics are: (Ciardhuain 2004).

- Collection and preservation of digital evidence.
- Validation.
- Identification.
- Analysis and Interpretation.
- Documentation.
- Presentation.

The above listed elements can be combined into four groups which are known as phases of forensic investigation framework, these phases are:

- **Preparation Phase:** This phase of an investigation process mainly deals with validation and testing of all computer system resources, verifying the integrity and security of the original data, making a working copy, selection of investigation tools and developing the search list.
- **Extraction Phase:** The purpose of this phase is to extract data that might be relevant to a forensic request from search data leads list.
- **Identification Phase:** The outcome of the identification phase basically depends on the extracted data list; this phase is concerned with the identification of items in the extracted data list. At this stage new data lists are developed such as the relevant data list, the new source of data list. Also this phase requires great coordination with the requester.
- **Analysis Phase:** Analysis phase addresses questions like who, when, how what, and produces a coherent story about the event. Forensic reporting which is very important depends on the outcome of the analysis phase. (Carroll and Brannon 2008).

A process overview of these phases is illustrated in Figure 1.

Due to the fact that the above mentioned forensic investigation phases provide all required steps in a computer forensic investigation process, in other words these phases provide means by which to create and establish a forensic investigation framework, the emphasis of the rest of this chapter will be on developing the investigation framework or model.

It is important to understand that performing these steps comes after a request and forensic data are obtained.

FORENSIC INVESTIGATION FRAMEWORK

The forensic investigation framework presented in this chapter is an investigation model that provides guidelines and key points to be considered in computer forensic investigations. The purpose of these guidelines which are industry best practices is to help organizations and investigators to identify what has happened to a system and addresses the question of how to approach a forensic investigation process.

To sum up, the forensic investigation framework or model provides step by step instructions on how to search, collect, protect and analyze evidence that might be used in a court of law.

Figure 1. Forensic investigation process overview

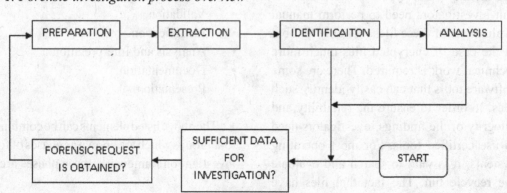

Figure 2. Preparation phase

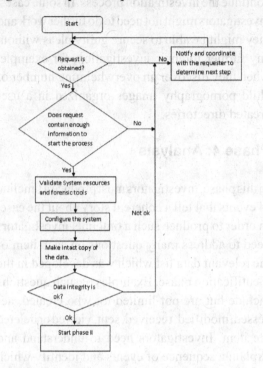

Figure 3. Data extraction phase

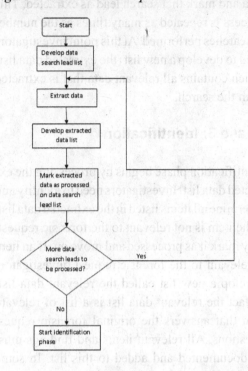

Phase 1: Preparation

The first step in any forensic investigation is to ensure that all computer system resources are functioning properly. This step is known as validation. The question is: How frequently should system resources be tested and validated? There is no clear answer, but all experts in the forensic community agree that at a minimum, all systems recourses should be validated after they were purchased and before they are used. Also all hardware devices and software programs must be retested after any update, patch, or reconfiguration. (Carroll and Brannon 2008). Before validating the system under question, investigators need to make sure there is enough information to proceed and a clear request is in hand. If anything is missing they must coordinate with the requester. Otherwise they continue and set up the process. The next step for investigators assuming that they have received the original copy of the data and verified its integrity is to make a working copy

of the original. In order make sure the copy they made (a bit for bit copy of the data) is intact and unaltered, investigators need to verify a hash or digital signature of the evidence. In case there are any problems, they must coordinate with requester about how to proceed. Otherwise they continue to develop a plan to extract data.

Phase 2: Data Extraction

At this stage of the process, investigators organize the forensic request into questions they can answer and the forensic tools required are selected. Initially based on the forensic request, investigators have some general ideas of what to search and look for. The next step for investigators at this stage is to develop a search list, as new leads are developed, investigators need to add them to the search list called the data search list. Investigators often repeat this step since the new findings may indicate a new lead to be investigated. For each search lead and findings, investigators extract relevant data and mark that search lead as extracted. This process is repeated as many times as the number of searches performed. At this point investigators need to develop a new list (the extracted data list) which contains all relevant data that is extracted from the search.

Phase 3: Identification

Identification phase begins by processing the extracted data list. Investigators need to identify and determine all items listed in the extracted data list. If the item is not relevant to the forensic request, they mark it as processed and move on. If an item is relevant to the forensic request, investigators develop a new list called the relevant data list. In fact the relevant data list is a list of relevant data that answers the original forensic request questions. All relevant items and findings must be documented and added to this list. In some cases an investigator might come across an item that is incriminating, but outside the scope of the forensic request. In this case investigator needs to stop all forensics activities and notify appropriate agencies and the requester as well. (Carroll and Brannon 2008).

A forensic investigation can lead to many different types of evidence and sources, examples include but are not limited to finding evidence that leads to stored files on an external hard disk drive or discovering a new e-mail account that was created or used by the target. In such cases investigators must notify the requester as well as appropriate agencies and document all these new findings on a list called the new source of data list. When the extracted data list is processed, investigators might need to go back to any new leads that are developed or any new source of data that is discovered during investigation process.

At this point in the investigation process, investigators must inform the requester of their initial findings and discuss with the requester what they think depending on their findings and what the return on investment will be if they agree to

continue the investigation process. In some cases, investigators might not need to do further work and they might be able to secure guilty pleas without any further forensic investigation, for example, when they discover an overwhelming number of child pornography images organized in a user created directories.

Phase 4: Analysis

In this phase, investigators must produce a timeline of events that tell a coherent story about the case. In order to produce such a timeline, investigators need to address many questions on each item of the relevant data list which was developed in the identification phase. Examples of such questions include but are not limited to: who created, accessed, modified, received, sent, viewed or deleted the item. Investigators need to understand and explain a sequence of events and identify which events happened at the same time. In other words, investigators need to connect all the dots and paint a complete picture of the event. When the investigators have cycled through investigation phases enough times they need to develop and produce a final list called the analysis result list.

The analysis result list is a list containing all investigation related information and data that answers questions like who, when, how, where, what and all other related information. In general this list must satisfy and respond to the forensic request. In some cases even at this late stage of the process, new data search leads or new sources of data leads might be generated. In this case investigators need to add these new leads to the appropriate lists and must go back to examine them fully according the investigation framework that was previously explained. See Figure 5.

Finally, after applying the above illustrated steps, investigators need to prepare the forensic report. The forensic report is a report of all the meaningful data that must satisfy the forensic request. A very important point investigators need to consider when developing a forensic report is

Figure 4. Data identification phase

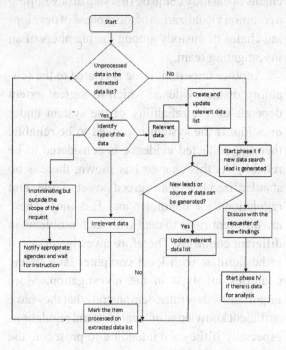

Figure 5. Data analysis phase

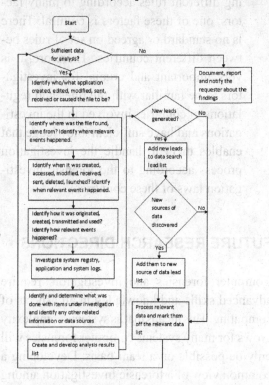

the fact that it should be prepared and organized in a way that makes it understandable and usable by the requester.

Another important factor to be considered carefully in all phases of the whole investigation process is the return on investment especially if the requester is considering submitting the case to a court of law. Also it is crucial for investigators as well as the requester to decide when to stop the investigation process. If sufficient evidence for prosecution is obtained, there is no need to continue the investigation and it must be stopped immediately. Doing that helps to reduce significantly the overall cost of investigation.

At the end of this chapter it is crucial to point out the fact that the forensic investigation process depends heavily on many factors, but the most important factors are:

- **Investigator's Skills:** The investigation process requires far more skill than just the ability to retrieve data, especially when a criminal case is involved. That is when the

investigator will need to testify as to what they did to the system under question. Also the court will need to know investigators level of education, training and experience in the field of computer and digital forensics. Therefore it is very important that investigators conducting the forensic investigation are properly skilled in this trade.

- **Forensic Tools:** The authenticity and reliability of the collected evidence depends to great extent on the used forensic tools. If used tools are not reliable, the evidence produced by these tools will not be considered reliable. Hence the use of certified tools is a decisive factor for the whole investigation process.

- **Computer Crimes and the Law:** Computer forensics is new science and hence the laws associated with this science and all digital crimes are evolving in most countries. Different countries are developing different rules according to many factors; one of these factors is cultural. There is no standard or agreed on set of rules between different countries. Therefore, it is very important and crucial for investigators to be familiar with the rules and regulations of countries involved in the investigations and have sufficient knowledge that enables them to handle the investigation process according to the forensic investigation laws of these countries.

FUTURE RESEARCH DIRECTIONS

Computer forensics and investigators require advanced skills and knowledge in all aspects of computing. This means that as systems complexity grows for many systems computer forensics will only be possible on a team basis. Developing a common view of a forensic investigation among the member of an investigation team becomes a significant challenge as system complexity grows and will require a formalized approach.

Identifying the role of the system under investigation in the attack is crucial since it narrows down the evidence collecting process and significantly reduces the effort required, the duration and overall cost of the investigation process. Classifications of systems to assist this process could save significant effort.

Due to the fact that the data evidence collected from computers, computer related resources and digital materials is fragile, the investigators should be conscious about the integrity and reliability of this evidence especially if they are considering to submit it to a court of law. Investigators need to develop and maintain a clearly defined chain of custody with the purpose of proving the authenticity of the collected evidence. Evidence is considered trustworthy if the chain of custody demonstrates that it is collected from the system under investigation and is stored and managed without alteration. Algorithms for developing

chains of custody could be first step in developing a common visualization of the process of developing chains of custody among the members of an investigating team.

Another important issue is related to the reliability of the evidence which to a great extent depends on the reliability of the system under question. If the system is proved to be reliable, then the collected evidence is considered to be reliable. As this chapter has shown, there is no standardized law or an agreed on set of rules and regulations for computer and E-crimes. There are different rules to deal with such problems in different countries. Therefore investigators need to be familiar with local computer laws of the countries involved in the investigation. More importantly, they must demonstrate that they have sufficient knowledge of local laws and regulations especially if they are intending to prosecute the attacker. In a globally interconnected world much more effort needs to go into developing training for professionals engaged in computer forensics in the laws pertaining to computer forensics in countries other than their own when forensic investigations cross national boundaries.

CONCLUSION

As a starting point for the development of a common visualization of the forensics process by the members of an investigating team this chapter has provided algorithms which give guidance and step by step instructions on how to deal with computer forensics and the investigations they carry out. As this chapter demonstrated, these algorithms cover different aspects of computer forensics and address key elements to be considered when attacked systems are investigated. Algorithms are unlikely to be created that provide a complete model of the forensics process but they are a starting point from which additional guidance can be provided to analysts on the basis of their particular expertise that leverages their existing understanding of the workspace.

REFERENCES

Agarwal, A., Gupta, M., Gupta, S., & Gupta, S. (2011). Systematic digital forensic investigation model. [IJCSS]. *International Journal of Computer Science and Security*, 5(1).

Ballora, M., Giacobe, N., Hall, D., & McNeese, M. (2011). Information fusion and computer network defense. In Onwubiko, C., & Owens, T. J. (Eds.), *Situational awareness in computer network defense: Principles, methods and applications*.

Carroll, O., & Brannon, S. (2008). *Computer forensics: Digital forensic analysis methodology*. United Stated Department of Justice.

Ciardhuain, S. (2004). An extended model for cybercrime investigations. *International Journal of Digital Evidence*, 3(1).

Crime, C. (n.d.). *Website*. Retrieved March 10, 2011, from http://www.cybercrime.gov

Forensics, C. (n.d.). *Home page*. Retrieved March 14, 2011, from http://www.computerforensics.com

Harris, S. (2010). *CISSP certification* (5th ed.). McGraw Hill.

Hawrylak, P., Hale, J., Papa, M., Daily, J. IV, & Greer, D. (2011). Attack graphs and scenario driven wireless computer network defense. In Onwubiko, C., & Owens, T. J. (Eds.), *Situational awareness in computer network defense: Principles, methods and applications*.

ISACA. (2011). *CISM review manual 2011*. ISACA.

Koloodgy, C. (2010). *Unified and automated situational awareness*. IDC.

Lang, L., Chunlei, W., & Guoqing, M. (2010). A framework for network security situational awareness based on knowledge discovery. *2nd International Conference on Computer Engineering and Technology*, (pp. 226-231).

Li, J., Ou, X., & Rajagopalan, R. (2009). *Uncertainty and risk management in cyber situational awareness*. Paper presented at ARO Workshop on Cyber Situational Awareness.

Onwubiko, C. (2011). Modelling situation awareness information and system requirements for the mission using goal-oriented task analysis approach. In Onwubiko, C., & Owens, T. J. (Eds.), *Situational awareness in computer network defense: Principles, methods and applications*.

Ruiz, M. E., & Redmond, R. (2011). Cyber command and control: A military doctrinal prospective on collaborative situation awareness for decision making. In Onwubiko, C., & Owens, T. J. (Eds.), *Situational awareness in computer network defense: Principles, methods and applications*.

Tan, T., Ruighaver, T., & Ahmed, A. (2003). *Incident handling: Where the need for planning is often not recognised*. Paper presented at 1st Australian Computer, Network & Information Forensic Conference.

Vacca, J. (2009). *Computer forensics: Computer crime scene investigation* (2nd ed.). Charles River Media, Inc.

Weise, J., & B. Powell, B., (2005). *Using Computer Forensics When Investigating System Attacks*. Sun Microsystems, Inc.

Yong, Z., Xiaobin, T., & Hongsheng, X. (2007). A novel approach to network security situation awareness based on multi-perspective analysis. *International Conference on Computational Intelligence and Security* (pp. 768-772).

ADDITIONAL READING

Berinato, S. (2007). The Rise of Anti Forensics. Retrieved February, 20, 2010, from http://www. csoonline.com/article/221208/The_Rise_of_ Anti_Forensics

Carrier, B. Digital forensics tool testing images. http://dftt.sourceforge.net/

Erbacher, R. F., Christensen, K., & Sundberg, A. (2006). Visual Forensic Techniques and Processes. *Proceedings of the 9th Annual NYS Cyber Security Conference Symposium on Information Assurance*, Albany, NY, pp. 72-80.

Johnson, T. A. (2006). *Forensic Computer Crime Investigation*. Connecticut: CRC Press.

Nelson, B., Phillips, A., & Steuart, C. (2009). *Guide to Computer Forensics and Investigations* (4th ed.). Course Technology.

NIST Computer Forensics Tool Testing Project. http://www.cftt.nist.gov.

Philipp, A., Cowen, D., & Davis, C. (2009). *Hacking Exposed Computer Forensics, Second Edition: Computer Forensics Secrets & Solutions, Second Edition*. McGraw-Hill Osborne Media.

Ren, W. (2006). Modeling Network Forensics Behavior. *Journal of Digital Forensic Practice*, *1*(1), 57–65. doi:10.1080/15567280600631932

Solomon, M. G., Rudolph, K., Tittel, E., Neil Broom, N., & Barrett, D. (2011). *Computer Forensics JumpStart* (2nd ed.). Sybex.

Volonino, L., & Anzaldua, R. (2008). *Computer Forensics For Dummies, For Dummies Carvey, H. (2009). Windows Forensic Analysis DVD Toolkit* (2nd ed.). Syngress.

Volonino, L., Anzaldua, R., & Goodwin, J. (2006). *Computer Forensics: Principles and Practices*. Prentice Hall.

KEY TERM AND DEFINITION

Computer Forensics: "The use of scientifically derived and proven methods toward the preservation, collection, validation, identification, analysis, interpretation, documentation and presentation of digital evidence derived from digital sources for the purpose of facilitating or furthering the reconstruction of events found to be criminal" (Carroll and Brannon 2008).

Compilation of References

Aalo, V., & Viswanathan, R. (1989). On distributed detection with correlated sensors: Two examples. *IEEE Transactions on Aerospace and Electronic Systems*, *25*, 414–421. doi:10.1109/7.30797

Aboba, B., & Simon, D. (2008). *Extensible authentication protocol (EAP) key management framework*. RFC 5247, IETF, August.

Acharya, S., & Ablitz, M. Mills., B., Znati, T., Wang, J., Ge, Z., & Greenberg, A. (March, 2007). OPTWALL: A hierarchical traffic-aware Firewall. In *Proceedings of 14th Annual Network & Distributed System Security Symposium*.

Acharya, S., & Znati, T. (May, 2009). *Dynamic traffic driven architectueres and algorithms to secure networks*. Security Technology Response, Symantec Corporation.

Acharya, S., Ge, Z., Greenberg, A., & Wang, J. (2006). *Methods and apparatus for optimizing Firewalls*. US Patent Docket Number: 2005-0520.

Acharya, S., Wang, J., Ge, Z., Greenberg, A., & Znati, T. (April, 2006). Simulation study of firewalls to improve performance. In *the 39th Annual Simulation Symposium*, Alabama, USA.

Acharya, S., Wang, J., Ge, Z., Znati, T., & Greenberg, A. (June, 2006). *Traffic-aware Firewall optimization strategies*. In IEEE International Conference on Communications, Istanbul, Turkey.

Acharya, S., Wang, J., Ge, Z., Znati, T., & Greenberg, A. (September, 2005). *Traffic-aware framework and optimization strategies for large-scale enterprise networks*, (pp. 1-20). Technical Report, University of Pittsburgh.

Adams, C., & Lloyd, S. (1999). *Understanding PKI. Concepts, standards, and deployment considerations* (2nd ed.). Addison-Wesley.

Agarwal, A., Gupta, M., Gupta, S., & Gupta, S. (2011). Systematic digital forensic investigation model. [IJCSS]. *International Journal of Computer Science and Security*, *5*(1).

Agarwal, R., & Joshi, M. V. (2000). *PN rule: A new framework for learning classifier models in data mining (a case-study in network intrusion detection). (Tech. Rep. RC 21719), IBM Research report*. Computer Science/ Mathematics.

Ager, B., Dreger, H., & Feldmann, A. (2005). *Exploring the overhead of DNSSEC*. Retrieved September 2010 from http://www2.net.informatik.tu-muenchen.de/~anja/feldmann/ papers/ dnssec06.pdf

Albrechtsen, E. (2008). *Friend or foe? Information Security management of employees*. Ph.D. dissertation. NTNU, Trondheim, March 2008.

Allen, J. H. (2001). *The CERT guide to system and network security practices*. Redwood City, CA: Addison-Wesley.

Alrabady, A., & Mahmud, S. (2005). Analysis of attacks against the security of keyless-entry systems for vehicles and suggestions for improved designs. *IEEE Transactions on Vehicular Technology*, *54*(1), 41–50. doi:10.1109/TVT.2004.838829

Al-Shaer, E., & Hamed, H. (April, 2004). Modeling and management of Firewall policies. *IEEE Transactions in Network and Service Management*, *1*(1).

Ammann, P., Wijesekera, D., & Kaushik, S. (2002). Scalable, graph-based network vulnerability analysis. In *Proceedings of the 9th ACM Conference on Computer and Communications Security* (pp. 217-224).

Amoroso, E. (1999). *Intrusion detection*. Intrusion.net Books, New Jersey.

Anderson, H. H. K., & Hauland, G. (2000). Measuring team situation awareness of reactor operators during normal operation: A technical pilot study. *Proceedings of the First Human Performance, Situation Awareness, and Automation Conference*, Savannah, 2000.

Anderson, J. R., & Lebiere, C. (1998). *The atomic components of thought*. Hillsdale, NJ: Lawrence Erlbaum Associates.

Anderson, J. R., & Lebiere, C. (2003). The Newell test for a theory of mind. *The Behavioral and Brain Sciences*, *26*(5), 587–639. doi:10.1017/S0140525X0300013X

Anderson, R. (2008). *Security engineering: A guide to building dependdable distributed systems* (2nd ed.). Indianapolis, IN: Wiley Publishing, Inc.

Andriole, S. J., & Halpin, S. M. (1991). *Information Technology for command and control: Methods and tools for systems development and evaluation* (pp. 1–576). IEEE Press.

Antonakakis, M., Dagon, D., Luo, X., & Lee, W. (2010). *Anax: A monitoring infrastructure of improving DNS security*. International Symposium on Recent Advances in Intrusion Detection, (RAID). Berlin, Germany: Springer Verlag.

Antony, R. (2008). Data management support to tactical data fusion. In Liggins, M. E., Hall, D. L., & Llinas, J. (Eds.), *Handbook of multisensor data fusion: Theory and practice* (2nd ed., pp. 619–653). Boca Raton, FL: CRC Press. doi:10.1201/9781420053098.ch24

Arends, R., Austein, R., Larson, M., Massey, D., & Rose, S. (2005a). *DNS security introduction and requirements*. IETF RFC 4033.

Arends, R., Austein, R., Larson, M., Massey, D., & Rose, S. (2005b). *Protocol modifications for the DNS security extensions*. IETF RFC 4035.

Arends, R., Austein, R., Larson, M., Massey, D., & Rose, S. (2005c). *Resource records for the DNS security extensions*. IETF RFC 4034.

Ariyapperuma, S., & Mitchell, C. J. (2007). Security vulnerabilities in DNS and DNSSEC. *Second International Conference on Availability, Reliability and Security*, (pp. 335-342).

Arkko, J., & Haverinen, H. (2008). *Extensible authentication protocol method for 3rd generation authentication and key agreement (EAP-AKA)*. RFC 4182, IETF, January.

Artz, M. L. (2002). *NetSPA: A network security planning architecture*. Unpublished M.S. thesis, Massachusetts Institute of Technology, Cambridge, MA.

Asnar, Y., & Giorgini, P. (2010). Multi-dimensional uncertainty analysis in secure and dependable domain. *International Conference on Availability, Reliability and Security*, (pp. 148-155).

Aven, T. (2007). A unified framework for risk and vulnerability analysis covering both safety and security. *Reliability Engineering & System Safety*, *92*, 745–754. doi:10.1016/j.ress.2006.03.008

Azaiez, M. N., & Bier, V. M. (2007). Optimal resource allocation for security in reliability systems. *European Journal of Operational Research*, *181*, 773–786.

Baboescu, F., & Varghese, G. (2001). Scalable packet classification, *Proceedings of ACM SIGCOMM*.

Baker, W. H., Hylender, D. C., & Valentine, A. J. (2008). Four years of forensic research: More than 500 cases: One comprehensive report. *Verizon Data Breach Investigation Report*, (pp. 2-27).

Ballora, M. Pennycook, B., Ivanov, P. Ch., Glass, L., & Goldberger, A. L. (2004). Heart rate sonification: A new approach to medical diagnosis. *Leonardo*, *37*, 41–46. doi:10.1162/002409404772828094

Ballora, M., Giacobe, N., Hall, D., & McNeese, M. (2011). Information fusion and computer network defense. In Onwubiko, C., & Owens, T. J. (Eds.), *Situational awareness in computer network defense: Principles, methods and applications*.

Banks, D. L., & Anderson, S. (2006). Combining game theory and risk analysis in counterterrorism: A smallpox example. In Wilson, A. G., Wilson, G. D., & Olwell, D. H. (Eds.), *Statistical methods in counterterrorism* (pp. 9–22). New York, NY: Springer-Verlag.

Bares, D. (2010). *A tactical framework for cyberspace situational awareness*. 15th ICCRTS, The Evolution of C2, C2 Assessment Metrics and Tools, Paper #196, Air Force Institute of Technology, 2010.

Barey, M., & Johnson, D. (1978). *Computer and intractability*. San Francisco, CA: Freeman.

Barford, P., Dacier, M., Dietterich, T. G., Fredrikson, M., Giffin, J., & Jha, S. … Yen, J. (2009). Cyber SA: Situational awareness for cyber defense. In S. Jajodia, P. Liu V. Swarup & C. Wang (Eds.), *Cyber situational awareness: Issues and research (Advances in information security)*.

Barford, P., Dacier, M., Dietterich, T. G., Fredrikson, J., Griffin, S., & Jajodia, S. (2010). Cyber SA: Situational awareness for cyber defense - Issues and research. In Jajodia, S., Liu, P., Swarup, V., & Wang, C. (Eds.), *Cyber situational awareness* (pp. 3–14). New York, NY: Springer. doi:10.1007/978-1-4419-0140-8_1

Barnes, J. E. (2008). Pentagon computer networks attacked. *Los Angeles Times*.

Bass, T. (1999). Multisensor data fusion for next generation distributed intrusion detection systems. *IRIS National Symposium on Sensor and Data Fusion* (pp. 24-27).

Bass, T. (2000). Cyberspace situational awareness demands mimic tradition command requirements. *AFCEA Signal Magazine*, 2000.

Bass, T. (2000). Intrusion detection systems and multisensor data fusion. *Communications of the ACM, 43*(4). doi:10.1145/332051.332079

Bell, M. I., & Bates, E. A. (2005). Analysis for network centric warfare in the navy. In *Analytical Support to Defence Transformation Meeting Proceedings*, (pp. 19-1-19-14). RTO-MP-SAS-055, Paper 19, Neuilly-sur-Seine, France, 2005.

Bernstein, D. J. (2005). *A state-of-the-art message-authentication code*. Retrieved September 2010 http://cr.yp.to/mac.html

Bernstein, D. J. (2006). Curve25519: New Diffie-Hellman speed records. *Ninth International Conference Theory and Practice of Public Key Cryptography*, (pp. 229-240).

Bernstein, D. J. (2007). *Snuffle 2005: The Salsa20 encryption function*. Retrieved September 2010 from http://cr.yp.to/snuffle.html

Bernstein, D. J. (2009a). *Cryptography in NaCl*. Retrieved September 2010 from http://cr.yp.to/highspeed/naclcrypto-20090310.pdf

Bernstein, D. J. (2009b). *DNSCurve*. Retrieved September 2010 from http://dnscurve.org.

Bernstein, D. J. (2009c). *DNSCurve: Usable security for DNS*. Retrieved September 2010 from http://cr.yp.to/talks/2008.08.22/slides.pdf

Bernstein, D. J. (2009d). *High-speed cryptography and DNSCurve*. Retrieved September 2010 from http://cr.yp.to/talks/2009.06.27/slides.pdf

Besnard, D., & Arief, B. (2004). Computer security impaired by legitimate users. *Computers and Security 23*(3), 253-264. doi:10.1.1.95.9210

Bier, V. M., & Azaiez, M. N. (2008). *Game theoretic risk analysis of security threats*. Berlin, Germany: Springer-Verlag.

Bier, V. M., Nagaraja, A., & Abhichandani, V. (2005). Protection of simple series and parallel systems with components of different values. *Reliability Engineering & System Safety, 87*, 315–323.

Biros, D. P. (2004). Scenario-based training for deception detection. *InfoSecCD Conference*, Kennesaw, GA, October 8, (pp. 32-36). doi:10.1145/1059524.1059531

Blais, C. L. (2005). Modelling and simulation for military operations other than war, naval postgraduate school. *Proceedings of the Interservice and Industry Training, Simulation and Education Conference (I/ITSEC)*, 2005.

Blasch, E. P., & Plano, S. (2002). JDL level 5 fusion model: User refinement issues and applications in group tracking. [SPIE]. *Proceedings - Society of Photo-Optical Instrumentation Engineers, 4729*, 270–279.

Blasch, E., Kadar, I., Salerno, J., Kokar, M., Powell, G. M., & Corkill, D. D. (2006). Issues and challenges in situation assessment (level 2 fusion). *Journal of Advances in Information Fusion, 1*(2), 122–139.

Block, J., & Rogaway, P. (2002). A block-cipher mode of operation for parallelizable message authentication. *Advance in Cryptology—EUROCHRYPT 2002* [Springer–Verlag.]. *LNCS, 2332*, 384–397.

Bloedorn, E. C., Christiansen, A. D., Hill, W., Skorupka, C., Talbot, L. M., & Tivel, J. (2001). *Data mining for network intrusion detection: How to get started.* Retrieved June 15, 2011, from http://citeseerx.ist.psu.edu/viewdoc/download?doi=10.1.1.102.8556.pdf

Bloom, B. (1970). Space/time trade-offs in hash coding with allowable errors. *Communications of the ACM, 7*(13), 422–426. doi:10.1145/362686.362692

Blum, R., Kassam, S., & Poor, H. (1997). Distributed detection with multiple sensors- Part II: Advanced topics. *Proceedings of the IEEE*, 64–79. doi:10.1109/5.554209

Bolchini, D., & Mylopoulos, J. (2003). *From task-oriented to goal-oriented Web requirements analysis.* Fourth International Conference on Web Information Systems Engineering (WISE'03), Roma, Italy, 10-12 December 2003.

Boni, W., & Kovacich, G. L. (2000). *Netspionage: The global threat to information.* Boston, MA: Butterworth-Heinemann.

Borja, A. T. (2003). *Integrating usability engineering in the iterative design process of the land attack combat system (LACS) human computer interface.* San Diego, CA: Space & Naval Warfare Systems Center.

Bowden, M. (2010, June). The enemy within. *The Atlantic Monthly.* Retrieved from http://www.theatlantic.com/magazine/archive/2010/06/the-enemy-within/8098/

Boyd, J. (1987). *Organic design for command and control.* Presentation Slides, May 1987. Retrieved from www.ausairpower.net/JRB/organic_design.ppt

Boyd, J. (Col.). (1987). *Organic design for command and control.* Presentation Slides, May 1987. Retrieved from www.ausairpower.net/JRB/organic_design.ppt

Boyd, J. R. (1995). *The essence of winning and losing.* Retrieved from http://www.danford.net/boyd/essence.htm

Brafman, O., & Beckstrom, R. A. (2008). *The starfish and the spider: The unstoppable power of leaderless organizations* (p. 240). Penguin Group USA.

Bregman, A. (1990). *Auditory scene analysis: The perceptual organization of sound.* Cambridge, MA: MIT Press.

Breiman, L., Friedman, J. H., Olshen, R. A., & Stone, C. J. (1984). *Classification and regression trees.* Belmont, CA: Wadsworth.

Breton, R., & Rousseau, R. (2003). *Situation awareness: A review of the concept and its measurement.* DREV, TR-2001-220, Defence Research Establishment, 2003.

Broad, W. J., & Sanger, D. E. (November 18, 2010). Worm was perfect for sabotaging centrifuges. *New York Times.* Retrieved Nov. 19, 2010, from http://www.nytimes.com/2010/11/19/world/middleeast/19stuxnet.html?_r=1

Bryl, V., Massacci, F., Mylopoulos, J., & Zannone, N. (2006). Designing security requirements models through planning. *Proceedings of the CAiSE 2006, LNCS 4001,* (pp. 33-47). Springer-Verlag, 2006.

Builder, C. H., Bankes, S. C., & Nordin, R. (1999). *Command concepts: A theory derived from the practice of command and control* (pp. 1–144). Washington, DC: RAND Corporation.

Campbell, C., Dawkins, J., Pollet, B., Fitch, K., Hale, J., & Papa, M. (2003). On modeling computer networks for vulnerability analysis. In Gudes, E., & Shenoi, S. (Eds.), *Research directions in data and applications security* (pp. 233–244). Boston, MA: Kluwer Academic Publishers.

Candey, R. M., Schertenleib, A. M., & Diaz Merced, W. L. (2005, December). *Sonification prototype for space physics.* Presentation at American Geophysical Union, Fall Meeting 2005, abstract #ED43B-0850, San Francisco, CA.

Cardenas, A. A., Amin, S., & Sastry, S. (2008, July). Research challenges for the security of control systems. In *Proceedings of 3rd USENIX workshop on Hot Topics in Security* (HotSec). USENIX Association Berkeley, CA, USA

Cardenas, A. A., Amin, S., Sinopoli, B., Giani, A., Perrig, A., & Sastry, S. S. (2009, July). Challenges for securing cyber physical systems. In *Proceedings of Workshop on Future Directions in Cyber-Physical Systems Security.*

Cardenas, A., Amin, S., & Sastry, S. S. (2008). Secure control: Towards survivable cyber-physical systems. In *Proceedings of 28th International Conference on Distributed Computing Systems (ICDCS)*, (pp. 495–500).

Carin, L., Cybenko, G., & Hughes, J. (2008). Cybersecurity strategies: The QuERIES methodology. *Computer*, *41*(8), 20–26.

Carnegie Mellon. (2005). *SILK: System for Internet level knowledge (SILK)*. Carnegie Mellon SEI, CERT NetSA Security Suite, 2005. Retrieved March 29, 2011, from http://tools.netsa.cert.org/silk/

Carroll, O., & Brannon, S. (2008). *Computer forensics: Digital forensic analysis methodology*. United Stated Department of Justice.

Castro, J., Kolp, M., & Mylopoulos, J. (2002). Towards requirements-driven Information Systems engineering: The Tropos project. [Amsterdam, The Netherlands: Elsevier.]. *Information Systems*, *27*, 365–389. doi:10.1016/S0306-4379(02)00012-1

CERT. (2011). *Denial of service*. Retrieved May, 2011, from http://www.cert.org/homeusers/ddos.html

Chafe, C., & Leistikow, R. (2001, July). *Levels of temporal resolution in sonification of network performance*. Paper presented at the 2001 International Conference on Auditory Display, Helsinki University of Technology, Espoo, Finland.

Chair, Z., & Varshney, P. K. (1986). Optimal data fusion in multiple sensor detection systems. *IEEE Transactions on Aerospace and Electronic Systems*, *22*(1), 98–101. doi:10.1109/TAES.1986.310699

Chambers Dictionary. (1997). *Chambers 21st century dictionary*. Retrieved from http://www.chambersharrap.co.uk/chambers/features/chref/chref.py/main

Chan, P. K., & Stolfo, S. (1993). Toward parallel and distributed learning by metalearning. In *Working Notes AAAI Work, Knowledge Discovery in Databases,* Portland, OR, (pp. 227–240). AAAI Press.

Chang, S. E., & Lin, C. S. (2007). Exploring organizational culture for information security management. *Industrial Management + Data Systems, 107*(3), 438-458.

Chang, S. C., Chen, H. H., & Fong, I. K. (1990). Hydro-electric generation scheduling with an effective differential dynamic programming algorithm. *IEEE Transactions on Power Systems*, *5*(3), 737–743.

Chawla, N. V., Bowyer, K. W., Hall, L. O., & Kegelmeyer, W. P. (2002). Smote: Synthetic minority over-sampling technique. *Journal of Artificial Intelligence Research*, *16*, 321–357.

Checkpoint. (2011). *NGX firewall*. Retrieved May, 2011, from http://www.checkpoint.com

Chen, E. (2010). *W32.Stuxnet dossier (official blog)*.

Chen, G., Nocetti, F., Gonzalez, J., & Stojmenovic, I. (2002). Connectivity based k-hop clustering in wireless networks. *Proceedings of the 35th Annual Hawaii International Conference on System Sciences (HICSS)*. IEEE Computer Society.

Chen, K., Tsai, H. C., Fabian, B., Liu, Y., & Shuler, J. (2009 July). A radiofrequency identification (RFID) temperature-monitoring system for extended maintenance of nuclear materials packaging. *Proceedings of the 2009 ASME Pressure Vessels and Piping Division Conference* (pp. 109-115). ASME.

Chen, Y.-S., & Lei, C.-L. (2010). Filtering false messages en-route in wireless multi-hop networks. *IEEE Wireless Communications and Networking Conference (WCNC)*, Sydney, Australia, (pp. 1-6).

Chen, G., Shen, D., Kwan, C., Cruz, J. B. Jr, Kruger, M., & Blasch, E. (2008). Game theoretic approach to threat prediction and situation awareness. *Journal of Advances in Information Fusion*, *2*(1), 35–48.

Chen, X., Makki, K., & Pissinou, N. (2009). Sensor network security: A survey. *IEEE Communications Surveys & Tutorials*, *2*(11), 52–73. doi:10.1109/SURV.2009.090205

Ciardhuain, S. (2004). An extended model for cyber-crime investigations. *International Journal of Digital Evidence*, *3*(1).

Cisco Systems Inc. (2011). Cisco ASA 5500 series adaptive security appliances. Retrieved from http://www.cisco.com/ en/US/prod/ collateral/ vpndevc/ ps6032/ ps6094/ ps6120/prod _brochure0900aecd80285492.pdf

Clancy T., & Tschofenig, H. (2008). *EAP generalized pre-shared key*. RFC 5433, IETF, November 19.

Clark, K., Tyree, S., Dawkins, J., & Hale, J. (2004, June). Quantitative and qualitative analytical techniques for network security assessment. *Proceedings of the 2004 IEEE Workshop on Information Assurance and Security* (pp. 321-328). IEEE.

Clark, K., Tyree, S., Lee, C., & Hale, J. (2007, June). Guiding threat analysis with threat source models. *Proceedings of the 2007 IEEE Workshop on Information Assurance* (pp. 262-269). IEEE.

Clark, V., & Hagee, M. W. (2005). FORCEnet: A functional concept for the 21st century. Retrieved March 28, 2011, from http://forcenet.navy.mil/concepts/fn-concept-final.pdf

Clarke, R. A., & Knake, R. (2010). *Cyber war: The next threat to national security and what to do about it* (pp. 1–304). Washington, DC: Harper Collins.

Clark, R. M. (1996). *Intelligence analysis: Estimation and prediction*. Baltimore, MD: American Literary Press.

Clayton, M. (2010). Stuxnet malware is 'weapon' out to destroy...Iran's Bushehr nuclear plant? *Christian Science Monitor*. Retrieved from http://www.csmonitor.com/USA/2010/0921/Stuxnet-malware-is-weapon-out-to-destroy-Iran-s-Bushehr-nuclear-plant

Cohen, W. W. (1995). Fast effective rule induction. *Proceedings of 12th International Conference on Machine Learning*, (pp. 115—123).

Conrad, D. (2001). *Indicating resolver support of DNSSEC*. IETF RFC 3225. Crypto++ 5.6.0 Benchmarks. (2009). *Speed comparison of popular crypto algorithms*. Retrieved October 2010 from http://www.cryptopp.com/benchmarks.html

CPS Week. (2010). Retrieved from http://www.cpsweek2010.se/

Crime, C. (n.d.). *Website*. Retrieved March 10, 2011, from http://www.cybercrime.gov

D'Amico, A., & Whitley, K. (2007, October). *The real work of computer network defense analysts*. Paper presented at the Workshop on Visualization for Computer Security (VizSEC 2007), Sacramento, CA.

D'Amico, A., & Whitley, K. (2007). *The real work of computer network defense analysts: The analysis roles and processes that transform network data into security situation awareness*. *VizSEC 2007* (pp. 19–37). Mathematics and Visualization.

Damas, J., & Neves, F. (2008). *Preventing use of recursive nameservers in reflector attacks*. IETF RFC 5338.

D'Amico, A., & Kocka, M. (2005). *Information assurance visualisation for specific stages of situational awareness and intended uses: Lessons learned*. Workshop on Visualisation for Computer Security, USA, 2005.

D'Amico, A., & Kocka, M. (2005, October 26). *Information assurance visualizations for specific stages of situational awareness and intended uses: lessons learned*. Paper presented at the IEEE Workshop on Visualization for Computer Security (VizSEC 05), Minneapolis, Minnesota.

D'Amico, A., Whitley, K., Tesone, D., O'Brien, B., & Roth, E. (2005, September 26-30). *Achieving cyber defense situational awareness: A cognitive task analysis of information assurance analysts*. Paper presented at the Human Factors and Ergonomics Society 49th Annual Meeting, Orlando, FL.

DARPA. (2009). *Intrusion detection evaluation dataset*. Retrieved October 16, 2009, from http://www.ll.mit.edu/IST/ideval/data/data_index.html

Delarue, J. (1962). *Historie de la gestapo*. Paris, France: Fayard.

Dempsky, M. (2009). *DNSCurve: Link-level security for the Domain Name System*, draft-dempsky-dnscurve-01.

Denial of Service Attack. (2011). *Website*. Retrieved May, 2011, from http://en.wikipedia.org/wiki/Denial-of-service_attack

Department of Defense (DoD). (2000). *Joint vision 2020. America's Military - Preparing for tomorrow*. Washington, DC, Summer 2000. Retrieved March 25, 2011, from http://www.dtic.mil/doctrine/jel/jfq_pubs/1225.pdf

Dhillon, G., & Backhose, J. (2001). Current directions in IS security research: Towards socio-organizational perspectives. *Information Systems Journal, 11*(2), 127–153. doi:10.1046/j.1365-2575.2001.00099.x

Distributed Denial of Service. (2011). *Website*. Retrieved May, 2011, from https://www.cert.org/homeusers/ddos.html

Douligeris, C., & Mitrokotsa, A. (2004). DDoS attacks and defense mechanisms: Classification and state of the art, *in Computer Networks, 44*(5), 643-666.

Drakopoulos, E., & Lee, C. C. (1991). Optimum multisensor fusion of correlated local. *IEEE Transactions on Aerospace and Electronic Systems, 27*, 593–606. doi:10.1109/7.85032

Dubendorfer, T., Wagner, A., & Plattner, B. (2004). An economic damage model for large-scale Internet attacks. In *Proceedings of the 13ᵗʰ International Workshop on Enabling Technologies*.

Dutt, V., & Gonzalez, C. (2011). Cyber situation awareness: Modeling the security analyst in a cyber attack scenario through instance-based learning. In *Proceedings of the 20th Behavior Representation in Modeling & Simulation (BRIMS) Conference*. Sundance, Utah, USA.

Dutt, V., Ahn, Y., & Gonzalez, C. (2011). *Cyber situation awareness: Modeling the security analyst in a cyber-attack scenario through instance-based learning*. Manuscript submitted for publication.

Dutt, V., Cassenti, D. N., & Gonzalez, C. (2010). Modeling a robotics operator manager in a tactical battlefield. In *Proceedings of the IEEE Conference on Cognitive Methods in Situation Awareness and Decision Support* (p. xx). Miami Beach, FL.

Eastlake, D., & Kaufman, C. (1997). *Domain name system security extensions*. RFC 2065. eSTREAM. (2008). *The ECRYPT stream cipher project*. Retrieved September 2010 from www.ecrypt.eu.org/stream/salsa20.html

Eiland, E. E., & Liebrock, L. M. (2006). An application of information theory to intrusion detection. *Proceedings of the Fourth IEEE International Workshop on Information Assurance (IWIA '06)* (pp. 119-134). Washington, DC: IEEE Computer Society Washington.

El-Atawy, A., Samak, T., Al-Shaer, E., & Li, H. (2007). *Using online traffic statistical matching for optimizing packet-filtering performance*. IEEE INFOCOM.

Emmerich, W. (2000). *Engineering distributed objects*. London, UK: John Wiley & Sons, Ltd.

ENABLE. (2006). *Requirements, scenarios and initial architecture. Deliverable D1.1*. Project IST ENABLE.

ENABLE. (2007). *Service authorization and control for fast/smart handover*. Project IST ENABLE Deliverable D4.3, December.

Endsley, M. R. (1996). Automation and situation awareness. *Automation and Human Performance: Theory and Applications*, (pp. 163-181).

Endsley, M. R., Selcon, S. J., Hardiman, T. D., & Groft, D. G. (1998). *A comparative analysis of SAGAT and SART for evaluations of situation awareness*. 42nd Annual Meeting of the Human Factors & Ergonomics Society. Chicago, IL.

Endsley, M. R. (1995). Toward a theory of situation awareness in dynamic systems. *Human Factors Journal, 37*(1), 32–64. doi:10.1518/001872095779049543

Endsley, M. R. (2000). Errors in situation assessment: Implications for system design. In Elzer, P. F. K. R. H. B. B. (Ed.), *Human error and system design and management (Lecture Notes in Control and Information Sciences* (Vol. 253, pp. 15–26). London, UK: Springer-Verlag. doi:10.1007/BFb0110451

Endsley, M. R. (2000). Theoretical underpinnings of situation awareness: A critical review. In Endsley, M. R., & Garland, D. J. (Eds.), *Situation awareness analysis and measurement* (pp. 3–30). Mahwah, NJ: Lawrence Earlbaum Associates.

Endsley, M. R., & Garland, D. J. (Eds.). (2000). *Situation awareness analysis and measurement*. Mahwah, NJ: Lawrence Erlbaum Associates.

Eronen, P., & Zitting, J. (November, 2001). An expert system for analyzing firewall rules. In *Proceedings of the 6th Nordic Workshop on Secure IT Systems (NordSec)*, (pp. 100–107). Copenhagen, Denmark.

ESRI. (2008). *Public safety and homeland security situational awareness*. An ESRI White Paper, February 2008. Retrieved from www.esri.com

ETSI Standard EN 302 304. (2004)., *ETSI standard*, November.

European Network of Excellence in Cryptology II (ECRYPT II.) (2009). *D.SPA.7: ECRYPT2 yearly report on algorithms and keysizes* (2008-2009).

Evans, R., Kearney, P., Stark, J., Caire, G., Carijo, F. L., Gomez, J., … Massonet, P. (2001). *MESSAGE: Methodology for engineering systems of software agents*. AgentLink Publication, September 2001.

Evans, S. C., & Barnett, B. (2002, October). *Network security through conservation of complexity.* Paper presented at IEEE Military Communications Conference (MILCOM) 2002, Anaheim, CA.

Falliere, N. M. (2011). *W32.Stuxnet dossier.* Retrieved May 11, 2011, from http://www.symantec.com/content/en/us/enterprise/media/security_response/whitepapers/w32_stuxnet_dossier.pdf

Fan, X., & Yen, J. (2007). R-CAST: Integrating team intelligence for human-centered teamwork. In

Feldmann, A., & Muthukrishnan, S. (March, 2000). *Tradeoffs of packet classification*. In IEEE INFOCOM.

Fink, G. A., North, C. L., Endert, A., & Rose, S. (2009). *Visualizing cyber security: Usable workspaces.* Workshop on Visualization for Cyber Security - VizSec.

Firewall Computing. (2011). *Wikipedia*. Retrieved May, 2011, from http://en.wikipedia.org/wiki/Firewall_computing

Folker, R. D. Jr. (2000). *Intelligence analysis in theater joint intelligence centers: An experiment in applying structured methods*. Joint Military Intelligence College.

Foo, B., Wu, Y. S., Mao, Y. C., Bagchi, S., & Spafford, E. (2005, June). *ADEPTS: Adaptive intrusion response using attack graphs in an e-commerce environment*. Paper presented at International Conference on Dependable Systems and Networks, Yokohama, Japan.

Foo, B., Glause, M. W., Howard, G. M., Wu, Y.-S., Bagchi, S., & Spafford, E. H. (2008). Intrusion response systems: A survey. In Qian, Y., Joshi, J., Tipper, D., & Krishnamurthy, P. (Eds.), *Information assurance: Dependability and security in networked systems* (pp. 377–412). Burlington, MA: Morgan Kaufmann.

Forensics, C. (n.d.). *Home page*. Retrieved March 14, 2011, from http://www.computerforensics.com

Forrest, S., Hofmeyr, S. A., & Somayaji, A. (1997). Computer immunology. *Communications of the ACM*, *40*(10), 88–96. doi:10.1145/262793.262811

Fracker, M. L. (1991). *Measures of situation awareness: Review and future directions.* Armstrong Laboratories, Wright-Patterson Air Force Base, OH.

Francillon, A., Danev, B., & Capkun, S. (2010). *Relay attacks on passive keyless entry and start systems in modern cars* (Rapport technique). Cryptology ePrint Archive, Report 2010/332.

Fry, R. (2010, July). Fighting wars in cyberspace. *Wall Street Journal*.

Fulp, E. (2005). Optimization of network firewalls policies using directed acyclic graphs. In *Proceedings of the IEEE Internet Management Conference*.

Fulp, E. (2006). *Parallel firewall designs for high-speed networks*. In IEEE INFOCOM High Speed Networking Workshop.

Furnell, S. (2007). IFIP workshop: Information security culture. *Computers & Security*, *26*(1), 35. doi:10.1016/j.cose.2006.10.012

Garba, D. M., & Howard, S. K. (1995). Situation awareness in anaesthesiology. *Human Factors*, *37*(1), 20–31. doi:10.1518/001872095779049435

Gardner, H. (1987). *The mind's new science: A history of the cognitive revolution*. New York, NY: Basic Books.

Garrancho, B., Pinto, E., Sousa, L., & Loureiro, N. (2009). *Vanishing point: Resilient DNSSEC key repository*. Retrieved September 2010 from http://dev.sig9.net/files/ResearchProject.pdf

Gilfix, M., & Couch, A. (2000, December). *Peep (the network auralizer): Monitoring your network with sound.* Paper presented at the 14th Systems Administration Conference (2000 LISA XIV), New Orleans, LA.

Giorgini, P. (2010). *Tropos: Basic, agent oriented software engineering course. Laurea Specialistica in Informatica, Dipartimento Ingegneria e Scienza* (pp. 2009–2010). Italy: University of Trento.

Giorgini, P., Massacci, F., Mylopoulos, J., & Zannone, N. (2005). *Modelling security requirements through ownership, permission and delegation. Proceeding of Requirements Engineering (RE'05)* (pp. 167–176). IEEE Press.

Giorgini, P., Massacci, F., Mylopoulos, J., & Zannone, N. (2005b). *Modelling social and individual trust in requirements engineering methodologies. Proceedings of iTrust '05, LNCS 3477* (pp. 161–176). Springer-Verlag.

Goldman, J. (2008). *Introducing IEEE802.11r* [Online]. Retrieved from http://www.wi-fiplanet.com/news/article.php/3776351

Goldstone, R. L., Day, S., & Son, J. Y. (2010). Comparison. In B. Glatzeder, V. Goel, & A. von Müller (Eds.), *On thinking: Volume II, towards a theory of thinking* (pp. 103-122). Heidelberg, Germany: Springer Verlag.

Gonzalez, C., Dutt, V., & Lejarraja, T. (2011). *How did an IBL model become the runners-up in the market entry competition?* Manuscript in preparation.

Gonzalez, C., & Dutt, V. (2010). Instance-based learning: Integrating decisions from experience in sampling and repeated choice paradigms. *Psychological Review, 118*(4).

Gonzalez, C., Lerch, J. F., & Lebiere, C. (2003). Instance-based learning in dynamic decision making. *Cognitive Science, 27*(4), 591–635. doi:10.1207/s15516709cog2704_2

Grabowski, M., Ayyalasomayajula, P., Merrick, J., Harrald, J. R., & Roberts, K. (2007). Leading indicators of safety in virtual organizations. *Safety Science, 45*, 1013–1043. doi:10.1016/j.ssci.2006.09.007

Grégoire, M., & Beaudoin, L. (2005). Visualisation for network situational awareness in computer network defence. In *Visualisation and the Common Operational Picture Meeting Proceedings* (pp. 20-1 – 20-6). (RTO-MP-IST-043, Paper 20). Neuilly-sur-Seine, France.

Gu, Y., McCallum, A., & Towsley, D. (2005). Detecting anomalies in network traffic using maximum entropy estimation. *ICM '05 Proceedings of the 5th ACM SIGCOMM Conference on Internet Measurement*, (pp. 345-350). Berkeley, CA: USENIX Association.

Gupta, P., & McKeown, N. (August, 1999). Packet classification using hierarchical intelligent cuttings. In *Proceedings of Hot Interconnects*.

Gupta, P., Prabhakar, B., & Boyd, S. (2000). *Near optimal routing lookups with bounded worst-case performance*. In IEEE INFOCOM.

Gupta, P., & McKeown, N. (2001). Algorithms for packet classification. *IEEE Network, 15*(2), 24–32. doi:10.1109/65.912717

Hagen, J. M. (2007). *Evaluating applied information security measures: An analysis of the data from the Norwegian Computer Crime Survey, 2006,* (pp. 1-66). Norwegian Defense Research Establishment (FFI), FFI-rapport 02558

Hagen, J. M. (2009). *The human factor behind the security perimeter. Evaluating the effectiveness of organizational information security measures and employees' contributions to security*. Doctoral Dissertation, Faculty of Mathematics, University of Oslo.

Hagen, J. M., & Spilling, P. (2009). Do organisational security measures contribute to the detection and reporting of IT-system abuses? In *Proceedings of the Third International Symposium on Human Aspects of Information Security & Assurance*, (pp. 71-81).

Hagen, J. M., Albrechtsen, E., & Hovden, J. (2008). Implementation and effectiveness of organizational information security measures. *Journal of Information Management and Computer Security, 16*(4), 377–397. doi:10.1108/09685220810908796

Hagen, J. M., Sivertsen, T. K., & Rong, C. (2008). Protection against unauthorized access and computer crime in Norwegian businesses. *Journal of Computer Security, 16*, 341–366.

Haines, J., Ryder, D., Tinnel, L., & Taylor, S. (2003). Validation of sensor alert correlators. *IEEE Security & Privacy, 1*(1), 46–56. doi:10.1109/MSECP.2003.1176995

Hale, A. I., & Glendon, O. (1987). *Individual behavior in the control of danger*. Amsterdam, The Netherlands: Elsevier.

Hall, D. H., & McMullen, S. A. H. (2004). *Mathematical techniques in multi-sensor data fusion* (2nd ed.). Artech House.

Hall, D. L., & Jordan, J. (2010). *Human centered information fusion*. Norwood, MA: Artech House.

Hall, D. L., & McMullen, S. A. H. (2004). *Mathematical techniques in multisensor data fusion* (2nd ed.).

Hamed, H., & Al-Shaer, E. (March, 2006). *Dynamic rule-ordering optimization for high-speed firewall filtering.* In ASIACCS.

Hamed, H., El-Atawy, A., & Al-Shaer, E. (April, 2006). *Adaptive statistical optimization techniques for firewall packet filtering.* In IEEE INFOCOM.

Harkins, D., Ohba, Y., Nakhjiri, M., & Lopez, R. (2007). *Problem statement and requirements on a 3-party distribution protocol for handover keying.* Internet Draft (work in progress), IETF, March.

Harris, S. (2010). *CISSP certification* (5th ed.). McGraw Hill.

Hausken, K. (2002). Probabilistic risk analysis and game theory. *Risk Analysis, 22*(1), 17–27.

Hausken, K. (2008). Strategic defense and attack for series and parallel reliability systems. *European Journal of Operational Research, 186,* 856–881.

Haverinen, H., & Salowey, J. (2006). *Extensible authentication protocol method for global system for mobile communications (GSM) subscriber identity modules (EAP-SIM).* RFC 4186, IETF, January.

Hawrylak, P. J. (2006). *Analysis and development of a mathematical structure to describe energy consumption of sensor networks.* Unpublished doctoral dissertation, University of Pittsburgh, Pittsburgh, PA.

Hawrylak, P. J., Cain, J. T., & Mickle, M. H. (2007). Analytic modeling methodology for analysis of energy consumption for ISO 18000-7 RFID Networks. *International Journal of Radio Frequency Identification Technology and Applications, 1*(4), 371–400. doi:10.1504/IJRFITA.2007.017748

Hawrylak, P. J., Cain, J. T., & Mickle, M. H. (2009). Analysis methods for sensor networks. In Misra, S., Woungang, I., & Misra, S. C. (Eds.), *Guide to wireless sensor networks* (pp. 635–658). New York, NY: Springer. doi:10.1007/978-1-84882-218-4_25

Hawrylak, P., Hale, J., Papa, M., Daily, J. IV, & Greer, D. (2011). Attack graphs and scenario driven wireless computer network defense. In Onwubiko, C., & Owens, T. J. (Eds.), *Situational awareness in computer network defense: Principles, methods and applications.*

Hayden, M. V. (2011). The future of things "cyber." *Strategic Studies Quarterly.* Maxwell AFB, AL: Air University Press. Retrieved from http://www.au.af.mil/au/ssq/2011/spring/hayden.pdf

Heidari, M. (1970). *Water resources systems analysis by discrete differential dynamic programming.* Department of Civil Engineering, University of Illinois at Urbana-Champaign.

Henderson, P. (2007). *On open systems and openness.* University of Southampton, October 30th 2007. Retrieved April 26, 2011, from http://pmh-systems.co.uk/OpenSystems/OpenSystems.pdf

Hermann, T. (2002). *Sonification for exploratory data analysis.* Unpublished doctoral dissertation, Bielefeld University, Germany.

Hertwig, R., Barron, G., Weber, E. U., & Erev, I. (2004). Decisions from experience and the effect of rare events in risky choice. *Psychological Science, 15*(8), 534–539. doi:10.1111/j.0956-7976.2004.00715.x

Hinrichs, S. (2005). Integrating changes to a hierarchical policy model. In *Proceedings of 9th IFIP/IEEE International Symposium on Integrated Network Management,* Nice, France.

Holley, I. B. (2004). *Technology and military doctrine: Essays on a challenging relationship* (pp. 1–160). Air University Press.

Homer, J., Varikuti, A., Ou, X., & McQueen, M. A. (2008). Improving attack graph visualization through data reduction and attack grouping. *Proceedings of the 5th International Workshop on Visualization for Computer Security* (pp. 68-79). ACM.

Höne, K., & Eloff, J. H. P. (2002). Information security policy: What do international security standards say? *Computers & Security, 21*(5), 402–409. doi:10.1016/S0167-4048(02)00504-7

Howard, M., & Leblanc, D. (2003). *Writing secure code.* Redmond, WA: Microsoft Press.

Howard, R. A. (1971). *Dynamic probablistic systems: Vol. 1. Markov models.* New York, NY: John Wiley & Sons, Inc.

Huber, M., Kowalski, S., Nohlberg, M., & Tjoa, S. (2009). Towards automating social engineering using social networking sites. *Computational Science and Engineering, CSE '09,* (vol. 3, pp. 117-123). doi: 10.1109/CSE.2009.205

Idaho National Laboratory. (2009, October). *National SCADA testbed substation automation report.*

IEEE P1363 Standards. (2009). *Standard specifications for public-key cryptography.*

IEEE Standard 802.11r. (2008). *Information Technology - Telecommunications and information exchange between systems - Local and metropolitan area networks - Specific requirements – Part 11: Wireless LAN Medium Access Control (MAC) and Physical Layer (PHY) specifications - Amendment 2: Fast BSS Transition.* IEEE, January.

IEEE Standard 802.16e. (2005). *IEEE standard and metropolitan area networks: Part16: Air interface for fixed and mobile broadband wireless access systems.* IEEE, December 7.

IEEE802.21 Draft P802.21/D00.05. (2006). *Standard and metropolitan area networks: Media independent handover services.* IEEE, March.

In *Proceedings of the 2010 IEEE/IFIP International Conference on Dependable Systems and Networks (DSN)* (pp. 211 - 220). Hong Kong, China: IEEE Press.

İnce, A. N. (1997). *Planning and architectural design of modern command control communications* (p. 301). Springer. Jackson, W. (2009). DOD creates cyber command as U. S. strategic command sub-unit. *Federal Computer Week.* Washington, DC. Retrieved from http://fcw.com/Articles/2009/06/24/DOD-launches-cyber-command.aspx?p=1

Ingols, K., Chu, M., Lippmann, R., Webster, S., & Boyer, S. (2009). Modeling modern network at-tacks and counter-measures using attack graphs. In *2009 Annual Computer Security Applications Conference* (pp. 117--126).

Ingols, K., Lippmann, R., & Piwowarski, K. (2006, December). Practical attack graph generation for network defense. *Proceedings of the 22nd Annual Computer Security Applications Conference* (pp. 121–130). IEEE.

Intel. (2005). *Intel active management technology quick reference.* Retrieved May 11, 2011, from http://download.intel.com/support/motherboards/desktop/sb/amt_quick_start_guide1.pdf

Intel. (2011). *Intel AMT frequently asked questions.* Retrieved May 11, 2011, from http://software.intel.com/en-us/articles/intel-active-management-technology-frequently-asked-questions/?wapkw=(active+management+technology)

ISACA. (2011). *CISM review manual 2011.* ISACA.

ISO IEC 27002. (2005). *Information technology – Security techniques – Code of practice for information security management.*

ISO/IEC 27001. (2005). *Information technology – Security techniques – Information security management systems – Requirements.*

Iwata, T., & Kurosawa, K. (2002). OMAC: One-key CBC MAC. *Pre-proceedings of Fast Software Encryption* [Springer-Verlag.]. *FSE, 2003,* 137–161.

Izguierdo, A., Hoeper, K., Golmie, N., & Chen, L. (2008). Using the EAP framework for fast media independent handover authentication. *Proceedings of the 4th Annual International Conference on Wireless Internet,* Maui, Hawaii, (pp. 1-8).

Jacobson, D., & Mayne, D. (1970). *Differential dynamic programming.* New York, NY: Elsevier.

Jajodia, S., Noel, S., & OBerry, B. (2005). Topological analysis of network attack vulnerability. *Managing Cyber Threats,* (pp. 247-266).

Jajodia, S., Liu, P., & Swarup, V. (2009). *Cyber situational awareness: Issues and research* (p. 249). Springer.

Jajodia, S., Liu, P., Swarup, V., & Wang, C. (2010). *Cyber situational awareness.* New York, NY: Springer.

Jajodia, S., Liu, P., Swarup, V., & Wang, C. (Eds.). (2009). *Cyber situational awareness: Issues and research (Advances in Information Security).* Springer.

Jariyakul, N., & Znati, T. (April, 2005). On the Internet delay-based clustering. *Proceedings of the 38th Annual Simulation Symposium.*

Jariyakul, N., & Znati, T. (December, 2005). A clustering-based selective probing framework to support Internet quality of service routing. *Distributed Computing - IWDC, Proceedings of the 7th International Workshop*, Kharagpur, India.

Jin, S., & Yeung, D. (2004). A covariance analysis model for DDoS attack detection. *IEEE International Communication Conference (ICC04)*, vol. 4 (pp. 20-24).

Jina, S., & Yeunga, D. S., & XizhaoWangb. (2007). Network intrusion detection in covariance feature space. *Pattern Recognition*, *40*, 2185–2197. doi:10.1016/j.patcog.2006.12.010

Johnson-Laird, P. (2006). *How we reason*. London, UK: Oxford University Press.

Joint Chiefs of Staff. (2006). *Personnel support to joint operations*. US Department of Defense Joint Publication. Department of Defense.

Joint Chiefs of Staff. (2007). *Joint publication 2-0 joint intelligence*. US Department of Defense Joint Publication. Department of Defense.

Joint Chiefs of Staff. (2010a). *Command and control for joint land operations*. US Department of Defense Joint Publication. Department of Defense.

Joint Chiefs of Staff. (2010b). *Joint publication 3-30 command and control for joint air operations*. US Department of Defense Joint Publication. Department of Defense.

Joint Chiefs of Staff. (2010c). *Department of Defense dictionary of military and associated terms*. US Department of Defense Joint Publication. US Department of Defense.

Jones, R. E. T., Connors, E. S., Mossey, M. E., Hyatt, J. R., Hansen, N. J., & Endsley, M. R. (2010). Modelling situation awareness for army infantry platoon leaders using fuzzy cognitive mapping techniques. *Proceedings of the 19th Conference on Behaviour Representation in Modelling and Simulation*, Charleston, SC, 21 - 24 March 2010.

Jones, A., Kovacich, G. G., & Luzwick, P. G. (2002). *Global information warfare: How businesses, governments, and others achieve objectives and attain competitive advantages* (pp. 3–75). New York, NY: Auerbach Publications. doi:10.1201/9781420031546

Jones, M. D. (1995). *The thinkers toolkit*. New York, NY: Three Rivers.

Joshi, M. V. (2002). On evaluating performance of classifiers for rare classes. *Proceedings of the 2002 IEEE International Conference on Data Mining* (pp. 641-644).

Joshi, M. V., Agarwal, R. C., & Kumar, V. (2001). Mining needles in a haystack: Classifying rare classes via two-phase rule induction, *Association for Computing Machinery Special Interest Group on Management of Data, 30*(2).

Juarez-Espinosa, O., & Gonzalez, C. (2004). *Situation awareness of commanders: A cognitive model*. Carnegie Mellon University, Department of Social and Decision Sciences, Papers 85. Retrieved from http://repository.cmu.edu/sds/85

Juniper Networks. (2011). *IGS series integrated security gateway*. Retrieved April 25, 2011, from http://www.juniper.net/us/en/local/pdf/datasheets/1100036-en.pdf#xml=http://kb.juniper.net/ index?page=answeropen&type=open&searchid=1255112038522 &answer-id= 16777216&iqaction =6&url= http%3A%2F%2Fwww.juniper.net% 2Fus%2Fen%2 Flocal%2Fpdf %2Fdatasheets%2F1100036-en.pdf& highlightinfo= 18875208,1477, 1492

Juvenal. (100). *Satires* (vol. 6). Rome.

Kam, M., Zhu, Q., & Gray, W. (1992). Optimal data fusion of correlated local decisions in multiple sensor detection systems. *IEEE Transactions on Aerospace and Electronic Systems, 28*, 916–920. doi:10.1109/7.256317

Karlof, C., & Wagner, D. (2003). Sensor network protocols and applications. *Proceedings of the First IEEE Secure Routing in Wireless Sensor Networks: Attacks and Countermeasures*, (pp. 113-127).

Karyda, M., Kiountouzis, E., & Kokolakis, S. (2005). Information systems security policies: A contextual perspective. *Computers & Security, 24*(3), 246–260. doi:10.1016/j.cose.2004.08.011

Keating, M., & Bricaud, P. (2002). *Reuse methodology manual for system-on-a-chip designs*. Boston, MA: Kluwer Academic Publishers.

Keeney, M., Kowalski, E., Capelli, D., Moore, A., Shimeall, T., & Rogers, S. (2005). *Insider threat study: Computer system sabotage in critical infrastructure sectors*, (pp. 2-45). Carnegie Mellon, Software Engineering Institute.

Kendall, K. (1999). *A database of computer attacks for the evaluation of intrusion detection systems*. Unpublished dissertation, Massachusetts Institute of Technology, USA.

Kessler, O., Askin, K., Beck, N., Lynch, J., White, F., & Buede, D. (1991). *Functional description of the data fusion process*. Warminster, PA: Office of Naval Technology, Naval Air Development Center.

Klein, G. A. (1989). Recognition-primed decisions. In Rouse, W. B. (Ed.), *Advances in man-machine system research* (*Vol. 5*, pp. 47–92). Greenwich, CT: JAI Press.

Kolkman, O. M. (2005). *Measuring the resource requirements of DNSSEC*. Technical report, RIPE NCC / NLnet Lab. Retrieved September 2010 from http://www.ripe.net/docs/ripe-352.html

Kolkman, O., & Gieben, R. (2006). *DNSSEC operational practices*. IETF RFC 4641.

Koloodgy, C. (2010). *Unified and automated situational awareness*. IDC.

Kometer, M. W. (2010). *Command in air war: Centralized versus decentralized control of combat airpower* (p. 348). Maxwell AFB, AL: Air University Press.

Koscher, K., Czeskis, A., Roesner, F., Patel, S., Kohno, T., & Checkoway, S. … Savage, S. (2010, May). *Experimental security analysis of a modern automobile*. Paper presented at the 2010 IEEE Symposium on Security and Privacy, Oakland, CA.

Kraemer, S., Carayon, P., & Clem, J. (2009). Human and organizational factors in computer and information security: Pathways to vulnerabilities. *Computers & Security*, *28*(7), 509–520. doi:10.1016/j.cose.2009.04.006

Kramer, G. (Ed.). (1994). *Auditory display: Sonification, audification, and auditory interfaces*. Santa Fe Institute Studies in the Sciences of Complexity (*Vol. 18*). Reading, MA: Addison Wesley.

Krawczyk, H., Bellare, M., & Canetti, R. (February, 1997). *HMAC-keyed-hashing for message authentication*. Internet Engineering Task Force, Request for Comments (RFC) 2104.

Kruegel, C., Toth, T., & Kirda, E. (March, 2002). Service specific anomaly detection for network intrusion detection. In *Proceedings of the Symposium on Applied Computing (SAC)*. ACM Press. Spain.

Krulak, C. C. (1996). Command and control. *Marine Corps Doctrinal Publication, 6* (pp. 1-156). Washington, DC: Wildside Press LLC. Retrieved January 30, 2011, from http://books.google.com/books?id=FiyX-ARjwDMC&pgis=1

Kubat, M., Holte, R. C., & Matwin, S. (1997). Learning when negative examples abound: One sided selection. *Proceedings of the Ninth European Conference on Machine Learning* (pp. 146-153).

Lakkaraju, K., Yurick, W., & Lee, A. J. (2004). *NVisionIP: NetFlow visualizations of system state for security situational awareness*. NVisionIP, VizSEC/DMSEC'04, October 29, 2004, Washington, DC, USA.

Lambert, D. A., Bosse, E., Breton, R., Rousseau, R., Howes, J. R., Hinman, M. L., … White, F. (2004). *Information fusion definitions, concept and models for coalition situation awareness*. (TTCP C31 Group, TR-C31-AG2-1-2004).

Lan, L.-N., Liu, X.-Y., & Yang, T.-H. (2009, 10-11 July 2009). *Multi-layer and multi-aspect design of CA system security*. Paper presented at the International Conference on Information Engineering, 2009 (ICIE '09), Taiyuan, Shanxi, China.

Lane, T., & Brodley, C. E. (1999). Temporal sequence learning and data reduction for anomaly detection. *ACM Transactions on Information and System Security*, *2*(3), 295–331. doi:10.1145/322510.322526

Lang, L., Chunlei, W., & Guoqing, M. (2010). A framework for network security situational awareness based on knowledge discovery. *2nd International Conference on Computer Engineering and Technology*, (pp. 226-231).

Laurie, B., Sisson, G., Arends, R., & Blacka, D. (2008). *DNS security (DNSSEC) hashed authenticated denial of existence*. IETF RFC 5155.

Lawson, J. (1981). Command control as a process. *IEEE Control Systems Magazine*, *1*(1), 5–11. doi:10.1109/MCS.1981.1100748

Lee, E. A. (2006). *Cyber-physical systems – Are computing foundations adequate?* Department of EECS, UC Berkeley, NSF Workshop on Cyber-Physical Systems: Research Motivation, Techniques and Roadmap, October 16-17, 2006.

Lee, W., Stolfo, S. J., Chan, P. K., Eskin, E., Fan, W., Miller, M., et al. (2000). Real time data mining-based intrusion detection. *Second DARPA Information Survivability Conference and Exposition, IEEE Computer Society*, (pp. 85-100).

Lee, W., Fan, W., Miller, M., Stolfo, S., & Zadok, E. (2000). *Toward cost-sensitive modeling for intrusion detection and response. Tech. Rep. No. (CUCS-002-00). Computer Science*. Columbia University.

Lefebvre, J. H., Grégoire, M., Beaudoin, L., & Froh, M. (2005). *Computer network defence situational awareness information requirements*. Defence R&D Canada – Ottawa, Technical Memorandum, DRDC Ottawa TM 2005-254, December 2005.

Lejarraga, T., Dutt, V., & Gonzalez, C. (in press). Instance-based learning: A general model of decisions from experience in repeated binary choice. *Journal of Behavioral Decision Making*.

Lemos, R. (2004). *Msblast epidemic far larger than believed*. Retrieved May, 2011, from http://news.com/msblast

Levitin, G. (2007). Optimal defense strategy against intentional attacks. *IEEE Transactions on Reliability*, *56*(1), 148–157.

Li, J., Ou, X., & Rajagopalan, R. (2009). *Uncertainty and risk management in cyber situational awareness*. Paper presented at ARO Workshop on Cyber Situational Awareness.

Liang, Y., Wang, H., & Lai, J. (2007, August). *Quantification of network security situational awareness based on evolutionary neural network*. Paper presented at 2007 International Conference on Machine Learning and Cybernetics, Hong Kong, China.

Libwhisker. (n.d.). *Website*. Retrieved March 16, 2009, from rfp@wiretrip.net/libwhisker

Li, D., & Ng, W. L. (2000). Optimal dynamic portfolio selection: Multiperiod mean-variance formulation. *Mathematical Finance*, *10*(3), 387–406.

Liggins, M. E., Hall, D. L., & Llinas, J. (Eds.). (2008). *Handbook of multisensor data fusion: Theory and practice* (2nd ed.). Boca Raton, FL: CRC Press.

Li, J., Ou, X., & Rajagopalan, R. (2010). Uncertainty and risk management in cyber situational awareness. In Jajodia, S., Liu, P., Swarup, V., & Wang, C. (Eds.), *Cyber situational awareness: Issues and research* (pp. 51–67). New York, NY: Springer. doi:10.1007/978-1-4419-0140-8_4

Linux IPChains. (2011). *Website*. Retrieved May, 2011, from http://people.netfilter.org/rusty/ipchains

Linux. (2011). *IPChains*. Retrieved May, 2011, from http://people.netfilter.org/rusty/ipchains

Lippmann, R. P., Fried, D. J., Graf, I., Haines, J. W., Kendall, K. R., & McClung, D. … Zissman, M. A. (2000). Evaluating intrusion detection systems: The 1998 DARPA off-line intrusion detection evaluation. *Proceedings of the 2000 DARPA Information Survivability Conference and Exposition (DISCEX)*, vol. 2 (pp. 12-26). Los Alamitos, CA: IEEE Computer Society Press.

Lippmann, R., Ingols, K., & Lincoln Lab, M. I. T. (2005). *An annotated review of past papers on attack graphs*. Massachusetts Institute of Technology, Lincoln Laboratory.

Liu, P., & Zang, W. (2003, October). *Incentive-based modeling and inference of attack intent, objectives, and strategies*. Paper presented at the 10th ACM conference on Computer and communications security (CCS'03), Washington, DC.

Liu, X., Wang, H., Lai, J., & Liang, Y. (2007, November). *Network security situation awareness model based on heterogeneous multi-sensor data fusion*. Paper presented at 22nd International Symposium on Computer and Inormation Sciences, Ankara, Turkey.

Li, W., Mei, S., & Jun-de, S. (2008). An efficient hierarchical authentication scheme in mobile IPv6 networks. *Journal of China Universities of Posts and Telecommunications*, *15*(1), 9–13.

Llinas, J., & Hall, D. L. (1998, 31 May-3 June). *An introduction to multi-sensor data fusion.* Paper presented at the IEEE International Symposium on Circuits and Systems (ISCAS '98), Monterey, CA.

Lobree, B. (2002). Impact of legislation on information security management. *Security Management Practices,* (November/December), 41-48.

Luo, Y., Szidarovszky, F., & Liu, J. (2011). *Simulation study on the prediction of the attacker's possible moves based on latent social network.* Unpublished working paper, Systems and Industrial Engineering Department, University of Arizona, Tucson.

Luo, Y., Szidarovszky, F., Al-Nashif, Y., & Hariri, S. (2009a, May). *A game theory based risk and impact analysis method for intrusion defense systems.* Paper presented at the Seventh ACS/IEEE International Conference on Computer Systems and Applications (AICCSA 2009), Rabat, Morocco.

Luo, Y., Szidarovszky, F., Al-Nashif, Y., & Hariri, S. (2009b, June). *Game tree based partially observable stochastic game model for intrusion defense systems (IDS).* Paper presented at IIE Annual Conference and Expo (IERC 2009), Miami, FL.

Luo, Y., Szidarovszky, F., Al-Nashif, Y., & Hariri, S. (2010). Game theory based network security. *Journal of Information Security, 1,* 41–44.

Lute, J. H., & McConnell, B. (2011). *A civil perspective on cybersecurity.* Retrieved February 28, 2011, from http://www.wired.com/threatlevel/2011/02/dhs-op-ed/

Lye, K., & Wing, J. (2005). Game strategies in network security. *International Journal of Information Security, 4,* 71–86.

Mahoney, M. V., & Chan, P. K. (2001).*Detecting novel attacks by identifying anomalous network packet headers.* Florida Institute of Technology. (Tech. Rep. No. CS- 2001-2).

Mahoney, M. V., & Chan, P. K. (2002). *Learning non stationary models of normal network traffic for detecting novel attacks.* The Eighth Association of Computing Machinery Special Interest Group Knowledge Discovery and Data Mining International Conference on Knowledge Discovery and Data Mining.

Mahoney, M. V., & Chan, P. K. (2001). *Detecting novel attacks by identifying anomalous network packet headers. Tech. Rep. No. (CS- 2001-2).* Florida, USA: Florida Institute of Technology.

Manning, B. (2003). *DNSSEC & operations.* Retrieved September 2010 from http://www.nordunet2003.is/smasidur/presentations/Manning.pps

Matheus, C. J., Kokar, M. M., & Baclawski, K. (2003). A core ontology for situation awareness. *Proceedings of the Sixth International Conference on Information Fusion* (pp. 545-552).

Mathew, S., Shah, C., & Upadhyaya, S. (2005, 23-24 March 2005). *An alert fusion framework for situation awareness of coordinated multistage attacks.* Paper presented at the Third IEEE Workshop on Information Assurance, College Park, Maryland.

Matulevičius, R., Mayer, N., Mouratidis, H., Dubois, E., Heymans, P., & Genon, N. (2008). Lecture Notes in Computer Science: *Vol. 5074. Adapting Secure Tropos for security risk management in the early phases of Information Systems development. Advanced Information Systems Engineering* (pp. 541–555).

Mazu Networks Inc. (2011). *Website.* Retrieved May, 2011, from http://www.mazunetworks.com

McAulay, A., & Francis, P. (1993). Fast routing tables lookup using cams. *Proceedings IEEE INFOCOM.*

McCarthy, K., Zabar, B., & Weiss, G. (2005). Does cost-sensitive learning beat sampling for classifying rare classes? *First International Workshop on Utility-Based Data Mining* (pp. 69-77).

McCumber, J. (2004). *Assessing and managing security risk in IT systems: A structured methodology.* Boca Raton, FL: Auerbach Publications. doi:10.1201/9780203490426

McGuinness and L. Foy. (2000). A subjective measure of SA: The crew awareness rating scale (CARS). *Proceeding of the First Human Performance, Situation Awareness, and Automation Conference, Savannah, Georgia,* 2000.

McGuinness, B., & Foy, L. (2000). A subjective measure of SA: The crew awareness rating scale (CARS). *Proceedings of the First Human Performance, Situation Awareness, and Automation Conference,* Savannah, Georgia, 2000.

McHugh, J., Christie, A., & Allen, J. (2000, Sep/Oct.). Defending yourself: The role of intrusion detection systems. *IEEE Software, 17*(5). doi:10.1109/52.877859

McNeese, M. D. (1986). Humane intelligence: A human factors perspective for developing intelligent cockpits. *IEEE Aerospace and Electronic Systems Magazine, 1*(9), 6–12. doi:10.1109/MAES.1986.5005199

Meyer, C. H., & Matyas, S. M. (1982). *Cryptography: A new dimension in computer data security*. John Wiley & Sons.

Mirkovic, J., Prier, G., & Reiher, P. (November, 2002). Attacking DDoS at the source. *Proceedings of ICNP*.

Mirkovic, J., & Reiher, P. (2004). A taxonomy of DDoS attack and DDoS defense mechanisms. *Computer Communication Review, 34*(2), 39–52. doi:10.1145/997150.997156

MIT Lincoln Laboratory. (2008). *Network security: Plugging the right holes. MIT Lincoln Laboratory, Cyber and Systems Technology*. Lexington, MA: MIT Lincoln Laboratory.

Mitnik, K. D., Simon, W. L., & Wozniak, S. (2002). *The art of deception: Controlling the human element of security*. John Wiley & Sons.

Mockapetris, P. (1987a). *Domain names – Concepts and facilities*. IETF RFC 1034.

Mockapetris, P. (1987b). *Domain names – Implementations and specification*. IETF RFC 1035.

Mölsä, J. (2005). Mitigating denial of service attacks: A tutorial. *Journal of Computer Security, 13*, 807–837.

Moore, D., Paxson, V., Savage, S., Shannon, C., Staniford, S., & Weaver, N. (2003). *Inside the Slammer Worm*. IEEE Security and Privacy.

Morimoto, J., Zeglin, G., & Atkeson, C. G. (2003, August). *Minimax differential dynamic programming: Application to a biped walking robot*. Paper presented at *SICE Annual Conference*, Fukui University, Japan.

Morris, D. J. (1983). *Communication for command and control systems* (p. 506). Pergamon Press.

Mouratidis, H. (2004). *A security oriented approach in the development of multiagent system: Applied to the management of the health and social care needs of older people in England/* PhD Thesis, University of Sheffield, 2004.

Mouratidis, H., Giorgini, P., & Manson, G. (2003). An ontology for modeling security: The Tropos approach. In *the Proceedings of the 7th International Conference on Knowledge-Based Intelligent Information & Engineering Systems (KES 2003), 2003*.

Mouratidis, H., & Giorgini, P. (2007a). Secure Tropos: A security-oriented extension of the Tropos methodology. *International Journal of Software Engineering and Knowledge Engineering, 17*(2), 285–309. doi:10.1142/S0218194007003240

Mulgund, S., Rinkus, G., Illgen, C., & Zacharias, G. (1997). *Situation awareness modelling and pilot state estimation for tactical cockpit interfaces*. Presented at HCI International, San Francisco, CA, August 1997.

Murray, D., & Yakowitz, S. (1979). Constrained differential dynamic programming and its application to multireservoir control. *Water Resources Research, 15*(5), 1017–1027.

Murray, D., & Yakowitz, S. (1981). The application of optimal control methodology to nonlinear programming problem. *Mathematical Programming, 21*, 331–347.

Mussabbir, Q. B. (2010). *Mobility management across converged IP-based heterogeneous access networks*. Unpublished doctoral thesis, Brunel University.

Muzea, G. (2005). *The vital few. The trivial many. Invest with the insiders. Not the masses* (pp. 200–203). John Wiley and Sons.

Nahin, P. J., & Pokoski, J. L. (1980). NCTR plus sensor fusion equals IFFN or can two plus two equal five? *IEEE Transactions on Aerospace and Electronic Systems, AES-16*(3), 320–337. doi:10.1109/TAES.1980.308902

Nakhjiri, M. (2007). *Keying and signaling for wireless access and handover using EAP (EAP-HR)*. Internet Draft (work in progress), IETF, April.

Narayanan V., & Giaretta, G. (2007). *EAP-based keying for IP mobility protocols*. Internet Draft (work in progress), IETF, November 16.

Narayanan, V. and Dondeti, L., (2008). *EAP extensions for reauthentication protocol.* RFC 5296, IETF, March 29.

Narayanan, V., & Dondeti, L. (2007). *EAP extensions for efficient re-authentication.* Internet Draft (work in progress), IETF, January.

NCCS. (2006). *Mørketallsundersøkelsen om datakriminalitet 2006 (The Norwegian Computer Crime Survey 2006).* Oslo, Norway: Næringslivets sikkerhetsråd (in Norwegian).

Newton-Evans Research Company. (2008). *Substation automation report.*

Noel, S., & Jajodia, S. (2004, October). Managing attack graph complexity through visual hierarchical aggregation. *Proceedings of the 2004 ACM Workshop on Visualization and Data Mining for Computer Security* (pp. 109-118). ACM.

Norman, D. A. (1990). The 'problem' with automation: Inappropriate feedback and interaction, not 'over-automation'. *Philosophical Transactions of the Royal Society of London. Series B, Biological Sciences, 327*(1241), 585–593. doi:10.1098/rstb.1990.0101

Ohba, Y., & Das, S. (2007). *An EAP method for EAP extension.* Internet Draft (work in progress) July.

Onwubiko, C. (2008). Data fusion in security evidence analysis. *Proceeding of the 3rd International Conference on Computer Security and Forensics,* 2008.

Onwubiko, C. (2009). Functional requirements of situational awareness in computer network security. *Proceeding of the IEEE International Conference on Intelligence and Security Informatics, IEEE ISI 2009,* 8-11, June 2009, Dallas, Texas, USA.

Onwubiko, C., & Owens, T. J. (2010). *Situational awareness in computer network defence: Principles, methods and applications.* Hershey, PA: IGI Global, USA. Retrieved from http://www.wikicfp.com/cfp/servlet/event.showcfp?eventid=11783&copyownerid=16539

Onwubiko, C. (2008). *Security framework for attack detection in computer networks.* VDM Verlag.

Onwubiko, C. (2011). Modeling situation awareness information and system requirements for the mission using goal-oriented task analysis approach. In Onwubiko, C., & Owens, T. J. (Eds.), *Situational awareness in computer network defense: Principles, methods and applications.*

Onwubiko, C. (2011b). Designing Information Systems and network components for situational awareness. In Onwubiko, C., & Owens, T. J. (Eds.), *Situational awareness in computer network defense: Principles, methods and applications.*

Orlikowski, W. J., & Iacono, C. S. (2001). Research commentary: Desperately seeking "IT" in IT research - A call to theorizing the IT artifact. *Information Systems Research, 12*(2), 121–134. doi:10.1287/isre.12.2.121.9700

Osterweil, E., Massey, D., & Zhang, L. (2007). *Observations from the DNSSEC Deployment.* 3rd Workshop on Secure Network Protocols (NPSec).

Osterweil, E., Ryan, M., Massey, D., & Zhang, L. (2008). Quantifying the operational status of the DNSSEC deployment. *In Internet Measurement Conference '08: Proceedings of the 8th ACM SIGCOMM Conference on Internet Measurement,* (pp. 231–242).

Ou, X., Boyer, W. F., & McQueen, M. A. (2006). A scalable approach to attack graph generation. In

Palser, B. (2005). *Hurricane Katrina: Aftermath of disaster.* Bloomington, IN: Compass Point Books.

Papadopoulos, C., Lindell, R., Mehringer, J., Hussain, A., & Govindan, R. (2003). *Cossack: Coordinated suppression of simultaneous attacks.* DARPA Information Survivability Conference and Exposition, Washington, DC.

Paxson, V. (1999). Bro: A system for detecting network intruders in real-time. *Computer Networks, 31*(23), 2435–2463. doi:10.1016/S1389-1286(99)00112-7

Perrow, C. (1999). *Normal accidents: Living with high-risk technologies: with a new afterword and a postscript on the Y2K problem.* Princeton, NJ: Princeton University Press.

Perusich, K. A., & McNeese, M. D. (2006). Using fuzzy cognitive maps for knowledge management in a conflict environment. *IEEE Systems. Man and Cybernetics, 36*(6), 810–821.

Philips, C., & Swiler, L. P. (1998). A graph-based system for network-vulnerability analysis. *Procedings of the 1998 Workshop on New Security Paradigms* (pp. 71-79). ACM.

Pinker, S. (1999). *How the mind works*. New York, NY: W.W. Norton & Company.

Proceedings of the 13th ACM Conference on Computer and Communications Security (pp. 336–345). Alexandria, VA: ACM.

Proceedings of Twenty-Second AAAI Conference on Artificial Intelligence (pp. 1535 – 1541). Vancouver, British Columbia, Canada.

Proctor, P. (2001). *Practical intrusion detection handbook*. Upper Saddle River, NJ: Prentice Hall PTR.

PSU. (2011). *Center for cyber-security, Information Privacy, and Trust*. Retrieved March 1, 2011, from http://cybersecurity.ist.psu.edu/research.php.

Qian, J., Hinrichs, S., & Nahrstedt, K. (2001). ACLA: A framework for access control list (ACL) analysis and optimization. In *Proceedings of IFIP Conference on Communications and Multimedia Security.*

Qiao, L., & Xiangsui, W. (2002). *Unrestricted warfare: China's master plan to destroy America* (p. 197). Panama City, Panama: Pan American Publishing Company.

Qin, T., & Burgoon, J. (2007). An investigation of heuristics of human judgment in detecting deception and potential implications in countering social engineering. *Intelligence and Security Informatics, 2007 IEEE*, (pp. 152-159). Doi: 10.1109/ISI.2007.379548

Qiu, L., Varghese, G., & Suri, S. (2001). Fast firewall implementations for software based and hardware-based routers. In *Proceedings of the ACM SIGMETRICS International Conference on Measurement and Modeling of Computer Systems*, (pp. 344–345). New York, NY: ACM Press.

Quinlan, J. R. (1993). *C4.5: Programs for machine learning*. Morgan Kaufmann.

Qureshi, Z., & Urlings, P. (2002). Situation awareness and automation: Issues and design approaches. *Proceedings Information. Decision and Control, 1999*, 605–610.

Racicot, J. (2008). *U.S Army infected by worm.* Retrieved from http://cyberwarfaremag.wordpress.com/2008/11/20/us-army-infected-by-worm/

Raymond, D. R., Marchany, R. C., Brownfield, M. I., & Midkiff, S. F. (2009, January). Effects of denial-of-sleep attacks on wireless sensor network MAC protocols. *IEEE Transactions on Vehicular Technology, 58*(1), 367–380. doi:10.1109/TVT.2008.921621

Ren, K., & Zhang, Y. (2008). LEDS: Providing location-aware end-to-end data security in wireless sensor networks. [TMC]. *IEEE Transactions on Mobile Computing, 5*(7), 585–598. doi:10.1109/TMC.2007.70753

Richardson, J., Ormerod, T. C., & Shepherd, A. (1998). The role of task analysis in capturing requirements for interface design. [Elsevier.]. *Interacting with Computers, 9*, 367–384. doi:10.1016/S0953-5438(97)00036-2

Ritchey, R., & Ammann, P. (2000). Using model checking to analyze network vulnerabilities. *Proceedings of the 2000 IEEE Symposium on Research on Security and Privacy* (pp. 156–165). IEEE Computer Society.

Riverhead Networks Inc. (2011). *Website*. Retrieved May, 2011, from http://www.riverheadnetworks.com

Roads, C. (1996). *The computer music tutorial*. Cambridge, MA: MIT Press.

Rossey, L. M. (2002). *LARIAT: Lincoln adaptable real-time information assurance testbed*. IEEE Aerospace Conference. Big Sky, MT: IEEE.

Roughan, M., Greenberg, A., Kalmanek, C., Rumsewicz, M., Yates, J., & Zhang, Y. (2002). Experience in measuring backbone traffic variability: Models, metrics, measurements and meaning. In *Proceedings of the 2nd ACM SIGCOMM Workshop on Internet Measurement*, (pp. 91–92). New York, NY: ACM Press.

Rowe, R. (2001). *Machine musicianship*. Cambridge, MA: MIT Press.

Ruighaver, A. B., Maynard, S. B., & Chiang, S. (2007). Organizational security culture: Extending the end-user perspective. *Computers & Security, 26*(1), 56–62. doi:10.1016/j.cose.2006.10.008

Ruiz, M. E., & Redmond, R. (2011). Cyber command and control: A military doctrinal prospective on collaborative situation awareness for decision making. In Onwubiko, C., & Owens, T. J. (Eds.), *Situational awareness in computer network defense: Principles, methods and applications.*

Saha, S., & Lagutin, D. (2009). *PLA-MIH: A secure MIH transport signaling scheme.* IEEE International Conference on Wireless and Mobile Computing, Networking and Communications, WIMOB 2009.

Salerno, J. (2008). Measuring situation assessment performance through the activities of interest score. *2008 11th International Conference on Information Fusion* (pp. 1-8).

Salerno, J., Hinman, M., & Boulware, D. (2002). Building a framework for situation awareness. In V. S. Naipaul (Ed.), *Proceedings of the Fifth International Conference on Information Fusion, 2002* (pp. 680-686). Sunnyvale, CA: International Society of Information Fusion.

Salerno, J., Hinman, M., Boulware, D., & Bello, P. (2003). Information fusion for situational awareness. *Proceedings of the Sixth International Symposium on Information Fusion (Fusion 2003),* Cairns, Queensland, Australia (pp. 507-513).

Salerno, J., Hinman, M., & Boulware, D. (2004). *Building a framework for situation awareness. AFRL/IFEA.* Rome, NY: AF Research Lab.

Salmon, P., Stanton, N., Walker, G., & Green, D. (2006). Situation awareness measurement: A review of applicability for C4i environments. *Applied Ergonomics, 37*(2), 225–238. doi:10.1016/j.apergo.2005.02.001

Salter, C., Saydjari, O., Schneier, B., & Wallner, J. (1998). Toward a secure system engineering methodology. In *Proceedings of New Security Paradigms Workshop* (pp. 2-10). Charlottesville, VA: ACM.

Saltzer, J., Reed, D., & Clark, D. (1984, November). End-to-end arguments in system design. *ACM Transactions on Computer Systems, 2*(4). doi:10.1145/357401.357402

Samuelson, P. A. (1970). The fundamental approximation theorem of portfolio analysis in terms of means, variances and higher moments. *The Review of Economic Studies, 37*(4), 537–542.

Sandom, C. (1999). Situational awareness through the interface: Evaluating safety in safety-critical control systems. *IEE Proceedings of People in Control – An International Conference on Human Interfaces in Control Rooms, Cockpits and Command Centres, University of Bath,* UK, 21-23 June 1999.

Sarter, N. B., & Woods, D. D. (1991). Situation awareness: A critical but ill-defined phenomenon. *The International Journal of Aviation Psychology, 1,* 45–57. doi:10.1207/s15327108ijap0101_4

Schneier, B. (1999, December). Attack trees: Modeling security threats. *Dr. Dobb's Journal,* December, 21–29.

Schneier, B. (1996). *Applied cryptography* (2nd ed.). John Wiley & Sons.

Schneier, B. (2004). *Secrets and lies: Digital security in a networked world, with new information about post-9/11 security* (2nd ed.). Wiley Publishing.

Schummer, T., & Lukosch, S. (2007). *Patterns for computer mediated interaction.* Hoboken, NJ: Wiley.

Sekar, R., Guang, Y., Verma, S., & Shanbang, T. (1999). A high-performance network intrusion detection system. In *Proceedings of the 6th ACM Conference on Computer and Communications Security.*

Shen, D., Chen, G., Blasch, E., & Tadda, G. (2007, October). *Adaptive Markov game theoretic data fusion approach for cyber network defense.* Paper presented at IEEE Military Communications Conference (MILCOM 2007), Orlando, FL.

Shen, D., Chen, G., Cruz, J. B., Jr., Haynes, L., Kruger, M., & Blasch, E. (2007). A Markov game theoretic data fusion approach for cyber situational awareness. *Proceedings of SPIE,* vol. 6571.

Shen, D., Chen, G., Haynes, L., & Blasch, E. (2007). *Strategies comparison for game theoretic cyber situational awareness.* Retrieved from http://www.dtic.mil/cgi-bin/GetTRDoc?AD=ADA521036&Location=U2&doc=GetTRDoc.pdf.

Shen, D., Chen, G., Cruz, J. B. Jr, Blasch, E., & Pham, K. (2009). An adaptive Markov game model for cyber threat intent inference. In Er, M. J., & Zhou, Y. (Eds.), *Theory and novel applications of machine learning* (pp. 317–334).

Shepard, R. N. (1962b). The analysis of proximities: Multidimensional scaling with an unknown distance function: Part II. *Psychometrika*, *27*, 219–246. doi:10.1007/BF02289621

Sheyner, O., Haines, J., Jha, S., Lippmann, R., & Wing, J. M. (2002). Automated generation and analysis of attack graphs. *Proceedings of the 2002 IEEE Symposium on Security and Privacy* (pp. 273–284). IEEE Computer Society.

Shneiderman, B. (1996, September). *The eyes have it: A task by data type taxonomy for information visualizations*. Paper presented at the 1996 IEEE Symposium on Visual Languages, Boulder, CO.

Sideman, A. (2011). *Agencies must determine computer security teams in face of potential federal shutdown.* Retrieved March 1, 2011, from http://fcw.com/articles/2011/02/23/agencies-must-determine-computer-security-teams-in-face-of-shutdown.aspx

Siever, W. M., Miller, A., & Tauritz, D. R. (2007, April). *Blueprint for iteratively hardening power grids employing unified power flow controllers*. Paper presented at SoSE' 07 IEEE International Conference on System of Systems Engineering, San Antonio, TX.

Simon, H. A., & March, J. G. (1958). *Organizations*. New York, NY: Wiley.

Singh, S., Baboescu, F., Varghese, G., & Wang, J. (2003). *Packet classification using multidimensional cutting*. In ACM SIGCOMM.

Siponen, M. T., & Oinas-Kukkonen, H. (2007). A review of information security issues and respective research contributions. *The Data Base for Advances in Information Systems*, *38*(1), 60–81.

Skaperdas, S. (1996). Contest success functions. *Economic Theory*, *7*, 283–290.

Smith, J. O. (1992). Physical modeling using digital waveguides. *Computer Music Journal*, *16*(2), 74–91. doi:10.2307/3680470

Smith, K., & Hancock, P. A. (1995). Situation awareness is adaptive, externally directed conciousness. *Human Factors*, *37*(1), 137–148. doi:10.1518/001872095779049444

Snort. (2009) *Snort manual*. Retrieved October 16, 2009, from www.snort.org/docs/snort_htmanuals/htmanual_260

Sommers, J., Yegneswaran, V., & Barford, P. (2001). *Toward comprehensive traffic generation for online IDS evaluation. Tech. Report*. Department of Computer Science, University of Wisconsin.

Sonnenreich, W., Albanese, J., & Stout, B. (2006). Return on security investment (ROSI): A practical quantitative model. *Journal of Research and Practice in Information Technology*, *38*(1), 55–66.

Spears, J. L., & Robert, J. C. (2006). A preliminary investigation of the impact of the Sarbanes-Oxley Act on information security. *Proceedings at the 39th Hawaii International Conference on System Sciences*, (p. 218.c). doi: 10.1109/HICSS.2006.24

Srinivasan, V., Suri, S., & Varghese, G. (1999). Packet classification using tuple space search. *In Proceedings of SIGCOMM*. ACM Press.

Srinivasan, V., & Varghese, G. (1999). Fast address lookups using controlled prefix expansion. *ACM Transactions on Computer Systems*, *17*(1). doi:10.1145/296502.296503

Stakhanova, N., Basu, S., & Wong, J. (2007). A taxonomy of intrusion response systems. *International Journal of Information and Computer Security*, *1*(1/2), 169–184.

Stanton, N. A., Chambers, P. R. G., & Piggott, J. (2001). Situation awareness and safety. *Safety Science*, *39*(3), 189–204. doi:10.1016/S0925-7535(01)00010-8

Steinberg, A. N., Bowman, C. L., & White, F. E. (1999). Revisions to the JDL data fusion model. In B. V. Dasarathy (Ed.), *Sensor Fusion, Architectures, Algorithms and Applications III, Proceedings of the Society of Photo-Optic Instrumentation Engineers (SPIE)*, *3719*, (pp. 430-441). Bellingham, WA: SPIE Publications.

Stewart, B. (2010). *Skating on stilts, why we aren't stopping tomorrow's terrorism, No. 591*. Stanford, CA: Hoover Institution Press.

Stockhausen, K. (1965). *Mikrophonie I, no. 15, for tamtam, 2 microphones, 2 filters and potentiometers*. Vienna, Austria: Universal Edition.

Straub, D. W., Carlson, P. J., & Jones, E. H. (1992). Deterring highly motivated computer abusers: A field experiment in computer security. In Gable, G. G., & Caelli, W. J. (Eds.), *IT security: The need for international cooperation* (pp. 309–324). Holland: Elsevier Science Publishers.

Sudit, M., Stotz, A., & Holender, M. (2005, March 28). *Situational awareness of a coordinated cyber attack.* Paper presented at the SPIE Conference on Data Mining, Intrusion Detection, Information Assurance, and Data Networks Security, Orlando, FL, USA.

Sudit, M., Stotz, A., Holender, M., Tagliaferri, W., & Canarelli, K. (2006). *Measuring situational awareness and resolving inherent high-level fusion obstacles.* Paper presented at the SPIE Conference on Multisensor, Multisource Information Fusion: Architectures, Algorithms, and Applications, Orlando, FL.

Sweller, J., Van Merrienboer, J., & Paas, F. (1998). Cognitive architecture and instructional design. *Educational Psychology Review, 10*(3), 251–296. doi:10.1023/A:1022193728205

Symantec Security Response. (2004). *w32.sasser.worm.* Retrieved May, 2011, from https://securityresponse.symantec.com/avcenter/venc/data/w32.sasser.worm.html

Symantec. (2010). *Internet threat report.* Retrieved May, 2011, from http://symantec.com

Symantec. (2011). *Internet security report.* Retrieved May, 2011, from https://eval.symantec.com

Szidarovszky, F., & Luo, Y. (2011). Optimal protection of computer networks against random attacks. Submitted to *Applied Mathematics and Computation* (Unpublished results).

Tadda, G. P. (2008). Measuring performance of cyber situation awareness systems. *2008 11th International Conference on Information Fusion* (pp. 1-8).

Tadda, G., Salerno, J. J., Boulware, D., Hinman, M., & Gorton, S. (2006, April 19). *Realizing situation awareness within a cyber environment.* Paper presented at the SPIE Conference on Multisensor, Multisource Information Fusion: Architectures, Algorithms, and Applications, Orlando, FL, USA.

Tadda, G. P., & Salerno, J. S. (2010). Overview of cyber situation awareness. In Jajodia, S., Liu, P., Swarup, V., & Wang, C. (Eds.), *Cyber situational awareness* (pp. 15–35). Springer, US. doi:10.1007/978-1-4419-0140-8_2

Tan, T., Ruighaver, T., & Ahmed, A. (2003). *Incident handling: Where the need for planning is often not recognised.* Paper presented at 1st Australian Computer, Network & Information Forensic Conference.

Tapscott, D., & Williams, A. D. (2008). *Wikinomics: How mass collaboration changes everything* (pp. 1–368). Portfolio Hardcover.

Tarsa, S., & Fulp, E. (2005). Trie-based policy representations for network firewalls. In *Proceedings of the IEEE International Symposium on Computer Communications.*

Taylor, F. W. (1911). *The principles of scientific management.* New York, NY: Harper.

Templeton, S., & Levitt, K. (2001). A requires/provides model for computer attacks. In *Proceedings of the 2000 Workshop on New Security Paradigms* (pp. 31--38).

Thomas, C., & Balakrishnan, N. (2008, July). *Performance enhancement of intrusion detection systems using advances in sensor fusion.* Paper presented at the 11th International Conference on Information Fusion, Cologne, Germany.

Thomas, C., & Balakrishnan, N. (2008b). Improvement in minority attack detection with skewness in network traffic. In V. Dasarathy (Ed.), *Proceedings of the SPIE Defense and Security Symposium: Vol. 6973* (pp. 242-253).

Thomas, C., Sharma, V., & Balakrishnan, N. (2008a). Usefulness of DARPA data set for intrusion detection systems evaluation. In V. Dasarathy (Ed.), *Proceedings of the SPIE Defense and Security Symposium: Vol. 6973,* (pp. 137-150).

Thoms, G. A. (2003). Situation awareness - A commander's view. *Proceedings of the Sixth International Symposium on Information Fusion (Fusion 2003),* Cairns, Queensland, Australia (pp. 1094-1101).

Thomson, K.-L., & von Solms, R. (2006). Towards an information security competence maturity model. *Computer Fraud & Security, 5,* 11–15. doi:10.1016/S1361-3723(06)70356-6

Thottan, M., & Ji, C. (2003). Anomaly detection in IP networks. *IEEE Transactions on Signal Processing, 51*(8), 2191–2204. doi:10.1109/TSP.2003.814797

Tian, J., Zhao, W., Du, R., & Zhang, Z. (2005, December). *D-S evidence theory and its data fusion application in intrusion detection.* Paper presented at Sixth International Conference on Parallel and Distributed Computing, Applications and Technologies, Dalian, China.

Tidwell, T., Larson, R., Fitch, K., & Hale, J. (2001). Modeling internet attacks. In *Proceedings of the 2001 IEEE Workshop on Information Assurance and Security* (vol. 59).

Toth, T., & Kruegel, C. (2002, December). *Evaluating the impact of automated intrusion response mechanisms.* Paper presented at 18th Annual Computer Security Applications Conference (ACSAC), Las Vegas, NV.

Trist, E., & Bamforth, K. W. (2001). Some social and psychological consequences of the longwall method of coal getting. *Human Relations, 4*(1), 3–38. doi:10.1177/001872675100400101

Trusted Computing Group. (2011). *TPM main part 1 design principles.* (D. Grawrock, Ed.) Retrieved from http://www.trustedcomputinggroup.org/resources/tpm_main_specification

Tsai, H. C., Chen, K., Liu, Y., Norair, J. P., Bellamy, S., & Shuler, J. (2008). Applying RFID technology in nuclear materials management *Packaging, Transport. Storage and Security of Radioactive Material, 19*(1), 41–46. doi:10.1179/174651008X279000

Tversky, A. (1977). Features of similarity. *Psychological Review, 84*, 327–352. doi:10.1037/0033-295X.84.4.327

US FAA. (1991). Aeronautical decision making. *U.S. Federal Aviation Administration (FAA) Advisory Circular (AC),* 60-122.

Vacca, J. (2009). *Computer forensics: Computer crime scene investigation* (2nd ed.). Charles River Media, Inc.

van Creveld, M. L. (1985). *Command in war* (pp. 1–339). Cambridge, MA: Harvard University Press.

Vaughn, R., & Evron, G. (2006). *DNS amplification attacks.* ISOTF, Tech.

von Clausewitz, C. (1832). *On war: Vom Kriege.* Forgotten Books. Retrieved from http://books.google.com/books?id=eVjotAEMyRwC&pgis=1

Von Solms, B. (2001). Information security: A multidimensional discipline. *Computers & Security, 20*(6), 501–508. doi:10.1016/S0167-4048(01)00608-3

Vosniadou, S., & Ortony, A. (1989). *Similarity and analogical reasoning.* New York, NY: Cambridge University Press. doi:10.1017/CBO9780511529863

Walker, G., Stanton, N. A., & Salmon, P. M. (2009). *Command and control: The sociotechnical perspective* (p. 198). Ashgate Publishing, Ltd.

Wang, A. J. A., & Yestko, K. (2005). Building reusable information security courseware. *Information Security Curriculum Development Conference,* September 23-24, Kennesaw, GA, USA. doi: 10.1145/1107622.1107642

Wang, H., Lai, J., & Liu, X. (2007, August). *Network security situational awareness based on heterogeneous multi-sensor data fusion and neural network.* Paper presented at Second International Multi-Symposiums on Computer and Computational Sciences (IMSCCS), Iowa City, IA.

Wang, H., Liu, X., Lai, J., & Liang, Y. (2007). Network security situation awareness based on heterogeneous multi-sensor data fusion and neural network. *Second International Multi-Symposiums on Computer and Computational Sciences. IMSCCS, 2007,* 352–359.

Wang, L., Noel, S., & Jajodia, S. (2006). Minimum-cost network hardening using attack graphs. *Computer Communications, 29*(18), 3812–3824. doi:10.1016/j.comcom.2006.06.018

Ward, P., & Smith, C. (2002). The development of access control policies for information technology systems. *Computers & Security, 21*(4), 365–371. doi:10.1016/S0167-4048(02)00414-5

Watson, D. R. (2008). The Honeynet project: Data collection tools, infrastructure, archives and analysis. *Information Security Threats Data Collection and Sharing, 2008* (pp. 24-30). Amsterdam, The Netherlands: WISTDCS '08 (WOMBAT Workshop).

Weise, J., & B. Powell, B., (2005). *Using Computer Forensics When Investigating System Attacks*. Sun Microsystems, Inc.

Whitten, A., & Tygar, J. D. (2005). Why Johnny can't encrypt: A usability evaluation of PGP 5.0. In Cranor, L., & Simson O'Reilly, G. (Eds.), *Security and usability: Designing secure systems that people can use* (pp. 679–702).

Wickens, C. D. (1992). *Engineering psychology and human performance* (2nd ed.). New York, NY: Harper Collins.

Winkler, I. S. (1996). The non-technical threat to computing systems. *Computing Systems, 9*(1), 3–14.

Wohl, J. G. (1981). Force management decision requirements for Air Force tactical command and control. *IEEE Transactions on Systems, Man, and Cybernetics, 11*(9), 618–639. doi:10.1109/TSMC.1981.4308760

Woo, T. (March, 2000). A modular approach to packet classification: Algorithms and results. *In Proceedings of IEEE INFOCOM.*

Wood, B. J., Saydjari, O. S., & Stavridou, V. (2000). *A proactive holistic approach to strategic cyber defense*, (p. 2). Menlo Park, CA: SRI International. Retrieved November 3, 2008, from http://www.cyberdefenseagency.com/publications/A_Proactive_Holistic_Approach_to_Strategic_Cyber_Defense.pdf

Writer, S. (2010). War in the fifth domain. *Economist, 396*(8689), 25–28.

Wu, H., Seigel, M., Stiefelhagen, R., & Yang, J. (2002). Sensor fusion using Dempster-Shafer theory. *IEEE Instrumentation and Measurement Technology Conference* (pp. 21-23).

Xiang, Y., & Zhou, W. (October, 2005). Intelligent DDoS packet filtering in high-speed networks. *Lecture Notes in Computer Science,* vol. 3758. Berlin, Germany: Springer.

Xie, P., Li, J. H., Ou X., Liu, P., & Levy, R. (2010). Using Bayesian networks for cyber security analysis.

Yakowitz, S. (1989). Algorithms and computational techniques in differential dynamic programming. In Leondes, C. T. (Eds.), *Control and dynamical systems: Advances in theory and applications, 31* (pp. 75–91). San Diego, CA: Academic Press, Inc.

Yan, H., Osterweil, E., Hajdu, J., Acres, J., & Massey, D. (2008). *Limiting replay vulnerabilities in DNSSEC*. 4th IEEE ICNP Workshop on Secure Network Protocols (NPSec).

Yang, H., & Lu, S. (2004). Commutative cipher based en-route filtering in wireless sensor networks. In *Proceedings of 60th IEEE Vehicular Technology Conference Fall* Los Angeles, CA, vol. 2, (pp. 1223-1227).

Yang, H., Ye, F., & Arbaugh, W. (2005). Toward resilient security in wireless sensor networks. *In Proceedings of The Sixth ACM International Symposium on Mobile Ad Hoc Networking and Computing* (MobiHoc), Urbana-Champaign, Illinois, USA, (pp. 34-45).

Yang, S. J., Byers, S., Holsopple, J., Argauer, B., & Fava, D. (2008, June 17-20). *Intrusion activity projection for cyber situational awareness.* Paper presented at the IEEE International Conference on Intelligence and Security Informatics (ISI 2008). Tapei, Taiwan.

Yang, H., Osterweil, E., Massey, D., & Zhang, L. (2010). Deploying cryptography in Internet-scale systems: A case study on DNSSEC. *IEEE Transactions on Dependable and Secure Computing, 7*(2).

Ye, F., Luo, H., & Zhang, L. (2004). Statistical en-route filtering of injected false data in sensor networks. In *Proceedings of the 23th IEEE International Conference on Computer Communications,* Hong Kong, China, (pp. 2446-2457).

Yen, J., McNeese, M. D., Mullen, T., Hall, D. L., Fan, X., & Liu, P. (2010). RPD-based hypothesis reasoning for cyber situation awareness. In Jajodia, S., Liu, P., Swarup, G., & Wang, C. (Eds.), *Cyber situational awareness: Issues and research* (pp. 39–49). New York, NY: Springer. doi:10.1007/978-1-4419-0140-8_3

Yin, X., Yurick, W., & Slagell, A. (2008). *VisFlowConnect-IP: An animated link analysis tool for visualising netflows.* SIFT Research Group, National Centre for Supercomputing Applications, University of Illinois at Urbana-Champaign, 2008.

Yong, Z., Xiaobin, T., & Hongsheng, X. (2007). A novel approach to network security situation awareness based on multi-perspective analysis. *International Conference on Computational Intelligence and Security* (pp. 768-772).

Yu, E. (1995). *Modelling strategic relationships for process reengineering.* PhD Thesis, Department of Computer Science, University of Toronto, Canada, 1995.

Yu, L., & Li, J. (2009). Grouping-based resilient statistical en-route filtering for sensor networks. *In Proceedings of the 28th IEEE International Conference on Computer Communications,* Rio de Janeiro, Brazil, (pp. 1782-1790).

Yurick, W. (2005). Visualising netflow for security at line speed: The SIFT tool suit. *Proceedings of the 19th Usenix Large Installation System Administration Conference (LISA),* (pp. 169-176).

Yu, Z., & Guan, Y. (2010). A dynamic en-route filtering scheme for data reporting in wireless sensor networks. [TON]. *IEEE/ACM Transactions on Networking, 18,* 150–163. doi:10.1109/TNET.2009.2026901

Zhang, Y., Fan, X., Xue, Z., & Xu, H. (2008, November). Two stochastic models for security evaluation based on attack graph. In *The 9th International Conference for Young Computer Scientists,* (pp. 2198-2203). Washington, DC: IEEE Computer Society.

Zhang, Z., & Ho, P. (2009). Janus: A dual-purpose analytical model for understanding, characterizing and countermining multi-stage collusive attacks in enterprise networks. *Journal of Network and Computer Applications, 32*(3), 710–720.

Zhao, X., & Sun, J. (November, 2003). A parallel scheme for IDS. *Proceedings of the Second Internatonal Conference on Machine Learning and Cybernetics.*

Zhu, S., & Setia, S. (2004). An interleaved hop-by-hop authentication scheme for filtering of injection false data in sensor networks. *IEEE Symposium on Security and Privacy,* Berkeley, CA, USA, (pp. 259-271).

Zhuang, J., & Bier, V. M. (2007). Balancing terrorism and natural disasters—Defensive strategy with endogenous attacker effort. *Operations Research, 55*(5), 976–991.

About the Contributors

Cyril Onwubiko is a leading information security expert and founder of Research Series in London, UK where he leads on intelligence and security assurance, Cyber security, and situational awareness in computer network defense. Prior to Research Series, he was an information security consultant at British Telecommunications, CLAS consultant at Cable & Wireless Worldwide, and a security analyst at COLT Telecommunications. He holds a PhD degree in Computer Network Security from Kingston University, London, UK. Dr. Onwubiko has authored several books, including "Security Frameworks for Attack Detection in Computer Networks," and has published over 30 academic articles in reputable journals, conference proceedings, and edited books. He is a member of the IEEE, Institute of Information Security Professionals (IISP), and CESG Listed Advisor Scheme (CLAS).

Thomas Owens obtained his PhD in Electrical and Electronic Engineering from Strathclyde University in 1986. In 1987 he joined as a Lecturer the Department of Electronic and Electrical Engineering, Brunel University, which was eventually absorbed into the School of Engineering and Design in 2004, in which he is now a Senior Lecturer. He was the project coordinator of the IST FP5 STREP Project CONFLUENT, of the IST FP6 Integrated Project INSTINCT, and of the FP6 SSA Project PARTAKE. He was dissemination manager of the IST Policy Support Project DTV4All. He is the author of more than 90 papers in journals, conference proceedings, and edited books.

* * *

Subrata Acharya is an Assistant Professor in the CIS Department at Towson University. Before joining Towson University, she completed her Ph.D. from the CS Department (Major: Network Security) University of Pittsburgh in December 2008. She has collaborated on various cutting edge research projects with AT&T, Symantec, and IBM Research Laboratories. Her research interests are in the areas of cyber security, health information security, and trust worthy computing. She has contributed to projects in secure networks (S-CITI project, NSF), future Internet design (Securing-NGI, NSF), computer science education – MHEC-BRAC, DoD IASP, et cetera. Her research has been published in various international conferences and journals, namely, NDSS, ICC, IEEE ANSS, IEEE TC, IEEE TPDS, et cetera. She has served as a NSF panel review member on Trustworthy Computing and Cross Cutting Programs in Computer and Network Security. She has also served as a reviewer and program committee member for various noteworthy conferences and journals.

Khidir Mohamed Ali holds a BSc in Computer Science, an MSc in Electronics and Automation and an MSc with distinction in Telecommunications and Computer Network Engineering. He obtained his PhD from Brunel University in 2006 for his research in Wireless Security. Prior to that Dr. Ali joined the Hewlett-Packard Company in 1996, where he spent 4 years as a computer network consultant. In 2006 he joined Jubail University College as a Senior Lecturer in the Department of Computer Science and Engineering, where he is currently the head of the department, which he has held since 2008. His research interest include computer security and, in particular, the security of WLANs and digital forensics. Dr. Ali teaches Data Communications, Computer Network Systems, Information Security, and Forensic Computing. Dr. Ali is a reviewer, editor, and the author of many journal papers and textbooks.

Marios Anagnostopoulos holds a B.Sc in Computer Science from Computer Science Department of the University of Crete. He received a M.Sc. degree in Information and Communication Systems Security in 2010 from the Department of Information and Communication Systems Engineering of the University of the Aegean. His Master's thesis was in the area of DNS security. He is currently a PhD candidate at the Department of Information and Communication Systems Engineering, University of the Aegean. His research interests are in the fields of network security, DNS security, applications of cryptography in communications systems, and network services and applications.

N. Balakrishnan obtained his PhD from the Indian Institute of Science, Bangalore, India. He is currently serving as the Associate Director of the Indian Institute of Science, Bangalore, India. He was awarded Padmasree by the President of India in 2002. He has fellowships in Third World Academy of Sciences, Indian National Science Academy, Indian Academy of Sciences, Indian National Academy of Engineering, and Institution of Electronic and Telecommunication Engineers. He is also an Honorary Professor of Jawaharlal Nehru Centre for Advanced Scientific Research and National Institute of Advanced Studies. He is the Editor-in-Chief of the *International Journal of World Digital Libraries* and also a member of the editorial board of many international journals. He has, to his credit, more than two hundred research papers in referred international journals, international conference proceedings, and book chapters. His research interests include the fields of network security, numerical electromagnetics, multi-parameter radars, and signal processing.

Mark Ballora is Associate Professor of Music Technology at Penn State University, where he teaches courses in audio/music production, musical acoustics, history of electroacoustic music, and software programming for musicians. He studied theatre arts at UCLA, and Composition and Music Technology at NYU and McGill University. He is author of the textbook "Essentials of Music Technology" (Prentice Hall, 2003), has written columns for *Electronic Musician* magazine, and has published articles describing sonification, His work includes sound designs and electroacoustic scores for modern dance, theatre, animated films, and radio dramas. His work has been presented at the International Conference on Auditory Display, Computers in Cardiology, the Society for Electro-Acoustic Music in the United States (SEAMUS), and the Society for Arts in Healthcare.

Erik Blasch received his B.S. in Mechanical Engineering from MIT and MS in Mechanical and Industrial Engineering from Georgia Tech and MBA, MSEE, from Wright State University, and a PhD from WSU in EE. Dr. Blasch also attended University of Wisconsin for an MD/PhD in Mech. Eng until being called to Active Duty in the United States Air Force. Currently, he is a Fusion Evaluation Tech Lead for the Air Force Research Laboratory, Adjunct Professor at WSU, and a reserve Maj. with the Air Force Office of Scientific Research. Dr. Blasch was a founding member of the International Society of Information Fusion (ISIF) and the 2007 ISIF President. Dr. Blasch has focused on Automatic Target Recognition, Targeting Tracking, and Information Fusion research compiling 300+ scientific papers and book chapters. He is active in IEEE and a SPIE fellow.

Uri Blumenthal obtained his MS in Applied Mathematics from Odessa State University in 1981. He worked at IBM Research Center on Network Management and Security projects, and co-authored User-based Security Model for SNMPv3 protocol. In 2000 he joined Lucent/Bell Labs to work on Wireless Security, and performed extensive modeling and simulation-based analysis of IPsec impact on performance and user experience in context of TCP/IP network in general, and cellular data networks such as EVDO, in particular. In 2004 he joined Intel Research Labs to work on Security Architecture of Intel products such as iAMT, and proposed several improvements that were implemented. In 2007 he joined MIT to work on Security Analysis and Design of distributed systems. He is a co-author of 20 publications and 18 patents.

Genshe Chen received the BS and MS in Electrical Engineering, PhD in Aerospace Engineering, in 1989, 1991, and 1994 respectively, all from Northwestern Polytechnical University, Xian, P. R. China. Currently Dr. Chen is an Independent Consultant Professional. He was the CTO of DCM Research Resources LLC, Germantown, MD, and the Program Manager in Networks, Systems and Control at Intelligent Automation, Inc. He was a Postdoctoral Research Associate in the Department of Electrical and Computer Engineering of The Ohio State University from 2002 to 2004. He worked at the Institute of Flight Guidance and Control of the Technical University of Braunshweig (Germany) as an Alexander von Humboldt research fellow and at the Flight Division of National Aerospace Laboratory of Japan as a STA fellow from 1997 to 2001. He did postdoctoral work at the Beijing University of Aeronautics and Astronautics and Wright State University from 1994 to 1997.

Jeremy Daily, before graduating in 2001 from Wright State University in Ohio with a BS degree in Mechanical Engineering, served six years in the U.S. Air Force, where he maintained flight-line navigation aids and meteorological systems. In June of 2006, he received a PhD in Engineering after completing a dissertation in fatigue and fracture based on his research conducted at the U.S. Air Force Research Laboratory, and is a registered professional engineer. He coauthored a textbook titled "Fundamentals of Traffic Crash Reconstruction" published by the Institute for Police Technology and Management. Jeremy continues with active research in traffic crash reconstruction, which has led to an advanced shot marker system, analytical sensitivity analysis, refinements of the Monte Carlo simulation method, a portable crash test system, and studies on accuracy of event data recorders. He has provided expert testimony in civil and criminal cases involving traffic crashes and digital forensic data on vehicles.

Varun Dutt is a PhD candidate (ABD), Department of Engineering and Public Policy, Carnegie Mellon University. He has also a Master's degree in Engineering and Public Policy and a Master's degree in Software Engineering from Carnegie Mellon University. Prior to coming to Carnegie Mellon, Varun worked as a Software Engineer in India's top IT firm, Tata Consultancy Services. He is also the

Knowledge Editor of the English daily, *Financial Chronicle*. His current research interests focus on environmental decision making, dynamic decision making, situation awareness, cyber situation awareness, and modeling of human behavior. Varun has published in journals of international repute, including *Journal of Behavioral Decision Making, Journal of Applied Cognitive Psychology, Games, Computers in Human Behavior*, and *Psychological Review*.

Xinwen Fu is an Assistant Professor in the Department of Computer Science, University of Massachusetts Lowell. He received his BS (1995) and MS (1998) in Electrical Engineering from Xi'an Jiaotong University, China and University of Science and Technology of China respectively. He obtained his PhD (2005) in Computer Engineering from Texas A&M University. From 2005 to 2008, he was an Assistant Professor with the College of Business and Information Systems at Dakota State University. In summer 2008, he joined University of Massachusetts Lowell as a faculty member. His current research interests are in network security and privacy.

Nicklaus A. Giacobe is a researcher studying cyber security situational awareness. He is interested in how to increase the awareness that a cyber security analyst has of events happening on the network. He uses the concepts of visualization, multi-sensor data fusion, and other techniques to address the questions of cognitive issues related to the analyst. His dissertation will be focused on the use of systems to develop situational awareness for security analysts. This work has three parts - (1) leveraging existing "sensors," (2) applying fusion algorithms, and (3) representing the fusion system in an HCI/representation that reduces cognitive load and increases situational awareness.

Cleotilde Gonzalez is Associate Research Professor, Department of Social and Decision Sciences, Carnegie Mellon University. Prior to joining Carnegie Mellon, Cleotilde completed her Ph.D. from Texas Tech University in Management Information Systems. Her research interests include the study of human decision making in dynamic and complex environments. She is the founding director of the Dynamic Decision Making Laboratory, Carnegie Mellon. She is affiliated faculty at HCII, CCBI, and CNBC. She is in the Editorial board of the *Human Factors Journal* and Associate Editor of the *JCEDM*. Cleotilde has published in journals of international repute, including *Journal of Behavioral Decision Making, Journal of Applied Cognitive Psychology, Games, Computers in Human Behavior, Organizational Behavior and Human Decision Processes, Journal of Cognitive Psychology, System Dynamics Review, Human Factors*, and *Psychological Review*.

Stefanos Gritzalis is a Professor at the Department of Information and Communication Systems Engineering, University of the Aegean, Greece and the Director of the Laboratory of Information and Communication Systems Security (Info-Sec-Lab). He also serves as the Special Secretary for the Administrative Reform at the Greek Ministry of Interior, Decentralization and Electronic Government. He holds a BSc in Physics, an MSc in Electronic Automation, and a PhD in Information and Communications Security from the Dept. of Informatics and Telecommunications, University of Athens, Greece. He has been involved in several national and EU funded R&D projects. His published scientific work includes 30 books or book chapters, 90 journals, and more than 120 international refereed conference and workshop papers. The focus of these publications is on information and communications security and privacy. His most highly cited papers have more than 1,000 citations. He has acted as Guest Editor in 22 journal special issues, and has been involved in more than 30 international conferences and workshops as General Chair or Program Committee Chair. He has served on more than 230 program committees of international conferences and workshops. He is an Editor-in-Chief or Editor or Editorial Board member for 15 journals and a Reviewer for more than 40 journals. He has supervised 10 PhD dissertations. He was an elected Member of the Board (Secretary General, Treasurer) of the Greek Computer Society. His professional experience includes senior consulting and researcher positions in a number of private and public institutions. He is a Member of the ACM and the IEEE.

John Hale is a Professor of Computer Science and faculty researcher in Information Security at the University of Tulsa. He received his Bachelor of Science in 1990, Master of Science in 1992, and Doctorate degree in 1997, all in Computer Science from the University of Tulsa. Dr. Hale has overseen the development of the premier information assurance curriculum in the nation. In 2000, he earned a prestigious National Science Foundation CAREER award for his education and research initiatives at iSec. His research interests include cyber attack modeling, analysis and visualization, enterprise security management, secure operating systems, distributed system verification, and policy coordination.

Joshua W. Haines is an Assistant Group Leader in the Cyber Systems & Technology Group at MIT Lincoln Laboratory. He is responsible for managing research and development of technology and systems in support of national cyber missions. Focus areas include system analysis, architecture engineering for robustness and security, development of network-centric cyber systems for situation awareness and decision support, automated analysis of network vulnerabilities, blue-team assessment of DoD programs, and development of testbed-based cyber assessments.

Janne Merete Hagen holds a Master of Science in Industrial Engineering and Management from Linköping Institute of Technology, Linköping, and a Master of Management from the Norwegian School of Management, Executive School, Oslo. She received her PhD degree in Computer Science from the University of Oslo in 2009. Hagen's research has focused on critical infrastructure protection and national emergency preparedness. She has been working at the Norwegian Defense Research Establishment (FFI) since 1996. The research has been cited in several Governmental White Papers and contributed to important improvements in national emergency preparedness. In 2010 she received the ITAKT award for her research on vulnerabilities and emergency preparedness in the Internet and telecommunication sector. Before she started at FFI, she was employed as researcher at the Institute of Transport Economics, where she conducted research on logistics, Electronic Data Interchange, and goods transportation.

David L. Hall is Dean of Penn State's College of Information Sciences and Technology. Author of more than 175 papers, reports, books, and book chapters, he has delivered numerous lectures on his research, research management, and artificial intelligence. Hall's research has covered stellar structures, celestial mechanics, digital signal processing, software engineering, and automated reasoning. Multisensor data fusion is a particular focus for Hall, and his work in this area is recognized both nationally and internationally. Hall has conducted and led research projects for such sponsors as NASA, the Defense Advanced Research Projects Agency, Naval Research Lab, Office of Naval Research, U.S. Air Force Rome Air Development Center, the Department of Defense, and private aerospace corporations. Courses taught at both the undergraduate and graduate level include Advanced Physics, Modern Physics, Astronomy, Celestial Mechanics, Artificial Intelligence and Knowledge-Based Systems, Information Systems and Project Management, and information fusion.

Peter J. Hawrylak is an Assistant Professor in the Electrical Engineering department at The University of Tulsa (TU), is Vice-Chair of the AIM RFID Experts Group (REG), and Chair of the Healthcare Initiative (HCI) sub-group of the AIM REG. Dr. Hawrylak is a member of The University of Tulsa's Institute for Information Security (iSec), which is a NSA (U.S. National Security Agency) Center of Excellence. Peter has four (4) issued patents in the RFID space and numerous academic publications. Peter's research interests are in the areas embedded system security, RFID, embedded systems, and low power wireless systems. He is Associate Editor of the *International Journal of Radio Frequency Identification Technology and Applications* (IJRFITA), published by InderScience Publishers, which focuses on the application and development of RFID technology.

Georgios Kambourakis received the Diploma in Applied Informatics from the Athens University of Economics and Business in 1993 and the Ph.D. in Information and Communication Systems Engineering from the Department of Information and Communications Systems Engineering of the University of the Aegean. He also holds a M.Ed. from the Hellenic Open University. Currently Dr. Kambourakis is a Lecturer at the Department of Information and Communication Systems Engineering of the University of the Aegean, Greece. His research interests are in the fields of mobile and wireless communication systems security and privacy, VoIP security, security protocols, public key infrastructure, DNS Security, and mLearning, and he has more than 80 publications in the above areas. He has been involved in several national and EU funded R&D projects in the areas of information and communication systems security. He is a reviewer of several IEEE and other international journals and has served as a technical program committee member in numerous conferences.

Elisavet Konstantinou holds a B.Sc. in Informatics from the University of Ioannina, a M.Sc. in Signal and Image Processing Systems, and a PhD in Theory and Applications of Elliptic Curve Cryptosystems from the University of Patras, Department of Computer Engineering and Informatics. She is currently a Lecturer in the Department of Information and Communication Systems Engineering, University of the Aegean. She was a research fellow in the Computer Technology Institute and participated in several EC funded projects (such as the IST projects ASPIS and FLAGS), as well as in several national projects. She has published several papers in international conferences and journals. Her research interests include elliptic curves cryptosystems and generation of their parameters, public key cryptosystems, group key agreement protocols, algorithm engineering, and algebraic number theory. She is a member of the IEEE Computer Society.

Jie Lin is a Ph.D. candidate in Computer Science and Technology from the Xi'an Jiaotong University of China. He received the BS degree from Department of Computer Science and Technology at Xi'an Jiaotong University in 2009. His main research interests include wireless sensor networks security and cyber-physical systems security.

George Louthan IV is a Master's Degree Research Assistant at the University of Tulsa's Institute for Information Security working in cyber-physical systems and formal modeling with a focus on attack graphs. His research interests also touch network security, novel user interfaces, visualization, and secure collaboration. He is currently working to extend existing, well-studied formal security models into the continuous domain and along with researchers across several fields to build the formal underpinnings of a real-time network vulnerability analysis and visualization engine suitable for large-scale multi-touch environments.

Yi Luo received the Ph.D. degree in Systems and Industrial Engineering Department from University of Arizona, Tucson, AZ, in 2011. His research interests include decision making under uncertainty, agent-based modeling, dynamical systems theory, game theory, optimization, adaptive learning, forecasting, data mining, simulation, and their applications in cyber security, supply chain management, sustainable systems, et cetera. He is the author of fifteen papers in international conferences and professional journals.

Eric X. McMillan is a Doctoral student in the College of Information Sciences & Technology at The Pennsylvania State University. Eric's research focuses on how the use of formal analytical methods impacts cyber situation awareness and problem solving. Prior to embarking upon his graduate career, Eric spent over a decade in industry designing enterprise scale Information System architectures and eight years in the US military as an intelligence analyst.

Michael McNeese examines issues bridging computer science and cognitive studies. McNeese received the first interdisciplinary Ph.D. awarded by Vanderbilt University. He is widely published, and among his most recent works is a book, titled, "New Trends in Collaborative Activities: Dynamics in Complex Systems." McNeese has taught at The Ohio State University and Wright State University. McNeese studies human interaction with Information Technology in complex environments, particularly collaborative systems that bring together the confluences of cognition, computation, collaboration, and context for given fields of practice – deriving advanced human-computer interfaces through innovations of affective computing, artificial intelligence, and computer-supported cooperative work perspectives. McNeese is a scholar in the area of learning sciences and is an advocate and practitioner of problem-based learning and computer- supported cooperative learning. As such, his methodological interests and activities are wide-ranging, spanning from ethnographic field study to experimental designs to protocol analysis to cognitive modeling to scaled-world simulations.

Qazi Bouland Mussabbir received his Ph.D degree in Electronic & Computer Engineering from Brunel University in 2010. At Brunel, he was a part of the Centre for Networks and Multimedia Communications. Currently he is a consultant for one of largest IT consultancy/technology firms in the world. His research interests are wireless network security, IPv6 mobility across heterogeneous networks, bootstrapping and service authentication, and network architecture.

Gerald C. O'Leary is currently a senior staff member in the Cyber Systems and Technology Group. He joined the technical staff of MIT Lincoln Laboratory in 1977. He has worked in the areas of satellite communications, speech processing, digital networking, and information security. He has served as Associate Leader of the Cyber Systems and Technology Group from 1984 to 1998 and of the Tactical Communications Systems Group from 1998 to 2000. Prior to joining the Laboratory, he worked at MITRE Corp. in the Advanced Radar Techniques Department and Signal Processing Systems, Inc., in the area of programmable digital processors for communications applications. He is a member of the IEEE. Mr. O'Leary received S.B. and S.M. degrees in Electrical Engineering and the Electrical Engineer degree from MIT in 1964 and 1966.

Mauricio Papa is an Associate Professor for the Department of Computer Science at The University of Tulsa. He also serves as Faculty Director of the Institute for Information Security, which supports a multi-disciplinary program of study and research tackling cyber security issues on a global scale. Dr. Papa received his Bachelor of Science in Electrical Engineering from Universidad Central de Venezuela in 1992 and his Master of Science in Electrical Engineering and Doctorate degree in computer science from TU in 1996 and 2001, respectively. His primary research area is critical infrastructure protection. Propelled by a world-class research program in SCADA network security, Dr. Papa and his team designed and constructed a novel process control network test bed to address cyber security needs for the critical infrastructure. He also conducts research in distributed systems, network security, cryptographic protocol verification, and intelligent control systems.

Michael E. Ruiz is a researcher and consultant at Deloitte Consulting, LLP, as well as, Affiliated Faculty for the Department of Information Systems in the School of Business at Virginia Commonwealth University. Mr. Ruiz served in the US Army as an analyst and software engineer. With 20 years of IT experience within academia, commercial, and public sectors, Mr. Ruiz advises executive level government officials on the outlook of Information Technology strategies and trends. Mr. Ruiz also leads internal research and development projects in the area of information sharing, enterprise governance, and cyber security. Mr. Ruiz is currently pursuing his PhD in Engineering with a focus on Cyber Analytics at Virginia Commonwealth University's School of Engineering.

Richard Redmond is Chairman and Associate Professor, of the Department of Information Systems in the School of Business at Virginia Commonwealth University. He received a Doctorate of Business Administration with a major in decisions sciences in 1983. His recent publications and research have been in the areas of software engineering, database systems, expert systems, agent-based systems, and applications of AI to business. More recently his focus has turned toward the Semantic Web and multi-agent based systems.

William Streilein is an Assistant Group Leader in the Cyber System Assessments Group at MIT Lincoln Laboratory. His current research interests include the investigation and development of machine learning analysis capabilities that support cyber situational awareness. Other areas of interest include understanding how mission-oriented behaviors are mapped to computer network infrastructure, the analysis of next-generation IPv6 network architectures, and the investigation of issues associated with the security and privacy of network-based databases. Prior to joining the Cyber Group, Dr. Strelein was a staff member in the Sensor Exploitation Group, where his research focused on the exploitation of multi-sensor fused imagery in interactive automatic learning and recognition environments. He holds a B.A. degree in Mathematics from Austin College, an M.M. in Electronic and Computer Music from the University of Miami, and a Ph.D. degree in Cognitive and Neural Systems from Boston University. He has been at Lincoln Laboratory since 1998.

Ferenc Szidarovszky received his education in Hungary, where he has earned two PhD degrees, one in Mathematics, the other in Economics. The Hungarian Academy of Sciences has awarded him with the degrees of "Candidate in Mathematics" and "Doctor of Engineering Sciences." Between 1973 and 1986 he was an investigator in several joint research projects between Hungarian and American researchers, and in 1988, he became a Professor with the Systems and Industrial Engineering Department of the University of Arizona. His research interests are decision making under uncertainty, multicriteria decision making, game theory, conflict resolution, and their applications in natural resource management, economics, and cyber security. He is the author of 18 books and over 300 refereed journal publications in addition to numerous conference presentations and invited lectures. He is regularly invited to give short courses in Game Theory in several countries of Europe and Asia.

Ciza Thomas obtained her PhD in Network Security from the Indian Institute of Science, Bangalore, India. She is serving as Professor in the Electronics and Communication Department, College of Engineering, Trivandrum, India. She was honored with an appreciation award in 2010, by the Higher Education Department of State Government of Kerala for implementing institutional repositories and e-learning systems for all the Government Engineering and Polytechnic Colleges in the State of Kerala. She has, to her credit, twenty five research papers in referred international journals, international conference proceedings, and book chapters. She serves as a reviewer to international journals in the field of network security and signal processing. She has also edited two books, titled "Sensor Fusion and its Applications," published by Sciyo books, and "Sensor Fusion: Foundation and Applications," by InTech Books. Her research interests include the fields of network security, sensor fusion, signal processing, data mining, information and communication technologies, et cetera.

Michael Tyworth is a Post-Doctoral Fellow at the College of Information Sciences and Technology at The Pennsylvania State University. Michael is currently leading a team of researchers and graduate students conducting applied and basic research into situation awareness in the cyber-security domain as part of an ongoing Multidisciplinary University Research Initiative sponsored by the US Army Research Office. In addition to the ongoing project, Michael's research has focused on the development of integrated Information Systems for law enforcement, inter-organizational collaboration, organizational identity, and socio-technical theory. Michael received his Ph.D. from the College of Information Sciences & Technology in December, 2009.

Xinyu Yang received the Diploma in Computer Science and Technology from the Xi'an Jiaotong University of China in 2001 and the BS, MS, and PhD degrees from Xi'an Jiaotong University in 1995, 1997, and 2001, respectively. He has held positions with the Department of Computer Science and Technology at the Xi'an Jiaotong University, where he is a Professor teaching in the Department of Computer Science and Technology. His main research interests are in the areas of wireless communication, mobile ad hoc networks, network security, and cyber-physical systems security.

Wei Yu is an Assistant Professor in the Department of Computer and Information Sciences, Towson University, Towson, MD 21252. Before that, He worked for Cisco Systems Inc. for almost nine years. He received the BS degree in Electrical Engineering from Nanjing University of Technology in 1992, the MS degree in Electrical Engineering from Tongji University in 1995, and the PhD degree in computer engineering from Texas A&M University in 2008. His research interests include cyber space security, computer network, and distributed systems.

Index

A

access router (AR) 228, 241
access service authoriser (ASA) 226
access service provider (ASP) 226, 241
advanced persistent threat 88
air traffic controller 34
asymmetric warfare 31, 141-142
authentication, authorization and accounting (AAA) 241
authorization and bootstrapping information request (ABIREQ) 230
authorization and bootstrapping information response (ABIRES) 230
average residence time (AVR) 237

B

backward process 56, 59, 64
battlefield 30-31, 86-87, 138, 264
bootstrapping client identifier (BCID) 230
bootstrapping configuration agent (BCA) 230, 241

C

channel binding (CB) 232
Chebyshev Inequality 166, 171-172, 180
cognitive factors 129
cognitive Instance-based learning 125
collaboration services 40-41
collaborative situation awareness for decision making 29, 37, 355
command and control and situation awareness theory 29
commercial and military environments 29
common operating picture 30, 37-38, 40-41
complete learning cycle 130
comprehension 2-4, 32, 34, 39, 46, 72, 74, 79, 85, 98, 106-107, 114-115, 125-127, 130, 149, 200, 343

computation 39, 43, 49-50, 57, 69, 76, 110, 190, 269
computation process 49
computer network defense 1-2, 4-5, 7-8, 23, 49, 67, 71-81, 86, 88, 92, 122, 141, 161, 259-260, 284, 344, 355
computer network security 2, 8, 48, 105, 107, 109, 112, 116, 122, 260
context-aware collaboration 40
control requirements 36, 293
crowd sourcing 37-38, 42
CSA-DM 37, 43
cyber analysts 30, 34
cyber c 30-37, 39, 41, 43
cyber command and control 29-30, 32, 35-36, 41, 43, 355
cyber doctrine 31
cyber-infrastructure 127-128
cybersecurity 46, 48, 68, 125-126, 138-139, 219
cyberspace 16, 29, 44, 74-75, 78-81, 115, 122, 140, 256, 259
cyber warriors 31

D

DARPA 99, 101, 162, 172-174, 179, 198, 296, 302-313, 315-318, 342
data collection services 38
data exfiltration 92
data fusion 8-9, 39, 69, 74, 79, 82-83, 109, 114-115, 120-122, 141-145, 147-149, 154-155, 158-159, 161-164, 168, 178-179, 260-262, 281, 315-318
data mining 39, 83, 100, 150, 160, 167, 178-179, 184, 298, 316-318
decision-point nodes 88
defensive 21, 29, 48, 50-51, 55, 59-60, 67, 70, 95, 98, 151-154, 253-254, 291, 296
defensive and operational capabilities 29
degree of reliability 88

detection and reporting of incidents and near-miss
    incidents 11
detection of malicious behavior 95
discrete time 51, 60
discrete-time dynamic evolutionary game 49
discrete-time stochastic control problem 48
doctrinal aspects 31
dynamic host control protocol v6 (DHCPv6) 227
dynamic programming 48, 50, 53-55, 68-70

E

EAP extended master session key (EMSK) 229
EAP re-authentication protocol (ERP) 228
enhance situational awareness 5, 48-49, 67, 108,
    119-120, 245
enterprise network 98, 102, 320, 322, 327, 330, 340
equilibrium analysis 51
equilibrium approach 49
extensible authentication protocol (EAP) 221-222,
    238-239, 241

F

Facebook 21
fast mobile IPv6 (FMIPv6) 222
field flight plan 34
forward process 56, 59, 62, 64
f-score 166, 173-174, 176-177, 180
fusion model 32, 161, 163

G

game theory 49, 68, 70, 287
guest OS 96

H

hacking 14, 16-17, 27, 94, 102, 154, 356
handover key response (HKResp) 231
handover key server (HKS) 231
honeynet 98, 101-102
honeypot 102
human decision-making 87
human endeavor 86
human relations 10, 26
human resources security 13
human role and the theoretical relationship 20

I

importance of properly educating IT-users 13
information element (IE) 230

information key (IK) 231
information master key (IMK) 231
information security 1-4, 8-28, 68-69, 78, 82, 86-87,
    89-90, 100-101, 108, 195-196, 255, 260, 344
information security incident management 13, 17
information security policy 13, 25, 27-28
insider threat 11, 25
internalization of security policies 17
internet engineering task force (IETF) 222, 241
internet service provider (ISP) 195, 242
intrusion detection systems 3, 5, 16, 74, 82, 101,
    107, 114-115, 117, 120, 148, 161-163, 165-166,
    172, 179-180, 183-185, 199, 261, 302-305,
    309, 316-319, 321-322, 341
ISO 27001 15, 22
ISO 27002 15
IT abuse incidents 16
IT security 19, 23, 26, 101, 285, 348
IT systems 10, 12, 15, 28, 139, 249, 340

J

JDL 32, 74, 142, 147-148, 153, 155, 159, 161, 163-
    164
joint chiefs of staff and military service leadership
    29
joint director's laboratories 32

K

kinetic worlds 92
knowledge, attitudes and behaviour 18

L

local area network 89, 202, 293
logging host 89
long-term memory 34, 39-40, 46, 154

M

maritime domain awareness 30
McAfee 33
MDA 30
media independent handover function (MIHF) 225
media independent handover (MIH) 221-222
medium access control (MAC) 230, 239, 242
message integrity key (MIK) 231
military industrial complex 29-30
military operation 31, 104
mobile IPv6 (MIPv6) 222, 240
mobile node (MN) 222, 242
mobility service authorizer (MSA) 226, 242

mobility service provider (MSP) 226, 242
multi-player sequential decision making models 49

N

national cybersecurity 125
network access server (NAS) 224, 242
network security 2-5, 8-9, 48, 68-70, 73, 78-79, 81, 88, 101-102, 105-109, 112, 114, 116, 122, 129, 148, 151, 154-155, 160-163, 184, 200, 219, 241, 246, 252-253, 260, 281, 297, 299, 301, 322, 326-328, 330, 343, 355
nominal stage 64
nonlinear objective functions 50
Norwegian Centre for Securing Information 21
Norwegian Computer Crime Survey 12, 15-16, 25-26
numerical experiment 48, 62
numerical stability 60

P

passive asset detection system 115
passive operating system fingerprint 115
point of attachment (PoA) 222, 226
probability of inertia 131, 136
protective monitoring 5, 105, 108-109, 113-114, 119, 252, 255, 258
protocol for carrying authentication for network access (PANA) 223, 240

Q

quality of service (QoS) 242

R

recognition-primed decision 76, 126
root master key (RMK) 229

S

sanctions and punishment 11, 15
Scandinavia 11
security awareness 10-11, 14, 16-18, 21, 28, 253
security controls 19
sensor fusion 163, 165-169, 176, 178-180, 254, 302-304, 309-311, 314, 318-319
service request identifier (SRID) 230
situational awareness 1-2, 4-5, 7-17, 20, 22-24, 28, 30, 32, 40, 42, 44-45, 48-49, 67, 71-72, 79, 82-84, 86-88, 92, 98, 100-109, 111-116, 118-122, 139-142, 148, 152, 156, 159-160, 162-164, 176, 181, 186-187, 197, 200, 202, 221-222, 245-247, 250, 253-257, 259-262, 264, 281, 289, 299, 303, 320-321, 343-344, 355
social networks 11, 21, 24
socio-technical theory 10-11, 15, 22-24, 72

T

the-need-to-know principle 11
threat to information security 10, 14
training in information security 12, 18, 23

U

unintentional threats 11
usage specific root key (USRK) 229

V

variable workload 117
voice over IP (VoIP) 222

W

wiki leaks 14
Windows Vista 12
WireShark 98-99